The Routledge International Handbook of Higher Education

The Routledge International Handbook of Higher Education

Edited by Malcolm Tight, Ka Ho Mok,
Jeroen Huisman, and Christopher C. Morphew

Routledge
Taylor & Francis Group

NEW YORK AND LONDON

First published 2009
by Routledge
270 Madison Ave, New York, NY 10016

Simultaneously published in the UK
by Routledge
2 Park Square, Milton Park, Abingdon, Oxon OX14 4RN

Routledge is an imprint of the Taylor & Francis Group, an informa business

© 2009 Taylor & Francis

Typeset in Minion by
RefineCatch Limited, Bungay, Suffolk
Printed and bound in the United States of America on acid-free paper by
Sheridan Books, Inc.

Library of Congress Cataloging in Publication Data
The Routledge international handbook of higher education / edited by Malcolm Tight . . . [et al.].
    p. cm.
    Includes bibliographical references and index.
    1. Education, Higher.   2. Education, Higher—Cross-cultural studies.   I. Tight, Malcolm.   II. Title: International handbook of higher education.
    LB2322.2.R677 2009
    378—dc22
    2008039009

ISBN10: 0–415–43264–2 (hbk)
ISBN10: 0–203–88222–9 (ebk)

ISBN13: 978–0–415–43264–1 (hbk)
ISBN13: 978–0–203–88222–1 (ebk)

Contents

List of Contributors

Gerlese S. Åkerlind Centre for Educational Development and Academic Methods, Australian National University, Australia.

Bettina Alesi International Centre for Higher Education Research, Kassel, Germany.

Phil Allen Office of Economic Development, University System of Georgia, USA.

Paul Ashwin Department of Educational Research, Lancaster University, UK.

Angela Brew Faculty of Education and Social Work, University of Sydney, Australia.

Jennifer M. Case Department of Chemical Engineering, University of Cape Town, South Africa.

Kelly Coate Centre for Excellence in Learning and Teaching, National University of Ireland, Galway, Ireland.

Jan Currie School of Education, Murdoch University, Australia.

Lars Owe Dahlgren Department of Behavioural Sciences, Linkoping University, Sweden.

Madeleine Abrandt Dahlgren Department of Behavioural Sciences, Linkoping University, Sweden.

Trine Danø NIFU STEP, Oslo, Norway.

Maryann Feldman Rotman School of Management, University of Toronto, Canada.

Marybeth Gasman Graduate School of Education, University of Pennsylvania, USA.

Colin Green Management School, Lancaster University, UK.

Tamsin Haggis Institute of Education, University of Stirling, UK.

Tony Harland Higher Education Development Centre, University of Otago, New Zealand.

Matthew Hartley Graduate School of Education, University of Pennsylvania, USA.

Jeroen Huisman School of Management, University of Bath, UK.

Håkan Hult Department of Behavioural Sciences, Linkoping University, Sweden.

Merle Jacob Research Policy Institute, School of Economics and Management, Lund University, Sweden.

Michael Jaeger Hochschul-Informations-System, Hanover, Germany.

Kristina Johansson Department of Behavioural Sciences, Linkoping University, Sweden.

Geraint Johnes Management School, Lancaster University, UK.

D. Bruce Johnstone State University of New York, Buffalo, USA.

Glen A. Jones University of Toronto, Canada.

Carole Kayrooz Pro-Vice-Chancellor, University of Canberra, Australia.

David Kember University of Hong Kong, Hong Kong.

Kerri-Lee Krause Institute for Higher Education, Griffith University, Australia.

Anna Kwan Open University of Hong Kong, Hong Kong.

Jenny J. Lee Centre for the Study of Higher Education, University of Arizona, USA.

Iryna Lendel Center for Economic Development, Cleveland State University, USA.

Tania Lewis Faculty of Education, Monash University, Australia.

Ranald Macdonald Learning and Teaching Institute, Sheffield Hallam University, UK.

Pamela N. Marcucci State University of New York, Buffalo, USA.

Simon Marginson Centre for the Study of Higher Education, University of Melbourne, Australia.

Delia Marshall Department of Physics, University of the Western Cape, South Africa.

Coralie McCormack Centre for the Enhancement of Learning, Teaching and Scholarship, University of Canberra, Australia.

Ka Ho Mok Hong Kong University, Hong Kong.

Christopher C. Morphew Institute of Higher Education, University of Georgia, USA.

Ruth Neumann Vice-Chancellor's Office, Macquarie University, Australia.

Dominic Orr Hochschul-Informations-System, Hanover, Germany.

Colin Pilbeam School of Management, Cranfield University, UK.

John T.E. Richardson Institute of Educational Technology, The Open University, UK.

Massimo Savino Educational Policy Institute, Toronto, Canada.

Astrid Schwarzenberger Hochschul-Informations-System, Hanover, Germany.

Peter Scott Vice-Chancellor, Kingston University, UK.

Helene Hård af Segerstad Department of Behavioural Sciences, Linkoping University, Sweden.

Sabine Severiens RISBO, Erasmus University, The Netherlands.

Theresa Shanahan Faculty of Education, York University, Canada.

Ilana Snyder Faculty of Education, Monash University, Australia.

David Soo Graduate School of Education, University of Pennsylvania, USA.

Bjørn Stensaker NIFU STEP, Oslo, Norway.

John Taylor Centre for Higher Education Management and Policy, University of Southampton, UK.

Malcolm Tight Department of Educational Research, Lancaster University, UK.

Alex Usher Educational Policy Institute, Toronto, Canada.

Lesley Vidovich Graduate School of Education, University of Western Australia, Australia.

Julie Vultaggio Graduate School of Education, University of Pennsylvania, USA.

Naomi Rosh White School of Political and Social Inquiry, Monash University, Australia.

Rick Wolff RISBO, Erasmus University, The Netherlands.

Mantz Yorke Department of Educational Research, Lancaster University, UK.

I
Introduction

1

Editorial Introduction

Malcolm Tight

Aim

The Routledge International Handbook of Higher Education aims to provide a critical account of the state of higher education, and higher education research, internationally at the beginning of the twenty-first century. That is, of course, a bold aim. How have we set out to achieve it? Well, there are strategies we have opted to follow, and others we have considered but then rejected. Let us start with the latter.

One strategy we have not attempted to follow is to be comprehensive. Even in a volume of 37 chapters, it is not possible to cover every country, or every discipline—though this kind of approach has been attempted by others (Clark and Neave 1992, Forest and Altbach 2006)—and, even if we had, the information would date fairly rapidly. Another, related, strategy we rejected early on was to be overly descriptive, to attempt to provide a snapshot picture in words of higher education in 2008.

Rather than being comprehensive and descriptive, we have aimed to make the *Handbook* thematic, critical and comparative. Thus, the organisation of the *Handbook* is thematic, structured in terms of the key issues and questions facing higher education, and those who research it. This thematic organisation is outlined and explained in the next section.

The approaches taken by the contributing authors to their themes are critical, exploring what is less well understood as well as what is. This critical approach explains why the focus of the *Handbook* is as much on the state of higher education research as on higher education. To better understand the issues facing higher education we need to appreciate how we go about trying to understand them.

In aiming to be comparative, we have sought to move beyond single-nation case studies to critical accounts of generic issues facing higher education systems across the globe, informed wherever possible by examples of responses from different systems.

In order to meet this aim and strategy, I approached and persuaded three co-editors—from different parts of the world, and with different expertise and contacts—to work with me: Jeroen Huisman, Ka Ho Mok, and Christopher C. Morphew.

Structure

The thematic structure adopted for the *Handbook* builds upon my own recent research mapping the current state of higher education research (Tight 2003, 2004). In analysing what was being published on higher education in 2000, this work identified eight key themes for higher education research, as follows:

- Teaching and Learning: including approaches to studying, learning styles, pedagogical styles.
- Course Design: including assessment, competencies, critical thinking, learning technologies, portfolios, postgraduate study, reflection, writing.
- The Student Experience: including access, counselling, diversity, employment, motivation, multiculturalism, non-completion.
- Quality: including evaluation, grading, outcomes, qualifications, standards.
- System Policy: including economies of scale, funding, globalisation, massification, national policy, returns on investment.
- Institutional Management: including autonomy, departments, governance, management, marketisation, mergers.
- Academic Work: including careers, induction, mobility, professionalism, training, writing.
- Knowledge: including disciplinarity, forms of knowledge, research.

Of course, other classifications are possible, and there are obvious overlaps or close relationships between the themes identified. This eightfold categorisation has, however, proved to be reasonably robust, both in previous research and in the organisation of the present *Handbook*.

Contents

The *Handbook* is organised, then, in eight sections, one for each of the themes identified. Each section contains four or five chapters, which aim to address many, if inevitably not all, of the subthemes or issues identified. Some chapters, of course, relate to more than one theme, and some of these connections are outlined in the introductions to each section.

The chapters have been sourced in two related ways. Thus, the majority have been specially commissioned from authors with expertise in the particular fields concerned, and the ability to work within the framework chosen for the *Handbook*. To these specially commissioned chapters we have added further chapters that have been recently published in article form. In some cases, these obviated the need to commission further chapters, while in others they were chosen so as to complement the specially commissioned chapters.

References

Clark, B. and Neave, G. (eds) (1992) *The Encyclopedia of Higher Education*. Oxford: Pergamon: four volumes.
Forest, J. and Altbach, P. (eds) (2006) *International Handbook of Higher Education*. Dordrecht: Springer.
Tight, M. (2003) *Researching Higher Education*. Maidenhead: Open University Press.
Tight, M. (ed.) (2004) *The RoutledgeFalmer Reader in Higher Education*. London: RoutledgeFalmer.

II
Teaching and Learning

Research on teaching and learning has evolved rapidly, as the chapters in this section readily demonstrate. This is a function of the complexity of the topic, and of the myriad ways in which researchers approach it. While there is general agreement on what constitutes learning and, more specifically, "deep" approaches to learning, there is less agreement on why students learn (or don't learn) in and out of the classroom, and on what institutional and cultural features may play a role in the phenomenon of learning. The chapters in this section provide a broad—if not exhaustive—perspective on the topic.

In the first chapter, Case and Marshall provide a historical analysis of the evolution of approaches to understanding learning. Early approaches, led by educational psychologists, have given way to more qualitative and naturalistic inquiries, which in turn have moved aside for work that focuses on what constitute deep—rather than surface—approaches to learning (Entwistle, 1998). The newest approaches focus on student experiences and their relationship to learning, the subject of dissonance—illogical relationships between approaches to learning and perceptions of context (Meyer et al, 1990)—and disciplinary contexts.

Haggis empirically examines leading non-North American higher education journals to assess what types of learning research have dominated the field. Her chapter highlights some of the important differences between research in higher education and adult education. Her study's findings highlight the problematic dominance of approaches to learning research, and questions why these journals publish so much of this type of research.

Moving beyond conventional applications of cognitive psychological learning theory, Ashwin and the other chapter authors delve into how interactions between student and instructor may affect learning and perspectives on learning. Ashwin points out—importantly—how research on learning that focuses on perceptions (student) or practices (academic) has "the unintended consequence of separating academics and students within teaching and learning interactions". The obvious implication is that researchers studying learning would do well to incorporate these interactions into their conceptual models.

Kember's chapter on Asian students builds on Ashwin's analysis by exploring the "paradox of the Chinese learner" (Watkins & Biggs, 1996), and the misperception of the Asian student as a rote learner. Kember's work also notes the importance of the relationship between learner and teacher. Research on how Asian students learn documents their adoption of approaches that are consistent with curricular and evaluative requirements. Tang's (1991) work on Hong Kong students, for example, demonstrates how students moved from deep approaches to learning to rote memorisation, because assessment techniques and requirements gave credit for the latter type of learning. Likewise, the misperception that Asian students are passive learners is also likely a response of students to their learning environment and the demands of instructors.

Investigating ethnic minority students, Severiens and Wolff focus on several factors that may work together to limit the depth of these students' experiences. The growth of minority students in tertiary systems in many countries is prevalent, and research on the factors that affect their achievement is growing in importance. This chapter uses frameworks provided by Tinto (1997) and Thomas (2002) to explore how concepts such as "institutional habitus" may interact with other demographic and institutional features to limit ethnic minority student achievement.

References

Entwistle, N.J. (1998). Approach to learning and forms of understanding. In B. Dart & G. Boulton-Lewis (eds) *Teaching and learning in higher education* (pp. 72–101). Melbourne, Australia: ACER Press.

Meyer, J.H.F., Parsons, P. & Dunne, T.T. (1990). Individual study orchestrations and their association with learning outcome. *Higher Education, 20*(1), 67–89

Tang, K.C.C. (1991). Effects of different assessment methods on tertiary students' approaches to studying. Unpublished Ph.D. Dissertation, University of Hong Kong.

Thomas, L. (2002). Student retention in higher education: the role of institutional habitus. *Journal of Education Policy, 17*(4), 423–442.

Tinto, V. (1997). Classrooms as communities. Exploring the educational character of student persistence. *Journal of Higher Education, 68*(6), 600–623.

Watkins, D. & Biggs, J.B. (eds) (1996). *The Chinese learner: Cultural, psychological and contextual influences.* Melbourne and Hong Kong: Australian Council for Educational Research and the Comparative Education Research Centre, University of Hong Kong.

2

Approaches to Learning

Jennifer M. Case and Delia Marshall

The new lecturer in the university of the twenty-first century who seeks to improve their teaching is faced with a bewildering array of questionnaires which promise to deliver useful information about their students and their learning. Some of these refer to "approaches to learning", others to "learning styles", still others to "learning patterns" and "study orchestrations". Can these provide answers to the complex challenges that currently present themselves in higher education learning contexts?

Coffield, Moseley, Hall and Ecclestone (2004) set out to assess the potential value of these tools, picking 13 commonly used questionnaires for the focus of their study, representing a range of learning theories. In short, they identify the ASSIST (Entwistle, 1997a), which measures "approaches to learning" as most appropriate for use, cautioning however that it could be "used by teachers without in-depth understanding of its underlying implications" (p. 25). What are these implications? This chapter provides an overview of key aspects of the approaches to learning theory. The review is necessarily selective, and where appropriate we refer readers to other resources for further details. Our focus is on the distinctive contributions that this research programme has generated over some three decades; we have attempted to identify particular insights that could be of value both to educators and to researchers.

The Origins of Approaches to Learning

Starting in the late 1960s, the experiences and voices of university students took on new levels of prominence in public life, and it is therefore not surprising that this era also saw new developments in research on student learning. In English-speaking countries, most of these researchers had backgrounds in educational psychology, and there was therefore substantial interest in developing questionnaires (termed "inventories") which were aimed at uncovering factors which could predict academic performance (for example, Biggs, 1970; Entwistle and Entwistle, 1970). Early work had focused mainly on traditional psychological attributes such as personality and motivation, but increasingly interest started to be directed towards the complex interaction between students and their environments.

Around this time, a research team in Sweden struck out on a new direction and, in a ground-breaking study, qualitatively examined students' responses to a "real" task which required them to read a piece of text in order to be able to respond to questions that would later be posed (Marton and Säljö, 1976a). This research approach had distinctive features that set it apart from the typical methodologies that were dominant in educational psychology at the time (Entwistle, 1997b). Firstly, it used a naturalistic setting which aimed to approximate a real educational situation. Secondly, it aimed to understand the individual participants' own perspectives of the situation[1] rather than aiming for the perspective of an "objective" outside observer. Marton and Säljö analysed participants' explanations of how they approached the reading task, and identified two distinctly different approaches: the "deep" approach to learning,[2] in which students focused on understanding the text, and the "surface" approach to learning, in which students did not focus primarily on understanding the text but rather on memorising text in order to be able to answer the questions.

Entwistle has been described as the first person in the English-speaking countries to grasp the importance of this Swedish work (Ramsden, 2005). Based in the UK, he and colleagues had turned their attention towards the "natural setting" of real university contexts and had conducted interviews with students about their experiences of studying. For this shift they credit the influence of key North American qualitative studies of student learning such as Becker, Geer and Hughes (1968) and Perry (1970). Using the work of Marton and Säljö (1976a) they were able to identity deep and surface approaches but they also noted the presence of what was considered to be a third approach, the strategic approach, where students were aiming towards top achievement, using whichever of the deep or surface approach was deemed necessary.

Entwistle's inventory was thus reframed using these new concepts and the "Approaches to Studying Inventory (ASI)" was shown to be a useful tool for identifying these three distinct approaches to learning[3] (Entwistle and Ramsden, 1983). In order to further communicate this new research on student learning, both English and Swedish researchers published a collected volume which is still considered a definitive text and is now in its second edition (Marton, Hounsell and Entwistle, 1984, 1997).

In parallel work in Australia, Biggs (1978) published an analysis of student responses to his Study Processes Questionnaire (SPQ) in which he noted the similarity of two of his categories to Marton and Säljö's (1976a) deep and surface approaches. In fact, his full set of three categories showed an even closer correspondence with Entwistle's work, including a third strategic approach.[4] Biggs characterised approaches to learning as "congruent motive-strategy packages", each comprising a motive and related strategy (Biggs, 1987a). He defined the surface motive as "extrinsic to the real purposes of the task" while the deep motive is "to engage the task properly, on its own terms . . . founded on an intrinsic interest in that task" (Biggs, 1993, pp. 6–7). Based on each of these motives, students will use a congruent strategy towards that end.

Following the methodological mix represented in the early studies, approaches to learning have continued to be identified mainly in natural settings using either qualitative interview or quantitative inventory studies, with the vast majority of studies in the literature falling in the latter category. The most widely used inventories (Richardson, 2004) are successive versions of Biggs' Study Processes Questionnaire, the SPQ (Biggs, 1987b; Biggs, Kember and Leung, 2001) and Entwistle's Approaches to Study Inventory, the ASI (Entwistle, 1997a; Entwistle and Ramsden, 1983; Entwistle and Tait, 1995). The origins of these two inventories as described in this section are summarised in Figure 2.1 below. Other key inventories are reviewed in Entwistle and McCune (2004) and Coffield et al. (2004).

Characteristics of Approaches to Learning

As noted above, a third approach to learning, the "strategic approach", emerged in Entwistle's interviews and was later incorporated into the ASI. The same approach was represented in the early versions of the SPQ. Recent versions of both of these inventories have dropped the strategic approach as an "approach" *per se*, and Entwistle and colleagues have replaced it with scales that

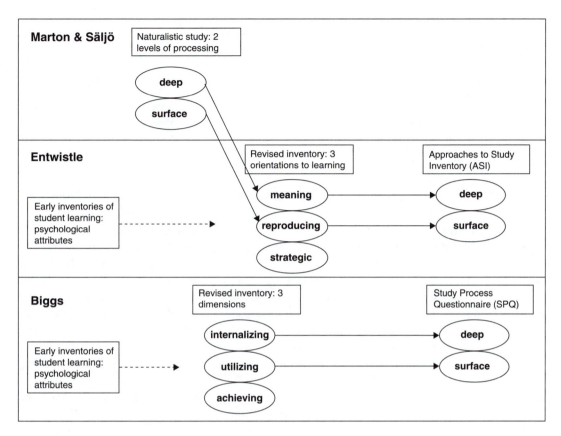

Figure 2.1 The Origins of Key Approaches to Learning Inventories.

measure "organised studying" and "effort management", as well as a fifth scale which measures "monitoring studying" and which is empirically related to the deep approach (Biggs et al., 2001; Entwistle et al., 2002). These aspects of learning bear considerable relation to the constructs of metacognition and self-regulation as represented in the educational psychology literature, particularly in North America (for example, Pintrich, 2004). Some of the newer inventories (for example, Vermunt and Vermetten, 2004) have specifically drawn on this literature to include these dimensions of learning. In short, all of these developments recognise that the "strategic approach" is not really a fundamentally distinct approach as are the deep and surface approaches. In this chapter we will therefore focus primarily on the "deep/surface dichotomy" which forms the focal point of the approaches to learning theory.

Entwistle (2004) provides a helpful summary of the learning strategies and processes used in the deep and surface approaches, reproduced as Table 2.1 below.

In reflecting on the key features of the deep approach, Entwistle (1997a) points out that "relating ideas" and "looking for patterns" can be seen as equivalent to Pask's (1976) notion of "comprehension learning" and similarly that "checking evidence" and "examining logic" define Pask's "operation learning". Both of these strategies were argued by Pask to be necessary for the development of a thorough understanding.

The deep approach is defined by a search for understanding, using whatever strategy can meet this end. Significant elaboration on the nature of the deep approach and of the processes by which students reach understanding, was provided by research on the so-called "Paradox of the Chinese

Table 2.1 Learning Strategies and Processes (Entwistle, 2004)

Deep approach	Surface approach
• relating ideas to previous knowledge and experience • looking for patterns and underlying principles • checking evidence and relating it to conclusions • examining logic and argument cautiously and critically • memorising whatever is essential to understanding • monitoring understanding as learning progresses	• treating the course seen as unrelated bits of knowledge • routinely memorising facts and carrying out procedures • focusing narrowly on the minimum syllabus demands • seeing little value or meaning in the course or set tasks • studying without reflecting on either purpose or strategy

Learner". The paradox is such: Chinese students on average were generally known to perform better academically than "Western students" and indeed tended to produce high deep approach scores on standard inventories. However, it is also well known that memorisation (or rote learning) is valued highly in Chinese culture and is used widely in teaching contexts. This seems to contradict a commonsense view on approaches to learning, which would associate memorisation with a surface approach. Marton, Dall'Alba and Tse (1996) solved this paradox by showing that for Chinese students, there is a fine distinction between "mechanical memorisation" and "memorisation with understanding", with the former being used in a surface approach and the latter strategy in a deep approach. Subsequent work attempted to establish the precise relationship between memorisation and understanding in a deep approach, and early work with high school students suggested that they were sequentially ordered, either memorisation followed by understanding, or understanding followed by memorisation (Marton, Watkins and Tang, 1997). Most recently, in a longitudinal study with Chinese university students, it has been established that these relatively mature learners use memorisation and understanding in a simultaneous manner (Marton, Wen and Wong, 2005). They explain as follows: "The logic of seeing memorisation and understanding as simultaneous is that in the case of repeated encounter with an object of learning, something is always invariant and something is varied. What is invariant (repeated) is supposed to enhance memorisation and what is varied is supposed to enhance understanding" (p. 297).

Another important study which produced further insights on the nature of the deep approach was conducted by Entwistle and Marton (1994), who investigated the ways in which understanding is developed by students who are revising for final examinations. From descriptions of these experiences, it appeared that students created "tightly integrated bodies of knowledge", which Entwistle and Marton termed "knowledge objects". These appeared as "quasi-sensory" experiences, with an awareness of aspects of knowledge beyond the margins of the current focus.

A recent study which investigated students' approaches to achieving understanding identified two interesting variations of the deep approach, termed "holding" and "moving" (Fyrenius, Wirell and Silén, 2007). The "holding" approach centres on the achievement of a fixed goal for understanding, and involves strategies of structuring and control. The "moving" approach, by contrast, involves an ongoing intention to continuously develop understanding with an open-ended outlook, and involves strategies which offer a change in perspective and deliberate variation.

The characteristics of the deep approach to learning can be seen to reflect what are generally held to be the aims of higher education (cf. Barnett, 1990). Indeed, an early study by Entwistle and colleagues found that although lecturers' espoused intentions focused on the kind of learning characterised by the deep approach, the actual demands of their courses were more in line with a surface approach (Entwistle and Percy, 1973). Subsequent work together with Ramsden was therefore focused on identifying the kinds of educational contexts that could better promote the ideals of higher education.

Relationships Between Approaches to Learning, Learning Outcomes, Educational Contexts and Student Backgrounds

Ramsden's work provided an elaboration of the role of context in determining approaches to learning. He characterised approaches as "relational", meaning that they arise out of the relationship between students and their environments. This he illustrated in the following model of the relations between students' perceptions of the educational context, their approaches to learning, and their learning outcomes[5] (see Figure 2.2).

The link on the right-hand side of the diagram between approaches to learning and learning outcomes forms the foundational justification for the theory and was in fact the focus of the original Marton and Säljö study (1976a). Students who were identified as using a deep approach were also seen to have qualitatively superior learning outcomes, as well as greater recall of facts. Svensson (1977) analysed the performance of this same group of students in the natural setting of a university course and found that students who used a deep approach were generally more successful than those who used a surface approach. Van Rossum and Schenk (1984) conducted a text-based naturalistic experiment somewhat similar to Marton and Säljö but used Biggs and Collis's (1982) SOLO taxonomy to classify learning outcomes. They found that students using a surface approach to learning never obtained more than a "multi-structural" level of learning outcome, in which facts are presented in an unconnected manner. The majority of students using a deep approach reached the "relational" level, in which ideas are presented as a coherent whole. In the context of a first year physics course, Prosser and Millar (1989) showed that students with a deep approach to learning demonstrated a greater degree of conceptual change towards more sophisticated conceptions.

The left-hand side of the diagram can be considered to represent those key aspects which influence the choice of approaches to learning,[6] and this forms the major focus of Ramsden's work. At the heart of his model are student perceptions, which mediate between educational context, student background and approaches to learning.

Regarding the impact of student background, rather than focusing on personality characteristics or motivation, it has been shown that a very useful characterisation of what students bring with them from prior learning experiences is the notion of "conceptions of learning", first established by Säljö (1979) and later expanded on by Marton, Dall'Alba and Beaty (1993). At the lower end of the range of conceptions of learning are "reproductive" notions such as an increase in knowledge, memorising and an acquisition of facts, while in the higher end they start with an abstraction of meaning, moving to an interpretive process aimed at understanding reality, and ending with learning as changing as a person.[7] Van Rossum and Schenk (1984) were first to explore the relationship

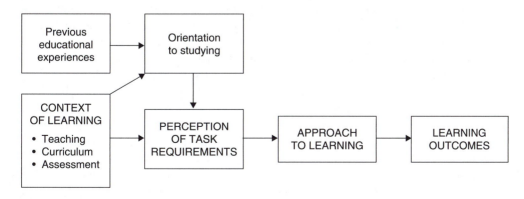

Figure 2.2 Student Learning in Context (Ramsden, 2003, p. 82).

between conceptions of learning and approaches to learning. As one would expect, they found a strong correlation, with students at the lower end of the conceptions of learning hierarchy tending towards a surface approach, and those at the upper end tending towards a deep approach.

A key finding of Entwistle and Ramsden's (1983) research established aspects of educational contexts which were related to the adoption of surface approaches to learning. These included high workloads, lack of flexibility and unclear goals and standards, and a high focus on examination preparation. The Course Experience Questionnaire, CEQ (Ramsden, 1991), emerged later from this work and continues to be used to measure students' perceptions of context. Thomas and Bain (1984) focused in more detail on students' perceptions of assessment and found that deep approaches were associated with open-ended written assignments, while surface approaches were common in multiple-choice and short-answer examinations. An important study in this area was conducted by Eley (1992), who analysed the inventory responses of a group of students who had just completed two concurrent courses in which the teaching approaches and course design were quite distinct. It was found that the same student could use slightly different approaches in different courses at the same point in time. When followed on a course basis, it was found that surface approach was linked to courses with an emphasis on performance in formal assessment, whereas the deep approach was linked to courses perceived as offering support, structure and cohesion, a focus on metacognitive development and independence in learning.

We have reviewed here a careful selection of studies which have illustrated the key linkages in the model given above, focusing on those which in our opinion have actually illuminated the nature of these relationships. There have been many more which have presented further quantitative verifications of these links. In fact, Biggs had already noted in 1993 that the relationships between all the variables in this model had been "heavily researched" (p. 9). We therefore contend that at this stage, after a further decade of ongoing industry, this line of enquiry should now be considered closed. It is not clear what repeated studies of these "variables" and their interrelationships are adding to knowledge on student learning.

Dissonance?

Groups of students whose inventory responses show illogical relationships between approaches to learning and perceptions of context were first identified by Meyer and colleagues and the phenomenon was termed "dissonance" (Meyer, Parsons and Dunne, 1990)[8]. For example, consider a student who is shown to adopt a surface approach and who states a preference for examinations which require detailed factual answers as expected, but who also ticks a statement which indicates a preference for assessments which require them to display their own thinking (Entwistle, Meyer and Tait, 1991). These evidently random responses were found to be associated with academically weak students and were considered as manifestations of a certain kind of student experience. In an early assessment of this new empirical finding, Entwistle et al. (1991) called for further research which might illuminate the reasons for these apparently illogical patterns. In response to the possibility that the main reason for the phenomenon of dissonance might be students' careless or unthinking engagement with the inventory, Entwistle et al. (1991) contend that this is not the case, based on the internal consistency of the item responses.

Research on dissonance has since mushroomed, although with maybe less critical interrogation of the actual meaning of this apparent phenomenon than might have been hoped for. One exception is an interesting study by Lindblom-Ylänne (2003), which interviewed students who had given "dissonant" inventory responses. With more detail in hand these responses become far more understandable, for example a student who scores highly on deep and surface approaches turns out to be someone who knows that his existing strategies are not working and is fully aware that he is trying, with mixed success, to implement a new strategy. Other examples include students who did not follow the instructions closely and who reported on their studies across all courses, not the course in question, and those on the other hand who focused on one particular situation in the course. Although Lindblom-Ylänne does not suggest such an interpretation, we would consider this research to be pointing directly to the limitations of inventory-generated data, especially considering the interpretations that current-day students with diverse linguistic backgrounds might place on the relatively arcanely worded inventory items (Richardson, 2004; Setlogelo, 2008).

The Importance of Context

No matter whether derived from naturalistic studies, student interviews or responses to inventories, approaches to learning were fundamentally defined as relating to a particular context. They were seen as students' responses to a context, whether a programme of study or course or a particular task, and were distinctly different to other constructs in the educational psychology literature which were more closely linked to personality and individual preferences. One such construct is that of "learning styles", which enjoys to this day substantial prominence in higher education literature, particularly in North America (for example, Felder, 1994). Learning styles claim to represent students' inherent preferences for learning and are not defined as a response to a context (Biggs, 1993) and therefore should not be conflated with approaches to learning, even though there is substantial evidence of this in the literature (Cassidy, 2004; Coffield et al., 2004).

This focus on context should be considered the substantial contribution of this research field. It is also the one area in which there has possibly been the most conceptual slippage as the theory has moved out into popular usage; most tellingly in references made to "deep learners" or "surface learners" (Biggs, 1993). In approaches to learning there can be no such thing as a "deep learner"; all one can identify is a student who is using an approach to learning in a particular context.

Chambers (2002) suggests that it is the predominance of quantitative inventory data collection methods that has led to such deviations from the original intentions of this theory. These studies, she argues, have tended to place the "spotlight" on students rather than teachings and teaching, and in the tendency to "sloganisation" it has become too easy to characterise students as deep or surface learners and thereby to shift blame in their direction. Haggis (2003) moves beyond a focus on methods to considerations of methodology. She highlights the epistemological assumptions that have underpinned much approaches to learning research, where a gradual reification of the constructs has led to an overwhelming focus on quantitative confirmation of the relationships between a set of variables, referred to by Malcolm and Zukas as a "relentlessly positivist orientation" (2001, p. 35).

What is needed is a return to the origins of approaches to learning research which turned towards interpretivist methodologies in order to understand the impact of students' perceptions of context. Both quantitative and qualitative data collection methods can be employed, although it becomes likely that qualitative analysis will play an important role. In the remainder of the chapter we review studies that use an interpretivist methodology. The chief focus for most of these studies has been on whether one can modify a context in order to promote a deep approach to learning, and the following section focuses here. A related consideration concerns the characteristics of approaches to learning in particular disciplinary contexts, and this will be dealt with in turn.

Understanding the Influence of Context on Approaches to Learning

Marton and Säljö's original work, which first identified deep and surface approaches to learning and established their relationship to learning outcomes (1976a), turned immediately to the obvious question of whether it is possible to promote a deep approach to learning through modification of the educational context (1976b). Their attempts to induce deep and surface approaches by inserting particular questions in the text pointed directly to the complexity of this challenge. As was expected, the superficial questions did elicit surface approaches to the task, but the "deep" questions were not always related to deep approaches, with some students performing a "technification" of the task and focusing in fact rather simplistically on the answering of the questions rather than on the underlying meaning of the text.

Ramsden, Beswick and Bowden (1986) reported on a learning skills programme which intended to increase the use of deep approaches. They were surprised to find that the students who attended did not perform any better or worse than their contemporaries who had not attended the programme, and furthermore that they actually increased their reported use of surface learning strategies, and marginally decreased their use of deep ones. This startling result is explained by the view that students extract from such programmes what is useful to them, with "what is useful" being fundamentally determined by their perceptions of the requirements of their courses. In this particular instance, student interview comments showed that their courses were perceived to be requiring the use of surface learning strategies.

Many studies have in fact shown that as students progress through their tertiary studies there is an increased prevalence of surface approaches (Biggs, 1987a; Gow and Kember, 1990; Watkins and Hattie, 1985). Biggs (1993) suggests a systems approach to understanding the complex relationship between context and student approach to learning, with students progressively attempting to achieve an "equilibrium" between themselves and the system. If they are increasingly adopting surface approaches, then these are implicitly what the system is perceived as requiring from them. Biggs (1999) later developed these ideas into the notion of "constructive alignment", where curricula can be designed such that they "demand" deep approaches of students and do not allow for the possibility of using surface approaches. This is certainly an attractive theory but given that one is always dealing with students' perceptions of the educational context rather than any objectively defined view of such a context, it is clear that this might be somewhat more challenging to enact in practice.

In a review of the literature in this area, Cope and Staehr (2005) note that there have been very few studies that give empirical assessments of attempts to induce deep approaches through structured modifications of the educational context. Newble and Jaeger (1983) report on a new ward-based assessment in a medical programme which was introduced in order to emphasise the importance of clinical skills. However, from the students' perspective it turned out this assessment was easier to pass, and so they spent more time in the library studying for their feared theoretical examination. The effect of the change was therefore exactly opposite to what was intended. Working in the context of the subject of anatomy in the early years of a medical programme, Eizenberg (1988) implemented a wide-ranging set of interrelated changes to all of curriculum, teaching and assessment, all focused towards the promotion of deep approaches to learning, in a subject area which is typically perceived as a vast amount of facts which will need to be reproduced. After exposure to two years of this newly presented subject, just fewer than half of students stated that they had used a deep approach to learning, although nearly all of them had intended to do so at the beginning of the year. In interpreting this finding, Eizenberg points to the impact of the other subjects in this demanding programme, which together resulted in these pragmatic responses.

Case and Gunstone (2002) report on modifications that were made to a second year chemical engineering course involving a reduction in content, changes to teaching style, the introduction of weekly journal tasks, and a greater focus on conceptual knowledge in the course assessment. The study focused in depth on the experiences of a small group of students as they went through the course, and showed that although a deep approach to learning was essential for success in the course, students really struggled to make changes to their approach while in a demanding and stressful programme. Cope and Staehr (2005) conducted an action research project where over the period of five years they made successive changes to an information systems course, aimed at increasing the number of students reporting deep approaches to learning. They identified the central issue as being students' perceptions of workload. In their final iteration they managed to reach a point where they had reduced the workload where students perceived that there was enough time to use a deep approach to learning, but where there was still sufficient content to satisfy the requirements of the course. They nonetheless conclude that there are severe limitations as to what can be achieved by a single lecturer working in a single course that forms part of a broader programme that is unchanged.

Struyven, Dochy, Janssens and Gielen (2006) report on a study which again shows that the interactions between perceptions of context and approaches to learning are complex and that counterintuitive effects can often be observed. They compared students in a traditional lecture-based course with those in a "student-activating" setting. This latter modification involved assignments which were collaborative and intended to get students involved as "active" learners who could construct their own knowledge, along the lines of the problem-based learning methodology. Both groups of students had similar approaches at the start of the course, but at the end of the course they found that the group in the "student-activating" setting showed a shift to a surface approach, also with lower scores on the strategic approach. It would appear that the perceptions of workload associated with this course design worked against the adoption of deep approaches to learning.

Approaches in Disciplinary Contexts

In some of the early work on approaches to learning it was clearly stated that approaches to learning might have different manifestations in different academic specialisations, in line with the context-dependency of these approaches (Ramsden, 1984). It was suggested that in some science tasks a deep approach would initially demand a narrow focus on details, which taken on its own might appear to be a surface approach. By contrast, in the humanities a deep approach would usually involve establishing a personal meaning from the very beginning of a task. It is an unfortunate consequence of the excessive focus on inventory studies that there has been relatively little attention paid to this important dimension of the research. Indeed, there are some inventory studies where items have been modified better to match the discipline, but this does not allow the researcher to fully engage with the nuances of context.

The few qualitative in-depth studies which have been open to identifying the particular forms that approaches to learning take in particular disciplinary contexts have delivered rather interesting results. For example, Booth (1992) investigated students as they were learning to write computer programs, and identified four distinctly different approaches to learning in this context: an "expedient" approach in which a previous program was identified which would suit the purposes of the current task; a "constructual" approach, where elements from their previously written programs were cobbled together for a solution; an "operational" approach, which focused on what the program was going to have to do; and a "structural" approach, which focused initially on the problem rather than the program specifications. The first two of these approaches Booth considered to be surface approaches, while the latter two approaches she classified as deep. Similarly, in a group of students undertaking a fashion design project Drew identified a set of distinct approaches appropriate to that context (Drew, Bailey and Shreeve, 2002). In our work with engineering students we have identified two types of "procedural approaches", intermediate to traditional deep and surface approaches. Procedural approaches involve students focusing on the solving of problems, sometimes at the expense of understanding (Case and Marshall, 2004). In recent work, McCune and Hounsell (2005) introduce the term "ways of thinking and practising" to describe in a particular discipline what might be the outcome of students' engagement with the field. For example, in final year biology courses, they identified working with primary literature and experimental data and learning to communicate in the biosciences as key dimensions of ways of thinking and practising in that context.

Conclusion

In this chapter it has been shown that the approaches to learning theory represented a significant shift in orientation for student learning researchers, particularly in moving away from an exclusive focus on individual characteristics and incorporating a focus on educational context. We have noted that an interpretivist methodology is the more productive research approach for exploring the influence of context. Nonetheless, the characterisation of the student that it presents is still very much conditioned by its origins in cognitive psychology. One is presented with an "asocial construction of the learner", an "anonymous, decontextualised, degendered being" (Malcolm and Zukas, 2001, p. 33, 38) who, rationally and freely, can choose between alternative approaches. Some approaches to learning researchers have incorporated perspectives similar to those in social psychology which recognise students' reasons for choosing to enter higher education and the role of collaborative learning within peer groups (for example, Gibbs, Morgan and Taylor, 1984; Vermunt, 2005; Yan and Kember, 2004), but this still fails to take account of the full impact of the social world on the individual experience.

In some ways approaches to learning can be seen as a description of what can be readily observed in almost any higher education context, but as a theory it doesn't offer much explanation for what underlies these approaches. Insights are needed into why some students appear to be unable—or unwilling—to engage with the aims of higher education (Haggis, 2003). Rather than locating the fault with the student, perspectives from social theory point to the ways in which the structures of power operate in order to perpetuate educational inequalities. Approaches to learning theory has been surprisingly insulated from these perspectives, which have had a profound impact on the broader field of educational scholarship (Coffield *et al.*, 2004; Haggis, 2003; Malcolm and Zukas, 2001). These perspectives are further reviewed in the following chapter.

In conclusion, then, we would like to suggest that the approaches to learning theory has opened up the area of student learning research for a whole new community of academic developers, many of whom did not necessarily have backgrounds in psychology or social science. It has given a view into what is going on in the higher education classroom, one which is immediately recognisable to practitioners (Entwistle, 1997c). It places at least some responsibility on educators to create learning environments oriented towards deep approaches to learning. It can also be a useful starting framework for those beginning to engage in the "scholarship of teaching and learning". However, for education researchers who wish to seriously engage with trying to understand students' experience of higher education, this framework on its own is arguably limited. There is a definite need to engage more widely with the broad range of perspectives that are available both in the theory of education and in social science more generally.

Notes

1. This is termed a second-order perspective (Marton, 1981).
2. These were originally termed "levels of processing" but later were termed "approaches to learning" (Marton and Säljö, 1984).

3. These were originally termed "orientations to studying" to indicate that they referred to general experiences of studying at university rather than a response to a particular task; they later adopted the term "approaches to studying" (Entwistle and Tait, 1995) to maintain this distinction, recent work refers to "approaches to learning and studying" (Entwistle, McCune and Hounsell, 2002).

4. These were originally termed internalizing, utilizing and achieving dimensions but later reworded as deep, surface and strategic approaches to learning (Biggs, 1987a).

5. This model was based on the "3P" model originally put forward by Duncan and Biddle (1974).

6. Note that key writers such as Biggs (1993) have stressed that all relationships in this model can be considered to work in both directions.

7. This final category was only identified in the later study by Marton, Dall'Alba, and Beaty (1993).

8. Initially these were referred to as "disintegrated" study orchestrations (Meyer, 1991) but this has been later replaced by use of the term "dissonant" (Meyer, 2000).

References

Barnett, R. (1990). *The idea of higher education*. Milton Keynes: SRHE and Open University Press.

Becker, H.S., Geer, B. and Hughes, E.C. (1968). *Making the grade: The academic side of college life*. New York: John Wiley and Sons.

Biggs, J.B. (1970). Personality correlates of certain dimensions of study behaviour. *Australian Journal of Psychology*, *22*(3), 287–297.

Biggs, J.B. (1978). Individual and group differences in study processes. *British Journal of Educational Psychology*, *48*, 266–279.

Biggs, J.B. (1987a). *Student approaches to learning and studying*. Melbourne: Australian Council for Educational Research.

Biggs, J.B. (1987b). *Study Process Questionnaire manual*. Melbourne: Australian Council for Educational Research.

Biggs, J.B. (1993). What do inventories of students' learning processes really measure? A theoretical review and clarification. *British Journal of Educational Psychology*, *63*, 3–19.

Biggs, J.B. (1999). *Teaching for quality learning at university: What the student does*. London: Society for Research into Higher Education and Open University Press.

Biggs, J.B. and Collis, K.F. (1982). *Evaluating the quality of learning: The SOLO taxonomy*. New York: New York Academic Press.

Biggs, J.B., Kember, D. and Leung, D.Y.P. (2001). The revised two-factor Study Process Questionnaire: R-SPQ-2F. *British Journal of Educational Psychology*, *71*(1), 133–149.

Booth, S. (1992). *Learning to program: A phenomenographic perspective*. Gothenburg, Sweden: Acta Universitatis Gothoburgensis.

Case, J.M. and Gunstone, R.F. (2002). Metacognitive development as a shift in approach to learning: an in-depth study. *Studies in Higher Education*, *27*(4), 459–470.

Case, J.M. and Marshall, D. (2004). Between deep and surface: Procedural approaches to learning in engineering contexts. *Studies in Higher Education*, *29*(5), 605–615.

Cassidy, S. (2004). Learning styles: An overview of theories, models and measures. *Educational Psychology*, *24*(4), 419–444.

Chambers, E. (2002). Understanding students' learning "from the inside": The early work of Alistair Morgan. In T. Evans (ed.), *Research in Distance Education 5: Revised papers from the 5th Research in Distance Education Conference*. Deakin University, Geelong.

Coffield, F., Moseley, D., Hall, E. and Ecclestone, K. (2004). *Should we be using Learning Styles? What research has to say to practice*. London: Learning and Skills Development Agency.

Cope, C. and Staehr, L. (2005). Improving students' learning approaches through intervention in an information systems learning environment. *Studies in Higher Education*, *30*(2), 181–197.

Drew, L., Bailey, S. and Shreeve, A. (2002). Fashion variations: Student approaches to learning in fashion design. In A. Davies (ed.), *Enhancing curricula: Exploring effective curriculum practices in art, design and communication in Higher Education* (pp. 179–198). London: Centre for Learning and Teaching in Art and Design.

Duncan, M.J. and Biddle, B.J. (1974). *The study of teaching*. New York: Holt, Rinehart & Winston.

Eizenberg, N. (1988). Approaches to learning anatomy: Developing a programme for preclinical medical students. In P. Ramsden (ed.), *Improving learning: New perspectives* (pp. 178–198). London: Kogan Page.

Eley, M.G. (1992). Differential adoption of study approaches within individual students. *Higher Education*, *23*, 231–254.

Entwistle, N.J. (1997a). The Approaches and Study Skills Inventory for Students (ASSIST). *Centre for Research on Learning and Instruction, University of Edinburgh*.

Entwistle, N.J. (1997b). Contrasting perspectives on learning. In F. Marton, D. Hounsell and N. Entwistle (eds) *The experience of learning* (2nd ed., pp. 3–22). Edinburgh: Scottish Academic Press.

Entwistle, N.J. (1997c). Reconstituting approaches to learning: A response to Webb. *Higher Education*, *33*(2), 213–218.

Entwistle, N.J. (2004). Teaching-learning environments to support deep learning in contrasting subject areas. Talk at University of Leeds.

Entwistle, N.J. and Entwistle, D. (1970). The Relationships between Personality, Study Methods and Academic Performance. *British Journal of Educational Psychology*, *40*, 132–143.

Entwistle, N.J. and Marton, F. (1994). Knowledge objects: understandings constituted through intensive academic study. *British Journal of Educational Psychology*, *64*, 161–178.

Entwistle, N.J. and McCune, V. (2004). The conceptual bases of study strategy inventories. *Educational Psychology Review*, *16*(4), 325–345.

Entwistle, N.J., McCune, V. and Hounsell, J. (2002). *Approaches to studying and perceptions of university teaching-learning environments: Concepts, measures and preliminary findings*. Edinburgh: University of Edinburgh.

Entwistle, N.J., Meyer, J.H.F. and Tait, H. (1991). Student failure: Disintegrated patterns of study strategies and perceptions of the learning environment. *Higher Education*, *21*(2), 249–261.

Entwistle, N.J. and Percy, K.A. (1973). Critical Thinking or Conformity? An Investigation of the Aims and Outcomes of Higher Education. *Research into Higher Education*, 1–37.

Entwistle, N.J. and Ramsden, P. (1983). *Understanding student learning*. London: Croom Helm.

Entwistle, N.J. and Tait, H. (1995). *The Revised Approaches to Study Inventory*. Edinburgh: Centre for Learning and Instruction, University of Edinburgh.

Felder, R.M. (1994). Reaching the second tier—learning and teaching styles in college science education. *Journal of College Science Teaching*, *23*(5), 286–290.

Fyrenius, A., Wirell, S. and Silén, C. (2007). Student approaches to achieving understanding—approaches to learning revisited. *Studies in Higher Education*, *32*(2), 149–165.

Gibbs, G., Morgan, A. and Taylor, E. (1984). The world of the learner. In F. Marton, D. Hounsell and N. Entwistle (eds), *The Experience of Learning* (pp. 165–188). Edinburgh: Scottish Academic Press.

Gow, L. and Kember, D. (1990). Does higher education promote independent learning? *Higher Education*, *19*, 307–322.

Haggis, T. (2003). Constructing images of ourselves? A critical investigation into "approaches to learning" research in higher education. *British Educational Research Journal*, *29*(1), 89–104.

Lindblom-Ylänne, S. (2003). Broadening and understanding of the phenomenon of dissonance. *Studies in Higher Education*, *28*(1), 63–78.

Malcolm, J. and Zukas, M. (2001). Bridging pedagogic gaps: conceptual discontinuities in higher education. *Teaching in Higher Education*, *6*(1), 33–42.

Marton, F. (1981). Phenomenography—Describing conceptions of the world around us. *Instructional Science*, *10*, 177–200.

Marton, F., Dall'Alba, G. and Beaty, E. (1993). Conceptions of learning. *International Journal of Educational Research*, *19*, 277–300.

Marton, F., Dall'Alba, G. and Tse, L. K. (1996). Memorizing and understanding: The keys to the paradox? In D. Watkins and J.B. Biggs (eds), *The Chinese learner: Cultural, psychological, and contextual influences* (pp. 69–83). Hong Kong: Comparative Education Research Centre.

Marton, F., Hounsell, D. and Entwistle, N. (eds) (1984). *The experience of learning*. Edinburgh: Scottish Academic Press.

Marton, F., Hounsell, D. and Entwistle, N. (eds) (1997). *The experience of learning* (2nd edn). Edinburgh: Scottish Academic Press.

Marton, F. and Säljö, R. (1976a). On qualitative differences in learning: I—Outcome and process. *British Journal of Educational Psychology*, *46*, 4–11.

Marton, F. and Säljö, R. (1976b). On qualitative differences in learning: II—Outcome as a function of the learner's conception of the task. *British Journal of Educational Psychology*, *46*, 115–127.

Marton, F. and Säljö, R. (1984). Approaches to learning. In F. Marton, D. Hounsell and N. Entwistle (eds) *The experience of learning* (pp. 36–55). Edinburgh, UK: Scottish Academic Press.

Marton, F., Watkins, D. and Tang, C. (1997). Discontinuities and continuities in the experience of learning: An interview study of high-school students in Hong Kong. *Learning and Instruction*, *7*(1), 21–48.

Marton, F., Wen, Q. and Wong, K.C. (2005). "Read a hundred times and the meaning will appear . . ." Changes in Chinese University students' views of the temporal structure of learning. *Higher Education*, *49*(3), 291–318.

McCune, V. and Hounsell, D. (2005). The development of students' ways of thinking and practising in three final-year biology courses. *Higher Education*, *49*(3), 255–289.

Meyer, J.H.F. (1991). Study orchestration: the mainfestation, interpretation and consequences of contextualised approaches to studying. *Higher Education*, *22*, 297–316.

Meyer, J.H.F. (2000). The modelling of "dissonant" study orchestration in higher education. *European Journal of Psychology of Education*, *15*(1), 5–18.

Meyer, J.H.F., Parsons, P. and Dunne, T.T. (1990). Individual study orchestrations and their association with learning outcome. *Higher Education*, *20*(1), 67–89.

Newble, D.I. and Jaeger, K. (1983). The effect of assessment and examinations on the learning of medical students. *Medical Education*, *17*, 25–31.

Pask, G. (1976). Styles and strategies of learning. *British Journal of Educational Psychology*, *46*, 128–148.

Perry, W.G. (1970). *Forms of intellectual and ethical development in the college years*. New York: Holt, Rinehart & Winston.

Pintrich, P. (2004). A conceptual framework for assessing motivation and self-regulated learning in college students. *Educational Psychology Review*, *16*(4), 385–407.

Prosser, M. and Millar, R. (1989). The "how" and "what" of learning physics. *European Journal of Psychology of Education*, *IV*(4), 513–528.

Ramsden, P. (1984). The context of learning. In F. Marton, D. Hounsell and N. Entwistle (eds) *The experience of learning* (pp. 144–164). Edinburgh: Scottish Academic Press.

Ramsden, P. (1991). A performance indicator of teaching quality in higher education: The Course Experience Questionnaire. *Studies in Higher Education*, *16*(2), 129–150.

Ramsden, P. (2003). *Learning to teach in higher education* (2nd edn). London: Routledge.

Ramsden, P. (2005). Foreword. *Higher Education*, *49*(3), 199–203.

Ramsden, P., Beswick, D.G. and Bowden, J.A. (1986). Effects of learning skills interventions on first year university students' learning. *Human Learning*, 5, 151–164.

Richardson, J.T.E. (2004). Methodological issues in questionnaire-based research on student learning in higher education. *Educational Psychology Review*, 16(4), 347–358.

Säljö, R. (1979). *Learning in the learner's perspective. I. Some common-sense conceptions.* Gothenburg, Sweden: Institute of Education, University of Gothenborg.

Setlogelo, D. (2008). *An investigation of the impact of approaches to learning and cultural capital on student success.* Unpublished MPhil, University of Cape Town, Cape Town, South Africa.

Struyven, K., Dochy, F., Janssens, S. and Gielen, S. (2006). On the dynamics of students' approaches to learning: The effects of the teaching/learning environment. *Learning and Instruction*, 16, 279–294.

Svensson, L. (1977). On qualitative differences in learning: III—Study skill and learning. *British Journal of Educational Psychology*, 47, 233–243.

Thomas, P.R. and Bain, J.D. (1984). Contextual dependence of learning approaches: The effects of assessments. *Human Learning*, 3, 227–240.

Van Rossum, E.J. and Schenk, S.M. (1984). The relationship between learning conception, study strategy and learning outcome. *British Journal of Educational Psychology*, 54, 73–83.

Vermunt, J.D. (2005). Relations between student learning patterns and personal and contextual factors and academic performance. *Higher Education*, 49(3), 205–234.

Vermunt, J.D. and Vermetten, Y. (2004). Patterns in student learning: Relationships between learning strategies, conceptions of learning, and learning orientations. *Educational Psychology Review*, 16(4), 359–384.

Watkins, D.A. and Hattie, J. (1985). A longitudinal study of the approach to learning of Australian tertiary students. *Human Learning*, 4, 127–142.

Yan, L. and Kember, D. (2004). Avoider and engager approaches by out-of-class groups: the group equivalent to individual learning approaches. *Learning and Instruction*, 14(1), 27–49.

3
Student Learning Research
A Broader View

Tamsin Haggis

Case and Marshall's reference (in their chapter in this book) to the limitations of relying on approaches to learning theory, or phenomenography, "on its own" points to the dominance of this theoretical model of learning in many of the literatures of higher education. Although this dominance does not extend to North America, it can be seen in the main UK-based journals, which are widely used in British, European, Australian, South African and Hong Kong higher education contexts. These are therefore referred to as "non-North American" higher education contexts (see Tight, 2007). This chapter focuses on student approaches to learning as defined in this area of the literature, with comparative reference to trends in North America.

The first section reports on a review of article titles relating to student learning over four decades in three non-North American journals and two North American journals, in order to test the claim that one approach dominates so much of the field. The results of this review are discussed in relation to a summary of broad theoretical moves in psychology and sociology over the same period, and then in relation to research in higher education published in the fields of adult education and sociologuistics. It is argued that the research published in higher education journals is generally at least one, if not two, decades behind educational research in other relevant fields.

Four Decades of Student Learning Research

According to Richardson, "the basic distinction between deep and surface approaches has been confirmed . . . not only in Europe, but in other parts of the world as well" (2000: 27). He suggests that this way of understanding student learning is so established that it has become "perhaps even a cliché in discussions about teaching and learning in higher education" (*ibid.*). Although this state of affairs may seem to suggest that the basic "problem" of understanding student learning has been solved, it could be argued that such statements simply reflect an advanced stage of development in one particular theoretical and methodological strand of research. This chapter is not concerned with mounting a critique of approaches to learning research (for this, see Haggis, 2003). Instead it asks what the effect of the dominance of this perspective may have been, in terms of the neglect of other possible approaches to the study of human learning.

Methodology

In order to test the claim that approaches to learning research has dominated thinking about learning in non-North American higher education contexts up to now, a review of articles on student learning was first carried out in three key non-North American higher education journals, covering the period from the 1970s to the present day (this was a review of titles only). The journals reviewed were *Higher Education, Studies in Higher Education* and *Teaching in Higher Education*. In terms of location and status, Tight (2007) has suggested that the journal *Higher Education* (*HE*) is generally regarded as "the leading non-North American international" higher education journal, and that *Studies in Higher Education* (*SHE*) is "the leading UK-based" journal (2007: 239). *Teaching in Higher Education* (*THE*), a more recent journal that has only been published since the late 1990s, was reviewed as well in order to compare a newer, initially less prestigious journal with the two more established ones.

In each journal, for each decade, a content analysis was performed on the language used in article titles relating to student learning. The six categories generated in relation to these titles were "cognitive psychology", "approaches to learning", "curricular innovation", "social context/student experience", "critical perspectives" and "discourse/writing". The categories were not restricted to areas such as "theory" or "methodology", but used a wider range of concepts in an attempt to capture the different areas of focus represented by the titles. Some of these could be classified as relating to specific theoretical approaches (e.g. "cognitive psychology", "approaches to learning", "discourse analysis"), but others, such as "curricular innovation" and "social context/student experience" were not, or only partially so. Three passes through the total data set were performed in order to cross-reference and confirm the categories.

That it was not possible to group the articles into solely theoretical areas is interesting. Though many of the perspectives categorised as "social context", for example, are clearly broadly socio-logical, "the student experience" aspect of this category can also incorporate a range of political agendas, as well as methodological approaches linked to quite specific (e.g. critical and emancipa-tory) strands of sociology. The category "curricular innovation" represents a broad-based area of activity that might draw on any number of different theories, or possibly even have very little theoretical basis. For example, ideas such as "peer-learning", "problem-based learning" and "self-regulated learning" could be seen to have developed as much in relation to cultural trends and value-positions as to research or theory. The discourse/writing category often reflects theoretical discourse analysis approaches, but also includes discussion of essay writing and writing skills.

Each category could be said to be attempting to answer a particular question. For example, cognitive psychology and approaches to learning might be said to be asking: "what can we discover about how individuals learn?" Key words in *cognitive psychology* include: personality, attainment, ability, motivation, information-retrieval, type, learning style/strategy, personal meaning, experi-ment, behaviour, orientation, achievement, performance, preference, study orchestration, process-ing, effectiveness and learning outcome. *Approaches to learning* includes phrases such as: approaches to study, approaches to learning, student perceptions, student conceptions, misconceptions, deep learning, dissonant conceptions, student ways of thinking, orientations to learning, and deep and surface. Although initially seen as distinct from cognitive psychology, approaches to learning work arises within the cognitive tradition, and as time goes on titles indicate a blurring of the distinction between them. For example, in 1996, an article titled "metacognitive, cognitive and affective aspects of learning styles and strategies: a phenomenographic analysis" appeared, and, in 2002, one titled "validation of a free response test of deep learning about the normal swallowing process".

Curricular innovation might be said to be asking the question: "what are the implications of our knowledge about individual learning for classroom teaching and curriculum design?" Key phrases in this category include: project work, peer learning, small group discussions, collaborative learning, problem-based learning, learning for self-direction, action learning, continuous assessment, increased student participation, task-based learning, negotiated learning, computer conferencing and resource-based learning. Article titles that were focused on teaching, instruction or teacher action were not included in the analysis. Although this category appears to focus on "teaching methods", titles here were only included if they focused on creating new kinds of learning experience.

Social context/student experience perspectives initially ask: "what is going on outside the class-room which might impact upon learning outcomes?", and "what do students themselves have to say about learning?" Later this focus extends to "how does what is done in the classroom impact upon work and life prospects?", and finally to issues such as "how can classroom experience serve the agenda of lifelong learning?" Key phrases here include: mature students, problems of adjustment, student stress, students with disabilities, students and social class, cultural and social capital, gender and inequality, international students, the student experience, integrating study with work and difference. Article titles which referred to participation statistics or organisational aspects of access policies were not included.

Critical perspectives ask questions such as: "what are the limitations of our current positions and views about learning?" These perspectives were often indicated by a question mark, in combination with words such as critical/critique, challenge, hidden curriculum, transformation, power, tensions, transgression and ethics. *Discourse and writing* perspectives are an extension of both social/student experience and critical perspectives. These perspectives might ask questions such as "what is the effect of particular types of language use in relation to student learning outcomes?", or "how does the way we speak, and what we ask students to write, create impediments to students' learning?" Key phrases here include: writing skills training, writing as a tool for learning, disciplinary discourses, writing experiences, academic literacies, genre effects/analysis, writing styles and gender/achievement, dialogic behaviour, problems of communicating feedback, participating in academic discourse.

The categories are listed above in the order that they appear in higher education journals through time. For example, there are no titles deemed to belong to the discourse/writing category in the 1970s; and social context and critical perspective titles become more prevalent throughout the decades.

Articles on Learning: 1970–2007

Figure 3.1 summarises the relative proportions of the different categories in each journal for each decade.

In the 1970s the main focus of *HE* in relation to learning appears to be the building of a knowledge base about individual student learning (cognitive psychology), and the development of a particular extension of this approach (approaches to learning). A smaller proportion of articles explore the application of this knowledge to practice (curricular innovation), and only a very small proportion of articles indicate an interest in understanding the effect of what goes on beyond the classroom (social context/student experience). *SHE*, by contrast, appears relatively unconcerned with building or discussing the knowledge base, but is very interested in considering the implications of research ideas about learning for practical teaching.

In the 1980s, the interest in learning research and theory has increased in *SHE*, whilst in *HE* it remains proportionally the same. Learning research in *HE*, however, has slightly less of a focus in this decade upon approaches to learning perspectives. Social and critical perspectives are increasing, particularly in *SHE*, with the combined effect of these increases resulting in a reduction in

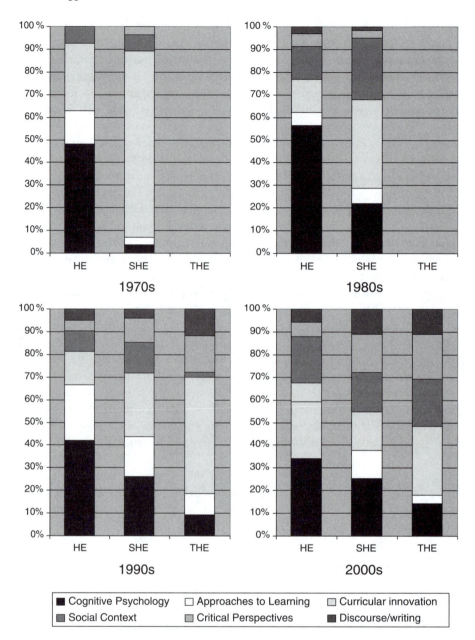

Figure 3.1 Content Comparison through the Decades.

consideration of experimental approaches to teaching and the curriculum. Titles suggest that interest in learning is still overwhelmingly focused at the level of the classroom.

In the 1990s, *HE*'s interest in building up a knowledge base about individual learning has increased very slightly, but is proportionally largely unchanged since the 1970s. Approaches to learning research, however, now makes up a much larger proportion of this focus. In the 1990s *HE* is only marginally more interested in asking "what's going on outside the classroom which might impact upon learning outcomes?" (social context/student experience) than it was in the 1970s, and is *less* interested in this question than it was in the 1980s. It is also apparently slightly less interested in critiquing its perspectives than it was in the previous decade, though discourse/writing perspectives have increased. *SHE*, though more prepared to engage in critique, also appears to be less interested in asking what is going on for students beyond the classroom than it was in the 1980s. Both journals show an increase in cognitive/approaches to learning approaches, and a corresponding reduction in curricular innovation and social perspectives. *THE*, a new journal in this decade, goes against these trends, returning to the much earlier interest in curricular innovation, and also developing critical and discourse perspectives to a greater degree.

By the 2000s, the three journals appear to have settled into a pattern in terms of distribution of focus. *HE* continues to publish the largest amount of psychologically-based research and theory; *THE* publishes the least; and *SHE* is between the two. Approaches to learning perspectives have reduced in both *SHE* and *THE*, but not in *HE*. All three journals are now less interested in discussing classroom practice than in considering social and critical perspectives.

Comparison with North American Trends in the Same Period

The two North American journals which will now be considered were also considered by Tight (2007). Both the *Journal of Higher Education* (*JHE*) and *Research into Higher Education* (*RHE*) were analysed across the same period as the non-North American journals considered so far (1970–2007).

The trends observable in article titles focused on learning in these two journals are somewhat different to those identified in non-North American contexts. Across the same period *JHE*, for example, has far fewer articles devoted to discussion of curricular innovation, even in the 1970s, and less of a focus on approaches obviously based in cognitive psychology (the titles for this journal, however, although indicating general areas of interest such as "college adjustment" or "cultural barriers", often give less away in terms of psychological or sociological orientation). Approaches to learning are almost nowhere to be seen (it is hard to tell, for example, whether occasional reference to "perceptions" might have been influenced by approaches to learning work). In this journal a large number of titles reflect various types of "social context" perspective, although this focus does not necessarily indicate a sociological perspective. Reflecting the reality of a mass higher education system attempting to attract and retain a wide variety of students, this journal's engagement with issues of race, colour and "the disadvantaged" is prevalent from the beginning of the 1970s, whereas in the UK-based journals race/ethnicity are mentioned quite rarely, and then only in the 2000s. *JHE* also focuses increasingly throughout the decades on issues of persistence, withdrawal and retention, very often explicitly in relation to variously described "non-traditional" students.

RHE has a similar focus in terms of the three areas identified in *JHE* (cognitive psychology, "the disadvantaged", and persistence/withdrawal/retention). Within cognitive psychology, there does not appear to be a dominance of any one area of interest, and only minimal direct influence of approaches to learning work. In the 1990s, however, when the influence of approaches to learning in the non-North American journals is at its peak, the learning titles in *RHE* suggest a similar type of focus, expressed in phrases such as approaches to learning, learning style, beliefs about the nature of knowledge, and in particular "epistemological beliefs" and "epistemological styles".

In contrast to *HE*, the non-North American journal with the most predominantly psychological approach, in the following decade (2000s) *RHE* develops a broad range of psychological interests rather than privileging the development of approaches to learning-type work. However, although this indicates a broader approach within the cognitive tradition, closer investigation suggests that this breadth of topics may be the result of an overall psychological orientation towards *all* learning topics, including those in the "social context" category, which in the non-North American journals are increasingly being analysed using sociological, critical and discourse approaches. From its predominantly psychological position, *HE*, in the non-North American context, privileges approaches to learning research; whereas in *RHE*, the dominant area of interest in this decade is persistence/withdrawal/retention.

Although apparently restricted to this largely psychological approach, at the same time *RHE* shows a much earlier interest than the non-North American journals in considering how aspects of institutional culture and practice might be affecting student learning. By the 2000s, however, when this area of interest in the non-North American journals is being explored using reflexive forms of critique and discourse analysis, the titles in *RHE* continue to indicate more psychological and measurement-based approaches. Overall, and also somewhat paradoxically, considering this general psychological bias, the titles in both *RHE* and *JHE* (although they actually mention "learning" relatively infrequently) suggest a somewhat broader view of learning than the non-North American journals. For example, these journals quite regularly discuss the idea of growth and development (personal, intellectual and vocational), and start discussing and attempting to measure the long-term social and economic benefits of higher education at quite an early stage.

Four Decades of Higher Education Research in its Wider Theoretical and Disciplinary Context

The trends outlined in the journals discussed will now be compared with key theoretical moves in psychology and, to a lesser extent, sociology (see Figure 3.2).

1970s

In the 1970s, the non-North American journals arguably take an individualistic approach to the study of student learning, which is rooted in both behaviourist and cognitive psychology. Within this overall orientation, there is some quite radical thinking, demonstrated by titles such as "a course without a structure", and "freedom in the selection of course content". The focus, however, is still predominantly upon answering the questions "what can we discover about how individuals learn?" and "what are the implications of our knowledge about individual learning for classroom teaching and curriculum design?"

In this decade, the discipline of psychology is developing a much wider range of cognitive perspectives. Potentially relevant, among many others, are the social and interactional perspectives of Bandura and Leont'ev, and the philosophical perspective of John Dewey. In addition, humanistic psychologists such as Abraham Maslow and Carl Rogers, and psychoanalytic theorists such as Erikson and Freud, are developing ideas which are being rapidly taken up by those who teach adults in contexts other than universities.

1980s

In the 1980s, the non-North American higher education journals continue to take a predominantly individualistic approach to the study of student learning, demonstrated most clearly by the overall increase in cognitive and approaches to learning perspectives. The potentially radical questioning of the 1970s in relation to curricular innovation appears to become reined in during this decade, particularly in *HE*, with discussions of self-managed and structure-free learning giving way to discussion of more manageable technologies, such as peer teaching and problem-based learning. In this decade social context perspectives also begin to increase, but these are arguably limited to attempts to answer the question "what's going on outside the classroom which might impact upon learning outcomes?" The focus of titles in this category is largely limited to a concern for the effects of access movements, and the resulting influx into higher education of "non-standard" entrants,

1970s →	1980s →	1990s →	2000s
PSYCHOLOGY (individual/ interactional): behaviourism/objectives (Bloom); cognitivism, including interactional perspectives (Dewey, Bruner, Bandura, Leont'ev) and developmental theories (Piaget, Kohlberg, Erikson); humanism (Rogers, Maslow); psychoanalysis (Freud, Fromm, Lacan)	**PSYCHOLOGY (individual/ interactional/ social):** All previous perspectives plus cognitive constructivism; social constructivism; multiple & triarchic theories of intelligence; socio-cultural approaches (e.g. activity theory); community psychology (radical social justice perspective, e.g. Burman); discourse perspectives; neural networks; connectionism	**PSYCHOLOGY (individual/ interactional/ social/distributed/evolutionary):** All previous perspectives plus development of collaborative, cooperative and discursive approaches; perspectives from neuroscience (cognitive neuropsychology); ecological and dynamic systems theories (Maturana & Varela; Fogel; Bosma & Kunnan); sociogenetics (Valsiner); evolutionary perspectives	Continuing development of **social/ interactional, distributed, networked,** and **emergentist** perspectives in both psychology and social theory. Increasing amounts of **interdisciplinary** work, and perspectives which try to overcome the perceived boundaries between **social/biological/technological**
SOCIOLOGY/SOCIAL THEORY (social): neo-Marxism; interactionism/interpretivism; sociology of knowledge, post-modern critique	**SOCIOLOGY/SOCIAL THEORY (social):** agency, meaning, interaction, structure (Goffman, Giddens); class, capital, power (Habermas, Bourdieu); "minority standpoint epistemologies": gender, race, sexuality & disability; post-modern/ post-structuralist critique (Foucault, Lyotard)	**SOCIOLOGY/SOCIAL THEORY interactional/social/distributed/ evolutionary/individual:** All previous perspectives continue and are joined by complexity theory and actor network theory (Latour, Byrne, Law & Urry); morphogenetic theory (Archer)	
HIGHER EDUCATION			
Individual: personality, attainment, motivation, information-retrieval, student type, approaches to study, perceptions, student learning processes	**Individual:** affect, anxiety, self-directed learning readiness scale, locus of control, skills, conceptions, approaches, perceptions, individualised learning, problem-based learning, independent study	**Individual:** study orchestrations, learning outcomes, study deficiencies, gender & learning style, learning behaviour, learning strategies, approaches & mature students/ gender, perceptions, conceptions, self-directed learning, problem-based learning, reflection	**Individual:** individual differences/styles, motivation, text & learner variables, learning outcomes, student type, threshold concepts, attrition, metacognition, dissonance, achievement, approaches, perceptions, conceptions, orientations, alienation/ belonging, active learning, self-directed learning, experiential learning, learning journals.
Social: access, mature students	**Social:** access, comparative achievements of conventional/non-traditional students, student experience, gender, mature students, social class, social disadvantage, groupwork	**Social:** mature students, class, gender, social inequality, adult learning, student experience, international students, disability	**Social:** mature students, academic & social integration, diversity, student debt, disabled students, adults, networked learning, web-mediated discussion (socio-culturally appropriate methodologies, university culture, work-related learning, power distance, complexity, uncertainty)

Figure 3.2 Comparison of Broad Theoretical Shifts in Psychology, Sociology and Higher Education Research through Four Decades.

though a small number of articles reflect an interest in the "minority standpoint epistemologies" of gender, race, sexuality and disability which are developing at this time in sociology (Ball, 2004).

In the 1980s in psychology itself, cognitive and constructivist approaches are developing into a range of social and interactional perspectives, which explore the relationship between individual and "context" in a variety of much more complicated and nuanced ways. Social constructivist approaches in general, and particular socio-cultural approaches such as activity theory, begin to consider the implications of not thinking of the individual as at the centre of all that might be designated "learning". This is a radical conceptual departure which is still almost completely absent in the higher education journals by 2007. In addition, the 1980s sees the development of more politically radical branches of psychology, such as community psychology, which critique and challenge mainstream psychology from a sociological perspective. In sociology, major theoretical work in relation to the relationship between the individual and society is being carried out by theorists such as Giddens, Habermas and Bourdieu, and a range of critical perspectives are being developed from feminist and post-modern positions.

1990s

The relative absence of this more nuanced and critical approach to the theorisation of individual and society continues, although to differing degrees, in the HE journals throughout the 1990s. Apparently largely uninterested in developments in psychology and sociology, *HE* in particular maintains its focus on the more individualistic and static aspects of cognitive psychology, and in this decade significantly increases its coverage of approaches to learning research. Although the other two non-North American journals are slightly more interested in critical and/or social perspectives, these are largely confined to critiquing new teaching methodologies and/or discussing generalised (and often psychologised) notions of gender, class and the student experience (exceptions are one article in *HE* which mentions cultural and social capital, two articles in *SHE* which mention Bourdieu and Freire respectively, and one article in *THE* which mentions post-modernism).

Whilst *HE* is focusing in this decade largely upon developing the concerns it identified in the 1980s (with limited critique of such concerns), the fields of psychology and sociology are witnessing the emergence of additional new theoretical developments. Resulting partly from increasingly cross-disciplinary flows of critique and ideas, these developments arguably have the potential to reframe the very foundations of the social sciences, and to liberate research thinking in hitherto unimaginable directions. In developmental psychology, for example, ideas from ecological and dynamic systems theories begin to create a range of fluid, dynamic and de-centred notions of self and society. In sociology, actor network theory creates new possibilities for a simultaneous framing of the social, biological and technological in networked relations through time, while complexity theory offers a radically contingent and dynamic perspective from which to consider the emergence of adaptive specificity and difference across a range of disciplines.

2000s

As these new perspectives in psychology and sociology are continuing to develop throughout the 2000s, the higher education journals apparently show little awareness of their existence. There is not yet even much discussion of theorists such as Habermas and Bourdieu and, in *HE* and *SHE*, there is a very limited amount of self-referential critique. *THE* is the journal most influenced by critical perspectives in sociology, but it too shows little sign of any interest in the ecological, dynamic systems and network theorisations occurring in other fields. In all of the journals there is some discussion of networks in relation to web-based and online learning, but this review of titles, at least, gives no indication of any of the radical questioning of conventional epistemologies and ontologies which is being explored in other disciplines.

Compared to other disciplines over this period, then, when it comes to discussions about learning (with some notable exceptions; see for example Webb, 1997; Terenzini, 1999; Mann, 2001), it can be seen that the higher education journals, and *HE* in particular, focus on a very narrow range of possible perspectives and methodologies. These are not only narrow in the sense that they are restricted to a predominantly psychological approach to learning (Malcolm & Zukas, 2001), but also narrow in terms of the field of psychology itself. Even in the 2000s, a great deal of discussion about learning in higher education is still focused upon the same basic questions that arose in the 1970s; "what can we discover about how individuals learn?", "what are the implications of our knowledge about individual learning for classroom teaching and curriculum design?", and "what is going on outside the classroom which might impact upon learning outcomes?". *THE* is the only journal which regularly explores questions such as "what is the effect of particular types of language use in relation to student learning outcomes?", or "how does the way we speak, and what we ask students to write, create impediments to students' learning?" in any detail. Thus, *HE*, and to a lesser extent also *SHE* (the two most prestigious non-North American journals), are usually at least one, and sometimes two, decades behind research in the two fields which have most directly informed the development of educational theory.

This lack, or, in the case of *SHE* and *THE*, relatively late, engagement with critical and social perspectives in the mainstream higher education journals does not, however, mean that no critical or social research has been carried out in the context of higher education. Relevant and challenging work has been taking place in two other disciplinary areas, those of adult education and sociolinguistics. Researchers in these fields do occasionally publish in higher education journals (see, for example, Boud & Lee, 2005; Lillis & Turner, 2001), but in the main this work has been published in the specialist journals of each field.

Adult Education

A comparison of the review of higher education journals with the leading UK-based journal in the field of adult education, *Studies in the Education of Adults (SEA)*, for the 2000s shows that *SEA* is dominated by the perspectives that are relatively limited in the higher education journals (see Figure 3.3). Although UK-based, this journal represents perspectives of North American, European, South African and Australasian researchers, as well as writers from the UK.

Adult education has been much more influenced throughout the decades by the changes and shifts in the wider intellectual worlds of the social sciences and the humanities. For example, in the 1970s and 1980s, when humanistic psychology is developing in psychology, adult learning theory begins to experiment with a wide range of ideas from humanism (e.g. self-actualisation, facilitation, self-direction, experience, reflection). The reflexive critique, which can be seen in the 1970s in fields such as sociology, begins to affect adult education by the 1980s, as researchers such as Brookfield (1993) and Boud (1990) bring critical reflexivity to bear not only on new teaching ideas and methodologies, but also on the field of adult education itself. By the 1990s, when the two main higher education journals are only just beginning to develop critical perspectives, adult education is critiquing every one of its central concepts, including the "adult" in adult education, and the policy contexts (such as "lifelong learning") within which its activities are embedded. At this time, adult education is also engaging with a range of issues related to learning for and in work, and drawing upon a range of socio-cultural and post-modern/post-structural theories.

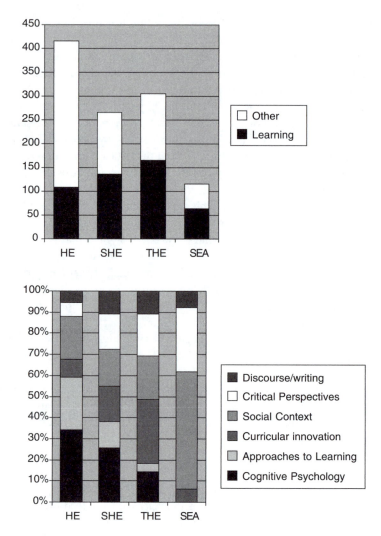

Figure 3.3 Comparative Balance of Article Focus in Three Leading Higher Education Journals and the Leading Adult Education Journal (2000s).

By the 2000s, adult educators have been critiquing their own field from Marxist/neo-Marxist, post-modern/post-structural and feminist perspectives for a number of decades. In contrast to *HE*'s apparent ongoing attempt to establish a robust, "evidence-based" theory of individual learning, in adult education the influence of post-modernism/post-structuralism and critical theory is by now raising questions about the nature of knowledge, and considering the implications of seeing knowledge itself as de-centred, contingent, distributed and social. A comparison of article titles focused on learning in the most recent volumes of *SHE* and *SEA* available online at the time of writing gives an indication of the differing content of these two journals today (see Figure 3.4).

Sociolinguistics

The discourse/genre work arising out of the second area, sociolinguistics, is grounded in the tradition of new literacy studies (Thesen & van Pletzen, 2006), exemplified by the work of Barton,

| *Studies in Higher Education* Vol 32 2007 | *Studies in the Education of Adults* Vol 38 2006 |

1

- Using concept maps to measure deep, surface and non-learning outcomes
- The interplay of perceptions of the learning environment, personality and learning strategies: a study amongst International Business Studies students
- Not belonging? What makes a functional learner identity in undergraduate mathematics?
- Identity and placement learning: student accounts of the transition back to university following a placement year

2

- Student approaches to achieving understanding—approaches to learning revisited

3

- Student conceptions of oral presentations
- Approaches to learning, course experience and examination grade among undergraduate psychology students: testing of mediator effects and construct validity
- Scaffolding through the network: analysing the promotion of improved online scaffolds among university students

4

- Improving the quality of students' academic writing: an intervention study
- Reading and writing tasks on different university degree courses: what do the students say they do?

1

- Beyond the moorland? Contextualising lifelong learning
- Learning habits and the dynamics of lifelong learning
- From critical vision to critical practice: exploring the process of critical transformational learning among archaeologists
- Consuming metaphors: stimulating questions for everyday learning

2

- Just do it: literacies, everyday learning and the irrelevance of pedagogy
- Adults' use of computers and the Internet for self-education
- Learning in a border country: using psychodynamic ideas in teaching and research
- "Invisible other": understanding safe spaces for queer learners and teachers in adult education

Figure 3.4 Comparative Titles of Articles on Learning in the most Recent Volumes of *SHE* and *SEA* (those available online in August 2007).

Gee, Ivanic and Street (see Barton et al., 2000). Arguing for a view of literacy practices as social, context-specific, patterned by power relations, historically situated and dynamic, this work brings together the socio-cultural concerns of contemporary approaches in the social sciences and post-structural/discourse approaches in the humanities. The research from this perspective which focuses specifically on higher education has become known as "academic literacies".

Academic literacies research first starts to make an appearance in the higher education context in the late 1990s, with the publication of an article by Lea & Street in *SHE*, and the books *Student Writing in Higher Education* (Lea & Stierer) in 2000, and *Student Writing* (Lillis) in 2001. As far as can be seen from the review of titles, *HE* publishes no research related to this tradition, with the exception of a very interesting article by Francis and Hallam in 2000, and Mann's (2000) paper on the student experience of reading. *SHE* publishes a very small number of articles in the following years; notably Francis et al. in 2001, and Robson et al., and Lea, in 2004. *THE*, on the other hand, publishes a range of articles taking an academic literacies approach, focusing on issues such as critical approaches to text, and the analysis of communication and discourse.

Despite its extraordinary relevance for developing a wider range of understandings of teaching and learning, and, even more importantly, as a source of potentially generative/transformative critique of higher education cultures and practices, most academic literacies research is not published in the main higher education journals being examined here. Whilst some academic literacy researchers are on the editorial boards or review for *SHE* and *THE*, most of their work is not published in these journals, with the result that staff in higher education who might benefit from this work are very likely not aware that it exists. They will probably never see, for example, the special issue of the *Journal of Applied Linguistics* which came out in 2007, or the recent work in South Africa collected together in Thesen and van Pletzen (2006).

Looking to the Future

The results of the survey of higher education journal titles undertaken in this study appear to support the claim that approaches to learning research, as a sub-set of cognitive psychological learning theory, has dominated non-North American higher education contexts until very recently. Whilst acknowledging the enormous importance and impact of this approach to the study of student learning, it has been suggested that this focus has been developed at the expense of a range of other approaches to research which potentially have a great deal to contribute to the many research questions generated by contemporary higher education contexts.

As well as the academic literacy work discussed above, adult education research has a long history of debate around the "new" teaching technologies which are currently being adopted by higher education (e.g. self-directed learning, experiential learning, learning contracts and individual learner profiling). It also has a long history of engagement with workplace and work-based learning, and learning for work, which could provide a wealth of research and practice-based perspectives on the issues becoming of concern to higher education, in relation to the increasingly work-focused agenda which is being imposed on the sector. In relation to these wider contexts and purposes, the North American research potentially also has much to offer in terms of understanding the challenges created by more recent shifts in other areas of the world towards mass higher education systems.

In relation to research in other fields, currently "missing" perspectives from sociology and psychology have the potential to open up new ways of thinking about learning in higher education. Although some writers have begun to engage with sociological and critical theory (see Archer et al., 2003; McLean, 2006), higher education overall has barely begun to grapple with the implications of shifting from an individual to a social approach to learning. This means that it has not yet begun to engage with the problems and limitations of "social" perspectives such as those represented by theorists such as Habermas and Bourdieu. Socio-cultural learning theories such as situated learning (Lave & Wenger, 1991) and activity theory (Engeström, 1987) have had even less influence on theorising learning in higher education to date.

As higher education begins to engage with the "social" perspectives listed above, a considerable amount of theorising in sociology and psychology is already leaving such approaches far behind. Post-modern and post-structuralist perspectives point to issues of diversity, particularity and connectivity; but these issues are also emerging as important from a much wider range of areas. Fields as far apart as evolutionary biology, artificial intelligence, environmental planning and public health have long been engaging with a range of ecological and dynamic perspectives, which have profound implications for educational theory and research (see, for example, Bosma & Kunnan, 2001, and Fogel et al., 1997, in psychology, or Davis & Sumara, 2006, in education).

In relation to these perspectives, there are many aspects of learning that are still not well understood, and which the currently dominant ontologies and epistemologies struggle to investigate and represent (see Haggis, 2008). For example, research into learning is still not able to deal well with "the fleeting", "the distributed", "the multiple" and "the complex" (Law & Urry, 2003: 10):

> Processes constitute the world of human experience—from nature to social reality to cognition itself. However, by and large, the centrality of processes does not appear to be reflected in theoretical descriptions of nature and the human domain (Seibt, 2003: vii).

As far as I am aware, there is as yet very little research that attempts to document different types of dynamic interaction and process through time in relation to "learning" situations in higher education. For example, there are very few ethnographies (for an important exception, see Nespor, 1994), although academic literacies research has begun one strand of work from this perspective.

References

Archer, L., Hutchings, M. and Ross, A. (2003). *Higher Education and Social Class*. London: Routledge.
Ball, S. (ed.) (2004). *The RoutledgeFalmer Reader in Sociology of Education*. London: Routledge.
Barton, D., Hamilton, M. and Ivanic, R. (2000). *Situated Literacies: Reading and writing in context*. London: Routledge.
Bosma, H. and Kunnan, E.S. (eds) (2001). *Identity and Emotion*. Cambridge: Cambridge University Press.
Boud, D. (1990). Assessment and the promotion of academic values. *Studies in Higher Education, 15*(1), 101–111.
Boud, D. and Lee, A. (2005). "Peer learning" as pedagogic discourse for research education. *Studies in Higher Education, 30*(5), 501–516.
Brookfield, S. (1993). Self-Directed Learning, Political Clarity and the Critical Practice of Adult Education. *Adult Education Quarterly, 43*(4), pp. 227–242.
Davis, B. and Sumara, D. (2006). *Complexity and Education*. Mahwah, NJ: Lawrence Erlbaum Associates.
Engeström, Y. (1987). *Learning by expanding: an activity-theoretical approach to developmental research*. Helskinki: Orienta-Konsultit.
Fogel, A., Lyra, M. and Valsiner, J. (1997). *Dynamics and Indeterminism in Developmental and Social Processes*. Mahwah, NJ: Lawrence Erlbaum Associates.
Francis, B., Robson, J. and Read, B. (2001). An Analysis of Undergraduate Writing Styles in the Context of Gender and Achievement. *Studies in Higher Education, 26*(3), 313–326.
Francis, H. and Hallam, S. (2000). Genre effects on higher education students' text reading for understanding. *Higher Education, 39*, 279–296.
Haggis, T. (2003). Constructing images of ourselves? A critical investigation into "approaches to learning" research in higher education. *British Educational Research Journal, 29*(1), 89–104.
Haggis, T. (2008). "Knowledge must be contextual": exploring some possible implications of complexity and dynamic systems theories for educational research. *Educational Philosophy and Theory, 40*(1).
Lave, J. and Wenger, E. (1991). *Situated Learning*. Cambridge: Cambridge University Press.
Law, J. and Urry, J. (2003). *Enacting the Social*. Lancaster, Department of Sociology and the Centre for Science Studies, Lancaster University. Available at: http://www.lancs.ac.uk/fass/sociology/papers/law-urry-enacting-the-social.pdf
Lea, M. (2004). Academic literacies: a pedagogy for course design. *Studies in Higher Education, 29*(6), 739–756
Lea, M. and Stierer, B. (2000). *Student Writing in Higher Education*. Buckingham: Open University Press
Lillis, T. (2001). *Student Writing: Access, regulation and desire*. London: Routledge.
Lillis, T. and Turner, J. (2001). Student Writing in Higher Education: contemporary confusion, traditional concerns. *Teaching in Higher Education, 6*(1), 57–68.
Malcolm, J. and Zukas, M. (2001). Bridging pedagogic gaps: conceptual discontinuities in higher education, *Teaching in Higher Education, 6*, 33–42.
Mann, S. (2000). The students' experience of reading. *Higher Education, 39*(3), 297–317.
Mann, S. (2001). Alternative perspectives on the student experience: alienation and engagement. *Studies in Higher Education, 26*, 7–19.
McLean, M. (2006). *Pedagogy and the University: Critical theory and practice*. London: Continuum.
Nespor, J. (1994). *Knowledge in Motion: Space, time and curriculum in undergraduate physics and management*. London: Falmer.
Richardson, J. (2000). *Researching student learning*. Buckingham: Open University Press.
Robson, J., Francis, B. and Read, B. (2004). Gender, student confidence and communicative styles at university: the views of lecturers in history and psychology. *Studies in Higher Education, 29*(1), 7–23.
Seibt, J. (ed.) (2003). *Process Theories: Cross-disciplinary studies in dynamic categories*. London: Kluwer.
Terenzini, P. (1999) Research and practice in undergraduate education: And never the twain shall meet? *Higher Education, 38*(1), 33–48.
Thesen, L. and van Pletzen, E. (2006). *Academic Literacy and the Languages of Change*. London: Continuum.
Tight, M. (2007). Bridging the Divide: A comparative analysis of articles in higher education journals published inside and outside North America. *Higher Education, 53*(2), 235–253.
Webb, G. (1997). Deconstructing deep and surface: towards a critique of phenomenography. *Higher Education, 33*, 195–212.

4

Conceptualising Teaching and Learning Interactions in Researching Higher Education

Paul Ashwin

Fortunately most educational situations are interactive situations in which a developing, learning human being engages with a situation in ways designed to meet his [or her] learning needs. Part of that situation is another human being who has some resources for instruction and some capacity to adapt to the learner. It is this that makes education both endlessly challenging and deeply humane (McKeachie 1975, p. 49).

Introduction

I came across the above quote in "How Students Learn", a collection of readings put together in the mid-1970s to provide an introduction to theories of learning for those interested in examining teaching and learning in higher education. As the quote illustrates, what makes educational inter-actions so fascinating and complex is their interactional nature, the way in which academics and students respond to each other in teaching and learning situations, and the impact this has on students' engagement with the ideas they are encountering.

The focus of this chapter is on how to conceptualise such interactions between academics and students when researching teaching and learning in higher education. I will argue that whilst in school-based research there is a body of research that seeks to examine the ways in which knowledge is shared in classroom settings (van der Aalsvoort and Harinck 2000), within higher education there has been relatively little discussion of how to conceptualise the interactive nature of teaching and learning situations.

"Mainstream" Approaches to Researching Learning and Teaching in Higher Education

Within research into learning and teaching in higher education, there are two mainstream approaches to conceptualising the teaching and learning processes. These have both been examined in earlier chapters: the approaches to learning and teaching perspective, which was the focus of the chapter by Case and Marshall, and the social practice perspective, which would include the "academic literacies" approach discussed by Haggis in her chapter.

Both of these approaches have made a significant contribution to our understanding of teaching and learning processes within higher education. The approaches to learning and teaching research (for excellent summaries see Prosser and Trigwell 1999; Richardson 2005; Entwistle 2007) has given a clear indication of how students' and academics' perceptions of the teaching and learning environment are consistently related to the quality of their learning and teaching, and to the quality of students' learning outcomes. Research from a social practice perspective has provided insights into the issues that students face in understanding the cultural context of their programmes (Lea and Street 1998; Jones *et al.*, 1999; Mann 2000; Lillis 2001), and the impact that institutional and disciplinary contexts have on academics' understanding of their teaching (Trowler and Cooper 2002).

However, these approaches are less helpful for conceptualising what occurs in teaching and learning interactions involving students and academics. Within the approaches to learning and teaching perspective, the focus is on students' and academics' *perceptions* of the teaching and learning process. As such, this research views teaching and learning interactions from the perspective of academics and students and there is little sense of the way in which academics and students impact on each other in a particular interaction. As a result, when the relations between academics' approaches to teaching and students' approaches to learning are examined, they are linked in a fairly distant manner, largely through the examination of the relation between students' and academics' scores on questionnaire inventories (Trigwell *et al.*, 1999; Vermunt and Verloop 1999). Thus, whilst the separation of the perceptions of academics and students has been important in correcting the assumption that because an academic is teaching their students are learning, it is less helpful when trying to conceptualise the teaching and learning situations as dynamic and interactive processes, in which academics and students have an ongoing but shifting impact on each other.

Within social practice approaches to researching learning and teaching in higher education, research tends to focus on learning practices or the practice of students (Lea and Street 1998; Mann 2000; Lillis 2001), or teaching practices or the practice of teachers (Trowler and Cooper 2002). This approach has again been important in demonstrating that students can have very different experiences of the cultures of higher education institutions, and that these experiences are very different from the experiences of their academic teachers. However, when one is trying to understand the way in which academics and students interact in teaching and learning situations, this approach again becomes problematic. This is for two reasons. First, when foregrounding social practices it becomes clear that academics and students are engaging in different types of practices. Whilst an academic might be involved in the practices involved in the designing a module, setting the assessment and marking the assessment, students on that module might be engaged in practices related to particular learning tasks, and to preparing their assessed work. Thus, the language of practices *tends* to lead to a primary focus on academics *or* students. Second, social practices are seen to be fairly durable ways of approaching particular tasks that are largely taken for granted by those who engage in them (Trowler 2005). This means that, in foregrounding social practices, there does not tend to be a focus on how the practices of students and academics impact on each other, and play out in distinctive ways in particular social interactions.

It is in this way that I am arguing that both of these ways of conceptualising teaching and learning processes are not particularly helpful in thinking about teaching and learning interactions in higher education. This is because conceptualising teaching and learning interactions in terms of "perceptions" or "practices" has the unintended consequence of separating academics and students within teaching and learning interactions. This leads to the tacit assumption that, within such interactions, academics teach and assess, whilst students learn and are assessed, which has the effect of splitting a single social process into four pedagogic roles. In this way, both of these ways of conceptualising learning and teaching in higher education tend to underplay the interactive processes in which students and academics have an ongoing impact on how a particular teaching and learning interaction develops and tend to produce static accounts of the teaching and learning process.

Alternative Ways of Conceptualising Teaching and Learning Interactions

So far in this chapter I have sought to show that it is important to find ways of conceptualising teaching and learning interactions in higher education. In the rest of this chapter I examine two: symbolic interactionism and activity theory. I selected these approaches because they both foreground the interaction between people within social encounters. Neither are commonly used to frame research into teaching and learning in higher education, but have been used in other areas of educational research to examine issues relating to teaching and learning. Symbolic interactionism was popular in research in compulsory education, particularly in the 1980s (Woods 1983), with activity theory being more commonly used in work-based contexts (for example, see Engeström 2001). I argue that each of these approaches offer insights into different aspects of the teaching and learning interaction.

It should be noted that, whilst both of these approaches offer a way of foregrounding teaching and learning interactions, neither take a position that everything that matters within a teaching and learning interaction is contained within the interaction. In different ways both approaches show how the meanings of teaching and learning interactions are the product of processes that occur outside of the immediate context of the interaction. It is important to emphasise this point, because a focus on teaching and learning interactions, and face-to-face interactions more generally, is sometimes criticised for naively assuming that everything that matters in social interactions is contained and generated within the local context of the interaction (for criticisms of this nature see, for example, Bourdieu 1977 and, from a actor network perspective, Nespor 1994; Latour 2005).

Symbolic Interactionism

Symbolic interactionism as an approach to researching social interactions rests on three assumptions (Blumer 1969, p. 2):

1. Human beings act towards things on the basis of the meanings that the things have for them.
2. The meanings of things arise out of the process of social interaction.
3. These meanings are modified through an interpretative process which involves self-reflective individuals symbolically interacting with one another.

Applying these assumptions to teaching and learning situations in higher education, the first assumption suggests that, within teaching and learning interactions within higher education, students and academics engage in these interactions on the basis of the meanings these interactions and the material under discussion have for them. This initial point is already recognised in the approaches to learning and social practices perspectives, which have examined the meaning of particular academic tasks for students and academics (Hounsell 1997; Mann 2000; Read *et al.*, 2001; Ashwin 2005, 2006). The second assumption situates the origins of these meanings within social interactions, and this is again generally recognised by mainstream approaches to researching learning and teaching in higher education. However, it is the third assumption, which emphasises the *changing* nature of these meanings *within* interactions that is not examined within these perspectives. It is perhaps worth noting that, as well as a conceptual issue, this is partly a methodological issue. Tight's (2003) analyses of research into higher education published in 2000 suggests that the vast majority of research into learning and teaching in higher education is based on data generated through the use of interviews or questionnaires. Given that such studies provide accounts generated outside of the immediacy of teaching and learning interactions, it is perhaps not surprising that the dynamic, shifting nature of such interactions is not focused upon. However, given symbolic interactionism's emphasis on the *meaning* of social interactions, it cannot be assumed that, on its own, observation of teaching and learning interactions provides a ready-made methodological solution to this issue.

As a research approach, symbolic interactionism is based on the US pragmatism of Dewey and Mead (Denzin 1992). Symbolic interactionism developed differently in the US and UK, and, as Atkinson and Housley (2003) show, there were also different paths of development within the UK. My comments will focus on how symbolic interactionism developed in studying UK schools, where it was closely bound up with the development of ethnography (Delamont 1983; Woods 1983, 1996; Hammersley 1999), and, to a lesser extent, further education (Bloomer 2001).

Woods (1983, pp. 5–15) identifies six "focusing concepts" of symbolic interactionism in relation to school education. The first is the idea that schools are made up of a number of *contexts* and situations, and pupils and teachers have different interpretations of these contexts. The second is that, through their *perspectives*, pupils and teachers make sense of these contexts and thus define and construct their social worlds. Third, these perspectives are derived from the pupil and teacher *cultures* that pupils and teachers construct in schools. Fourth, drawing on their perspectives and their reading of the constraints of the contexts and cultures of the school, pupils and teachers develop *strategies* to "cope" with the situation as they perceive it. The strategies of teachers and pupils are brought together through the concept of *negotiation*, which is focused on how pupil and teacher strategies interact, define and redefine the social interaction in the classroom. Finally, over time, pupils and teachers develop *careers*, which are understood as the changing perspective through which they make sense of their "selves" as a whole, that is how they understand their changing identities, within the context of the school, at a particular point in time.

The strength of symbolic interactionism as an approach to researching teaching and learning interactions in schools has been the way that it has contributed to an understanding of how such interactions are partially the product of the careers that teachers and pupils develop in response to the school environment. So, for example, in the edited collections of Woods (1980a; 1980b) and the work of Hargreaves (1972), Delamont (1983), Woods (1983) and Pollard (1982; 1985), a strong sense is given of pupils and teachers developing their identities in relation to their individual careers, and the pupil and teacher cultures of the school; and of the way that teachers and pupils negotiate a "working consensus" of the classroom, which allows teacher and pupils "to cope" with the classroom situation.

Symbolic interactionism studies give a strong sense of how the establishment of a particular classroom consensus might lead to a context in which pupils are more or less likely to be able to focus on the academic elements of their school work (for example, see Pollard 1985). They also can provide a sense of how the development of students' learning careers can impact on the way in which they approach the "learning opportunities" available to them in educational contexts (for example, see Bloomer 1997, 2001; Bloomer and Hodkinson 2000; Bloomer *et al.*, 2004). These accounts give a strong sense of the impact of, for example, social class on the ways in which pupils and teachers negotiate together, and the ways in which students' learning careers develop.

Where symbolic interactionism is less helpful is in understanding teaching and learning interactions *as teaching and learning interactions*. That is to say, whilst there is a convincing account given of how particular situations or learning careers might make pupil/student learning more or less likely, there is not a strong sense given of how particular interactions between teachers and pupils might enable pupils to develop a deeper understanding of the concepts that they are studying, and might also change teachers' understanding of these concepts. Rather the focus is on how pupils and teachers maintain and develop their careers in relation to the contexts and constraints that they experience.

To put this argument into the context of teaching and learning in higher education, symbolic interactionism is helpful in understanding how students and academics negotiate the meaning of particular teaching and learning interactions, and how such negotiations are informed by the careers of academics and students. However, it does not appear to be helpful in understanding how teaching and learning interactions can facilitate students' critical engagement with the discipline(s) they are studying in higher education, and how this might lead to changes in academics' understanding of these disciplines. One of the very few recent studies into teaching and learning in higher education adopting an interactionist perspective illustrates this point nicely. Fejes *et al.*, (2005) give a strong sense of how students and academics negotiate the function of the higher education seminar, but it is again unclear how interactions between academics and students might contribute to students' understanding of their discipline, or to a change in academics' understanding.

Activity Theory

The second approach for examining teaching and learning interactions that I examine is Engeström's (2001) version of activity theory. Whilst I argued that symbolic interactionism ended up losing a sense of teaching and learning interactions *as teaching and learning interactions*, Engeström explicitly situates activity theory as a way of understanding the way in which people learn in particular situations.

Engeström sees his work as part of the third generation of activity theory. The first generation, of which Vygotsky's work was the most significant, focused on the way in which tools or artefacts mediated the relation between subjects and objects—that is, the way in which people use tools to achieve their ends, and the way in which these tools impact on the consciousness of the people who used them. Thus, language is a tool that we can use to express ourselves, but it also shapes the terms in which we can talk and think. The second generation of activity theory Engeström situates in the work of Leont'ev (1978). For Engeström, Leont'ev placed Vygotsky's ideas in a collective context by distinguishing between "action" and "activity". Activity describes how people engage in collective tasks, with an intention that goes beyond the object of individual actions. The example Leonte'v uses is of going fishing, where the overall objective of the collective activity is to get food, but the individual actions of, for example, preparing the equipment in order to catch the fish are not directly related to getting food.

Figure 4.1 shows Engeström's diagrammatic representation of Leont'ev's ideas. In this diagram, the subject, mediating artefact, object triangle of Vygotsky is placed in the wider context of the rules, community and division of labour of the activity on which the subject is focused. Engeström (1996, p.67) explains the diagram in the following way:

The *subject* refers to the individual or subgroup whose agency is chosen as the point of view in the analysis. The *object* refers to the "raw material" or "problem space" at which the activity is directed and which is molded or transformed into *outcomes* with the help of physical and symbolic, external or internal *tools* (mediating instruments and signs). The *community* comprises multiple individuals and/or subgroups who share the same general object. The *division of labor* refers to both the horizontal division of tasks between members of the community and to the vertical division of power and status. Finally, the *rules* refer to the explicit and implicit regulations, norms and conventions that constrain actions and interactions within

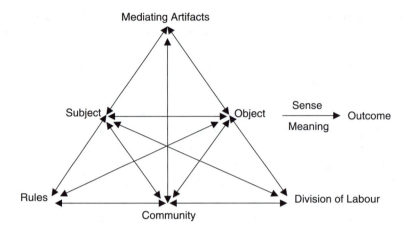

Figure 4.1 An Activity System (Engeström 2001).

the activity system. Between the components of an activity system, continuous construction is going on. (eg. agents modify tools, rules etc).

The third generation of activity theory, where Engeström situates his work, focuses on a minimum of two interacting activity systems. This focus emphasises the multi-voiced nature of activity. For example, Engeström (2001) reports on a project that was focused on getting greater understanding between the activity systems of hospital physicians, general practitioners and patients' families. In focusing on two or more activity systems interacting together, he argues that the objects of the activities system can change and lead to "expansive learning".

In summary, although—as is inevitable in developing a theory—Engeström's view of the crucial aspects of an activity system has changed (cf. Engeström 1987; 1996; 1999; 2001), the key aspects of his view of activity theory can be summarised as:

- The activity system as a whole should be taken as the unit of analysis. In doing so there is a rejection of the separation of individual perception and situated action from the system.
- Activity systems take shape and are formed over a lengthy period of time. Thus they have a history that shapes the way the activity is organised.
- Because they are collective, activity systems are made up of a multitude of voices and perspectives that can be in conflict with each other.
- Activity systems develop and change through contradictions within a particular activity system and between activity systems.
- These contradictions can be collectively harnessed by those within an activity system in order to generate expansive learning, and this can be encouraged by a developmental research agenda.

In applying activity theory to teaching and learning interactions in higher education, I argue that it is through a focus on the interacting activity systems of students and academics that activity theory offers a way of conceptualising the learning that takes place within educational interactions.

Although some studies have examined how academics move between different activity systems of their professional development and their teaching (see Fanghanel 2004; Knight *et al.*, 2006), in applying the ideas of activity theory to teaching and learning in higher education, it appears, in contrast to Engeström's work, to be common practice to conceptualise the degree programme or course as a single activity system (for example, Barab *et al.*, 2002; Coupland and Crawford 2002; Russell 2002; Berglund 2004; Havnes 2004). However, in a similar way to my argument in relation to social practices, within teaching and learning interactions it is not clear that students and academics are part of the same activity system. For example, it is not clear that students and academics have the same "object" in teaching and learning interactions, or that their activities are carried out in relation to the same community. Academics' activity is likely to be situated in the community of the rest of their department or disciplinary group (Henkel 2000), whilst the relevant community for students might consist of other students (Solomon 2007) and, possibly, other friends or members of their family. Given this, it would seem to make more sense to see student and academics as part of two different activity systems, with slightly different objects, mediating artefacts, communities, divisions of labour and rules. Gutiérrez *et al.*, (1999) have used such an approach to examine how local and official knowledge discourses in schools can lead to expansive learning.

Figure 4.2 attempts to illustrate how this might be applied to teaching and learning interactions in higher education. It shows the activity systems of an academic and a student, and shows how the activities of academics and students within teaching and learning interactions might involve different mediating artefacts, draw up different rules, be situated with reference to different communities and involve a different division of labour. Crucially, it demonstrates that the object of the interaction may be different for the academic and for the student (the shaded ovals of "learning object" and "teaching object"). As the student and academic engage in the teaching and learning interaction, their view of what the object of their interaction is then changes (learning object$_1$ and teaching object$_1$). This might involve the development of a shared object (object$_3$). Thus, this way of conceptualising teaching and learning interactions offers a way of thinking about students and academics as part of different activity systems, and illustrates how they might impact on each other's understanding of their discipline(s).

Although this is not the theoretical perspective that informs their research, this approach offers a way of conceptualising the processes examined in the "Production of University English" research project (Jones *et al.*, 2005; Bruce *et al.*, 2007). The accounts of the interactions between academics and students in these studies focus on how academics "reframe" students' contributions to discussion in terms of debates and critical issues in the discipline and, in doing so, they discuss the different roles of the students and academics in these discussions. Jones *et al.*, (2005, p. 258) examine how in an assignment brief on one module: "borders are crossed between academic and non-academic writing, between the seminar room and the world outside, and between different student identities." The notion of interacting activity systems seems to provide a framework in which to understand these processes, and how students and academics come together from distinctive positions in order to "produce" English as a discipline in a particular seminar encounter. In this way, activity theory can give a better sense than symbolic interactionism of how these interactions can

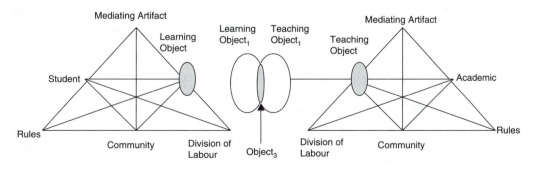

Figure 4.2 The Interacting Activity Systems of Students and Academics (after Engeström 2001).

lead to learning, in terms of a change in the ways that both academics and students might think about how a particular text relates to the debates and controversies within English as a discipline.

However, whilst activity theory casts light on how teaching and learning interactions can lead to learning for both students and academics, it is less helpful in relating this learning to student and academic identities or "careers". In discussing Figure 4.2, I focused on a generic individual student, but it was not clear whether this was an activity system for all students in a particular interaction, or whether each student was part of a different activity system. Similarly, although Engeström (2001) emphasises the multi-voicedness of activity systems, in practice the "subject" element of an activity system is denoted by a role such as "general practitioner", "hospital practitioner" or "parent" (Engeström 1995, 2001). This means that unlike symbolic interactionism, there is little sense of how the careers of particular students and academics shape, and are shaped by, teaching and learning interactions, and how these careers influence the way in which students and academics interpret their roles. Thus, within an activity theory perspective, whilst there is a clearer sense of how the interaction might lead academics and students to reinterpret the ideas they are discussing, there is less of a sense of how they negotiate the social interaction, and how this is informed by, and informs, their institutional careers.

Conclusions

We have seen that, in the two approaches to conceptualising teaching and learning interactions, symbolic interactionism foregrounds issues of how academics' and students' careers interact with their context, in order to lead to particular strategies being developed within teaching and learning interactions. However, whilst symbolic interactionism offers a strong sense of how these strategies played out in the social aspects of the situation, it can be difficult to get a sense of the situation as an interaction that leads to changes in the way that academics and students understand their disciplines. With activity theory, there is more of a focus on how the interactions between academics and students can lead to disciplinary learning, but the processes by which careers of academics and students affect, and are affected by, the interaction are very much in the background.

In conclusion, I do not want to argue that we should find a way to *combine* the insights of symbolic interactionism and activity theory into a single approach in order to be able to account for different aspects of teaching and learning interactions in higher education. This would be to over-simplify a complex interaction. Rather, I want to argue that we need to respect the complex nature of teaching and learning processes. Within research into teaching and learning in higher education, we can understand teaching and learning situations in many ways, but we need to adopt different approaches to understanding different aspects of the teaching and learning process. Thus, if we wish to foreground how students and academics approach their learning and teaching, and how this relates to students' learning outcomes, then we might adopt an approaches to learning perspective. If we are interested in foregrounding the ways in which different practices of students and academics are informed by their institutional and disciplinary settings, then we might adopt a social practice approach. Symbolic interactionism seems to provide a powerful way of foregrounding the careers of academics and students, and how these inform, and are informed by, teaching and learning interactions, whilst activity theory provides a sense of how teaching and learning interactions can change students' and academics' understanding of disciplinary knowledge.

This is not intended to be an exhaustive list; there are many other useful approaches. For example, Haggis (2006) argues that complexity theory offers a useful way of understanding students as "dynamic systems", and how their histories and different aspects of their lives impact on their narratives of their experiences in higher education. Hodkinson et al., (2008) draw on Bourdieu's concepts to argue for the notion of "learning cultures" as a way of understanding how students' learning in further education is situated within different institutional and political contexts. However, the point is that no single approach can deal with all of the complexity of teaching and learning processes: some are more useful for asking some questions rather than others because they foreground and background different aspects of teaching and learning processes. Thus, in the two additional examples given, different aspects of the teaching and learning process are put very much in the background. Haggis (2006, p. 12) argues that within her approach, "learning" "seemed to disappear as any kind of recognisable generic entity", whilst, within the approach of Hodkinson *et al.*, (2008), "teaching" is not discussed and learning takes centre stage.

This is not an argument that, in conceptualising teaching and learning processes in higher education, "anything goes". As I have shown, some ways of conceptualising teaching and learning processes are more helpful in understanding particular aspects of these processes than others. Rather it is an argument that we need a range of ways of conceptualising teaching and learning processes if we are to develop a deeper understanding of the complexity of these processes. It is in this way that we might develop a clearer sense of the "deeply humane" nature of teaching and learning interactions.

References

van der Aalsvoort, G. and Harinck, F. (2000). Studying social interaction in instruction and learning: methodological approaches and problems. In H. Cowie and G. van der Aalsvoort (eds) *Social Interaction in Learning and Instruction: The Meaning of Discourse for the Construction of Knowledge*. Amsterdam: Pergamon.

Ashwin, P. (2005). Variation in students' experiences of the Oxford tutorial. *Higher Education, 50,* 631–644.

Ashwin, P. (2006). Variation in academics' accounts of tutorials. *Studies in Higher Education, 31,* 651–665.

Atkinson, P. and Housley, W. (2003). *Interactionism: An Essay in Sociological Amnesia*. London: Sage

Barab, S., Barnett, M., Yamagata-Lynch, L., Squire, K. and Keating, T. (2002). Using activity theory to understand the systemic tensions characterising a technology rich introductory astronomy course. *Mind, Culture, and Activity, 9*(2), 76–107.

Berglund, A. (2004). A framework to study learning in a complex learning environment. *ALT-J, 12*(1), 65–79.

Bloomer, M. (1997). *Curriculum Making in Post-16 Education: The Social Conditions of Studentship*. London: Routledge.

Bloomer, M. (2001). Young lives, learning and transformation: some theoretical considerations. *Oxford Review of Education, 27*(1), 429–449.

Bloomer, M. and Hodkinson, P. (2000). Learning careers: continuity and change in young people's dispositions to learning. *British Educational Research Journal, 26*(5), 583–597.

Bloomer, M. Hodkinson, P. and Billet, S. (2004). The significance of ontogeny and habitus in constructing theories of learning. *Studies in Continuing Education, 26*(1), 19–43.

Blumer, H. (1969). *Symbolic Interactionism: Perspective and method*. Berkeley, CA: University of California Press.

Bourdieu, P. (1977). *Outline of a Theory of Practice*. Translated by R. Nice. Cambridge: Cambridge University Press.

Bruce, S., Jones, K. and McLean, M. (2007). Some notes on a project: democracy and authority in the production of a discipline. *Pedagogy: Critical Approaches to Teaching Literature, Language, Composition, and Culture, 7*(3), 481–500.

Coupland, M. and Crawford, K. (2002). Researching complex systems of activity. Paper presented at the *European Association for Research into Learning and Instruction, SIG 10, Current Issues in Phenomenography*, Canberra, Australia. Available online: http://www.anu.edu.au/cedam/ilearn/symposium/Coupland.doc (accessed on 24 August 2007).

Delamont, S. (1983). *Interaction in the Classroom*. 2nd edn. London: Methuen.

Denzin, N. (1992). *Symbolic Interactionism and Cultural Studies: The politics of interpretation*. Oxford: Blackwell.

Engeström, Y. (1987). *Learning by Expanding: An activity-theoretical approach to developmental research*. Available from: http://lchc.ucsd.edu/MCA/Paper/expanding/toc.htm (accessed on 22 August 2007).

Engeström, Y. (1995). Objects, contradictions and collaboration in medical cognition: an activity-theoretical perspective. *Artificial Intelligence in Medicine, 7*: 395–412.

Engeström, Y. (1996). Developmental studies of work as a testbench of activity theory: the case of primary care medical practice. In S. Chaiklin and J. Lave (eds) *Understanding Practice: Perspectives on activity and context*. Cambridge: Cambridge University Press.

Engeström, Y. (1999). *Learning by Expanding: Ten years after*. Introduction to German edition of *Learning by Expanding*. Available from: http://lchc.ucsd.edu/MCA/Paper/Engestrom/expanding/intro.htm (accessed on 22 August 2007).

Engeström, Y. (2001). Expansive learning at work: toward an activity theoretical reconceptualisation. *Journal of Education and Work, 14*(1), 133–156.

Entwistle, N. (2007). Research into student learning and university teaching. In N. Entwistle and P. Tomlinson (eds) *Student Learning and University Teaching*. Leicester: British Psychological Society.

Fanghanel, J. (2004). Capturing dissonance in university teacher education environments. *Studies in Higher Education, 29,* 576–590.

Fejes, A., Johansson, K. and Abrandt, M. (2005). Learning to play the seminar game: students' initial encounters with a basic working form in higher education. *Teaching in Higher Education, 10,* 29–40.

Gutierrez, K., Baquedano-López, P. and Tejeda, C. (1999). Rethinking diversity: hybridity and hybrid language practices in the third space. *Mind, Culture, and Activity, 6,* 286–303.

Haggis, T. (2006). Context, agency and time: looking at learning from the perspective of complexity and dynamic systems theory. Paper presented at Economic and Social Research Council Teaching and Learning Research Programme Thematic Seminar Series: *Contexts, communities, networks; Mobilising learner's resources and relationships in different domains,* University of Stirling, June 2006.

Hammersley, M. (1999). Introduction. In M. Hammersley (ed.) *Researching School Experience: Ethnographic studies of teaching and learning.* London: Falmer Press.

Hargreaves, D. (1972). *Interpersonal Relations and Education.* London: Routledge and Kegan Paul.

Havnes, A. (2004). Examination and learning: an activity-theoretical analysis of the relationship between assessment and educational practice. *Assessment and Evaluation in Higher Education, 29*(2), 159–176.

Henkel, M. (2000). *Academic Identities and Policy Change in Higher Education.* London: Jessica Kingsley Publishers.

Hodkinson, P., Biesta, G. and James, D. (2008). Understanding learning culturally: overcoming the dualism between social and individual views of learning. *Vocations and Learning, 1:* 27–47.

Hounsell, D. (1997). Contrasting conceptions of essay writing. In F. Marton, D. Hounsell and N.J. Entwistle (eds) *The Experience of Learning: Implications for teaching and studying in higher education.* 2nd edn. Edinburgh: Scottish Academic Press (also available at: http://www.tla.ed.ac.uk/resources/EoL.html).

Jones, C., Turner, J. and Street, B.V. (eds) (1999). *Students Writing in the University.* Amsterdam/Philadelphia: John Benjamin's Publishing Company.

Jones, K., McLean, M., Amigoni, D. and Kinsman, M. (2005). Investigating the production of university English in mass higher education: an alternative methodology. *Arts and Humanities in Higher Education, 4,* 247–264.

Knight, P., Tait, J. and Yorke, M. (2006). The professional learning of teachers in higher education. *Studies in Higher Education, 31*(3), 319–339.

Latour, B. (2005). *Reassembling the Social: An introduction to actor-network theory.* Oxford: Oxford University Press.

Lea, M. and Street, B. (1998). Student writing in higher education: an academic literacies approach. *Studies in Higher Education, 23,* 157–172.

Leont'ev, A. (1978). *Activity, Consciousness and Personality.* Englewood Cliffs, NJ: Prentice-Hall. Available at: www.marxists.org/archive/leontev/works/1978/index.htm (accessed on 17 January 2008).

Lillis, T. (2001). *Student Writing: Access, regulation and desire.* London: Routledge.

Mann, S. (2000). The student's experience of reading. *Higher Education, 39,* 297–317.

McKeachie, W. (1975). The decline and fall of laws of learning. In N. Entwistle and D. Hounsell (eds) *How Students Learn.* Lancaster: Institute for Research and Development in Post-Compulsory Education, Lancaster University.

Nespor, J. (1994). *Knowledge in Motion: Space, time and curriculum in undergraduate physics and management.* London: RoutledgeFalmer.

Pollard, A. (1982). A model of classroom coping strategies. *British Journal of Sociology of Education, 3,* 19–37.

Pollard, A. (1985). *The Social World of the Primary School.* London: Cassell Education.

Prosser, M. and Trigwell, K. (1999). *Understanding Learning and Teaching: The experience in higher education.* Buckingham: Open University Press.

Read, B., Francis, B. and Robson, J. (2001). "Playing safe": undergraduate essay writing and the presentation of the student "voice". *British Journal of Sociology of Education, 22*(3), 387–399.

Richardson, J. (2005). Students' approaches to learning and teachers' approaches to teaching in higher education. *Educational Psychology, 25,* 673–680.

Russell, D. (2002). Looking beyond the interface: Activity theory and distributed learning. In M. Lea and Nicoll K. (eds) *Distributed Learning: Social and cultural approaches to learning.* London: RoutledgeFalmer.

Solomon, Y. (2007). Not belonging? What makes a functional learner identity in undergraduate mathematics? *Studies in Higher Education, 32,* 79–96.

Tight, M. (2003). *Researching Higher Education.* Buckingham: Open University Press.

Trigwell, K., Prosser, M. and Waterhouse, F. (1999). Relations between teachers' approaches to teaching and students' approaches to learning. *Higher Education, 37,* 55–70.

Trowler, P. (2005). "A sociology of teaching, learning and enhancement: improving practices in higher education". *Revista de Sociologia, 76:* 13–32.

Trowler, P. and Cooper, A. (2002). Teaching and learning regimes: implicit theories and recurrent practices in the enhancement of teaching and learning through educational development programmes. *Higher Education Research and Development, 21,* 221–240.

Vermunt, J.D. and Verloop, N. (1999). Congruence and friction between learning and teaching. *Learning and Instruction, 9,* 257–280.

Woods, P. (1980a). Strategies in teaching and learning. In P. Woods (ed.) *Teacher Strategies: Explorations in the sociology of the school.* London: Croom Helm.

Woods, P. (1980b). The development of pupil strategies. In P. Woods (ed.) *Pupil Strategies: Explorations in the sociology of the school.* London: Croom Helm.

Woods, P. (1983). *Sociology and the School: An interactionist viewpoint.* London: Routledge and Kegan Paul.

Woods, P. (1996). *Researching the Art of Teaching: Ethnography for educational use.* London: Routledge.

5
International Students from Asia

David Kember

International Students

Governments in developed countries have made commitments to expand university entry to achieve the aim of mass, and eventually universal, higher education (Trow, 2006). However, they have been unwilling to maintain the same levels of per capita funding for the expanded intake. To maintain standards, universities have, therefore, been forced to seek funding from other sources.

One of the most popular has been that of recruiting overseas students, to the extent that many universities in Western countries now have substantial proportions of overseas students, and fees from them have become a major supply of revenue. In 2004 nearly 17% of students in Australia and 13% in the UK were international (Organisation for Economic Co-operation and Development, 2006). The most common source of overseas students has been countries in Asia, which still retain elite higher education systems. These countries have a substantial body of students unable to progress into university. A respect for education commonly results in frustration at the lack of opportunity at home. Buoyant economies in Asia provide both economic incentives to obtain a degree and the means for many to pursue their education overseas.

While the universities are very grateful for the source of finance, teachers have often perceived their Asian students to study in ways they are not used to, and which do not seem ideal for higher education. This chapter reviews work on the approaches to study, motivation and beliefs about learning and knowledge of Asian students. The aim is to help the many teachers who have Asian students in their classes to better understand commonly employed ways of learning and suggest underlying causes. Potential strategies for helping Asian students adapt their learning approaches will also be suggested.

Most of the work in this area has been on Chinese students. In addition, the general literature on the psychology of the Chinese people is more developed than that of other cultures in Asia. There has, though, been sufficient work in other parts of Asia to permit a degree of speculation on the extent to which conclusions can be extrapolated from the research into Chinese students to those from other parts of Asia.

Three caveats should be clearly stated at the outset. Firstly, even if some generalisations can be attempted, students from Asia are not homogenous in their characteristics. There is a rich and complex tapestry of variations arising from cultural distinctions, individual variations and background circumstances. Secondly, neither is there homogeneity within a cultural group. Any apparent differences between cultures are ones of degree, rather than distinctions which can be attributed to each individual within the particular cultural groups. Finally, no attempt is made to generalise to international students from other continents as there is little evidence that the phenomena discussed arise as a result of the students being international. Research into the study approaches of students not from Asia or the West is comparatively restricted, so there is a limited base for extrapolation.

The Paradox of the Chinese Learner

Perhaps the most commonly advanced perception of international Asian students is that they have a greater tendency towards rote learning than their Western counterparts. The observation has been widespread in anecdotal form, but affirmations in print are also quite common. I see no point in extensively reviewing this literature as I intend to draw upon the research which suggests that it is largely a misperception. The following quotation, from the official minutes of a course planning committee in one of the universities in Hong Kong, is sufficient to establish how entrenched negative perceptions of Asian students have been:

> Students in Hong Kong . . . expect lecturers to teach them everything that they are expected to know. They have little desire to discover for themselves or avail themselves of the facilities which are available to them within the teaching institution. They wish to be spoon fed and in turn they are spoon fed. Lecturers are under pressure to feed the student with a certain amount of academic and community needs information and the simplest way to do it . . . is to adopt the old and traditional approaches to teaching (Minutes of the [. . .] Course Planning Committee, 1989, p. 13).

This perception, though, has been seen as an inconsistency which has become known as the "paradox of the Chinese learner" (Watkins and Biggs, 1996). Rote learning is seen as an undesirable approach to learning, which when adopted by Western students has tended to be associated with poor learning outcomes. However, there is abundant evidence from international comparisons of students from Asia performing very well (see Stevenson and Lee, 1996, for a review). For example, the third Programme of International Student Assessment, organised by the Organisation for Economic Co-operation and Development, compared the performance of 15-year-olds in 57 countries and regions (Organisation for Economic Co-operation and Development, 2007). In science and reading, two of the top four spots went to Asian countries, while in mathematics they filled three of the top four places.

The negative perceptions also seem inconsistent with the lengths to which Western universities go to recruit Asian students. While the contribution of their fees to university revenue provides an obvious incentive, if their study approaches really were as impoverished as the above quotation implies, surely the desire to recruit students would have waned over time. Research into the paradox has produced two contributing explanations:

1. Research in Hong Kong and China has uncovered evidence of a set of approaches to learning, intermediate between pure surface and deep approaches, which combine memorisation and understanding. Observations of Asian students apparently attempting to memorise material could have been misinterpreted as rote memorisation, when actually the memorisation was combined with attempts to reach understanding, and was therefore not a surface approach.
2. When Asian students do employ a surface approach, it is likely to be a response to perceptions of contextual factors in the teaching and learning environment, rather than a characteristic of a cultural group or a predominant regional trait.

Approaches to Learning

The original characterisation of approaches to learning was essentially dichotomous. Marton and Säljö (1976) claimed that, when students were asked to read an academic text, they either adopted a deep approach, by trying to understand the underlying meaning intended by the author, or a surface approach, in which superficial features are committed to memory (research on approaches to learning is reviewed in the chapter in this book by Case and Marshall).

Intermediate Approaches to Learning

The characterisation of approaches to learning has been revised following research largely emanating from Hong Kong. Kember and Gow (1989, 1990) compared factor structures of data from questionnaires used to measure approaches to learning with those from elsewhere and interviewed students about their approaches to tackling specific academic tasks. Analysis suggested that memorisation might be occurring in conjunction with attempts to reach understanding in a "narrow approach". Students worked systematically through texts section by section, attempting to understand each new concept, and then commit it to memory, before proceeding to the next. The following quotation, from an interview with a Hong Kong student, illustrates the approach:

> I read in detail section by section. If I find any difficulties I try my best to solve the problem before I go onto the next section. . . . If you don't memorise important ideas when you come across them then you will be stuck when you go on. You must memorise and then go on— understand, memorise and then go on—understand, memorise and then go on. That is my way of studying (Kember and Gow, 1990, p.361).

Other intermediate approaches have subsequently been identified. Marton et al., (1996) reported two combinations of memorising and understanding, one of which took a different form to the narrow approach described above. The two variants were distinguished by whether the attempt to understand came before or after the memorisation. When memorisation came first, it was used as an attempt to reach understanding.

Tang (1993) found variants on a surface approach, in which Hong Kong school students made limited attempts to order or understand material to reduce the memorisation load. The students initially intended to memorise material, but found the memory load became such that some selection was necessary as they progressed through school. Watkins (1996) interpreted interviews with Hong Kong secondary school students as showing that students developed through a sequence of three or four stages. Initially their intention was to achieve through reproduction, by rote-learning everything. The students then passed to the next stage of rote-learning things perceived as more important. In the subsequent developmental stage, the students started to see the benefit of trying to understand material before committing it to memory.

Tang (1991) observed students initially employing a deep approach, by trying to understand concepts, but then committing the material to memory to satisfy assessment requirements. This intermediate approach was used by students who had a preference for seeking understanding, but recognised that their examinations normally required them to reproduce material. They, therefore, tried to understand the concepts, and then made sure the material was learnt so they could get a good grade in the examination.

Kember (1996, 2000a) suggested that the various forms of combining memorisation and understanding meant that approaches to learning might be better characterised as a continuum rather than the dichotomous deep and surface approaches. The positions upon the continuum are characterised by the intention and the strategy employed (see Table 5.1).

The existence of the intermediate approaches provides one explanation for the paradox of the Chinese learner. Western university lecturers could have observed Asian students appearing to try to commit material to memory. It is common, for example, to see them with cue cards of key facts before tests and examinations. They can also be observed rehearsing written speeches before presentations. To the Western observer these visible signs of attempts to memorise would normally be interpreted as rote learning or mechanical memorisation, as that is what such behaviour would commonly imply if the students were from the West. The assumption would, therefore, be that students displaying such behaviour were employing a surface approach to learning, and that that was a common trait among Asian students.

However, the discovery of the intermediate approaches means that the signs may not have been diagnostic of a surface approach—the students could have been combining memorisation with efforts to understand material, which is not consistent with either rote learning or a surface approach. Such behaviour could provide an explanation for the good performance of Asian students. Seeking understanding, or employing a deep approach, tends to be associated with positive academic outcomes. Assessment often requires little more than reproduction, so rewards those who have committed material to memory, in which case employing one of the combined approaches offers the best of both worlds.

Are Intermediate Approaches Culturally Specific?

It has yet to be established whether all positions on the spectrum are found universally or some are specific to Asia or Confucian-heritage countries. Evidence of the intention to both understand and memorise has also been found in mainland China (Marton *et al.*, 1996) and Japan (Hess and Azuma, 1991), so it may be quite widespread among Asian students. This has led to some interpretations that Chinese or Asian learners have distinct approaches to learning from those characterised in the West. There is, though, no clear evidence for this position.

The revised Study Process Questionnaire (R-SPQ-2F, Biggs *et al.*, 2001) was completed by large samples of university students in Sydney and Hong Kong (Leung *et al.*, in press). Multiple-group analyses using structural equation modelling showed configural invariance, implying that students from the two countries were employing the same conceptual frame of reference when responding to the R-SPQ-2F. This suggests that the continuum characterisation of approaches to learning is likely to be applicable for Western as well as Chinese subjects. The correlations between deep and surface

Table 5.1 Approaches to Learning as a Continuum between Deep and Surface Poles

APPROACH	INTENTION	STRATEGY
surface	memorising	rote learning
intermediate 1	primarily memorising	strategic attempt to reach limited understanding as an aid to memorisation
understanding and memorising	understanding and memorising	repetition and memorising to reach understanding seeking comprehension then committing to memory
intermediate 2	primarily understanding	strategic memorisation for examination or task after understanding reached
deep	understanding	seeking comprehension

approaches for universities in both Hong Kong and Sydney were negative (Hong Kong = −0.39, Sydney = −0.63). These substantial negative correlations are consistent with the continuum model of approaches to learning, as they imply that the deep and surface approaches can be envisaged as opposite ends of a spectrum.

Comparison of mean scores showed the Hong Kong sample to be higher on both deep and surface approaches, with the effect sizes for differences (d) on the surface approach being substantially larger than for the deep approach ($d = 0.75$ versus $d = 0.24$, respectively). The difference in mean scores suggested cultural differences in the extent to which particular approaches are employed. The Hong Kong sample seemed to have a greater propensity to employ combinations of approaches or intermediate approaches.

It is possible that Asian students are more inclined than their Western counterparts to employ the two central approaches in the row labelled "understanding and memorisation" in Table 5.1. The narrow approach (Kember and Gow, 1990) possibly results from studying in a second language. Those employing it lack the ability to skim through a text, searching for cues to key concepts, so instead systematically work through material, section by section, seeking to first understand then commit to memory. The other central approach features frequent repetition which results in material being committed to memory, and eventually leads to understanding (Marton et al., 1996). Kember (1996) has speculated that this approach may result from learning a character-based language, as these are traditionally learnt through constant repetition in order to remember the numerous characters. If this is the case, this approach is likely to be restricted to those countries which use character-based languages.

Other intermediate positions on the spectrum, though, seem more likely to be adopted as responses to prevailing learning and assessment contexts. They might then be somewhat more prevalent in Asia, as it is common there for assessment to be restricted to public examinations, and these assume great importance in elite educational systems, especially when parental expectations are high. There is some evidence, from the work of Entwistle and Entwistle (2003), that the intermediate positions close to the deep and surface poles of the continuum occur in the West. They identified a range of interpretations of understanding in Western students revising for examinations. Some of these showed signs of both memorising and understanding. Case and Marshall (2004) identified intermediate procedural approaches for problem-solving by engineering students in South Africa and the UK. Some cases were classified as surface procedural, as the students mechanically solved problems by using algorithms. There was also evidence of deep procedural approaches, when students intended to reach an understanding through application by solving problems.

Learning Approaches as Responses to Perceived Context

When Asian students do use a surface approach, it is commonly a response to the perceived context, as with students everywhere (see the chapter by Case and Marshall). In Asia there is often intense pressure to perform well in school-level examinations, because of restricted access to the latter part of secondary education and/or limited places in universities. Asian international students are normally from countries which retain elite educational systems. Progress towards mass higher education varies across the region, but Hong Kong can be used as a reasonably typical example. Currently only about one-third of an age group are able to obtain a place in form 6, for the final two years of secondary schooling (Education and Manpower Bureau, 2003). Only about 17% of an age group gain entry to one of the seven universities funded by the University Grants Committee of Hong Kong (University Grants Committee of Hong Kong, 2006). The percentages obtaining places in the more prestigious universities are obviously lower still, thus placing even more pressure on the many students who aim for the most prestigious programmes in the top universities.

In Hong Kong progression into the final years of secondary school, or entry to university, depends almost entirely on results in the externally set examinations. Examinations are of similar importance in most other Asian countries. The combination of the significance of the examinations and the elite educational systems naturally prompts both pupils and teachers to concentrate attention upon passing examinations. These pressures inevitably influence approaches to both teaching and learning, so practices such as coaching for examinations and remembering model answers are common.

These pressures are magnified because of the importance placed on education, which arises from the respect shown to education in Confucian-heritage societies, and from the potential economic benefits which tend to accrue to the better educated. Lee (1996) reviewed the writing of Confucius on the topic of education, and expressed the view that the term learning pervades the *Analects* to the extent that it might be interpreted as a book of learning. The Confucian philosophy became enshrined in China in a tradition of cultivation of the self and of scholarship to provide a preparation for government office.

As will be argued later, in Chinese and most Asian societies achievement motivation has a more family and societal orientation than in the West. This results in additional pressures from parents on their children. These pressures are often reinforced by expectations of social advancement through education. It is common for one generation of an extended family to make financial sacrifices to enable the next generation to receive a better education than they did. This creates a burden to both do well in studying to take full advantage of the opportunity provided, and also to ensure that results are good enough to obtain a prestigious well-paid position, which will enhance the status of the family and result in a financial dividend for the sacrifice.

The overall effect of the contextual influences on approaches to learning constitutes the second contribution to the paradox of the Chinese learner. If Chinese students are genuinely observed to be rote-learning or employing surface approaches to learning, this is not a manifestation of a predisposition by cultural groups or an inherent characteristic of Asian learners. It is, rather, a response to perceptions of contextual factors in the teaching and learning environment, magnified by systemic pressures and societal expectations.

Beliefs about Teaching, Learning and Knowledge

The importance of examinations in the elite educational systems, magnified by family and societal pressures, influence students' beliefs about the interconnected trio of conceptions of teaching, learning and knowledge. This trio of beliefs normally form a logically related and consistent set. Underlying conceptions have a marked impact upon behaviour, so beliefs about teaching and learning are a major determinant of how students behave in their studies.

Kember (2001) investigated the beliefs about teaching, learning and knowledge of two contrasting groups of part-time Hong Kong students: novices and experienced students. The novice interviewees were in their first year of part-time study, mostly studying part-time because they had been unable to gain a place in a full-time undergraduate degree in a UGC-funded university.

Analysis of the interviews revealed two contrasting sets of the trio of beliefs. The large majority of novice students held a trio of beliefs labelled "didactic/reproductive". They believed that the role of the teacher was to transmit or teach a body of knowledge. Their role as students was to absorb the knowledge decided as appropriate by the teacher or the examination authority. The outcome of the process of teaching and learning was judged by whether the students were able to reproduce the body of knowledge for the examinations and other assessment. They believed that knowledge is defined by an authority, so is either right or wrong. Where multiple opinions exist, an authority will eventually decide which is correct. The more experienced and sophisticated students held a different trio of beliefs called "facilitative/transformative".

Good Teaching

A highly significant consequence of the contrasting belief sets is that they resulted in very different conceptions of what constitutes good teaching (Kember *et al.*, 2003). Those holding the naïve belief set preferred teacher-centred forms of teaching. They wanted teaching in which a defined body of knowledge was transmitted to them; so they preferred didactic teaching. By contrast those with the facilitative/transformative set of beliefs thought that didactic teaching was poor teaching. The outcome is that the conceptions of good and poor teaching are diametrically opposite (see Figure 5.1).

The contextual, systemic and societal pressures described can act to influence Asian school students to cling to the naïve trio of beliefs. They then enter university with a set of beliefs which are not compatible with the ideals of higher education. Holding this set of beliefs would influence students to study and behave in class in ways which university teachers would construe as being inconsistent with achieving desired learning outcomes. If the previous schooling of international students has induced the naïve trio of beliefs, it could be a significant contributing cause to explain the behaviours of international students reported by their university teachers.

Passive Learners

A logical consequence of holding the naïve trio of beliefs is being passive in class. Active participation in class is inconsistent with a belief that learning is a process of absorbing and reproducing material delivered by the teacher. Other factors which could contribute to international students taking a passive role in class are:

- having been brought up in the Confucian tradition, which shows a high respect for teachers

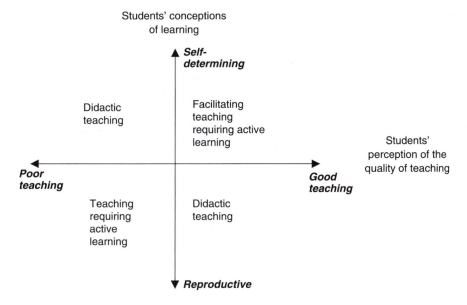

Figure 5.1 Contrasting Conceptions of Good Teaching.

- the tradition of filial piety, which results in an upbringing stressing orderly behaviour and respect for elders
- studying in a foreign cultural environment, and often one in which the locals seem more confident and assertive
- studying in a second language, and refraining from speaking out because of a lack of confidence in expressing oneself in the language of instruction.

Asian students can, though, be persuaded to engage in discussion and actively participate in class activities. Kember with McNaught (2007) contains material derived from award-winning university teachers, which includes techniques for managing and promoting discussion, which work well with both Asian and Western students. Firstly, it is important that the teacher makes an effort to establish a rapport with students, and uses icebreakers to get to know them. The technique for encouraging participation is to break the students into small groups of about four to discuss a topic, or question or work together on a set activity:

> You have to encourage them to speak more. Give them questions ahead of time and ask them to think about it in a small group. Usually they will respond as a group. They will say, "Our group believe this or that . . .", and they are less likely to say "I believe this or that . . .". If you give them preparation time, usually they are pretty good about it. Normally I give them a question to think about and ask them to respond a little bit later, after the break (David Ahlstrom—CUHK—Management, quoted in Kember with McNaught, 2007, p. 84).

When the small group technique is used in Hong Kong, rather than a deadly silence, the result is normally a lively buzz of discussion. Once the group has formulated an answer or opinion they will then be keen to tell the rest of the class; so there is no problem in getting a spokesperson to talk for the group. Discussion in small groups deals with inhibitions, and results in a strong commitment to the consensus achieved by the group. After holding a series of activities using a similar format, students start to feel confident about participating in class. The award-winning teachers all believed in active student participation:

> My perception is teachers generally talk too much. You can tell somebody's puzzled by the way they look. And you can tell if somebody is not paying attention, often because I'm talking too much. You can tell that somebody is subtly drifting off, that's the time to ask questions, to get them moving and to keep them in. It's monitoring what's going on really. I try and make it so that I don't talk more than 50 to 60 percent of the time at most. The rest of the time is students'. Whenever I teach, I have all these questions I'm going to ask them about (Gordon Mathews—CUHK—Anthropology, quoted in Kember with McNaught, 2007, p. 87).

Resistance to Active Learning

Another consequence of holding the naïve trio of beliefs is that students can seem reluctant to engage in active forms of learning, and appear resistant to innovative forms of teaching and learning. They conceptualise teaching as something in which the teacher conveys to them a defined body of knowledge, which they absorb and commit to memory. Forms of teaching and learning inconsistent with these beliefs are regarded as inferior.

Again it is possible to persuade students to adapt to more innovative forms of learning and appreciate that they result in better learning outcomes. For over five years I ran an inter-institutional initiative known as the Action Learning Project, which supported 90 action research projects within eight universities and colleges in Hong Kong (Kember, 2000b). In these projects teachers introduced a wide variety of innovative forms of teaching and learning into their courses—almost anything other than didactic lecturing—to supposedly passive students.

The Action Learning Project was evaluated with a multiple-method, multiple-voice approach. This included a questionnaire to all project participants. The substantial majority of the respondents believed that their projects had resulted in:

- improved teacher–student relationships
- improvements in students' attitude
- improvements in students' learning approaches
- improvements in students' performance.

Each of the projects was extensively evaluated, so these responses would have been informed by evaluation data. This would seem to provide evidence that Asian students can adapt to innovative teaching, can come to see the advantages of it and can benefit from it.

Helping Students to Change Beliefs and Approaches

In the preceding two sections it has been suggested that holding the naïve trio of beliefs can be a major contributor to Asian students being reluctant to engage in class discussion, and resisting the introduction of more innovative forms of teaching which involve student activity. Evidence has also been presented, however, of students being able to overcome an initial dislike of active involvement in class, and eventually participate willingly in learning activities. For this process to happen, it seems as though there must have been some shift in their beliefs about teaching and learning, as this seems to be either a pre-condition or an accompanying transition if students are to willingly contribute and participate in class.

More direct evidence of changes in beliefs about learning came from interviews with the experienced part-time students (Kember, 2001), who were asked to compare their learning experiences as full-time undergraduate students with their current practices as part-time students enrolled for higher degrees. These parts of the interviews provided rich evidence of a shift in beliefs about learning. One typical quotation is given below:

I think my learning method changed after my second year of university.
Q: From what to what?
Because from Hong Kong schools, I was trained to memorise, revise, not to think that much. And I tried the same method in first two years of university. My grade points weren't high enough because the exams are not oriented towards memorising everything. For example, the lecturer will give you a take-home exam. You know, you take your final exam home and you . . . and to give you one week to do your final exam. So, when I had it first outside yes, very easy. You know. But it was very hard. It was harder than writing an exam because there are no right answers. They make you think. And because I really thought it would be easy. But in fact, you would realise that there were no right answers. There will be no right answer at all. You have to think and analyse and how you present your thoughts. . . . And in my third and fourth year of my undergraduate course, I learnt to think and present my thoughts. And I wasn't memorising anymore. I understood what was happening. Memorising did not help (Kember, 2001, pp. 213–214).

This student made this conceptual change through exposure to a type of assessment incompatible with existing beliefs about learning, though earlier experiences had clearly raised doubts. There was also evidence of the other experienced postgraduate students in the sample holding more sophisticated beliefs. All of the sample went through the Hong Kong school system, which is likely to have influenced a significant proportion towards reproductive beliefs at some stage. Yet they must have developed away from these beliefs as the experienced students in the sample were clearly self-directing at the time of the interviews. The award-winning university teachers recognised the naïve trio of beliefs as a problem which needed to be dealt with:

> Unfortunately, in Hong Kong education, they are not trained to discuss and debate at primary and secondary levels. It's difficult for them to put down the old mode of learning and pick up discovery. . . . Students who grow up in Hong Kong however are generally frightened as they are so used to have model answers given to them in their secondary school training. "You just give me the model answers, tell me all about the author and I will memorise so that I can regurgitate during exams." There were times when students were really frightened and dissatisfied with the fact that I had not given them the absolute model answers. So, it takes rather a long time to convince the students that the teacher is not there to tell me everything or hand down knowledge. It is I myself who need to think independently, analyse, discover and eventually understand (Lo Wai Luen—CUHK—Chinese Literature, quoted in Kember with McNaught, 2007, p. 40).

This quotation makes it clear that changing deep-seated beliefs is never an easy process, especially when the beliefs in question are central to a person's role, as beliefs about teaching and learning are to students. The naïve trio of beliefs about teaching, learning and knowledge is clearly not suited to the ideals of university education, yet is hard, and even traumatic, to change, as it becomes entrenched through the years of schooling. Changing beliefs needs a challenge to one or more of the components of the trio, through exposure to practices consistent with more sophisticated beliefs. However, the exposure needs to be progressive and support should be provided. When students enter a programme believing that all questions have answers which are either right or wrong, activities and assessment might be planned so as to progress from relatively straightforward tasks at the outset to more open-ended ones as the programme progresses:

> So, my teaching will move from a more structured approach at the beginning to a more open-end one towards the end; the teacher will move away from readily providing answers to giving no concrete answers eventually. This is exactly what the real world is: no definite answers for questions. At the start, they will gain confidence from "getting the answers right". This confidence is important to enable them to gradually discover that there are no absolute concrete answers but a logic or framework of thinking based upon which they can formulate their viewpoints, judgments and predictions. Learning is about developing their own thinking rather than finding model answers (Andrew Chan—CUHK—Marketing, quoted in Kember with McNaught, 2007, p. 64).

The adult education movement has seen students developing self-direction as an important goal; so the literature can make a valuable contribution towards identifying ways to help learners become self-directing. Kember (2007) synthesised key principles from the contributions of the adult education literature:

1. The change needs to be progressive or gradual, rather than abrupt.

2. Change should be from the familiar or known territory to the unknown.
3. There needs to be a challenge to existing beliefs through exposure to contrary positions, which in this case means exposure to types of teaching and learning inconsistent with existing beliefs.
4. Exposure to contrary positions needs to leave students dissatisfied with their existing beliefs, in this case by showing that the alternative forms of teaching and learning lead to better learning outcomes.
5. Support needs to be provided for what can be a difficult, and even traumatic, process.

A Hong Kong example comes from Kember *et al.* (2001, ch. 10 in particular). This book reports courses which challenged learners' reproductive beliefs, by focusing towards the development of reflective practitioners. This posited the students' experience as a significant source of knowledge for the course. The courses were initially quite discomforting for the majority of the students. With support from the teachers and fellow students, though, most adapted to and eventually came to prefer reflective to reproductive learning. In the process they also became more self-directing.

Achieving Motivation

To this point the chapter has dealt with study approaches and behaviours about which there have been quite widespread negative perceptions of Asian students. This section and the next deal with motivation. This brings a contrast to the previous parts of the chapter, as Asian students have a reputation for being highly motivated, though there appears to be a degree of suspicion about the nature of their motivation and, in some quarters, a feeling that it is not the most desirable form for university study. Again, however, there may well be a degree of misunderstanding of the nature of motivation in Asian society.

Achievement motivation is assumed to drive Asian students to work hard, and often do well in their studies. To examine the assertions that Asian students have high levels of achieving motive, it is first necessary to look at a definition of it. The definition of the achieving motive scale incorporated within the Study Process Questionnaire is given by Biggs (1987, p. 11) as follows:

> Achieving motive is based on competition and ego-enhancement: obtain highest grades, whether or not material is interesting.

This definition is consistent with Western psychology texts which portray achievement motivation as an individual competitive drive. Hofstede (1980, 2001) examined individualism and collectivism by analysing IBM personnel surveys. Hofstede (2001, p. 215) has a table of individualism index values for 50 countries and three regions. The top four ranked countries are predominantly English-speaking Western countries: USA, Australia, UK and Canada. It is significant that much of the educational psychology literature has emanated from these countries. The nature of achievement motivation has been based on research predominantly from countries classified as highly individualist. However, the very large majority of Asian countries appear in the lower half of the table, as their societies are more collective in nature.

In a study of Chinese high school students, Yu (1974) found that Western measures of achievement motivation were not appropriate, as they characterised the motivation as individual. Hsu (1981) compared Americans and Chinese, and argued that the motivating force for the latter came primarily from the family and the clan. Yang and Yu (1988) argued that Chinese achievement motivation featured socially approved goals. Yu (1996) compared the Western traditional individual-oriented achievement motivation (IOAM) with social-oriented achievement motivation

(SOAM), which gave a better representation to the traditional Chinese form of motivation. In SOAM the goal is set by others rather than by the individual. The action necessary to achieve the goal and the evaluation of its attainment were also determined by others.

The greater degree of collectivism in many Asian societies implies that achievement motivation has been seen as having a more social or family orientation. This may be undermined to some extent by competitive examination systems or Western media. However, the degree of collectivism still seems to be such that characterising achievement motivation of Asians primarily as an individual drive and a competitive force is not appropriate.

Extrinsic Motivation

Biggs (1987) envisages approaches to learning as having motive and strategy components. Intrinsic motivation is the motive component of a deep approach, and extrinsic motivation that of a surface approach. There appears to be a quite widely held perception that Asian international students display high levels of extrinsic motivation, which is often seen as undesirable. These perceptions of high levels of extrinsic motivation may be accurate, but motivation through the potential benefits of a successful career entered on graduation does not seem to preclude intrinsic interest, and there is evidence that the two can be mutually reinforcing.

Kember et al. (in press) conducted an open naturalistic study to better characterise motivation in higher education. Open semi-structured individual interviews were conducted with 36 students from three universities in Hong Kong. Transcripts were coded with NVivo software so it was possible to perform checks on the incidence of coding in particular categories.

Every single one of the 36 interviewees had at least one coding related to career, job or financial considerations. The nature of the statements and their universal incidence casts doubt on the characterisation of the comments as consistent with narrowly extrinsic forms of motivation with negative connotations. Surely, the entire group of interviewees could not have entered university and worked through to their third year with negative goals and minimal aspirations.

There were 28 students with one or more coding related to interest in the subject studied; so all but eight students were coded for both interest and career-related aspirations. Detailed examination of transcripts produced many examples of career aspirations and interest in subject matter serving to mutually reinforce each other. The manifestation of both career- and interest-related motivation in the same interviews is evidence that the two can co-exist, and that intrinsic and extrinsic motivation are not mutually exclusive, as they are at times portrayed.

The career aspect of motivation was more consistent with the learning orientations formulated by Beaty et al. (2005). They included a vocational orientation with intrinsic and extrinsic sub-categories. The latter was distinguished by students aiming to obtain a qualification which would lead to a job. The intrinsic vocational orientation was defined by students seeking an education which would equip them well for their future careers.

Conclusion

International students from Asia have been seen as something of a mixed blessing. Universities value the revenue they provide to the extent that they contribute a major portion of the income of many universities. However, their teachers often seem perplexed by their study habits. It can appear to Western teachers that Asian students adopt study behaviours which are normally associated with poor or undesirable learning outcomes.

Yet there is evidence of Asian students performing well. In international comparison studies, students from Asia, particularly those from Confucian-heritage countries, are often among the most highly rated. Asian international students frequently obtain high grades in their overseas universities. This is in spite of them not usually being among the top ranked students in their home country. The best students win places in their country's universities, so have no need to seek an undergraduate degree overseas.

Research into the learning approaches and motivation of Chinese students suggests that Western interpretations of study behaviours of international students from Asia can often be misinterpretations. In other cases, such as passive behaviour and reluctance to engage in innovative forms of learning, their actions may be a consequence of beliefs about learning and teaching which have been acquired through years of schooling in elite educational systems which have high consequences for results in external examinations. The pressure to do well in examinations and gain one of the restricted number of places in universities is magnified by societal and family pressures because of the respect accorded to education.

Students can be helped towards more sophisticated beliefs about learning, teaching and knowledge, and with this transition comes a greater openness to study behaviours more consistent with the ideals of higher education. Many students who complete undergraduate degrees in their home countries clearly do make the transition to the more sophisticated belief set. High-ranking universities in the West have become keen to recruit research students from Asia. They would not do this, and those recruited would not succeed as research students, if they lacked high-order intellectual capabilities.

References

Beaty, L., Gibbs, G. and Morgan, A. (2005). Learning orientations and study contracts. In F. Marton, D. Hounsell and N. Entwistle (eds) *The Experience of Learning: Implications for teaching and studying in higher education* (pp. 72–86). 3rd (Internet) edn. Edinburgh: University of Edinburgh, Centre for Teaching, Learning and Assessment.

Biggs, J. (1987). *Student Approaches to Learning and Studying.* Melbourne: Australian Council for Educational Research.

Biggs, J., Kember, D. and Leung, D.Y.P. (2001). The revised two factor Study Process Questionnaire: R-SPQ-2F. *British Journal of Educational Psychology, 71,* 133–149.

Case, J. and Marshall, D. (2004). Between deep and surface: procedural approaches to learning in engineering education contexts. *Studies in Higher Education, 29*(5), 605–615.

Education and Manpower Bureau (2003). *Education Statistics.* Hong Kong: Education and Manpower Bureau.

Entwistle, N. and Entwistle, D. (2003). Preparing for examinations: The interplay of memorising and understanding, and the development of knowledge objects. *Higher Education Research and Development, 22*(1), 19–41.

Hess, R.D. and Azuma, M. (1991). Cultural support for schooling: Contrasts between Japan and the United States. *Educational Researcher, 20*(9), 2–8.

Hofstede, G.H. (1980). *Culture's Consequences: International differences in work-related values.* Beverley Hills: Sage.

Hofstede, G.H. (2001). *Culture's Consequences: Comparing values, behaviors, institutions, and organisations across nations.* Thousand Oaks: Sage.

Hsu, F.L.K. (1981). *Americans and Chinese: Passage to differences* 3rd edn. Honolulu: University of Hawaii Press.

Kember, D. (1996). The intention to both memorise and understand: Another approach to learning? *Higher Education, 31,* 341–351.

Kember, D. (2000a). Misconceptions about the learning approaches, motivation and study practices of Asian students. *Higher Education, 40*(1), 99–121.

Kember, D. (2000b). *Action learning and action research: Improving the quality of teaching and learning.* London: Kogan Page.

Kember, D. (2001). Beliefs about knowledge and the process of teaching and learning as a factor in adjusting to study in higher education. *Studies in Higher Education, 26*(2), 205–221.

Kember, D. (2007). *Reconsidering Open and Distance Learning in the Developing World: Meeting students' learning needs.* London: Routledge.

Kember, D. et al. (2001). *Reflective Teaching and Learning in the Health Professions.* Oxford: Blackwell Science.

Kember, D. and Gow, L. (1989). Cultural specificity of approaches to study. Paper presented the 6th Annual Conference of the Hong Kong Educational Research Association, Hong Kong.

Kember, D. and Gow, L. (1990). Cultural specificity of approaches to study. *British Journal of Educational Psychology, 60,* 356–363.

Kember, D., Hong, C. and Ho, A. (in press). Characterising the motivational orientation of students in higher education: A naturalistic study in three Hong Kong universities. *British Journal of Educational Psychology.*

Kember, D. with McNaught, C. (2007). *Enhancing University Teaching: Lessons from research into award winning teachers.* London: Routledge.

Kember, D., Jenkins, W. and Ng, K.C. (2003). Adult students' perceptions of good teaching as a function of their conceptions of learning—Part 1. Influencing the development of self-determination. *Studies in Continuing Education, 25*(2), 240–251.

Lee, W.O. (1996). The cultural context for Chinese learners: Conceptions of learning in the Confucian tradition. In D. Watkins and J.B. Biggs (eds). *The Chinese Learner: Cultural, psychological and contextual influences* (pp. 25–41). Melbourne and Hong Kong: Australian Council for Educational Research and the Comparative Education Research Centre, University of Hong Kong.

Leung, D.Y.P., Ginns, P. and Kember, D. (in press). Examining the cultural specificity of approaches to learning in universities in Hong Kong and Sydney. *Journal of Cross Cultural Psychology.*

Marton, F. and Säljö, R. (1976). On qualitative differences in learning, outcome and process I. *British Journal of Educational Psychology, 46*, 4–11.

Marton, F., Dall'Alba, G. and Kun, T.L. (1996). Memorising and understanding: the keys to the paradox? In D. Watkins and J.B. Biggs (eds). *The Chinese Learner: Cultural, psychological and contextual influences* (pp. 69–84). Melbourne and Hong Kong: Australian Council for Educational Research and the Comparative Education Research Centre, University of Hong Kong.

Organisation for Economic Co-operation and Development (2006). *Education at a Glance: OECD indicators for 2006.* Paris: Organisation for Economic Co-operation and Development.

Organisation for Economic Co-operation and Development (2007). *Assessing Scientific, Reading and Mathematical Literacy: A framework for PISA 2006.* Paris: Organisation for Economic Co-operation and Development.

Stevenson, H.W. and Lee, S.Y. (1996). The academic achievement of Chinese students. In M.H. Bond (ed.) *The Handbook of Chinese Psychology.* Hong Kong: Oxford University Press.

Tang, K.C.C. (1991). Effects of different assessment methods on tertiary students' approaches to studying. Unpublished Ph. D. Dissertation, University of Hong Kong.

Tang, T. (1993). Inside the classroom: The students' view. In J.B. Biggs and D.A. Watkins (eds). *Learning and Teaching in Hong Kong: What is and what might be* (pp. 35–52). Hong Kong: Faculty of Education, Hong Kong.

Trow, M. (2006). Reflections on the transition from elite to mass to universal access: Forms and phases of higher education in modern societies since WWII. In J.J.F. Forest and P.G. Altbach (eds) *International Handbook of Higher Education* (pp. 243–280). Netherlands: Springer.

University Grants Committee of Hong Kong. (2006). *Facts and Figures 2005.* Hong Kong: University Grants Committee Secretariat. Retrieved 16 August 2006, from http://www.ugc.edu.hk/english/documents/figures/

Watkins, D. (1996). Hong Kong secondary school learners: a developmental perspective. In D. Watkins and J.B. Biggs (eds). *The Chinese Learner: Cultural, psychological and contextual influences* (pp. 107–119). Melbourne and Hong Kong: Australian Council for Educational Research and the Comparative Education Research Centre, University of Hong Kong.

Watkins, D. and Biggs, J.B. (eds) (1996). *The Chinese Learner: Cultural, psychological and contextual influences.* Melbourne and Hong Kong: Australian Council for Educational Research and the Comparative Education Research Centre, University of Hong Kong.

Yang, K.S. and Yu, A.B. (1988). Social- and individual-oriented achievement motivation: Conceptualization and measurement. Paper presented at the symposium on Chinese personality and social psychology, 24th International Congress of Psychology, Sydney.

Yu, A.B. (1996). Ultimate life concerns, self, and Chinese achievement motivation. In M.H. Bond (ed.) *The Handbook of Chinese Psychology* (pp. 227–246). Oxford: Oxford University Press.

Yu, E.S.H. (1974). Achievement motive, familism and hsiao: A replication of McClelland-Winterbottom studies. Unpublished doctoral dissertation. University of Notre Dame.

6

Study Success of Students from Ethnic Minority Backgrounds:

An Overview of Explanations for Differences in Study Careers

Sabine Severiens and Rick Wolff

Introduction

Ethnic minority students record less study success in comparison with their peers from majority backgrounds. In this chapter, we attempt to find an answer to the question of why this is so, and what educational programmes can do to reduce these differences. Research in this area is divided into three sections with overlapping themes. In the first theme, Tinto's model is central along with the terms "social integration" and "academic integration". The second theme zooms in on explanations from the social domain, and the third explores research on factors in the learning environment.

The literature shows that an initial answer to the question of what universities can do involves dealing with differences. The performances of ethnic minority students improve in programmes in which the social integration of ethnic minority and majority students is good, in which contact with teachers is good, in which teachers refer to differences positively and use them in their teaching, and in which diversity is explicitly referred to as a positive value. A second answer involves, within the education system, promoting contact with their own community in combination with encouraging the maintenance of their cultural identity. Research has clearly shown that social support networks in their own community, and a feeling of awareness of one's own cultural identity, have a positive impact on the study success of ethnic minority students.

Diversity in Higher Education

Increasing Structural Diversity

In the past decade(s), higher education in Western societies has become ethnically more diverse. The "traditional student" who enters higher education straight from secondary education, who is on the brink of entering their twenties, who studies full-time and whose parents are highly educated with middle or high incomes is no longer the average student. Democratisation of higher education, in combination with the long-term effects of post-colonial and labour migration, has led to an increasing number of students in general, and an increase of ethnic minority students in particular.

More than 90% of the 1971 US freshman population was White/Caucasian. In 2006, their share decreased to just above 75%, due to the strong emergence of Asian-American/Asian (from 0.6% to 8.6%), Latina/o (from 0.6% to 7.3%) and multiracial (from 1.3% to 7.2%) students. The share of African-American, the largest minority group, also increased, though less spectacularly (from 7.5% to 10.5%: Pryor *et al.*, 2007).

In Europe, the number of first year students of non-Western descent in Dutch higher education, who in the Dutch context are considered as ethnic minority students, more than doubled, up to a total of almost 16,000 students, from 1997 to 2006. Though this number may seem small in absolute figures, in the relative sense this caused an increase from 8% non-Western influx of first year students in 1997 to 13% in 2006 for both forms of higher education in the Netherlands (higher vocational education and university education: Central Bureau of Statistics, Netherlands). In the UK some 14% of undergraduates were of an ethnic minority background in the academic year 2001 (Connor *et al.*, 2004). Although figures of previous years are not entirely reliable, due to changes in nationwide data collection and changes in ethnic categories through the years, the authors conclude that "in broad terms, the trend is likely to be upwards, as the figures suggest" (p. 41).

Although on a nationwide scale the ethnic diversity of the student population has increased, ethnic minority students are not evenly spread throughout the country. Ethnic minority students tend to enroll in less prestigious institutions (public institutions, vocationally oriented tracks) in areas with a relatively high proportion of ethnic minority residents (Connor *et al.*, 2004; European Monitoring Centre on Racism and Xenophobia, 2004). Moreover, this group of students seems to be concentrated in a limited number of disciplines. Ethnic minority students, as well as students from lower socio-economic backgrounds, more often choose "high status" subjects such as medicine, law and economics (Van de Werfhorst *et al.*, 2003; Wolff, 2007).

Less Success

These developments in the student population along ethnic lines raise the question of how well non-traditional groups of minority students are performing. Does access to higher education also mean that chances for success are more or less the same for both traditional and non-traditional groups of students? International data generally show that the study careers of minority students are less successful. They earn fewer credits in the same amount of time (Hofman and Van den Berg, 2003; Swail *et al.*, 2003; Severiens and Wolff, in press), they need more time to graduate, and retention rates among these students are lower compared with those of White students. In the North American case much evidence is available (see, for example, Bowen and Bok, 1998; Massey *et al.*, 2003). Recently published figures show that, by the age of 24, 6–7% of the low-income group students—a category with a relatively large number of African-American, Latina/o and Asian students (Pell Institute, 2005) attained a bachelor's degree, compared with 52% among high-income students (Mortensen, 2005).

In a recent study on the attainment of ethnic minority students in UK higher education, Richardson (2008) finds that Asian students have half the chance and Black students one-third of a chance of obtaining a "good" degree compared with White students. The author concludes that "even when the effects of . . . other variables are taken into account, students from ethnic minorities are substantially and significantly less likely to obtain good degrees than are White students" (p. 45). In the Netherlands, in higher vocational education 68% of White Dutch students graduate within six years, while at universities this percentage is 55%. For ethnic minority groups the rates are much lower: 50% in higher vocational education and around 40% at university level (Wolff, 2007).

In conclusion, the backgrounds of the student population are becoming more diverse, but ethnic minority students record less study success. Given this observation, we can ask what educational programmes can do to reduce the differences in school performances and to offer diverse groups of students equal opportunities. It is important to answer this question, not only from an egalitarian perspective but also from a pragmatic one. Because of ageing and the decreasing number of young people, it is becoming increasingly important to use all available talent to the full.

The Role of Teaching in Study Success

Given the central question of this chapter, we have selected the role that teaching plays in the study success of ethnic minority students as the perspective for seeking explanations. Our literature search indicated three relevant areas, namely:

- social and academic integration according to Tinto's model (1997, 1998)
- the social domain
- the learning environment.

These are not independent areas; they often overlap. The areas have different perspectives and different underlying theoretical assumptions. The concept of "social integration" from Tinto's educational model, for example, is also found in the social domain, from a more sociological perspective. Where Tinto's model takes the institution as a starting point, and zooms in on the way in which the instructional design of the programme either promotes the social integration of various groups of students or not, the starting point of the studies in the social domain is the students themselves. The social domain, for example, is more concerned with processes that take place in "peer groups", and that either promote study success or not. In Tinto's model, academic integration mainly involves the quality of the contact between teachers and students, and the quality of the lessons given. The studies that take the learning environment as their starting point, on the other hand, do not examine teaching and learning in themselves, but rather the underlying processes in the learning environment and its climate that affect study progress and achievement of students.

Social and Academic Integration

When I sit with an ethnic minority fellow student, I can open his bag with no problem. I wouldn't dare try that with Jan. With majority students, you deal in a business-like way. You go to meetings and do what you have to do. And then you go home. (Interview with an ethnic minority student, Severiens *et al.*, 2006: 153)

In Tinto's model, social integration refers to good social contact with teachers and fellow students. For most students, a group with whom they feel at home is an important deciding factor in the pleasure they experience in a programme, and it ultimately also determines the chances of whether they will record study success and complete the programme. Participating in all kinds of social activities, having many friends, feeling quite at home and enjoying study are all signs that students are socially well integrated.

When tests are marked, Dutch students more easily receive an additional tenth of a point. Example: last year, two Dutch youths achieved this in fifteen minutes while a youth from Cape Verde had to spend a whole day nagging for it. You don't want to say it's racism, but it looks like it. (Interview with an ethnic minority student, Severiens *et al.*, 2006: 144)

Academic integration refers to the extent to which students feel at home in the programme regarding the field, and the teachers and students who represent that field. Good academic integration means that students identify positively with the field concerned, that teachers talk to them about this and invite their students, as it were, to participate in the profession. An example is the extent to which students can ask (or dare to ask) their teachers questions (Severiens *et al.*, 2006).

The underlying idea of the studies that investigate social and academic integration, in groups of ethnic minority and majority students, is that a relatively minor degree of integration is related to mediocre study progress, or even to the decision to drop out of the study. However, this connection is not present in all the studies. For example, Nora and Cabrera (1996) describe several studies showing that ethnic minority students are relatively often faced with negative contact among their fellow students and teachers. In their own research they also find that ethnic minority students experience more prejudice and discrimination. Although these experiences have a negative effect on "academic experiences" and on social integration, no effect was found on study progress. In the study conducted by Berger and Milem (1999), significant connections were found between academic and social integration and study progress. Ethnic minority students tend to spend less time in programmes, due to lower academic and social integration, but this relationship was found to be a general mechanism. This means that no differences were found between students of diverse ethnic backgrounds and their social and academic integration. Eimers and Pike (1997) conducted another study about integration in relation to ethnicity. This study shows that a lack of academic integration has negative effects on study progress, particularly for ethic minority students.

In our own qualitative research (Severiens *et al.*, 2006), carried out among students at institutes for higher vocational education and at research universities, we saw that the experiences of ethnic minority students involving inequality in the programme, like being treated "differently" by fellow students and by teachers, and feeling less at home in the programme, had an influence on their social and academic integration. As the quotation above shows, this is expressed, for example, in the extra effort some ethnic minority students have to make to get a higher grade during the discussion of test results, compared with majority students in the same programme. Conversely, more equality in the programme, and more attention for diversity, seems to lead to an equal degree of social and academic integration and study progress for ethnic minority and majority students.

Another study conducted among teacher training programmes (Severiens *et al.*, 2007) revealed that, in programmes in which ethnic minority students performed relatively poorly, social integration appeared to take place in a "problematic" atmosphere. The quality of cooperation between students in such programmes is less when compared with programmes in which ethnic minority students perform relatively well. Furthermore, the best academic integration, in terms of contacts between teachers and students, both ethnic minority and majority, is achieved in programmes in which the differences in study progress are small. In other words, the quality of academic and social integration is related to the study progress of ethnic minority students. Where large differences exist to the disadvantage of ethnic minority students, there are also a relatively large number of complaints, particularly from ethnic minority students, regarding their interaction with fellow students and teachers.

To summarise, we can cautiously argue that research based on Tinto's model shows that ethnic minority students have less contact with their fellow students and teachers, and are therefore less well socially and academically integrated. This has an adverse effect on the study success of ethnic minority students. We put this cautiously because not all the research clearly points in this direction, and the connections are not always strong (Braxton, 2000; Severiens and Wolff, in press).

The Social Domain

The social domain refers to the social networks and the bonds of students that are related to their institutional or study experiences. This domain largely involves contacts that are maintained outside regular classes. This involves contact with fellow students, but the social domain can also involve, for example, support from parents and family or via contacts in other social situations (like clubs or societies).

Social Contacts as a Predictor of Study Success

Peers seem to play an important role in the extent to which students are able and willing to adapt to the demands that education makes of them (Astin 1993; Tinto, 1993), in the perseverance to continue and in ultimately obtaining school success (Terenzini and Pascarella, 2005). Peers can have either a positive or negative impact on study success. According to some authors, social aspects are particularly important for students from minority groups. In these groups, access to a support network is a better predictor of study success than are cognitive skills, for example (Fuertes and Sedlacek, 1994; Tracey and Sedlacek, 1985, 1987). Moreover, the social environment may have an influence on the choice of institution and course, and a social support network seems to be a major tool in remaining motivated at school or during a period of study (Wolff and Crul, 2003). Regarding the choice of school and study, ethnic minority students seem to have a lesser degree of access to a network that can help them further in their school career than is the case for majority students (Severiens et al., 2007).

Acting "White"

Steinberg (1996) also points to the role of peers as an important explanation of the difference in study success between Asian and African-American students in the US. This difference is attributed to the peers of Asian students more often finding education and performance to be important, while the peers of African-American students least often emphasise the importance of academic performances. Gloria et al. (2005) show that Latino peer groups help each other to "survive" in education. A concrete negative example of this is the domino effect regarding dropping out. In a study conducted at a number of teacher-training programmes for primary education (Severiens et al., 2007), several teachers and programme managers said that dropping out never seems to involve just one student. Once an atmosphere is created among students of "I won't make it", the chances are great that this view will spread across a larger group of students. The result is that a number of students drop out of the programme within a short space of time.

What is involved here are general mechanisms, but the interaction between peers may comprise ethno-cultural elements as well. An example of this is the ethnographical study into an ethnically mixed "middle-class high school" conducted by Ogbu (2003). This study was not conducted in higher education institutions, but is nevertheless discussed here as it uncovers the powerful relationship between social processes, identity and learning. Ogbu concluded that the social pressure within groups of African-American boys often had a negative effect on their study performances. We expect similar processes to occur in higher education. Studying hard is not cool, and is regarded as "White" behaviour. This seems to apply to boys in particular. Once a fellow student performs above the average, he or she is no longer welcome in the group. It is not so much the good grades that are rejected, but rather that the attitude and behaviour that is necessary to obtain good grades is regarded as "White". Some examples are speaking "proper" English, enrolling in honours classes, paying attention during lessons, raising your hand to answer questions put by the teacher and socialising with White peers. The reason why this "White" behaviour is rejected is that it is in conflict with a perceived African-American identity. Such an identity is regarded as being in opposition to the White identity, instead of being just different. Massey *et al.* (2003) refers to this process as the theory of oppositional identity.

> The working groups were annoying because all the other members of the group were Dutch and contact with them wasn't very good. Maybe because I come from another country . . . but I don't like them. They're very curious and not funny. I am not like them. But that's also because of me. I think that people find me antisocial because I don't talk very much. It would be different if I had just one other student from Aruba in my group. (Interview with an ethnic minority student, Severiens *et al.*, 2006: 92).

A comparative study of two "problem institutions" with many ethnic minority students (one in the Bronx and the other in the Bijlmer district of Amsterdam: Paulle, 2005) puts several points regarding these group attitudes and oppositional identities into perspective. Paulle encountered dominant "Black" student groups with an anti-school attitude at both institutions. After further study he observed, however, that "Black" is an ambiguous term that is interpreted by each pupil differently, and which definitely does not always refer to "race" or "ethnicity", that certainly not all ethnic minority students share the views of the dominant "Black" student groups, that "non-Black" students can also form part of these dominant student groups, and that the anti-school attitude of members of the dominant student group is mainly adopted in a group process. Individual contact with members of the dominant group revealed that they too were aware of the importance of good schooling.

Pride in One's Own Cultural Identity

Why is the role of peers so important in the social domain? This can be explained by means of the life-world that peers share. Fellow students recognise and identify with one another. They are facing the same school challenges (completing study assignments and studying for examinations and tests), and they often spend more time with each other, than, for example, with their parents or teachers. This communality can create strong bonds that ensure that peers take each other as examples, and therefore have more influence on each other than other people who are involved in their education.

In an ethnically diverse population, this shared life-world can ensure that students of the same origin are attracted to one other. Ethnic minority students often refer to a shared (family) background, a shared sense of humour and shared (educational) experiences that make them feel more closely bound to other ethnic minority students than to majority fellow students. Johnson *et al.* (2007) demonstrate this process. They found that, of all ethnic groups, Asian-Pacific-American students participate the most in ethnic as well as inter-ethnic meetings. This student group in particular seems to create bonds with the institution via "contexts . . . that emphasize and celebrate their ethnic identities" (p. 536). In other words, the Asian-Pacific-Americans group establishes bonds in its own specific way, namely by underscoring and being proud of their own ethnic identity in their contact with students from different ethnic backgrounds, and within the social domain of their education institution. This may be one of the explanations for the relatively good performances of Asian-Pacific-American students.

Pride in one's own identity can be reinforced by joining social organisations in one's own cultural community. Hurtado and Carter (1997), for example, found that Latino students who participate actively in their own community also integrate better into the education institution in which they are enrolled. Rhamie and Hallam (2002), in a study into successful African-Caribbean students in the UK, point out that a strong individual basis can be laid through a system of combined support from parents, the school and social organisations (sports clubs, the church, etc.). The positive support of parents and organisations in which the students are active can even compensate for a lack of support from the school (for example, discrimination and exclusion on the part of peers and teachers). Rhamie and Hallam argue that, through positive feedback, children learn which attitudes and behaviour generate success, which in part explains the success of the African-Caribbean students interviewed. Although the possible positive influences on school and study performances of access to a network via organisations and clubs are general mechanisms, the examples referred to show that this particularly applies in the case of specific ethnic groups.

We see the mechanism regarding "maintenance of one's own identity" in relation to study success reflected in a slightly different way in the study conducted by Phalet and Andriessen (2003). They present a contextual model in which the hypothesis is that maintenance of culture in the home situation has a supporting effect in the private domain, while adaptation in the context of school is related to good school performances. Their study partially confirms this hypothesis. Students of Turkish and Moroccan origins who perform well are much more aware of their own ethnic identity and background, and strongly resist adaptation to the dominant Dutch culture in the private sphere. On the other hand, in the context of school, the combination of maintenance of one's own culture and adaptation seems to deliver the most success. Phalet and Andriessen state that this is because the retention of culture serves as a psychological buffer at school: it protects students and ensures they perform well.

In short, the literature on the social domain shows that the various social networks (peers, parents, family, extended family, organisations) can have both an encouraging and inhibiting influence on school and study success. In part this involves general processes and bonds that apply to all students, and seem to extend to ethnic minority groups. But there also appear to be mechanisms with a specific cultural nature, of which "acting White" is an example.

The Learning Environment

Three areas of research explore the learning environment. The first area employs the concept of institutional habitus to investigate the role of the institute in the success of minority students. The second area compares students at historically Black colleges and universities (HBCUs) and predominantly White institutions (PWIs) to find out why learning environments in HBCUs are more stimulating for minority students. The third area refers to teacher expectations.

Institutional Habitus

Many studies reveal that ethnic minority students in general felt less at home in the programme, compared with their fellow students from the dominant culture. For example, various US studies show that African-American students and Asian-Pacific or Hispanic/Latino students feel less strongly that they belong in a programme than White American students (Hurtado and Carter, 1997; Johnson et al., 2007). A study by Read et al. (2003) focuses on the extent to which ethnic minority students actually do belong, and the degree to which "academia" is foreign to them. One result of this study was that ethnic minority students seek each other out to reinforce their sense of belonging. In addition, studies into dropping out show that, for ethnic minority students in particular, the lack of a feeling of belonging (referred to in terms of "not fitting in") is an important reason for dropping out (Zea et al., 1997; Just 1999, Hurtado et al., 1999; Swail et al., 2003; Nora and Cabrera, 1996).

In a recent study, we saw that non-Western, ethnic minority drop-outs from teacher-training programmes for primary education felt less comfortable in the programme compared with their majority fellow drop-outs (Severiens *et al.*, 2007). No less than 76% of the ethnic minority drop-outs had been faced with inequality.

> If you don't really feel comfortable, you can't perform optimally. I feel as if I'm being watched all the time. (Interview with an ethnic minority student, Severiens *et al.*, 2006: 154)

The question is why ethnic minority students feel less comfortable. The concept of "institutional habitus", as observed by Thomas (2002), provides insight into this issue.

Thomas uses the concept to describe the academic and social experiences of non-traditional students. Institutional habitus refers to the norms and practices of particular social classes or groups. Thomas was inspired by the work of Reay *et al.* (2001), who define "institutional habitus" as "the influence of a cultural group or social class on an individual's behaviour, as it is transferred through an organization" (para 1.3). The source for this concept was the work of Bourdieu, who views the educational system as the primary institution where class differences are reproduced. The curriculum is biased in favour of those things with which middle-class students are already familiar. The consequence is that the dominant group of students feels like fish in water (Bourdieu and Wacquant, 1992: 127). On the other hand, students from non-traditional backgrounds may feel like fish out of water.

Thomas's empirical research (2002), conducted at a British higher education institution with a high percentage of students from non-traditional groups (ethnic minorities, lower socio-economic backgrounds), points out that the relatively low drop-out rate at this institution can in part be attributed to the attitude of the teachers and guidance counsellors, who are aware of the differences in the cultural, social and educational backgrounds of their students, and incorporate this information into the way in which they teach and assess. The atmosphere among the students is also such that friendships and cooperation are not hindered by differences in home situations or personal background. Thomas concludes from her research that students from non-traditional backgrounds stand a greater chance of succeeding in higher education when they study in a habitus where diversity and differences are seen as enrichment, where they are valued and no group is denied access.

This result is also found in various other studies. The research shows that an institutional habitus in which differences have a positive meaning can ensure that students from minority groups can perform better (cf. Rendon *et al.*, 2000). Van Laar and Levin (in press) concluded in their study that, based on the experiences of African-American, Latino, South Asian and White American students at UCLA (University of California, Los Angeles), a positive campus climate in respect of racial diversity can play an important role for students from minority groups regarding their feeling of well-being and their study progress. They point out that an increase in the number of students from ethnic minority groups can lead to racial tension on campus. They therefore emphasise that:

> as institutions of higher education focus on achieving greater structural diversity, they must also make concerted efforts to communicate to students of all ethnic groups that the institution is devoted to their development.

Historically Black Colleges and Universities

Similar studies that connect institutional and programme culture to the ethnic backgrounds of students are mainly found in the US. An overview of studies into this area shows that African-American students who study at historically Black colleges and universities (HBCUs) experience more social and psychological support, are more content, feel more a part of the community and have a greater chance than African-American students studying at "White" universities of persevering with their studies and completing them successfully (Fleming, 2002; Hurtado *et al.*, 1999). Swail *et al.*, (2003) arrive at similar conclusions when they state the research shows that "HBCUs support campus climates that foster students' self-pride and confidence, and lead to academic and social success" (p.58). One characteristic that has remained constant throughout the history of HBCUs concerns the personal nature of the relationships between staff and their students.

Based on their overview, Hurtado *et al.*, (1999) constructed a framework aimed at reaching a better understanding of the education climate at institutions. According to them, this is determined by four interconnected dimensions: the historical legacy of institutions regarding the inclusion and exclusion of various ethnic minority groups; the structural diversity by numeric representation of these groups in both staff and the student population; the psychological climate of perceptions and attitudes; and a behavioural dimension characterised by group interactions and relationships.

Staff Expectancy

We have seen that support in the learning environment can play an important role in study success. A special and central feature in this environment concerns the expectations of teachers and faculty members. First of all, positive role models and mentors expecting excellent performance seem to be especially important for minority student success (Swail *et al.*, 2003). Conversely, low expectations among teachers seem to lead to low performance of students, referred to as the Pygmalion effect. Generally, teachers have lower expectations of their ethnic minority students, which results in few challenging questions and little challenging material. As a result, they perform less well. However, Ogbu (2003) is doubtful about the sequentiality of this effect. In his study he observed that Black students often indicate that teachers do not expect them to perform well, do their homework or pay attention in class. However, Ogbu observed few concrete examples of these low expectations, and the students themselves gave mainly hypothetical examples. He concluded that it is difficult to indicate what comes first: the low expectations of teachers or the attitudes and behaviour of the students. That a relatively large number of Black students do not do their homework and are not very focused during classes could also be the cause of the low expectations of teachers. This student behaviour may be a result of stereotype threat (Massey *et al.*, 2003; Steele and Aronson, 1995). The basic idea in this theory is that negative stereotypic expectations undermine the performance of members of the stereotyped groups.

To summarise, research that examines the learning environment exposes a number of processes and mechanisms that do not help to decrease differences in the study success of ethnic minority and majority students. Thomas's research into institutional habitus, and the analysis of HBCUs and teacher expectancy, however, also provide a basis for possibly restructuring this process.

Conclusions

To explain why the educational careers of ethnic minority students generally progress less smoothly, we searched for literature on the role of education itself. There is a large area of study that also offers explanations for differences that we do not discuss: the role of the tools (the capital) of the students themselves. We have not discussed what the role is, for example, of cognitive and learning skills (human capital), or the role of motivation and belief in one's own capabilities (identity capital). The role of parents, and the extent to which they can help their children find their way in education (cultural capital), was dealt with indirectly, as was the role of good networks and social support (social capital). The reason for not starting from capital theory to seek explanations from the individual perspective is that this approach offers fewer reference points for solutions. By explicitly focusing on research carried out from the perspective of the institution and the learning of students, the answer to the central question: "what can institutions and programmes do to reduce differences in school careers?" comes more quickly into focus.

We divided the research conducted in the past 15 years into three themes: Tinto's model is the central focus of the first theme; in the second the focus is on processes in the social domain; and the third theme looks at research that takes processes related to inequality in the learning environment as its starting point. The research into the differences in study performances and school careers, conducted using Tinto's model, explains these differences through the lower degree of social and academic integration of ethnic minority students. This means that, in general, ethnic minority students maintain poorer contact with their fellow students and teachers. The studies within the social domain give more background regarding social integration. For example, we see that peer support networks are of additional importance to ethnic minority students for good study performances. On the other hand, these peer networks can also have a negative impact. For example, Ogbu (2003) shows in an insightful manner how group processes, in which "Black" identity is defined in opposition to "White", handicap African-American students from doing their best and achieving good school performances.

The studies we discussed in the third theme, the learning environment, factually elaborate Tinto's academic integration. These studies oppose, more explicitly than Tinto does, the idea that students in minority positions have to integrate and insert themselves into the academic culture in order to be successful. Using the concept of "institutional habitus", Thomas (2002) shows how institutions that take the differences between students as their basis, instead of striving for homogeneity, ensure that ethnic minority students perform better. Teacher expectancy also plays a role in this: the low expectations of teachers, a poor learning attitude and poor school performances seem to have a reciprocal negative effect on one another.

The literature offers two clear reference points for answering the question of what institutions and programmes can do to reduce differences. The first answer involves dealing with differences. The performances of ethnic minority students improve in programmes in which social integration and contact with teachers of ethnic minority students is good, in which teachers regard differences as enriching and use them in classes, and in which diversity is explicitly referred to as a positive value. Such a diversity-friendly climate could, for example, be encouraged by designating diversity as a professional competency for teachers. Similarly, Rendon et al., (2000) argue that the greatest challenge for education institutions is to change their direction towards being truly multicultural institutions. The following quotation from a teacher expresses such a climate:

> We are open to all nationalities and cultures. We are an international programme and it is therefore normal that the focus is on cultural differences and how to deal with them. If you are unable to put yourself in someone else's culture, then you cannot practice your profession. (Interview with a majority teacher, Severiens et al., 2006: 134)

The second answer to the question of what education can do involves promoting contact in one's own community, in combination with encouraging the retention of one's own cultural identity in the education system. Research has clearly shown that social support networks and a feeling of awareness of one's own cultural identity have a positive impact on the performances of ethnic minority students. If universities or programmes succeed in making contact with these networks, this contact could then be used to distribute information: for example, to disseminate the message that a school or programme regards the diverse backgrounds of its pupil or student population as an enrichment and will actively use them in the curriculum. It is plausible that this would give minority groups a sense of recognition, which would probably have a positive effect on feeling comfortable and ultimately on school performances and study success. The quotation below is a good example of a teacher who works in this way:

> (We teach in a way that . . .) is specifically connected to the specific everyday lives of ethnic minorities, like unequal distribution of income and Turkey's entry into the EU. But also issues like segregation to which we have devoted three lectures. These are topical subjects, especially because we have many ethnic minorities here. (Interview with a majority teacher, Severiens *et al.*, 2006: 95)

One of the main conclusions of the studies by Severiens *et al.*, (2006, 2007) is that ethnic minority students are more dependent on the quality of teaching, while majority students rely on their more favourable starting point (on their "capital"). This result makes it even more important to translate the two directions referred to above into good and stimulating education for ethnic minority students.

References

Astin, A.W. (1993). *What Matters in College: Four critical years revisited.* San Francisco, CA: Jossey-Bass.
Berger, J.B. and Milem, J.F. (1999). The role of student involvement and perceptions of integration in a causal model of student persistence. *Research in Higher Education, 40*(6), 641–664.
Bowen, W.G. and Bok, D. (1998). *The Shape of the River: Long-term consequences of considering race in college and university admissions.* Princeton, NJ: Princeton University Press.
Bourdieu, P. and Wacquant, L. (1992). *An Invitation to Reflexive Sociology.* Chicago: Chicago University Press.
Braxton, J.M. (2000). *Reworking the Student Departure Puzzle.* Nashville: Vanderbilt University Press.
Connor, H., Tyers, C., Modood, T. and Hillage, J. (2004). *Why the Difference? A closer look at higher education minority ethnic students and graduates,* Research Report No. 552. London: Department for Education and Skills.
Eimers, M.T. and Pike, G.R. (1997). Minority and nonminority adjustment to college: differences or similarities? *Research in Higher Education, 38*(1), 77–97.
European Monitoring Centre on Racism and Xenophobia (2004). *Migrants, Minorities and Education. Documenting Discrimination and Integration in 15 Member States of the European Union.* Vienna: European Monitoring Centre on Racism and Xenophobia.
Fleming, J. (2002). Who will succeed in college? When the SAT predicts black students' performance. *Review of Higher Education, 25*(3), 281–296.
Fuertes, J.N. and Sedlacek, W.E. (1994). Using the SAT and noncognitive variables to predict the grades and retention of Asian American university students. *Measurement and Evaluation in Counseling and Development, 27,* 74–85.
Gloria, A.M., Castellanos, J., Lopez, A.G. and Rosales, R. (2005). An examination of academic nonpersistence decisions of Latino undergraduates. *Hispanic Journal of Behavorial Sciences, 27*(2), 202–223.
Hofman, W.H.A. and Van den Berg, M. (2003). Ethnic-specific achievement in Dutch higher education. *Higher Education in Europe, 28*(3), 371–389.
Hurtado, S. and Carter, D.F. (1997). Effects of college transition and perceptions of the campus racial climate on Latino students' sense of belonging. *Sociology of Education, 70,* 324–345.
Hurtado, S., Milem, J., Clayton-Pedersen, A. and Allen, W. (1999). Enacting diverse learning environments: improving the climate for racial/ethnic diversity in higher education. *ASHE-ERIC Higher Education Report, 26*(8), 1–140.
Johnson, D., Alvarez, P., Longerbeam, S., Soldner, M., Inkelas, K., Leonard, J. and Rowan-Kenyon, H. (2007). Examining sense of belonging among first-year undergraduates from different racial/ethnic groups. *Journal of College Student Development, 48*(5), 525–542.
Just, H.D. (1999). *Minority Retention in Predominantly White Universities and Colleges: The importance of creating a good "fit".* ERIC Report E 439 641.
Laar, van, C. and Levin, S. (in press). Minority ethnic groups and the university experience. In Sidanius, J., Levin, S., Van Laar, C. and Sears, D.O. (eds) *The Diversity Challenge: Social identity and intergroup relations on the college campus.* New York: Russell Sage.
Massey, D.S., Charles, C.Z., Lundy, G.F. and Fischer, M.J. (2003). *The Source of the River.* Princeton: Princeton University Press.
Mortensen, T. (2005). *Bachelor's Degree Attainment by Age 24 by Family Income Quartiles, 1970 to 2003.* Oskaloosa, IA: Postsecondary Opportunity.
Nora, A. and Cabrera, A.F. (1996). The role of perceptions of prejudice and discrimination on the adjustment of minority students to college. *Journal of Higher Education, 67*(2), 119–148.
Ogbu, J.U. (2003). *Black American Students in an Affluent Suburb.* Mahwah, NJ: Lawrence Erlbaum Associates.
Paulle, B. (2005). *Anxiety and Intimidation in the Bronx and the Bijlmer: An ethnographic comparison of two schools.* Amsterdam: Dutch University Press.

Pell Institute. (2005). *Indicators of Opportunity in Higher Education. 2005 Status Report* (http://www.pellinstitute.org/). Washington, D.C.: The Pell Institute.

Phalet, K. and Andriessen, I. (2003). Acculturation, motivation and educational attainment: a contextual model of minority school achievement. In Hagendoorn, L., Veenman, J. and Vollebergh, W. (eds) *Integrating Immigrants in the Netherlands: Cultural versus socio-economic integration.* Aldershot: Ashgate.

Pryor, J.H., Hurtado, S., Saenz, V.B., Santos, J. L. and Korn, W.S. (2007). Examining sense of belonging among first-year undergraduates from different racial/ethnic groups. *Journal of College Student Development, 48*(5), 525–542.

Read, B., Archer, L. and Leathwood, C. (2003). Challenging cultures? Student conceptions of belonging and isolation at a post-1992 university. *Studies in Higher Education, 28*(3), 261–277.

Reay, D., David, M. and Ball, S. (2001). Making a difference? Institutional habituses and higher education choice. *Sociological Research Online, 5,* 4.

Rendon, L., Jalomo, R.E. and Nora, A. (2000). Theoretical considerations in the study of minority student retention in higher education. In Braxton, J.M. *Reworking the Student Departure Puzzle.* Nashville: Vanderbilt University Press.

Severiens, S. and Wolff, R.P. (in press). A comparison of ethnic minority and majority students: social and academic integration and quality of learning. *Studies in Higher Education.*

Severiens, S., Wolff, R.P. and Rezai, S. (2006). *Diversiteit in leergemeenschappen: Een onderzoek naar stimulerende factoren in de leeromgeving voor allochtone studente in het hoger onderwijs.* Utrecht: ECHO.

Severiens, S., Wolff, R.P., Meeuwisse, M., Rezai, S. and de Vos, W. (2007). *Waarom stoppen zoveel allochtone studenten met de Pabo?* Den Haag: SBO.

Steele, C.M. and Aronson, J. (1995). Stereotype threat and the intellectual test performance of African Americans. *Journal of Personality and Social Psychology, 69,* 797–811.

Steinberg, L. (1996). *Beyond the Classroom: Why schools reform has failed and what parents need to do.* New York: Simon and Schuster.

Swail, W.S., Redd, K.E. and Perna, L.W. (2003). Retaining minority students in higher education: a framework for success. *ASHE-ERIC Education Report, 30*(2), I–187.

Terenzini, P.T. and Pascarella, E.T. (2005). *How College Affects Students: A third decade of research.* San Francisco, CA: Jossey-Bass.

Thomas, L. (2002). Student retention in higher education: the role of institutional habitus. *Journal of Education Policy, 17*(4), 423–442.

Tinto, V. (1993). *Leaving College: Rethinking the causes and cures of student attrition.* 2nd edn Chicago: The University of Chicago Press.

Tinto, V. (1997). Classrooms as communities. Exploring the educational character of student persistence. *Journal of Higher Education, 68*(6), 600–623.

Tinto, V. (1998). Colleges as communities. Taking research on student persistence seriously. *Review of Higher Education, 21*(2), 167–177.

Tracey, T.J. and Sedlacek, W.E. (1985). The relationship of noncognitive variables to academic success: A longitudinal comparison by race. *Journal of College Student Personnel, 26*(5), 405–410.

Tracey, T.J. and Sedlacek, W.E. (1987). Prediction of college graduation from noncognitive variables by race. *Measurement and Evaluation in Counseling and Development, 19,* 177–184.

Van de Werfhorst, H.G., Sullivan, A. and Cheung, S.Y. (2003). Social class, ability and choice of subject in secondary and tertiary education in Britain. *British Educational Research Journal, 29*(1), 41–62.

Wolff, R. and Crul, M. (2003). *Blijvers en uitvallers in het hoger onderwijs.* Utrecht: ECHO.

Wolff, R.P. (2007). *Met vallen en opstaan: Een analyse van instroom, uitval en rendementen van niet-westers allochtone studenten in het Nederlandse hoger onderwijs 1997–2005.* Utrecht: ECHO.

Zea, M.C., Reisen, C.A., Beil, C. and Caplan, R.D. (1997). Predicting intention to remain in college among ethnic minority and nonminority students. *The Journal of Social Psychology. 137*(2), 149–160.

III
Course Design

Course design is concerned with how we organise, deliver and assess the higher education curriculum. It is clearly closely related to both teaching and learning (discussed in Section II), which focuses on the approaches and strategies used day to day by lecturers and students, and the student experience (Section IV), which essentially examines the same issues as course design, but from the perspective of the student rather than the academic or institution.

Key contemporary issues of concern include: the use made of information and communication technologies (e.g. Laurillard, 2002); the employment of particular "curriculum delivery" strategies, such as problem-based learning (e.g. Savin-Baden, 2000) or work-based learning (e.g. Boud and Solomon, 2001); and how we cope with an increasingly heterogeneous student body.

The first of the four chapters in this section, by Kelly Coate, addresses the issue of curriculum head on. Starting from definitions of curriculum, she proceeds to consider how these vary in terms of level of study (undergraduate, postgraduate, doctoral) and regional, national or international orientations. Internationally, the Bologna Process is clearly having an impact, not only within Europe but beyond it as well, as is the virtual availability of curricula, as from MIT, anywhere in the world. Different conceptualisations of curricula are, of course, contested, both in terms of product and process, and in how well they are, or should be, constructively aligned to teaching, learning and assessment.

Coate then reviews three ways in which higher education curricula are currently developing: increasing internationalisation, moves to encourage greater civic engagement (see also the chapter in the section on institutional management by Hartley and Soo) and related efforts to develop social capital. She concludes by offering a schema for curricula involving the three domains of knowing, acting and being, emphasising the importance of the last of these.

Anna Kwan discusses one strategy for delivering the curriculum that has been particularly influential in recent decades, namely problem-based learning. Having outlined the nature and process of problem-based learning, Kwan compares it with more conventional approaches, such as subject, case and project-based learning. The theory behind the approach is then considered, along with the practical issues involved in designing and implementing a problem-based curriculum. Problem-based learning has been widely applied in different disciplinary contexts, but remains strongest in those with a professional or practice orientation, including medicine and health, social work, business studies and law. Kwan concludes by examining criticisms of, and challenges to, problem-based learning, and its likely future development.

In the third chapter in this section, Ilana Snyder, Simon Marginson and Tania Lewis look at the relationship between the use of information and communication technologies and change processes, focusing on the Australian higher education system. They identify two main paradigms in the use of information and communication technologies: the constructivist, which sees these technologies as another technique to be applied in the development of self-directed learners, and the corporate, which takes a top–down, managerial approach to their adoption across institutions.

Snyder and her colleagues completed 15 case studies in different disciplines and types of university, focusing on the educational, technological and organizational domains and their interactions. In all, 130 interviews of academics, managers and students were completed. Their findings are presented in terms of the use of information and communication technologies in three ways: to cultivate student-centred learning in social contexts, to implement transmission-based pedagogy, or to progress educational and organizational objectives simultaneously. Not surprisingly, they conclude that technological innovations work best when educational and organisational objectives are "in harmony", noting the importance of both discipline-based and central support and drivers.

The fourth and final chapter, by Marybeth Gasman and Julie Vultaggio, focuses on the impact of student diversity—in terms of race, ethnicity, class, gender and ability—on the university classroom. Historically, higher education has tended to privilege students (and staff) with particular physical and social characteristics: i.e. white, able-bodied men from the middle classes and above. Gasman and Vultaggio's concern is with how to enhance the learning in an equitable fashion of the much more diverse student groups that massification has now established as the norm.

References

Boud, D. and Solomon, N. (eds) (2001). *Work-based Learning: a new higher education?* Buckingham: Open University Press.
Laurillard, D. (2002). *Rethinking University Teaching: a conversational framework for the effective use of learning technologies.* London: RoutledgeFalmer.
Savin-Baden, M. (2000). *Problem-based Learning in Higher Education: untold stories.* Buckingham: Open University Press.

7
Curriculum

Kelly Coate

Curriculum

Most applications for any type of employment require a *curriculum vitae*: the standard document summarising major life achievements and literally meaning a "course of life". It is a purposive account, but not perhaps entirely authentic in faithfully representing every twist and turn of the course of a life, lived within the complexities of social and institutional relationships. The information presented on a *curriculum vitae* is selected from an array of possibilities, recast into a simplified but instructional form. The CV writer must communicate in a very particular and highly conventional manner, typically reducing years of experience into easily understood categories: "previous employment", "education", etc.

In a similar vein we can understand the construction of the higher education curriculum. The author of a typical curriculum, perhaps for a module or course, will select content from an enormous range of subject-specific knowledge. This content will be reconstructed into a format that again is highly conventional and well established within the discipline in question. Even non-specialists will understand the basics of a well-drafted curriculum document. A typical syllabus will include topics or themes grouped into particular categories, and it will be chronological or sequential, giving space to each topic or theme as the course progresses through its allotted time.

Although, on the surface, a typical curriculum document or syllabus appears to be a fairly straightforward matter of content organisation, there is much that is not known about the processes that shape the development of curricula. What considerations are taken into account when designing curricula? Even just a cursory attempt to understand curricula development will reveal that there is often a complex interplay between academic considerations, internal and external constraints, and power relationships between those with some sort of an investment in the course. Lying silently but powerfully underneath all of these issues are the very real concerns of the social and historical contexts in which curricula are developed. Here we see coming into view the values and social forces of the contemporary world (Cornbleth 2008).

These values and phenomena are wide-ranging and sometimes conflicting. Technological innovations, religion, citizenship, democracy, globalisation and multiculturalism are just a few of the social forces that might shape the curricula of various disciplines. Yet is the curriculum a reflection or mirror of contemporary concerns and state-of-the-art knowledge, or does it somehow reconstruct and reshape the knowledge available in society at any one time? Can it even be suggested that the higher education curriculum is in itself a social force, helping to define the values, morals and concerns of contemporary society? Any one of these concepts is enough on its own to assign a powerful role to the curriculum, and yet it may be possible that higher education curricula are playing all three roles.

In this chapter, some of the ways in which curricula have been conceptualised in higher education will be examined. From the outset, it is important to emphasise that the curriculum in higher education, in contrast to school-level curricula, is a relatively under-researched and theoretical concept. The autonomy of academics to construct curricula without interference, monitoring or evaluation has until relatively recently remained unchallenged in many higher education systems. Therefore, the curriculum has traditionally been the result of a private process; its results, or the "curriculum-in-action" (Barnett and Coate 2005), were also part of the private pedagogic transactions between academics and students. Recent decades have seen many changes and challenges to the autonomy of academics to write and deliver curricula, and as such there are new conceptualisations of curricula in view.

A General Overview

The Latin origin of the word curriculum is a "course of action". Most academics, when questioned about the meaning of the term curriculum, would probably imagine a plan, outline or syllabus for a module or other unit of instruction within a degree programme (Fraser and Bosanquet 2006). This "course of action" is the most basic understanding of curricula.

Beyond syllabi and course outlines, it becomes an impossible task to define "the" higher education curriculum. There are many different curricula in higher education: at undergraduate and postgraduate levels, in the enormous variety of disciplines and subject areas offered in higher education, and through curricula frameworks that have been developed at national and even supranational levels. There are also now "virtual" curricula. Let us look at some of these distinctions in turn, and in so doing introduce some important terminology in relation to curricula design.

Which Level of Curricula?

In comparison with school curricula, curricula in higher education institutions tend not to be subjected to as much influence or interference from the state. This is not to suggest that academics design curricula with total freedom (although historically, academic control over curricula was almost absolute in many countries) but there does seem to be a tendency for state control over curricula to be attenuated at the higher levels of study. Decisions about curricula—what is taught, when it is taught, how it is taught and to whom it is taught—seem to be made by academics with the greatest freedom at the highest levels of the education system. In other words, academics designing and developing undergraduate curricula tend to do so with less freedom than those developing postgraduate or doctoral-level curricula.

This diminishment of state interference in curricula at the higher levels of study occurs for many reasons, not least because at higher levels of study there are fewer people able to make specialist judgements about the content of courses or appropriate pedagogical approaches. At undergraduate level there are often many more practical constraints on curriculum design than at higher levels of study. Introductory courses, for instance, may involve large groups of students with concomitant timetabling issues in relation to lecture theatres or the availability of tutors to lead seminar groups. Teaching might take place in teams, in which case the control over content will be shared. Introductory or undergraduate level courses in the early years are also quite heavily defined by notions around "core" or "foundational" knowledge. What is the basic knowledge that a sociologist, or engineer, or chemist, needs to know before progressing to the higher levels of the discipline?

The core knowledge of a discipline is a remarkably enduring phenomenon. In most well-established disciplines, there are fairly stable views as to the content of the early stages of a degree programme, which can remain virtually unchanged for decades. From time to time there are various challenges to this core knowledge, as shifting paradigms, new social forces or new knowledge necessitate some form of change. For example, the critics of the "literary canon" in North American higher education were challenging a curriculum which they felt over-represented a Eurocentric, masculine worldview. The debates that ensued from these challenges provoked public discussions about large questions, such as the roles of universities in societies (see Bloom 1987; Readings 1996). The resulting diversification of many core curricula—the greater inclusion of black, Hispanic and women authors on introductory literature courses, for instance—suggests the powerful role that curricula can play in mirroring social forces in society at large.

These types of high-profile skirmishes are fairly rare. Generally, the least specialised levels of curricula (e.g. year one in an undergraduate degree programme) tend to be most strongly classified and framed (Bernstein 1971) levels of curricula, with the most stable knowledge content. Classification and framing are sociological terms used to denote the degree of stability around curricula in terms of agreed subject content and teaching approaches. Strong classification and framing suggests that there is less contestation over the knowledge and teaching methods deemed to be appropriate within a curriculum.

As the level of study advances, academic freedom to design curricula may increase as areas of specialisation within research might feature more substantially. The final year of an undergraduate degree may involve students undertaking research: a trend that is increasingly identified as "research-oriented teaching" (Jenkins *et al.*, 2007). There are disciplinary differences in the extent to which research is linked to teaching in the later years of undergraduate degrees (Coate *et al.*, 2001), but, nevertheless, it seems that curricula design might be more open and flexible at these stages. In addition, the introduction of students' research into curricula may be seen as a process of handing curricula "space" from the teacher to the student.

Further on, at postgraduate level, these trends increase. The core content of a professionally oriented master's degree, for instance, might be strongly shaped by external influences, yet there tends to be more "space" for student participation in the curriculum overall. The course developers also retain a large degree of control over curricular design decisions, such as the "mode" of study (distance, blended, problem-based learning, research) and the mix between core and optional modules on offer. In other areas of postgraduate-level teaching, the curriculum may largely reflect specialist academic research areas, and function more as a means of inducting students into the "mastery of a discipline" (Parker 2002), or even to introduce the "ultimate mystery" of a discipline (Bernstein 1977).

Mastery and mystery are two powerful terms that aptly describe doctoral-level curricula. It is at this highest level of study that students are expected, traditionally, to "master" the discipline: to become fully immersed within it, and to participate within the community of scholars who practise and shape it (Parker 2002). Paradoxically, this mastery of a discipline entails understanding the "mysteries" within it; in other words, the gaps, disputes and fissures within the knowledge being produced at the highest levels. In order to master a subject area, then, a student must understand how to contribute knowledge to it by identifying these mysterious outer reaches of a discipline where knowledge is contested and constructed.

Conventionally, this induction into academic knowledge production has been achieved through a PhD by research. In this mode of study, the curriculum was almost solely defined by the supervisor: the "course of action" of the student's programme (number of meetings, suggested readings, plans for research) would largely be within the control of one academic. In more recent years, various external agendas have been brought to bear on doctoral-level curricula, and, as such, there is more attention focused on design of curricula across doctoral programmes that share similar elements.

Policy drivers are enforcing certain changes in the doctorate: in Australia, the UK and Ireland, for instance, emphasis on the role that the doctorate plays within the creation of a knowledge economy has led to tighter structures within doctoral programmes (e.g. Neumann 2007). The Bologna Process has also now turned attention to the doctorate (or "third cycle"), and this is encouraging national-level discussions about the nature of doctoral programmes in many countries, particularly in relation to knowledge economy policies (European University Association 2005). The establishment of graduate schools with specified research training programmes is becoming a feature in doctoral studies in a number of countries (Powell and Green 2007). Professional doctorates, which include substantive modules and attached coursework, as well as a research-based thesis, are also gaining in popularity (Scott *et al.*, 2004).

The control, agency and power that individual academics possess to design and develop curricula can be eroded as external demands increase, and systematic controls are put into place over programmes of study. Why is this important? Historically, as mentioned above, most academics in universities held a great—almost total—degree of freedom to design and develop curricula as they deemed appropriate. At the highest levels of education, many academics have viewed this freedom as a hard-won, professional responsibility, and there is often resentment against increased interventions. An important element of academic work was the degree of trust placed with academics to design and control their curricula outputs, and greater external interventions, through such initiatives as generic research training programmes at doctoral level, are often perceived as indicating a lack of trust.

There are a number of other ways in which academic freedom is being eroded or is perceived to be diminishing. One of the factors in this perception of loss of control is a greater awareness of national and international standards, and the development of quality assurance systems and related qualifications frameworks. Curriculum developers are increasingly orienting their efforts towards national frameworks or international standards. Another complicating factor in terms of the development of curricula is, therefore, the potential tension between regional, national and international orientations.

Regional, National or International Orientations?

Most higher education institutions are caught up in complex interplays between regional, national and international interests. Curricula that are developed within them often become bound up within these different orientations. There are a number of ways in which these different concerns are reflected in curricula development, and it is useful to elaborate on a few of them here.

Curricula often reflect regional concerns and contribute substantially to the local communities in which they are based. My own university, for instance, is located in the Irish-language-speaking region of Ireland (the *gaeltacht*), and has a government mandate to promote the Irish language. Not only are there courses on offer that teach the Irish language and Irish culture, but there are specialist postgraduate courses for Irish-language journalists, teachers and translators, and courses within the undergraduate curricula taught through the medium of Irish. It is possible to learn French in Irish, for example. In terms of the regional role that curricula can play, these examples strongly suggest that curricula can be not just a reflection of society, but a social force that helps shape and develop local concerns.

The challenge for universities that play a strong regional role is that inevitably the curricula on offer have a limited appeal outside of the region. Here we can see that there might be considerations about curricula that go beyond individual academics, even beyond course teams and departments, to institutional, regional and national levels. It is at a national level, for instance, that NUI Galway is mandated to promote and develop the Irish language through its curricular provision. Ireland is not the only nation-state with similar expectations of its higher education curricula. Greek higher education, for example, has been steered by the state to promote Greek culture, and the transformation of the South African higher education system has been perceived to be an important part of national transformations.

At the national level, however, in many higher education systems, expectations of curricula that do not relate to cultural or regional roles of institutions are increasingly being developed. These expectations often stem from concerns with quality and transparency. The establishment of national quality assurance or enhancement mechanisms, and of qualifications frameworks or subject benchmarks, are encouraging academics to look towards these external frameworks to guide their curriculum development. In most higher education systems that are well developed, these frameworks and audit mechanisms are becoming more formalised.

There are undoubtedly many benefits to increased transparency and evaluation of curricula. Yet quality assurance and enhancement mechanisms have also been widely perceived as heralding a loss of academic control over curricula development (e.g. Morley 2003; Evans 2004). National systems for reviewing quality in universities are usually ascribed a bureaucratic or managerial role, rather than an academic role, and a certain lack of trust in academic autonomy has seemingly entered higher education systems where this has taken place. Yet, in some national systems that are small but newly expanding, a quality assurance mechanism can increase confidence in curricular offerings, as seen in South Africa, for instance, or Norway (e.g. McDonald and van der Horst 2007).

What are some of the ways in which external evaluations or quality review exercises can impact on curricula design? There may be accreditation bodies that evaluate certain aspects of curriculum design within particular subject areas. National systems for quality assurance, such as that in the UK, force another level of transparency or accountability onto curricula design, by ensuring that courses and degree programmes achieve a similar standard of outcomes. Subject benchmarks, for example, detail the learning outcomes expected from different programmes, and therefore curricula developers are encouraged (or required) to detail how their curriculum meets these expectations.

These expectations of curricula are not only occurring nationally, but are now developed and discussed at supra-national levels. The most obvious example is the Bologna Process, through which the ministers of higher education from 45 countries in and around Europe agreed to harmonise degree structures. The Bologna Process has had a substantial impact on some national systems, in terms of changes to length of degree programmes, and moves towards modularisation or semesterisation (Eurydice 2005). The European Credit Transfer System (ECTS) has increased awareness across different national systems of issues of standardisation of curricula outputs. In countries as diverse as Estonia and Portugal, for instance, academics are struggling to understand how the curricula they are designing translate into a 10 ECTS module, or over 250 hours of student effort. For many academics, this has marked a radical departure from previous practices, and there has inevitably been resistance and disgruntlement.

The Bologna Process is in some ways a (large) regional development, being centred within and on the peripheries of the European Union. It has gained attention even further afield, however, as the attractiveness of offering degree programmes that are seen to comply with a framework of international "standards" is strong for some universities and national higher education systems. This international orientation of curricula has existed for a long time, but may be increasing due to trends associated with globalisation. Academics in particular fields have historically tended to look towards reputable degree programmes elsewhere to assess their own standards on an informal basis. Now the influence of international developments is more keenly felt, when access to curricular documents has been drastically simplified by the internet.

An engineering lecturer in Iceland, for instance, may have studied for a period in the US and have become familiar with the engineering programmes in MIT. When designing courses in Iceland, knowledge of the "MIT approach" becomes one factor in how the curriculum is shaped (Geirsdóttir 2008). Now, it is possible for any academic or administrator in the world to log on to MIT's OpenCourseWare site and peruse the curricula on offer. Universities elsewhere are making access to curricula documents and artefacts easier. The Open University in the UK has an open courseware site, and other universities increasingly upload video recordings or podcasts of lectures onto special sections of their websites that are available for public use.

This "virtual" availability of curricula is an interesting phenomenon within a globalised higher education system. Whilst some staff in higher education institutions are positive about these changes, and believe that curricula should be openly shared and freely available, others are undoubtedly sceptical. Concerns over the legal ownership or copyright of curricula are sometimes expressed, which reveal a view of curricula as a product resulting from academic labour, much in the same way as academics produce books or other scholarly outputs. Certainly, curricula that have been developed specifically for online delivery are "written" or "authored" in a way that might suggest curricula such as these are being commodified. An online curriculum "package", for instance, can be delivered or even sold online as if it were a package holiday.

Now we can see that we need to turn attention not just to curricula internationally, but also curricula in a virtual world. The commodification of knowledge and curricula that can be bought and sold in a global marketplace is provoking interest, particularly given that some private, for-profit companies have been extremely successful at it, such as Kaplan Inc. in the US. One of the fears is that academia itself will become driven by economic demands to market and sell products to be delivered elsewhere, thereby removing much of the joy of teaching and learning that is gained through establishing personal contact with students through classroom interactions (e.g. Naidoo and Jamieson 2005). Are these concerns well founded?

Certainly the increased provision of for-profit private higher education, and the economic value of online degree programmes, is not in question, and the providers who have found a market for their products will continue to deliver them. There are, however, moves afoot to "subvert" the privatisation of higher education by opening up spaces for freely sharing curricular materials, such as MIT's OpenCourseWare site. In many respects, the "virtual" world of curricula is currently the most dramatic and radical reshaping of higher education curricula, as it has forced what was once a private, closed world out into an open, public space. What is more, it has enabled those who are willing to share their curricula freely to put into practice a public-spirited ethos about the role of higher education in society.

"Virtual" curricula may, therefore, be one way in which we can understand curricula as a social force, as its role in public life may be seen as shaping the knowledge society or fulfilling some of the aims of lifelong learning policies. Other aspects of its impact on traditional conceptions of curricula will be returned to. Indeed, all of the above issues are only touching upon some of the distinctions that need to be kept in mind when exploring curricula in higher education. At the very least, they raise questions as to whether we can discuss "the" higher education curriculum as if it were a single entity, or whether the complexities mentioned make it an impossible task. Beyond this, we can see that curricula are shaped by social forces, and may even play a part in shaping the values of society. Before we return to expand on some of these important issues, it is useful to first understand some ways in which curricula have been theorised in attempts to enable academics to understand, develop and enhance curricula.

Conceptualisations of Curricula: Contestations

An early and helpful discussion of curricula in higher education was produced by Goodlad (1984), in which he set out five different types of curricula: formal, ideal, perceived, operational and experiential. The formal curriculum is that set out in documentation such as a syllabus, whereas the ideal curriculum denotes those aspects of curricula over which there might be a struggle for control. The perceived curriculum represents academics' perspectives on what curriculum is or should be. The operational curriculum describes classroom processes, whereas the experiential curriculum represents the curriculum as perceived by students.

Goodlad's categorisations are helpful for this discussion in several respects. His categories can be seen to imply a distinction between curriculum-as-product and curriculum-as-process, as such:

- product (ideal, formal, perceived)
- process (perceived, operational, experiential).

The ideal, formal and perceived curricula are all indicative of a view of curriculum as a product, or an entity to be negotiated, produced and presented in a final format. The operational and experiential forms denote that the curriculum exists mainly as it is "in action": it is not a static entity but comes into being through the processes of designing and delivering it. The perceived curriculum is both product and process, given that it is possible to perceive curricula as both an entity and a continually evolving social construct.

Through Goodlad's distinction between product and process, a clearer understanding of curricula emerges. We can begin to conceptualise the *products* of curricula as the enduring elements of curricula design, such as the core knowledge in undergraduate degrees, or course outlines or syllabi. The ongoing *processes* of curricula design and delivery lie behind those products: such as the struggles over what types of knowledge can be included in curricula, and the experiences within the classroom as students encounter the curriculum.

An example will help to further illuminate these ideas. The MIT OpenCourseWare site is a useful place in which to peruse curricular offerings at a university that is generally perceived to be a standard-bearer for the "harder" disciplines within science and technology curricula. What counts as "ideal" in the MIT case is world-class excellence in these subjects. Yet a recent browse through the site uncovered a module called "Topics in Comparative Media: American Pro-Wrestling" (see: http://ocw.mit.edu/OcwWeb/Comparative-Media-Studies/CMS-997Spring2007/CourseHome/index.htm). The curriculum documents available on the site make it clear that this is a course that will enable students to think critically about a form of entertainment in America with roots in the carnival, which is highly specialised in form and now a huge economic success. Although anyone downloading the materials from the website will only see this curriculum "product", it is possible to speculate that the "processes" of curricula development behind it were extensive. Not only did the readings, lecture notes, blog and video recordings all have to be carefully designed or selected and put together into a package, but presumably many other behind-the-scenes negotiations took place. The topic of wrestling would raise eyebrows at many universities, and would probably even be rejected by those which have less confidence in their status in the world than MIT. The inclusion of such a topic at a place like MIT raises interesting issues about the boundaries around what is considered to be "legitimate" academic knowledge.

This module is just one example of how the product of curricula developments, such as materials on a website, do not give much of an insight into the processes behind and around the shaping of curricula. What debates took place when this module was proposed? Was the design of the module subsequently negotiated or modified, or did the curriculum designer have complete academic autonomy to develop the module as desired? How did the students experience the module, and what unexpected outcomes were there, if any? All of these questions would reveal fascinating insights into the processes of curricula development, but they would require a dedicated research project to uncover.

The curriculum products available on the web are, therefore, artefacts which offer only small glimpses into much bigger worlds. Arguably, the reason why these kinds of materials are being made freely available is because they enable only a superficial insight into the courses on offer: they do not give much indication of the quality of teaching, for example. The universities that offer curricula freely in this manner do not have much to lose because they are not giving much away.

The MIT example is also fascinating because it gives one insight into how the borders around legitimate knowledge, or ideal curricula, can be shaped by underlying social forces. The inclusion of knowledge in curricula that was not traditionally perceived to be legitimate for academic study can be read in two ways: either it is a liberating attempt to diversify and democratise an exclusive and elite curricula, or it can be viewed as a dangerous "dumbing down" of a university curricula that should be maintaining and preserving certain core knowledge, values and standards. Both points of view are vigorously debated at times of change within curricula, such as during the 1970s and 1980s, when political movements brought women's studies and black studies into university curricula. The more ubiquitous reference to the "dumbing down" of curricula through cultural studies and media studies provoked similar debates that centred on the politics of cultural relativism: is pro wrestling a topic as worthy of study as Shakespeare, for example? We should not lose sight here that both cultural studies and women's studies, at least in some countries, have struggled very hard to survive as subject areas in their own right, and may even be losing the battle.

These types of debates raise important questions about the nature of university knowledge. Is it in some ways special, requiring a sense of standing apart from the world? Or should curricula be in and of the world in which they are located; capable of reflecting a wide range of perspectives and engaging a student population of great diversity? The debate is an important one, for it prompts questions about the role of universities and higher education institutions in society. This brings us to an issue that should perhaps be at the heart of discussions about curricula: the intended outcomes for the students.

Conceptualisations of Curricula: Constructive Alignment

The discussion about curricula has been fairly abstract, but has hopefully illustrated the complexities of a topic that might not at first sight seem that contentious. However, there are ideas about curricula of a more practical nature, and that are intended to enable the enhancement or improvement of the student experience through curriculum development. These ideas turn attention to the outcomes of curricula, particularly in relation to student learning. One of the key points within this approach is that curriculum design should begin with an understanding of what the learning outcomes are for any particular module, course or programme.

One of the most influential approaches to curricula design has been Biggs' (1999) notion of *constructive alignment*. What Biggs has proposed is that the development of curricula should focus on ensuring that the teaching methods, learning activities and assessment requirements are aligned with the learning outcomes of the course. In other words, achieving alignment between these elements will help ensure that the students construct meanings from the course that lead to the intended outcomes. In an aligned curriculum, students are able to make sense of the teaching, learning and assessment activities because they are coherent and transparent. The entire "teaching system", if constructively aligned, should encourage students of all abilities to acquire the necessary skills to meet the desired objectives.

The learning outcomes of a module or course, therefore, become paramount when considering curriculum design within this framework. This focus on outcomes has enabled those who design and develop curricula to understand whether or not the learning activities and assessment methods actually achieve the desired results. For instance, does a three-hour, unseen, written examination at the end of a module actually measure the types of learning that the course designer intended? It has long been acknowledged within the teaching and learning literature that such examinations are often a poor measurement for a variety of intended learning outcomes, and yet they continue to be a major feature within many higher education systems. Constructive alignment is, therefore, one way of encouraging an approach to curricular design that focuses on how best to achieve and measure the intended learning outcomes (Rust 2007).

Learning outcomes are becoming an established feature within quality assurance mechanisms in many countries, and they are certainly prominent within the Bologna Process, given that the signatory countries are committed to developing their use in curricula design. Yet there are critics of an outcomes-based approach to curricular development, not in the sense that learning outcomes as such are undesirable, but more in the sense that an unduly technical discourse has entered the lexicon of curriculum design. The language of learning outcomes, which has become highly specialised in some curriculum frameworks, could be seen to be reductionist and overly goal-oriented. They have been promoted by external agencies (such as quality assurance mechanisms) as ways of monitoring curricula. Learning outcomes such as these tend to focus on learning that is measurable, rather than learning that is transformative or empowering (Parker 2003).

This is why debates and discussions around the wider purposes of curricula, which are often neglected in the higher education literature, are so important. Without these discussions, there can be a tendency for unduly narrow conceptualisations of curricula to come into play (Barnett and Coate 2005). It can be difficult, for instance, to feel any sense of creativity or autonomy within curricula design if specified learning outcomes must be produced. The language of learning outcomes can be perceived to be not much more than a litany of verbs describing measurable outcomes: e.g. synthesise, explain, apply, calculate, define. Whilst the clarity of such aims is valuable for students and staff, is there a danger that the non-measurable outcomes of higher education curricula might be downplayed? What if the learning outcomes are primarily that students are encouraged to take risks, be creative and increase their own sense of self-confidence and self-worth, or even are challenged to fundamentally alter their preconceived notions? These are aims that are not easily definable or measurable, but are implicitly the outcomes of what many would see to be a *higher* education.

This is not to suggest in any way that constructive alignment is itself a misguided concept. Educators such as Biggs, who wish to promote approaches to curriculum design that enable students to have valuable and affirming educational experiences, are perhaps too thin on the ground at the moment. In lieu of these articulations, ideas about curriculum development that are shaped by agendas of accountability, managerial auditing exercises or other bureaucratic requirements begin to creep into the discourse. It is against such technicist and bureaucratic approaches to curricula development that resistance is sometimes expressed (e.g. Hussey and Smith 2003).

New Curricular Spaces

However, there are other voices and ideas emerging about contemporary curricula that tap into the broader purposes of higher education and its role in society. These emerging ideas run counter to the more technicist vision of the outcomes-based curricula discussed above, by opening up different understandings of what it might mean to be a student in the twenty-first century. A brief overview of several of them—internationalised curricula, civic engagement and a social capital approach—will be provided before concluding with a proposed schema for opening up new curricula "spaces".

Internationalised Curricula

Discussions about internationalised curricula are currently gaining ground (e.g. De Vita and Case 2003; Jones and Killick 2007; Takagi 2007). In some ways this is not a new idea, as previous "versions" of internationalised curricula were proposed under the rubric of the multicultural curriculum, and even before that in the export of curricula overseas: for instance, through the University of London's external programme. Some definitions of the internationalised curricula echo this past, by emphasising the inclusion of international content. The Organisation for Economic Cooperation and Development (OECD) provided one such definition by highlighting an "international orientation in content" within curricula and aimed at the preparation of students for "performing (professionally/socially) in an international and multicultural context" (OECD 1996: 36). The idea of diversifying curricula to include a wider range of perspectives and knowledge has been mentioned, and, in the case of internationalisation of curricula it suggests this diversity comes from the inclusion of scholarly work from across the globe. This raises interesting questions for curriculum designers: is the "right" approach to an internationalised curricula a longer reference list that includes books from Asia, Latin America, or Africa? How can one academic become an expert on knowledge from all corners of the globe?

Hence, this early definition, which focuses on diversity in content, has been criticised as being overly simplistic and even unhelpful (De Vita and Case 2003; Brookfield 2007). More recent discussions have begun to emphasise the "processes" (values) of curricula development over the "product" (content) of curricula. These processes are what the second half of the OECD definition is beginning to hint at: the preparation of students for performing in an international context. The value behind such orientations is that, in an increasingly globalised world, students need to be equipped with the skills necessary to interact with and value a range of cultures and perspectives. These discussions are taking place at institutional levels and within disciplinary specialisations.

To give one recent example of a disciplinary approach, a report has been produced called *The Global Engineer* (Bourn and Neal 2008), which argues for the global dimension to be integrated into engineering curricula. Funded by the UK's Department for International Development, and produced by Engineers Against Poverty, the emphasis is on education for sustainable development and global citizenship. These are tall orders, and the authors note that one of the main challenges is convincing academics that there is curricula "space" for such projects, given that many engineering academics are opposed to a reduction in the core content of engineering curricula. Again, this suggests that the "product" or "content" view of curricula is still pervasive. Nevertheless, the ethical, moral and civic imperatives behind such initiatives may win out, and it is notable that these types of initiatives are being encouraged at institutional level in some cases.

Leeds Metropolitan University (LMU) in England, for instance, has produced a strategy to internationalise the curriculum, in which a key priority is to "develop students' international opportunities and global perspectives" (LMU 2004). The "ethos" of the university is described as aspiring to be international in orientation. In direct relation to the earlier comments about tensions between international and regional orientations of curricula, LMU has tackled this tension head on, by describing itself as a "world-class regional university with world-wide horizons". The development of an internationalised curriculum is one way in which LMU will be presented as having an international orientation.

University College London (UCL), in a similar fashion, has recently branded itself as "London's Global University", nicely capturing its local and international orientations in one short phrase. UCL has put forward a key strategic priority to educate its students for "global citizenship and leadership" (see http://www.ucl.ac.uk/global_citizenship/). These efforts go beyond "flavouring courses with a sense of the international and global", towards a more holistic understanding of an inclusive curriculum that has an international ethos embedded within it (De Vita and Case 2003: 394). UCL and LMU are just two examples of universities that are now taking steps to promote an internationalised curriculum, although there are differences in the terminology used. However, they both focus on the *processes* of internationalising the curriculum (rather than just a multi-cultural, content-focused product) in an attempt to address some of the challenges of globalisation. In this way, they are both reflecting the social forces that shape students' experiences in contemporary higher education, but also helping to shape the students' experiences to prepare them for these challenges.

Civic Engagement

Civic engagement is again a contemporary version of an older idea: the reassertion of the public role of universities in educating future citizens to participate within a civil society (Hollander 2007; Watson 2007). The concept of civic engagement centres around a terminology that differs between national contexts, but which denotes similar values: e.g. community, democracy, service, engagement and social capital. In the US, the "service" ethos has been strongly embedded within the higher education system since its inception, although some might suggest it has taken a back seat lately in favour of a more economic agenda for higher education (but see the chapter in this book by Hartley and Soo). The ethos behind civic engagement initiatives is that students and staff should not only "give back" to society some of the skills and knowledge they have, but also that, through doing so, they can enhance their own learning and development. Non-paid work within disadvantaged communities or within community organisations is particularly encouraged, but increasingly this is also done as part of the curriculum. Students might take a "service learning" module, for instance, in which they gain credit for the academic, scholarly work they produce as a result of voluntary work. Learning journals or reflective portfolios are often used for these purposes.

Curricula of civic engagement are almost entirely process-oriented. They are "lived" curricula, or "curricula-in-action": the curriculum unfolds as the student goes into communities or community-based organisations and works with them. This is not to suggest that curricula designers have no role in a service learning module. On the contrary, the planning of the "course of action" for a service learning module entails a huge raft of concerns, including the establishment of partnerships with community organisations, the safety of students, the guidelines for their engagement with communities, and the assessment requirements. Curricula designers of service learning courses must be cognisant of how to constructively align the learning objectives, student activities and learning outcomes, perhaps even more so than with conventional course design.

The most notable aspect of civic engagement or service learning is that curricula oriented towards these goals offer an ethical, moral and democratic justification for higher education in a climate that is increasingly driven by an economic profit motive. These initiatives engage students in a type of learning that goes beyond filling their heads full of knowledge, or giving them skills to gain a lucrative employment position, towards encouraging them to become citizens capable of participating in and actively shaping a democratic, civil society. That higher education has a key role to play in "active citizenship" is being recognised in countries outside of the US, such as the UK and Ireland (see McIlrath and Mac Labhrainn 2007). Again, we see the growing currency of terminology in relation to curricula around notions of citizenship and democracy, which are underpinned by more philosophical arguments about the broader purposes of curricula in higher education. These purposes are related to the development of theories of social capital as against human capital.

Social Capital

Theories about social capital gained broad appeal through Putnam's (2001) book *Bowling Alone*, in which he argues that American citizens have in recent decades become disengaged from political processes. Although Putnam's thesis is based on somewhat popularist notions of "community", his endorsement of active citizenship is echoed by other critical voices who increasingly see higher education as playing an important role in the maintenance and enhancement of civil society. Social capital is a term that denotes the value of social networks and cooperation, in contrast to human capital theory which focuses on economic gain. It is a term that resonates with those who believe higher education has an ethical and moral role to play within society. Walker (2006), for instance, draws on the work of the philosophers Sen and Nussbaum to argue for higher education pedagogies that develop the capabilities of humans to function in civil society.

An approach to curricula development that focuses on the capabilities of students to contribute to the "cultivation of humanity" and the "ideal of the world citizen" (Nussbaum 1997), or an education that enables personal freedom to achieve "well-being" (Sen 1992), is a fairly radical idea in the contemporary higher education climate. The dominant discourse from governments all over the world concerning the development of higher education systems is one of economic growth, the knowledge economy and global competitiveness. There are a few other voices: the proponents of liberal education in North American higher education, for instance, often place an emphasis on the values of an education that embraces civic and global engagement (e.g. Hoy and Meisel 2008). Social capital, as against economic or human capital, reminds us that higher education can contribute to the development of society and humanity, and not just the economy.

How might these aspirations be achieved through curricula? Service learning, civic engagement and internationalised curricula are arguably all versions of curricula underpinned by a philosophical and ethical argument in favour of a higher education focused on the cultivation of humanity, but there are other ways. One means by which attention can be turned towards social rather than economic capital is through the foregrounding, within curricula design, of the students' sense of their own identity and development. In Barnett and Coate (2005) we argued in favour of opening up "curricula spaces" which enable the student's sense of self to come into view. To conclude this chapter, I would like to summarise the schema we proposed for thinking about curricula in relation to this aim.

Conclusions: A Proposed Schema

It was suggested that, in the absence of debates and discussions, an unduly narrow conceptualisation of curricula may come to dominate our understandings of curriculum design. Curriculum design can be thought about in a fairly technical way, through the production of learning outcomes, alignment to national frameworks, calculations of credit weightings, and so on. These technical aspects of curriculum development are useful, but only in so far as they enable course designers to meet institutional, professional or national requirements.

One way, perhaps, of capturing some of the ideas behind the emerging curricula spaces, summarised above, is through an acknowledgement that curricula (and, indeed, higher education) should be about more than the acquisition of a certain core body of knowledge or key skills. To that end, we developed a schema (Barnett and Coate 2005) in which three curricular "domains" are proposed for curriculum designers to consider within their own courses: knowing, acting and being. These domains are represented in Figure 7.1.

There are a few key points about this schema. Firstly, it suggests that these three domains may vary in terms of their weighting within curricula. The domain of knowing (knowledge), for

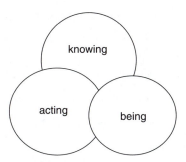

Figure 7.1 A Schema for Curricula.

example, might be fairly prominent within certain disciplines where the "core" knowledge of the subject is emphasised. In some curricula, the domain of acting might play a more prominent role, in terms of the skills or actions that students are expected to acquire and perform (in laboratories, for instance). In other types of curricula, the domain of being (or "self") might be more apparent, in terms of the development of students' identities (e.g. within particular professional areas that typically engage students in reflective practice, such as nursing studies).

Secondly, the schema denotes the possibility of overlap between the domains, so that some aspects of curricula are perceived as being interrelated. Here, we might think about skills that are embedded within disciplinary contexts, such as particular types of critical thinking associated with the acquisition of certain humanities subjects. Or there might be overlap between the acting and being domains, such that as students perform certain skills, their identities begin to evolve in particular ways. Thus, the students who begin to think like historians might begin to understand themselves to be historians.

The crucial aspect of this schema is the domain of "being": it denotes much more than "attitudes" or "attributes", which are terms sometimes used in professional qualifications frameworks. To develop curricula which engage with the student's sense of self is to acknowledge that higher education is about "being" in this world. It is a suggestion that higher education has a role to play in developing students' engagement with the world. Curricula in higher education are at the heart of this process.

It may be that some of the emerging forms of engaged curricula (socially, civically, globally) are struggling to find space amongst the more technical, instrumental modes of curricula development (frameworks, benchmarks, learning outcomes). Or it may be that these two conceptualisations of curricula can happily co-exist in the right climate. The challenge will be to encourage discussions about curricula design and development, a hitherto hidden world of academia. Indeed, it is the hidden nature of curricula development that is problematic, and not curricula as such; by initiating debates and discussions about the importance of curricula it may be possible to ensure that the values we might wish to promote through higher education are reflected within them.

References

Barnett, R. and Coate, K. (2005). *Engaging the Curriculum in Higher Education.* Maidenhead: Open University Press.

Bernstein, B. (1971). On the Classification and Framing of Educational Knowledge. In: M.F.D. Young (ed.) *Knowledge and Control.* London: Routledge and Kegan Paul.

Bernstein, B. (1977). *Class, Codes and Control,* Vol. *3,* 2nd ed. London: Routledge & Kegan Paul.

Biggs, J.B. (1999). *Teaching for Quality Learning at University.* Buckingham: Open University Press.

Bloom, A. (1987). *The Closing of the American Mind.* London: Penguin.

Bourn, D. and Neal, I. (2008). *The Global Engineer: Incorporating global skills within UK higher education of engineers.* London: Department for International Development, Engineers Against Poverty and the Institute of Education, London.

Brookfield, S. (2007). Diversifying curriculum as the practice of repressive tolerance. *Teaching in Higher Education, 12*(5–6): 557–568.

Coate, K., Barnett, R. and Williams, G. (2001). Relationships between teaching and research in higher education in England. *Higher Education Quarterly, 55*(2): 158–174.

Cornbleth, C. (2008). Climates of opinion and curriculum practices. *Journal of Curriculum Studies, 40*(2): 143–168.

De Vita, G. and Case, P. (2003). Rethinking the internationalization agenda in UK higher education. *Journal of Further and Higher Education, (27)*: 383–398.

European University Association. (2005). *Doctoral Programmes for the European Knowledge Society*. Brussels: European University Association.

Eurydice. (2005). *Focus on the Structure of Higher Education in Europe 2004/2005. National Trends in the Bologna Process*. Brussels: Eurydice.

Evans, M. (2004). *Killing Thinking: The death of the universities*. London: Continuum.

Fraser, S.P. and Bosanquet, A.M. (2006). The curriculum? That's just a unit outline, isn't it? *Studies in Higher Education, 31*(3), 269–284.

Geirsdóttir, G. (2008). We are caught up in our own world: Conceptions of curriculum within three different disciplines at the University of Iceland. Unpublished PhD Thesis: Iceland University of Education.

Goodlad, S. (1984). *Education for the Professions: Quis Custodiet?* Guildford: Society for Research into Higher Education and NFER-Nelson.

Hollander, E. (2007). Foreword. In McIlrath, L. and Mac Labhrainn, I. (eds) *Higher Education and Civic Engagement: International perspectives*. Hampshire: Ashgate Publishing Limited.

Hoy, A. and Meisel, W. (2008). *Civic Engagement at the Center: Building a democracy through integrated cocurricular and curricular experiences*. Washington: The Association of American Colleges and Universities.

Hussey, T. and Smith, P. (2003). The Uses of Learning Outcomes. *Teaching in Higher Education, 8*(3): 357–368.

Jenkins, A., Healey, M. and Zetter, R. (2007). *Linking Teaching and Research in Disciplines and Departments*. York: Higher Education Academy.

Jones, E. and Killick, D. (2007). Internationalisation of the curriculum. In E. Jones and S. Brown (eds) *Internationalising Higher Education*. London: Routledge.

Leeds Metropolitan University. (2004). *Leeds Metropolitan University Internationalisation Strategy 2004–2008*. Leeds: LMU.

McDonald, R. and van der Horst, H. (2007). Curriculum alignment, globalization, and quality assurance in South African higher education. *Journal of Curriculum Studies, 39*(1): 1–19.

McIlrath, L. and Mac Labhrainn, I. (eds) (2007). *Higher Education and Civic Engagement: International perspectives*. Hampshire: Ashgate Publishing Limited.

Morley, L. (2003). *Quality and Power in Higher Education*. Buckingham: Open University Press.

Naidoo, R. and Jamieson, I. (2005). Empowering participants or corroding learning? Towards a research agenda on the impact of student consumerism in higher education. *Journal of Education Policy, 20*(3): 267–281.

Neumann, R. (2007). Policy and practice in doctoral education. *Studies in Higher Education, 32*(4): 459–473.

Nussbaum, M. (1997). *Cultivating Humanity: A classical defense of reform in liberal education*. Cambridge, MA: Harvard University Press.

OECD. (1996). *Internationalization of Higher Education*. Paris: OECD.

Parker, J. (2002). A new disciplinarity: communities of knowledge, learning and practice. *Teaching in Higher Education, 7*(4): 373–386.

Parker, J. (2003). Reconceptualising the curriculum: from commodification to transformation. *Teaching in Higher Education, 8*(4): 259–543.

Powell, S. and Green, H. (2007). *The Doctorate Worldwide*. Maidenhead: Open University Press.

Putnam, R. (2001). *Bowling Alone: The collapse and revival of American community*. New York: Simon and Schuster.

Readings, B. (1996). *The University in Ruins*. Cambridge, MA: Harvard University Press.

Rust, C. (2007). Towards a scholarship of assessment. *Assessment and Evaluation in Higher Education, 32*(2): 229–237.

Sen, A. (1992). *Inequality Re-examined*. Oxford: Oxford University Press.

Scott, D., Brown, A., Lunt, I. and Thorne, L. (2004). *Professional Doctorates: Integrating academic and professional knowledge*. Maidenhead: Open University Press.

Takagi, H. (2007). Internationalisation of undergraduate curricula: the gap between the idea and practice. Paper presented at the Learning Together Conference, London: Institute of Education 22–24 July 2007.

Walker, M. (2006). *Higher Education Pedagogies*. Maidenhead: Open University Press.

Watson, D. (2007). *Managing Civic and Community Engagement*. Maidenhead: Open University Press.

8
Problem-based Learning

Anna Kwan[1]

1. Nature of PBL

Definition and Major Characteristics

Problem-based learning (PBL) is a form of enquiry-based learning, in which learning is driven by a process of inquiry (O'Rourke and Kahn, 2005). Definitions of PBL vary, but a comprehensive example would be a total education strategy based on the principle of using real-world problems as a starting point for the acquisition and integration of new knowledge. PBL is more than an instructional method, but a nurturing environment in which all curriculum elements are systematically aligned to help students achieve the learning outcomes. In a problem-based learning environment, several distinct characteristics may be identified and utilised in designing and implementing such curriculum (Barrows, 1985; Kwan, 2008; Stepien, Gallagher and Workman, 1993). These include:

1. Learners explore open-ended real-world problems as the starting point of learning.
2. Learners engage in self-directed learning, including planning, implementing and evaluating their overall learning process.
3. Learners work cooperatively in small groups to support each other to achieve the learning outcomes.
4. Teachers assume the role of facilitators and co-learners.
5. Learning outcomes emphasise not only content knowledge but also process skills and learning attitudes.

The problems in PBL primarily are vehicles for the development of clinical problem-solving skills (Barrows, 1996), but now the learning outcomes embedded in the problems include content knowledge and other important abilities like self-directed learning, critical thinking and reasoning, finding and using appropriate learning resources, communication, information and technology, teamwork and leadership skills, which are much demanded in the workplace.

PBL Process

In a PBL process, the real-world ill-structured problem is presented to students to start the learning sequence, before any preparation or study has occurred. Students work in a team to analyse the problem in a manner that allows their ability to reason and apply knowledge to be challenged, evaluated and developed. Students identify needed areas for learning all of which leads to individualised study. The skills and knowledge acquired are shared among team members, then applied back to the problem, to evaluate the quality of learning. To reinforce deep learning, students' learning in the process, including individualised study, is summarised and integrated into the students' existing knowledge and skills (Barrows and Tamblyn, 1980). To illustrate the steps in a PBL process, Woods (1994) has identified eight tasks for students:

1. Explore problems.
2. Identify learning issues.
3. Solve the problems with existing knowledge.
4. Identify the learning needs.
5. Set learning goals and allocate tasks.
6. Study individually.
7. Share and teach.
8. Assess and reflect on the whole process.

Students will generally follow these steps, but ensuring the quality of learning is most important. Students therefore may need to repeat certain steps, as indicated in the Figure 8.1.

2. Comparing PBL with Other Instruction Approaches

Conventional Approaches vs. Problem-based Learning

PBL differs fundamentally from conventional curricula. Compared with conventional modes, PBL has made a fundamental shift in the elements of course design, such as learning materials, the role of teachers and students. Figure 8.2 illustrates the differences.

To distinguish the differences between the lecture method and PBL, Shepherd and Cosgriff (1998) compared the role of instructor and student, the cognitive focus, the nature of problems used and the source of information for learning. The role of the instructor in a lecture environment is that of a transmitter who owns and shares knowledge. He or she also directs students' thinking and assesses students' achievements. In a PBL environment, the instructor takes the role of a coach who presents students with real-world problems, then fades in the background by facilitating and modelling at appropriate points. He or she is not the only assessor but the person to arrange assessment and ensure students receive feedback.

Students in lectures are generally passive receivers of information and knowledge. In PBL, students are active participants. By engaging in problem inquiry to formulate their own solutions, they develop knowledge and strategies for problem-solving and self-evaluation. In terms of cognitive focus, students in lectures normally receive knowledge then apply it in tests. In PBL, students acquire, integrate and apply knowledge but also develop metacognitive strategies to regulate their own learning.

In lectures, information is presented by the instructor and the problems are well structured for students to apply their learning. However, in PBL information is gathered and processed by students. Ill-structured daily life problems are used to stimulate the student's self-directed learning process.

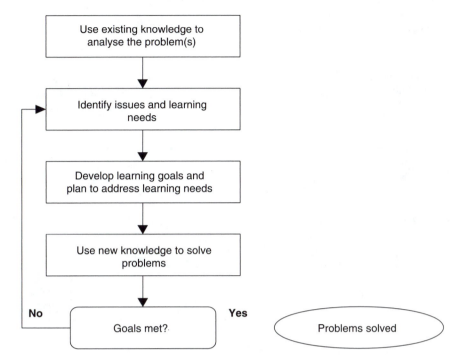

Figure 8.1 A Flowchart of PBL Process.

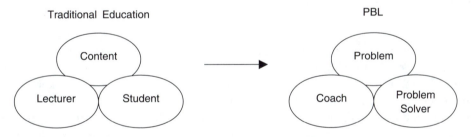

Figure 8.2 A Model of Curriculum Shift (Tan, 2003).

Subject-based Learning vs. PBL

Conventional teaching and learning is usually subject-based. Teachers may ask students to solve problems, but for most of the time, teachers teach students the subject contents and the concepts prior to giving them a problem to solve. The problem-solving process serves as a means for students to apply the subject contents learned. In PBL, however, the teacher will never start a PBL sequence by teaching the knowledge contents, but instead will present students with a problem to explore. Students apply their existing knowledge to analyse the problem, identify the issues and try to specify the possible solutions as steps for constructing their own learning. Figure 8.3 illustrates further the different activities and their sequences between subject-based learning and problem-based learning.

Case Method vs. PBL

Both the case method and PBL are problem-orientated approaches, using real-world scenarios or cases to develop students' abilities in analysing problems, identifying issues and formulating

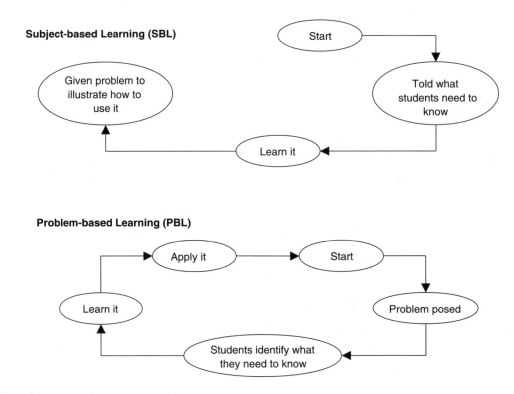

Figure 8.3 Differences Between SBL and PBL (Woods, 1994).

solutions. But they differ much in learning outcomes, contents, processes and assessment. In terms of learning outcomes, PBL also focuses on self-directed learning and lifelong learning abilities, cooperative teamwork skills, project management skills and the acquisition of new knowledge. For learning contents, PBL uses scenarios or cases as stimulus for students to pursue new knowledge on their own. In the case method, just like the conventional subject-based methods, theories and knowledge are usually taught and cases are used for students to apply the theories and knowledge learned (Bridges and Hallinger, 1995; Brown and Campione, 1981; Brown et al., 1983; Christensen, 1987).

During the case method learning process, the teacher may lead students in the discussion. In PBL, the students engage in self-directed learning, in which they take turns to lead the team to set goals and plans to achieve their goals. The teacher is the facilitator to assist the smooth implementation of the learning process and to check if students are on the right track. Guidance will be given only if it is necessary.

In term of assessment, the case method usually focuses on assessing the end product, while PBL also focuses on formative assessment to allow students to receive continuous feedback from peers and the teacher during the learning process.

Project-based Learning vs PBL

Both PBL and project-based learning are inquiry-based learning, which are based on constructivism, allowing students active exploration and building knowledge through experience. Both use open-ended questions to provide students with real-world context. Both advocate interdisciplinary learning, and emphasise inquiry skills and learning to learn. Both are student-centred approaches and provide students with flexibility in learning, in particular for PBL, emphasising activating students' previous knowledge while learning new knowledge to ensure deeper knowledge integration. Students focus on building new knowledge, and do not need to spend time to learn the knowledge they have learned before as in conventional approaches, particularly in large-class situations where flexibility for individual students is relatively low. Teachers in both situations should be facilitators to help students perform collaborative learning, performance assessment and reflective practice.

The differences between the two are related to the extent of implementation of the characteristics mentioned above. In general, PBL aims at establishing systematic structure and procedures to build a more stable learning environment/community to support longer-term student development (Kwan, 2004). PBL uses real-world problems to guide students to develop reasoning skills through analysing the problems and searching for appropriate solutions. Theoretically, the PBL can replace conventional teaching and learning for all subjects in classrooms, while project-based learning is generally used as a part of learning to support the whole. In PBL, scenarios are specially written for curriculum integration. Learning issues in different areas are interwoven to minimise compartmentalisation of learning. Teachers need to work together as a team in preparation, implementation and evaluation. The collaborative culture among colleagues is more explicit.

Some project-based learning may emphasise summative assessment, thus students are assessed on end products such as presentation, reports and artefacts. PBL on the other hand places greater emphasis on the development of students during the learning process. Formative and continuous assessment tasks are used to assess group and individual students' learning of contents, as well as attitude and skills in learning how to learn. Peer and self-assessment tasks are highly common.

In some project-based learning situations, students might not see the meaning of doing the project. First, the project topic is not a free choice but is assigned by the teacher. Occasionally, students can select a topic from the teacher-prescribed list. Also, students might be given just the project topic without background information, and do not know why they are doing the project. The lack of ownership may lead students to just look for materials generally related to the topics to put together a descriptive report for assessment. Some students may rely on cut-and-paste, thus the aim of project-based learning is defeated. Table 8.1 illustrates how PBL project work differs from typical project work in the learning process.

To summarise, the most distinctive characteristic of PBL is "problem-first". Compared with other instructional methods, its explicit goal is to empower students to become self-directed learners. Students work with peers on carefully selected and designed problems as a means to build up new knowledge, problem-solving capability, self-directed learning strategies and team skills. The teacher's role is to work with students to create a stimulating and nurturing learning environment for students to achieve these goals.

3. History, Rationale and Theoretical Foundations of PBL

Origin and Rationale for PBL

Many would argue that the concept of PBL can be traced to the progressive movement, especially to Dewey's belief that education should connect students' experiences outside of school so as to tap into students' natural instincts to investigate and create. However, PBL as we know it today, originated in 1965 with Howard Barrows, a medical educator at McMaster University in Hamilton, Ontario, Canada. He observed that the ways the conventional medical schools prepared doctors by didactic teaching, in which students were required to memorise a large amount of information and then to apply the information in clinical situations may not work best. The curriculum for the

Table 8.1 Differences between PBL Project and Typical Project Work (Chin and Chia, 2004)

PBL project work	Typical project work
• Problems are identified by students themselves, and inspired by real-life experiences.	• Problems are identified by students or given by the teacher. Sometimes, problems are contrived.
• Problems are ill structured, with sub-problems embedded in a multifaceted, overarching problem statement that presents a scenario.	• Problems may be well defined if given by teacher. • The problem is usually encapsulated in a clear and focused investigative question or topic at the outset.
• Questions emerge along the way.	• No role-playing is usually involved. If the problem is given, students may feel detached from it, and see their role as merely fulfilling the requirements of a task set by the teacher.
• Students role-play a character in the problem statement with whom they can identify.	
• Students are required to generate questions and identify learning issues (based on the problem statement) which then act as springboards for their inquiry and learning.	• Students are usually not explicitly required to pose questions and identify learning issues. However, questions may arise incidentally during the course of the investigation.
• Because students are required to offer a solution to a multifaceted, ill-defined problem, they are unable to use "copy-and-paste" strategies in the written report.	• Some projects allow descriptive reporting on specific topics. This may lead students to resort to "copy-and-paste" strategies in the written report.

newly established School of Medicine should aim at developing doctors' abilities to handle patients' health problems in a competent and humane way. To be able to do this, the doctors must master an essential body of knowledge, the ability to apply the knowledge, and the capacity to learn how to learn to extend and improve that knowledge to keep up in the ever-expanding field of medicine. To achieve this aim, Barrows developed PBL to invite students to work on a series of clinical problems that went beyond conventional case studies, allowing students to engage in acquiring new knowledge on their own, to integrate and apply the knowledge in the context of patients' problems as a means to cultivate students' clinical reasoning (Barrows, 1985).

The major rationale behind using PBL is the ineffectiveness of conventional approaches and the quest for deep learning and lifelong learning, which demands the reconsideration of the learning outcomes and processes for university education. In universities, learning is organised for students to acquire basic discipline knowledge in the early part of a course and apply this knowledge to diagnose and solve related problems in the later part. This conventional approach has been criticised for several reasons, such as: (a) creating an artificial divide between the basic and clinical parts of the discipline, (b) making the application of the acquired knowledge difficult, (c) wasting time in acquiring knowledge that is subsequently forgotten or found to be irrelevant, and (d) hampering students' learning motivation when the acquisition and retention of information that has no apparent relevance.

To promote effective and deep learning, students must be allowed to construct their own understanding in the process. Students also need opportunity to apply their prior knowledge to make sense of new knowledge. Students should be provided with group and individual learning experiences as well as flexibility during the learning process, including what to learn and how to learn it.

Rapid social changes have rendered our existing knowledge and skills outdated. To keep up with changes, professionals should be able to acquire new knowledge continuously. University education should therefore be able to empower students' self-directed learning attitudes and skills which can enable them to learn *life-wide and life-long*. To develop students' self-regulated skills, the power should be returned to students so that they can take whole responsibility of their own learning. The encouragement of active participation and collaboration will provide students with powerful sources of motivation and systematic peer learning opportunities. Students will acquire not only content knowledge but also process skills which are highly relevant to students' careers and later development.

Theoretically, PBL, with its learning outcomes and process, can avoid many of the problems with the conventional approaches. Basic knowledge and application are integrated throughout the curriculum. Learning occurs in context and builds on what students already know. This process can enhance learning retention, interest and motivation.

Theoretical Foundations of PBL

Although we are not sure if Barrows and colleagues had done a very comprehensive literature search prior to the formation of the PBL approach, as a user of PBL or other education approaches, we need to analyse critically the nature and theoretical base of the target approach before making a selection. We discover that PBL is well supported by a number of learning theories, including situated learning, constructivism, information processing, metacognition, self-directed learning and cooperative learning (Kwan, 2008).

Situated learning

From the situated learning perspective, knowledge does not exist on its own but within the learning context. Knowledge, just like tools used by humans, is a product of learners' interaction with the environment. When designing learning, we need to consider both the learners and the learning environment. Conventional instruction methods tend to rely on teachers to design materials and direct the learning processes. Gaps are often created between classroom learning and students' lives, hampering the extent of student involvement. Situated learning stresses the importance of learners' situations and needs. It calls for arranging appropriate learning situations which allow learners to interact with the environment to construct their own knowledge.

Constructivism

Constructivism asserts that knowledge is not a fixed object but is constructed by an individual through his or her own experience of that object (Sherman, 1995). The constructivist approach emphasises learners working on authentic projects in a collaborative manner. Just like in the real-world situation, learners take full responsibility to monitor and direct their own learning and performance.

PBL embraces both cognitive and social constructivist viewpoints shared by Piaget and Vygotsky. As summarised by Cobb (1993, cited in Duffy and Cunningham, 1996), the major elements of cognitive and social constructivist theories are being applied in PBL. For cognitive constructivism, the mind performs cognitive reorganisation of raw materials like primary data and interactive materials. Student autonomy allows students to take responsibility for their own learning, thus increasing ownership. Learning should be structured to address learners' personal views and experiences to add meaningfulness and personal motivation. Cognitive constructivism emphasises conceptual organisation, suggesting information should be structured around concepts, problems, questions and themes as well as interrelationships. All learning activities are thinking-related in nature, which should build upon students' prior knowledge and address misconceptions. Questioning, particularly with open-ended questions, encourages individual inquiry and question-asking behaviour.

From the social constructivists' points of view, the mind performs social transactions and emerges from acculturation into a community of practice; thus authentic problems should be used to mirror real-world complexities. Team choice allows learners to build learning on common interests and experiences within the team, making learning activities more relevant, meaningful, and both product and process oriented. Problems with multiple solutions lead to uncertainty and novelty, which demand social dialogue. Students are encouraged to give elaboration and justification for their viewpoints through discussion, questioning and sharing in presentations. Group processing and reflection promotes group processing of experiences. Teacher support focuses on illustrating the problem's steps and providing needed clarifications and hints. The culture of accepting multiple viewpoints encourages analysing a problem from different perspectives and practising this accommodating attitude.

Information processing

Basically, the information-processing perspective suggests that for better retention, new information received by the learner needs to go through an organisation and elaboration process. If the learner further engages in an encoding process, the information will transform into schema. Rehearsing will allow the knowledge to be stored in long-term memory for later retrieval.

Metacognition

Metacognitivists believe that the performance of the learner depends much on their ability to monitor, adjust and modify their own learning. Metacognition, as a component outside the intelligence framework, includes cognitive knowledge and cognitive modification. The former is the learner's understanding of their own cognitive process, and the latter is learners' ability to monitor, evaluate and modify their own cognitive processes. Developing students' metacognitive abilities and strategies can enhance students' capabilities in understanding, monitoring and solving problems in their own learning, helping them gradually become self-directed learners who can continue to learn lifelong.

Self-directed learning

Self-directed learning may stem from John Dewey, who believed learners have inborn potential to their own growth and development. The aim of education is to assist learners to grow. The teacher's major role is to invite students to engage in learning, thus intervention during the learning process should be minimised.

Some also suggest that the philosophy of self-directed learning is related to Maslow's concept of self-actualisation (1954) and Rogers' idea of experiential learning (1969, 1983; Rogers and Freiberg 1994). Maslow believed that we will increase our understanding of our own motivation through the self-transformation process. Rogers suggests ego drives our behaviours, creativity and core personality.

Self-directed learners know how to learn, how to change and make modification. They are able to set and implement their learning goals and plans as well as to assess the outcomes (Rogers, 1983). Self-directed learners are active, ready to take responsibilities, determined and persistent. Self-directed learners do not just work on their own but are able to use appropriate social networks and resources to facilitate self-growth. As Cranton (1996) has claimed, self-directed learning is a foundation of transformative learning. The learners are able to get beyond gaining factual knowledge to change themselves based on what they have learned.

Cooperative learning

Cooperative learning proposed that learning can be stimulated considerably through human interaction. In a team process, when members work together to attain their learning goals, communication, and the positive dependence and influence among members, can create powerful social and psychological support, which will enhance the learning results significantly (Johnson and Johnson, 1994).

4. Designing and Implementing PBL Curricula

When designing PBL curricula, as in designing other curricula, the expected learning outcomes should be specified. The learning outcomes should be related to capabilities such as applying particular content knowledge to solve problems. Once the learning outcomes are identified, learning activities, assessment tasks and feedback should be selected to organise an aligned learning environment.

PBL Implementation Models

In a total PBL environment, students work on problems to confront their existing knowledge and acquire new knowledge. Class time can be arranged into four meetings, as practised in some of the McMaster University programmes and the *Learning to Learn* course at City University of Hong Kong. This is indicated in Table 8.2.

In a hybrid PBL environment, students are also provided with other instruction support, such as lectures, tutorials and lab sessions (e.g. Armstrong, 1997; O'Kelly, 2005), as shown in Figure 8.4.

Formulating PBL Problem Statements

In a PBL course, the appropriateness of problem statements is critical to the success. According to Duch (2001), a good PBL problem should have the characteristics specified in Table 8.3.

Ensuring Successful Implementation of PBL

To ensure the successful implementation of PBL, we need to create an aligned learning environment and well-designed problems to help students achieve the expected learning outcomes. It is also crucial to prepare teachers (Little, 1997; Framer, 2004). For teachers, the preparation should include course design, the PBL procedures, writing PBL problems and, even more importantly, accepting role change and performing accordingly. Learning how to work with students and to facilitate the PBL process are the key for success in PBL implementation. Experiential staff development opportunities, including a practicum, reflection, sharing with colleagues and further practice are effective in helping teachers internalise their facilitator role and master related skills (Kwan, 2008). Since PBL excludes direct teaching, demands students take full responsibility in learning and uses more formative assessment, some students may feel frustrated. Communicating PBL rationale and

Table 8.2 The Four Meetings in Total PBL

	Meeting	Activities
1	*Exploration Meeting*	• Students explore the problem as a starting point of their learning. They also share their existing knowledge and identify their learning needs.
		Students engage in individual inquiry.
2	*Preparation Meeting*	• Students share and learn new knowledge from peers in their own small group.
3	*Teaching Meeting*	• Students teach and learn from their peers in the whole class.
4	*Assessment Meeting*	• Students reflect on the whole learning process and evaluate their success and seek directions for future improvement.

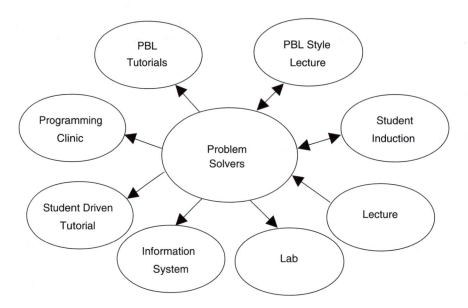

Figure 8.4 A Hybrid Model of PBL (O'Kelly, 2005).

Table 8.3 Characteristics of Good PBL Problems (Duch, 2001)

1. An effective problem must first engage students' interest and motivate them to probe for deeper understanding of the concepts being introduced. It relates to the reality of the student's world and interests.

2. Good problems induce students to make decisions or judgements based on facts, information, logic and/or rationalisation. They require students to justify decisions and reasoning based on the principles being learned.

3. Cooperation from all members of the group is necessary in order to effectively work through a good problem. The length and complexity of the problem is such that students realise that a "divide and conquer" effort will not solve the problem. For example, a series of "end of chapter" type questions would likely end up being divided by the group, assigned to individuals, and reassembled for a solution, in which case students gain little critical-thinking and problem-solving experience.

4. The initial questions in the problem have one or more of the following characteristics so that all students in the group are initially drawn into a discussion of the topic:

   a. open ended, not limited to one correct answer
   b. connected to previous learning
   c. controversial issues that will elicit diverse opinions.

   These characteristics keep the students functioning as a group, drawing on each other's knowledge and ideas rather than encouraging them to work individually at the onset of the problem.

5. The objectives and standards of the curriculum are incorporated into the problem. The problem also connects to concepts in other curriculum areas.

procedure to students at the beginning of a PBL programme and helping them to cope with change are particularly essential.

5. Disciplines Using PBL, Rationale and Impact

Since Barrows used PBL with his medical students in 1969, the application of PBL has been extended to different subject areas in higher education. By searching some PBL portals (e.g. Temasek Polytechnic), we can see that PBL has been applied to individual subjects and even in an integrated or cross-disciplinary manner, for example in architectural design, biology, chemistry, engineering, family healthcare, geography, law, language and communication, nurse education, teacher education and others. Some examples are illustrated further below.

Medical Science, Nursing and Dental Education

PBL has been widely used in medical science, nursing and dental education. The major rationale, as stated by Creedy and Alavi (1997), is that PBL mirrors the real world and thus enhances the students' preparation and broadens their learning. The specific clinical situation in PBL provides the stimulus for identifying what is necessary learning in order to understand and manage the situation. Concepts and skills can be introduced, practised and reinforced within an environment which is safe and supportive. Evidence of PBL impact is strong. Khoo et al. (2008) conducted a systematic analysis of 13 previous studies on the effects of PBL during medical school. PBL was found to have positive effects on physician competencies after graduation, especially in the social and cognitive dimensions. However, there is absence of evidence of positive effects of PBL on physician competencies in the technical and teaching dimensions. This is likely to be because these dimensions require psychomotor skills, which are more effectively instilled using deliberate practice methods, including formal procedural skills training and preceptorships. In the knowledge dimension, there was strong evidence that PBL graduates rated themselves as possessing less medical knowledge than graduates in the control groups. The evidence from the objective assessment, however, did not support this finding.

Political Science

The PBL approach has been incorporated into a pair of upper-level courses in political science in the University of Delaware for over seven years (Burch, 2001). The rationale for using PBL is that PBL problems mirror the complexity, richness and ambiguity of problems that confront policy-makers. Students' interactions within their study groups mimic the contingencies and uncertainties of all manner of politics. Also, PBL group dynamics simulate political life and democratic practices. Group interactions model the practices of participatory, pluralistic democracy because all members have to participate by drawing on their diverse knowledge and experiences. PBL heightens participation and students can learn from the wider and richer range of views and the diversity of others' experiences and impressions. PBL problems require a response and an action aimed at addressing the problem, thus providing opportunities for improvement in critical thought and collective social action. PBL learning requires students to confront problems, conceive the possible, and construct alternatives, thus fostering skills which enable students to articulate their own goals and nurture a vision of social justice for all groups to work constructively towards the end. Research drawn from 20 years of PBL experience concludes that PBL has done no harm in terms of conventional tests of knowledge, and that students may show better problem-solving skills (Albanese and Mitchell, 1993; Vernon and Blake, 1993). Students retain information longer and recall it more quickly and accurately (Barrows, 1996). However, some students may feel frustrated, particularly those who dualistically define "learning" as the collection of concrete right-or-wrong "facts".

Social Work

PBL when applied to social work education evolved into the "issue-based approach" to learning (Bolzan and Heycox, 1997). The issue-based approach appears to some degree in all social work courses in the state of New South Wales, Australia, including University of New South Wales, University of Sydney and University of Newcastle. The wide use of the issue-based approach helps to enhance students' capacity to transfer knowledge and skills across different contexts and levels of intervention, from interpersonal to societal. The flexibility of the issue-based approach enables new situations to be devised in line with current developments in the welfare field. Attention is focused on students' own world views and life experiences in recognition of the use of self in social work. Partnerships involve an exchange of resources, knowledge and experience.

However, several challenges in implementation have been reported. It is resource-intensive and a high level of commitment by both educators and the institution is demanded. It is necessary to prepare students to engage in this style of learning (e.g. life experience, maturity, level of competence). Students' willingness to explore the breadth of social work beyond their particular practice preference is also an issue.

Business Studies

The effectiveness of PBL in business education varies the greatest as compared with other disciplines. The effectiveness of PBL depends on both the social-financial-political environment and the subjects. Using the situation in England and the Netherlands as an example, Gilbert and Foster (1997) illustrated how the social-financial-political environment affected the effectiveness of PBL. In England and the Netherlands, institutions are often dissatisfied with or doubt the educational value or effectiveness of PBL in tertiary education in comparison with more conventional methods. Hesitancy about PBL often centres on efficiency issues and perceptions of students' extrinsic motives and rapidly increasing student numbers. PBL has been undergoing more challenge in England because of the financial climate of English tertiary education, where the need for cost–benefit analysis is evident in the context of "privatization and the efficiency squeeze" (Gilbert and Foster, 1997; Boud and Feletti, 1997; Drinan, 1997). The growth in distance learning programmes and development of internet degrees also present real challenges for PBL.

The subjects also have significant impact on the implementation of PBL. Business and economics faculty are oriented towards efficiency (as compared with their medical counterparts). Conventional methods like lecturing to large classes look efficient compared with meeting large numbers of small groups. Faculties of business studies are often less positive about PBL, since their academic future is largely determined by research and publication lists, not by how well they learn to tutor PBL groups.

Investigating the difference between the benefits gained from PBL in accounting and statistics disciplines, Siaw (2000) found that the PBL scores for statistics were significantly lower than those for accounting. Students seemed to gain more benefits in accounting PBL tutorials than in statistics PBL tutorials. Siaw explained that PBL may not suitable for statistics due to the existence of abstract concepts that needed to be mastered first before attempting to solve applied problems. The lack of understanding about the fundamental concepts was a possible hazard for students to interact actively in the group, and consequently PBL becomes less effective. The unpredictable ability of the students, their prior knowledge about statistics, and the time constraints of the available tutorial hours also made it difficult to implement PBL activities successfully. On the other hand, accounting students may have absorbed a mass of worldwide information through the media, thus acquired related modes of reasoning, and some of them were working in the field, so it was easier to implement PBL successfully in this discipline.

Gerald (2005) presents a comparative analysis of PBL likely benefits for medical and management education, and suggests that although PBL is not a promising way of undertaking all aspects of management education. Selective implementation of PBL will offer considerable educational benefits, such as improving students' managerial thinking skills.

Legal Education

Schön (1987) claims that some of the most eminent law schools have realised the need to develop competencies that go beyond thinking like a lawyer, for example skills in trail work, client relations, negotiation, advocacy, and legal ethics. The PBL approach helps to achieve this by having students regard problems in a holistic manner. They must be prepared to approach the problem from a variety of angles rather than trying to fit the problem into a narrow box or pigeon-hole. In analysing the major factors contributing to effective PBL, Winsor (1997) suggests (a) the need to highlight the role(s) of instructors and provide clear guidelines for these roles available both to instructors and students, (b) the need for materials to be shorter, non-repetitious and of the highest quality in order to maintain enthusiasm and motivation, and (c) constant and adequate feedback on ongoing performance.

Hee and Lim (2000) conclude from their experience in Temasek Polytechnic at Singapore, that using PBL as a full curriculum approach may lead to gaps in knowledge about substantive law subjects and may leave students short of rule-oriented knowledge in many subjects. There must be a balance of the training in process skills with training in relevant and current legal knowledge and skills. Year 1 is a transitional year when students adjust from life and study at secondary school to tertiary education. The law school decided Year 1 would be used to prepare the students for PBL. Full PBL implementation only begins with all the substantive law subjects in Year 2.

Learning to learn

In 1996 City University of Hong Kong established a course, *Learning to Learn*, to help first-year students to be effective students. The course adopted PBL as the learning environment to develop students in self-directed learning in 1999. In this 39-hour credit-bearing course, students meet three hours a week to work with peers on problems which address issues on time management, team-work, critical and creative thinking, whole-personal development and lifelong learning. Kwan and Ko (2004a, 2004b) reported very positive results. Students improved their attitude and skills in learning and became deep learners. According to the pre- and post-test data, formative assessment in the course, the end-of-course evaluation and student post-course interviews, students also improved significantly in metacognitive strategies as well as critical thinking dispositions. Students enjoyed learning in a PBL environment and attained better academic results than their non-course peers. Some graduates of the university suggest that the course is one among the very few most useful courses in their university study, since they have transformed their attitude towards learning in the stimulating and supportive PBL environment created by the tutor and themselves. The positive impact on their study approach and whole personal development lasts with time. The course team attributes their success to selection of enthusiastic facilitators, comprehensive preparation for facilitators and students, as well as good communication and the strong support for them throughout the course.

Literature and colleagues' experiences suggested that PBL can make a very positive impact on students, but this requires at least three important conditions. The first condition is a good facilitator who is effective in communicating the learning outcomes and expectations to students, and in working with the students to create a nurturing environment to support the development of the expected attitudes and abilities in students.

A second condition is the provision for helping students to analyse their strengths and limitations in study approaches (Biggs 1987) and learning strategies (Weinstein and Palmer 2002). Helping students to appreciate the richness of a PBL environment and take initiatives to maximise their development within is highly essential.

A further condition involves sufficient opportunities for developing specific learning outcomes

(Kwan 2008). For example, to develop students in self-regulated learning, they need to internalise the importance of a proactive learning attitude and the value of total involvement. Students are willing to participate actively in discussion with their peers to identify their cognitive gaps, thus learning needs. During the PBL inquiry process, students need to engage seriously in making inquiry plans, collecting, analysing, integrating and evaluating information, as well as reviewing the whole process. Students should have the opportunity to experience several learning cycles so that the mastery of self-learning and the formation of the plan-do-review habit become possible.

To develop problem-solving and thinking abilities among students demands ample opportunities for analysing authentic problems, formulating hypotheses, evaluating knowledge, materials and experiences, and relating the appropriate solutions to the problem being solved. The engagement in self- and peer-assessment, recurrent reflection and discussion are crucial. Through interacting with others, students will be able to deepen their understanding of the problems to be solved. They also need to familiarise themselves with the PBL procedures and follow through the steps to develop and master systematic problem-solving strategies. The opportunity for performing brainstorming activities is vital for students to develop open-mindedness and fluency in creative thinking.

For facilitating knowledge acquisition, students need to articulate existing knowledge and to apply existing knowledge to solve the problem. Conducting inquiry, drawing on knowledge from different sources and integrating knowledge at different points of time are powerful processes for constructing a broad and flexible knowledge foundation.

To develop teamwork skills, students should enjoy the opportunity to share knowledge and experience to support peer learning. By sharing responsibilities among team members, students will learn how to cooperate. Taking turns to assume the role of leader and providing psychological, social and technical support to peers are necessary conditions for nurturing leadership skills.

6. Major Criticisms, Issues of PBL and Its Likely Future Development

Criticisms and Challenges

The major criticisms of PBL focus on its efficiency and effectiveness. Some research suggests that PBL curricula cover about 80% of what might be accomplished in a conventional curriculum in the same period. Another concern is, in some situations, students learning in a PBL environment may not be doing as well as students from traditional schools, for example in the basic science component of the US National Board Examinations (e.g. Kalaian, Mullan and Kasim, 1999; Shenouda, Swenson and Fournier, 2003). A further concern voiced is that PBL is costly, in demands of staff time and resources. Other criticisms include that PBL can be stressful for both students and staff, particularly at the beginning when they have to cope with unfamiliarity. Some have also questioned whether students can really know what might be important for them to learn, particularly in areas which students have no prior knowledge. Staff may need to cope with heavier teaching loads and the discomfort of being a facilitator who may be asked by students from time to time to comment on materials they have never seen before. PBL can be very challenging to implement, as it requires a great deal of planning and hard work from the teacher.

However, one can also argue that most of these criticisms may not stand. If we judge the success of an educational approach by the extent it achieves its learning outcomes, PBL has been very successful in developing self-directed learners who may not be good at remembering factual knowledge in examination situations, but good in solving authentic problems systematically in a real-world context. They have also developed the habit and the ability to monitor their own learning process, which are crucial prerequisites for lifelong learning. PBL, as other deep learning approaches, would demand more time and resources. We need to decide to go for quantity or quality and how to strike a balance. Changing a conventional learning environment to PBL, just like implementing any innovations, can create stress. A thorough plan and good preparation, including piloting, can reduce such stress. Students not knowing what are the most important areas to learn when they do not have prior knowledge is not a problem in PBL, since students come to explore and construct learning, including developing metacognitive and problem-solving skills. In designing PBL problems, students' prior knowledge has been taken into consideration. The implementation of PBL can create considerable workload at the beginning; team effort is important in this regard. To assume the role of co-learner will allow teachers to learn from students and to demonstrate lifelong learning attitudes.

Recently, PBL and other minimal guided instruction approaches were criticised for ignoring the structure that constitutes human cognitive architecture (Kirschner, Sweller and Clark, 2006). According to cognitive load theory, learners' working memory is limited in duration and capacity when processing novel information, thus they may find it difficult to process a large amount of information in a short period of time. Active problem-solving activities may become a challenge for novice learners at the beginning. Thus doubt is cast on the research that suggested that people learn best in an unguided or minimally guided environment. Novice learners should be given direct instruction on the concepts and procedures essential in a particular discipline, rather than letting them discover by themselves (e.g. Cronbach and Snow, 1997; Klahr and Nigam, 2004; Mayer, 2004; Shulman and Keisler, 1996; Sweller, 2003). However, the views of Kirschner, Sweller and Clark (2006) have been challenged for judging learning success mainly based on recall of facts and solving structured problems, ignoring the demands of contemporary education and failing to acknowledge the social dimension of learning and constructivism, which are well supported by empirical research in the past half-century.

Issues and the Likely Future Development of PBL

PBL has been around for more than three decades and its impact has been increasingly recognised. While effort has been extended to different disciplines in higher education and success has been reported, its implementation is still far more prosperous in professional education. This phenomenon can be explained by three reasons: (a) PBL fits well with professional education since it was originally designed for nurturing students to be professionals, (b) professional education is more responsive to public accountability, thus there is a pressing need for revisiting learning outcomes, leading to more attempts in curriculum innovations and applying PBL, and (c) successful examples generate more attempts for implementing PBL. As innovations in any areas, the practitioners are often stimulated by real examples of success. Well-documented research in these areas provides strong evidence leading to more rapid development in professional education. According to this trend, PBL will be gradually used in areas other than professional education when it fits well with the nature of the subjects. The wide use of PBL is perhaps just a matter of time.

To make that day come earlier, several issues may need to be addressed. The first thing we need to do may be to make explicit how PBL can address the practical aspects of higher education. For example, the trend of decreasing resources among universities and increasing class size. More work should be done on applying PBL in large classes with its rigour well maintained. To examine carefully the appropriateness of using tutorless PBL groups and PBL online may be possible areas to explore.

Another area deserving our concern is the less systematic document of the impact of PBL. Although we have a great deal of research studies reporting positive results of implementing PBL, it has been difficult to conduct meta-analysis on the effectiveness of PBL due to too many variations of PBL and some of the studies not being well documented (Newman, 2004). To collect more useful data to support the merits of PBL, wider collaborative effort of different disciplines and across countries is needed to start an international project and put together existing studies. For the benefits of the higher education advancement, university academic staff development should be more rigorous to include action research preparation.

To anticipate the likely development for PBL in the future, although it seems that professional education will still be the champion, PBL is also spreading into non-professional subject areas. The dissatisfaction with conventional approaches should be the biggest driving force for changing the learning outcomes for higher education. Capabilities beyond subject knowledge such as self-directed learning and problem-solving will be demanded, leading the search for better alternatives. Towards this, PBL should have much to contribute.

Note

1. The author wishes to thank Professor Donald Woods and Professor Luis Branda for their invaluable guidance and support in her journey of pursuing PBL.

References

Albanese, M., and Mitchell, S. (1993). Problem-based learning: a review of the literature on its outcomes and implementation issues. *Academic Medicine*, 68(1), 52–81.

Armstrong, E.G. (1997). A hybrid model of problem-based learning. In D. Boud and G. Feletti (eds) *The Challenge of Problem-based Learning*. 2nd edn. London: Kogan Page, 137–150.

Barrows, H.S. (1985). *Now to Design a Problem-Based Curriculum for the Preclinical Years*. Springer Series on Medical Education. New York: Springer.

Barrows, H.S. (1996). Problem-based learning in medicine and beyond: A brief overview. *New Directions for Teaching and Learning*, 68, 3–11.

Barrows H.S. and Tamblyn, R.M. (1980). *Problem-Based Learning: An approach to medical education*. New York: Springer.

Biggs, J. (1987). *Learning Process Questionnaire (LPQ): Manual*. Hawthorn, Vic.: Australian Council for Educational Research.

Bolzan, N., and Heycox, K. (1997). Use of an issue-based approach in social work education. In D. Boud and G. Feletti (eds), *The Challenge of Problem-based Learning*. 2nd edn. London: Kogan Page, 194–202.

Boud, D. and Feletti, G. (eds) (1997). *The Challenge of Problem-based Learning*. (2nd edn). London: Kogan Page.

Bridges, E. and Hallinger, P. (1995). *Implementing Problem-based Learning in Leadership Development*. Eugene, OR: ERIC Clearinghouse.

Brown, A., Bransford, J., Ferrara, R. and Campione, J. (1983). Learning, remembering and understanding. In J. Flavell and E. Markman (eds), *Carmichael's Manual of Child Psychology* (1). New York: Wiley, 77–166.

Brown, A.L. and Campione, J.C. (1981). Inducing flexible thinking: A problem of access. In M. Friedman, J.P. Das and N. O'Connor (eds), *Intelligence and Learning*. New York: Plenum, 515–529.

Burch, K. (2001). PBL, politics, and democracy. In B.J. Duch, S.E. Groh and D.E. Allen (eds) *The Power of Problem-based Learning*. Sterking: Stylus.

Chin, C. and Chia, L.G. (2004). Implementing project work in biology through problem-based learning. *Journal of Biological Education*, 38(2), 69–75.

Christensen, C. (1987). *Teaching and the Case Method: Text, cases and readings*. Boston: Harvard Business School.

Cranton, P. (1996). *Professional Development as Transformative Leaning: New perspectives for teachers of adults*. San Fransisco: Jossey-Bass.

Creedy, D. and Alavi, C. (1997). Double-blind peer reviewed paper. Problem-based learning – a case for infection control. *British Journal of Infection Control*, 6(6), 16–19. 2005

Cronbach, L.J. and Snow R.E. (1997). *Aptitudes and Instructional Methods: A handbook for research on interactions*. New York: Irvington.

Drinan, J. (1997). The limits of problem-based learning. In D. Boud and G. Feletti (eds), *The Challenge of Problem-based Learning*. 2nd edn. London: Kogan Page, 333–339.

Duch, B. (2001). Writing problems for deeper understanding. In B. Duch, S. Groh and D. Allen (eds) *The Power of Problem-based Learning*. Virginia: Stylus.

Duffy, T. and Cunningham, D. (1996). Constructivism: implications for the design and delivery of instruction. In D.H. Jonassen (ed.) *Handbook of Research for Educational Communications and Technology*. New York: Simon and Schuster, 170–198.

Framer, L.A. (2004). Faculty development for problem-based learning. *European Journal of Dental Education*, 8(2), 59–66.

Gerald, F.S. (2005). Problem-based learning: can it improve managerial thinking? *Journal of Management Education* 29, 357–378.

Gilbert, A. and Foster, S.F. (1997). Experiences with problem-based learning in business and management. In D. Boud and G. Feletti (eds), *The Challenge of Problem-based Learning*. 2nd edn. London: Kogan Page, 244–252.

Hee, S.Y. and Lim, P.B. (2000, December). Law's Odyssey. *Problem-Based Learning: Educational innovation across disciplines*. The 2nd Asia Pacific Conference on PBL, Temasek Polytechnic, Singapore

Johnson, D.W. and Johnson, R.T. (1994). *Cooperative Learning in the Classroom*. Association for Supervision and Curriculum Development. Alexandria: Virginia.

Kalaian, H.A., Mullan, P.B. and Kasim, R.M. (1999). What can studies of problem-based learning tell us? Synthesizing and modeling PBL effects on National Board of Medical Examination performance: hierarchical linear modeling meta-analytic approach. *Advances in Health Sciences Education*, 4, 209–221.

Khoo, G.C., Khoo, H.E. and Koh, D. (2008). The effects of problem-based learning during medical school on physician competency: a systematic review. *Canadian Medical Association Journal*, 178, 34–41.

Kirschner, P.A., Sweller, J. and Clark, R.E. (2006). Why minimal guidance during instruction does not work: An analysis of the failure of constructivist, discovery, problem-based experiential and inquiry-based learning. *Educational Psychologist*, 41(2), 75–86.

Klahr, D. and Nigam, M. (2004). The equivalence of learning paths in early science instruction: effects of direct instruction and discovery learning. *Psychological Science*, 15, 661–667.

Kwan, A.S.F. (2004). Is problem-based learning effective in promoting learners' creativity? *Journal of Youth Studies*, 7(2) 68–79.

Kwan, A.S.F. (ed.) (2008). *Problem-Based Learning: Rationale and implementation*. Hong Kong: Education Development Office, City University of Hong Kong.

Kwan, A.S.F. and Ko, E.I. (2004a). Learning how to learn. In J. Jones, O. Kwo and T. Moore (eds), *Developing Learning Environments*. Hong Kong: Hong Kong University Press, 77–100.

Kwan, A.S.F. and Ko, E.I. (2004b). *Helping Secondary Students to Learn How to Learn*. Paper presented at the 29th International Conference on Improving University Learning and Teaching, Bern.

Little, S. (1997). Preparing tertiary teachers for problem-based learning. In D. Boud and G. Feletti (eds) *The Challenge of Problem-based Learning*. 2nd edn. London: Kogan Page, 117–136.

Maslow, A. (1954). *Motivation and Personality*. New York: Harper

Mayer, R. (2004). Should there be a three-strikes rule against pure discovery learning? The case for guided methods of instruction. *American Psychologist*, 59(1), 14–19.

Newman, M. (2004). *The Effectiveness of Problem-based Learning: A pilot systematic review and meta-analysis*. Teacher and Learning Research Programme, Cambridge.

O'Kelly, J. (2005). Designing a hybrid problem-based learning (PBL) course: a case study of first year computer science in NUI, Maynooth. In T. Barrett, I. Mac Labhrainn and H. Fallon (eds) *Handbook of Enquiry and Problem-based Learning*. Galway: CELT.

O'Rourke, K. and Kahn, P. (2005). Understanding enquiry-based learning. In T. Barrett, I. Mac Labhrainn and H. Fallon (eds), *Handbook of Enquiry and Problem-based Learning; Irish case studies and international perspectives*. Galway: AISHE and NUI Galway.

Rogers, C.R. (1969). *Freedom to Learn*. Columbus, OH: Merrill

Rogers, C.R. (1983). *Freedom to Learn for the 80s*. Columbus, OH: Merrill.

Rogers, C.R. and Freiberg, H.J. (1994). *Freedom to Learn*. 3rd edn. Columbus, OH: Merrill/Macmillan.

Schön, D. (1987). *Educating the Reflective Practitioner*. San Francisco: Jossey Bass.

Shenouda, N.S., Swenson, R.L. and Fournier, J.T. (2003). The impact of a newly implemented PBL curriculum on the National Board of Chiropractic Examiners Part I Examinations at the National University of Health Sciences. *Teaching and Learning in Medicine*, 15(4), 233–237.

Shepherd, A. and Cosgriff, B. (1998). Problem-based learning: a bridge between planning education and planning practice. *Journal of Planning Education and Research*, 17(4), 348–357.

Sherman, L.W. (1995). A postmodern, constructivist pedagogy for educational psychology, assisted by computer mediated communications. In Prodeedings of the ACM Conference on Computer Supported Cooperative Work (CSCL'95), Bloomington, Indiana.

Shulman, L. and Keisler, E. (eds) (1966). *Learning by Discovery: A critical appraisal*. Chicago: Rand McNally.

Siaw, I.S.C. (2000). Fostering self-directed learning readiness by way of intervention in business education. *Proceedings at the 2nd Asia Pacific Conference on Problem-Based Learning: Education Across Disciplines, Singapore*, December 4–7.

Stepien, W.J., Gallagher, S.A. and Workman, D. (1993). Problem-based learning for traditional and interdisciplinary classrooms. *Journal for the Education of the Gifted*, 4, 338–345.

Sweller, J. (2003). Evolution of human cognitive architecture. In B. Ross (ed.) *The Psychology of Learning and Motivation*. Volume 43. San Diego: Academic Press.

Tan, O.S. (2003). *Problem-based Learning Innovation: Using problems to power learning in the 21st century*. Singapore: Thomson Learning.

Vernon, D.T.A. and Blake, R.L. (1993). Does problem-based learning work? A meta-analysis of evaluative research. *Academic Medicine* 68, 550–563.

Weinstein, C.E. and Palmer, D.R. (2002). *Learning and Study Strategies Inventory 2nd edn*, Clearwater, FL: H and H Publishing.

Winsor, K. (1997). Applying problem-based learning to practical legal training. In D. Boud and G. Feletti (eds), *The Challenge of Problem-based Learning*. 2nd edn. London: Kogan Page, 224–243.

Woods, D.R. (1994). *Problem-based Learning: How to gain the most from PBL*. Hamilton, ON: McMaster University.

9

"An Alignment of the Planets":
Mapping the Intersections Between Pedagogy, Technology and Management in Australian Universities[1]

Ilana Snyder, Simon Marginson and Tania Lewis

The research interrogates the connections between information and communication technologies' (ICTs) use and change processes in Australian higher education. The empirical investigation focuses simultaneously on three domains of practice: the educational, the technological and the organizational, with a particular interest in their overlaps and intersections. There were 15 case studies, covering three discipline clusters (Medicine/Health Sciences, Economics and Business, English/Cultural Studies/Communications) in each of five different types of Australian university. The main research technique was semi-structured interviews with academic, executive and administrative staff, supplemented by focus groups with students and the study of curriculum and strategy documents. The main findings of the study were that the most effective use of ICTs in universities occurs when educational and organizational objectives are in harmony; when ICTs innovations are dominated by corporatist objectives at the expense of pedagogical objectives, benefits are limited and tensions evident; and pedagogical initiatives by discipline-based ICTs "champions" require central support if they are to add value on a sustained basis. The optimal conditions for ICTs innovations in teaching and learning are disciplinary independence and capacity, conditions present in only one of the 15 case studies.

In Australian higher education, as in most of the developed world, information and communication technologies are playing a growing part in teaching, learning and administration. Although some writers warn against naïvely promoting technology as the simple solution to complex educational and organizational processes (Cunningham *et al.*, 1998; Newman and Johnson, 1999; Peters 2002; Wajcman, 2002), others continue to declare that technology will revolutionize higher education by enhancing accessibility, quality and cost-effectiveness (e.g. West, 1997–8). Indulging in what Woolgar (2002, p. 6) calls "sweeping grandiloquence", technology boosters welcome ICTs as the universal catalyst and panacea for all needs and problems.

New technologies in any sphere are often accompanied by uncritical boosterism, as if to clear the way for the new while conferring a special authority on advocates of the new. But although technologies can have profound implications in higher education, those implications are not always benign or transparent, and they are always connected with social, cultural, organizational and political exigencies. Technology is not a straightforward driver of change, free of social relations and the sole element in innovation. It is people who make changes to higher education amid dynamic social and cultural relationships and practices (Lewis *et al.*, 2005).

We need to ask questions still not commonplace in the ICT-related literature. For whom and what purposes are ICTs introduced? In what ways are they associated with different practices? Under what conditions? To explore these questions empirically we need to focus on people's everyday professional experiences with ICTs across a range of sites.

Paradigms in ICTs Innovations

In the fields of higher education studies, school education, education management, educational computing and educational psychology, there is much discussion of ICT-associated innovations. But many claims about ICTs are inadequately supported by research, and existing research is often evaluation orientated. Although evaluation studies can produce useful data, such as classifications of innovations and insights into the interaction between organizational and educational factors (e.g. Gunn, 1999; Reeves and Laffey, 1999), these studies are often characterized by the absence of research questions and "talking up" of ICTs and institutional "re-engineering" (Snyder, 1997). Similarly, conferences on ICTs and pedagogical innovation proliferate, but are often "show-and-tell" reports of teaching practices and efforts to engender change (Collis and Moonen, 2001). Grounded investigations represent a small fraction of the total literature.

There are two broad paradigms providing alternative conceptions of the use of ICTs in the context of pedagogy and organization (Lewis, 1999; Privateer, 1999; Dutton and Loader, 2002). The two paradigms are associated with distinctive purposes and approaches to people and social relations in higher education. We refer to them as the e-constructivist paradigm and the e-corporate paradigm.

The e-constructivist paradigm has emerged directly out of the teaching and learning context. Constructivism, which evolved independently of and prior to the use of ICTs, understands the desired form of learning as "a process of socially based active co-construction of contextualized knowledge" (Salomon and Almog, 1998, p. 229). While there is no canonical form of constructivism, and emphases on the role of the individual vis-à-vis group learning vary (Bonk and Cunningham, 1998), constructivism highlights the proactive, reflective, self-regulated learner, and seeks to develop the use of ICTs so as to enhance these aspects of pedagogy. Here computer-mediated communication is seen to augment the potential for collaboration; and the design and manipulation of web-based media are seen to foreground student initiative, self-regulation and self-motivation (Laurillard, 1993; Looi, 1998; Gunn, 1999; Lin *et al.*, 1999).

The e-corporate paradigm is focused on the potential of ICTs, particularly online ICTs, to bring higher education to a larger student population, while reducing per capita costs, standardizing systems, creating saleable product and enhancing the competitiveness of the institution, corporation or academic unit. It gestures towards student-centredness, but it foregrounds the proactive student as consumer rather than as collaborator or critical reflector (Giroux, 2005) and the principal mode is transmission. Associated with increased managerial control and declining academic autonomy, this paradigm tends to emphasize standardized curricula in the form of intellectual property. There is also a tendency to technological determinism as reflected in assumptions that ICTs in themselves develop cognition, initiative and collaboration (Fabry and Higgs, 1997). This pedagogically lightweight paradigm is strongly criticized by many scholars (cf. Andrews, 2004). On the other hand, its proponents see it as key to the survival and advance of institutions in an increasingly marketized and efficiency-driven mass higher educational environment.

The two paradigms are characterized by different constellations of concepts, values, bodies of research, bodies of practice and social–institutional interests. Each paradigm has a normative element, and an observable purchase in real-world settings that can be tracked empirically. But it is a mistake to see the two paradigms as monolithic, hermetically sealed and wholly oppositional. The points of intersection and overlap are just as interesting as evidence of a divide. Academics and administrators in universities are continually negotiating and working across and between the two paradigms.

The Study

The study was supported by a 2001–03 Australian Research Council Large Grant. Data analysis continued into 2005. This is the first overall summation.

Research Questions

Specifically, the study examines whether the use of ICTs is associated with more "student-centred" learning, meaning self-regulated and reflective, and with increased administrative efficiency. It is framed by three research questions:

1. To what extent does the use of ICTs facilitate the cultivation of student-centred learning in social contexts?
2. To what extent does the use of ICTs facilitate the implementation of transmission-based pedagogy?
3. What are the implications for ICTs innovations of coincidence between educational objectives and organizational objectives?

Domains of Investigation

The study investigates these questions via observations conducted in three domains: the educational, the technological and the organizational. We are particularly interested in what happened at the points of overlap and intersection between the domains. The technological domain connects to both of the other domains. It is most interesting to study what happens when all three domains are in play at once.

The educational domain encompasses both professional teaching and student learning (Ramsden, 1992). Teaching is affected by professional academic requirements and practices, disciplinary cultures, demographics such as the age of staff, institutional staffing policies, conditions of work and the balance of roles between academic staff and general staff (Marginson and Considine, 2000). Both policy statements and scholarly studies about ICTs evidence wide expectations of a paradigm shift in teaching and learning, in which students determine their own learning to a greater degree (e.g. Bates, 2000). This forms part of diverse and sometimes contrary discourses, from democratic notions of learning to the modelling of students as consumers and education as a business. Actual research-based evidence for changes in student learning is elusive. Evidence on student attitudes is stronger than evidence on learning outcomes (Dillon and Gabbard, 1998). Online learning foregrounds student capabilities, in that the immediate presence of the teacher is weaker (Salomon and Almog, 1998). However, notions that students have a universal preference for ICT-based learning have no research backing (Ryan, 1998). Students have a variety of needs and responses. It seems that the potential of ICTs to meet varying needs remains underdeveloped (Bates, 2000).

While some studies bring educational and technological factors into conjunction with the organizational (e.g. Yetton, 1997; Harris, 2000), the organizational domain is often seen as given or prior to the educational. We prefer to treat each domain as a relatively autonomous field with its own set of rules and practices, but with the potential to interact with the other domains in complex and sometimes unplanned ways. In the educational domain, changes associated with the use of technology are driven primarily by academic objectives. In the organizational domain changes associated with the use of technology are often driven by institutional objectives, such as cost reduction, the broadening of modes of delivery and/or the implementation of new systems of research management, personal accountability or task control. There is something of a fit between the educational/organizational distinction and our two paradigms in the sense that e-constructivist practices are more likely to be centred in the educational domain and e-corporate practices in the organizational domain. The fit is not precise or limiting. Both paradigms can arise in each domain of higher education and may be present concurrently.

The Case Work

For empirical investigation we used a case-study methodology (Stake, 1995). The study comprised 15 individual cases, representing three discipline clusters, in five Australian universities. The five universities and the three disciplines are of contrasting types:

- Disciplines: Marginson and Considine (2000) identify three broad "families" of disciplines in Australian higher education, with distinctive missions and pedagogical dynamics: (a) professional training, (b) general-vocational training, and (c) the "basic" disciplines. The three discipline clusters chosen for the study were Medicine/Health Sciences, Business Studies and English/Communications. It was expected that these would evidence contrasting receptions of ICTs, from close pedagogical applications, to a special interest in application to mass delivery, to reticence. So it proved.
- University types: the locations of the case studies were distributed across the five types of Australian universities identified by Marginson (1997) (see also Marginson and Considine, 2000): Sandstones; Redbricks; Gumtrees; Unitechs; and New Universities.

Conduct of the Studies

At each site, we interviewed academic and administrative managers with the technology portfolio, deans, academics said to be using ICTs in "innovative" ways and focus groups of students. We also interviewed some institutional leaders, managers and support staff from outside the particular academic units. The interviews were semi-structured and focused on the participants' views, experiences and ICT-mediated teaching and learning practices in the formal education context. Participants were asked about the pedagogical and organizational aspects of ICTs innovations. The interviews canvassed the origins and preconditions of the innovations, including infrastructure, resources and funding, and the responses of academic peers inside and outside the institution. We asked if the innovations had changed over time and, if so, how the changes might be explained. We were particularly interested in exploring whether the innovations had met pedagogical and organizational objectives and, if not, what had been the obstacles. The research produced 130 separate interviews ranging from 30–90 minutes in length. In addition focus groups with students were conducted in each university. We also collected relevant documents, including curricula and university plans and strategies.

Findings in Relation to the Three Research Questions

Using ICTs to Facilitate the Cultivation of Student-centred Learning in Social Contexts

The most sustained and far-reaching example of the use of ICTs to promote student-centred learning was at the Sandstone Faculty of Medicine. In the mid-1990s a problem-based learning (PBL) approach to postgraduate medical education was initiated:

> There were essentially three major factors of change. One was converting from an under-graduate to a graduate entry. The second was adopting PBL as the method. And thirdly, the IT—that it would be heavily based in IT. So you can see, any one of those can be a major change for a faculty, particularly if you think of medicine . . . a very traditional course for so many years. (Senior Lecturer, Department of Medical Education, Sandstone)

This represented a curriculum-driven, ICT-mediated change in the direction of e-constructivist learning. When the Internet became widely available in the mid-1990s, students had electronic access to the weekly "problems", other web-based resources, their tutors and each other via an electronic forum: "an enriched environment that students can access from anywhere". Despite "all sorts of cases of typical resistance", the consensus was that the technology-mediated curriculum was successful. Both the PBL approach and the use of ICTs were seen as pivotal to the success of the programme. In the words of the faculty Head of Medical Education: "The students are well pre-pared . . . more outspoken . . . tend to be much more proactive . . . they tend to do things." Medically, "these students are much better prepared for their clinical responsibilities than in the past", although a few critics of the programme complained that the students "don't know much basic science when they come out".

The innovation had been initiated by a "champion" (Schon, 1963), who retired just as it got going. However, the commitment to education-driven change she had generated continued (cf. Taylor, 1998):

> The basic tenet of how we run this course is that the educational needs drive IT; IT does not drive education . . . We had a sort of conjunction of the planets, if you like, an alignment: we were introducing a new course at the right time, when this technology had been shown to be stable. (Sub-Dean IT, Faculty of Medicine, Sandstone)

The change was controlled at the faculty level and largely independent of central university man-agement and financial support. The relationship with the university centre and its broader ICTs agenda was devolved:

> They've watched with interest. They haven't interfered. They haven't said "no". But they haven't pressed either. It's not been the result of some Vice-Chancellorial edict that we did that. I'd say peaceful co-existence. We haven't looked to them for much financial help . . . they haven't changed their allocation to us. It's calculated in exactly the same way as it was. (Professor, Faculty of Medicine, Sandstone)

At the Redbrick and the Gumtree universities, the Faculties of Medicine had different approaches to the use of ICTs. Though it was moving to a similar PBL approach, the Redbrick medical faculty had decided not to go "high tech". Part of the explanation lay in the culture of the university, which prioritized a high-quality, "on-campus" experience. Many of the interviews indicated a negative view of "online delivery": for them, "online equated with Distance Education (DE), and that DE was inferior to the on-campus experience". Another part of the explanation, as perceived by the Head of the Teaching Research Unit, was that even though the Pro-Vice-Chancellor Education was in favour of developing IT capabilities, the money hadn't "really been forthcoming".

Perhaps the most significant part of the explanation was offered by the Dean of Medicine:

> Institutionally the changes have been measured. It's not an institution that goes through wild pendulum swings.

Forces for change were beginning to mobilize but they weren't coming from within:

> The need for change came from without . . . [as] the graduates of traditional medical courses were seen as not being very good communicators and perhaps didn't have the societal focus they should have. (Head of the Teaching Research Unit)

Despite examples of innovation in the faculty—the digitizing of resources for online databases that facilitated more independent learning—the Dean's sense was that technology would not play a central role in the curriculum change. Its use was not seen as intrinsic to what he described as the faculty's pedagogical goal: "to develop students' capabilities as self-regulated learners".

The Gumtree Faculty of Medicine, where a PBL programme begun in the 1970s was still "flourishing", also prided itself on promoting self-regulated learning without the integration of technology. In a university with a high degree of faculty autonomy and stretched finances, there was little evidence of a push from the centre to increase the use of ICTs for teaching and learning. Nor was there a push from within the faculty. This was perhaps ironic, as in the early days the Faculty of Medicine had boasted a Computer-assisted Instruction Unit. A version of the unit was still in existence but it persisted in using computers for their capacity for programmed learning, rather than for developing an e-constructivist approach to PBL. The PBL cases were paper-based in contrast to their online delivery at the Sandstone. The explanation was the lack of resources to support such a change. However, students were communicating electronically and live video link-ups were used with remote students. As with Medicine at both the Sandstone and the Redbrick, the old DE model of education provision for students at a distance, formerly paper-based but now online, was identified as a continuing incentive for the use of ICTs, but regarded as a solution to a problem of geography rather than as a favoured option.

Overall, Medicine appeared to be more amenable to the use of ICTs than the other discipline clusters. This is probably explained by financial and infrastructural factors, as much as by characteristics of the discipline: medical faculties are more likely to have the resources to engage in major innovations in approaches to teaching and learning that are both technology-mediated and under their own control.

Wealthier medical faculties are in a position to customize their own ICTs systems and platforms, enabling a fuller expression of disciplinary autonomy in initiating innovations. The study also highlighted the reality that less wealthy medical faculties do not have that same capacity for independent initiatives.

The pattern was somewhat similar in the Sandstone and Redbrick universities for Business Studies. The Sandstone University Faculty of Business had invested heavily in Blackboard Instructional Management software five years before the university centre decided to purchase the market alternative, WebCT. As the Dean explained: "We had to get a robust IT platform into place." Despite the incentive of a centrally paid for and supported management system, he decided to continue with Blackboard: "I'd want to be assured that any centrally provided server was both comfortable and reliable". Many people interviewed at the Redbrick Faculty of Commerce and Economics believed that the university had been rather slow in entering online education, and that this wasn't necessarily a bad thing. At the Gumtree, the Management Faculty had again been slow to take up technology, more so than the Medical Faculty.

The English/Communication departments at the Sandstone and the Redbrick (and the other three university types), where they used ICTs, made do with centrally provided management software whether WebCT or Blackboard.

Further evidence of changes to curriculum and pedagogical practices associated with the use of ICTs was in isolated pockets and connected with "champions" across the universities and discipline clusters. The Redbrick had a number of examples. One enthusiast was an Associate Professor in the English Department who had won an IT Fellowship offered by the Pro-Vice-Chancellor Education, which was almost the only example we saw there of institutional support for an ICT-mediated innovation. He valued the Fellowship as "invigorating and re-enthusing", providing an opportunity for him to "rethink pedagogical issues". He also emphasized the importance of central support for the initiative's potential long-term success.

Leading the way in technology-mediated innovations at the New University was the Faculty of Human Development. This faculty had the highest rate of uptake of WebCT and offered two online courses. The Dean attributed this to grassroots developments rather than central direction: "staff have gone and done professional development training courses . . . so they know what it is and they've got ideas about what it can be used for", while emphasizing that the university's support for WebCT had also contributed.

By contrast, at the Unitech, it was difficult to find evidence of the use of ICTs to promote student-centred learning across the three clusters of disciplines. More than at the other sites, the e-corporate paradigm was in the ascendancy. There were individual teachers struggling with large workloads and still managing to design and run innovative programmes, but they were isolated and often worn down by the lack of institutional support. In the words of one lecturer at the Unitech: "Psychologically, I felt whipped", and of another:

> I was in charge of 500 students online without any support plus my usual load . . . there's no doubt about the aim . . . it's basically efficiency . . . masqueraded as a better medium . . . the Nirvana of the New Age.

Overall, in the 15 case studies there was just one example of a major technology-mediated curriculum change that unequivocally generated more student-centred or self-regulated student learning. It seems that unless a number of basic conditions are present—financial capacity, financial independence, academic autonomy, a devolved administrative structure and tolerance from the university centre—such initiatives are difficult to organize and sustain. It does not seem coincidental that this example was at the Sandstone university in the discipline of Medicine. The more common scenario across the five universities and the three discipline clusters were instances of highly motivated individuals and small teams of enthusiastic technology-savvy academics working to construct ICT-mediated learning environments that were designed to promote independence in their students, based more or less on e-constructivist principles. But they were scattered, often unconnected, and weary from the increased work demands associated with the innovations. Where supportive institutional strategies were absent, these individuals did not always work with others, and sometimes their efforts were resisted by colleagues (cf. Hannan *et al.*, 1999).

Using ICTs to Facilitate the Implementation of Transmission-based Pedagogy

At the Unitech the imagined potential of distance-based ICTs to support future markets in international education was a powerful driver of institutional policy. This was despite the absence of clear-cut evidence of international demand for online education at scale and the failure of previous global "e-U" ventures (Cunningham *et al.*, 1998; Marginson, 2004). The position of the Unitech in this regard was distinctive. In the other institutions, interviewees were more wary of the promised dividends of e-learning, though all were taking advantage to different degrees of ICTs online delivery to remote students.

At this point it should be emphasized that our findings in relation to the Unitech were specific to the time of the case study in the early 2000s: since then there have been two subsequent Vice-Chancellors and major changes in ICTs and organization. We mention the Unitech example because at that stage it was a sharply realized case of the corporatist paradigm in ICTs innovation. The Unitech was widely described by interviewees at all levels, as "fragmented", "disorganized", "diverse" and comprising "different tribes". In pursuit of greater standardization and coherence, the institution's then executive was working to gain more central control. A principal means for achieving this was:

> the corporate learning management system . . . integrated with the academic management system, integrated with the knowledge management system and the timetable system. (Director, Learning Technology Services Unitech)

Part of the plan was the teaching and learning strategy:

> It's about managing the relationship between the lecturer, the tutor and the students in a way that ensures all students are getting the level of service the university wants them to get . . . We're trying to find that balance between teacher effectiveness . . . and efficiencies and cost effectiveness'. (Director, Learning Technology Services Unitech)

Also part of the plan was the aim to develop every course in the university in online form, including the courses for which there was never any intention of online teaching: the cost-efficient strategy would develop potentially saleable intellectual property while securing central institutional ownership of courseware. It would standardize and render transparent the entire body of curriculum and "retool" all teachers as online course developers without paying the full costs of professionals. As such, the highly centralized ICT-mediated teaching and learning strategy was shaped by the e-corporate paradigm more directly than at the other four universities:

> Our teaching and learning strategy is based on a belief that the whole is greater than the sum of the parts. And this involves a radical departure from the traditional view that academics have of their role in the university. Most academics are discipline focused, their self image as an academic is very much centred around their role in their discipline . . . One of the fundamental precepts is that as an academic you have to surrender your autonomy as a discipline expert and become part of a group that is collectively responsible for the overall intellectual development of the student. Some of my less charitable colleagues accuse me of being not all that totally removed either personally or politically from the Stalinist view of forced collectivization. (University Manager, Learning Technologies, Unitech)

Although managers acknowledged that centralizing processes needed to be balanced with scope for innovation at the level of the academic unit, academics across the three discipline clusters, particularly at the junior to middle level, believed that the DLS had been imposed rather than allowed to grow organically and noted poor communication between the centre and the periphery. There was broad-based hostility towards the innovation enterprise. For example, in the large Unitech Business Faculty there was resistance to what was interpreted as a command from the centre to move to online delivery, though the move was already gradually taking place. The lecturer, who was managing 500 online students without any administrative or teaching support, described the Unitech's online strategy as "economically driven". Life Sciences, in particular Nursing, was less advanced in the move to online teaching, but its incipient resistance had been met with a firm response from the centre: it was being pushed into change. Students and staff complained that they were not prepared and that infrastructure and support services were inadequate or absent. In Applied Communication there was a different approach that took more account of the disciplinary needs. There, however, even one early adapter was critical of the DLS. While noting that the university had tried to accommodate diversity, he argued that the centralized system was "lacking in flexibility", hampering rather than encouraging innovation.

The students at the Unitech, across the three disciplines, did not express a preference for ICT-based learning. Although some appreciated increased opportunities for data retrieval, inter-student communication and electronic assessment, or some applauded the time–space flexibility of online learning (cf. Lockyer *et al.*, 1999), others regretted the loss of contact with teachers and each other, and expressed concerns about the potential for greater surveillance associated with online teaching (cf. Swartz and Biggs, 1999; Kitto, 2003). The potential of the use of ICTs to meet varying needs was under-developed at the Unitech and indeed at most of the sites. Technology strategies did not always connect with students' uses of technology. Students were pursuing their own e-constructivism that was quite separate from the university's e-corporatist technology strategy:

It doesn't seem to have deeply penetrated their approach to university. If they're on the Internet, it's a different box from uni work. They're very skilled on it sometimes. You know they're publishing, communicating, doing amazing things, but nothing to do with getting a degree. (Technology Leader, Academic Unit, Unitech)

Implications for ICTs Innovations of Coincidence Between Educational Objectives and Organizational Objectives

An ICT-mediated educational innovation, located in a supportive and benign university environment, with a clear agenda, carefully formulated and based on consultation and planning, seems most likely to succeed. More than at any other site we investigated, the Sandstone University Faculty of Medicine's radical curriculum change, based on e-constructivist principles, embodied these characteristics. With some dissent, both academics and students confirmed that the venture had been successful. By contrast with the Unitech's lack of institutional coherence and mounting tension between the centre and the faculties, the Sandstone operated on a principle of "give and take". The centre was attempting to instigate a universal teaching and learning platform, but in keeping with its "collegial spirit" preferred "people-centred" approaches to change rather than imposition from above. The Vice-Chancellor told us that the centre's role was to induce change through "incentives not by regulation": the members of the senior executive regarded a degree of autonomy as intrinsic to the production of innovations in teaching and learning. As a senior manager told us:

No matter how vertically integrated an institution like a university is, you can't rule by fiat . . . it doesn't work.

The institution's apparently democratic sensibility provided conditions for ICT-mediated innovation to thrive.

At the same time, some characteristics of the e-corporate paradigm had begun to take hold at the Sandstone. Evidence of tension between the centre and the disciplines was emerging. Decentralization did not in itself provide every Sandstone unit with the same freedom to act. Faculties that chose to work outside the central system were not provided with technology infrastructure or support services, and not all had the same resource capacity. This was much better for Medicine than for academic units in poorer faculties such as Arts. While the Sandstone Arts Faculty as a unit took advantage of the central provision of IT software and support, the English Department was openly resistant to online forms of education and most of its academics ignored the IT resources on offer. In the Sandstone University's Business Faculty, with its own networked Blackboard technology that was set up prior to the central WebCT initiative, many academics with little pressure from above chose to use the software, but as in Business faculties in most other universities, "teaching with ICTs" often meant little more than putting course outlines and notes on the Web.

The complexity of the issue of local autonomy versus central control is evident. While devolution at the Sandstone brought with it the opportunity for major disciplinary driven innovation, only Medicine seemed to have sufficient funds to support this. In other faculties, most academics seemed to agree with the central university managers about the need to centralize ICTs for teaching and learning. Self-determination cost too much.

As in the Sandstone, the Redbrick ran along devolved collegial lines with the faculties and deans exercising considerable power. At the time of data collection, there were moves afoot to strengthen the role of the centre via the appointment of a "CEO" Information Services to manage IT strategic directions for the whole university. One explanation given was that few initiatives were emerging spontaneously. Overall, the Redbrick was trying to balance a conservative, gradualist approach to the use of ICT while recognizing that students liked the flexibility of online options. The university was being pulled in a number of directions. It wanted to prioritize the on-campus experience but was increasingly aware of competition from other universities on the "flexible" path.

Financial constraints at the Gumtree limited the extent of central initiatives in IT. The school in which English was located had constructed its own central computing system, chosen mainly because it was cheap: there were terminals on academics' desks, but with the software centrally located and controlled. The managers saw it as a wonderful initiative because it did not cost much. However, there was resistance to the standardized hardware and software within the school. One academic, who had come from a better-resourced Sandstone university, and for whom ICTs was integral to his teaching, was no longer using technology. For him, the system was a step backwards. The Gumtree acknowledged the importance of central planning and control in IT operations, but financial constraints combined with democratic traditions to make it difficult to achieve. The university had to make do with pockets of innovation, which, given strong disciplinary autonomy, was also the line of least resistance, and still left space for ritualistic claims to excellence:

> We're probably the leanest central administration in the country. Our IT budget is miniscule compared with many others. Our nominal amount to be spent on IT infrastructure in a year is $2 million. [We] don't put in crazy PeopleSoft systems at $25 million a pop because we can't afford it . . . [But] I think we're up with them in terms of what we do. Maybe not in the width of what we do but in terms of the quality (University Manager, Learning Technologies, Gumtree).

The New University was also trying to balance central control and a coherent organizational structure with faculty autonomy. The approach to technology had been a mixture of ad hoc initiatives by individuals, some faculty decisions and some strategies and guidelines from the centre. The Vice-Chancellor's group had taken a "let's wait and see" attitude to the integration of ICTs. It had been cautious in adopting a networked student administrative system. The lack of coherent IT policy was reflected in the fact that at the time of data collection the New University had two parallel websites containing slightly different information. However, certain strategies for the implementation of ICTs across the university were being put in place.

Final Comments

In sum, the main findings of the study are:

1. The most effective use of ICTs in universities occurs when educational and organizational objectives are in harmony.
2. When ICTs innovations are dominated by corporatist objectives at the expense of pedagogical objectives, benefits are limited and tensions evident.
3. Pedagogical initiatives by discipline-based ICTs "champions" require central support if they are to add value on a sustained basis.
4. The optimal conditions for ICTs innovations in teaching and learning are comprised by academic and financial autonomy, and academic and financial capacity. These conditions were present in only one of the 15 case studies.

The research suggests that in the first years of the twenty-first century in Australia the frequency of technology-mediated innovations in higher education was increasing. This can be explained at least partly by institution-level strategies and management. Nevertheless, most innovations we found had their origins within academic disciplines and were designed to improve teaching and cater for a more diverse student population. A smaller number were driven by university reorganization or the need to raise income. When institution-driven innovations worked outside academic cultures this sometimes resulted in tension between managerial and academic practices.

In the case studies the universities were often negotiating between e-constructivist and e-corporate approaches. Academics and managers referred to features of these paradigms when discussing their own ICTs strategies and practices. Academics' pedagogical innovations seldom occurred in a context free from institutional and managerial imperatives. Management spoke of oganizational strategies in relation to both corporate agendas and teaching and learning agendas. However, the meanings and organizational implications of the two paradigms were at times rather different, depending upon the particular agendas of different people in the organizations. For instance, in the discourse and practices accompanying teaching and learning strategies we saw some evidence of efforts to develop self-regulated and self-motivated learners. We also saw some evidence of the discourse of student-driven learning articulated to market-driven models of students as consumers, an approach which tended to be more concerned with administrative scope and efficiences than with critical pedagogical outcomes.

Given the centrality of academic practices to the productivity, standing and identity of universities, it is to be expected that reforms in which institutional innovation is drawn into synergy with academic innovation are likely to be the most effective. Another lesson garnered from the study is that technology-mediated pedagogical initiatives by "champions" can be generalized in lasting fashion only when supportive institutional strategies are in place: when there is "an alignment of the planets". This conclusion is consistent with literature on technological change elsewhere (cf. Lankshear *et al.*, 2000), which finds that complementarity between innovations in different parts of institutional and inter-institutional systems enables optimum development. If so, the key question for universities, and their academic units, is how to establish the resources, systems, discursive practices and other conditions that facilitate complementarity.

The case studies suggest a number of basic requirements for the effective use of ICTs. To secure fruitful synergies in academic/management partnerships, each needs to articulate and communicate compatible (though not necessarily identical) goals and values. There needs to be a division of labour between the two elements in which the managers provide enabling work conditions while academics deploy autonomy creatively and productively. However, one bottom line is that unless institutions and units are financially strong, the integration of ICTs remains a challenge whether driven from the centre or within units.

Note

1. Snyder, I., Marginson, S. and Lewis, T. (2007) "An Alignment of the Planets": Mapping the intersections between pedagogy, technology and management in Australian universities. *Journal of Higher Education Policy and Management*, 29(2), 187–202. Reprinted by permission of the publisher.

References

Andrews, R. (ed.) (2004). *The impact of ICT on literacy education*. London: Routledge.
Bates, A.W. (2000). *Managing technological change*. San Francisco, CA: Jossey-Bass.
Bonk, C.J. and Cunningham, D.J. (1998). Searching for learner-centred, constructivist, and sociocultural components of collaborative educational learning tools. In C.J. Bonk and K. King (eds) *Electronic collaborators: learner-centered technologies for literacy, apprenticeship, and discourse*. Boston, MA: Lawrence Erlbaum Associates.
Collis, B. and Moonen, J. (2001). *Flexible learning in a digital world: experiences and expectations*. London: Kogan Page.
Cunningham, S., Tapsall, S., Ryan, Y., Stedman, L., Bagdon, K. and Flew, T. (1998). *New media and borderless education: a review of the convergence between global media networks and higher education provision*. Canberra: Department of Employment, Education, Training and Youth Affairs, Evaluations and Investigations Program, Higher Education Division.
Dillon, A. and Gabbard, R. (1998). Hypermedia as an educational technology. *Review of Educational Research*, 68(3), 322–349.
Dutton, W. and Loader, B. (eds) (2002). *Digital academe: new media and institutions in higher education and learning*. London: Routledge.
Fabry, D. and Higgs, J. (1997). Barriers to the effective use of technology. *Journal of Educational Computing Research*, 17(4), 385–395.
Giroux, H. (2005). Academic entrepreneurs: the corporate takeover of higher education. *Tikkun*, 20(2), 18–22, 28.
Gunn, C. (1999). They love it, but do they learn from it? *Higher Education Research and Development*, 18(2), 185–199.
Hannan, A., English, S. and Silver, H. (1999). Why innovate? *Studies in Higher Education*, 24(3), 279–289.
Harris, M. (2000). Virtual learning and the network society. *Information, Communication and Society*, 3(4), 580–596.
Kitto, S. (2003). Translating an electronic panopticon: educational technology and the re-articulation of lecturer–student relations in online learning. *Information, Communication and Society*, 6(1), 1–23.
Lankshear, C., Snyder, I. with Green, B. (2000). *Teachers and technoliteracy: managing literacy, technology and learning in schools*. Sydney: Allen and Unwin.
Laurillard, D. (1993). *Rethinking university teaching: a framework for the effective use of educational technology*. London: Routledge.
Lewis, R. (1999). The role of technology in learning. *British Journal of Educational Technology*, 30(2), 141–150.
Lewis, T., Marginson, S. and Snyder, I. (2005). The network university? Technology, culture and organisational complexity in contemporary higher education. *Higher Education Quarterly*, 59(1), 56–75.
Lin, X., Hmelo, C., Kinzer, C. and Secules, T. (1999). Designing technology to support reflection. *Educational Technology Research and Development*, 47(3), 43–62.
Lockyer, L., Patterson, J. and Harper, B. (1999). Measuring effectiveness of health education. *Higher Education Research and Development*, 18(2), 233–246.
Looi, C. (1998). Interactive learning environments for promoting inquiry learning. *Journal of Educational Technology Systems*, 27(1), 3–22.
Marginson, S. (1997). Competition and contestability in Australian higher education. *Australian Universities Review*, 40(1), 5–14.
Marginson, S. (2004). Don't leave me hanging on the Anglophone: the potential for online distance education in the Asia-Pacific region. *Higher Education Quarterly*, 58(2–3), 74–113.
Marginson, S. and Considine, M. (2000). *The enterprise university*. Cambridge: Cambridge University Press.
Newman, R. and Johnson, F. (1999). Sites of power and knowledge? Towards a critique of the virtual university. *British Journal of Sociology of Education*, 20(1), 79–88.

Peters, M. (2002). The university in the knowledge economy. In S. Cooper, J. Hinkson and G. Sharp (eds) *Scholars and entrepreneurs: the universities in crisis.* Melbourne: Arena Publications.

Privateer, P.M. (1999). Academic technology and the future of higher education. *Journal of Higher Education, 70*(1), 60–79.

Ramsden, P. (1992). *Learning to teach in higher education.* London: Routledge.

Reeves, T. and Laffey, J. (1999). Design, assessment and evaluation of a problem-based learning environment in undergraduate engineering. *Higher Education Research and Development, 18*(2), 219–232.

Ryan, Y. (1998). Time and tide: Teaching and learning online. *Australian Universities Review, 41*(1), 14–19.

Salomon, G. and Almog, T. (1998). Educational psychology and technology. *Teachers College Record, 100*(1), 222–241.

Schon, D. (1963). Champions for radical new innovations. *Harvard Business Review,* March–April, 77–86.

Snyder, I. (ed.) (1997). *Page to screen: taking literacy into the electronic era.* Sydney: Allen and Unwin.

Stake, R.E. (1995). *The art of case study research.* Thousand Oaks, CA: Sage.

Swartz, J. and Biggs, B. (1999). Technology, time and space. *Journal of Educational Computing Research, 20*(1), 71–85.

Taylor, P. (1998). Institutional change in uncertain times: lone ranging is not enough. *Studies in Higher Education, 23*(3), 269–279.

Wajcman, J. (2002). Addressing technological change: the challenge to social theory. *Current Sociology, 50*(3), 347–363.

West, R. (1997, 1998). *Learning for life, Vols. 1 and 2.* Canberra: Australian Government Publishing Service.

Woolgar, S. (ed.) (2002). *Virtual society: technology, cyberbole, reality.* Oxford: Oxford University Press.

Yetton, P. (1997). *Managing the introduction of technology in the delivery and administration of higher education.* Canberra: Australian Government Publishing Service.

10
Diverse Student Groups:
Teaching with a Goal of Inclusivity

Marybeth Gasman and Julie Vultaggio

College and university classrooms comprise diverse learners with diverse needs. Too often, faculty members forget that such diversity exists, teaching in monolithic ways and failing to, or opting not to, vary their instruction in the classroom. According to Kuh *et al.*, (2005), "students flourish when their prior learning is valued and their preferred learning styles are recognized" (p. 285). Thus, the purpose of this chapter is to provide an overview of diverse student learners based on an examination of available research. Though there are many different aspects of student diversity, we focus on issues of race and ethnicity, class, gender and ability. In addition, we consider how teaching and learning strategies can be adapted to enhance the learning process for these students. In order to counteract the exclusion of particular groups from consideration in the classroom, research shows that students should be given ample opportunity to self-reflect and "interrogate assumptions and bias"—thus helping them feel included in the learning process (Mayhew and Fernandez, 2007, p. 58). In the words of higher education scholar and pioneer Arthur Chickering, "we need to learn how to recognize, respect, and respond to the wide-ranging individual differences among our diverse learners. If we do this—and it is a big if—then many more of our students will achieve learning that lasts" (2006, p. 11).

Diverse Learner Experiences

Issues of Race and Ethnicity

One of the hallmarks of Western higher education is competition, stemming from European academic traditions and supported by the Protestant ethic. However, for many students of colour and women, "co-operation rather than competition is highly valued" in academic endeavours (Morey, 2000, p. 32). In many non-Western cultures, working together towards a common goal is stressed, and collective efforts—as opposed to individual efforts—are emphasized. Notably, this approach can have an adverse impact in classrooms that are shaped by Western thought and an emphasis on individualism. For example, the notion of collectivism is much more important than individualism for Latino, American Indians and indigenous peoples, and Asian students, which has important learning implications (Castellanos and Jones, 2003; Lynch, 1997; Morey, 2000; Tatum, 1997). Latino students foster strong ties to their immediate and extended families, and often rely on these relatives for support through the educational process. American Indian students tend to place similar emphasis on the importance of family; as Tatum (1997) describes: "as with Latinos (who often share Indian ancestry), extended family and kinship obligations are considered very important. Consequently, group needs are more important than individual needs" (p. 145). Many Asian cultures also stress collectivism over the American ideal of individualism (Pratt, 1991). Considering these points, students from these diverse racial and cultural backgrounds may excel in more collaborative learning environments and on assignments that emphasize group interaction (Tatum, 1997).

In recent years, researchers interested in the experiences of all students in college and university classrooms have also explored how "Whiteness" manifests in these settings. According to Maher and Tetrault (1997), "A necessary part of perceiving how the assumption of Whiteness shapes the construction of classroom knowledge is understanding its centrality to the academy's practices of intellectual domination, namely, the imposition of certain ways of constructing the world through the lenses of traditional disciplines" (p. 4). Often times, both faculty and students are unaware of the way Whiteness permeates classroom discussions. As a result, faculty members pursuing a *laissez-faire* model of classroom participation—for example, allowing a few outspoken students to dominate the classroom discussion—may become unwitting accomplices of White domination (Maher and Tetrault, 1997). Along these lines, faculty members sometimes display a lack of intellectual support for culturally-based research and discussion (Margolis and Romero, 1998). For instance, research papers that focus on minority issues may be considered "unworthy" by some White faculty (Pruitt and Isaac, 1985, p. 534). These phenomena leave many students of colour feeling ignored and in effect silenced.

According to Gasman *et al.*, (2004), students of colour often feel academically isolated in the classroom due to the lack of alignment between their viewpoints and those of their White professors. Moreover, according to Carter and Wilson's (1995) research, faculty members ask questions of "greater complexity and give more complete answers to mainstream (white) students than to students from underrepresented/minority groups" (p. 33). In addition, students of color often frequently feel discouraged from participating in class discussions if there are no other minority students in the classroom (Pruitt and Isaac, 1985). Research also shows that students of color tend to be viewed as the "token" representative of their race in classrooms with few minorities, which generates feelings of anger and frustration that may prevent these students from participating in group conversations (Jackson, 2003; Taylor and Antony, 2000). This sense of tokenization is not limited to peer stereotyping; faculty members often unwittingly hold expectations of students from certain racial backgrounds, such as Asian Americans, who are seen as the "model minority" (Chang and Kiang, 2002; Tatum, 1997). Furthermore, due to the "risky" nature of racial issues, faculty members may not feel comfortable addressing these concerns in the classroom (Gasman *et al.*, 2004). This, of course, is unfortunate as research shows that faculty members play the most critical role in facilitating learning and interaction for diverse learners (Mayhew and Fernandez, 2007).

According to the literature, students of colour frequently sense that their perspectives are not valued in the classroom. For example, Gasman *et al.*, (2008) found that Black students at a highly selective school of education felt that their voices were not fairly represented in course discussions, or expressed difficulty relating to conversations in the classroom. In addition, students in the study described their course readings and classroom environments as overwhelmingly Eurocentric. These finding are substantiated by other research related to Blacks and students of color in general (Cheatham and Phelps, 1995; Gasman *et al.*, 2004; Pruitt and Isaac, 1985).

Building on Gasman *et al.*'s (2008) findings, research shows that many faculty members and institutions have historically privileged Eurocentric knowledge on their syllabi and in the classroom. Due to the lack of inclusion of alternative racial and ethnic perspectives, this prevalent

Eurocentrism often creates an inhospitable environment for students of colour (Gasman *et al.*, 2004). For example, in their study of 26 female students of colour in a sociology program, Margolis and Romero (1998) noted that the academic experience "simultaneously reproduces gender, race, class, and other forms of inequality" (p. 2). According to the authors, there are two aspects of racism that occur in college curricula: 1) the "weak" form, which takes place in the specific courses required to complete the program and 2) the "strong" form, which systematically "acts to reproduce stratified and unequal social relations" (Margolis and Romero, 1998, p. 2). To illustrate this subtle discrimination, one participant in Gasman et al.'s (2008) study stated: "The same three or four Black authors are accessed in my experience (Audre Lourde, bell hooks, and Gloria Ladson-Billings). I've never been in a class where any Afrocentric literature is interrogated for usefulness. I guess the majority of Black people aren't qualified to intelligently discuss the state of black education and the needs of black children (hint: I'm being ironic and a little cynical here)". The lack of racial representation on college and university syllabi not only limits students' exposure to diverse perspectives on important issues, but also creates frustration that could spill over into classroom discussions—which could consequently silence students of color or discourage them from playing an active role in the learning process.

Despite having ample research on what works well in terms of educating diverse learners, some classrooms continue to maintain a hidden curriculum or the "unstated but clearly enforced rules about knowledge and behaviours valued in the classroom" (Morey, 2000, p. 33). Through this hidden curriculum, faculty members often unknowingly propagate "an ideology, thought, and action that works to perpetuate power relationships, cultural hegemony, and political relationships", that puts a damper on the progress of all students, especially diverse learners (ibid). In turn, this can prevent students from developing thoughts and research that challenge the dominant social structure, which is an educational goal for many learners.

Issues of Gender

Although often ignored, gender shapes students' classroom experiences in several ways (Baxter Magolda, 1998; Severiens and ten Dam, 1994). For example, research shows that women tend to excel in classrooms that offer greater socio-emotional support, though they also perform well on independent research projects. Men, on the other hand, tend to work better in teams, yet they don't need the same kinds of emotional support as their female counterparts (Harrop *et al.*, 2007; Robson *et al.*, 2004; Sutton and Henry, 2005).

Frequently, issues of gender intersect with issues of race in college and university classrooms. In her study of Black women attending various institutions, Jackson (2003) found that participants struggled to be recognized for both elements of their identity, as faculty and administrators often focus on race and neglect gender. Women of colour need support in both arenas, and one strategy for doing so is creating curricula that contain more female and racial minority perspectives. This call for inclusive curricula is encouraged by several other authors (hooks, 1994; Schmitz *et al.*, 2001). Expanding on this intersection of race and gender, Sadker and Sadker (1992) found that "White male students are most likely to be involved in classroom discussions while underrepresented/minority group students and white women tend to be quieter and to assume a less powerful role in discussions. When women do speak, they are more likely than men to be interrupted" (p. 33). Moreover, faculty members tend to maintain greater eye contact with White male students, and are more inclined to remember their names (Morey, 2000; Sadker and Sadker, 1994). Of greater concern is Sadker and Sadker's (1992) finding that faculty members allow more time for White male students to respond to questions, and give more positive reinforcement or praise for their responses.

Issues of Class

Much like race, ethnicity, and gender, class plays a significant role in the classroom and in the learning experiences of diverse students. Although class is often ignored or rendered invisible in discussions, it permeates the daily lives of students. According to Ohmann (2003), "To notice or make a fuss about class would, then, spoil the illusion; it would remind all that they came to a selective college in part to preserve or upgrade their class standing. It would call into question their individuality, uniqueness, and freedom. So they enact class without allowing its reality" (p. 11). While class is frequently unseen and unaddressed in the classroom, research studies and national surveys have consistently found a "correlation between academic achievement and socio-economic status" (Howard, 2001, p. 7). Conversations that assume all students belong to a specific class, or the dominant class, can be alienating. For instance, hooks (1994) describes how the perception that loud, passionate or emotional comments in the classroom are often "associated with being a member of the lower classes" (p. 178). As a result, "students are often silenced by means of their acceptance of class values that teach them to maintain order at all costs" (p. 178). Thus, much like the silencing of students of color, students from low-income backgrounds may feel that their opinions are not respected in classrooms that emphasize conventional middle- to upper-class values. In addition, belonging to a specific class and having it hold them back can make learning a frustrating experience.

Students from low-income backgrounds may also suffer in the classroom because they spend too many hours working part-time or full-time jobs. Most of these students are forced to hold down jobs to support their education, and find themselves torn between studying and being able to fund it (Walpole, 2003). The majority of students in Walpole's study were working up to 16 hours per week, and low-income students were less involved in the classroom and had underdeveloped study habits compared with their middle- and high-income counterparts. Due to time committed to working, these students are also less likely to participate in individual projects with faculty members or visit them outside of class—two activities that tend to lead to greater intensity of learning and participation in graduate school.

Compared with the issues of race and gender, class receives virtually no attention in the scholarly literature pertaining to college students (Karabel and Astin, 1975; Karen, 1991; Pascarella and Terenzini, 1991; Trow, 1992; Walpole, 2003). However, there is considerable overlap between these different aspects of students' identities. As described by Castellanos and Jones (2003), for example, class plays a significant role in the educational experiences of Latina/o students. The authors cite numerous empirical studies showing that financial concerns, including time spent working, produced increased levels of stress for these students, which may inhibit their ability to complete readings and course assignments, and in turn, their involvement in class discussions.

Issues of Disability

Another group that has been enrolling in greater numbers in colleges and universities is students with disabilities. These disabilities range from speech impediments to hearing difficulties to health-related issues. However, according to Scott et al., (2003), 41 percent of student disabilities pertain to learning. As the authors describe, "common accommodation procedures require that a student with a disability self-identify as having a disability to the class instructor within the first weeks of class, provide documentation to authorized campus disability professionals that verifies eligibility for accommodations, request specific accommodations based on the disability, and wait for adjustments to be implemented" (p. 40). Yet even when faculty members follow these procedures and accommodate students with disabilities, this may not be enough. All students need to be welcomed into the classroom and the course discussions in meaningful ways. Often times, students with disabilities, especially those with hearing and speech conditions, report feeling ignored and over-looked in the classroom by both faculty and student peers (Barga, 1996; Holmes-Siedle, 1994; Kame'enui and Carnine, 1998; Scott *et al.*, 2003). Some students with disabilities fear being labeled as "deviants" by faculty and fellow students (Luna, 2002).

According to research conducted by Luna, students with disabilities consider their relationships with peers and professors to be essential for learning, and an important strategy for success. For example, one of the participants in Luna's study noted that she learned better and retained more when she had the opportunity to talk through course content with the professor or her classmates. Luna found that learning disabled students may also benefit from more time to think through concepts in the classroom. Several participants in her study noted that thinking is a visual process for them and takes "more time than the pace of most classroom discussion allows" (p. 600). Finally, Luna found that students with learning disabilities suffered greatly when asked to conform to standard test-taking rules, especially timed tests. These students left the exam feeling "stupid" and in many cases "stopped trying" once they experienced failure.

Based on this research, it is clear that students' classroom experiences vary according to their race, gender, class, and ability. Though some of these elements may be concealed, it is important for faculty to recognize and acknowledge that different learners have different academic needs based on the complex intersection of their identities. In addition to including all students' voices in the classroom, faculty should be cognizant of developing curricula that reflect the perspectives of students' diverse personalities. The next section offers practical suggestions on how to achieve these goals.

Approaches to Enhancing Learning in the Classroom

Instruction

According to Morey (2000), "the instructional component of a course can be made inclusive by incorporating teaching strategies and learning activities that provide opportunities for personal participation and growth, capitalize on student experiences, and learning strengths" (p. 31). Thus, in addition to becoming more cognizant of diverse learners and their individual needs, faculty should make efforts to use inclusive teaching methods. As described by hooks (1994), one way to be more egalitarian in the classroom is to move the discussion around the room, giving each student an opportunity to talk and contribute significantly. In addition, she, as well as Maher and Tetrault (1997), remind faculty members not to let white males dominate the classroom conversa-tion. Sadker and Sadker (1992) also suggest being cognizant of answering everyone's questions, giving people equal time to speak, and not letting people interrupt, which seems to be a particular issue for women.

bell hooks (1994) advocates an "engaged pedagogy", one in which the faculty member uses a holistic approach and treats students "as whole human beings with complex lives and experiences rather than simply as seeking after compartmentalized bits of knowledge" (p. 15). Building on this point, it is important for faculty to recognize that students have different learning styles, but also realize that their personal characteristics combine to create a unique whole. For this reason, faculty should refrain from addressing only one characteristic of students without acknowledging all of the other qualities that form their identities and influence their experience in the classroom. These issues are exacerbated for female students of color, students of color with disabilities, or any combination of the characteristics discussed above. According to Morey (2000), faculty members "send powerful messages about their valuing or devaluing of diversity by how they initiate and respond to student questions, comments, and behaviours" (p. 33). Thus, in delivering lectures or conversing in the classroom, faculty should remember to address questions and concerns from all students without preferencing one particular group.

Classroom Environment

As suggested in the previous section, classroom dynamics are an important aspect of the learning process, particularly for diverse learners (Kitano, 1997; Morey, 2000). According to Luna (2002), diverse students often have difficulty in classrooms with rigidly defined hierarchical power relationships between students and professors, and feel that the hierarchy constrains their role in shaping and contributing to their own educational experiences. To combat this effect, Luna suggests that faculty members allow students to "participate in shaping academic contexts", and develop "shared understandings of what counts as learning in the classroom and creative strategies for demonstrating that learning" (p. 603). Morey (2000) concurs, noting that in an inclusive classroom, "dynamics include the challenging of biased views and the sharing of diverse perspectives within an environment of mutual respect. Students are equal participants in the learning process" (p. 29). In addition, she asserts that faculty members in this type of classroom "share power within the limits of responsibility and reality", and learn from students. They also use instructional approaches that center on the "experiences and knowledge that students bring and can include critical pedagogy and issues-oriented approaches" (Morey, 2002, p. 29).

Translating this research to practice, faculty members must be willing to negotiate their power status in order to create an inclusive classroom environment (Gasman *et al.*, 2004). One approach that faculty can use is to ask students to lead a class discussion, or perhaps ask students to prepare questions for a class discussion, in effect, letting them steer the direction of the class. According to Rong (2002), "Inviting students to participate in class planning, organizing class activities, and other related decision-making begins the process of student empowerment. Small group activities also give many nontraditional students or underrepresented groups voices that might be lost within the large group" (p. 135). She also notes that when power is shared: "Students tend to take a closer look at the materials selected for class, and they listen more thoughtfully because their own insights have been valued" (p. 135)

Curricula

While faculty members' teaching strategies and classroom behaviors are overt indicators of their dedication to inclusivity, curricula and course syllabi should be equally reflective of this commitment. According to Morey (2000), an inclusive course that fosters student learning "covers traditional views and adds alternative perspectives" (p. 29). Thus, curricula and syllabi should incorporate readings, topics and authors that address issues of race, gender, class and ability (Gasman *et al.*, 2008; Jackson, 2003; Renn, 2000). In doing so, faculty not only emphasize the value of diverse perspectives in the classroom—which could effectively prevent the "silencing" of many underrepresented students—but also expose all learners to different types of material and viewpoints based on authors' individual identities. These varying opinions may help students personally connect to the material, which could promote a more positive and engaged learning experience.

In considering how to develop more inclusive curricula and course syllabi, research suggests several different approaches that are modifiable, based on the needs of the faculty member as well as the structure of the academic department or institution. For instance, while many institutions support programs and courses on specific racial groups (i.e. Black Studies, Latino Studies, Asian Studies, and Native American and Indigenous Studies), other colleges and universities may prefer to address racial issues in the broader arena of Ethnic Studies, which can serve as a department or a group of interrelated courses (Hu-DeHart, 2002). Along these lines, issues of gender may be addressed through a course on women's studies, or simply by incorporating gender and sexuality issues into existing courses on sociology, history, literature or writing (Renn, 2000; Schmitz *et al.*, 2001). For example, faculty should update current syllabi and curricula to include topics of race, gender, class and ability; adding a lecture (or multiple lectures), discussion questions and readings by diverse authors can send a clear message to students that the faculty member values diversity and supports the needs and opinions of all learners.

Assignments and Assessment

In addition to creating more inclusive curricula, Morey (2000) suggests that "an inclusive course utilizes different types of assessments for students to demonstrate their mastery over the content, and ensures consideration of individual differences in expressing knowledge" (p. 29). Thus, faculty members should use alternative assessment practices that "support knowledge acquisition on the part of all students" (p. 32). By including non-traditional or innovative assessments and assignments in their courses, faculty can incorporate the learning styles of more diverse students, and increase their sense of control over their work as well as their motivation (McKeachie and Svinicki, 2006).

Based on her research, Luna (2002) asserts that diverse students may benefit from writing exercises that allow them to explore thoughts and ideas, rather than assignments that simply focus on the mechanics of writing. Diverse learners have particular difficulty when they are not given opportunities to "demonstrate strengths such as leadership, creativity, and hands-on problem solving" (p. 602). Faculty members should provide more open-ended assignments that allow diverse learners to explore topics that interest and engage them in a holistic learning experience. In addition, faculty members should permit unique and non-traditional methods that allow students of all backgrounds to draw upon their talents. For instance, students could be given the option to write a collaborative paper for a shared grade, which would speak to the learning styles of those from cultures that value collective efforts as described earlier (Tatum, 1997). Faculty members could also allow students to use non-traditional reporting methods, such as story-telling, lyric-writing or photography, which could also speak to students' diverse learning strategies based on race, culture, gender and ability. Mayhew and Fernandez (2007) found that diverse students who reflected on course materials examined these materials from multiple perspectives, and "applied this knowledge to analyzing societal problems consistently gained a better understanding of themselves and issues related to diversity, regardless of course content" (p. 75). Most importantly, faculty should support students' ideas for papers and projects. As mentioned earlier, studies have shown that diverse learners are often discouraged from pursuing research on controversial issues such as race and ethnicity (Margolis and Romero, 1998; Pruitt and Isaac, 1985). In doing so, faculty members not only deprive students of their voice in creating the project, but of the joy and pride in researching a topic of personal significance.

Conclusion

Students from diverse backgrounds—including, but certainly not limited to, race, gender, class and ability—enter the classroom with different needs and learning styles that faculty may unwittingly neglect. However, this is not to say that faculty members are completely at fault; in most cases, they do not receive training on how to embrace diverse learners in the classroom, nor are there outlets for discussing these issues (hooks, 1994). In the words of Adam Howard (2001), "the majority of faculty members have not had the necessary training to create teaching and learning environments that respond to different levels of academic skill and knowledge, and to students as individuals" (p. 8). Faculty members need to make conscious efforts to recognize students' different needs in the classroom, and address them in non-discriminatory manners. This involves advancing our instruction techniques, classroom environments, curricula and assessments/assignments to be inclusive of all learners. By adopting these changes, faculty can integrate a "flexible, responsive pedagogy based on an educational discourse that values diversity [and] may help us accommodate a wide range of students' abilities" (Luna, 2002, p. 602). Consequently, faculty members can enhance the classroom learning experience for students of all backgrounds.

References

Barga, N.K. (1996). Students with learning disabilities in education: Managing a disability. *Journal of Learning Disabilities*, *29*(4), 413–421.

Baxter Magolda, M. (1998). Learning and gender: Complexity and possibility. *Higher Education*, *35*, 351–355.

Carter, D.J. and Wilson, R. (1995). *Minorities in higher education: 1993 Twelfth Annual Status Report*. Washington, D.C.: American Council on Education.

Castellanos, J. and Jones, L. (2003). *The majority in the minority: Expanding the representation of Latina/o faculty, administrators, and students in higher education*. Sterling, VA: Stylus Publications.

Chang, M.J. and Kiang, P.N. (2002). New challenges of representing Asian American students in U.S. higher education. In W.A. Smith, P.G. Altbach and K. Lomotey (eds) *The racial crisis in American higher education: Continuing challenges for the twenty-first century* (revised edition). Albany, NY: State University of New York (SUNY) Press, 137–158.

Cheatham, H. and Phelps, C. (1995). Promoting the development of graduate students of color. In A. Pruitt and P. Issac (eds) *Student services for the changing graduate student population*. San Francisco, CA: Jossey-Bass, *72*(4), 91–99.

Chickering, A.W. (2006). Every student can learn—if. . . . *About Campus*, May/June, 9–15.

Gasman, M., Gerstl-Pepin, C., Anderson-Thompkins, S., Rasheed, L. and Hathaway, K. (2004). Negotiating power, developing trust: Transgressing race and status in the academy. *Teachers College Record*, *106*, 689–715.

Gasman, M., Hirschfeld, A. and Vultaggio, J. (2008). "Difficult yet rewarding": The experiences of African American graduate students in education at an Ivy League institution. *Journal of Diversity in Higher Education*, forthcoming.

Harrop, A., Tattersall, A. and Goody, A. (2007). Gender matters in higher education. *Educational Studies*, *33*(4), 385–396.

Holmes-Siedle, J. (1994). Design for disability: Creating universal design. *Architects' Journal*, *199*(6), 35–41.

hooks, b. (1994). *Teaching to transgress: Education as the practice of freedom*. New York: Routledge.

Howard, A. (2001). Students from poverty: Helping them make it through college. *About Campus*, 5–12.

Hu-DeHart, E. (2002). Ethnic studies in U.S. higher education: History, development, and goals. In W. Banks and B. Banks (eds) *Handbook of research on multicultural education*. San Francisco, CA: Jossey-Bass, 869–881.

Jackson, J. (2003). Toward administrative diversity: An analysis of the African-American male educational pipeline. *Journal of Men's Studies*, *12*(1), 43–60.

Kame'enui, E.J. and Carnine, D. (1998). *Effective teaching strategies that accommodate diverse learners*. Upper Saddle River, NJ: Prentice Hall.

Karabel, J. and Astin, A.W. (1975). Social class, academic ability, and college quality. *Social Forces*, *53*, 381–398.

Karen, D. (1991). The politics of class, race, and gender: Access to higher education in the United States, 1960–1986. *American Journal of Education*, *99*, 208–237.

Kitano, M. K. (1997). What a course will look like after multicultural change. In A.I. Morey and M. Kitano (eds) *Multicultural course transformation in higher education: A broader truth*. Boston, MA: Allyn and Bacon, 18–30.

Kuh, G., Kinzie, J., Schuh, J., Whitt, E. and Associates (2005). *Student success in college: Creating conditions that matter*. San Francisco, CA: Jossey-Bass.

Luna, C. (2002). Learning from diverse learners: (Re)writing academic literacies and learning disabilities in college. *Journal of Adolescent and Adult Literacy*, *45*(7), 596–605.

Lynch, E.W. (1997). Instructional strategies. In A.I. Morey and M. Kitano (eds) *Multicultural course transformation in higher education: A broader truth*. Boston, MA: Allyn and Bacon, 56–70.

Maher, F. and Tetrault, M. (1997). Learning in the dark: How assumptions of Whiteness shape classroom knowledge. *Harvard Educational Review*, *67*(2), 1–25.

Margolis and Romero (1998). "The department is very male, very white, very old, and very conservative": The functioning of the hidden curriculum in graduate sociology departments. *Harvard Educational Review*, *68*(1), 1–32.

Mayhew, M.J. and Fernandez, S.D. (2007). Pedagogical practices that contribute to social justice outcomes. *The Review of Higher Education*, *31*(1), 55–80.

McKeachie, W.J. and Svinicki, M. (2006). *McKeachie's teaching tips: Strategies, research, and theory for college and university teachers*. Boston, MA: Houghton Mifflin Company.

Morey, A.I. (2000). Changing higher education curricula for a global and multicultural world. *Higher Education in Europe*, XXV (1), 25–39.

Ohmann, R. (2003). Is class an identity? *Radical Teacher*, *68*, 10–12.

Pascarella, E. and Terenzini, P. (1991). *How college affects students*. San Francisco, CA: Jossey-Bass.

Pratt, D. (1991). Conception of self within China and the United States: Contrasting foundations for adult education. *International Journal of Intercultural Relations, 15,* 285–310.

Pruitt, A.S. and Isaac, P.D. (1985). Discrimination in recruitment, admission, and retention of minority graduate students. *Journal of Negro Education, 54*(4), 526–536.

Renn, K.A. (2000). Including all voices in the classroom: Teaching lesbian, gay, and bisexual students. *College Teaching, 48*(4), 129–135.

Robson, J., Francis, B. and Read, B. (2004). Gender, student confidence and communicative styles at university: The views of lecturers in history and psychology. *Studies in Higher Education 29*(1), 7–23.

Rong, X. (2002). Teaching with differences and for differences: Reflections of a Chinese American teacher educator. In L. Vargas (ed.), *Women faculty of color in the White classroom.* New York: Peter Lang Publishing, 125–143.

Sadker, M. and Sadker, D. (1994). *Failing at fairness: How schools cheat girls.* New York: Simon and Schuster.

Schmitz, B., Butler, J.E., Guy-Sheftall, B. and Rosenfelt, D. (2001). Women's studies and curriculum transformation in the United States. In W. Banks and B. Banks (eds) *Handbook of research on multicultural education.* San Francisco, CA: Jossey Bass.

Scott, S.S., McGuire, J.M. and Foley, T.E. (2003). Universal design for instruction: A framework for anticipating and responding to disability and other diverse learning needs in the college classroom. *Equity and Excellence in Education, 36*(1), 40–49.

Severiens, S. and ten Dam, G.T.M. (1994). Gender differences in learning styles: A narrative review and quantitative meta-analysis. *Higher Education, 27*(4), 487–501.

Sutton, P. and Henry, A. (2005). An exploration of student learning experiences and approaches to learning. *Psychology Teaching Review, 11*(1), 42–52.

Tatum, B. (1997). *Why are all the Black kids sitting together in the cafeteria? And other conversations about race.* New York: Basic Books.

Taylor, E. and Antony, J.S. (2000). Stereotype threat reduction and wise schooling: Towards the successful socialization of African American doctoral students in education. *Journal of Negro Education, 69*(3), 184–198.

Trow, M. (1992). Class, race, and higher education in America. *American Behavior Scientist, 35,* 585–605.

Walpole, M. (2003). Socioeconomic status and college: How SES affects college experiences and outcomes. *The Review of Higher Education, 27*(1), 45–73.

IV
The Student Experience

This section focuses on the student's experience of higher education, and how it fits into their lives. It takes what might be called an opposite perspective to that in the previous section, on course design, which focused on how and what higher education institutions provide for students. And the perspective is broader than that in the second section of the handbook, dealing with teaching and learning, which focused in very tightly on the educational experience.

Seen in this way, the topic of the student experience potentially covers everything from what leads students to enrol on particular courses in particular higher education institutions, to what they subsequently do with their higher education after (hopefully successfully) completing their programmes (e.g. Schomburg and Teichler, 2000). In between these points, we may also consider, for example:

- how they respond at the time to their higher education experience (e.g. Silver and Silver 1997)
- how it relates to their home and working lives (bearing in mind the increasing numbers of students who work their way through college)
- the use made of other aspects of the university (e.g. sporting and social facilities)
- how the student experience varies for different kinds of student (e.g. in terms of gender, class, ethnicity and age: Archer *et al.*, 2003).

The student experience is, therefore, a broad theme, which is necessarily covered selectively in the four chapters included in this section.

In the first of these chapters, Naomi Rosh White focuses on the undergraduate student experience at a time of changing funding arrangements, in her case in Australia. She interviewed 79 full-time undergraduates, taking a psychodynamic perspective. The picture she paints is a somewhat disturbing one, of students feeling marginalised and anonymised in a massified higher education system. She concludes that contemporary universities are suffering from "task corruption", a defensive state involving the loss or distortion of aspects of the institution's previous and accepted way of operating.

Pamela Marcucci and Bruce Johnstone examine more specifically changes in students' tuition fee policies, taking an international comparative perspective. They note the varied legal position in different countries on whether fees can be charged, what level of charge is acceptable, and how this varies between institutional (e.g. public and private) and student (e.g. home or international) types.

Tuition fee policy is clearly related to national conceptions of parental financial responsibility: thus, policies of deferred or no tuition fees assume no parental responsibility. Curiously, tuition fees are only rarely directly related to the actual costs of the tuition provided. The trend is clearly, however, moving away from government support towards family, student or employer funding.

Madeleine Abrandt Dahlgren and her colleagues examine the learning trajectories that students engage in, or are engaged in, in moving between the statuses of senior student and novice worker. Their longitudinal study involved interviewing 36 students who had studied at a Swedish university on two separate occasions: in their final year of study, and after 18 months' work experience. The sample was split between three different programmes—in political science, psychology and mechanical engineering. They conclude that different approaches were taken to managing this transition, with the psychology programme showing the greatest continuity in practice between studying and work, while the other two programmes remained much more explicitly academic in nature.

Finally, Coralie McCormack moves beyond the undergraduate experience to discuss how postgraduate research students cope with their higher education experience, and what might be done by higher education institutions to help them cope better. Having noted that postgraduate research is following undergraduate study in becoming a more common, if not yet massified, experience, she presents accounts (stories) of 23 Australian research students to illustrate "commonly recognised critical moments in candidature". She then considers how this experience might be improved, and how such developments fit in with changing ideas about the nature and purpose of the PhD.

References

Archer, L., Hutchings, M. and Ross, A. (2003). *Higher Education and Social Class: issues of exclusion and inclusion.* London: RoutledgeFalmer.

Schomburg, H. and Teichler, U. (2006). *Higher Education and Graduate Employment in Europe: results from graduate surveys from twelve countries.* Dordrecht: Springer.

Silver, H. and Silver, P. (1997). *Students: changing roles, changing lives.* Buckingham: Open University Press.

11
Tertiary Education in the Noughties
The Student Perspective[1]

Naomi Rosh White

The psychodynamics of learning and teaching at a time of changing funding arrangements and priorities are explored and discussed through students' accounts of their experience of university. The contextual, organizational and socio-political characteristics implicated in these psycho-dynamic processes are considered. Among the psychodynamic issues that emerged from students' accounts were organizational distancing, expressed in the physical and symbolic distance between students and teachers as well as a perceived distance between lecturers and their teaching responsibilities, and transference evident in the students' struggle between dependence and independence.

Australian universities have been undergoing significant changes over the past two decades. Institutions solely responsible for teaching have been merged with universities whose mandate includes both teaching and research. The number of students entering university has increased while government spending on education has been falling in real terms (King, 2001). Universities are now responsible for securing an increased proportion of their funding from a range of sources (Marginson and Considine, 2000, pp. 56–7; King, 2001). Although the greatest percentage of universities' income is still generated through government funding for undergraduate student places, an increasing proportion is now required to be independently raised through matching government funds for externally awarded research grants, postgraduate degree completions and publications. All students are now charged fees. Higher levels of local and international full-paying students, consulting and funded research and casual staff, and decreased administrative support provide the only leverage points for boosting and manipulating university financial resources.

The changed funding arrangements have been accompanied by shifts in organizational culture, understandings of universities' primary tasks, and how education is to be delivered. Throughput, attracting funding and efficiency have become key university performance indicators. The emerging culture of the university is one in which education is a commodity (Delucchi and Smith, 1997; Delucchi and Korgen, 2002; Smith, 2000) and universities are seen as corporate entities or "enterprise" institutions selling educational "products" (Marginson and Considine, 2000). Priorities have been reordered, with the consequence that funded research and postgraduate teaching have pushed undergraduate teaching to the margins. A range of policies and practices suggest this diminution of status. These include institutional incentives rewarding the introduction of mediated, web-based learning (Marginson and Considine, 2000, p. 59), large classes accompanied by overall reductions in staff–student ratios, the use of research funds to "buy" permanent academic staff out of teaching and an increased percentage of casual teaching staff to whom core teaching activities such as tutorials, marking of student work as well as lecturing are delegated. The loadings various professional activities attract and the adoption of research output rather than teaching quality or performance as the primary criterion for academic promotion also suggest the lower organizational status of teaching (McInnis, 1995; King, 2001). Student patterns of engagement in university life are also changing, with increased workforce participation rates and attenuated time spent on campus (McInnis, 2001). Student attrition rates are also high. Recent figures show that 21.2% of commencing undergraduate students dropped out of university in 2002 (Department of Education, Science and Training, 2004, p. 3). Sitting within the context of the broader politics and economics of university governance and associated changes in university culture are the everyday practices of, and relationships between, teachers and students. These practices and relationships are informed by, and given meaning within the context described above. Furthermore, this milieu is one in which the generic underlying contradictions, struggles and tensions inherent in the teaching–learning interaction must be managed at both organisational and individual levels, despite diminishing resources being allocated to this task.

As the previous discussion suggests, students' experience of university is embedded in a complex environment made up of diverse interdependent elements. Student-related characteristics represent one set of elements. These include life-stage issues and changing patterns of engagement in paid work and study. Organizational factors, such as how teaching and learning are structured, and institutional priorities comprise another set. Organizational features are, in turn, framed and formed by broader socio-political priorities. Together these elements create the environment for the production and consumption of tertiary education by teachers and students. Of interest to the present study are the psychodynamics of the relationships between teachers and students as fore-grounded in students' accounts of their experiences of being at university in this new social and cultural context. The psychodynamics are explored and discussed in relation to some of the contextual organizational and socio-political characteristics that may be implicated in these processes.

The following questions guided the study: first, how do undergraduate students experience university teaching and learning? Second, how might the underlying psychodynamics of these institutional experiences be understood? Third, how does the current socio-cultural climate and structure of universities enhance or militate against the effective and productive management of these processes? The data obtained in response to the questions were considered through the framework of psychoanalytic theory.

Conceptual Issues

One of the central and widely shared fantasies is of teacher omnipotence in education. Linked to this is the view that there is a direct link between teaching and learning, and that teaching and student learning are rational outcomes of the teacher's conscious efforts (Britzman, 1998, p. 41). Both students and teachers share this fantasy. If, however, we take a critical stance in relation to this assumption, then our attention can shift to a different set of relevant processes, namely how unconscious processes are differentially contained and expressed through organizational structure, culture and interactions.

The psychoanalytic approach to organizational analysis examines the unconscious processes that give meaning to interactions in organizational settings. One significant entry point to these processes is individuals' articulations of their experience of institutional practices and structure. Another important entry point is the identification of the relevant features of these institutional structures and, where appropriate, the broader cultural context in which both the individuals and the organizations are embedded. This approach enables attention to be given simultaneously to different levels of analysis. That is, the theory provides a framework for considering organizational practices and what people say about them in relation to the underlying tensions and fantasies that arise from these practices and also give them particular meaning.

Adopting this perspective enables us to view universities not simply in relation to how well or poorly they achieve their core tasks, but as structures which through their practices and policies manage teacher and student fantasies and the anxieties, avoided or denied feelings and the perceptions of their members (Jacques, 1955; Hinshelwood, 1987, p. 72). The psychoanalytic perspective also enables us to consider the ways in which students, teachers and the institutions in which they operate can protect themselves from the anxieties generated by their roles and interactions through the adoption of blocking and distorting defences, such as denial or transference, for example. Defensive processes that become entrenched as organizational culture can act as powerful constraints that prevent organizations from achieving their core tasks. Core tasks may be seen as too difficult, resulting in a drift away from them, and a simultaneous move towards seemingly achievable, but less relevant, tasks.

At the personal and interpersonal level, learning and teaching are characterized by ambivalence, uncertainty and anxiety. The anxiety arises out of, among other things, uncertainty, frustration and the potential for shame, as well as the struggles around dependence and independence, authority and control. Central to this anxiety is the process of transference. Tension is inherent in the transference and countertransference in relationships between teachers and their students. For the student transference can occur because as a person in authority the teacher unconsciously reminds them of parental authority. This process simultaneously evokes dependency needs and feelings, resistance to this dependency and the desire to share in the authority figure's imagined omnipotence. As a student, one puts oneself in the hands of the teacher. In so doing, students surrender their authority and autonomy to that of the teacher. The dependence associated with this deferral and surrender can entail the shifting of responsibility for student learning from student to teacher. The process of learning also entails deferral of another kind, namely the deferral of gratification provided in the form of teacher feedback. These engender a dependence that is simultaneously resisted and embraced by both the student and teacher. Its reward for students is an imagined sharing in the teacher's status or omnipotence, sometimes just by virtue of association. Consider how students gain status by having been taught by a Nobel prize-winning scientist or a "celebrity" academic. There is also the potential to share in the teacher's omnipotence (or displace him or her) through the acquisition of knowledge. As Britzman (1998) puts it, "the student desires to be as important and as all knowing as s/he imagines the teacher to be; the student desires the teacher's omnipotent position" (p. 34).

For the teacher, the omnipotence associated with student surrender is a powerful status marker, as well as an attribution and expectation that produce considerable teacher anxiety. The anxiety rests on a sense that one is not quite what students or peers imagine one to be, or what one projects oneself to be. The anxiety is also associated with a diminution of professional status through institutional practices and priorities that are driven by a "customer/service provider" managerial model. Rather than "having authority", teachers become planners or facilitators whose relationship with students is increasingly administrative. Alongside the contradictions inherent in teacher omnipotence is the potential for the teacher's own development to be played out in his or her relations with individual students, the body of knowledge being taught and through relationships with peers. A process of transference may also occur for the teacher, by which the teacher projects his or her childhood conflicts on to the student. One example of how this is manifested is in some teachers' discomfort with immature learners, because immature learners remind teachers of their former selves and their present failings (Bernfeld, 1973). Taken together, the countervailing forces described above provide fertile ground for submerged and/or overt adversarial relationships. These, together with the changing structure of tertiary education, have the potential to contribute to staff and student disaffection and anxiety. As Arthur Jersild (1955) has claimed, the history of education is in part a history of people's efforts to face anxiety.

Method

Seventy-nine full-time Victorian undergraduate students, obtained using a purposive snowball sampling technique, participated in the study. Excluded from the sample were first-year students, mature-age students, postgraduate or honours students and international students. These categories of students were excluded because their status had the potential to raise additional and extraneous status-specific issues.

Although gender has not been found to be a significant variable in perceptions of university experience (Kerridge and Matthews, 1998; Brady and Eisler, 1999), an equal number of male and female interviewees were included in the sample. The degree programmes in which students were enrolled were Arts (40 students, 13 of whom were enrolled in Arts as part of a double degree) and professional degrees (39 students), such as medicine, law, business, journalism, IT, engineering and nursing. The students were enrolled in a range of universities in Victoria. Eighty-three per cent of the students interviewed held paid jobs, with 60% of the total sample working for 11 hours or more per week. A significant percentage of the sample (34%) were paying their HECS fees upfront, with four of these being full-fee students.

The students were interviewed using a semi-structured interview schedule. The interviews lasted between 20 minutes and 1 hour and focused on how students experienced the university learning–teaching environment, their views about the purposes and outcomes of entering university and the role of peers. When completed, the interviews were transcribed in preparation for thematic coding. The analysis of the interviews was conducted with a view to identifying the clusters of responses that illuminated the perceptions and underlying psychodynamic processes pertinent to the experience of being an undergraduate student in the current university environment.

The analysis was conducted principally with reference to the theoretical issues guiding the study. While there were many general statements made by students about their university experience—neutral, positive or negative—not all of these were articulated in ways that permitted analysis with reference to those theoretical issues. Bryman argues that qualitative research follows a theoretical, rather than statistical logic, stating that it "should be couched in terms of the generalizability of cases to *theoretical* propositions rather than to *populations* or universes" (Bryman, cited in Silverman, 2000, p. 105). Furthermore, qualitative methodologists argue that analysis should be conducted in relation to "the wider universe of social explanation in relation to which [one has] constructed [one's] research questions" (Mason, cited in Silverman, 2000, p. 106). In line with this approach, the data analysis for the present study was not conducted with a view to documenting the frequencies of responses. Rather, the intent was to conduct an intensive analysis using cases of interest, choosing them because they illustrated the feature or process constituting the focus of study and its social context (Denzin and Lincoln, 1994; Silverman, 2000).

The Defensive Organization

Undergraduate students feel they don't matter. The responses of the students interviewed suggest that they experience university as a distancing and, in psychodynamic terms, defensive organization. This defensive posture has various manifestations. One is the distance between students and their teachers—a distance that is both physical and symbolic. A second manifestation is the perceived distance between lecturers and their teaching responsibilities.

Maintaining Distance: Teachers and Students

Almost all students interviewed spoke about their placement in large classes. Large classroom or lecture situations were seen to have two negatively valued consequences. The first was that students feel they have no identity in the organization, and secondly, large classrooms act as barriers to meaningful relationships between students and their teachers. Students spoke about lecturers not knowing their names and of their sense of being part of an anonymous mass:

> When you walk into a lecture theatre and there's 500 people of which 100–200 aren't even interested—they're just sitting there as rabble . . . Students are perceived as a flock of sheep through university's eyes. I mean, we are just a bunch of numbers and letters. They treat you like you're in a bank or something. I think I get treated better in a bank, and that's a terrible standard to be compared to (male, Commerce).

Associated with the sense of a mass education was a perception that lecturers want students to take the role of passive attendees rather than that of active participants:

> Lecturers expect a great deal of patience . . . In terms of the actual lecture process, that's really time to shut up and listen to what the lecturer has to say. (male, Arts)

This state of affairs stands in stark contrast with student expectations. The students interviewed spoke about how they wanted their teachers to focus on them as people. They felt more involved if they were known by, or had some sense of a relationship with, their lecturers. This, they believed, contributes to a good university experience and to the motivation to learn: they will "try harder":

> There are some lecturers I've never spoken to. But if you have actually spoken . . . it's them who I actually feel I want to do well for. I don't want to waste their time (female, Arts).

Universities have always adopted the practice of large lecture groups at undergraduate level. However, the current situation is distinctive, in that funding constraints and the prioritisation of research and postgraduate teaching have meant that large-group teaching is no longer routinely supported by small-group tutorials, and where tutorials are offered, they are frequently or solely taught by sessional staff who are rarely contactable outside class hours. In such circumstances, these defensive practices take on particular significance. While some universities are attempting to overcome this problem through the assignment of mentors to first-year students and to students who have been achieving poor grades, the system overall defends teachers from having to confront what one writer has called students' "ordinary fragilities" as learners (Jersild, 1955). Examined from the perspective of the psychodynamics of organizational life, this reliance on large-group teaching without tutorial and small-group teaching can be seen to constitute a practice designed to manage teacher anxiety. That is, large classes can be seen to preserve a structured, organizationally sanctioned distance between teachers and students, protecting teachers from having to deal at a personal level with their students in circumstances that are less than optimal for promoting student learning.

The anonymity, depersonalized relationships and mass grouping described by the students interviewed is similar to that identified by Isabel Menzies (1970), in her classic study of nursing in a London teaching hospital. In this study, Menzies showed how the nursing system was structured and partly functioned to evade the anxiety of caring for patients. Among the defences evident were depersonalization and denial of the significance of the individual by splitting up the nurse–patient relationship, so that no one nurse was particularly responsible for any patient. These defences were deeply ingrained in the system and very difficult to change.

Distance from Task: Teachers and Teaching

Accompanying the sense of student distance from their teachers is students' perception of lecturers' distance from their work. Students' remarks suggest an awareness of organizational priorities and their impact on how lecturers approach their undergraduate teaching responsibilities. These students recount their experiences with lecturers who, they believe, have little interest in teaching, and for whom research is paramount:

> [I want lecturers to] not be there because they're there for their research—and lecturing is just a second part to what they do. Because a lot of them are there for research and some of them don't actually care what they are saying (female, Arts).

Students' perceptions are matched by lecturers' priorities. Research has shown that while most academics have an interest in both teaching and research, twice the proportion who say they are primarily interested in teaching also say they have a much stronger career interest in research, and the clear majority would prefer to spend more time on research if they could (McInnis, 1999, p. 50). Furthermore, there has been a significant decline in the proportion of time given to teaching (McInnis, 1999).

Further evidence of students' tacit understanding that undergraduate teaching has been marginalized is evident in students' belief that lecturers' effectiveness is measured with reference to the size of their classes (i.e. how many students they attract) and students' results, rather than with reference to the quality of their teaching. These priorities are felt by them to affect how lecturers treat them:

> It's more of a mass education than anything else. It's more aimed at results and examination scores. I think they push you through and don't worry about the quality so much (male, Arts).

It is also evident in the resentment they express about people who are not fluent in English (particularly, it seems, in business courses), or who have come from professional backgrounds and have no experience or knowledge of how to teach or to assess student work, but who are placed before them as lecturers:

> Some of our lecturers, all they have done is they've been in industry for all their life and instead of retiring they've decided to lecture for a few years. They've got no real idea academic-wise what's good and what isn't (male, Engineering).

The perceived teacher detachment from task might be a contributor to both students' (Schroeder, 1993) and teachers' need for a high degree of structure and detail with respect to course requirements. This need for structure is maintained and reinforced by widely adopted practices such as the ubiquitous use of reading packages, lecture notes online, extensive reading lists and tightly specified assessment tasks. While teacher guidance and clearly articulated expectations might be regarded by many as intrinsic to good teaching practice, these institutional practices could also be read as an encroachment into student initiative and responsibility. Approaching these practices with a view to understanding their psychodynamics, one could argue that there is an obsessive quality to "over-preparation" by teachers. From this view, the practices can be seen as mechanisms by which attention is deflected from the teacher–student relationship and the process of teaching/learning to what has been committed to paper: if the instructions and reading packages ensure that everything has been covered, then the teacher (or the institution) can't be held responsible for students who for one reason or another fall between the cracks or fail to perform satisfactorily. As argued by Bain *et al.* (1992), while the ostensible reason for producing this material for students is to promote learning, it may in fact have the opposite, unconscious effect, that of preventing the real work taking place (p. 34). The generation of paper, not learning–teaching, becomes the work.

Who "Owns" What Problem? Transference, Dependence and Independence

Teachers determine the subject-matter and teaching mode and, during classes, control who talks and when. Confirmation that learning has occurred is provided by teachers. This is a situation that has the potential to generate considerable student resentment and resistance. It is an arena for the expression of students' struggle with dependence and independence, the simultaneous desire for surrender and need for control. These are struggles of particular significance in early adulthood.

The Matter of Responsibility

One manifestation of students' struggles is an ambivalent stance towards responsibility. The contradictory attributions of responsibility are illustrated by the following student comments:

> It gets kind of frustrating when [the lecturers] are down the front and if they can't hold my attention. I don't understand why they should be so high and mighty and tell me off for keeping myself amused . . . I'm always the one in the class who gets picked on by a lecturer, but it's their own fault if they can't hold my attention and do an interesting lecture (male, Accounting).

> A lecturer for one of my subjects doesn't put anything on the web. I find that very frustrating and almost treating us like kids, that if we can't get to a lecture and if I can't get the notes off anyone, then I'm left information-less. There's no resources I can go to; there's no notes that came with the lecturers' books . . . When I can't get the information for skipping a lecture, I find that very frustrating. I don't think it's rude of me not to go to every single one. [The lecturer] wouldn't know. I think it's an unreasonable expectation. The learning is not in my court anymore; it's him trying to control how I learn (male, Science).

> [Lecturers should] make the students have an idea of what's going to be on the exam. . . . That should be summarised . . . at the end of semester. Because often during the year, the lecturers will say this question is going to be on the exam, and if you don't show up to that lecture, then you're disadvantaged (male, Arts/Science).

Students speak about what they most want from their teachers: "passion." Being passionate about teaching was mentioned by almost every student interviewed as the quality most valued in lecturers. Students are very keenly attuned to this "passion" or involvement in their teachers, and its absence is readily recognized by them:

> [I] want a passionate heart that is willing to teach and willing to share (female, Arts).

> You want your lecturers to be enthusiastic. You don't want them to stand up there and mumble (male, Arts/Law).

Clearly, a charismatic, clear communicator is a more effective teacher than a mumbling, inarticulate one. Academics who convey their discomfort with or disinterest in teaching will not heighten the motivation of their students. Lecturers do have a responsibility to make clear, informative, well-structured presentations and to encourage student participation and involvement. Research has shown that teacher behaviours such as poor presentation skills, lack of enthusiasm and bad choice and organization of material are potential demotivators (Ditcher and Tetley, 1999).

However, the students' desire for evidence of *teacher* commitment and passion is not matched by their *own* commitment to their university studies. Student responses revealed a passivity that raises fundamental questions about how students see themselves as learners:

> I need a bit more motivation . . . Basically, I don't want to study. I'm lazy . . . I want [the lecturers] to excite me and make me want to be passionate about learning that subject . . . If it doesn't grab my attention, I'll just doze off, even though I might not be tired. My attention span is severely lacking in a subject that doesn't grab my attention at all. My overall experience at uni, I'd have to say, probably six out of ten lecturers have actually made me want to keep studying. . . . [The others] lack charisma (male, Arts).

In contrast to their expectations regarding the scope of lecturers' responsibilities, more than half the students interviewed described themselves as "lazy" or not "good students". They reported that the time they allocated to study ranged from 0% to 5% of the week for most of the study period and increased to 80% or 90% when assignments were to be submitted. Of those interviewed, 65% reported spending on average approximately 35% or less of their week on university work. They also reported that they did not complete weekly prescribed reading, did not continually and regularly attend to their university work and that they left completion of assignments or studying for exams until the last minute.

The gap between student expectations of themselves and the expectations they have of their teachers may have several sources. Some of these are structural. For instance, full-time students are showing increased workforce participation rates (McInnis, 2001). University studies are viewed as secondary to the commitment to paid work (Levine and Cureton, 1998, p. 6; McInnis, 2001). The students interviewed for this study conformed to these patterns, reporting that approximately 65% of their week was split between paid work and social activities:

> I think a lot of people are frustrated with pressures with part-time work and things like that. So they find themselves in a position where they can't put enough time into uni and this makes them frustrated with their marks (male, Arts).

Second, life-stage factors are relevant. Undergraduate university studies most often coincide with the transition to adulthood. Social life at university has been identified as very important to students in other research (Levine and Cureton, 1998), as well as to the students interviewed for this study. They come to university to broaden their experience with people from different backgrounds. University offers an interregnum during which to identify personal directions and consolidate a sense of self:

> I didn't really have an idea what I wanted to do, so I thought going into a course, a general sort of course, would give me an opportunity and a bit more time to think about what I wanted to do, bide my time a bit (female Arts/Education).

> You're so young when you get to uni. You've been so sheltered for all your life. You're really building your social skills, independent of your family and independent of everything else. You've go to figure out what sort of person you really are (female, Business).

Third, underlying unconscious processes may be contributing to student deflection of responsibility. In the comments above, the perceived rights of one group (students) have become the duties and responsibilities of another (teachers). The comments are evocative of Shaw's (1995) theory that teaching is often elided with mothering, with the corollary being that "being taught" may be elided with "being mothered". A particular form of caring comes to be assumed encoded into educational practice (Yeatman, 1995). Another feature of the teaching–learning process might also be relevant to these students' understandings of responsibility. Anna Freud has said that education is a form of interference and resistance a consequence of this interference (see Britzman, 1998, p. 11). The self-reported minimal effort put into university studies by a majority of students and the deflection of responsibility could be read as a resistant response to this "interference". It might also mirror students' marginalized institutional status and the alienation they perceive in their teachers. That is, at the unconscious level the absence of student commitment might mirror the organization's, and by default lecturers', perceived indifference to student needs and expectations.

Finally, the deflection of responsibility evident in students' remarks can be interpreted in relation to the changing context of education. Underlying their remarks is a shift in authority such that academics are being held accountable for student learning outcomes and for meeting students' wants in ways that signal the emergence of the student as customer and what has been called the new "contractualism" (Yeatman, 1995).

The Meaning of Grades

The discourse around grades is a rich source of information about the anxieties, contradictions and tensions inherent in university practice and teacher–student relations. Movement between student independence and dependence, passivity and agency finds clear expression here. It is evident in the simultaneously held views that grades and teacher evaluations are at once important and irrelevant, in reference to "rights" with respect to the award of grades and in the deflection of responsibility for student achievement to teachers. Two main issues emerged from students' responses: first, the significance of being evaluated, and second, the conferring of authority to evaluate.

The meaning of teacher evaluations and expectations varied. On the one hand, grades were valued by students: that is, they were taken by students to indicate their level of proficiency and learning. Grades (rather than learning) were seen by almost 80% of the students to be the key indicator of whether they were putting sufficient effort and time into university study. Grades were also understood to inform students of the standard of their work. As one student said:

> You come to uni to get a professional to evaluate you, not for a self assessment (male, Performing Arts).

Students were keen to receive lecturer evaluations and, as has been shown in previous research, expressed a need and desire for frequent feedback (Schroeder, 1993). On the other hand, an almost cavalier attitude to lecturer expectations was evident in many of the students' remarks:

> I do take into consideration what [lecturers] think, but I basically go about my own way of doing things and if they don't like that, well that's their bad luck (female, Arts).

> I don't really think that it's up to the lecturer to validate someone's work. You can take or leave the marks that they give you (male, Performing Arts).

Such views are confirmed by the uncollected piles of marked, end-of-semester essays gathering dust in university offices across the country. Given the relative anonymity of the learning–teaching situation and the absence of meaningful or sustained personal contact between teachers and students discussed earlier, students' views may be associated with the absence of a personal teacher authority to internalize (Craib, 1994, p. 109). That is, students do not "take in" teachers as part of themselves because the structure of the teaching–learning situation militates against it. Menzies-Lyth (1985) elaborates on this idea in her argument that some organizations are structured in such a way to inhibit the provision of models with which students can identify. Put another way, these contradictory attitudes might mirror lecturers' perceived indifference to student expectations.

The second broad theme evident in students' remarks about grades dealt with how grades should be awarded. Many of the students asserted that "effort" should be rewarded and many also stated they were hoping to obtain high grades. Roughly two-thirds of the students interviewed stated that they felt it acceptable to challenge or query a grade when the desired grade was not achieved:

> At the end of the day the lecturers are providing us a service and if we feel hard done by or we think there's a lack of understanding then we have a right as students to express our concerns [about grades] (male, Arts).

The reasons the students gave for these challenges ranged from a genuine sense of having been unfairly assessed, to needing a higher grade for entry into another course, to simply trying it on:

> If I put in a lot of work, if I've done my best, I'd like to see that rewarded with a good score . . . Another factor is that a lot of students just want to get that good mark cause it means maybe the scholarship that they need, the good report their parents might need, if they are overseas students . . . Getting a good mark is important maybe to specialise later, if they want to do a Master's or anything like that, or even when you get a job (female, Dental Science).

These views and aspirations were expressed against a background of reports by the majority of interviewees that they made minimal effort with their university work, except in the last minute.

These contradictory expectations and behaviours have many possible explanations. Grading is an anxiety-arousing process for both teachers and students. It is anxiety-arousing for teachers because ultimately, explicated criteria notwithstanding, conclusively justifying a grading decision can be a difficult if not impossible task. For students, the process can be experienced as ritualized or routinized shaming. When seeking to understand students' remarks in relation to the conceptual issues outlined earlier, several possible explanations emerge. Students' views suggest transference processes, namely the fusing of dependency needs and need for affirmation with resistance to these needs, and the desire to share in the authority figure's (in this case, the teacher's) imagined omnipotence while preserving one's own. That is, the comments overall can be read to reveal the contradictory struggle between the desire for dependence on authority, the desire to *be* that authority while at the same time wishing to be *free* of that same authority.

These underlying struggles occur in the context of educational practices that might be contributing to student attitudes to grades. The increasing distance between students and their teachers means the management of shame and containment of attendant anxiety is more difficult to achieve. Academic standards are understood differently by individual lecturers, a situation made more complicated when marking of student work is conducted by increasing numbers of sessional teachers and tutors. With high teaching loads cross-marking becomes an increasingly unrealistic option. Variations in standards are further exacerbated by occasional exhortations for academic staff to award their more able students, in particular, higher marks so that departments and faculties can successfully attract honours and higher degree students, and so that their students receive a competitive edge in the award of Commonwealth Scholarships.

Finally, there may be lecturer self-interest involved. Research has suggested that grade leniency is the most significant factor in positive evaluation of teaching (Greenwald and Gilmore, 1997; Marsh and Roche, 2000). These pressures may be resulting in grade inflation by some teachers and departments, and concomitantly, unrealistic student expectations with respect to the marks they should be awarded. The role of marks in university selection might also affect student attitudes to grades. The majority of undergraduate students enter university from schools that have pushed them through the sieve of a pressured qualifying examination primarily if not solely directed to the achievement of the highest possible grades. Finally, broader cultural factors might also contribute to attitudes to grades. In individualistic and narcissistic cultures such as our own, people are sensitive to positive self-enhancing information. Control of grades, evaluations of one's own performance in order to maintain a sense of mastery/control, are cultural, as well as personal, issues.

Concluding Remarks

Marginalization of undergraduate university studies can occur at two levels: at the institutional level in teaching and learning practice, and in the everyday lives of students where university studies compete with paid work and the personal exploration and development occurring at this life stage. The findings of the present study suggest that undergraduate students are aware of their institutional marginalization. Many of the teaching practices mentioned by the students interviewed for this study are not new. Large classes have been an enduring feature of some university teaching practices. Academics have always conducted research. Teachers have always held the dual role of contributing to and judging student development. Students have always simultaneously juggled dependence on their teachers and the requirement to demonstrate independence of them.

However, what is new is the context and social climate within which these practices and processes occur, the shifting university culture within which undergraduate teaching is embedded. Students are now described as "customers"; teachers have become service providers (Levine and Cureton, 1998; Coats *et al.*, 2000). Being a "customer" rather than a "learner" is a disengaged position. It is also a position that relies on others to satisfy and to deliver (goods or services). This is consistent with a passivity and dependence that is antithetical to what we understand to be conducive to learning.

The students' comments here suggest what Jane Chapman (1996) has called "task corruption". By task corruption, she means a defensive institutional or individual process that entails either conscious or unconscious avoidance or "destruction" of the institution's primary task (Chapman, 1996, pp. 7–8). One form of corruption is "amputation", where "parts of the task are 'lopped off' or neglected in favour of other parts of the task". This is succinctly illustrated by the comments of one of the students interviewed:

> I personally believe that the way universities are run today is not necessarily in the best interests of students, but rather in securing numbers to generate a wealthy university and to establish research programs and post graduate programs rather than focusing on the majority of students who come to study in undergraduate degrees (male, Law/ Science).

A second form of corruption, "simulation", occurs when "the system or individual adopts the appearance of task engagement, precisely in order to avoid [this] engagement" (Chapman, 1996, p. 8). "Task corruption" is most likely to occur in professions where the quality of service is not easily defined or measured, and where the incentives are stacked to reward "numbers of units supplied" and against maintaining the service at a high standard. The students' comments suggest that the quality of the learning process at universities has been amputated and replaced with measurable output units. They also suggest an awareness of task corruption through simulation, namely the appearance (rather actuality) of task engagement on the part of individual teachers. In this process, the integrity of the task and what it ought to be is subverted and destroyed.

Hinshelwood's articulation of the problems faced by individuals in defensive organisations is relevant here. In such organizations there is a sense of "a gap, an emptiness at the core of things", an absence of anything with which to form an allegiance (Hinshelwood, 1987, p. 129). Organizational and societal characteristics are implicated in psychodynamic processes as they provide the ideological, economic and "emotional" context in which these processes occur, as well as framing the parameters of potential individual and organizational responses. The challenge facing universities today is how to deal with these issues in increasingly straitened circumstances. The alternatives to prevailing practice described below offer one starting-point for discussion about how this challenge might be met:

> Because my course is quite small, I know most of my lecturers on a first name basis . . . [Being] on a more personal level with my lecturers has been a great help . . . Because it's more of a personal relationship with your lecturers, by failing or not trying your hardest you feel you're letting down not only yourself, but the lecturers as well, because they've put in that much effort to helping you. So you feel you need to pay them back by putting in that effort (female, Health Sciences).

> They encourage us to branch out as much as we can and to be as different and creative as we want to be . . . The way the students and teachers interact. Everyone sits around in a circle and you have discussions and bring up subjects and your voice is just as important as the teachers, and everybody has as much credibility as each other. I think you learn a lot from the people around you because everyone is from so many different walks of life and you all come together for the same reason . . . You know your teacher and the teacher knows you, that adds a whole new dimension to it (female, Creative Arts).

Acknowledgements

I gratefully acknowledge the comments made on an earlier draft of this paper made by Chris Lloyd, Ruth Rosh and Peter White. I would also like to thank the anonymous reviewers for their suggestions and comments.

Note

1. Rosh White, N. (2006) Tertiary education in the noughties: the student perspective. *Higher Education Research and Development*, 25(3), 231–246. Reprinted by permission of the publisher.

References

Bain, A., Long, S. and Ross, S. (1992). *Paper houses: The authority vacuum in a government school. Australian Institute of Social Analysis Report*. Ringwood: Collins Dove.
Bernfeld, S. (1973). *Sisyphus, or the limits of education.* Trans. Frederic Lilge. Berkeley, CA: University of California Press.
Brady, K.L. and Eisler, M. (1999). Sex and gender in the college classroom: A quantitative analysis of faculty–student interactions and perceptions. *Journal of Educational Psychology*, 91(1), 127–145.
Britzman, D.P. (1998). *Lost subjects, contested objects: Toward a psychoanalytic inquiry of learning.* New York: State University of New York Press.

Chapman, J. (1996). *Hatred and corruption of task* (Australian Institute of Social Analysis Working Paper No. 3). Carlton: AISA.

Coats, D., Stevenson, K., King, M. and Sander, P. (2000). University students' expectations of teaching. *Studies of Higher Education, 25*(3), 309–323.

Craib, I. (1994). *The importance of disappointment.* London: Routledge.

Delucchi, M. and Smith, W.L. (1997). A postmodern explanation of student consumerism in higher education. *Teaching Sociology, 25*(4), 322–327.

Delucchi, M. and Korgen, K. (2002). "We're the customer—we pay the tuition": Student consumerism among undergraduate sociology majors. *Teaching Sociology, 30*(1), 100–107.

Denzin, N. and Lincoln, Y. (eds) (1994). *Handbook of qualitative research.* Thousand Oaks, CA: Sage.

Department of Education, Science and Training. (2004). *Higher education attrition rates 1994–2002: A brief overview* (Research Note No. 1). Canberra: DEST.

Ditcher, A. and Tetley, J. (1999). Factors influencing university students' academic success: What do students and academics really think?" In Higher Education Research and Development Society of Australasia (ed.), *Cornerstones: What do we value in higher education? Proceedings, July 12–15, Melbourne, Australia.* Canberra: Higher Education Research and Development Society of Australasia.

Greenwald, A.G. and Gilmore, G.M. (1997). "No pain no gain": The importance of measuring course workload in student ratings of instruction. *Journal of Educational Psychology, 89*(4), 743–751.

Hinshelwood, R.D. (1987). *What happens in groups: Psychoanalysis, the individual and the community.* London: FAB.

Jacques, E. (1955). Social systems as a defence against persecutory and depressive anxiety. In M. Klein, P. Heimann and R. Money-Kyrle (eds), *New directions in psycho-analysis.* London: Tavistock.

Jersild, A. (1955). *When teachers face themselves.* New York: Simon and Schuster.

Kerridge, J.R. and Mathews, B.P. (1998). Student ratings of courses in higher education: Further challenges and opportunities. *Assessment and Evaluation in Higher Education, 23*(1), 71–82.

King, S.P. (2001). The funding of higher education in Australia: Overview and alternatives. *Australian Economic Review, 34*(2), 190–194.

Levine, A. and Cureton, J. (1998). Collegiate life: An obituary. *Change, 30*(3), 12–19.

Marsh, H.W. and Roche, L.A. (2000). Effects of grade leniency and low workload on students' evaluations of teaching: Popular myth, bias, validity or innocent bystanders? *Journal of Educational Psychology, 92*(1), 202–228.

Marginson, S. and Considine, M. (2000). *The enterprise university: Power, governance and reinvention in Australia.* Cambridge: Cambridge University Press.

McInnis, C. (1995, November). *Change and diversity in the work patterns of Australian academics. Seminar on Human Resources and Staff Development in Higher Education (OECD Programme on Institutional Management in Higher Education).* Hong Kong: Hong Kong Baptist University.

McInnis, C. (1999). *The work roles of academics in Australian universities: Department of Education, Training and Youth Affairs.* Retrieved October 5, 2004, from http://www.detya.gov.au/archive/ highered/eippubs/eip00_5/fullcopy.pdf.

McInnis, C. (2001). *Signs of disengagement? The changing undergraduate experience in Australian universities.* Retrieved October 5, 2002, from http://www.cshe.unimelb.edu.au/downloads/ InaugLec23_8_01.pdf.

Menzies, I.E.P. (1970). *The functioning of social systems against anxiety: A report on a study of the nursing service of a general hospital.* London: Tavistock Institute of Human Relations.

Menzies-Lyth, I. (1985). The development of the self in children in institutions. *Journal of Child Psychotherapy, 11*(1), 49–64.

Schroeder, C. (1993). New students, new learning styles. *Change, 25*(5), 21–27.

Shaw, J. (1995). *Education, gender and anxiety.* London: Taylor and Francis.

Silverman, D. (2000). *Doing qualitative research: A practical handbook.* Thousand Oaks, CA: Sage.

Smith, W.L. (2000). Teaching in a consumeristically charged environment. *Michigan Sociological Review, 14*(1), 58–72.

Yeatman, A. (1995). Interpreting contemporary contractualism. In J. Boston (ed.) *The state under contract.* Wellington: Bridge William Books.

12

Tuition Fee Policies in a Comparative Perspective
Theoretical and Political Rationales[1]

Pamela N. Marcucci and D. Bruce Johnstone

As governments are increasingly turning to cost-sharing in order to meet the growing demand for, and decreasing government investment in, public higher education, the choice among different tuition fee policies becomes of great importance. Tuition fee policies and the financial assistance policies that accompany them are critical both for the very considerable revenue at stake and for the potential impact on higher education accessibility and the implications for equity and social justice. This chapter looks at tuition fees in an international comparative perspective in the context of this rich mixture of finance, ideology and politics.

Introduction

The charging of tuition fees by higher education institutions is a critical component in any cost-sharing strategy and one that has become increasingly salient as more and more countries turn to cost-sharing in an effort to meet growing demand for, and offset decreasing government investment in, higher education. The immediate issue addressed in a country's tuition fee policy is the division of the burden of higher education's instructional costs between the student and his/her family and the government, or taxpayer, as well as the accompanying financial assistance policies/programmes that are adopted to ensure that the implementation of tuition fees does not reduce access to higher education for students from lower socio-economic backgrounds. Thus, the policies by which tuition fees are established (or opposed or rejected) are critical both for the very considerable revenue at stake, as well as for the potential impact on higher education accessibility and the implications to equity and social justice. This chapter will look at tuition fees in an international comparative perspective in the context of this rich mixture of finance, ideology and politics. In the US, "tuition" is a fee charged for instruction. In the UK and in English language usage in most of the rest of the world, the word "tuition" means instruction, and a fee charged must therefore be called a tuition fee. We will follow the UK practice and refer to the tuition fee.

The distinction between such a tuition fee and other kinds of fees is imprecise and is sometimes even deliberately intended to hide what could just as well be termed a tuition or a tuition fee because of either legal obstacles or political opposition to the very idea of such a fee. However, a tuition fee generally refers to a mandatory charge levied upon all students (and/or their parents) covering some portion of the general underlying costs of instruction. A fee, on the other hand, generally refers to a charge levied to recover all or most of the expenses associated with a particular institutionally provided good or service that is frequently (although not always) partaken of by some but not all students and that might, in other circumstances, be privately provided. Thus, charges to cover some or all of the costs of food and lodging, or of health and transportation services, would normally fall under the category of fees, as might the charges to cover some special expenses associated with instruction such as consumable supplies in an art class or transportation associated with a special internship experience.

Less precisely distinct from a tuition fee because they are usually levied on all students but are nonetheless based on the actual expense of the particular institutionally provided good or service, and which therefore might be referred to as fees as opposed to tuition or tuition fees, could be charges levied to cover the cost of processing admission applications or of providing student Internet access or recreational programmes. Finally, charges levied on all students that are associated with non-instructional programmes or services and that the students themselves have a major hand in allocating among competing programmes and services (usually through an elected student government) are generally referred to as fees.

Further to the definition of a tuition fee, this chapter will not make a major distinction between a tuition fee that is charged *up front* (that is, payable at the time of matriculation and thus most frequently paid for by parents, in so far as they are financially able) and a tuition fee that is *deferred* (regardless of whether this deferred obligation, or *loan*, is to be repaid on a predetermined fixed schedule or on a schedule that is based on the graduate's later earnings or income). The distinction is not unimportant. But it is not that one or the other form of obligation is or is not a tuition fee—as both forms are mandatory payments to cover part of the expenses of instruction, and thus both are indeed tuition fees. Rather, the important distinction is which party—the parent or the student—is obliged to pay, a distinction to which we will return below (see Johnstone, 2004).

Historically, the development of many higher education systems (particularly in Western Europe, Central and Eastern Europe, Russia and the nations of the former Soviet Union and Francophone Africa) were developed based on an ideology of free tertiary education for qualified students. The argument for free higher education is based on several rationales:

- The returns to society from an educated population are very high.
- Education is (or should be) a fundamental right.
- Tuition fees may discourage the participation of students from low-income families, rural areas or ethnic minorities with negative impacts in terms of social equality and social benefits.
- The costs of student maintenance are high and already beyond the reach of many families, especially when coupled with the costs of forgone student earnings.

Moreover, the immediate beneficiaries of free public higher education have tended to be the politically powerful middle and upper classes that use these rationales to support their own interest in keeping higher education free.

In recent years, however, there has been a dramatic shift in the burden of higher education costs with students and their parents being asked to shoulder a larger share. The rationales for this shift include:

- Private returns to higher education (higher lifetime earnings, enhanced status, etc.) are substantial (and probably extend as well to parents of students).
- Free higher education is still enjoyed disproportionately by the children of middle and

upper classes, while the costs tend, in most countries, to be paid for by taxes that are at best proportional and frequently regressive. Thus, most economists view totally free higher education—especially to the extent that most parents would willingly pay a fee if one were levied, and even more so if there are means-tested grants for those unable to pay—to be effectively a redistribution of income from the poor to the wealthy.

- Students and families who pay tuition fees will demand accountability and, therefore, universities will have to be more consumer-orientated and efficient.
- The costs of higher education, with per-student costs rising at rates in excess of inflation, and magnified by increasing enrolments, are calling for extremely high annual increases in revenue. However, the increased difficulty of taxation, especially in low-income and transitional countries, plus increasing competition from other compelling public needs, such as healthcare and primary education, make increased tax revenues to higher education doubtful at best.

Whatever the arguments, the simple fact is that growing enrolments and decreasing government investment have translated into growing numbers of state policies that encourage, or at least allow, the charging of tuition fees.

Setting of Tuition Fee Policies

The tuition policy of a country is generally dependent on a law or other type of legal instrument that provides the basis for charging or for prohibiting tuition fees. The USA, Canada, Japan, India, South Korea, the Philippines and some of the Anglophone nations in Africa have national and/or state policies requiring moderate tuition fees in most or all public higher educational institutions (Johnstone, 1992). In China the 1998 Higher Education Law calls for the charging of tuition fees to all students.

Other countries have laws that prohibit the charging of tuition fees. In Central and Eastern Europe, Russia and the other countries of the former Soviet Union, free higher education is frequently guaranteed by their constitutions or framework laws. In Nigeria the government announced in May 2002 that the 24 federal universities were forbidden to charge tuition or other academic fees. In Ireland government efforts to reinstate tuition fees, abolished in 1996, met with failure in the summer of 2003.

In Germany, until recently, the federal framework law (HRG: Hochschulrahmengesetz) imposed restrictions on the authority of individual *Länder* (state) to charge tuition fees, and the Social Democratic government banned tuition fees for the first degree outright (Ziegele, 2003, 2005). Certain exceptions were made, and several states (Baden-Württemberg, Bavaria, Saxony, Berlin, Lower Saxony and Brandenburg) implemented the special forms of fees that were allowed, such as tuition fees for students who exceeded the normal duration of a certain programme, plus four semesters and tuition fees for students enrolled in a second degree. In January of 2005, after several years of emotional debate, the country's supreme court overturned the ban in a case brought by six *Länder* and ruled that individual *Länder* could introduce tuition fees. As of 2005, several *Länder* plan to pass enabling legislation and impose fees of about €500 per semester in the next couple of years, while others have no intention of changing their tuition policies.

The legal status of tuition fees is less clear in other countries. In Mexico, where public universities have charged, albeit inconsistently, very low tuition fees for the past 30 years, the constitution is ambiguous as to whether higher education is the sole responsibility of the state. The very public student protests in the late 1990s that accompanied the first (and fairly modest) increase in tuition fees at the Universidad Nacional Autónoma de México since 1948 illustrated the volatility and uncertainty surrounding this issue (Table 12.1).

The authority to set tuition fees at public higher education institutions is vested in different entities in different countries. In many countries, including Canada, India and the USA, tuition levels are set at the state or provincial level. In the US, the entity, or entities, responsible for setting tuition differs from state to state and may include the governor, legislature, state higher education coordinating or governing board, or the individual institution. It is often difficult to determine the exact mix of legal authority and political influence in the setting of tuition fees in US public institutions or higher educational systems. For example, if an institution (or the system), given the authority to set tuition fees, does so against the clear wishes of the governor and the legislature, the government may in turn effectively "retaliate" and undo the revenue effect of the tuition fee simply by reducing the state taxpayer allocation. In a similar "mix" of fee-setting authorities, the governing Board may have the sole authority to *establish* the tuition fee but only the state government may have the power to *appropriate the revenue raised therefrom.*

In other countries, including Hong Kong and the UK (until recently), the central government is responsible for setting tuition fee levels. And in others, such as Chile and South Korea, the individual institutions are authorized to set their own tuition fees. The new Higher Education Act in the UK, passed in 2004 amid great controversy, allows universities to charge "top-up" fees over and above the standard governmental fee up to a maximum of £3,000 (US $4,846). While much of the opposition from the political left was over the spectre of only a handful of the elite universities availing themselves of this authority—and thus of the "rich getting richer"—preliminary observations in 2005 are that most universities will charge the maximum allowable tuition fee. Similarly, in 2005, legislation was passed in Australia that gives universities the power to increase their tuitions by up to 25% above current levels.

In several countries tuition fee setting authority is split between the central and state governments or between the state and institutions. In The Netherlands, for example, the government sets tuition fees for those students eligible for student support and the institutions set tuition fees for the students who are not eligible (i.e. part-time students, students who have used up all of their entitlement for student support and students whose personal income exceeds the income limits for student support). Reforms to the higher education system have been proposed to Parliament, however, that, if accepted, would lead to a much more differentiated and market-based system and institutions would have considerably more latitude to set tuition levels (Jongbloed, 2005).

In Japan, a major reform in 2004 authorized the national universities to incorporate as public corporations and to set their own tuition fees. However, universities may not exceed 110% of the standard fee set by the Ministry of Education and the Ministry of Finance. The local authorities continue to determine the tuition fee levels at local public institutions.

In Nigeria, the federal government has forbidden the charging of tuition fees at the federal universities (though, as of July 2006, it is poised on the brink of changing this policy), but the 11 universities that are owned and financed by the states are allowed to set their own tuition fees. It is particularly interesting that in a country such as Nigeria, where explosive student protests against tuition fees have probably played a considerable role in the federal policy, there is not much opposition to the charging of tuition fees at the state level. It has been hypothesized that at the state level the community feels more involved in, and responsible for, their universities (Ishengoma, 2002).

Types of Tuition Fee Policies

The types of tuition fee policy adopted by a country are strongly related to its conception of parental financial responsibility for their children's higher education. *Up-front tuition policies* are

Table 12.1 Tuition Fees in Various Countries for First Degree, Recent Academic Year (National currencies converted to US dollar by Purchasing Power Parities)

Country	Low	Public Medium	High	Special fee-paying track
Australia (2005; 2004 PPP)	$3,500	$5,000	$5,850	$9,500
Austria (2002/03; 2003 PPP)	$800	$800	$800	NA
Canada (2003/04; 2004 PPP)	$1,460	$3,170	$4,375	NA
China (2004/05; 2003 PPP)	$1,640	$2,960	$3,820	NA
Ethiopia (2003/04; 2003 PPP)	$1,559[1]	$1,559	$1,559	NA
Hong Kong (2002/03; 2002 PPP)	$6,060	$6,060	$6,060	NA
Hungary (2000/01)	$0	$0	$0	$2,400
India (2001/02; 2001 PPP)	$20[2]	$85[3]	$37[4]	NA
Japan (2005; 2004 PPP)	$4,060	$4,060	$4,500	NA
Korea (2000/01; 2000 PPP)	$195	$1,404	$2,927	NA
Mexico (1999/2000; 1999 PPP)	$178	$535	$1,159	NA
Mongolia (2002/03; 2002 PPP)	$1,125	$1,125	$1,688	NA
Netherlands (2002/03; 2004 PPP)	$1,520	$1,520	$1,520	Set by institutions
Russia (1999/2000; 1999 PPP)	$0	$0	$0	$500
Scotland (2004/05; 2004 PPP)	$3,485	$3,485	$3,485	NA
Singapore (2005/06; 2003 PPP)	$1,340	$3,875	$4,800	NA
South Africa (2004; 2003 PPP)	$4,500	$7,000	$9,300	NA
UK (2005/06; 2004 PPP)	$0[5]	$1,000	$1,900	NA
United States (2004/05)	$4,350	$9,000	$12,400	NA
Vietnam (2002/03; 2002 PPP)	$0	$0	$0	$410–683

Notes: [1]Deferred payment: this amount includes payment for room and board, health services as well as tuition. [2]Central University. [3]State University. [4]University or Government College. [5]When residual family income is below £22,000 no tuition fees are charged. When income is between £22,010 and £32,742 some tuition fees are charged and when income is above £32,745, full tuition fees are charged.

based on the assumption that parents have a responsibility to cover some portion of their children's higher education costs and that they should pay according to their ability. In this case, the proportion of tuition fee to be paid or the amount of financial assistance available depends on a family's income. This is the case, for example, in Austria, Chile, the Netherlands, South Africa, the USA and the UK (through 2005).

Box 1 Austria: Introduction of Tuition Fees

After close to 30 years of free tuition, in the fall of 2000, the Austrian right-of-centre government announced the introduction of a €363 tuition fee per semester for students in universities and Fachhochschulen effective as of October 2001. While the introduction of tuition fees may have been useful in reducing the number of what are called "card index corpses" or those students who enrol just to avail themselves of student perks, but do not actually pursue their degree with any commitment, it appears not to have had as negative an impact as feared on enrolments (which dipped significantly in 2001/02, but grew in 2002/03, though not to previous levels). Many argue that it has had no real impact on the quality of education, since the government has simply reduced its contribution by what the universities are able to get from their students (Sully, 2000; Leidig, 2001; Potterton, 2001).

In those countries with *no tuition fees* (the Scandinavian countries) or with *deferred tuition policies* (the Higher Education Contribution Scheme in Australia, the Graduate Endowment Scheme in

Scotland and the Students' Allowance Scheme in New Zealand), there is the assumption that parents are not financially responsible for their children's higher education and that the children themselves cannot be expected to cover its cost while they are studying.

In Scandinavia, the state pays for all instructional costs for qualified students using the considerable resources collected from its taxpayers, while the students, as "financially independent adults", assume the burden of living costs through subsidized student loans. In Australia, parents can choose to pay the "up-front" tuition fees—with an incentive to do so—or they may also leave this burden on the children to be repaid with an income-contingent loan. In Scotland, the tuition fee is automatically deferred and repaid as a loan, but the parents may choose to cover some or all of the costs of student living.

Box 2 Australia and Scotland: Deferred Tuition Fee Policies

Since 1989, most Australian students contribute to the cost of their higher education through the Higher Education Contribution Scheme (HECS). Under the HECS programme, Commonwealth-funded students (i.e. those students who only make a contribution towards the cost of their education, while the Australian government contributes the majority of the cost) and their families have the option of paying their tuition fees up front (with a 25% discount, reduced to 20% for students starting their study in 2005) or accepting the terms of the income-contingent loan. In 1997, HECS was increased and differentiated into three cost bands based on a combination of the relative cost of course delivery and the relative profitability of certain programmes. The government directly pays the university the tuition fee for each HECS deferred student and assumes responsibility for collecting the loans once students have reached a certain income level after graduation.

Recent legislation has introduced a subsidized income-contingent loan programme (FEE-HELP) also for full fee-paying students (i.e. those students who pay tuition fees that are not subsidized by the Australian government) in public or eligible private institutions, whereby they will be able to defer payment of their tuition fees until their salary has reached the average Australian earning income.

The Graduate Endowment Scheme (GES) in Scotland was created in 2001 by legislation of the Scottish Parliament, wherein Scottish and EU students are liable to pay a fixed amount (£2,154 per year of study) at the end of their degree in recognition of the higher education benefits received. The contribution can be paid as a lump sum or income contingently once income has reached £10,000. A recent agreement in the Scottish Parliament enables the ministers (with the approval of Parliament) to set top-up fees for English students studying at Scottish universities.

In recent years, deferred tuition policies have come into vogue as a way to reconcile requiring students to contribute to their higher educational costs with their inability to do so while still studying. Income-contingent loans are one way of deferring the tuition fee to the future. Such loans carry "a contractual obligation to repay some percentage of future earnings . . . until the loan is repaid at a contractual rate of interest, or until the borrower has repaid either a maximum amount or for a minimum number of years" (Johnstone, 2005). Graduate taxes are a variant on the income-contingent loan "whereby the student (sometimes only the graduated student), in return for government subsidization of higher education in the form of low or no tuition fees, becomes obligated to an income surtax, generally for the rest of his or her earning lifetime" (Johnstone,

2005). While no country has introduced a formal graduate tax, the Scottish Graduate Endowment Scheme described above and the Ethiopian Graduate Tax described below have many common elements (Boxes 2 and 3).

Box 3 The United Kingdom: From Up-front to Deferred Tuition Fees

In the UK, a government White Paper was presented to Parliament in January 2003 that signalled a significant shift in tuition fee policy from an up-front tuition fee to a deferred income-contingent graduate contribution system. From 1998 to the present, means-tested contributions to up-front tuition fees ranged from zero contributions for families with income below £17,370 (US$28,061 using 2004 PPP rate of US$15.619) to £1,025 (US $1,655) for families with income above £28,000 (US $45,234). There was a system of income-contingent loans in place that allowed students to borrow to pay their up-front tuition fees. In 2004 legislation was passed that will abolish up-front tuition fees and introduce an income-contingent repayment obligation that students who start their study in 2006 will pay after graduation through the tax system. Institutions have been granted the right to set these student contributions between £0 and £3,000 (US $4,846).

A recent cross-party deal in the Welsh Assembly has concluded a long debate about tuition fees in Wales. As part of the agreement, Welsh students at Welsh universities will be exempt from top-up fees through the 2006/07 academic year and will pay the current flat rate means-tested deferred tuition fee of £1,200 (US $1,938). Welsh students studying in England, however, will have to pay the top-up fees. Starting with the 2007/08 academic year, higher education institutions in Wales can charge an annual deferred flexible fee of up to £3,000, but the increase will be offset for Welsh students by a non-means-tested fee grant of up to £1,800. English and Scottish students will have to pay the entire amount.

Box 4 Ethiopia: Introduction of a Graduate Tax

Until 2003, higher education in Ethiopia was free for the limited number of students who qualified for it based on their school-leaving certificate examinations.

In June of that year, the Higher Education Proclamation introduced a major policy shift indicating that cost-sharing would be a key component in financing Ethiopian higher education development. In September the Higher Education Cost-Sharing Council of Ministers Regulation introduced a graduate tax designed to recoup the government's full costs for student meals, accommodation and health services, plus 15% of estimated tuition costs. Payments will take place at a flat rate of 10% regardless of income category until the students' agreed-upon share is fully recovered (Saint, 2003). Students and their families who pay their contribution up front as a lump sum will receive a 5% discount, and those who pay as a lump sum in the first year after graduation will receive a 3% discount (Saint, 2003). Evening students will continue to pay their fees.

In many countries with either legal restrictions against, or strong popular resistance to, tuition fees, *dual-track tuition policies* are being implemented. In these countries a certain number of free (or very low-cost) university places are awarded by the government based on some criteria (usually scoring above a certain cut-off point on the secondary school-leaving examination) and other places are available to qualified, but lower-scoring, students on a tuition fee paying basis or special continuing education or professional courses are set up by universities for which they charge tuition fees.

Governments all over the world are implementing dual-track fee policies. In Australia, since 1998 universities have been able to offer fee-paying places to Australian undergraduates as long as they have met their enrolment target for Commonwealth-funded students. In 2003 legislation was passed that, starting in 2005, increased the proportion of full fee-paying students allowed to enrol in an institution from 25% to 35% of the total enrolments in each programme of study. In Hungary tuition fees have not been charged since 1998, except for those students whose scores are below average on the entrance exams. In Russia, where free higher education is guaranteed by the constitution, the 1996 Law on Education introduced the concept of higher education cost-sharing, and more than 25% of all university income is said to come from tuition fees paid by students who have passed the entrance exam, but have not scored high enough to qualify for state support (Bain, 2001). In the 2001/02 academic year over 50% of university students paid full tuition fees. In Russia the government has also started to experiment extensively with a new system of financing based on government individual financial obligations (GIFOs). GIFO is a voucher system that provides students with five levels of tuition fee subsidy (0% to 100%) based on their scores on a national entrance examination. In Uganda, where, as in much of sub-Saharan Africa, higher education is supposedly "free", 80% of Makerere University's 22,000 students pay an average yearly tuition fee of $700 (Wachira and Bollag, 2002).

One further variant on the dual-track tuition policy model is the practice of charging international students tuition fees that are even higher than those charged to domestic full-fee paying students. In Australia, for example, part of the higher tuition paid by international students (A$10,000 to 13,500 per year compared to A$8,000 for domestic students) is used for capital costs and for English language and student skills support. Some European Union countries have different tuition policies for international students from other EU countries and for international students from non-EU countries. Box 3 (describing the treatment of English and Scottish students in Wales) illustrates the complexity of the issue (Table 12.2).

Table 12.2

Up-front		No tuition	Dual track tuition fee	Deferred tuition fee
Austria	The Netherlands	Brazil	Australia	Australia
Belgium	Nigeria (State)	Denmark	Egypt	Scotland
Canada	Philippines	Finland	Ethiopia	New Zealand
Chile	Portugal	France[1]	Hungary	Ethiopia
China	Singapore	Francophone Africa	Kenya	England (as of 2006)
Hong Kong	South Africa	Germany[2]	Poland	Wales (as of 2007)
India	Spain	Greece	Romania	
Italy	Turkey	Ireland[3]	Russia	
Japan	England (now)	Luxembourg	Tanzania	
Kenya	United States	Malta	Uganda	
Korea	Wales (now)	Nigeria (Federal)	Vietnam	
Mexico		Norway		
Mongolia		Sweden		

Notes: [1]The 1958 French Constitution defines access to education as free; however, registration fees of approximately €230/year (US $256 using 2004 PPP conversion) are charged to cover administrative costs and health costs. [2]Recent legislative changes allow individual states to introduce tuition fees. [3]While Ireland's universities do not charge tuition fees, they do charge students a yearly student service fee of €750 (US $742 using 2004 PPP conversion) (2005).

Box 5 Kenya: Module II Academic Programmes

Higher education was historically free in Kenya. Eligible students paid no tuition fees and were given living allowances in exchange for their working in the public sector for three years following graduation. This changed in 1991, when tuition fees were introduced for all government-supported students and most government support for living expenses was eliminated in the face of financial austerity and growing enrolments.

Continued declines in government support for higher education has forced universities to continue to look for ways to generate additional income. Among other initiatives, in 1998, the University of Nairobi introduced the highly successful Module II programmes, academic programmes for privately sponsored students in which they pay full tuition fees. These programmes are run in parallel to the Module I Programmes (traditional student-supported programmes whereby students pay only 20% of tuition fees). By the 2002/03 academic year, of the close to 22,000 undergraduate students enrolled at the University of Nairobi, about half were in the Module II programmes, and since their creation, these programmes had raised over 3 billion Kenyan Shillings (US$130,000,000 using 2002 PPP estimate) (Kiamba, 2003).

How Are Tuition Fees Set?

A critical policy question, of course, is the proper level of tuition. This question is most usefully answered by positing an appropriate percentage of the underlying instructional costs that would be covered by a tuition fee. This, however, is not a simple matter. For example, costs vary substantially across institutions and sectors, and especially across programmes in accord with prevailing faculty–student ratios, equipment needs and other programme-specific costs, as, for example, among programmes in science, history or undergraduate teacher education. Furthermore, the calculation of instructional costs also depends on assumptions or accounting conventions: for example, how so-called indirect costs or institution-wide expenditures are apportioned among first-degree or graduate instruction, or how pension costs or the costs of health insurance or the costs of capital (i.e., debt service and depreciation) are handled.

The appropriate tuition fee may be thought to depend on the cost of the programmes. This is the case in Canada, China, South Africa and Vietnam, where programmes with higher costs charge higher tuition fees. In other cases, the appropriate tuition fee may be thought to depend on the private benefits believed to be attached to certain institutions or certain degree programmes. Regardless of the underlying instructional cost differences, it is commonly thought appropriate (or perhaps merely expedient, or just more feasible) to recover a higher percentage of these costs from those programmes and degrees believed to bring the greatest private return to the student (or parents), either in future earning capacity or in prestige and job security, or anything else valued in a profession or vocation. Thus in the world of private higher education, and in public higher education where tuition is permitted, tuition and associated fees for medical and other advanced health professional programmes are generally high, reflecting not only the greater instructional costs of such education, but the high market value of the degree (in turn reflecting the high income and high status associated with these professions). In Mexico, the USA and Vietnam, higher-prestige institutions or institutions belonging to more competitive categories (universities versus community colleges) charge higher tuition fees.

The establishment of a "proper tuition" is made even more complicated by the interaction and the inter-country variations between instructional costs and the presumed mix of public and private benefits. For example, it is conventionally thought that research, or "classical", universities are more costly per student than shorter-cycle, more vocationally orientated and less research-intensive institutions: thus, a common percentage of costs to be covered by a tuition fee would yield a higher tuition in the classical, research university. However, although the presumably higher unit costs of the classical university may be true for medicine, it is probably not true for certain other professional programmes, such as law or business, which are highly sought after and which bring considerable private benefits, but which can be rather inexpensively delivered, particularly at the first-degree level.

Further complicating the establishment of a proper tuition fee is the fact that a realistically expected family contribution cannot be derived simply from some *ex ante* rule of what parents at various income levels ought to pay, but of what parents seem in fact willing to pay at a particular time in a particular culture. Thus, the Swedish parent has become accustomed to paying very heavy taxes, but then to enjoying the benefit of "free" university education for their children; the imposition of tuition charges in Sweden could well be resisted, even by parents who by most measures could well afford the tuition. In contrast, Chinese parents, who probably have only one child to begin with, and who have probably always placed a very high value on education (or else the child would probably not be in a position even to contemplate higher education), are apparently willing to make considerable personal financial sacrifices for their child to go to a university (Box 6).

Parents may be thought to be more willing to pay in countries with substantial private education, where people are more used to paying for the higher (and sometimes the secondary) education of their children. This seems to be the case in the USA, where tuition at private colleges and universities may be well in excess of $20,000 a year, and total expenses in excess of $35,000—making even a moderately high public university tuition of $6,000–$8,000 seem quite modest and politically acceptable. (The same association of politically acceptable public sector tuition with an extensive private university sector, however, does not seem to hold in countries such as Japan, Brazil, India, Korea, and the Philippines that have extensive private sectors but which still feature low or no cost public classical universities.)

Finally, the very availability of need-based grants and loans as well as possibilities for part-time employment affect the level of tuition fees that can be charged in the public sector. In theory, a "need-based" grant, increasingly in conjunction with a student loan, substitutes for the missing parental contribution from the low-income family. However, grants and loans in most countries are generally rationed, usually by criteria of academic merit or preparedness having nothing to do with the ability of the family to provide financial support. Because academic merit or preparedness, at least as conventionally measured, is strongly correlated with socio-economic status, the more "merit" figures into the awarding of grants and subsidized loans—much of which (to the upper-middle class) is likely to have little or no impact on the student's enrolment decision—the less is apt to be available for low-income students, and the more the imposition of tuition is thus likely to be a barrier to higher educational participation.

Another type of tuition policy is one in which tuition fees are charged as a way of penalizing those students who have studied longer than the normal programme duration. In Hungary, tuition fees were abolished in 1998, except for those mentioned above who do not score high enough on the entrance exam and for those who take longer than the allotted five years to complete their degree. In the Czech Republic, the 1998 Higher Education Act allowed institutions to charge fees as a penalty for students who study beyond the standard length of the programme. In Germany, for example, the state of Baden-Württemberg charges a tuition fee of $500 per semester to students who have exceeded the normal programme duration.

Box 6 China: From Free Higher Education to Dual-track to Up-front Tuition Fees

China's tuition fee policy passed through several quite distinct stages. From 1949 through the mid-1980s, higher education was completely funded by the government, which was, in turn, responsible for making the enrolment and personnel plans. College graduates were assigned jobs by the government and there was little room for personal preference in terms of type or location. The monetary returns for a university education were extremely low. In 1985 a dual-track tuition fee policy was announced in the policy document, *Decision on Reform of the Educational Structure*. The document stated that higher education institutions could charge tuition fees to a small number of students who had scored below the cut-off point for public-supported students. In 1993, the Chinese government announced the introduction of a one-track enrolment policy wherein all students would be charged tuition fees. By 1997, all regular higher education institutions charged tuition. This policy was reiterated in the 1998 Higher Education Law of the People's Republic of China. At present, approximately 27% of the total recurrent higher education expenditure is covered by student's tuitions (Li, 2005).

Tuition Fees and Implications for Access and Enrolment Behaviour

It was mentioned in an earlier section of this chapter that arguments against free higher education often cite its regressivity, in that it benefits the middle and upper-middle socio-economic classes to which the great majority of students belong at the expense of the low-income taxpayers, whose children are not well represented in higher education, as a reason to charge tuition fees and implement means-tested grant and loan programmes. The counterargument to this rationale is that charging tuition fees or increasing tuition fees will have a negative impact on enrolment rates.

Research in this area in Australia, Canada, China, the Netherlands, New Zealand, the USA and the UK (Li and Min, n.d.; Leslie and Brinkman, 1998; Andrews, 1999; Heller, 1999, cited in Vossensteyn, 2000; Junor and Usher, 2002, 2004; Chapman and Ryan, 2003; La Rocque, 2003a, 2003b; Vossensteyn, 2005) suggests that at the macro level, demand for higher education is relatively inelastic in the face of price increases, but that in some countries (or at certain tuition fee levels) there may be a corresponding change in the proportion of students enrolled from different socio-economic groups. Interestingly, this appears to be the case in the US and the UK where net price changes appear to have a greater effect on students from lower socio-economic classes, but not in Australia and New Zealand where the introduction of tuition fees (albeit deferred) did not influence the composition of the student body (Chapman and Ryan, 2003; LaRocque, 2003a, 2003b).

Looking at the impact of a decrease in or elimination of tuition fees on student enrolment, a recent report by the Irish Department of Education and Science indicates that the introduction of the free fees initiative in 1995 had "little or no impact to date on promoting equity and broadening access to higher education for the lowest socio-economic groups" (Department for Education and Skills, 2003). While all socio-economic groups experienced actual increases in participation between 1991 and 2001, within the university sector, "the lower socio-economic groups represented an even smaller proportion of entrants in 2001 than they did in 1995" (Department for Education and Skills, 2003).

Macro-level enrolment data may also mask the changes in enrolment *behaviour* that result from the implementation of, or increases in, tuition fees. These changes could be students switching from full- to part-time programmes, taking time off for a period of time to earn money, working longer hours in off-campus employment and/or changing from more to less expensive institutions or majors, or to institutions closer to home. There is also evidence in the United States that, in the face of rising tuition fees, more students may be participating in the College Board's College-level Examination Programmes that culminate in a test that, when passed with a certain score, allow students to receive college credit from many public and private colleges and universities (Hebel, 2003).

In general, however, little is known empirically worldwide about the impact of cost-sharing (and tuition fees) on higher education accessibility and enrolment behaviour, or about the ameliorative efficiency of programmes such as means-tested grants and loans, and additional research is needed in order to inform higher education policy-making.

In an effort to shed more empirical light on the issue of causal links between affordability and accessibility, Usher and Cervenan (2005) conducted research in 16 countries and found that the links are far from simple. For example, some countries with substantial tuition fees, like the USA, Canada and the UK, do fairly well on accessibility measurements (participation rates, attainment rates and an educational equity index developed by Usher to capture the degree to which the student population reflects the socio-economic make-up of the general population and gender parities), while others with free higher education systems, like Austria and Germany, do not score particularly well on any of the accessibility measures.

Future Trends

Whatever one's personal perspective or ideological stance, it is clear that there is a worldwide trend for decreased government support for higher education and increased costs for students and families in the form of some type of tuition fee. Even countries like Germany, with a firm tradition of free higher education and a powerful student movement, are in the process of planning a move to across-the-board tuition fees for all students. It is also clear that given the financial austerity facing governments and the compelling competing public needs in terms of healthcare, primary education, housing and the environment, any expansion in higher education enrolment will have to come at the cost of increased investment by parents and students. The challenge, therefore, is to design efficient and effective student aid programmes that can offset any discouraging impact that tuition fees have on the participation of low-income students.

Note

1. Marcucci, P.N. and Johnstone, B.M. (2007). Tuition fee policies in a comparative perspective: theoretical and political rationales. *Journal of Higher Education Policy and Management, 29*:1, 25–40. Reprinted by permission of the publisher.

References

Andrews, L. (1999). *Does HECS deter? Factors affecting university participation by low SES groups.* Adelaide: Department of Education, Training and Youth Affairs, Higher Education Division.
Bain, O. (2001). The costs of higher education to students and parents in Russia: Tuition policy issues. *Peabody Journal of Education,* 76, 57–80.
Chapman, B. and Ryan, C. (2003). *The access implications of income contingent charges for higher education: Lessons from Australia (Discussion Paper No. 463).* Canberra: Australian National University, Center for Economic Policy Research.
College Board. (2004). *Trends in college pricing.* New York: College Board.
Department for Education and Skills. (2003). *The future of higher education.* London: DfES.
Hebel, S. (2003, December 13). Va. Governor wants to inject college into senior year of high school. *Chronicle of Higher Education.* Retrieved from: http://chronicle.com/

Heller, D. (1999). The effects of tuition and state financial aid on public college enrolment. *Review of Higher Education*, 23(1), 65–89.

Ishengoma, J. (2002). *Financing higher education in the Federal Republic of Nigeria: Developments and trends.* Buffalo, NY: International Comparative Higher Education Finance and Accessibility Project.

Johnstone, D.B. (1992). Tuition fees. In B.R. Clark and G. Neave (eds) *The encyclopedia of higher education, Vol. 2* (pp. 1501–1509). Oxford: Pergamon.

Johnstone, D.B. (2004). Cost-sharing and equity in higher education: Implications of income contingent loans. In P. Texteria, B. Jongbloed, D. Dill and A. Amaral (eds) *Markets in higher education* (pp. 37–59). Dordrecht: Kluwer Academic Publishers.

Johnstone, D.B. (2005). *Higher educational accessibility and financial viability: The role of student loans* (Prepared for the World Report on Higher Education: The Financing of Universities II International Barcelona Conference on Higher Education, Global University Network for Innovation (GUNI) Barcelona, Spain, May 24–25 and November 28–30, 2005). Buffalo, NY: University at Buffalo Center for Comparative and Global Studies in Education.

Jongbloed, B. (2005, March). Higher education funding in The Netherlands: Recent Developments. *IAU Horizons, World Higher Education News, 11*(1), 9.

Junor, S. and Usher, A. (2002). *The price of knowledge: Access and student finance in Canada.* Montreal: Canada Millennium Scholarship Foundation Research Series.

Junor, S. and Usher, A. (2004). *The price of knowledge 2004: Access and student finance in Canada* (Canada Millennium Scholarship Foundation Research Series). Ogdensburg, NY: Renouf.

Kiamba, C. (2003, September). *The experience of privately sponsored studentship and other income generating activities at the University of Nairobi.* Paper prepared for the World Bank Regional Training Conference on Improving Tertiary Education in Sub-Saharan Africa: Things that Work, Accra, Ghana.

LaRocque, N. (2003a). *Who should pay? Tuition fees and tertiary education financing in New Zealand.* Wellington: Education Forum.

LaRocque, N. (2003b, September 16). Top-up tales. *Guardian.* Retrived from: http://education.guardian.co.uk

Leidig, M. (2001, March 23). Austrian fee plan gets finishing touches. *Times Higher Education Supplement.* Retrieved from: http://thes.co.uk/

Leslie, L. and Brinkman, P. (1998). *The economic value of higher education.* New York: Macmillan Publishing Co.

Li, W. (2005, May). *Private expenditures, family contributions and financial aid. Need analysis in higher education.* Paper presented at the International Conference on Higher Education Finance: Cost, Access and Assistance, Huazhong University of Science and Technology, Wuhan, China.

Li, W. and Min, W. (n.d.). *Tuition, private demand and higher education expansion in China.* Peking: Peking University.

Potterton, L. (2001, November 16). Austrians petition for the right to free higher education. *Times Higher Education Supplement.* Retrieved from: http://thes.co.uk/

Saint, W. (2003). *Higher education development for Ethiopia: Pursuing the vision.* Washington, DC: World Bank.

Sully, M. (2000, October 6). Protesters fight plan to levy fees. *Times Higher Education Supplement.* Retrieved from: http://thes.co.uk/

Usher, A. and Cervenan, A. (2005). *Global higher education rankings. Affordability and accessibility in comparative perspective.* Washington, DC: Educational Policy Institute.

Vossensteyn, H. (2000, June). *A new look at price responsiveness.* Presented at the 13th CHER Annual Conference, Bowness-on-Windemere, UK.

Vossensteyn, H. (2005). *Perceptions of student price-responsiveness.* Enschede: CHEPS/University of Twente.

Wachira, K., and Bollag, B. (2002, June 12). A tale of rebirth: Makerere University survived a dictator's reign and is thriving again. *Chronicle of Higher Education.* Retrieved from: http://chronicle.com/

Ward, L. (2005, June 22). No top-up fees for Welsh students. *Education Guardian.* Retrieved from: http://education.guardian.co.uk

Ziegele, F. (2003). *Country report: HE finance and cost-sharing in Germany.* CHE Center for Higher Education Development.

Ziegele, F. (2005, April 21). Scottish MPs agree to top-up fees. *Education Guardian.* Retrieved from: http://education.guardian.co.uk

13

From Senior Student to Novice Worker

Learning Trajectories in Political Science, Psychology and Mechanical Engineering[1]

Madeleine Abrandt Dahlgren, Håkan Hult, Lars Owe Dahlgren, Helene Hård af Segerstad and Kristina Johansson

This longitudinal study focuses on the transition from higher education to working life. Research has hitherto described the transition in rather general terms, and there is still only limited knowledge about how graduates construe themselves as professionals, or how they experience the transition to the sociocultural contexts of working life. In this study, the transition is viewed as a trajectory between different communities of practice. Three different master's programmes at Linköping University are focused on and compared: Political Science, Psychology and Mechanical Engineering.

The specific aims are to: (i) identify aspects of identity and knowledge formation as reported by informants, both as senior students and later as novice workers with 18 months of work experience; (ii) identify features of discourses of knowledge and competence operating in the programmes and working life; and (iii) to relate the results to differences in the way the programmes are designed. The results indicate that the psychology programme prepares for working life in a rational way, that is, the generic skills and substantive knowledge acquired seem to correspond to the demands of professional work. The other programmes stand out as preparing for working life either by providing generic skills that need to be transformed in professional work, or by containing elements that mainly play a ritual role rather than corresponding to the demands of working life.

Introduction

In recent decades, the idea and role of universities as educational institutions has been debated intensely in relation to societal change and the changing demands of working life (Barnett, 1994). The percentage of students enrolled in higher education has multiplied several times during this period. The working forms in universities have also been debated and at times critiqued internally. The increasing interest in student-centred pedagogics in higher education over the last three decades could be seen as an expression of the universities' ways of responding to these demands.

Research in the area has shown that not only the content of educational programmes or working forms in the university may contribute to students' learning. The sociocultural contexts, in terms of the academic disciplines and their differences in ontological and epistemological standpoints, also impact on the design and delivery of university courses, which in turn influence students' learning processes (Snow, 1964; Becher, 1989, 1994; Abrandt Dahlgren, 2000, 2003; Neumann 2001; Abrandt Dahlgren and Dahlgren, 2002; Neumann *et al.*, 2002). Becher (1989) distinguishes between hard pure, soft pure, hard applied and soft applied fields of study. Neumann *et al.* (2002) build on this framework in their literature review on teaching and learning in their disciplinary contexts. They show that there are considerable differences in curriculum, assessment and cognitive purpose, as well as in characteristics of teachers, types of teaching methods and student learning requirements. The outcome of university programmes in terms of how graduates construe themselves as professionals, or how they experience the transition to the sociocultural contexts of working life is an area that has been paid less attention in previous research.

The aim of this chapter is to further examine and compare the transition from higher education to working life in three different study programmes at Linköping University: Political Science, Psychology and Mechanical Engineering. The specific aims are: (i) to identify features of discourses of knowledge and competence operating in the programmes and working life, and aspects of identity as reported by informants as senior students and later as novice workers with 18 months of work experience; and (ii) to relate the results of this comparison to differences in the way the programmes are designed. The results reported here constitute a part of a comprehensive joint research project between four research teams from Sweden, Norway, Germany and Poland. The project focuses on the transition between higher education and working life (project *Students as Journeymen between Communities of Higher Education and Work*, within the EU 5th Framework Programme, contract no. HPSE CT-2000-00068).

Research on Transition between Higher Education and Working Life

The relationship between higher education and working life is an area of research that has attracted increasing interest among researchers in recent years. In Brennan *et al.*'s (1996) review of research on the transition from higher education to working life they found that research has predominantly concerned either the systems level, with focus on the match between the output of higher education and the societal demands for academically trained manpower, or studies on the expediency of higher education as assessed retroactively by professional novices. They argue that the transition is often described in rather general categories, and there is little concern with the experienced impact of education or specific work task requirements.

A more recent review of the field by Johnston (2003) points out that there is still little information in the research literature on graduate employment from the graduates' perspective. There is a need for research focusing on experiences of graduates in their early employment years, she argues, particularly as regards their working conditions and culture. Other areas where she argues that more research is needed are on relationships between higher education and work, fulfilment issues such as the nature and extent of the graduates' job expectations, satisfaction and commitment, and relationships between employers' explicit expectations and graduates' experienced expectations.

Another complicating factor when assessing the feasibility of study programmes with regard to requirements in working life is the lack of stable forecasts about the nature of future tasks in working life and qualifications (Barnett 1994, 2000a). In a recent Swedish state survey on the new conditions for learning in higher education (SOU 2001:13), it is argued that work in qualified positions in contemporary working life requires a perspective on competence that, in addition to specific knowledge and skills, also includes abilities of independent learning. Furthermore, the ability to formulate, analyse and solve problems is emphasised. This includes an emphasis on accessibility, transferable skills, competency formation, modularisation, student profiling and the development of reflective practitioners (Symes and McIntyre, 2000). Becoming professional has been argued to include engagement in a wider set of discourses, which comprises a responsibility for the professional that moves beyond the limits of a local professional–client transaction (Barnett, 1997).

An example of research where the graduates' experiences of the transition to work life have been particularly attended to is a recent study by Kaufman and Feldman (2004) where a symbolic interactionist perspective is applied when researching senior students' experiences as regards the development of identity formation in their college years. The results show that the experience of college plays an important constitutive role in forming the self-perceived identities of students. This was particularly evident in three domains (i.e. intelligence and knowledgeability, occupation, and cosmopolitanism). Within the domain of occupation, interaction with peers stood out as an important feature in forming self-perceived occupational identities. Kaufman and Feldman argue that college provides students with the "situational contexts within which a variety of identities may be negotiated, experienced, and ultimately constructed" (p. 481). An interesting finding is that the experience of college for some students constituted a symbolic entitlement for certain occupations and careers, and that they perceived themselves as deserving the better jobs because they were highly educated.

The study by Kaufmann and Feldman does not, however, address particular circumstances within certain disciplines or professional fields that may have different knowledge traditions and cultures of learning. The present study makes an attempt at detailing the transition to work life from three different academic contexts—Political Science, Psychology, and Mechanical Engineering—taking into account these particular aspects from a sociocultural perspective. The three programmes could be viewed as representing a broad variety of knowledge traditions and cultures, from the classical liberal arts programme with a loose structure, to more professional programmes in which a particular profession is more or less clearly defined as the intended outcome.

Theoretical and Methodological Frame of Reference

Communities of Practice

In this study, the transition from higher education to working life is viewed as a trajectory from one community within academia, with a particular set of boundaries and traditions, to another community of practice within work life, with a different location and different boundaries, activities and traditions (Wenger, 1998). Trajectories are seen as motions over time, not necessarily following a predestined course, but open to interaction with and influence by a multitude of sources. A central source of identity formation in the community of practice is participation; the identity is constituted through the recognition of mutuality in relations of participation. Newcomers become part of a community of practice through the process of legitimate peripheral participation (Lave and Wenger, 1991), in which the sense of belonging is developed through the relationships between newcomers and old-timers. Another source complementary to participation in this process is reification. Reification refers to the abstractions such as tools, symbols, terms and concepts produced by the community to reify something in this practice in a congealed form.

Identity Formation

Bauman (1991) claims that, in the change to the modern, functionally differentiated society, individual persons are no longer firmly rooted in one single location or subsystem of society, but, rather, must be regarded as socially displaced. The individual needs to establish a stable and defensible identity to differentiate between the self and the outer world, but at the same time needs the affirmation of social approval.

Wenger (1998) describes identity formation in a community of practice as a nexus of multi-membership. As such a nexus, an identity is not a coherent unity, nor is it simply fragmented. Wenger claims that identities are at the same time one and multiple. We reason along the same lines as Wenger, and are aware that identities described in this study are only partial and contextually situated in the realm of studies and work.

Discourses

The concept of discourse could be defined as the use of language as a social practice or action that is both constituted and constituting (Winther Jørgensen and Phillips, 2000). The constituted aspect of the discourse is the different discursive practices, in higher education and work life, which are socially and historically situated, and in which participation and reification influence the inform-ants' ways of talking about their experiences. The constituting aspect of discourse is the use of language as an action that can influence these communities.

In this study, we have chosen three different study programmes, building on the assumption that their characteristics as communities of practice in the university vary. More specifically, we are assuming that educational design, expectations of knowledge formation and identity building in students will vary among the programmes. Similarly, it is our assumption that the graduates will enter different sectors of work life, with different demands on them as novices in working life that do not necessarily match the presupposed outcome of the study programme.

Methods

Design and Data Collection

Twelve students from each programme were interviewed on two occasions, the first time during their last year of studies (early 2002) and the second time after approximately 15–18 months of professional work (mid-2003). The sample is approximately a representative proportion in terms of gender of the population in each programme.

The age of the informants from the Political Science programme varies between 24 and 37 years of age. The majority of students/novices are in the age span of 24–26. The age of the informants from the Psychology programme varies between 24 and 46 years; more than half of them are between 24 and 26 years of age. The age of the informants from the Mechanical Engineering programmes varies between 24 and 31 years, with an average age of 27.

The interviews were taped and subsequently transcribed verbatim. The duration of each inter-view varied between 45 and 90 minutes.

Data Analyses

The methodology and analytical procedure applied in the project is multilayered. We are interested not only in the variation in individual constructions of various aspects of education expressed by the students, but also in what constitute the most common features of the constructions in each group studied, and could be understood as discourses operating in the programmes and in work life.

The primary analysis of interview data is inspired by the rigorous procedure of phenomenogra-phy, as a first step on the way towards understanding socially (institutionally) and culturally situated and constructed meanings. The initial phase can be described as *familiarisation*, and means that the transcriptions are carefully read with the aim of getting acquainted with the texts in detail. This is also necessary in order to make any corrections or editing. The analysis continues with a phase of *condensation*, in which the most significant statements are selected to give a short version of the entire dialogue concerning the phenomenon under study. The selected significant dialogue excerpts were then *compared* in order to find sources of variation or agreement. Taking into account the result of the previous steps, the next feature of the analysis was to *group* answers that appeared to have similarities. Based on this grouping, the categories that form the result were developed in the next step: *articulating*. Finally, the categories obtained were *contrasted* with regard to similarities and differences at a meta-level. The aim of a phenomenographic analysis is to arrive at a set of descriptive categories, portraying similarities and differences concerning how a certain phenomenon in question is conceived of by people (Marton, 1981; Dahlgren and Fallsberg, 1991). In our study, we are transcending the scope of phenomenography by viewing the categories obtained through the analysis as provisional, and as representing only the first stage of a process of analysis and interpretation.

In the second part of the analysis we have linked the individual and social constructions in data interpretation by a procedure designed on the basis of the methodologies of discourse analysis (cf. Gee, 1999; Talja, 1999). This means that we have searched for inconsistencies and contradictions in particular interviews, as they may reflect subject positions related to power structures and discourses operating. Secondly, we have also read the transcripts with a particular searchlight on recurrent tropes, i.e. descriptions, explanations, arguments, etc. that the informants use, and tried to articulate the assumptions that such tropes are built on. A third way of identifying discourses has been to look for utterances that attribute certain ideas to other locations than the personal, e.g. when an informant refers explicitly to ideas being transferred from peers, family, or a particular formal regulation.

The Context of the Study

Linköping University has four faculties, Engineering, Arts and Sciences, Educational Sciences and Health Sciences. About 20% of the students at Linköping University are enrolled in PBL (problem-based learning) programmes. The programmes chosen for this study are master's programmes in psychology, political science and mechanical engineering. Undergraduates in Sweden follow either a "Kandidatexamen" or a bachelor's degree, lasting three years, or a "Magisterexamen", or master's degree, lasting four to five years. The informants in the study are senior students, and later novices in working life.

Political Sciences

Political Sciences belongs to the Faculty of Arts and Sciences. The programme Political Science and Economics is claimed to provide the students with a broad knowledge of the social sciences. Students can choose to study political science as a separate subject for two years, or as a master's programme over four years. The development of a critical approach to various political and economic theories is emphasised as an important intended outcome of the programme. The most common working forms during the first years of study are lectures, exercises and seminars covering a range of different areas in political science and economics (Table 13.1). During the later parts of the studies, the students specialise in either political science or economics as their major field of study.

Table 13.1 Master's programme in Political Science. Sequence of courses

Year 1	40 weeks	Political Science (20 weeks), Economics (20 weeks)
Year 2	40 weeks	Statistics (10 weeks), Law (10 weeks), Economics (20 weeks) or Economics (20 weeks)
Year 3	40 weeks	Optional courses in Economics or Political Science (40 weeks).
Year 4	40 weeks	Optional courses in Economics or Political Science (20 weeks), BA thesis (10 weeks), MA thesis (10 weeks)

Table 13.2 Master's programme in Psychology. Thematic learning modules

	7 weeks	Introduction to psychology
Module I	23	Cognitive psychology and the biological bases of behaviour
Module II	40	Human development and educational psychology
Module III	56	Sociology, organisational psychology and group psychology
Module IV	47	Personality theory, psychopathology and psychotherapy
Module V	27	Research methodology and Master's thesis

Psychology

The educational programme for training psychologists belongs to the Faculty of Arts and Sciences, and is a five-year, problem-based programme. The overall characteristics are claimed to stimulate critical reflection through an emphasis on learning through problem-solving, experiential and self-directed learning. Theories, methods and problems in the field of psychology are dealt with from a research perspective. It is also claimed that since the scientific basis of the profession is rapidly developing and changing, it is important to develop the ability for lifelong and independent learning within the programme. Such a competence is defined as the students' ability to identify their own learning needs, choose, make use of and critically assess different sources of knowledge, and evaluate learning processes and their outcome. The students are also required to actively seek knowledge with the aim of developing into independent problem-solvers, capable of investigation and intervention. The programme is organised in larger learning modules (Table 13.2), where sub-disciplinary perspectives of psychology are moulded into themes. The dominant working form is small group tutorials, where emphasis also is put on communicative and evaluative fields. The students also have periods of clinical placement as a part of every module.

Mechanical Engineering

The mechanical engineering programme belongs to the Faculty of Engineering and comprises four and a half years. "Rapid advances in technology require an engineer to be capable in computation, design, production, economics and management" according to the university website (http://www.liu.se/en/education/study/ing/progsw?id=20). The first two and a half years of the mechanical engineering programme is designed to lay a basic foundation for the forthcoming studies (Table 13.3). After completing their basic studies, the mechanical engineering students can choose one of six branches of specialisation. This means that the content of the first part of the mechanical engineering programme is organised in a large number of both sequential and parallel courses. The working forms are typically lectures, exercises and laboratory work.

During the final two years, there are 10 optional profiles of engineering that students can choose from. The studies are conducted in project form, where theoretical learning is integrated with laboratory work, computer practice and field trips to industrial sites. A profile represents 20 weeks

Table 13.3 Master's programme in Mechanical Engineering

Year 1–2	60 weeks	Predefined curriculum for all students. Basic foundation studies. Introduction of various technologies.
Year 2	20 weeks	Choice of optional branch. Five general mandatory courses plus several electives for each branch.
Year 3	40 weeks	Continued studies within a chosen branch. Three general mandatory courses plus several electives for each branch.
Year 4	40 weeks	Selection of specialisation project work, 13 electives available (20 weeks). Elective courses (20 weeks).
Year 5	20 weeks	Master's thesis.

of study in the fourth year, including an 8–10-week project course. The concluding master's thesis is written in the specific area of specialisation chosen. The project work is predominantly conducted at companies in the industrial sector.

Results

The rationale for how the results are presented is that the informants' individual constructions, and the reifications in terms of educational design, are also considered to reflect features of discourses of knowledge and competence operating within the different programmes. Through the individual perspectives of the informants as students, and later as novices, we will also uncover some of the relationships of the educational programmes to the broader constellation of practices constituted by working life. We will also attempt to describe typical characteristics of the trajectories between the different communities of higher education and work.

First, we account for the different areas of employment of the graduates from the three programmes. This is followed by an analysis and interpretation of two dimensions of the trajectory from education to working life, i.e. aspects of identity formation and knowledge formation. The three programmes are then compared with respect to the characteristics of the educational design, and on a meta-level with respect to the respective relationships between education and work.

Political Science

Areas of Employment

Eight of the 12 novices are found in a variety of different work contexts within the public sector. Municipal administration, social welfare administration and the national migration authority are examples of such areas of operation. Two novices are working in private companies, one of the informants is still studying and one is unemployed.

Trajectory in Terms of Identity Formation

The political science programme could be claimed to prepare not for a specific professional activity, but for an academic way of being, developing a *homo academicus* as the outcome of the educational programme. The trajectory into working life for some of the political scientists could be described as being positioned as responsible interpreters of legislative texts. This responsibility is also linked to certain moral dilemmas, as one of the novice's expression illustrates:

How much influence you should have as a civil servant? What do I have the right to do and how much should I do? The higher up in the hierarchy you are or on different levels I think there are even more of these moral dilemmas. How much should ignorant politicians decide and how much should knowledgeable civil servants decide? So I guess that's a moral dilemma in political science (POL 13, Novice).

This is a typical trait of the political scientists in local, regional and state authorities. The situated identity as a *mediator* could also be interpreted as positioning political scientists so that they are squeezed between conflicting interests in the community of working life. The following quotation illustrates how such conflicting interests operate.

It works that way that we write a proposal [about the application for permission to serve alcohol], and then the person who has applied comes here. If it's a negative proposal the person who has applied comes here with a lawyer and talks in front of the politicians . . . So I realised very soon that if you can't be more explicit than the lawyer, the decision that you have proposed will not be approved by the social welfare office. That's one thing that I learned very fast, you were run over by the politicians in the beginning (POL 1, Novice).

Few of the novices see themselves as being in a position of power in relation to the political decision-making arena. This could reflect either an unawareness of the political dimension of the role of the political scientist, or indicate differences in exercising power in different organisations.

As a result of work experience, a new role and situated identity of the political scientist as a *negotiator* and a *mediator* crystallises as the awareness of the responsibility involved in being the advocate of the individual citizen increases. When describing this new role and identity, the novices' answers generally point out generic skills, both when asked what kind of knowledge they acquired through their education and what is required in their present work. This also constitutes the answer to the more general question about the knowledge required to be recognised as a good political scientist.

We had a lot of independent studies in political science, so [the most important] is probably to learn to become independent, sit at home and read . . . (POL 18, Novice).

The Trajectory in Terms of Knowledge Formation

The transition can be described as a *process of detailing* in a transformation from generic academic skills, i.e. the capacity to read and write academic texts, to skills in analysing and describing problems in combination with substantive skills, i.e. being knowledgeable about political systems and the institutions of democracy.

I think the studies give you a good basis but you must be aware that it is only a start. In my view it is a lifelong learning process and you can't say that now I am a political scientist when you have got your exam, but you always have to learn new things (POL 15, Senior student).

This particular combination of skills leads to the experience of a vague exit from the programme; there are signs of fragments of an identity as an *independent investigator* or *civil servant* developing at the end of the programme. Analytical and communicative skills are the most frequently mentioned abilities. A thorough understanding of the structure and functions of Swedish society is, furthermore, mentioned as a significant element of professional competence. A critical attitude is mentioned as desirable, not least when assessing data gathered for investigative or evaluative purposes. It is important to be able *to work independently and search for information*, as one of the novices expresses it (POL 20).

Psychology

Areas of Employment

All 12 novice psychologists work as clinical consultants. Fields of operation are hospitals, particularly the psychiatric area involving children, teenagers and adults, and schools.

Trajectory in Terms of Identity Formation

The psychology programme could be claimed to prepare for the requirements of clinical work. During the trajectory of the programme, the psychology students compose a kind of *professional fellow-being* character, comprising elements both from their private personality as well as their professional role. The concept comprises the meaning of the helper and the social engineer capable of moderating people's behaviour. Periods of clinical internship have made it necessary to separate the private and the professional sphere. A quotation from one of the informants illustrates this:

> It is important to be involved and empathic, without losing your critical attitude, to be able to keep a certain distance, even if you are very close ... It's in a way a basic condition for being able to do the job, to feel and to analyse, but also to be able to come home and not be a psychologist after work (PSY8, Senior student).

The typical characteristic of the discourses in working life about the professional role of a psychologist is the *ability to reflect*, both on the individual and the collective level. On the individual level, reflection constitutes both a way of synthesising and understanding the client's problems and a way of scrutinising their own thoughts and feelings.

> It is important that I dare to be a human being in the encounter with other people, it is not only about techniques, technical knowledge, facts and methods, but that I as a human being allow myself to be moved by the meeting with the clients, but also that I use my humanity to feel and reflect, to draw conclusions from the meeting. To develop in my professional role, it is clear to me that I also need to develop my personal identity (PSY10, Novice).

Reflection also stands out as a hallmark of a good psychologist at the collective level. Some statements in the interviews indicate that the ability to contribute valuable reflections to a discussion between the team or between colleagues gives a feeling of being professional.

> I feel like a good psychologist sometimes when I meet clients and I feel I can help them in some way ... or if I can contribute good reflections in treatment conferences where we are discussing various cases. I sometimes feel that I can contribute to someone else's case (PSY3, Novice).

The Trajectory in Terms of Knowledge Formation

Two ways of relating to the theoretical body of knowledge are discernible from the primary phenomenographic analysis. The *eclectic mode* means that fragments of knowledge from different theoretical schools are moulded ad hoc in the application to be applied in a specific case. The *pluralistic mode* means there is a repertoire of perspectives from which the professional selects a specific theoretical perspective for a specific case. The awareness of pluralism, i.e. the existence of competing theoretical schools of psychology and the application of these in clinical practice, stands out as the most important feature of the novices' answers to the questions about what kind of knowledge is acquired in the educational programme. The trajectory from the educational programme to working life is characterised by *continuity and confirmation* of the knowledge base acquired during the educational process. Some of the interviews are also very convincing as regards students' feeling of being prepared, of putting into practice the knowledge they have developed during their studies.

> I was surprised by, partly how easily I was entering the professional role and felt confident, and partly by that I could convey my knowledge to the people I met, I was a school psychologist, and there was no doubt about it (PSY 6, Novice).

The feeling of being put to the test, rather than socialised into the professional work, leads to a legitimate participation in the professional community shortly after entering working life, indicating a close power/knowledge relationship.

Mechanical Engineering

Employment Areas

Ten of the novice engineers were at the time of the interview working in medium-sized and large private enterprises. Two of them were enrolled in trainee progammes.

The novice engineers describe their work using the words calculating and constructing. Examples of areas of application are developing products and/or computer programs, certifying and evaluating processes and products.

Trajectory in Terms of Identity Formation

The discourse operating in the educational programme of what constitutes a mechanical engineer is typically that of being representatives of an *intellectual elite*, mastering complex theoretical problems with the task of *building society*. This is illustrated by the following quotations:

> Sometimes you get the feeling that they would like to have many top students, to kind of show off to other technical schools in Sweden and the rest of the world. It is not my point of view, but it seems to be important to them to get some kind of elite in certain ways . . . It is important with the career thing, it is mentioned already in the information brochures, it is very focused on careerists and that kind of person (ENG 21, Senior student).

> The engineers solve problems for the ordinary people. Engineers solve problems in their own ways, but it is for the benefit of all society. All products that we have, cars, telephones, are developed by engineers. So engineers make things easier for all society. That is what develops engineering itself too (ENG24, Senior student).

As novices, the typical interpretations of the discourses operating in working life concerning what constitutes a mechanical engineer have been replaced by that of an employable trainee with *generic problem-solving capabilities*. The mechanical engineer is also typically flexible and inter-changeable. The flexibility refers to the capabilities of entering a multitude of different projects, and the interchangeability that professional responsibility concerns only a delimited part of the project in question. The ability to be flexible is considered important, and in a way creates a dilemma in the novices' choices between specialisation, which would mean the acquisition of expertise within a certain area, but at the same time be to the detriment of generic flexibility.

The particularity of the discourses operating in working life about the professional role characteristics is that of being an *exclusive thinker*. The informants claim that there is a typical "engineering-thinking" that seeks the *optimal* and most *pragmatic solution* to any problem. Two informants give their notions of what this could mean:

> But what you are good at is above all to think like a mechanical engineer. Think about something, you see something and you not only look at the external, you also think about it in an engineering way, like, this can be changed. The most important thing is to learn a certain way of thinking about things (ENG 28, Novice).

> Critical thinking, the way engineers are thinking maybe . . . if one has a problem, to be able to sort it out, and divide it into different sub problems, which are actually possible to solve, because if one has a new problem, then one has to divide it to be able to find a solution and solve the problem (ENG 31, Novice).

However, the characteristics of the work task for most of the novices are typically that the novices get well-defined and limited tasks as parts of bigger projects, which they do not have a full understanding of or responsibility for. Only gradually do they get working tasks of a more complex nature.

The Trajectory in Terms of Knowledge Formation

The trajectory from education to working life appears to the mechanical engineers as a *discontinuity in scope and responsibility* of the professional role. This could be interpreted to mean that passing the programme leads to a formal legitimacy that in itself is a merit and, thereby, leads to a peripheral legitimate participation in the professional community of engineering. It also indicates that parts of the trajectory in terms of knowledge formation are ritual. The ritual feature of the programme is strongest at the beginning, where students are put to the hardest test by taking the massive initial courses.

> Engineers have a similar training, you have been through courses of similar difficulty, I think that is why you feel like an engineer, you have made it, there are several who don't think they will make it when they start on the programme, because it is really hard work. Very few really make it, and that is perhaps why you feel that you kind of are of the same kind (ENG29, Novice).

The experience of intensity in the programme decreases in the latter part as the students learn how to cope with the demands, and the ritual courses are less prevalent.

Educational Design and Process

In the following, we will relate the findings regarding students' views of the transitions to the structural and functional properties of the three programmes as displayed in course documents and the interviews.

Political Science

It seems as if the discourse about educational design in the early parts of the political science programme concerns conveying *basic descriptive knowledge* about political systems and theories. The students describe a cycle consisting of lectures, independent studies and seminars. As the programme progresses, the important aim becomes instead to develop the students' abilities to *investigate, analyse and compare* different political systems. This is reflected in the teaching forms used in the programme, with lectures and seminars dominating the early stages. The seminars follow a distinct structure, where the teacher plays a directive role and the *interactions between students are regulated* The latter stages of the programme are dominated by independent thesis work under supervision. Contact with the teachers is less prominent in the initial phase of the programme, and the students feel more anonymous as freshmen than they do as senior students. Furthermore, there seems to be a lack of contextualisation and meta-reflection throughout the educational programme since the programme concerns the study *of* politics rather than *in* politics, emphasising academic features of politics rather than encouraging students to acquire a particular political standpoint. In the terminology used by Neumann *et al.* (2002), political science would be viewed as a field of soft, pure knowledge, being reiterative, holistic, concerned with the particulars and having a qualitative bias.

Psychologists

The discourses concerning educational design operating in the psychology programme have a *professional and clinical focus* already from the outset of the programme. The use of real-life scenarios as the point of departure for learning contributes to this focus. There is also a *focus on the individual*; students are selected after individual interviews. The *interaction between fellow students*, which is emphasised from the outset of the programme in the small group tutorials, seems to have an impact as regards the ability to prioritise, look for causal relationships as well as relationships between parts and wholes. The feedback between students is considered very important, and students emphasise the importance of being well prepared and contributing to discussions. It is obvious that discourse about an engaged, talkative and capable student has a strong presence in the programme. There are two discourses about learning psychology operating in the programme, to learn and discern differences between the relevant theories, and to integrate them into themselves (the students) as persons. Clinical placements seem to have played a role in integrating the content learned with learning about one's own person. Applying the scheme cited in Neumann *et al.* (2002), the psychology programme could be categorised as a mix between a hard and soft applied field of knowledge, on the one hand concerned with the enhancement of professional practice, on the other hand outgoing, with multiple influences on both research and teaching.

Mechanical Engineering

Using the terminology of Neumann *et al.* (2002), the mechanical engineering programme could be categorised as a field of hard applied knowledge; indeed engineering is the very example used by the authors to typify this field, concerned with mastery of the physical environment and directed towards products and techniques.

Nevertheless, the discourse about educational design operating within the engineering programme resembles that in political science, in that the notion is to provide students with basic knowledge from the outset of the programme. The large number of specific and parallel courses, the large classes and the lecture format, contribute to forming a very competitive learning climate. Students have to prioritise their commitment and discern their individual focus and understanding of the field of engineering in the trajectory throughout the programme. The discourse about the knowledge base in engineering thus appears to be fragmented and multiple to the students.

Discussion

Identity and Knowledge Formation as a Process of Continuity, Discontinuity or Transformation

The psychology programme has the most obvious professional focus. There is a high degree of *continuity* between being a student and being a professional novice. The socialisation and transition to work is immediate; when the novices show evidence of professional skills in practice, this leads to a full legitimate participation in the professional community (Wenger, 1998). The emphasis on contextualisation to the diverse field of psychology throughout the programme may be a feature of the educational design that contributes to the feeling of preparedness for work, as it is a strong feature of problem-based learning. Positive impact on graduates' perceptions of communication, and generally on the feeling of preparedness for professional work, in PBL programmes has previously been shown in the field of medical education (Jones et al., 2002; Antepohl et al., 2003; Willis et al., 2003).

Both the other groups have experienced the transition from higher education to work as a process involving some kind of *discontinuity* or *transformation*. In the case of the political scientists, the transformation means recontextualising their general knowledge and generic skills to specific areas of work. Engineering novices achieve a formal legitimacy by passing the programme, which is an indicator of being able to learn fast and work hard, and thus functions as a door opener to the labour market. The character of the working tasks as delimited parts of larger projects could be seen as the novices reaching what in Wenger's (1998) terminology could be described as peripheral legitimate participation in the professional community.

Sequential, Parallel or Thematic Organisation of Content

The organisation of the content in the three programmes could be described as *sequential, parallel or thematic*. The political science programme has a typical academic focus; the sequential organisation is driven by the internal logic of the discipline, which maintains the idea of basic learning before analysis, comparison or application. This also contains the idea of stepwise progression in small parts leading to an eventual and gradual understanding of the field of knowledge, and the development of generic academic skills. The mechanical engineering programme resembles the political science programme in the sense of having an academic focus. This focus is, however, blurred by the parallel organisation of courses. For both groups, the contextualisation of knowledge to working life occurs, if at all, late in the programme, or is left to the novices to handle individually. The thematic organisation of the psychology programme, on the other hand, integrates the academic and professional foci. The potential for contextualisation seems to be enhanced through the use of real-life scenarios as the point of departure for learning.

Rational or Ritual Relationship between Higher Education and Work

The relationships between education and work could also be described in a more abstract way. It is reasonable to assume that the great majority of educational programmes include knowledge and skills that are *rational* in character, with regard to their relation to working life, in that they are preparing for a specific field of knowledge or professional field of work, which emphasises the utility value of knowledge. It is also reasonable to assume that programmes include knowledge and skills that are rather *ritual* in character, where the connection to a specific context of application is lacking, and the most important feature is instead the exchange value of knowledge. The impact of education could be claimed to encompass *substantive skills* that are content-specific and contextually situated. On the other hand, the impact of education may also comprise *generic skills*, which are transferable between different contexts. Such skills may likewise be acquired in various contexts and developed through different contents.

For political science, the relationship between higher education and working life could be described as rational, emphasising generic skills. The content of the studies appears to be relevant to the presumptive area of professional work for the graduates. Typically, the generic knowledge needs to be transformed and contextualised in order to be applicable in the individual case. Knowledge and skills of a ritual character seem to play a minor role in the educational programme.

In the case of the psychology programme, the relationships between higher education and working life could be described differently. A similarity is that the contents of the programme are mainly rational, but the emphasis is high both on generic skills, such as the ability to communicate and interact with clients, and on substantive knowledge. Here, substantive knowledge refers to the competing schools of knowledge within psychology and the consequences of their application in the individual case.

The mechanical engineering programme, on the other hand, displays yet another emphasis on the different aspects of knowledge. The exchange value of passing the programme is in all likelihood revealed by an emphasis on the ritual aspects of knowledge. At the same time, the content of the programme appears to be rational to enable students to develop the generic problem-solving skill that is seen as a hallmark of the competence of the professional engineer. The achievement of a formal legitimacy as a ritual door opener to the labour market could be compared with the symbolic entitlement to a certain career or occupation, as found in Kaufman and Feldman's study (2004).

There are suggestions in the literature that, if higher education were to respond to the demands from the labour market, this would lead to an emphasis on operational competence that would constitute a reductionistic perspective, and be to the detriment of traditions of knowledge and learning at universities (Barnett, 1994). On the other hand, too great an emphasis on the university traditions might lead to an academic competence that might be of less value in the labour market. The challenge for universities is to find ways to bridge these demands and find a way to prepare for a changing and supercomplex society (Barnett, 1994, 2000b) that is based on:

a view of human being located neither in operations and technique nor in intellectual paradigms and disciplinary competence but in the total world experience of human beings. (Barnett, 1994, p. 178)

The rational generic relationship between higher education and work as found in political science could be seen as one example of how academic competence is transformed through experiences of work. This result gives some support to Barnett's way of reasoning, that what constitutes an "academic" is not *a priori* given, but a matter of "dynamic relationships between social and epistemological interests and structures" (1994, p. 256). The rational substantive and rational generic relationships between higher education and work, found as an outcome of the PBL design in the psychology programme, could be viewed as one example of how operational and academic competencies are bridged. The differences between the programmes as regards design, i.e. the parallel, sequential and thematic structure, may be seen as reflecting the notions of professional preparedness embedded in the various discourses of higher education. The engineering and political science programmes instead expose different academic notions about what is characteristic of communities of practice encountered by professionals in their respective fields. The psychology programme represents an attempt at depicting the professional community of practice in the academic context, which is illustrated, for example, by the broad themes in the programme, which also correspond to professional specialities.

Note

1. Abrandt Dahlgren, M., Hult, H., Dahlgren, L.O., Hård af Segerstad, H. and Johansson, K. (2006, October). From senior student to novice worker: Learning trajectories in political science, psychology and mechanical engineering. *Studies in Higher Education, 31*(5), pp. 569–586. Reprinted by permission of the publisher.

References

Abrandt Dahlgren, M. (2000) Portraits of PBL: course objectives and students' study strategies in computer engineering, physiotherapy, and psychology, *Instructional Science*, 28, 309–329.

Abrandt Dahlgren, M. (2003) PBL through the looking glass: comparing applications in computer engineering, psychology and physiotherapy, *International Journal of Engineering Education*, 19, 672–681.

Abrandt Dahlgren, M. and Dahlgren, L.O. (2002) Portraits of PBL: students' experiences of the characteristics of problem-based learning in physiotherapy, computer engineering and psychology, *Instructional Science*, 30, 111–127.

Antepohl, W., Domeij, E., Forsberg, P. and Ludvigsson, J. (2003) A follow up of medical graduates of a problem-based learning curriculum, *Medical Education*, 37, 155–162.

Barnett, R. (1994) *The limit of competence. Knowledge, higher education and society* (Buckingham: Open University Press).

Barnett, R. (1997) *Higher education: a critical business* (Buckingham: Open University Press).

Barnett, R. (2000a) *Realizing the university in an age of supercomplexity* (Buckingham: Open University Press).

Barnett, R. (2000b) Supercomplexity and the curriculum, *Studies in Higher Education*, 25(3), 255–265.

Bauman, Z. (1991) *Modernity and ambivalence* (Oxford: Blackwell).

Becher, T. (1989) *Academic tribes and territories: intellectual enquiry and the cultures of disciplines* (Buckingham: Open University Press).

Becher, T. (1994) The significance of disciplinary differences, *Studies in Higher Education*, 19(2), 151–161.

Brennan, J., Kogan, M. and Teichler, U. (eds) (1996) *Higher education and work* (London: Jessica Kingsley).

Dahlgren, L.O. and Fallsberg, M. (1991) Phenomenography as a qualitative approach in social pharmacy research, *Journal of Social and Administrative Pharmacy*, 8(4), 150–156.

Gee, P. (1999) *An introduction to discourse analysis. Theory and method* (London and New York: Routledge).

Jones, A., McArdle, P.J. and O'Neill, P. (2002) Perceptions of how well graduates are prepared for the role of pre-registration house officer: a comparison of outcomes from a traditional and integrated PBL curriculum, *Medical Education*, 36, 16–25.

Johnston, B. (2003) The shape of research in the field of higher education and graduate employment: some issues, *Studies in Higher Education*, 28(4), 414–426.

Kaufman, P. and Feldman, K.A. (2004) Forming identities in college: a sociological approach, *Research in Higher Education*, 45(5), 463–496.

Lave, J. and Wenger, E. (1991) *Situated learning* (Cambridge: Cambridge University Press).

Marton, F. (1981) Describing conceptions in the world around us, *Instructional Science*, 10, 177–200.

Neumann, R. (2001) Disciplinary differences and university teaching, *Studies in Higher Education*, 26(2), 135–146.

Neumann, R., Parry, S. and Becher, T. (2002) Teaching and learning in their disciplinary contexts: a conceptual analysis, *Studies in Higher Education*, 27(4), 405–417.

Snow, C.P. (1964) *The two cultures and a second look. An expanded version of the two cultures and the scientific revolution* 2nd edn (Cambridge: Cambridge University Press).

SOU 2001:13 *Nya villkor för lärandet i den högre utbildningen*. [Swedish Government official report: New conditions for learning in higher education].

Symes, C. and McIntyre, J. (eds) (2000) *Working knowledge: the new vocationalism and higher education* (Buckingham: Open University Press).

Talja, S. (1999) Analyzing qualitative interview data: the discourse analytic method, *Library and Information Science Research*, 21(4), 459–477.

Wenger, E. (1998) *Communities of practice: learning, meaning and identity* (Cambridge: Cambridge University Press).

Willis, S.C., Jones, A. and O'Neill, P. (2003) Can undergraduate education have an effect on the ways in which pre-registration house officers conceptualise communication? *Medical Education*, 37(7), 603–608.

Winther Jørgensen, M. and Phillips, L. (2000) *Diskursanalys som teori och metod* [Discourse analysis as theory and method] (Lund: Studentlitteratur).

14

Postgraduate Research Students' Experience

It's All About Balancing Living

Coralie McCormack

Introduction

This chapter responds to three questions:

- Who are today's postgraduate research students?
- What is their experience of candidature?
- How can this experience better prepare current and future students?

The first section of the chapter sets the scene for the stories to follow by foregrounding the commonality in today's research student cohort across countries, while acknowledging national diversity. Australian students' stories of their research experience, told in their own words, extend our understanding of the emotionality of the lived experience of postgraduate research. Their stories demonstrate the complexity and diversity of the postgraduate experience, and suggest strategies to successfully negotiate this complexity. The final section looks to the future to consider research student experience in a globally complex and competitive doctoral education environment. It is suggested that the learning emerging from the lived experiences of individual research students' stories can support future students' journeys "across complex terrain with heavy baggage" (Miller and Brimicombe, 2004, p. 405).

Today's Postgraduate Research Students

Internationally, doctoral education has undergone a fundamental reshaping over the last two decades. This reshaping has been characterised by both commonality and diversity (Kehm, 2007). Powell and Green (2007), reporting surveys of doctorates in 17 countries, note differences in elements of the doctoral experience, as well as common understandings and areas where there are common issues being addressed.

Massification of the undergraduate higher education system ("the rising tide of access to and participation in, higher education": Enders, 2004, p. 420) has been followed by an expansion in the number of students undertaking a higher degree by research (and the number of degrees awarded). In Canada the number of doctoral candidates rose by 106% during the decade 1991 to 2001 (Williams, 2005). In Finland, there was a 50% increase in enrolments in the 1980s and a 120% increase in the 1990s (Powell and Green, 2007). In China, the number of doctoral candidates increased from 18 in 1983 to 188,000 in 2003 (Zhuang, 2007). The percentage of the population enrolled in doctorates is highest in Europe, North America and Australia, and lowest in Asia and Africa (Powell and Green, 2007).

Accompanying the growth in student numbers has been the diversification of the research student population in terms of gender, age on graduation, levels of preparation, work experience and patterns of study. While the proportion of men students remains well above that of women students in some countries (eg France, Germany, Japan, South Africa), more women now participate in higher education as research students. The proportion of women students approximately equals that of men students in many countries (including Australia, Canada, Poland, UK, USA: Bawa, 2005; Pearson *et al.*, 2007; Kehm, 2005; Nyquist, 2002; Williams, 2005). In a few countries, such as Brazil, women constitute more than half of the doctoral student population (Ribeiro, 2007).

Where doctoral students begin study immediately after an undergraduate degree, most candidates are under 30 years of age (Powell and Green, 2007). In countries where an increasing number of students are over 30 years at the beginning of their candidature, average age on completion of doctoral study is later. In the UK the average age on completion is 32 years; in Germany it is 33 years; in Canada and Australia it is slightly higher, 36 years and 37 years respectively (Kehm, 2005; Powell and Green, 2007). The average age of doctoral completers in most Nordic countries is 37–38 years (Guomundsson, 2005).

Although the expansion of higher education has been accompanied by a growth in some aspects of diversity, other aspects remain unchanged (Meek and Wood, 1998). While the number of Maori students receiving doctorates in New Zealand increased from 3 in 1997 to 17 students in 2000 (Melrose, 2003), they, like African Americans and Hispanic students in the USA (Woodrow Wilson National Fellowship Foundation, 2005) and indigenous Australian students (Evans, 2007), are under-represented in doctoral enrollment and achievement. Bawa (2005, p. 12) notes with concern that addressing "the overwhelming race imbalances" is essential to the future of South African doctoral education.

Today's research students bring with them expectations and motivations that will take them beyond the traditional research graduate career path, which in the past led into academia. Research graduates are increasingly finding employment in industry and other sectors outside the academy (Bazeley, 1999; Enders, 2004; Kehm, 2005; Nerad, 2006; Powell and Green, 2007).

Stories of Postgraduate Research Students' Experiences

The Student Storytellers

The Australian students' stories of postgraduate research presented in this section are drawn from my doctoral research (McCormack, 2001), a longitudinal study of postgraduate research students' experience of their candidature, and from earlier research (McCormack and Pamphilon, 2000) focusing on women academics' experience of research candidature. The characteristics of these students capture the diversity of today's student population. Twenty-three students, across five Australian universities, across four fields of study (communication, education, politics and management, and sciences) tell their stories.

Choosing the Stories

Students' stories were collected, analysed and re-presented though a narrative inquiry framework of storying stories (McCormack, 2001, 2004). Storying stories both seeks personal experience stories and generates stories by composing stories about those experiences. In this process interview transcripts are viewed through multiple lenses—active listening, narrative processes, language, context and moments—to highlight both the individuality and the complexity of a life. The views highlighted by these lenses are then used to write interpretive stories of individuals' experiences. Interpretive stories are the experiences of "real" people told in their own words, as they experienced the events the stories portray.

Interpretive stories extend our understanding of the research student experience because they invite the reader to "live their way into" the experiences they are reading (Denzin, 1994, p. 506). Viewing experiences through students' eyes reveals the commonalities and differences experienced across individuals. More importantly, however, interpretive stories expose for the reader the "experiential, embodied" knowledge (Clandinin, 1985, p. 363) that "we usually keep to ourselves" (Grumet, 1991, p. 70). That is, the personal practical knowledge of students negotiating their everyday postgraduate experience: stories of times of feeling "in the right space" (comfortable and confident), and times of "unhomliness" (Bhabha, 1994—feeling uncertain, uncomfortable and unsure of whether they are, or could ever be, in the "right" place). Interpretive stories also provide readers "with the reflective space necessary to reimagine" their lives now and in the future (Neumann and Peterson, 1997, p. 8). "And through re-imagining, [students] can see the possibility of constructing alternative stories of their experience" (McCormack, 2001, p. xviii).

The interpretive stories included in this chapter were chosen to illustrate research students' experience of commonly recognised critical moments in candidature. Research is "full of critical moments that disrupt [the] process" (Byrne-Armstrong et al., 2001, p. vii; see also Comber, 1999; McCormack, 2001; Salmon, 1992). It is at such times that the experience of being a postgraduate research student is most visible, and available to be vicariously experienced by others. Two particular problematic aspects of candidature—relationships with supervisors and thesis-related writing—are illustrated in these stories. Also illustrated in the stories are the critical moments of candidature when students experienced a crisis of confidence, a stage that "many doctoral students seem to experience" (Kiley and Wisker, 2008).

Most of the stories have been deliberately positioned as pairs, that is, stories that offer differing perspectives of the same critical moment in candidature. For example, Barbara and Miranda's (all names are pseudonyms) stories of changing supervisors, Lisa and Grace's stories of writing and Myra and Miranda's stories of having nothing to "show" for hours/days/weeks of work. The paired stories re-present a time of loss and trauma, and a time when the same critical moment was experienced positively. All stories were chosen because they clearly illustrate a diversity of strategies; strategies to negotiate trauma and strategies to build on positive experiences. What makes these strategies particularly valuable is that they have been "road tested" by students in their everyday lives.

The stories that follow are also those research students themselves observe are missing from "how to" guidebooks which generally give "inadequate attention to the matter of how to handle emotional challenges and the stress induced by juggling too many identities and responsibilities" (Miller and Brimicombe, 2004, p. 411). As observed by Grace (one of the storytellers), the stories below are those "they don't tell you in the thesis preparation course" (McCormack, 2001, p. 392). They are not told because they are not neatly pleated stories but, rather, messy stories of contradictions and contingencies, turning points and tensions. They are stories about the joys and fears of beginning research (Ashley, Grace), and about the contradictions of candidature (Lisa, Anna,

Judy, Myra, Miranda, Lydia and Barbara). And they are stories that, as Barbara concludes, are all about balancing living. Balancing living involves balancing contradictory emotions—pleasure (moments of achievement and confidence) and pain (moments of uncertainty, tension, isolation and powerlessness)—within life's broad tapestry.

Individual Stories, Common Dilemmas

Ashley: You Have to Love What You're Researching

I was quite elderly by the time I got round to doing my PhD. I was 51 by the time I'd finished my PhD, so I wasn't any spring chicken by any stretch of the imagination, but I felt, "Oh what the heck I'm doing this for me. I'm not doing it for anyone else." It was a personal drive and the passion for the topic that got me enrolled. I really never seriously contemplated a PhD until this topic came up. It was so relevant to me and I just really felt that something needed to be done about it.

And now I'm finished I know that I have made a difference, and that's such a wonderful feeling. I made a difference because I loved what I was doing and something had to be done. I always tell anyone who is going to do a master's by research or a PhD that they have to love what they're researching, because if they don't love it they probably won't finish it.

Grace: Overcoming the Fears of a Novice Researcher

I feel like I'm going into an area where, sure I know my topic inside out, but I don't know about the how to get to where I want to go. I feel like quite a novice in terms of doing research. It feels like I'm out on a limb. It requires me to step out of my comfort zone.

I went to a national conference in November. That was about my lowest point really. I was thinking of giving up my thesis. I was not feeling that well, and then I got there and I listened to all these papers, and I thought, "Well yes, some of them are great, some of them are pretty ordinary." "Well you can't say that if you don't get out and do it yourself." I had been saying for a while that I should do a conference paper, and people had been asking me for ages to do it. So I thought, "Yes, I can do it." So I decided to look for the next conference and it was a Queensland conference so I thought, "Right, I am going to do one there." But I was nervous: Would it be good enough? How would it be received by academics? How can I talk about this stuff? Can I match up academically? Then once I started writing it became really difficult to keep it small. It was really exciting once I started writing. So by the time I got there I was really excited and wanted to do it. I felt I knew my material so well I just really enjoyed being up there and talking through my slides. My paper was really well received. It was an overview of my thesis so people, academic midwives, were really excited about the work and saying, "Yes, yes this is a really good place to go." So now I'm all fired up and want to do another one.

Lisa: Writing is a Contradictory Process

At the beginning I was feeling confident about what I wanted to say academically. I gave my first conference paper and I felt really good. Just getting my ideas out into an audience of strangers and not having them run out of the room in horror or shoot me down in flames gave me confidence. It helped me focus a lot of my ideas. I enjoyed the process. I think a conference experience helps to open up other avenues, to meet people and to get your work published. I submitted my paper to a journal and it was accepted, which is fantastic.

The following year everything changed because I realised "I've got to write chapters". I'm supposed to be writing one draft chapter every two months. I've just handed in the first one to my supervisors and that was the scariest thing I have ever done. Talk about a PhD being a life-changing experience! The whole thing of putting yourself down on paper has totally changed my life. It freaked me out totally. Then after I got the comments and criticisms (all of them well founded) back from my supervisors I totally fell apart. This is me on paper and I knew it wasn't as good as I wanted it to be. That first experience of writing a chapter wasn't like writing the conference paper. Writing a chapter was so exposing.

And there were other things happening in my life too. Everything else wasn't going well and that translated into my thesis. It was definitely things feeding into each other. It was one of those periods when as a student you think "I can't do this, it's too hard, my writing's not good enough, I'm not good enough." I've realised the actual writing process is incredibly hard and nothing had prepared me for it.

Now, I'm entering a new phase of the PhD. I'm getting used to writing. I'm training myself to be a better writer. I am doing four or five days' writing each week. I wrote myself a proper work schedule. It's sort of 8.30 to 10 o'clock sit at my computer and not get up for anything except to go to the toilet. At 10 o'clock I have a cup of tea and then back to the computer and so on through the day. If I didn't have my writing schedule I would just go off and do other stuff, like reading or doing internet research. I try to give myself one or two days a week when I don't write. I don't work after 8 o'clock at night. My brain just doesn't work at night. Then I realised I could be a bit more flexible. I could call my partner from the garden, sit and be idle for a short while and then go back to work. You have to spend some time working out how you work best, learning about yourself, what writing strategies work for you.

Anna: I Feel Like a Second-rate Person in my Department

Ever since I started studying it's been like, I was a second-rate person, just because of the topic that I was doing, it wasn't science. The other students in my department had a journal club, they got funding for their research and funding for equipment and to go to conferences, and the academics were all really interested in what they were doing. I felt as though, well, you know, I wanted to look after the environment, and I couldn't, there was no funding at all. I couldn't have a desk. I couldn't have anything and nobody had ever asked me the whole time, in a year and a half, they never asked me what I was doing. I suppose that got to me after a while. It made me think I was a second-rate person.

Judy: I Feel Well Supported by My Department

My supervisor is really excited about my topic and I feel really well supported by my department, having done my undergraduate and honours study there. I know the department is looking at transdisciplinary research at the moment, and the head is really keen to set this up. So it's good timing. It's like "Come into our fold because we need you, we need people to think about the environment." We have a meeting every Friday with all of the postgraduates in our department, and that is a very pleasurable thing. We bounce ideas off each other and it's a lovely social place as well as an intellectual exercise. Sometimes we have lunch together afterwards.

Myra: Some Days It Feels Like I Haven't Done a Thing

Some days you feel like you're never really getting to the task. In the morning you come in with a particular task in mind but then a whole lot of other demands are placed on you during the day. And suddenly it's time to go and pick up the kids. When you get home you want to continue the thought process you had started before you left uni, you want to turn on the computer and type up something, but the kids need to have afternoon tea and then you need to start making dinner. At the end of the day you may have done a myriad of things but because you haven't done that task that you really wanted to do, you don't have that sense of satisfaction.

The strategy I came to employ to try and get over the sense of never achieving anything is to write everything down. I just have a document open on the computer and I put thoughts there with the date. So when I run through the document later I can see "Oh I was thinking about. . . ." Another thing that works for me is self-monitoring. To make an effort to counteract that feeling of "I've done nothing today", I take time during the day to consciously remind myself that "I'm doing as much as I can with this hour, there's not much more I could have packed into it". That helps me think at the end of the day, "Whoa, I couldn't have done any more".

Miranda: You Can't Compare Yourself to Other People

I think in some ways I feel as though I have done a lot and then I think, "Oh no, I'm at the same stage." But I'm not. I think of the hours and hours I've spent doing analyses of the transcripts, and there will be tonnes more to come, and I think "Well you have done all that." Just because you're not constantly on it all the time you feel guilty.

I talked to another friend the other night and she's written 40,000 words, and we started the same year and I think "Oh how depressing", but she has more time to do it. Today I was talking to a PhD student who finished a couple of years ago, and he said "Just keep plodding along", but he used to put dreadful hours into it. Every night he worked, all the holidays and stuff. And I thought "Well I can't survive like that, I've got to have breaks, I've got to have holidays and I've got to have leisure."

I think there's actually a natural level at which you can progress, like absorbing ideas, thinking through your ideas. And sometimes you can't speed that up. So things I thought about two months ago I might think differently about now, because you had that time to think it through. You can't really compare yourself to other people. You've got to have your own sort of time line, and your own way of dealing with it, and be confident of that.

Lydia: I Don't Really Know What the Role of a Supervisor Is

A problem I find with being a student in the same university as my supervisor is I know what's happening to her time. So I'm less likely to demand her time. We've only had one meeting in the last year. Either she's busy, or I couldn't make it. She has Fridays set aside but Fridays aren't always suitable for me. So yes it's a mismatch really, finding the time.

I don't know if scheduling meetings is meant to come from me or her. Like, I feel I need her to motivate me. But I don't know whether her heart's in it. If her heart's not in it mine's not either. If your supervisor is not that interested in what you're doing then it doesn't allow the passion to bubble up as much. She's a fairly new academic and focused on career advancement. In many respects you're better to have someone who has done their career advancing, and they're willing to mentor people. They don't have any other agendas and they can give you their time.

But yeah, I don't know what to expect. I don't know what supervisors can do, or do do. I haven't got anything to compare with. It might be that I've just got to do it myself. I don't know what the role of the supervisor is to be quite honest.

Barbara: Changing Supervisors Worked for Me

Within months of transferring into the PhD my initial supervisor took a position in Queensland, and she felt it was appropriate that I stayed here and not follow her. She organised for Suzanne to become my new primary supervisor.

There was quite a big shift needed. It was a transfer of a whole relationship and a whole history, and I don't think we did enough transferring stuff and so I lost ground. Things went funny for quite a while, but then it got back on track. Suzanne and I—we then took off and it worked perfectly. It was a reshaping of my PhD so that it utilised her skills better. That was what was really needed. My initial supervisor and I had designed something that brought the two of us together beautifully, but then, when she went, Suzanne and I picked up the same process and tried to do it but you can't. It took us quite a while to realise that it wasn't working, and I don't know that we've even named it together yet but I think we acknowledged it. Together we redesigned the PhD to use her skills more. I don't think both Suzanne and I realised how huge that was but we got through it. Since then I've had a uniquely supportive path through postgrad.

Miranda: I Wouldn't Want to Change Supervisors Again

When you change supervisors you do sometimes think "I've been there before." My first primary supervisor and I had long discussions about whether I should interview students. Initially I was going to and then we came to the conclusion that I wouldn't. But then once again with Belinda, she was really pushing that I should interview students. And you think "I've been through all this and I've discussed it and I've explained why," and all of a sudden you've got to go through it all again with the new supervisor. It just feels as though you've gone backwards. It just annoyed me. It made me angry actually. I wouldn't want to change supervisors again.

Having said that I wouldn't want to change supervisors again, six months later I find myself doing just that. After I did my progress seminar I was discussing some of my comments with Belinda, and it made me realise that she didn't really know what I was trying to do, and didn't or couldn't understand conceptually the theoretical approach I was using. And she realised that too. So we both came to the same conclusion that she wasn't the most appropriate supervisor. We tried to think of people who might be more appropriate, but we couldn't come up with anyone. So then I raised the idea of transferring to another university. So I went to another university and talked to Fronz and just talking to him, within five minutes, it was just amazing, he completely understood where I was at. I almost burst into tears. So I moved institutions. And that was a draining process in itself, so many forms to fill in! Eventually the approval came through and I started with my new primary supervisor. I feel as though I lost another six months in this second change of supervisors. But it also felt like I was going forwards, as finally I had found the right supervisor.

Barbara: It's Really All about Balancing Living

My son was diagnosed with multiple sclerosis last year. That was the time when I thought "What am I doing?" That's the time when you sort of wanted to stop everything. I also felt that no matter what I said to him, if I stopped things in my life he'd know that and that would be even harder for him to handle. So I sat up in hospital next to him with the laptop computer and this was actually really good. He actually sat with only one hand working typing my PhD. In actual fact it was a really strong moment in our family life. It was also horrendous, but the fact that we sort of pulled together to help him through that first attack, and part of that was him helping me do the PhD.

It made me realise that juggling those things actually teaches you something about the complexity of life, and that there's always competing values, and that part of your job in life is to be thinking and rethinking. I'd learned some skills of hard-nosed thinking and then heart-felt thinking about my priorities, and that's what is at the heart of the balancing act. At first I thought I was really only balancing my role as academic and the research side of things, but they don't separate out that easily. It's really all about balancing living.

Learning from Students' Experiences

This section contextualises the emotions of students' stories presented in the previous section within the wider student experience literature on emotionality and research candidature. It then highlights the learning drawn from the emotional rollercoaster of students' experience.

"Certain qualities are needed to do a research degree and the main ones are emotional in nature" (Vilkinas, 2005b). Research students report a range of emotions during their candidature (Nyquist et al., 1999; Parsons, 1999; Salmon, 1992; Vilkinas, 2005a). Different stages of candidature, Parsloe (1993) suggests, are characterised by different emotions. The excitement of beginning research and collecting data can be rapidly overtaken by feelings of confusion and anxiety. Writing up and thesis examination can be times of both pleasure and anxiety. Lee and Williams (1999) note the trauma of research student experience, likening it to a "trial by fire". Lamm (2004, p. 12) reports the "agony of cultural dislocation" for a student who felt "torn between the culture of the thesis, home and studies". Students commonly draw on metaphors to help them make sense of these emotions (Appel and Dahlgren, 2003; Bartlett and Mercer, 1999). The strength of students' emotional investment in their research, and their experience of candidature, emerges as a key finding from this literature, suggesting the role of emotion in postgraduate research student experience as a topic for further investigation.

The students' stories told in this chapter tell of times of intense, often conflicting, emotions; times of feeling "at home" (feeling balanced) and times of "unhomliness" (feeling unbalanced). There were times when students felt comfortable and confident with their topics, their time management, their progress and their writing. Students experienced "unhomliness" at times of: struggle to come to terms with the mismatch of institutional values and expectations with their own; receiving mixed messages or overtly negative messages regarding support for their research; or when self-doubt and a sense of being alone (invisible, isolated, without voice or connection) overtook them.

Interaction with supervisors is one context where students experience "a range of heightened emotions" (Lamm, 2004, p. 1). Increasing the visibility of these emotions, and the strategies students employ to negotiate them, is particularly important in today's doctoral research context, because it has been suggested that the quality of the supervisor–student interactions can directly influence the quality of the doctoral experience and its outcomes for students. "A good match between student and adviser makes the relationship mutually fruitful and satisfying" (Golde and Dore, 2001, p. 35). Unsatisfactory supervisory relationships have been implicated in student withdrawal or failure to complete (Latona and Browne, 2001; Lovitts, 2001). Shorter completion time has been associated with keeping the same supervisor throughout, keeping the same dissertation topic, developing a close relationship with the supervisor, meeting frequently with the supervisor, a fast turnaround time for material submitted to supervisors and collaborating with the supervisor on papers (Seagram et al., 1998).

In the stories of candidature reported in this chapter, the heart of the research student experience, the supervisor–student relationship, illustrates how common dilemmas (such as developing relationships with supervisors, meeting with supervisors, changing supervisors, supervisor absence or lack of support) are played out in individuals' experiences, and made visible through their emotional rollercoaster ride. The emotional ups and downs of changing supervisor, for example, were evident in Miranda's account of feeling like she was going backwards, then forwards, then backwards again and finally going forwards. When students needed their supervisor's support, supervisors were often noticeable by their absence, as when Anna sought conference funding, or when she sought her supervisor's support when she discovered another student was plagiarising her work: "There was nobody I could go and talk to about it. So I just had to put up with it. My supervisor didn't really get involved" (McCormack, 2001, p. 312). Supervisors were noticeably absent from Grace's experience of presenting her first conference paper, an experience she described as being out on a limb where fears of not being good enough weighed heavily on her, but also an experience of excitement and validation of her topic and her self as a researcher.

All of the students' stories speak of feeling the need to consciously and continually rebalance following times of becoming unbalanced. Looking across their experiences this rebalancing can be seen at two levels: at the big picture (rethinking the experience) and at the small picture (chipping away). Each of the small things by themselves may not look particularly important, but, as Jo said, they make an enormous difference, when taken together, to balancing work, postgraduate study and other life spheres.

The Future for Postgraduate Research Students

Globally, the traditional beliefs and practices of doctoral education have been, and will continue to be, challenged by changing student demographics, the changing knowledge economy, and its expectations of universities as knowledge producers, and of doctoral students as knowledge workers, the internationalisation of doctoral education, the explosion of communication technology, and continuing demands for accountability (Enders, 2004; Nerad, 2006; Park, 2005; Pearson, 1999; Williams, 2005).

In a discussion of globalisation and its impact on research education, Nerad (2006) has noted that, in today's changing knowledge economy, the knowledge of interest is that related to economic performance and this interest, she observes, is reflected in the global expansion of doctoral awards in science and engineering. In 2002, for example, she notes that 60% of PhDs awarded in the USA, New Zealand, France and Germany were in the fields of science and engineering. Science and engineering PhD graduates were even more common in China, where two-thirds of awards were granted to students in these fields. Immediately, the question that comes to mind is: whose knowledge is being valued in a rapidly globalising world, and what is the future for students whose knowledge is not valued? In the knowledge economy of the future, the potential exists for doctoral education to become a site of heightened tension regarding what constitutes legitimate doctoral knowledge outcomes. Will the PhD continue to be primarily a site of knowledge discovery, or will the PhD of the twenty-first century be a site for preparation of knowledge workers rather than knowledge creators? While this tension is not necessarily new to doctoral educators or students in industrial economies, such as Australia, Europe, USA and the UK, its resolution will become a topic of more urgent debate for all economies.

Associated with this growing concern over the nature and purpose of the PhD has been (and will continue to be) increased international and national attention on student time to completion, student attrition and the quality of supervision (Bawa, 2005; Golde, 2006; Holdaway, 1996; Kehm, 2005; McAlpine and Norton, 2006; McCormack, 2005; Neumann, 2007; Taylor, 2006; Visser et al., 2007). Even though the quality of supervision is among the key global concerns, there seems to be little regulation of "who can supervise" at a national level. Powell and Green (2007, p. 252) report that, in Japan, "supervision appears to be far more regulated at a national level than in other countries" (with the possible exception of China). Across the European Community it is being suggested that all countries adopt a common performance review framework for supervisors

(European University Association, 2007). More often, however, individual institutions establish their own system of supervisor accreditation or registration. Supervisor skill development programmes have been evident in association with registration and accreditation systems in Australia and the United Kingdom (Brew and Peseta, 2004; McCormack and Pamphilon, 2004; Neumann, 2007; Park, 2005). Conceptualising and implementing supervisor training challenges programme developers to consider the current and future role of supervisors, and the purpose of supervision, but will this flurry of supervisor "training" flow on to improved supervision and enhanced student experience? Also, in focusing on systems of regulation and training of supervisors, are we focusing on the "easy" changes, while consigning to the "too hard" basket important issues around complexity and the diversity of the individual student/supervisor experience?

While there is commonality globally in the broad areas of challenge, calls for "more studies on the impact of globalization locally" have emerged (Nerad, 2006, p. 11). Local research by Neumann (2007) suggests that the global demand for accountability in research education, reflected nationally in Australia in changing government policies, has driven change in three areas: the nature of research topics, supervision practices and selection of students into research programmes. In the humanities and social science disciplines, in the institutions participating in her research, the focus was "on 'do-able' projects within the government's specified time frame of three years' (p. 465). Evans et al. (2005b) have also noted the tendency to "risk manage" the doctoral experience by encouraging students "to take 'outcome insurance' by keeping to safe territory" (p. 10). Changes in supervisory practices observed by Neumann (2007) include the emergence and normalisation of "fast supervision" (Green and Usher, 2003), where the emphasis of the supervisor is on timely completion.

For individual students globalisation has brought both benefits and risks. Inter-institution mobility of students is beginning, and more opportunities for students to engage internationally are slowly emerging. New types of doctorate are emerging, such as professional doctorates, industry-based doctoral programmes, doctorates by project, publication or portfolio (Clerke and Lee, 2008; Kehm, 2006; Leonard et al., 2006; Park, 2005). New communication technologies (such as blogs) will create further opportunities for students to communicate across time and space.

However, researchers have also noted some risks for particular student groups. Pearson et al. (2008) note that the tendency in a global economy to classify, categorise and normalise research students within homogenous statistical groupings, such as age or enrollment status, masks the diversity within these groupings. In Australia, Evans et al. (2005a) and Neumann (2007) have suggested that the increased selectivity in student recruitment for those student groups most likely to complete raises social justice and equity concerns. Neumann (2007) noted that, in science and engineering, "the unspoken policy was to give preference to full-time students" (p. 471).

That postgraduate research can be a time of personal transformation is evident in the doctoral education literature (Bartlett and Mercer, 1999; Heinrich, 2000; Kapitzke, 1998; Lamm, 2004; McCormack, 2001; Ngunjiri, 2007). Leonard et al. (2004) found UK research students were as concerned with personal growth as with vocational development. Also in the UK, Butterfield (1997) noted an emphasis on personal outcomes (curiosity, fulfillment and challenge). In a recent Australian study of doctoral graduates (Western et al., 2007), intrinsic reasons (such as personal satisfaction) were strong drivers for all graduates, but especially for women and students in the humanities, arts and social sciences. However, as Brew (2001, p. 13) suggests, research "as a process of personal and social learning is left out of the economic model" dominating today's doctoral education contexts. Will students with such a conception of research become, like dinosaurs, extinct in the (doctoral) landscape? If such students are missing from the future research student population, does this matter?

If the dilemma of future doctoral education is, as described by Enders (2004, p. 427), "how to be simultaneously standardized and pluralized, large and small, formal and informal", then research students will be positioned in the liminal in-between space (Bhabha, 1994) of the contact zone, a space "where disparate cultures meet, clash, and grapple with each other, often in highly asymmetrical relations of domination and subordination" (Pratt, 1992, p. 4). The stories told in this chapter suggest strategies that will support future research students to effectively negotiate the emotional rollercoaster, and the stresses of juggling multiple life roles, amidst the challenges and opportunities of this contested space.

References

Appel, M.L. and Dahlgren, L.G. (2003). Swedish doctoral students' experiences on their journey towards a PhD: obstacles and opportunities inside and outside the academic building. *Scandinavian Journal of Educational Research*, 47(1), pp. 89–110.

Bartlett, A. and Mercer, G. (1999). Cooking up a feast: finding metaphors for feminist postgraduate supervisions. *Australian Feminist Studies*, 14(30), pp. 367–375.

Bawa, A. (2005). The PhD and South Africa's research capacity. Paper presented to the conference *Forces and Forms of Change in Doctoral Education Internationally*, organised by the Centre for Innovation and Research in Graduate Education, 6–9 September 2005, Seattle, USA. Available online at: http://depts.washington.edu/cirgeweb/c/global-network/forces-and-forms-global-network/forces-and-forms-i/commissioned-papers/ (accessed 29 April 2008).

Bazeley, P. (1999). Continuing research by PhD graduates. *Higher Education Quarterly*, 53(4), pp. 333–352.

Bhabha, H. (1994). *The location of culture* (London and New York: Routledge).

Brew, A. (2001). *The nature of research. Inquiry into academic contexts* (London: Routledge).

Brew, A. and Peseta, T. (2004). Changing postgraduate supervision practice: A programme to encourage learning through reflection and feedback. *Innovations in Education and Teaching International*, 41(1), pp. 5–22.

Butterfield, S. (1997). "Making a difference": purposes and perspectives on part-time research degree students in Education. *British Journal of In-service Education*, 23(3), pp. 363–374.

Byrne-Armstrong, H., Higgs, J. and Horsfall, D. (2001). *Critical moments in qualitative research* (Oxford: Butterworth).

Clandinin, D.J. (1985). Personal practical knowledge: a study of teachers' classroom images. *Curriculum Inquiry*, 15(4), pp. 361–385.

Clerke, T. and Lee, A. (2008). Mainstreaming the doctoral portfolio. Paper to the *8th Quality in Postgraduate Research Conference: Research Education in the New Global Environment*, 17–18 April 2008, Adelaide, South Australia.

Comber, B. (1999). Shifting gears: learning to work the discourses of academic research, in: A. Holbrook and S. Johnston (eds) *Supervision of postgraduate research education* (Coldstream, Victoria, Australia, Australian Association for Research in Education), 131–136.

Denzin, N.K. (1994). The art and politics of interpretation, in: N.K. Denzin and Y.S. Lincoln (eds) *Handbook of qualitative research* (Thousand Oaks: Sage), 500–515.

Enders, J. (2004). Research training and careers in transition: a European perspective on the many faces of the Ph.D. *Studies in Continuing Education*, 26(3), pp. 419–429.

European University Association (2007). *Doctoral programmes in European universities: achievements and challenges*. Report prepared for European Universities and Ministers of Higher Education. Available online at: http://www.eua.be/fileadmin/user_upload/files/Publications/Doctoral_Programmes_in_Europe_s_Universities.pdf (accessed 12 December 2007).

Evans, B. (2007). Doctoral education in Australia, in: S. Powell and H. Green (eds) *The doctorate worldwide* (Buckingham: Open University Press), 105–119.

Evans, T., Evans, B. and Marsh, H. (2005a). International doctoral conference commissioned paper: Australia. Paper presented to the conference *Forces and Forms of Change in Doctoral Education Internationally*, organised by the Centre for Innovation and Research in Graduate Education, 6–9 September 2005, Seattle, USA. Available online at: http://depts.washington.edu/cirgeweb/c/global-network/forces-and-forms-global-network/forces-and-forms-i/commissioned-papers/ (accessed 29 April 2008).

Evans, T., Lawson, A., McWilliam, E. and Taylor, P. (2005b). Understanding the management of doctoral studies in Australia as risk management. *Studies in Research*, 1, pp. 1–11.

Golde, C.M. (2006). Preparing stewards of the discipline, in: C.M. Golde and G.E. Walker, and associates (eds) *Envisioning the future of doctoral education. Preparing stewards of the discipline* (San Francisco, CA, Jossey-Bass), 3–20.

Golde, C.M. and Dore, T.M. (2001). *At cross purposes: what the experiences of doctoral students reveal about doctoral education* (Philadelphia, PA: Pew Charitable Trusts).

Green, P. and Usher, R. (2003). Fast supervision: changing supervisory practice in changing times. *Studies in Continuing Education*, 25(1), pp. 37–50.

Grumet, M.R. (1991). The politics of personal knowledge, in: C. Witherall and N. Noddings (eds) *Stories lives tell. Narrative and dialogue in education* (New York: Teachers College Press), 66–77.

Guomundsson, H.K. (2005). Doctorates and doctoral studies in the Nordic countries. A short overview. Paper presented to the conference *Forces and Forms of Change in Doctoral Education Internationally*, organised by the

Centre for Innovation and Research in Graduate Education, 6–9 September 2005, Seattle, USA. Available online at: http://depts.washington.edu/cirgeweb/c/global-network/forces-and-forms-global-network/forces-and-forms-i/commissioned-papers/ (accessed 29 April 2008).

Heinrich, K.T. (2000). The passionate scholar: a mid-life, woman doctoral student's quest for a voice. *International Journal of Qualitative Studies in Education, 12*(1), pp. 63–83.

Holdaway, E.A. (1996). Current issues in graduate education. *Journal of Higher Education Policy and Management, 18*(1), pp. 59–74.

Kapitzke, C. (1998). Narrative in a doctoral narrative: reflections on postgraduate study and pedagogy. *Australian Educational Researcher, 25*(2), pp. 95–111.

Kehm, B.M. (2005). Forces and forms of change: doctoral education in Germany within the European framework. Paper presented to the conference *Forces and Forms of Change in Doctoral Education Internationally*, organised by the Centre for Innovation and Research in Graduate Education, 6–9 September 2005, Seattle, USA. Available online at: http://depts.washington.edu/cirgeweb/c/global-network/forces-and-forms-global-network/forces-and-forms-i/commissioned-papers/ (accessed 29 April 2008).

Kehm, B.M. (2006). Doctoral education in Europe and North America: a comparative analysis. Wenner Gren International Series, 83, pp. 673–78. Available online at: http://www.portlandpress.com/pp/books/online/fyos/083/0067/0830067.pdf (accessed 28 April 2008).

Kehm, B.M. (2007). Quo vadis doctoral education? New European approaches in the context of global changes. *European Journal of Education, 42*(3), pp. 307–319.

Kiley, M. and Wisker, G. (2008). "Now you see it, now you don't": identifying and supporting the achievement of doctoral work which embraces threshold concepts and crosses conceptual thresholds. Abstract for a paper presented at the second biennial Symposium on Threshold Concepts, June 18–20 2008, Queens University, Kingston, Ontario, Canada. Available online at: http://thresholdconcepts.appsci.queensu.ca/documents/MargaretKiley.doc (accessed 22 April 2008).

Lamm, R. (2004). Learning and affect in the research higher degree. Paper to the *Australian Association for Research in Education Conference: Doing the Public Good*, November 28–December 2, 2004, Melbourne, Australia.

Latona, K. and Browne, M. (2001). Factors associated with completion of research higher degrees. *Higher Education Series*, 37, Department of Education, Training and Youth Affairs, Canberra, Australia.

Lee, A. and Williams, C. (1999). "Forged in fire" narratives of trauma in PhD supervision pedagogy. *Southern Review, 32*(1), pp. 6–26.

Leonard, D., Becker, R. and Coate, K. (2004). Continuing professional and career development: the doctoral experience of education alumni at a UK university. *Studies in Continuing Education, 26*(3), pp. 269–386.

Leonard, D., Metcalfe, J., Becker, R. and Evans, J. (2006). Review of the literature on the impacts of working context and support on the postgraduate research student learning experience. Available online at: http://www.npc.org.uk/whatiswherecanifindhowdoi/Useful_Documents/DoctoralExperienceReview.pdf (accessed 25 April 2008).

Lovitts, B.E. (2001). *Leaving the ivory tower. The causes and consequences of departure from doctoral study* (London: Rowman and Littlefield).

McAlpine, L. and Norton, J. (2006). Reframing our approach to doctoral programs: an integrative framework for action and research, *Higher Education Research and Development, 25*(1), pp. 3–17.

McCormack, C. (2001). *The times of our lives: women, leisure and postgraduate research.* Doctoral dissertation, University of Wollongong, Australia.

McCormack, C. (2004). Storying stories: a narrative approach to in-depth interview conversations. *International Journal of Social Research Methodology, 7*(2), pp. 219–236.

McCormack, C. (2005). Is non-completion a failure or a new beginning? Research non-completion from a student's perspective. *Higher Education Research and Development, 24*(3), pp. 233–247.

McCormack, C. and Pamphilon, B. (2000). Paths, phases, juggling and balancing acts: how women academics understand their personal experience of postgraduate study, in: M. Kiley and G. Mullins (eds) *Quality in postgraduate research: making ends meet* Conference Proceedings (Adelaide: The Advisory Centre for University Education, The University of Adelaide), 191–202.

McCormack, C. and Pamphilon, B. (2004). More than a confessional: postmodern groupwork to support postgraduate supervisors' professional development. *Innovations in Education and Teaching International, 41*(1), pp. 23–37.

Meek, L.V. and Wood, F.Q. (1998). Managing higher education diversity in a climate of public sector reform (Canberra: Department of Education, Employment and Youth Affairs, Commonwealth of Australia).

Melrose, M. (2003). *The history of postgraduate education in New Zealand: where have we been and where are we likely to go from here?* A paper to the Higher Education Research and Development Society of Australasia Conference Learning for an Unknown Future, University of Canterbury, Christchurch, New Zealand, 6–9 July 2003.

Miller, N. and Brimicombe, A. (2004). Mapping research journeys across complex terrain with heavy baggage. *Studies in Continuing Education, 26*(3), pp. 405–417.

Nerad, M. (2006). Globalization and its impact on research education: trends and emerging best practices for the doctorate of the future, in: M. Kiley and G. Mullins (eds) *Quality in postgraduate research: knowledge creation in testing times* (Canberra: Australian National University), 5–12.

Neumann, R. (2007). Policy and practice in doctoral education. *Studies in Higher Education, 32*(4), pp. 459–473.

Neumann, A. and Peterson, P.L. (1997). Researching lives: women, scholarship and autobiography in education, in: A. Neumann and P.L. Peterson (eds) *Learning from our lives: women, research and autobiography in education* (New York: Teachers College Press), 1–17.

Ngunjiri, F.W. (2007). Painting a counter-narrative of African womanhood: reflections on how my research transformed me.

Journal of Research Practice, 3(1). Available online at: http://jrp.icaap.org/index.php/jrp/article/viewArticle/53/76 (accessed 24 July 2007).

Nyquist, J.D. (2002). The PhD. A tapestry of change for the 21st century. *Change*, Nov/Dec, pp. 13–20.

Nyquist, J.D., Manning, L., Wulff, D.H., Austin, A.E., Sprague, J., Fraser, P.K., Calcagno, C. and Woodford, B. (1999). On the road to becoming a professor. The graduate student experience. *Change*, May/June, pp. 18–27.

Park, C. (2005). New variant PhD: the changing nature of the doctorate in the UK. *Journal of Higher Education Policy and Management*, 27(2), pp. 189–207.

Parsloe, P. (1993). Supervising students for higher degrees by research in a social work department. *Journal of Further and Higher Education*, 17(3), pp. 49–60.

Parsons, M. (1999). The dark side of a Ph.D: learning the lessons that supervisors don't teach, in: A. Bartlett and G. Mercer (eds) *Postgraduate research supervision. Transforming (R)elations* (New York: Peter Lang) pp. 189–193.

Pearson, M. (1999). The changing environment for doctoral education in Australia: implications for quality management, improvement and innovation. *Higher Education Research and Development*, 18(3), pp. 269–287.

Pearson, M., Evans, T. and Macauley, P. (2007). Growth and diversity in doctoral education: assessing the Australian experience. *Higher Education*. Available online at: http://www.springerlink.com.ezproxy2.canberra.edu.au/content/p121u24645683qp4/fulltext.pdf (accessed 6 January 2008).

Pearson, M., Cumming, J., Evans, T., Macauley, P. and Ryland, K. (2008). Problematising diversity in doctoral education and the implications and for policy and practice. Symposium at the *8th Quality in Postgraduate Research Conference: Research Education in the New Global Environment*, 17–18 April 2008, Adelaide, South Australia.

Powell, S. and Green, H. (2007). Conclusions, in: S. Powell and H. Green (eds) *The doctorate worldwide* (Maidenhead: Open University Press), 231–260.

Pratt, M. (1992). *Imperial eyes. Travel writing and transculturation* (London and New York: Routledge).

Ribeiro, R.J. (2007). Doctoral education in Brazil, in: S. Powell and H. Green (eds) *The doctorate worldwide* (Maidenhead: Open University Press), 144–154.

Salmon, P. (1992). *Achieving a PhD—ten students' experience* (Stoke-on-Trent, Trentham Books).

Seagram, B.C., Gould, J. and Pyke, S.W. (1998). An investigation of gender and other variables on time to completion of doctoral degrees. *Research in Higher Education*, 39(3), pp. 319–335.

Taylor, C. (2006). Heeding the voices of graduate students and postdocs, in: C.M. Golde and G.E. Walker, and associates (eds) *Envisioning the future of doctoral education. Preparing stewards of the discipline* (San Francisco, CA: Jossey-Bass), 46–61.

Vilkinas, T. (ed.) (2005a). *The thesis journey: tales of personal triumph* (Frenchs Forest, Pearson Education).

Vilkinas, T. (2005b). Emotional encounters of the PhD kind. Available online at: http://www.unisa.edu.au/unisanews/2005/April/emotional.asp (accessed 26 April 2008).

Visser, M.S., Luwel, M. and Moed, H.F. (2007). The attainment of doctoral degrees at Flemish universities: a survival analysis. *Higher Education*, 54, pp. 741–757.

Western, M., Kubler, M., Western, J., Clague, D., Boreham, P., Laffan, W. and Lawson, A. (2007). *PhD graduates 5 to 7 years out: employment outcomes, job attributes and the quality of research training* (Canberra, Department of Education, Science and Training).

Williams, G. (2005). *Doctoral education in Canada 1900–2005* (Ottawa: Canadian Association for Graduate Studies).

Woodrow Wilson National Fellowship Foundation (2005). *Diversity and the PH.D. A review of efforts to broaden race and ethnicity in U.S. doctoral education.* Executive summary. Available online at: http://www.woodrow.org/images/pdf/resphd/WW_Diversity_PhD_ExecSum.pdf (accessed 8 January 2008).

Zhuang, L. (2007). Doctoral education in China, in: S. Powell and H. Green (eds) *The doctorate worldwide* (Maidenhead: Open University Press), 155–167.

V
Quality

Any reasonable discussion of how quality in higher education can, should be and is determined must be nuanced. As the chapters in this section illustrate, there are many ways by which quality is currently gauged within higher education and in the popular press. As Usher and Savino note in their chapter, these differences are often a reflection of the reason for determining quality in the first place. The goal may be a kind of popular ranking for the use of prospective students, such as produced by *McLeans* or *The Times Higher Education Supplement*. Or, quite differently, the goal may be the development of a kind of self-generating "quality culture", as described by Dano and Stensaker. Or the goal may simply be the maintenance of minimum standards, as is typically the case with conventional forms of accreditation.

Quality is a term that is often used by those inside and outside higher education to describe very different things. In the chapters by Usher and Savino, and Dano and Stensaker, the type of quality assurance being analysed is likely a product of what Neave (1988) terms as "the rise of the evaluative state", or, as Taylor describes in his chapter, the need for new means of governmental monitoring in an era of neo-liberalism and increased massification.

Quality assessment can be carried out at the student, institutional, national or supra-national level. The first two chapters of this section focus on the level of the student learner. In the first chapter, Richardson discusses the role of student evaluations and, in the process, identifies several reasons why students are asked to evaluate their courses, instructors, and institutions. While teaching evaluations have been in place for a long time, new advances in student evaluation, such as the National Survey of Student Engagement in the US, highlight different reasons to seek student input into quality monitoring. Ultimately, however, the vagaries and ambiguities of the teaching and learning experience make it very difficult to measure students' experience inside and outside the classroom. Nonetheless, factors such as institutional culture are often powerful predictors of how students will describe their experiences.

Yorke's discussion on grading is illuminating because, as he points out, grading is so ubiquitous and normative in higher education that, paradoxically, it may seem unworthy of analysis. The chapter highlights our acceptance of the subjectivity of grading, even as it documents our investigation of related topics such as grade inflation. This may be, as Yorke highlights, because even when standards and rubrics are formally applied by instructors, there is significant disciplinary and institutional variation in grading that is exacerbated by the instructor's sense of "quality".

Taylor's chapter moves the lens to the problem of national monitoring, and highlights how changing realities have brought with them an increased focus on auditing quality at the national level. He identifies privatisation and massification as two examples, and points out how new types of monitoring also provide new means for higher education institutions to communicate their distinctiveness and quality to important external constituents. In this sense, national monitoring can be seen as part of the new competitive marketplace in many countries where little competition existed previously.

The relationship between accountability and improvement is the focus of the chapter by Dano and Stensaker. They provide a survey of quality assurance policies in four of the five Nordic countries, in an attempt to determine how different countries' policies may both ensure accountability and produce improvement. The push for harmonisation and compatibility that is illustrated by movements like Bologna highlights the importance of this chapter. At the same time, the difficulty of constructing and applying equitable standards across institutional types remains an ongoing concern.

The final chapter provides a comprehensive analysis of university rankings and league tables. In this chapter, Usher and Savino show how the differences in the criteria used by the various ranking organisations are a function of very different ideas about what constitutes quality. That university rankings can produce very different results—with the exception of a small number of elite universities—suggest that these tools are both institutionally constructed and varied in their conception of how laypersons and those inside higher education identify quality.

Reference

Neave, G. (1988). On the cultivation of quality, efficiency and enterprise: an overview of recent trends in higher education in Western Europe, 1986–88. *European Journal of Education, 23*(1–2), 7–28.

15

What Can Students' Perceptions of Academic Quality Tell Us?

Research Using the Course Experience Questionnaire

John T. E. Richardson

In higher education, student feedback is collected for a wide variety of purposes. Sometimes, students are asked to provide evaluations of individual teachers or course units. Marsh and Dunkin (1992) identified four purposes for collecting such evaluations: diagnostic feedback to teachers about the effectiveness of their teaching; a measure of teaching effectiveness to be used in administrative decision-making; information for students to use in the selection of course units and teachers; and an outcome or process measure for use in research on teaching. The routine collection of students' evaluations does not in itself lead to any improvement in the quality of teaching (Kember *et al.*, 2002), but it can help in the professional development of individual teachers, particularly when supported by an appropriate process of consultation and counselling (Roche and Marsh, 2002). Nevertheless, evaluations of this sort provide little information about the students' experience of their programmes or institutions as a whole.

Several questionnaires have been devised to obtain feedback from students about their institutions or degree programmes. Two such instruments are widely used across the United States. The National Survey of Student Engagement is administered annually to first-year and final-year students at four-year colleges (Kuh *et al.*, 2001, pp. 55–72, 163–180); here, the idea of engagement is defined as "the quality of effort students themselves devote to educationally purposeful activities that contribute directly to desired outcomes" (Hu and Kuh, 2002, p. 555). The Noel-Levitz Student Satisfaction Inventory is based upon consumer theory: it measures students' expectations and satisfaction with regard to different aspects of their programmes, and it is administered in all years of undergraduate programmes at 800 institutions (*National Student Satisfaction and Priorities Report*, 2007). In England, Wales and Northern Ireland, the National Student Survey was introduced in 2005 to obtain student feedback from all final-year undergraduate students on the quality of their programmes (Richardson *et al.*, 2007).

The instrument that has been most widely used for quality assurance purposes is the Course Experience Questionnaire (CEQ), which since 1993 has been used in annual surveys of recent graduates from Australian universities. In the first part of this chapter, I shall argue that in its original forms the CEQ is a robust tool that can be used in a variety of countries, in a variety of institutions, in a variety of disciplines and with a variety of student populations. In the second part,

I shall refer to different studies that show how students' responses to the CEQ reflect important characteristics of their academic context and are systematically related to their approaches to studying, their academic engagement and their personal development.

The Course Experience Questionnaire

The CEQ was devised by Ramsden (1991a) as a performance indicator for monitoring the quality of teaching on individual programmes of study at Australian universities. In the light of preliminary evidence, a national trial of the CEQ was commissioned by a group set up by the Australian Commonwealth Department of Employment, Education and Training to examine performance indicators in higher education (Linke, 1991). In this national trial, usable responses to the CEQ were obtained from 3,372 final-year undergraduate students at 13 Australian universities and colleges of advanced education (see also Ramsden, 1991b).

The instrument used in this trial consisted of 30 items in five scales which had been identified in previous research as reflecting different dimensions of effective instruction: good teaching (8 items); clear goals and standards (5 items); appropriate workload (5 items); appropriate assessment (6 items); and emphasis on independence (6 items). The defining items of the five scales (according to the results of the national trial) are shown in Table 15.1. In addition, three of the items in the Appropriate Assessment scale could be used as a subscale to tap students' perceptions of the importance of rote memory as opposed to understanding in academic assessment.

The respondents were instructed to indicate their level of agreement or disagreement (along a scale from "definitely agree", scoring 5, to "definitely disagree", scoring 1) with each statement as a description of their programme of study. Half of the items referred to positive aspects, whereas the other half referred to negative aspects and were to be scored in reverse. This means that the instrument as a whole controlled for any systematic response biases, either to agree with all of the items or to disagree with all of the items (unfortunately, the items to be scored in reverse were not distributed equally across the five CEQ scales).

As a result of this national trial, it was determined that the Graduate Careers Council of Australia (GCCA) should administer the CEQ on an annual basis to all new graduates through the Graduate Destination Survey, which is conducted a few months after the completion of their degree programmes. The survey of the 1992 graduates was carried out in 1993, and obtained usable responses to the CEQ from more than 50,000 graduates from 30 institutions of higher education (Ainley and Long, 1994). Subsequent surveys have covered all Australian universities, and have typically obtained usable responses to the CEQ from more than 80,000 graduates, reflecting overall response rates of around 60% (Ainley and Long, 1995; Johnson, 1997, 1998, 1999; Johnson et al., 1996; Long

Table 15.1 Defining Items of the Scales in the Original Course Experience Questionnaire

Scale	Defining item
Good Teaching	Teaching staff here normally give helpful feedback on how you are doing.
Clear Goals and Standards	You usually have a clear idea of where you're going and what's expected of you in this course.
Appropriate Workload	The sheer volume of work to be got through in this course means you can't comprehend it all thoroughly.*
Appropriate Assessment	Staff here seem more interested in testing what we have memorised than what we have understood.*
Emphasis on Independence	Students here are given a lot of choice in the work they have to do.

Note. Items with asterisks are negatively worded and are to be coded in reverse.

and Hillman, 2000). However, in the GCCA surveys, the original version of the CEQ has been modified in certain respects.

First, in response to concerns about the employability of graduates, a Generic Skills scale was added to "investigate the extent to which higher education contributes to the enhancement of skills relevant to employment" (Ainley and Long, 1994, p. xii). This contained six items that are concerned with problem-solving, analytic skills, teamwork, communication and work planning. The items in the Generic Skills scale are somewhat different from those in the rest of the CEQ, insofar as they ask respondents to evaluate the skills that they have gained from their programmes rather than the quality of the programmes themselves.

Second, to compensate for this and to reduce the length of the questionnaire still further, the Emphasis on Independence scale was dropped. This was a curious decision, since most academics would agree that a key aim of higher education was to foster independent thinking in students. A further seven items were removed on the grounds that they had shown only a weak relationship with the scales to which they had been assigned in Ramsden's (1991a; 1991b, p. 6) analysis of the data from the Australian national trial. This produced a revised, short form of the CEQ consisting of 23 items in five scales.

Third, two other items were employed but not assigned to any of the scales. One measured the respondents' general level of satisfaction with their programmes, and this has proved to be helpful in validating the CEQ as an index of perceived academic quality. An additional item in the first two surveys was concerned with the extent to which respondents perceived their programmes to be overly theoretical or abstract. This was replaced in the next three surveys by reinstating an item from the Appropriate Assessment scale that measured the extent to which feedback on their work was usually provided only in the form of marks or grades. In subsequent surveys, this in turn was replaced by a wholly new item concerned with whether the assessment methods required an in-depth understanding of the syllabus. In practice, however, the responses to these additional items have not shown a strong relationship with those given to other items from the Appropriate Assessment scale, and so they have not been used in computing the respondents' scale scores.

Given that there are two different versions of the CEQ, the original 30-item version and the revised 23-item version, which one should researchers and practitioners use? Wilson et al. (1997) proposed that, for research purposes, the original version of the CEQ should be augmented with the Generic Skills scale to yield a 36-item questionnaire. They presented findings obtained using the short, 23-item version and this 36-item version with successive cohorts of graduates from one Australian university, and both seemed satisfactory. Many researchers also include the general satisfaction item, not as part of the CEQ, but as a 37th item to validate the CEQ as a measure of students' perceptions of quality.

The CEQ was originally devised to measure graduates' perceptions of the quality of their degree programmes. Even so, it can also be used to monitor the perceptions of currently enrolled students (Ginns et al., 2007). In the same way, the National Student Survey was originally intended to be used with recent graduates in England, Wales and Northern Ireland, but for practical reasons was turned into a survey of final-year students (Richardson et al., 2007). The CEQ has also been used to collect feedback on particular course units (Gibbs and Lucas, 1996; Lawless and Richardson, 2002; Lucas et al., 1997; Richardson, 2003, 2005a).

The CEQ was also originally devised to measure the purely academic quality of degree programmes. It did not contain any items concerned with the pastoral, physical or social support of students. Indeed, Wilson et al. (1997) found that students' satisfaction with their institution's facilities was only a weak predictor of their general satisfaction with their programmes. Nevertheless, McInnis et al. (2001) devised six additional scales intended to measure perceptions of student support, learning resources, course organisation, learning community, graduate qualities and intellectual motivation. Richardson (2005a) found that, when used along with the original CEQ scales, the new scales tended to dominate the students' responses. This suggests that they perceive the extended CEQ to be concerned with informal aspects of higher education (such as learning resources and support systems), rather than the more formal aspects of the curriculum that usually define teaching quality.

Even so, the new scales have been incorporated into the national quality assurance process in Australia. Since 2002, universities have been required to use the Good Teaching scale, the Generic Skills scale, and the general satisfaction item in surveys of their graduates. They may also include up to eight additional scales: Appropriate Assessment, Appropriate Workload, Clear Goals and Standards, Graduate Qualities, Intellectual Motivation, Learning Community, Learning Resources and Student Support. However, results from subsequent surveys suggest that the reliability of some of these scales is relatively low, and that the new scales are not clearly differentiated from the old ones. There is also some concern that some institutions are not adopting uniform procedures in distributing the survey (Coates, 2006).

Psychometric Properties of the CEQ

For the rest of this chapter, I discuss research findings obtained using either the 30-item or the 36-item version of the CEQ. If these questionnaires are to be used as research instruments, then it is important to know about their reliability and validity. Evidence concerning these properties of the 30-item version of the CEQ was obtained in the Australian national trial (Ramsden, 1991a, 1991b), and in research carried out in individual universities in Australia (Trigwell and Prosser, 1991) and Britain (Richardson, 1994). Evidence concerning the 36-item version of the CEQ was obtained in the study by Wilson *et al.* (1997).

An instrument is *reliable* to the extent that it would yield consistent results if used repeatedly under the same conditions with the same participants, and is therefore relatively unaffected by errors of measurement. This is measured by a number of different coefficients of reliability, all of which vary in principle between zero (reflecting total *un*reliability) and one (reflecting perfect reliability). The most obvious way to establish the reliability of an instrument is to measure its *test–retest reliability*: this involves calculating the correlation coefficients between the scores that are obtained by the same individuals on two successive administrations of the same instrument. However, this suffers from two kinds of problem:

- With relatively short intervals between the two administrations, the participants will become familiar with the instrument and may even recall the responses that they gave at the first administration; as a result, its test–retest reliability may be spuriously high. This problem can be ameliorated by constructing equivalent or "parallel" forms of the same instrument for administration on the different occasions, but this is not a solution that has been adopted in the case of student feedback questionnaires.
- In contrast, with relatively long intervals between two administrations of the same instrument, the participants are more likely to be exposed to contextual influences that lead to changes in the personal qualities being measured; as a result, the instrument's test–retest reliability may be spuriously low. In this situation, the correlation coefficient between the scores obtained at the two administrations is more a measure of its stability than its reliability, and variability in the scores obtained on different occasions need not cast doubt on the adequacy of the instrument. Moreover, longitudinal studies of this sort are hard to carry out because of the high probability of attrition: the participants may decline to participate in the follow-up session, or they may no longer be available for inclusion

(for instance, in the case of students who have withdrawn from their studies in the interim). As a result, the participants who contribute data from the follow-up session may be unrepresentative of the original sample.

An alternative approach is to estimate an instrument's reliability by examining the consistency among the scores obtained on its constituent parts at a single administration (it is also clearly less arduous to administer an instrument on a single occasion than on two separate occasions). The most common measure of internal consistency is Cronbach's (1951) coefficient alpha. This estimates the reliability of an instrument by comparing the variance of the total scores with the variances of the scores on the constituent items. This is generally felt to be a useful indicator of the reliability of a test instrument, although low values of internal consistency may arise *either* because the scale in question is unreliable *or* because it is not measuring a single personal quality or trait. Of course, the CEQ is supposed to be measuring several dimensions that may or may not combine to reflect a single overarching quality. The internal consistency of the scales in both versions of the CEQ is generally satisfactory.

The other fundamental requirement of a research instrument is that it should be *valid* in the sense that it measures the personal qualities or traits that it purports to measure. This can be judged in a number of different ways. One approach is to examine the wording or structure of the constituent items; this is known as *face validity*. The items in the CEQ originated in statements made by real students in research interviews, and so this requirement seems to be met. Of course, this technique is limited in so far as it relies upon subjective and qualitative judgements rather than objective procedures.

Another approach is to examine the relationships among the scores obtained by a sample of participants on the constituent parts of an instrument. This is known as *construct validity* and is usually addressed by means of factor analysis. This can provide evidence that the instrument measures one or more distinctive traits or constructs. In both the 30-item and the 36-item versions of the CEQ, most items load on factors that reflect the scales to which they have been assigned, although there is a consistent tendency for a few items on the Good Teaching scale and the Emphasis on Independence scale to load on other factors.

Two studies have identified a possible further problem with the Good Teaching scale. Broomfield and Bligh (1998) confirmed the scale structure of the CEQ, except that the Good Teaching scale was reflected in two separate factors: one was defined by three items concerned with classroom instruction; the other was defined by two items concerned with the feedback given to the students on their work. Kreber (2003) obtained similar results when she asked students to evaluate particular course units. My own interpretation of these results is that the quality of instruction is likely to depend on the competence of individual teachers, whereas the quality of feedback (in particular, its form and punctuality) is likely to depend more on institutional practices (Richardson, 2005a).

These analyses provide evidence of the construct validity of the individual scales in the CEQ. Students' responses to the individual items in each scale can then be averaged to yield scores on the scales themselves, between a minimum of 1 and a maximum of 5. Factor analyses can then be carried out on students' scores on the constituent scales to provide evidence of the construct validity of the whole instrument. These analyses usually produce a single factor on which all of the scales show salient loadings (e.g. Richardson, 1994). It is plausible to interpret this as a global measure of perceived academic quality. The Appropriate Workload scale typically shows the lowest loadings on this factor, and there has been some debate as to whether this scale should be taken to define a separate dimension (Ainley, 1999; Richardson, 1997).

A further approach is to examine the correlations between the scores on an instrument and the scores obtained on some independent criterion. This is known as *criterion* (or *criterion-related*) *validity* and yields coefficients varying between zero (reflecting a total lack of validity) and one (reflecting perfect validity). The criterion may be measured at the same time as the instrument is administered (*concurrent validity*), or it may be measured at some later point, so that the instrument is essentially being used to predict the criterion in question (*predictive validity*). The criterion validity of the CEQ as an index of perceived quality can be evaluated by examining the correlations between students' scale scores and their responses to the additional item concerned with their general satisfaction. Typically, students' scores on all of the CEQ's scales show statistically significant correlations with their ratings of general satisfaction. Once again, however, their scores on the Appropriate Workload scale often show the weakest association with their general satisfaction ratings.

Another form of validity is *discriminative validity*: the extent to which an instrument yields different scores on groups of participants who would be expected to differ from one another on the underlying trait or traits. In the case of students, the groups might differ on demographic characteristics (such as age, gender or educational background) or on contextual characteristics (such as their academic discipline, department or institution). The Australian graduate surveys have consistently shown that students' scores on the constituent scales of the CEQ vary across different academic disciplines, and across different institutions of higher education offering programmes in the same discipline.

These surveys have also identified apparent differences related to the demographic characteristics of the respondents, including gender, age, first language and ethnicity. However, the authors of the annual reports from these surveys have been at pains to point out that these effects could simply reflect the enrolment of different kinds of student on programmes in different disciplines, with different teaching practices and different assessment requirements. In other words, observed variations might arise from the respondents taking different programmes rather than from inherent characteristics of the respondents themselves.

Research studies with large samples of students taking the same course units have found statistically significant effects of age, gender and prior qualifications. Nevertheless, these effects are typically small in magnitude and inconsistent from one study to another (Richardson, 2006). In the National Student Survey in England, Wales and Northern Ireland, effects of demographic characteristics such as age, gender and ethnicity have been obtained, but once again these are small in magnitude and only attain statistical significance because of the extremely large number of respondents (more than 170,000 in 2005: see Surridge, 2006).

One final point to emphasise is that reliability and validity are not absolute properties of a questionnaire, but properties of a particular set of responses to the questionnaire when it has been administered in a particular context. It follows that the reliability and the validity of the CEQ (or any other instrument) have to be confirmed from scratch in each specific context.

Research Studies Using the CEQ

Here are just four examples of research studies that have used the CEQ to monitor students' perceptions of the academic quality of their courses and programmes in higher education.

Sadlo (1997) used the CEQ to compare programmes of occupational therapy at six schools in different countries. Two of the schools used traditional, subject-based curricula. Two employed innovative curricula based on the principles of problem-based learning. The two remaining schools were hybrids in these terms: one employed a curriculum that was subject-based but directed towards the professional needs of the students; the other employed a curriculum that was problem-based but retained formal lectures. Sadlo found that students who received a problem-based curriculum produced higher scores on the CEQ than students who received a subject-based curriculum. Students at the hybrid schools produced CEQ scores that were intermediate, suggesting that the effect of problem-based learning is (as clinicians would say) "dose-dependent": the more of it there is in the curriculum, the better.

Richardson *et al.* (2004) administered the CEQ to students who were deaf and also to hearing students who were taking the same programmes at two British universities. They found that the students who were deaf rated their programmes just as positively as did the hearing students. Indeed, the deaf students who preferred to communicate by sign language, or by speech accompanied by sign language, produced higher scores on the Generic Skills and Emphasis on Independence scales. Richardson *et al.* attributed this to the extra tutorial support that these students were receiving with regard to their study skills and their English language skills. Despite these tutorial sessions taking up additional time, the students did not produce lower scores in terms of the appropriateness of their workload.

In Australia, the CEQ has been distributed to all graduates, including those who have studied by distance learning. However, some of the items refer to "lecturers" or to "teaching staff", and there is a serious issue of how graduates who have studied by distance learning would make sense of these. Richardson and Woodley (2001) adapted the 35-item version of the CEQ for use in distance education by amending these items to refer either to the course materials or to the tutors. Their results confirmed the intended structure of the CEQ, except that the Good Teaching scale split into two separate scales concerned with good materials and good tutoring, respectively. This is not, of course, surprising, because this reflected exactly how the relevant items had been reworded.

Subsequent research showed that the adapted version of the CEQ was a reliable and valid instrument for monitoring the experience of distance-learning students (Lawless and Richardson, 2004; Richardson, 2005b). Price *et al.* (2007) gave this version to students who were taking two versions of the same course, both by distance learning. One version of the course was supported with face-to-face tuition, but the other was supported by wholly online tuition. The two groups of students produced identical profiles of CEQ scores, except that the students who received online tuition produced somewhat lower scores on the Good Tutoring scale than did the students who received face-to-face tuition. Price *et al.*, suggested that both tutors and students needed guidance in making the most effective use of online tuition, given the absence of the para-linguistic cues that support face-to-face interactions.

The Individual Student Experience

Thus far, I have only described the use of the CEQ to monitor the experience of entire groups of students. Entwistle (1989) and Ramsden (1989) suggested that students taking the same programme, or students in the same department, would be likely to experience their academic environment in a similar way. This turns out to be totally false: several investigations have found considerable variations in how different students experience the same courses of programmes, judged by their scores on the various scales of the CEQ.

Just as one example, Richardson (2003) surveyed students who had taken a particular course by distance learning with the Open University entitled "Learning Online: Computing with Confidence". This course was presented twice a year, ran for just 12 weeks and earned 10 credit points (i.e. 1/12 of a year's full-time study) at an introductory level. The materials were delivered through a website, computer conferencing, CD-ROMs, supplementary printed information and practice learning materials. The students communicated with their tutor and with other students by e-mail and computer conferencing, and participation in online group work was an obligatory part of the course.

A total of 178 students completed the adapted version of the CEQ in a postal survey carried out at the end of one presentation of this course. Table 15.2 shows their scores on the seven scales (including separate Good Materials and Good Tutoring scales), as well as an average score across all

Table 15.2 CEQ Scores of 178 Students Taking a Course on "Learning Online"

Scale	Mean	Standard deviation	Correlation with general satisfaction
Appropriate Assessment	4.17	0.77	0.33
Appropriate Workload	3.48	1.01	0.51
Clear Goals and Standards	3.47	0.97	0.59
Generic Skills	3.77	0.88	0.65
Good Materials	3.96	0.86	0.71
Good Tutoring	3.57	0.93	0.47
Student Choice	3.01	0.79	0.42
Overall perceived quality	3.63	0.61	0.77

Note. Adapted from Richardson (2003, p. 437).

seven scales as a measure of overall perceived quality. The correlation coefficients with their ratings of general satisfaction are also shown. These ratings were most strongly related to scores on the Good Materials and Generic Skills scales. In this study, they were least strongly related to scores on the Appropriate Assessment scale, which may be due to a ceiling effect: the latter scores were approaching the logical maximum of 5, which will have reduced their possible variation (the phenomenon of "restriction of range").

The main reason for presenting these data is to point out that the mean scores were roughly 3 on a scale from 1 to 5 and that the standard deviations were roughly 1. In most datasets, one would expect the vast majority of scores to fall within two standard deviations either side of the mean, which in this case is 3 ± 2 or between 1 and 5. In other words, this sample of students, who were all taking the same course, generated scores on the CEQ that spanned the entire logical range. Clearly, different students can vary markedly in terms of their perceptions of the same academic environment. Table 15.2 also shows that the scores obtained by individual students on the CEQ were correlated with their satisfaction with the course. What other aspects of students' experience might be associated with their CEQ scores?

Several studies have investigated the link with students' approaches to studying. In the 1970s, interview-based research found that students adopted three main approaches to studying in higher education: a deep approach based on understanding the meaning of the course materials; a surface approach based on memorising the course materials for the purposes of assessment; and a strategic approach based on obtaining the highest possible marks or grades (see the chapter in this volume by Case and Marshall). The same students may exhibit different approaches, depending on the demands of different courses, the quality of teaching and the nature of the assessments. However, different students may exhibit different approaches within the same courses, depending upon their perceptions of the content, the context and the demands of those courses (see Richardson, 2000, chap. 2, for a review).

Richardson (2005b) obtained responses to the CEQ and another questionnaire, the Revised Approaches to Studying Inventory (RASI), from more than 2,100 students who were taking distance-learning courses. Figure 15.1 shows the relationship between their overall scores on the CEQ and their scores on the Deep Approach, Strategic Approach and Surface Approach scales of the RASI. Their scores on the CEQ were positively correlated with their use of a deep approach and positively correlated with their use of a strategic approach, but they were negatively correlated with their use of a surface approach (that the scores on Strategic Approach were so high was simply because there are more items contributing to that scale in the RASI). Richardson found that the students' scores on the two questionnaires shared 61% of their variance. Other studies have yielded similar results (Richardson, 2007).

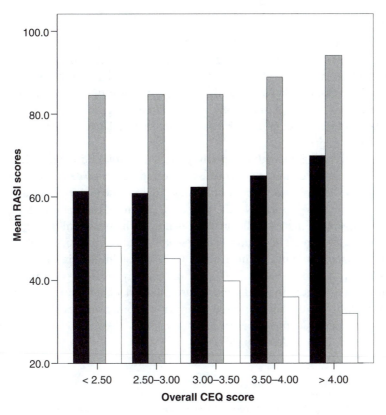

Figure 15.1 Relationship between CEQ Scores and Approaches to Studying. The black bars show students' scores on Deep Approach, the grey bars show their scores on Strategic Approach and the white bars show their scores on Surface Approach. Adapted from Richardson (2005b).

Another aspect of the student experience is academic engagement. It is generally agreed that involvement in both the academic domain and the social domain is important for enhancing student engagement. Richardson *et al.* (2003) obtained responses to the CEQ and an Academic Engagement Form from 404 students with and without a hearing loss who were taking courses with the Open University. In distance education, the idea of engagement seemed to depend on students' relationships with their tutors and peers, and their own identity as learners. Students who showed higher levels of academic engagement tended to produce higher scores on the CEQ, as well as higher ratings of general satisfaction, and the students' scores on the two questionnaires shared 83% of their variance.

A further aspect of the student experience is the extent to which students feel that they have developed as a result of taking their degrees. Lawless and Richardson (2004) developed a Personal and Educational Development Inventory (PEDI), in which graduates rated the extent to which their studies had enabled them to develop in each of 26 areas or competences. They obtained responses to the PEDI and the CEQ from over 3,000 recent Open University graduates. An analysis of responses to the PEDI yielded four scales, which were concerned with cognitive skills, mathematical skills, self-organisation and social skills. The graduates who reported a greater amount of personal development tended to produce higher scores on the CEQ, and their scores on the two questionnaires shared 65% of their variance.

Conclusions

The CEQ appears to be a robust and reliable instrument that can be used to evaluate students' experiences both at the course unit and programme levels. It can provide useful comparative data across different curricula, modes of course presentation and subgroups of students. CEQ scores show wide variation across students taking the same course or programme. The CEQ scores produced by individual students are intimately related to their approaches to studying, academic engagement and personal development. Even so, they show relatively little systematic variation with demographic variables.

The CEQ was originally intended as a performance indicator, and for practical purposes it is probably most useful in the context of quality assurance. In Australia, data at the programme level are published for prospective students and other stakeholders to compare institutions offering the same subjects (in England, Wales and Northern Ireland, data from the National Student Survey are made available in a similar manner). In practice, within each subject, most institutions produce similar scores, with a few producing relatively high scores and a few producing relatively low scores.

The CEQ is probably too blunt an instrument to be of use in itself in bringing about specific improvements in the student experience. It may well identify areas of good practice or areas of concern, but it will not identify the underlying causes. Instead, data from surveys such as the CEQ or the National Student Survey should be used, together with other sources of information (external examiners' reports, staff–student meetings and other kinds of course evaluation), to provide a more detailed picture of the student experience.

References

Ainley, J. (1999, August). *Using the Course Experience Questionnaire to draw inferences about higher education*. Paper presented at the conference of the European Association for Research on Learning and Instruction, Göteborg, Sweden.

Ainley, J. and Long, M. (1994). *The Course Experience Survey 1992 graduates*. Canberra: Australian Government Publishing Service.

Ainley, J. and Long, M. (1995). *The 1994 Course Experience Questionnaire: A report prepared for the Graduate Careers Council of Australia*. Parkville, Victoria: Graduate Careers Council of Australia.

Broomfield, D. and Bligh, J. (1998). An evaluation of the "short form" course experience questionnaire with medical students. *Medical Education, 32*, 367–369.

Coates, H. (2006). *Enhancing the GCA national surveys: An examination of critical factors leading to enhancements in the instrument, methodology and process*. Parkville, Victoria: Graduate Careers Australia.

Cronbach, L.J. (1951). Coefficient alpha and the internal structure of tests. *Psychometrika, 16*, 297–334.

Entwistle, N. (1989). Approaches to studying and course perceptions: The case of the disappearing relationship. *Studies in Higher Education, 14*, 155–156.

Gibbs, G. and Lucas, L. (1996). Using research to improve student learning in large classes. In G. Gibbs (ed.) *Improving student learning: Using research to improve student learning* (pp. 33–49). Oxford: Oxford Centre for Staff Development.

Ginns, P., Prosser, M. and Barrie, S. (2007). Students' perceptions of teaching quality in higher education: The perspective of currently enrolled students. *Studies in Higher Education, 32*, 603–615.

Hu, S. and Kuh, G.D. (2002). Being (dis)engaged in educationally purposeful activities: The influences of student and institutional characteristics. *Research in Higher Education, 43*, 555–575.

Johnson, T. (1997). *The 1996 Course Experience Questionnaire: A report prepared for the Graduate Careers Council of Australia*. Parkville, Victoria: Graduate Careers Council of Australia.

Johnson, T. (1998). *The 1997 Course Experience Questionnaire: A report prepared for the Graduate Careers Council of Australia*. Parkville, Victoria: Graduate Careers Council of Australia.

Johnson, T. (1999). *Course Experience Questionnaire 1998: A report prepared for the Graduate Careers Council of Australia*. Parkville, Victoria: Graduate Careers Council of Australia.

Johnson, T., Ainley, J. and Long, M. (1996). *The 1995 Course Experience Questionnaire: A report prepared for the Graduate Careers Council of Australia*. Parkville, Victoria: Graduate Careers Council of Australia.

Kember, D., Leung, D.Y.P. and Kwan, K.P. (2002). Does the use of student feedback questionnaires improve the overall quality of teaching? *Assessment and Evaluation in Higher Education, 27*, 411–425.

Kreber, C. (2003). The relationship between students' course perception and their approaches to studying in undergraduate science courses: A Canadian experience. *Higher Education Research and Development, 22*, 57–75.

Kuh, G.D., Hayek, J.C., Carini, R.M., Ouimet, J.A., Gonyea, R.M. and Kennedy, J. (2001). *NSSE technical and norms report*. Bloomington, IN: Indiana University, Center for Postsecondary Research and Planning.

Lawless, C.J. and Richardson, J.T.E. (2002). Approaches to studying and perceptions of academic quality in distance education. *Higher Education*, 44, 257–282.

Lawless, C.J. and Richardson, J.T.E. (2004). Monitoring the experiences of graduates in distance education. *Studies in Higher Education*, 29, 353–374.

Linke, R.D. (1991). *Performance indicators in higher education: Report of a trial evaluation study commissioned by the Commonwealth Department of Employment, Education, and Training*. Canberra: Australian Government Publishing Service.

Long, M. and Hillman, K. (2000). *Course Experience Questionnaire 1999: A report prepared for the Graduate Careers Council of Australia*. Parkville, Victoria: Graduate Careers Council of Australia.

Lucas, L., Gibbs, G., Hughes, S., Jones, O. and Wisker, G. (1997). A study of the effects of course design features on student learning in large classes at three institutions: A comparative study. In C. Rust and G. Gibbs (eds) *Improving student learning through course design* (pp. 10–24). Oxford: Oxford Centre for Staff and Learning Development.

Marsh, H.W. and Dunkin, M.J. (1992). Students' evaluations of university teaching: A multidimensional perspective. In J. C. Smart (ed.), *Higher education: Handbook of theory and research*, vol. 8 (pp. 143–233). New York: Agathon Press.

McInnis, C., Griffin, P., James, R. and Coates, H. (2001). *Development of the Course Experience Questionnaire (CEQ)*. Canberra: Department of Education, Training and Youth Affairs.

National student satisfaction and priorities report (2007). Coralville, IA: Noel-Levitz.

Price, L., Richardson, J.T.E. and Jelfs, A. (2007). Face-to-face versus online tutoring support in distance education. *Studies in Higher Education*, 32, 1–20.

Ramsden, P. (1989). Perceptions of courses and approaches to studying: An encounter between paradigms. *Studies in Higher Education*, 14, 157–158.

Ramsden, P. (1991a). A performance indicator of teaching quality in higher education: The Course Experience Questionnaire. *Studies in Higher Education*, 16, 129–150.

Ramsden, P. (1991b). Report on the Course Experience Questionnaire Trial. In R.D. Linke, *Performance indicators in higher education: Report of a trial evaluation study commissioned by the Commonwealth Department of Employment, Education, and Training. Volume 2: Supplementary papers*. Canberra: Australian Government Publishing Service.

Richardson, J.T.E. (1994). A British evaluation of the Course Experience Questionnaire. *Studies in Higher Education*, 19, 59–68.

Richardson, J.T.E. (1997). Students' evaluations of teaching: The Course Experience Questionnaire. *Psychology Teaching Review*, 6, 31–45.

Richardson, J.T.E. (2000). *Researching student learning: Approaches to studying in campus-based and distance education*. Buckingham: Open University Press.

Richardson, J.T.E. (2003). Approaches to studying and perceptions of academic quality in a short web-based course. *British Journal of Educational Technology*, 34, 433–442.

Richardson, J.T.E. (2005a). Instruments for obtaining student feedback: A review of the literature. *Assessment and Evaluation in Higher Education*, 30, 387–415.

Richardson, J.T.E. (2005b). Students' perceptions of academic quality and approaches to studying in distance education. *British Educational Research Journal*, 31, 1–21.

Richardson, J.T.E. (2006). Investigating the relationship between variations in students' perceptions of their academic environment and variations in study behaviour in distance education. *British Journal of Educational Psychology*, 76, 867–893.

Richardson, J.T.E. (2007). Variations in student learning and perceptions of academic quality. In N. Entwistle, P. Tomlinson and J. Dockrell (eds) *Student learning and university teaching* (*British Journal of Educational Psychology, Monograph Series II*, No. 4) (pp. 61–71). Leicester: The British Psychological Society.

Richardson, J.T.E., Barnes, L. and Fleming, J. (2004). Approaches to studying and perceptions of academic quality in deaf and hearing students in higher education. *Deafness and Education International*, 6, 100–122.

Richardson, J.T.E., Long, G.L. and Woodley, A. (2003). Academic engagement and perceptions of quality in distance education. *Open Learning*, 18, 223–244.

Richardson, J.T.E., Slater, J.B. and Wilson, J. (2007). The National Student Survey: Development, findings and implications. *Studies in Higher Education*, 32, 557–580.

Richardson, J.T.E. and Woodley, A. (2001). Perceptions of academic quality among students with a hearing loss in distance education. *Journal of Educational Psychology*, 93, 563–570.

Roche, L.A. and Marsh, H.W. (2002). Teaching self-concept in higher education: Reflecting on multiple dimensions of teaching effectiveness. In N. Hativa and P. Goodyear (eds) *Teacher thinking, beliefs and knowledge in higher education* (pp. 179–218). Dordrecht: Kluwer.

Sadlo, G. (1997). Problem-based learning enhances the educational experiences of occupational therapy students. *Education for Health*, 10, 101–114.

Surridge, P. (2006). *The National Student Survey 2005: Findings*. Bristol: Higher Education Funding Council for England.

Trigwell, K. and Prosser, M. (1991). Improving the quality of student learning: The influence of learning context and student approaches to learning on learning outcomes. *Higher Education*, 22, 251–266.

Wilson, K.L., Lizzio, A. and Ramsden, P. (1997). The development, validation and application of the Course Experience Questionnaire. *Studies in Higher Education*, 22, 33–53.

16

Grading Student Achievement in Higher Education
Measuring or Judging?

Mantz Yorke

A "Natural" Activity

Grading attracts less attention than it merits because it involves practices which almost everyone will have experienced in one way or another. It is a "natural" part of the educational landscape. There is hence a tendency for assessors and users of assessments to believe that they understand grading and, perhaps, to place an unwarranted belief in the robustness of the grades that are awarded. Grading probably receives less attention in pedagogic development programmes than is merited when its significance for students is taken into account.

From time to time grading has been subjected to critique (e.g. Milton *et al.*, 1986; Yorke, 2008), though the force of such critiques has hitherto become dissipated against the breakwaters of tradition. Continuing the critique, this chapter argues that grading is in general more complex and less precise than many take to be the case. For these reasons it is necessary to consider the merits of the reliance that is typically placed on grades, and how some of the problems with grading might be addressed.

The Significance of Grades to Society

The Importance Assigned to Grades

Grading scales of one form or another pervade higher education, apart from in a handful of institutions (such as Alverno College in the US) where student achievement is described in qualitative rather than quantitative terms. Grade-point averages [GPAs] and degree classifications are of importance to students. A GPA of 3.00 or an upper second class honours degree opens doors to graduates that would otherwise remain closed. The "first sift" undertaken by employers is often on the basis of the overall index of the graduate's performance, and applicants for postgraduate awards in the UK almost inevitably need to have gained an "upper second".

Grade Inflation

Despite the weight that society places on grades there are persistent claims of grade inflation, and hence some scepticism about the worth of grades. There is a substantial literature, mainly from the US, arguing whether or not grade inflation exists. The argument is made complex by the variation in the way that "grade inflation" has been defined (see Hu, 2005, and Yorke, 2008, p.108ff).

Stone (1995), Rosovsky and Hartley (2002), and Johnson (2003) are amongst those who have argued that grade inflation is a significant feature of higher education in the US, whereas Adelman (2008), who has examined grades on a large number of transcripts, argues that the proponents' case is itself inflated, and that the general level of grades in the US has remained much the same over a period of 20 years. Adelman suggests that the allegations of grade inflation are based on a highly selective reading of the evidence, in which performances in elite institutions drown out those from the less prestigious institutions. Following his review of the literature, Hu (2005) arrives at an intermediate assessment of the position.

In the UK there has been a steady rise in the proportion of "good honours degrees" (i.e. first and upper second class honours degrees) in recent years, which has predictably excited press comment (from Clark, 2008, amongst others) about the "dumbing down" of standards. Yorke (2008) found, from a study of awards made between 1994 and 2002, that grades were tending to rise more quickly in elite institutions than in others in the UK—a finding that is consistent with Adelman's reading of US data.

Grade inflation is not a primary focus of this chapter, but Hu (2005) and Yorke (2008, chapter 5) provide convenient starting points from which to approach the issues involved. In particular, they point out the difference between pernicious grade inflation and a rise in grades that may be attributed to causes that are not necessarily deplorable, such as changes in the ways in which curricula are designed and implemented, and in approaches to the assessment of student achievement.

Standards

Standards are based on disciplinary and/or professional norms, implying often a qualitative judgement on the part of the assessor (based on sedimented understandings of what the expected standards are) as to whether the student has reached a particular level of achievement. Evidence from reviews in UK higher education, whilst painting a generally very positive picture of provision, has nevertheless consistently pointed to weaknesses in the area of assessment. There are relevant summary observations in Quality Assurance Agency (QAA) publications (2004, paras 13–14), while the archive of reports on the QAA website (found by navigating from www.qaa.ac.uk/reviews/academicReview/default.asp) provides plenty of more detailed evidence on this point.

Standards are difficult to pin down with precision—the fuzziness of constructs relating to standards and criteria has been noted by a number of writers (e.g. Sadler, 1987, 2005; Webster et al., 2000; Tan and Prosser, 2004; Woolf, 2004). If standards and criteria are fuzzy, then grading against them cannot be other than a fuzzy process. Earlier writers, encouraged by the "instructional objectives" approach that was stimulated in the second half of the twentieth century, argued for the specification of achievements in precise terms, with Mager (1962) being a prominent advocate. The apotheosis of this approach was arguably the system of National Vocational Qualifications [NVQs] in England and Wales, whose assessment schemes involved evidencing performance to such a fineness of detail across a variety of contexts that they proved unsustainable in the manner envisaged by Jessup (1991). Whilst many practical achievements at the basic NVQ Level 1 can be evidenced with precision (see www.qca.org.uk/14–19/qualifications/index_nvqs.htm for general descriptions of Levels 1 to 5), most of those desired of higher vocational levels (and a fortiori of higher education) are inherently fuzzier.

Assessment Criteria and Standards

Lists of assessment criteria and assessment rubrics (for samples of the latter, see Walvoord, 2004: Appendix A) are common in higher education. They are intended to make clear to both students and assessors the standards that are expected. However, assumptions of interpretability may be rather too easily made. Wolf (1995), amongst others, has shown that statements of expectation and criteria need to be accompanied by exemplifications if meaning is richly to be communicated.

Assessment criteria are often specified with reference to excellence (as would be expected for the particular point in the programme reached by the student), which means that a low level of pass can be indexed against a set of negativities. The following example illustrates the expectation, in one UK institution, regarding the standard of third class honours at bachelor's level:

Third class (40–49%)
A basic understanding of the main issues but not coherently or correctly presented

Third class answers demonstrate some knowledge or understanding of the general area but a third class answer tends to be weak in the following ways:

- descriptive only;
- does not answer the question directly;
- misses key points;
- contains important inaccuracies;
- covers material sparsely, possibly in note form;
- assertions not supported by authority or evidence.

(Higher Education Quality Council, 1997a, p. 26)

One could be forgiven for not understanding why a performance of this kind would actually merit an honours degree.

There is a broader weakness in the use of lists of performance descriptors. Performances rarely fit neatly into the "boxes" which define levels of achievement. A student may achieve above the specified level in one aspect of their work, and underachieve in respect of another. The assessor is faced with making a judgement about the general level of the work, which may not be achieved satisfactorily by adding up points for various components, as in "menu marking". Sadler (2005) suggests subdividing criteria into categories of primary and secondary importance, but this does not provide an unequivocal solution to the problem, because of the unevenness of performances and the implicit restriction on achievements that are worth valuing but fall outside the formal specification. Studies, such as that by Saliu (2005), have been undertaken using a "fuzzy set" approach to grading, which allows that a performance can exhibit, simultaneously, different "degrees of membership" of the various assessment categories. However, whilst the logic of the approach has much to commend it, the challenges of implementing it seem insurmountable in practice.

Grade Distributions

Normativeness pervades grading. It lies in the background when topics and items for assessment are being selected. It comes to greater prominence whenever doubts are expressed about the frequency with which high grades are being awarded, since there is often an underlying presumption that grades should approximate a statistically normal distribution. Yet any curriculum which is based on a conception of "mastery learning" is likely to give rise to a distribution which is negatively skewed (i.e. the bulk of the grades lie towards the upper end of the scale, accompanied by a thinner "tail" of lower grades) and not "normal". This may be a contributory factor where a rise has been observed in awarded grades. When the curriculum is specified in terms of "expected learning outcomes" (or similar, rather than in more general terms), the students know what is expected of them and can target their efforts appropriately. This shifts upward the likelihood of obtaining a high grade—indeed, there should be no objection in principle to all students obtaining the highest grade for their work, since they could all show that they have achieved to a high standard the specified learning outcomes (the price may be a limitation on the amount of non-specified study undertaken by the student, but that is a matter that will not be pursued here). However, some external examiners and assessment boards look askance at such "top-ended" distributions of grades. Further, a problem arises in the computation of GPA and the like when the study units taken by a student are a combination of those with a bias towards norm-referencing in their grading practice and those where the bias is towards criterion-referencing.

The "Measurement Assumption"

There is a widespread—often implicit—belief that assessments of student achievement are tantamount to measurements, even if, at the time of their award, they are seen by markers as general signals of the level of achievement. The "measurement assumption" is made wherever grades are treated statistically, as if they are from measurement scales with common properties (such as when they are summed or averaged). Disciplinary and departmental cultures invest grades with particular meanings which undercut an implicit assumption of commonality in scalar properties. For example, does a percentage of 55 carry the same meaning in law (where, in the UK, grades tend to be low) and in some aspects of healthcare (where they can often be quite high)? Superficially similar, the scales on which such grades were recorded are in practice likely to be quite different. As Knight (2006, p. 438) pointedly put it: "True measurement carries invariant meanings." The variance inherent in the use of grading scales means that grades cannot be treated as if they are measurements akin to those of physical properties such as mass and length (see also Dalziel, 1998, on this point).

Certifying

Knight and Yorke (2003) argued that considerations of reliability, validity and generalisability raised questions about the extent to which institutions could certify, or warrant, their students' achievements:

- Some achievements can be assessed cheaply and reliably: these are often to be found at the lower taxonomic levels.
- Some achievements can be assessed with tolerable reliability, but only if the assessments cover a variety of situations. The costs that tolerable reliability implies may not be fully appreciated. An assessment centre may be better placed, in resource terms, to undertake some aspects of assessment on behalf of a putative employer.
- Some achievements, especially those that are complex, cannot be assessed reliably by an institution (e.g. placement performance), and all that may be possible is for the institution to attest that the student has undertaken the activity. It would be for the student to

represent their achievements to an interested party, perhaps drawing on a self-constructed portfolio of relevant evidence.

Not every educational achievement that is valued is susceptible to formal grading, since the grading is likely to lack technical robustness.

Knight (2006) further argues that much summative assessment is context-bound and hence "local" in nature, thus prejudicing its generalisability (formative assessment is likewise "local", but its generalisability is of considerably less significance).

Grading Practice

There are many sources of variability in grading, whose interconnectedness cannot receive justice in a necessarily linear narrative. Many of these sources are to be found within individual institutions, whereas others reflect origins that are more broadly social in character (for a schematisation, see Hu, 2005, p. 11).

The Fragility of Grading

The disquiet expressed by some commentators regarding grade inflation relates in the main to overall indexes of student achievement. Rather less disquiet is evident at the level of the component grades that are aggregated in some way to provide an overall index. Yet a consideration of the practices involved in grading the work produced by students suggests that grading is a more fragile operation than many take to be the case. This may not matter very much when the purpose of the grading is formative—i.e. that it is intended as a signal to students of the level of their achievement (accompanied, one would hope, by some indication of ways in which the student might do better next time). It is when the grade acts as a summative statement of achievement that the fragility becomes a matter of particular concern. In the discussion that follows, the focus is on summative assessment at the level of the bachelor's degree, though much of the argument applies, *mutatis mutandis*, to other levels of study.

Sampling from the Curriculum

What is assessed is a sample from the range of possibilities inherent in a curriculum or curricular component. Some intended learning outcomes are more challenging than others—for example, analysis, evaluation and creativity (at the upper end of Anderson and Krathwohl's, 2001, revision of Bloom's, 1956, *Taxonomy of Educational Objectives*) are generally more demanding than remembering, understanding and applying. The grades gained by students will be influenced by the assessment tasks that are specified. One cannot interpret what a grade might signify unless one knows what was being assessed. Not only is sampling from the curriculum an issue here, but so are the circumstances governing the extent to which the student's performance was helped by a pre-structuring of the task (in contrast to the student independently having to work out an appropriate structure for tackling it).

The type of performance being assessed needs to be factored into an interpretation of the awarded grade. Evidence from the UK (e.g. Bridges *et al.*, 2002) indicates that coursework assignments tend to attract higher grades than do formal examinations. This is not surprising, since the completion of an assignment in a student's own time allows for access to supporting resources that are not available unless the examination is "open book" (of course, supporting resources are not an unalloyed blessing—they may be used in a proper academic manner or plagiarised). Placements and practicums are difficult to grade (for reasons that are discussed later), and often are assessed on a pass/fail basis.

Approaches to Grading

There are, perhaps, two main kinds of approach to grading: holistic and additive. Holistic assessment takes place "from the top down", in that the work is first appraised as a whole, this often being followed by a refining as it is weighed against whatever more detailed criteria may have been specified. Additive assessment takes place "from the bottom up", in that the work is sequentially graded against a set of criteria and the overall grade is determined by addition of the separate grades (which are quite often weighted relative to the importance of the criteria). The difficulty—as those who have used both approaches can attest—is that the two approaches do not necessarily give the same overall grade. Studies show that assessors sometimes juggle the grades they give for components of the task until they arrive at an overall grade which they believe does the student justice (Baume *et al.*, 2004; Hawe, 2003; Sadler, 2008). These assessors are reconciling what the additive approach tells them with their holistic appreciation of the merits of the work (and, perhaps occasionally, of the student).

Matters are complicated where the assessor brings into play criteria additional to those specified in order to take into account aspects of the work that are worthy of acknowledgement (see Sadler, 2008, and, for empirical evidence regarding the assessment of dissertations, Webster *et al.*, 2000). The less tightly the task is specified (particularly an issue where creativity is involved), the more problematic becomes assessment.

Walvoord and Anderson, for example, suggest the use of:

> a "fudge factor" of 10 percent or so that you can award to students whose work shows a major improvement over the semester. Or you may simply announce in the syllabus and orally to the class that you reserve the right to raise a grade when the student's work shows great improvement over the course of the semester. (Walvoord and Anderson, 1998, p. 99)

This conflates two purposes of assessment—to index actual achievement and to encourage students.

Assessors, perhaps particularly in the nurturing professional areas, are quite often reluctant to fail students because they want to give them a further chance to demonstrate that they can satisfy the requirements of the course (see, for example, Brandon and Davies, 1979; Hawe, 2003). A reluctance to fail students can also occur because of the assessor's awareness of the economic consequences for the institution or organisational unit, or because the assessor is aware of the commitment of time and energy that would be needed in respect of an appeal against the decision to fail (Newstead, 2002).

Assessors who are expert in both their discipline and assessment practice may be able to judge the general standard of a piece of work using a holistic approach, though they may find difficulty in mapping their judgement on to the specified assessment criteria. The difficulty arises, in part, from the desire to include non-specified criteria, and from the "intersections" between different criteria (see, for a critical review, Sadler (forthcoming). For a holistic approach to grading to be effective, it seems necessary for the assessor to be able to demonstrate the level of expert behaviour that is described by Dreyfus and Dreyfus (2005). The less experienced may find the additive approach helpful in assessing—and in developing their capability as assessors. Where the assessment specification covers both subject content and more "generic" matters (for example, the ability to give an effective presentation), an assessor may have differential expertise across the specified requirements.

The use of the additive approach has an advantage where the assessor may be called to account, such as in institutional quality assurance processes, or when a student lodges an appeal against a grade. Of some relevance to the point, Hodges *et al.* (1999) found, in a study of medical practitioners, that junior personnel obtained higher scores for their use of a diagnostic checklist than did their more experienced colleagues—presumably because the juniors "followed the script", whereas the more senior were able to apply learning from their experience to get to the heart of the diagnosis more quickly.

Finally, there is a slew of personal circumstances (some of which are noted by Pascarella and Terenzini, 2005, p. 66) that can affect an individual assessor's grading, including:

- the number of pieces of work that have to be marked;
- the time available for marking;
- the order in which the submitted pieces of work are marked;
- their level of concentration on the task; and
- how tired they are.

Disciplinary Variation

There is plenty of evidence that grades vary across subject disciplines, in terms of means and distributions, whether one looks at the study unit or the overall index: evidence on the point can be found in Yorke *et al.* (1996), Kuh and Hu (1999), Johnson (2003), Adelman (2008), Yorke (2008a), and on the website of the Higher Education Statistics Agency (HESA) in the UK. In the UK experience, for example, high grades have consistently been hard to attain in Law (see Yorke *et al.*, 1996, for data at module level and, by navigating via "view statistics online" at www.hesa.ac.uk, the tabulation of bachelor's degree awards for 2005–06 published by HESA). At bachelor's level in 2006, and not untypical of the previous decade, 5.4 per cent of UK graduates in Law were awarded a first class honours degree. The corresponding percentages for Social Studies, Historical and Philosophical Studies, and Engineering and Technology were 9.0, 12.7 and 18.2, respectively. Whilst entry qualifications across these subject areas differ, it is highly unlikely that they account for the wide variation observed.

The reasons for this variation are not transparent, but are likely to involve, *inter alia*, the kind of assessment task, the extent to which the task admits of an unequivocally correct response (thereby encouraging the use of the full grading scale), the approach taken to grading and the extent to which assessors adopt a "psychological set" in which encouragement or the valuing of a student's progress is to the fore.

Complex Achievements

"Graduateness"

An overall index of achievement masks the profile of achievements of a student, in which some aspects are generally superior to others (whether this is judged by grades or by qualitative criteria). The former Higher Education Quality Council (HEQC) in the UK was challenged by government in the mid-1990s to investigate academic standards. The challenge arose because of concerns emanating from Asia about the robustness of academic standards. The threat to recruitment to institutions in the UK led to HEQC establishing the *Graduate Standards Programme*. The Programme's report (HEQC, 1997b) indicated the complexity of the standards issue, illustrating it with a grid in which the concept of "graduateness" was elaborated under the five main headings of subject mastery, intellectual/cognitive, practical, self/individual and social/people. It implied that students would vary in the profiles that would be judged as reaching an acceptable standard of graduateness, and that different kinds of profile might be valued according to how the student intended to exploit the bachelor's degree qualification.

"Wicked" Competences

Consistent with "human capital" perspectives on higher education (see Becker, 1975, for the original proposition), there is increasing political interest in constructs like employability and workforce development. Such constructs highlight the complexity of achievements in so-called "real world" settings, and demand the display of what Knight (2007) called "wicked" competences. "Wicked" competences have quite a lot in common with the so-called "soft skills" that are valued by employers (such as the application of emotional intelligence in teamworking and other situations). Knight (ibid, p. 2) described them as:

> achievements that cannot be neatly pre-specified, take time to develop and resist measurement-based approaches to assessment.

Such achievements often take longer than an individual module of study to develop, and may more appropriately be assessed over a complete study programme. This requires the assessor to resolve a "part-whole conundrum", which demands a response to the question "what is the relationship between the learning outcomes specified for the programme as a whole, and those specified for its component parts?" A summary grade built up from a number of module grades (e.g. a GPA) may not do adequate justice to learning outcomes that are specified for the entire programme (see, for example, Sadler, 2007, pp. 389–90).

Problems outside the academy, such as those that can be met in work placements, practicums and the like, are often "messy" and unbounded, requiring more than a mono-disciplinary approach to their solution in circumstances in which the information base is less than ideal. In such circumstances there are some similarities with the "mode 2" approach to the production of knowledge that is described by Gibbons *et al.* (1994): however, some placements turn out to involve little more than menial tasks.

The assessment of complex achievements is challenging, but Knight (2007) provides some empirical evidence for academics believing that such assessment is not particularly problematic. Students' effectiveness in dealing with complexity will be contingent on the prevailing circumstances. Assessments are therefore judgements rather than measurements (which, in reality, are no more than quasi-measurements at best). In Knight's (2006) terms such judgements are "local", and hence cannot be force-fitted into a specified list of assessment criteria. Grades can signal in only broad terms the strengths and weaknesses of such multi-faceted achievements, and an overall grade might obscure a significant weakness. A pass/fail approach to grading, supported by a commentary on strengths and weaknesses, may be more informative.

Transcripts and Portfolios

An approach to assessment that relates more to professional judgement than measurement does not fit with the ways in which students' overall achievements are typically represented (in grade-point averages or in honours degree classifications), and pass/fail grades are typically dropped from calculations of indexes of achievement. The "measurement problem" may be mitigated by disaggregating achievements, as in transcripts.

Transcripts of achievements in study units have been a commonplace in US higher education for a long time, though they were adopted rather more recently in the UK, as has been the diploma supplement across Europe. These "flesh out" overall indexes of achievement. However, and as noted above, the gradings in particular study units are subject to a variability in which disciplinary norms are influential. A way of dealing with the problem of variability, albeit not wholly satisfactory for various technical reasons, is to set a student's grade against the generality of grades attained by the relevant cohort. Hence 55 per cent shows up as relatively high when the cohort modal percentage is 50, but as relatively weak when the modal percentage is 65. Other approaches of varying degrees of complexity have been proposed (e.g. Morrison *et al.*, 1995; Johnson, 1997; Felton and Koper, 2005). However, they introduce what many might see as a statistical obfuscation, Johnson's approach being particularly susceptible to such an objection.

In the UK, there is an expectation that, during their programmes, students complete "Progress Files" (see especially www.qaa.ac.uk/academicinfrastructure/progressFiles/guidelines/progfile2001.asp). These, originally recommended in the Dearing Report (National Committee of Inquiry into Higher Education, 1997, para 9.48), have two components: an official transcript of achievements, and a personal compendium through which "students can monitor, build and reflect upon their own personal development", and on which they can draw when presenting themselves, for example, to potential employers. The compendium is the place in which students can record, and reflect upon, their experiences—particularly in the more open circumstances of placements and the like. If institutions are unable to certify some kinds of achievement, it falls to the student to make claims for them and to support them with the evidence that they have compiled. The personal compendium is a private document, and not for public presentation—indeed, any recruiter would recoil from a heap of such documents attached to job applications.

Institution-level Considerations

Brumfield (2004) conducted a survey of the way in which institutions in the US derived GPAs from the collections of grades achieved by students in curricular components. This indicated that, whilst there was some generality of approach to the computations (and also to the award of honours), there were some quite considerable variations in institutional practice. A smaller survey of 35 varied institutions in the UK (Yorke *et al.*, submitted) and a survey of Australian universities (Australian Vice Chancellors Committee, 2002) also showed marked variation within the respective national systems.

In the UK-based study, for example, sources of variation included the following:

- the study units whose grades "count" in the determining of an overall index of achievement (for example, although students have to obtain the specified number of credits for the award, "award algorithms" vary regarding the number of module grades that have to be included in the computation of the honours classification);
- rules governing the inclusion of grades for modules that have had to be retaken;
- the weighting of performances at different levels of the programme when computing the honours classification; and
- the handling of students' claims for discretionary treatment because of personal circumstances that may have affected their performance.

It is readily apparent that interpretation of a GPA or an honours degree classification risks being simplistic, since "local" considerations (Knight, 2006) influence what is reported.

An issue which may be of more significance in the UK than elsewhere is the near-complete use of institution-wide assessment regulations. This has evolved as institutional review activity undertaken by the Quality Assurance Agency for Higher Education (QAA) has asked institutions with varied regulations for different subject groupings why this should be so, and has made critical comment where divergence has been evident (critical comment in the educational press may also have been a potent driver of institutional change).

"Translation" between Systems

A further issue is the difficulty associated with "translating" grades achieved in one national system into the grading system of another. The way in which percentage grades are awarded in the US, Australia and the UK indicates differing assumptions: percentages tend to be highest in the US and lowest in the UK. Any inference that students in the US are more able than their peers in Australia and the UK is however unwarranted. Karran (2005) conducted a survey of overall indexes of achievement in Europe (where the Bologna Process—see www.europeunit.ac.uk/bologna_process/index.cfm—stresses the harmonisation of programme structures), and showed a diversity of scaling that makes problematic "translation" between one system and another.

Professional Development for Assessment

Approaches to the grading of work vary (e.g. Ekstrom and Villegas, 1994; Yorke et al., 2000; Hornby, 2003), with some of the variance being attributable to disciplinary norms. Most of the sample questioned by Yorke et al had learned their assessment practice from colleagues, a number had attended developmental workshops on the topic, and a few relied on their experience of having been assessed earlier in their lives. They had mixed views regarding the accuracy with which they could grade work, some pointing to "double marking", moderation or some reliance on external examiners as providing a safety-net against rank injustice to the student. For various technical, social and structural reasons, such a safety-net has a much wider mesh than those who rely on it probably appreciate.

Relatively few academics have made a systematic study of assessment, and hence the institutional (and system-wide) capacity to support colleagues in respect of assessment is limited, despite the growth of teaching development centres in a number of higher education systems. Inexperienced assessors need to undergo a period of induction into assessment within their subject discipline. The development of institutional capacity in assessment should not be left to chance, and it is poor practice to leave the induction process to happen "naturally": Johnston's (2004, pp. 405–6) vignette presents a vivid picture of a person struggling to work out how to adjust her assessment practice to suit a context with which she was unfamiliar.

The induction process has to deal with the language in which achievements are represented, since there is plenty of scope for misunderstanding. Students do not necessarily share academics' understandings of specifications of expected learning outcomes (see Maclellan, 2001), nor do they always understand the quasi-legal phraseology of regulations relating to assessment. Webster et al. (2000) pointed to the different meanings given by academics within a broad subject area to terms like "analysis" and "evaluation". The potential for variation is increased as one crosses subject discipline boundaries; "analysis" has different connotations in, say, English, Law and Computer Science. Webster et al also pointed to the occasional lack of coherence between the grade awarded and the words used alongside, as in the following two examples (p. 76):

- "Real awareness of the various perspectives" (46% awarded); and
- "this is a clear, well presented [dissertation] ... which fulfils its specific aims" (49% awarded).

What should a student make of such apparent contradictions?

Inherent Ambiguity

This chapter supports the contention that grades are "inherently ambiguous evaluations of performance with no *absolute* connection to educational achievement" (Felton and Koper, 2005, p. 562: emphasis added), and provides a basis for understanding the inherent ambiguity. However one goes about grading, the excellent student (according to the chosen assessment criteria) will end up at the top of the lists of performances, and the very weak student at the bottom. It is between the two extremes that the picture is haziest. Two students may end up in the same broad band of grading, but for very different reasons. To be useful, assessment information needs to be more finely grained than a single index. Users *need* detail if they are to make optimal judgements, as in recruitment: it is a different question as to whether they actually want it.

Walvoord (2004) gave her book the main title *Assessment Clear and Simple*. Making allowance for the fact that "assessment" in American usage has broader connotations than in the UK (since it encompasses programme evaluation), this chapter has shown that grading is neither clear nor simple, and that the path of developmental work stretches far into the distance.

References

Adelman, C. (2008). Undergraduate grades: a more complex story than "inflation". In L.H. Hunt (ed.) *Grade inflation and academic standards.* Albany, NY: State University of New York Press.

Anderson, L.W. and Krathwohl, D.R. (2001). *A taxonomy for learning, teaching and assessing.* New York: Addison Wesley Longman.

Australian Vice Chancellors Committee (2002). Grades for Honours Programs (concurrent with pass degree), 2002. At www.avcc.edu.au/documents/universities/key_survey_summaries/Grades_for_Degree_Subjects_Jun02.xls (accessed 26 January 2008).

Baume, D. and Yorke, M. with Coffey, M. (2004). What is happening when we assess, and how can we use our understanding of this to improve assessment? *Assessment and Evaluation in Higher Education, 29*(4), pp. 451–77.

Becker, G.S. (1975). *Human capital.* Chicago: Chicago University Press.

Bloom, B.S. (1956). *Taxonomy of Educational Objectives, Handbook 1: Cognitive domain.* London: Longman.

Brandon, J. and Davies, M. (1979). The limits of competence in social work: the assessment of marginal work in social work education. *British Journal of Social Work, 9*(3), pp. 295–347.

Bridges, P., Cooper, A., Evanson, P., Haines, C., Jenkins, D., Scurry, D., Woolf, H. and Yorke, M. (2002). Coursework marks high, examination marks low: discuss. *Assessment and Evaluation in Higher Education, 27*(1), pp. 35–48.

Brumfield, C. (2004). *Current trends in grades and grading practices in higher education: results of the 2004 AACRAO survey.* Washington, DC: American Association of Collegiate Registrars and Admissions Officers.

Clark, L. (2008). First-class degrees double in a decade amid "dumbing down" claims. *The Daily Mail,* 10 January 2008. At www.dailymail.co.uk/pages/live/articles/news/news.html?in_article_id=507442&in_page_id=1770 (accessed 26 January 2008).

Dalziel, J. (1998). Using marks to assess student performance: some problems and alternatives. *Assessment and Evaluation in Higher Education, 23*(4), pp. 351–66.

Dreyfus, H.L. and Dreyfus S.E. (2005). Expertise in real world contexts. *Organization Studies, 26*(5), pp. 779–92.

Ekstrom, R.B. and Villegas, A.M. (1994). *College grades: an exploratory study of policies and practices.* New York: College Entrance Examination Board.

Felton, J. and Koper, P.T. (2005). Nominal GPA and real GPA: a simple adjustment that compensates for grade inflation. *Assessment and Evaluation in Higher Education, 30*(6), pp. 561–69.

Gibbons, M., Limoges, C., Nowotny, H., Schwartzman, S., Scott, P., and Trow, M. (1994). *The new production of knowledge: the dynamics of science and research in contemporary societies.* London: Sage.

Hawe, E. (2003). "It's pretty difficult to fail": the reluctance of lecturers to award a failing grade. *Assessment and Evaluation in Higher Education, 28*(4), pp. 371–82.

Higher Education Quality Council (1997a). *Assessment in higher education and the role of "graduateness".* London: Higher Education Quality Council.

Higher Education Quality Council (1997b). *Graduate Standards Programme: final report* (2 vols.). London: Higher Education Quality Council.

Hodges, B., Regehr, G., McNaughton, N., Tiberius, R. and Hanson, M. (1999). OSCE checklists do not capture increasing levels of expertise. *Academic Medicine*, 74(10), pp. 1129–34.

Hornby, W. (2003). Assessing using grade-related criteria: a single currency for universities? *Assessment and Evaluation in Higher Education*, 28(4), pp. 435–54.

Hu, S. (2005). *Beyond grade inflation: grading problems in higher education [ASHE Higher Education Report 30(6), whole issue]*. San Francisco, CA: Jossey-Bass.

Jessup, G. (1991). *Outcomes: NVQs and the emerging model of education and training*. London: Falmer.

Johnson, V.E. (1997). An alternative to traditional GPA for evaluating student performance. *Statistical Science*, 12(4), pp. 251–69.

Johnson, V.E. (2003). *Grade inflation: a crisis in college education*. New York: Springer.

Johnston, B. (2004). Summative assessment of portfolios: an examination of different approaches to agreement over outcomes. *Studies in Higher Education*, 29(3), pp. 395–412.

Karran, T. (2005). Pan-European grading scales: lessons from national systems and the ECTS. *Higher Education in Europe*, 30(1), pp. 5–22.

Knight, P.T. (2006). The local practices of assessment. *Assessment and Evaluation in Higher Education*, 31(4), pp. 435–52.

Knight, P. (2007). Fostering and assessing "wicked" competences. At http://www.open.ac.uk/cetl-workspace/cetlcontent/documents/460d1d1481d0f.pdf (accessed 26 January 2008).

Knight, P. and Yorke, M. (2003). *Assessment, learning and employability*. Maidenhead: Open University Press.

Kuh, G. and Hu, S. (1999). Unraveling the complexity of the increase in college grades from the mid-1980s to the mid-1990s. *Education Evaluation and Policy Analysis*, 21(3), pp. 297–320.

Maclellan, E. (2001). Assessment for Learning: the differing perceptions of tutors and students. *Assessment and Evaluation in Higher Education*, 26(4), pp. 307–18.

Mager, R.F. (1962). *Preparing instructional objectives*. Palo Alto, CA: Fearon.

Milton, O., Pollio, H.R. and Eison, J. (1986). *Making sense of college grades*. San Francisco, CA: Jossey-Bass.

Morrison, H.G., Magennis, S.P. and Carey, L.J. (1995). Performance indicators and league tables: a call for standards. *Higher Education Quarterly*, 49(2), pp. 128–45.

National Committee of Inquiry into Higher Education (1997). *Higher education in the learning society*. Norwich: Her Majesty's Stationery Office.

Newstead, S.E. (2002). Examining the examiners: why are we so bad at assessing students? *Psychology Learning and Teaching*, 2(2), pp. 70–75.

Pascarella, E.T. and Terenzini, P.T. (2005). *How college affects students. Volume 2: A third decade of research*. San Francisco, CA: Jossey-Bass.

Quality Assurance Agency (2004). *Academic review of subjects in HEIs—2002–04: summary report*. At www.qaa.ac.uk/reviews/academicReview/summaryreport04/report.asp (accessed 22 January 2008).

Rosovsky, H. and Hartley, M. (2002). *Evaluation and the academy: are we doing the right thing?* Cambridge, MA: American Academy of Arts and Sciences.

Sadler, D.R. (1987). Specifying and promulgating achievement standards. *Oxford Review of Education*, 13(2), pp. 191–209.

Sadler, D.R. (2005). Interpretations of criteria-based assessment and grading in higher education. *Assessment and Evaluation in Higher Education*, 30(2), pp. 176–94.

Sadler, D.R. (2007). Perils in the meticulous specification of goals and assessment criteria. *Assessment in Education: Principles, Policy and Practice*, 14(3), pp. 387–392.

Sadler, D.R. (2008). Transforming holistic assessment and grading into a vehicle for complex learning. In G. Joughin (ed.) *Assessment, learning and judgment in higher education: critical issues and future directions*. Dordrecht: Springer.

Sadler, D.R. (forthcoming) Indeterminacy in the use of preset criteria for assessment and grading. *Assessment and Evaluation in Higher Education*.

Saliu, S. (2005). Constrained subjective assessment of student learning. *Journal of Science Education and Technology*, 14(3), pp. 271–84.

Stone, J.E. (1995). Inflated grades, inflated enrollment, and inflated budgets: an analysis and call for review at the state level. *Education Policy Analysis Archives*, 3(11). At http://epaa.asu.edu/epaa/v3n11.html (accessed 26 January 2008).

Tan, K.H.K. and Prosser, M. (2004). Qualitatively different ways of differentiating student achievement: a phenomenographic study of academics' conceptions of grade descriptors. *Assessment and Evaluation in Higher Education*, 29(3), pp. 267–81.

Walvoord, B.E. (2004). *Assessment clear and simple: a practical guide for institutions, departments, and general education*. San Francisco, CA: Jossey-Bass.

Walvoord, B.E. and Anderson, V.J. (1998). *Effective grading: a tool for learning and assessment*. San Francisco: Jossey-Bass.

Webster, F., Pepper, D. and Jenkins, A. (2000). Assessing the undergraduate dissertation. *Assessment and Evaluation in Higher Education*, 25(1), pp. 71–80.

Wolf, A. (1995). *Competence-based assessment*. Buckingham: Open University Press.

Woolf, H. (2004). Assessment criteria: reflections on current practices. *Assessment and Evaluation in Higher Education*, 29(4), pp. 479–93.

Yorke, M. (2008). *Grading student achievement in higher education: signals and shortcomings*. Abingdon: Routledge.

Yorke, M. (2008a). Faulty signals? Inadequacies of grading systems and a possible response. In G. Joughin (ed.) *Assessment, learning and judgment in higher education: critical issues and future directions*. Dordrecht: Springer.

Yorke, M., Bridges, P., Woolf, H. *et al.* (2000). Mark distributions and marking practices in UK higher education. *Active Learning in Higher Education*, 1(1), pp. 7–27.

Yorke, M., Cooper, A., Fox, W., Haines, C., McHugh, P., Turner, D. and Woolf, H. (1996). Module mark distributions in eight subject areas and some issues they raise. In N. Jackson (ed.) *Modular higher education in the UK*. London: Higher Education Quality Council, pp. 105–07.

Yorke, M., Woolf, H., Stowell, M., Allen, R., Haines, C., Redding, M., Scurry, D., Taylor-Russell, G., Turnbull, W. and Walker, L. (submitted) Enigmatic variations: Honours degree assessment regulations in the UK.

17
National Monitoring of Higher Education
Motives, Methods and Means

John Taylor

Introduction

Throughout the world, the political and popular profile of higher education has never been higher. Aware of the growing needs of the knowledge economy and the knowledge society, governments have sought to increase participation in higher education in order to meet the demand for knowledge workers and have encouraged the development of innovation and technology transfer in order to create competitive economic advantage. With massification has also come increasing socio-economic awareness of higher education, an expectation that access for higher education is to be provided. Even in countries where demographic factors are threatening to slow the continued expansion in student numbers, such as Japan or Ireland, governments are looking to increase participation by addressing particular issues of demand by age, socio-economic background, ethnicity, gender, disability, mode of delivery and geography.

However, with growth and expansion, and with increasing complexity, have come new approaches to funding and management. Governments, recognising the importance of higher education, and often conscious of the electoral consequences of increasing participation, have sought to direct or steer the organisation and delivery of higher education. Even in a nation such as the United States, with little tradition of federal government involvement in higher education, the Spellings Report published in 2006 marks a new level of national concern with higher education (Spellings, 2006). Ideas of new public management, with an emphasis on target setting, devolved responsibility for delivery and strict accountability, have found expression within higher education in many European countries.

Debates persist regarding the role of higher education as a public good or a private good, or both, and attention focuses on the consequent implications for the funding of education and research. Above all, issues of competition and marketisation have arisen. Governments, keen to encourage the expansion of higher education, but unable or reluctant to find the necessary resources, have promoted the expansion of private sectors in higher education. Within the public sector, governments have sought to foster competition in order to promote choice and efficiency. New funding models have emerged, commonly with an element of private funding through fees, again intended to develop competition as well as to reflect the private benefits of higher education and to compensate for inadequate public resources.

A consistent theme running through all these changes is the need to monitor higher education. In 1997, Power discussed the inter-relationship between accountability verification and risk reduction in his influential book *The Audit Society: Rituals of verification* (Power, 1997). This theme was described earlier in higher education by Neave as the "rise of the evaluation state" (Neave, 1988). Whether it is a government looking to ensure that quality is maintained, especially at times of expansion, or that national policy objectives have been achieved, or that value for money has been achieved, or whether it is the student faced with a dazzling array of choices about institutions of higher education, entrance requirements, subjects of study, modes of learning and the costs of study, there is a demand for some objective evidence or criteria upon which to make the necessary judgements. In effect, as the importance of higher education to economies and societies around the world has grown and has been more openly recognised, so the need to monitor and to evaluate has been reinforced. Moreover, in seeking to respond to these challenges, higher education institutions (HEIs) have themselves looked to enhanced monitoring as an effective tool in order to understand more fully their internal operations. As a result, important questions must be faced about the purposes and methodology of monitoring, and about the impact of such monitoring on the actual delivery of education and research.

Objectives of Monitoring

Monitoring is an activity that is common to all kinds of procedures and practices across the world. Referring to the need for audit, Flint writes that the essential pre-requisite is "that there is a relationship of accountability or a situation of public accountability" (Flint, 1988: 23). This certainly applies in the world of higher education where universities and colleges may be responsible for the expenditure of very considerable sums of public money or where government feels a responsibility to safeguard the interests of the population or to regulate an area of strategic significance. However, monitoring is also related to concepts of trust and may be required "when accountability can no longer be sustained by informal relations of trust alone but must be formalised, made visible and subject to independent validation" (Power, 1994: 9–10). This last point was especially apparent in the UK during the 1980s and 1990s when many new tools for monitoring higher education were introduced at a time when the historic relationship of mutual trust between government and the universities was challenged by Margaret Thatcher's government.

Accountability to stakeholders, including government, students, employers and society in general, is clearly a driving force behind monitoring of higher education. This is explicit in the purposes set out by the Quality Assurance Agency (QAA) in the UK:

> To achieve its mission, QAA works in partnership with the providers and funders of higher education, staff and students in higher education, employers and other stakeholders, to:
>
> - safeguard the student and wider public interest in the maintenance of standards of academic awards and the quality of higher education;
> - communicate information on academic standards and quality to inform student choice and employers' understanding, and to underpin public policy-making;
> - enhance the assurance and management of standards and quality in higher education;
> - promote wider understanding of the nature of standards and quality in higher education, including the maintenance of common reference points, drawing on UK, other European and international practice.
>
> (QAA, 2008)

As with the UK example, the motivation behind monitoring in other countries is commonly multi-faceted. Most significantly, monitoring is often associated with quality enhancement. This may take the form of feedback to the institution itself and/or the wider communication of good practice. Thus, for example, the audits undertaken by the Finnish Higher Education Evaluation Council (FHEEC) are intended:

> ... to collect and disseminate best QA practices and promote their adoption within the HEIs. The aim of the audit process and public reporting on the HEI system is to activate the debate on quality issues, as well as the interaction between the HEIs and their stakeholders.

More specifically, the FHEEC states the aim of each institutional audit to be:

- to establish the qualitative objectives set by the HEI for its own activities;
- to evaluate what procedures and processes the HEI uses to maintain and develop the quality of its education and other activities;
- to evaluate whether the HEI's quality assurance works as intended, whether the QA system produces useful and relevant information for the improvement of its operations and whether it brings about effective improvement measures.

(FHEEC, 2007, p. 10)

In Australia, the Australian Universities Quality Agency (AUQA) is responsible for the quality audit of higher education institutions, including a system of periodic auditing intended to consider the quality of academic activities, including attainment of standards of performance and quality assurance arrangements intended to maintain and elevate that quality and compliance with criteria set out in national protocols. For the first cycle of audits, completed in 2007, whole-of-institution audits were undertaken, based on a self-assessment and site visit. A specific objective of the monitoring undertaken by AUQA is that "through AUQA's work, there will be an improvement in public knowledge of the relative standards of Australian higher education and an increase in public confidence in Australian higher education" (AUQA, 2008).

Another consistent theme running through these examples is the perceived importance of monitoring in communicating information and understanding about higher education. Power notes that "audits are usually justified as enhancing the transparency of individual and corporate actions to those parties who have an interest in the nature and effects of those actions. In other words, they are thought to shift power; from professionals to the public, from experts to stakeholders" (Power, 1994: 18). Thus, monitoring of higher education may be seen as one aspect of the consumerisation of higher education, the shift from higher education as a supply-driven function to higher education as a demand-driven activity. Transparency is often advocated in higher education as a device that can lead to better understanding of policy and decision-making for staff and to wider choice and influence for students. However, whether monitoring procedures have succeeded in broadening and deepening the appreciation of higher education is much less clear. On the one hand, it is apparent that individual students have a new sense of their rights and expectations, with examples of litigation increasing; on the other hand, there is little evidence that the outcomes of monitoring are significantly influencing student choice of institutions or effective involvement in institutional governance (see, for example, HEFCE (2008)). A strong note of caution may be struck: "transparency alone does not empower, and paradoxically, may even serve to pacify and neutralise other possible forms of accountability, such as those based on answerability. At the extreme, audits which have become tightly interwoven in regulation programmes can do more to promote obscurity than transparency" (Power, 1994, p. 21).

Monitoring may also be used as a device in order to inform, influence and drive change in higher education. Sometimes change may be an explicit objective; on other occasions, the desire to encourage change is more implicit or may even be disguised. Of particular significance is the preparation of comparative information, whether it be within an institution, across institutions or between countries. The development of performance indicators and of benchmarking are key stages in monitoring. At one level, they inform institutions and their stakeholders of relative performance over time or between institutions and countries, thereby showing areas of relative strength or weakness. Thus, indicators may show relatively more expensive activities (for example, cost per student) or may measure relative success or failure (for example, research income per member of staff or applications per place). Such management information may be used to identify issues for attention or to force change. However, at another level, such information, especially when published or widely disseminated, unleashes a competitive reaction, within institutions and among policy-makers; publication of the outcome of monitoring may have a significant impact on enhancing or retaining a university's much-cherished reputation and brand, or may help to make or break the reputation of a particular department. In this way, monitoring may have very serious consequences for higher education, underlining the importance of ensuring both that information is collected and analysed with skill and accuracy, and that interpretation is fair and balanced. In this way, monitoring is a tool which may inform change, by highlighting issues or suggesting possible lines of action; monitoring should prompt questions and debate, but, in itself, it does not provide answers and does not lend itself to the application of policy in a slavish, formulaic way, either within institutions or across national systems.

In Portugal, the use of monitoring as an instrument for change is explicit. Since 1994, both public and private institutions have been required by law to undertake quality assessments of their educational processes, with the following objectives:

- to stimulate and to improve quality of all university activities;
- to inform and to show society how the university is organised and how the inputs and outputs of its educational system are processed;
- to promote dialogue among different schools;
- to contribute to the reorganisation of the actual network of higher education institutions.

As a result, "Government can implement some positive and negative measures, namely, by reinforcing or cutting financial support for the target institutions" (Pile and Teixeira, 1997: p. 5).

In Germany, the sense of competition stimulated by the monitoring process is equally apparent, although the consequences for funding are less direct. Whilst the federal government is becoming increasingly involved in research strategy at national level, including the identification of centres of excellence, most quality assessment and monitoring is undertaken at the level of the *Länder*. Hartwig draws some important conclusions about monitoring in Germany that reinforce the link with competition and change:

Everywhere, quality assessment responds to a political call for action. The development of quality assessment is not only connected to the expansion of the higher education sector, but also to the limited amount of public resources provided for it and to the demands of internationalisation and international competition . . . One important effect of quality assurance is that departments have to become clear about their needs regarding their priorities and their future development. They have to clarify which international trends they want to follow. Universities feel obliged to introduce quality assessment in order to enhance the quality of their institutions in a highly competitive global market for teaching and research. Quality assessment is expected to highlight the particular strengths and weaknesses of the evaluated department as well as standards and aims to be met. It should lead to a better self-awareness of the overall performance of the department under review (Hartwig, 2003, p. 80).

In Germany, there is no direct link at the level of the *Länder* between monitoring and resource allocation. This reflects a recognition of the need to retain teaching in some key subject areas and to reflect differences by discipline in research activity. Elsewhere, however, monitoring of activity may lead directly to funding outcomes. Thus, the Research Assessment Exercise (RAE) in the UK, an occasional review of research activity, first undertaken in 1985–86 and most recently undertaken in 2007–08, leads to ratings that contribute directly to the allocation of funds to individual universities for research. For the UK Higher Education Funding Councils, the RAE is first and foremost a methodology to inform the allocation of funds. However, it has also had more profound effects on UK higher education, facilitating the concentration of research funding in departments identified to be of the highest quality and successfully encouraging a strongly competitive approach to the management and delivery of research in UK universities.

Monitoring of higher education may therefore be undertaken with different objectives in mind, for accountability, to enhance quality, to encourage wider understanding and awareness, to promote change, to stimulate competition and comparisons, and to inform the allocation of resources. Often, monitoring is undertaken not for a single reason but for a combination of motives. Brennan draws attention to some other motives for the establishment of quality agencies, including the undertaking of quality checks on new (sometimes private) institutions, the award of institutional status and the support of student mobility (often through the international comparison of qualifications) (Brennan and Shah, 2000, p. 32).

The objectives of monitoring may therefore vary widely depending on the context and rationale. Similarly, the response of stakeholders to the increasing levels of scrutiny also varies widely. In countries with a tradition of strong institutional autonomy, active monitoring has often been viewed as an intrusion, an imposition, often initiated by government, that threatens to erode self-determination and independence. In the UK, for example, new forms of monitoring have often been greeted with deep unease by universities. For some institutions, monitoring has raised profound questions of principle. For others, the main unease has been a practical one, reflecting concern about the additional workload often imposed on institutions through monitoring or about the use made of monitoring by outside bodies, most notably the press. Whilst many institutions have publicly criticised the growth of monitoring, it is also important to note that, commonly, these same institutions have readily adopted monitoring for their internal management and self-regulation. Thus, the monitoring of performance at all levels within institutions—college, school, department, centre, service and individual member of staff—have become commonplace, driven by the same objectives that have underpinned the emergence of monitoring more generally. Such trends are clear in the UK, but have also been witnessed in North America and Australia. For these universities, therefore, the main issue is less the element of change implied by monitoring and more the fear of external control.

By contrast, Brennan describes the stronger traditions of state regulation that have characterised many other countries in continental Europe, leading to higher levels of conformity in areas such as curriculum, employment and financial management and assumed equivalence between institutions. For such institutions, monitoring has been a key instrument for change, opening up new sources of information and stimulating new forms of comparison and competition. Monitoring has been part of the increasing deregulation of higher education witnessed in countries such as Austria, Croatia and Hungary and of a transfer of responsibilities from state to institutions (Brennan and

Shah, 2000, p. 27). In continental Europe, therefore, and, in practice, in other parts of the world, including in particular Latin America, monitoring has been challenged mainly as an agent of change and less from concern about institutional control.

Monitoring clearly raises issues of control and change. For individual members of academic staff, it also raises issues of academic freedom. The ability to teach and research without direct, detailed control of methods and content is a freedom much cherished in many countries across the world. At one level, monitoring can mean some degree of oversight; such oversight might be supportive as well as adversarial. At another level, some staff fear that teaching and research will be subject to control. Monitoring can be used to inform the selective allocation of resources which may support some individuals and deny funds to others. Monitoring may also tend to favour quantitative assessment rather than qualitative assessment. In teaching, monitoring may encourage staff to be more cautious and less experimental. For individuals, therefore, monitoring can be an uncomfortable and disconcerting process, and may discourage risk-taking and innovation for fear of failure. There is clearly a risk that monitoring may lead to control and caution by academic staff. In reality, however, this is less a problem of monitoring in itself and more an issue of how such monitoring is implemented, by whom and why. It is therefore necessary to address some of the different forms of monitoring now prevalent in higher education.

Forms of Monitoring

In the same way that the motivation for monitoring of higher education can vary, so the form taken by the monitoring process may also vary widely. The most simple distinction is between monitoring that is externally driven and that which is internal to the higher education institution. External monitoring may, in turn, be either formal, undertaken as part of a national regulatory framework, or informal, possibly involving processes outside of the control or influence of either government or institutions. Similarly, internal monitoring within institutions may also be either formal or informal. These distinctions are of considerable significance since there are often important consequences for universities arising from these different forms of monitoring.

As far as formal external monitoring is concerned, it is necessary also to distinguish between what Van Vught (1991) identified as the two primary traditions in government steering of higher education: the state control model, or the interventionary state, and the state supervisory model, or the facilitating state:

> The state control model treats higher education as a homogeneous enterprise, with government attempting to regulate all aspects of the dynamics of the higher education system: access, curriculum, degree requirements, the examination system, appointments and remuneration of academic staff, and so on. This model does not recognise the loosely coupled, multi-dimensional character of higher education. In contrast, in the state supervisory/facilitatory model, the influence exercised by the state is weak, with many of the basic decisions on such matters as curriculum, degrees, staff recruitment, and finance, left to the institutions themselves. The state sets the broad parameters in which higher education operates, but fundamental decisions about missions and goals are the province of the system and its individual institutions. (Goedegebuure et al., 1997, p. 621)

Monitoring is often feared as an instrument of government control. Yet, paradoxically, formal monitoring is often relatively weak in systems where state control is strongest. Thus, for example, in the countries of Eastern Europe where, until the last 15 years, higher education was closely controlled by the state, there was little tradition of monitoring or assessment; in effect, controls were such that monitoring was not needed and any assessment process would, in practice, have been examining the role of the state itself.

Monitoring, therefore, is more often a characteristic of the state supervisory model. The precise form of the evaluation may vary, the key difference being between monitoring as a tool for assessment and monitoring as a tool for assurance. Assessment has been familiar within UK higher education since the 1980s. In 1986, the first Research Selectivity Exercise was undertaken, followed in 1989, 1992, 1996, 2001 and 2008 by further Research Assessment Exercises (RAE). In each case, data is collected on staffing, funding for research, research students and selected outputs (normally publications), supplemented by text-based commentaries and further information. The information is collected by 67 units of assessment that equate loosely to subjects or disciplines and is assessed on a peer review basis. Ratings are then awarded to each university submitting under that unit of assessment. In 2001 assessments were given on a seven-point scale (1, 2, 3b, 3a, 4, 5 and 5*, with 5* the highest rating), but for 2008 a more sophisticated approach has been adopted based on profiles showing the proportion of activity rated as 1*, 2*, 3* and 4*, with 4* representing the highest level of international quality. The RAE has been a crucial factor in shaping UK higher education over two decades. Essentially a device to ensure that government block grant funding for research is directed to the university departments perceived to be of highest quality, the RAE has been much criticised for creating an overemphasis on research at the expense of teaching, for becoming an end in itself, and thereby distorting research activity, and for its costs, both direct and in terms of staff time; further, more technical issues have also provoked vigorous debate, such as the consequences for academic staff development, equal opportunities, interdisciplinary research, publishing practice, criteria used, definitions for ratings and "game playing". At the same time, however, it is also suggested that the RAE has encouraged the better management of research in UK universities and enhanced rewards for leading researchers, and has therefore underpinned the widely acknowledged success of UK research relative to international competitors.

Assessment was also applied to teaching and learning in the UK. In June 1992, the Government indicated that the new Higher Education Funding Council for England (HEFCE) was to develop an approach to assessment, the outcomes from which were to be "in a form which can be used to inform funding allocations". Hence, from 1993, a process of assessments began, based on peer review, which identified provisions as "excellent", "satisfactory" or "unsatisfactory". Following an internal self-assessment, external assessors could decide whether or not they wished to accept the self-categorisation proposed; if not, or if in doubt, the assessors would visit the institution concerned. From 1995, this system evolved, following consultation with universities, into an assessment process where all departments would be visited and a new grading scale applied based on six core aspects of quality; curriculum design, content and organisation; teaching, learning and assessment; student progression and achievement; student support and guidance; learning resources; and quality assurance and enhancement. For each aspect, a score of 1–4 could be achieved, giving a highest maximum score of 24. Like the RAE, this system of teaching quality assessment received much criticism, especially for the labour-intensive nature of the assessment visits, for "game playing" by institutions, who swiftly became extremely adept at preparing the necessary paperwork and at coaching their staff and students, for grade inflation and for the absence of a clear formative element; in particular, as with the RAE, universities were unhappy that both exercises had created crude, oversimplified "scores" that were enthusiastically used by the press for institutional comparison. The system effectively came to an end in 2001 when, under pressure from leading universities in particular, the Government announced a new "lighter touch" and a new system emerged without an explicit numerical rating and with a greater emphasis on quality enhancement and audit.

The UK experience through the assessment-based monitoring of both research and teaching reveals much about the impact of external monitoring:

- Monitoring, especially when linked to published "scoring" systems, rapidly and inevitably leads to vigorous competition and preparation of comparative "league tables".
- Such competition will lead to professionalisation and improvements in university management, especially in preparing data for external submission.
- As far as possible, procedures should be transparent and fair, with clear criteria and involving the use of peer review in order to moderate and explain shortcomings in data.
- Monitoring should be cost-effective and efficient, both on the part of those doing the monitoring and those being monitored, and should be as non-intrusive as possible.
- Assessment-based monitoring can lead to real improvements, such as those in research management or in university procedures for teaching and learning, but that such improvements will diminish over time.
- Monitoring can have unforeseen consequences—for example, none of the individuals involved in the initial development of the RAE foresaw its emergence as a central element of higher education policy in the UK.

The UK illustrates how monitoring for assessment may develop. Elsewhere, the main driver for monitoring has been quality assurance and improvement rather than assessment. In Sweden, the National Agency for Higher Education (the Högskoleverket) has undertaken a regular programme of institutional audits since 1995. The emphasis is primarily on quality assurance processes and the extent to which they yield results in the form of improvement. A new round of audits, begun in 2007, assumes that institutions now have in place necessary systems and therefore concentrates on results and outcomes:

> Short-term effects of quality assurance routines may be reallocation of resources, more teachers with research qualifications, new syllabuses, updated reading lists, enhancement of teacher qualifications, new teaching methods, more satisfied students and improved throughput. More long-term effects may relate to student perceptions of their programmes after qualification, their possibilities of then finding work and what employers think of the programme and the knowledge acquired by students. General aspects of quality such as promoting student influence, gender equality, diversity, internationalisation, co-operation and sustainable development will also be appraised. Here too the audits focus on results and outcomes (Högskoleverket, 2008).

Over a six-year period, the Högskoleverket reviews the quality of all degree programmes and also monitors the quality procedures of all higher education institutions. The evaluation of subjects and programmes involves the following stages:

- Departments carry out self-evaluation.
- The Högskoleverket compiles an overall national survey of more extensive subject areas. These describe the programmes subject to evaluation in any given year.
- A sample of subjects, programmes or individual courses is made. This sample is based on an appraisal of the self-evaluations, key statistics and other factual material.
- The programmes selected are then subject to in-depth evaluations. In these cases a panel of assessors is appointed, which makes site visits.

Panels of assessors consist of individuals with academic and teaching skills from higher education institutions in Sweden and abroad. In addition, there will be a student member and assessors with labour market experience may be added. Visits take as a starting point the self-evaluation, supplemented by meetings with programme staff, senior representations of the university, other teaching staff, support staff and students. After the visit, a report is written, with recommended improvements. Three years later, a follow-up enquiry is conducted to determine how the recommendations have been dealt with.

The methodology of the Swedish system is based heavily on self-evaluation, a common feature of more formative, less assessment-based systems. Here, the key assumption is that monitoring is a process of self-reflection and self-improvement rather than a tool for external assessment. The role of external advisors is more for their specialist input and advice within this process rather than as detached assessors. Other important features include student participation—a further indicator of the emphasis placed on improvement—and the report, with subsequent follow-up, but without the explicit ratings and scorings that have been a feature of more assessment-based systems.

External monitoring may also represent a form of control and quality assurance. This can be illustrated by the process of accreditation that exists in many countries. In the USA, for example, whilst the Federal Department of Education does not accredit institutions or programmes, the Secretary of Education is required by law to publish a list of nationally recognised accrediting agencies. These agencies are private educational associations of regional or national scope that have developed evaluation criteria and procedures intended to ensure that the education provided by institutions of higher education meets acceptable levels of quality. The functions of this form of monitoring are:

- Verifying that an institution or program meets established standards;
- Assisting prospective students in identifying acceptable institutions;
- Assisting institutions in determining the acceptability of transfer credits;
- Helping to identify institutions and programs for the investment of public and private funds;
- Protecting an institution against harmful internal and external pressure;
- Creating goals for self-improvement of weaker programs and stimulating a general raising of standards among educational institutions;
- Involving the faculty and staff comprehensively in institutional evaluation and planning;
- Establishing criteria for professional certification and licensure and for upgrading courses offering such preparation; and
- Providing one of several considerations used as a basis for determining eligibility for Federal assistance.

The normal accrediting procedure involves six stages:

1. Standards: The accrediting agency, in collaboration with educational institutions, establishes standards.
2. Self-study: The institution or programme seeking accreditation prepares an in-depth self-evaluation study that measures its performance against the standards established by the accrediting agency.
3. On-site Evaluation: A team selected by the accrediting agency visits the institution or programme to determine first-hand if the applicant meets the established standards.
4. Publication: Upon being satisfied that the applicant meets its pre-accreditation status, lists the institution or programme in an official publication with other similarly accredited or pre-accredited institutions or programmes.
5. Monitoring: The accrediting agency monitors each accredited institution or programme

throughout the period of accreditation granted to verify that it continues to meet the agency's standards.

6. Re-evaluation: The accrediting agency periodically re-evaluates each institution or programme that it lists to ascertain whether continuation of its accredited or pre-accredited status is warranted. (US Department of Education, 2008).

Accreditation can take various forms. However, Campbell and Rozsnayai suggest that "while accreditation has different definitions, forms and functions, it generally has the following character-istics: it provides proof (or not) that a certain standard is being met in a higher education course, programme or institution. The standard met can either be a minimum standard or a standard of excellence; it involves a benchmarking assessment; judgements are based solely on quality criteria, never on political characteristics and always yes/no; the emphasis is on accountability" (Campbell and Rozsnyai, 2002: 31).

Similar pressures are seen elsewhere in the world. For example, in Japan, as of 2004, government law has required all public and private universities, junior colleges and colleges of technology to be accredited by an evaluation organisation authorised by the national government. Accreditation is seen as a necessary response to the globalisation of higher education, and especially concerns about quality within international markets. However, accreditation and monitoring also offers a form of ongoing control by the Ministry of Education in Japan following the deregulation of government authorisation for the establishment of new higher education institutions (Yonezawa, 2005). In India, the National Assessment and Accreditation Council (NAAC) undertakes a series of institutional assessments using both self-evaluation and peer review. In the Netherlands, quality assurance is undertaken by the Association of Universities in the Netherlands (USNU) and involves assessments based on self-evaluation and peer review visits. However, a further level of review is undertaken on behalf of the Ministry of Education, Culture and Science by its own inspectors. These inspections occur every two years and, potentially, can lead to the withdrawal of funding in cases of failure.

Such formal procedures normally result in the publication of reports and guidance. Mostly, any comparative analysis or rankings is undertaken by third parties, normally the press or the uni-versities themselves. However, some rankings are undertaken by formal bodies themselves. Thus, the Higher Education Commission in Pakistan issues its own rankings of universities and so does the National Accreditation Centre in the Ministry of Education and Science in Kazakhstan. In both cases, the impetus is towards quality improvement by encouraging competition and wider aware-ness of institutional strengths.

External Monitoring: Some Informal Approaches

Formal monitoring of higher education, as has been demonstrated, is motivated in part by the intention to reassure stakeholders in higher education of quality and standards, including students, prospective students, families and employers. In an increasingly market-driven world of higher education, monitoring also serves to provide some of the information necessary for markets to operate, or, at least, for some element of market principles to apply. The same can be said of the forms of informal monitoring that have now developed in many parts of the world. Most of these informal approaches to monitoring take the form of rankings which aim to compare the perform-ance at different universities according to various criteria. Most are also associated with newspapers or publishing companies and a less charitable view of their production would suggest these rank-ings have more to do with circulation and sales than with providing a public service. Nevertheless, rankings are now an established form of monitoring that cannot be ignored.

The first example of college and university rankings was the assessments made in the US by the magazine *US News & World Report*, which launched its rankings of US universities in 1983 and has published them annually since 1985. The precise methodology used by *US News* has varied over time, but may be summarised as follows:

- peer assessment, using a survey of reputation among staff (faculty) and administrators
- retention and graduation rates
- quality of intake as measured by test scores, high school class results and the proportion of applicants accepted
- resources including average class size, staff (faculty) salaries, staff (faculty) qualifications, staff (faculty)–student ratios and proportions of full-time academic staff
- expenditure per student
- alumni giving.

Similar rankings have emerged in many other countries. In Canada, another news magazine, *Maclean's*, produces an annual ranking of Canadian universities based on factors including student characteristics, teaching staff, finances, teaching resources and reputation. Rankings are made for institutions that are primarily undergraduate, those that are comprehensive and those that are medical and doctoral institutions. In the UK, there is a range of league tables, including *The Times, Sunday Times* and *Guardian*; in addition, a wide range of books are published, such as the *Times Good University Guide* (2008). The oldest established rankings, compiled by *The Times* newspaper, uses a range of factors:

- student satisfaction, taken from the UK National Student Survey
- research quality, taken from the Research Assessment Exercise
- entry standards
- resources, including student–staff ratios, library and computing spending and facilities spending
- proportion of students graduating with good honours degrees and completion rates
- employment prospects.

The *Guardian* does not use research standing and uses the following factors:

- student assessments, from the UK National Student Survey
- spending per student
- student–staff ratios
- employment
- value-added, which attempts to relate degree results with entrance qualifications
- entrance qualifications.

National rankings, both of whole institutions and of different subject areas, are now a feature of higher education around the world. They are the subject of vigorous debate and criticism, especially of the methodologies used. This form of monitoring may be criticised for many reasons:

- These rankings involve the formulaic combination of various factors, often entailing the use of weightings that are highly subjective and lacking "any defensible empirical or theoretical basis".
- The averaging process commonly applied leads to a final "result" that is meaningless as a base for true comparisons.

- In some countries, such as the UK, rankings compare in a single table institutions with widely differing missions and objectives, leading to the charge of comparing "apples with pears".
- Rankings are widely criticised for effectively presenting listings of relative wealth between universities.
- Methodologies change frequently, leading to distortions and fluctuations in results.
- Use of opinion and reputation surveys is often criticised for bias and for favouring out-dated and possibly incorrect perceptions of the standing of particular institutions.
- Mixing of research and teaching criteria within a single assessment.
- Inability to cope successfully with concepts such as "value-added".

Such criticisms have led some universities in some countries to withdraw co-operation with this form of monitoring. In the US, in 2007, the Annapolis Group of colleges decided not to participate in reputational rankings, in the UK, three universities have refused to allow *The Times* to have access to data and in Canada several universities have also refused to take part in the *Maclean's* survey. At the same time, this form of external monitoring has also become more sophisticated, at least in part to answer some of these central criticisms and to meet the needs of users. Thus, in Germany, the Centre for Higher Education Development (CHE) introduced ratings based on surveys of students and professors that allow users to design their own rankings according to personal preferences and academic interests. In December 2007, the CHE also introduced "excellence" rankings for master's and doctoral programmes.

However, in practice, such informal monitoring continues to develop, with many forms of "alternative" rankings. Indeed, it may be argued that it is this continuing growth in the number of rankings that has actually begun to dilute the impact of this type of monitoring. It is sometimes said that it is a poor university president or vice-chancellor who cannot claim that their university is not top of at least one ranking.

Another relatively recent development is the emergence of global rankings of universities. In 2003, the Shanghai Jiao Tong University Institute of Higher Education began to produce its inter-national ranking of universities. In this case, the initial motivation was to monitor how the rapidly developing Chinese universities compared with their international competitors. The factors used in compiling this ranking are:

- number of Nobel prizes and Fields Medals
- number of articles and citations in scholarly journals (data from Thomson ISI)
- number of academic staff.

Thus, the ranking is, deliberately, research-based; ratings are produced by broad disciplinary group-ings as well as by institution.

A year later, in 2004, the *Times Higher Education Supplement* (now *Times Higher Education*) produced a second set of international rankings, intended to be more broadly based. This included a significant reputational element based on a survey of academic staff and a survey of global employers. Further elements include the proportion of international students, the proportion of international staff, student–staff ratios (used as a proxy for teaching quality) and citation performance.

Again, there is already a proliferation of such tables. In the US, *Newsweek* magazine has pub-lished a Top 100 Global Universities and in Spain the Cybermetrics Laboratory of the National Research Council has produced a Webometrics Ranking of World Universities based on web pres-ence and web publication.

As with national rankings, this form of international monitoring is subject to heavy criticism. The use of citations strongly favours institutions where the primary medium of research is the English language and the use of opinion surveys represents a highly subjective element within such analysis and is subject to extremely low response rates; moreover, the availability of accurate, comparable international data is very limited. Here, such rankings fail to achieve many of the key requirements for effective monitoring, most notably transparency and credibility.

However, of particular concern is the growing evidence of the impact of such informal monitoring on institutional management. Marginson points to the danger that "rankings, especially reputational rankings, become an end in themselves and protected from critical scrutiny, without regard to exactly what they measure, whether they are solidly grounded or whether their use has constructive effects. The desire for rank ordering overrules all else. Often institutions are rank ordered even where differences in the data are not statistically significant. Moreover, the illusion is created that all institutions have the same capacity to succeed even though their circumstances are often vastly different" (Marginson, 2007, p. 8). Frequently, apparently "casual" comments about being in the "top ten" or the "Global Top 100" begin to take on a motivational reality.

A study of league tables undertaken for the Higher Education Funding Council for England (HEFCE) concluded that "league tables and the individual indicators used to compile them appear to be having a significant influence on institutions' actions and decision-making, although institutions themselves are reluctant to acknowledge this, league tables are being used by many institutions as key performance indicators and in some cases strategic targets. They are being used by some senior management teams and governing bodies as one of several drivers for internal change" (HEFCE, 2008: 6). The HEFCE study highlights how league tables may conflict with other national and institutional priorities, such as widening participation, community engagement and the provision of socially valued subjects.

This tension reflects a belief within institutions that such rankings have a clear influence on student recruitment, especially of high-quality and international students, and on the external profile of institutions with key stakeholders, especially governments and key funding organisations. Failure to cope with this tension tends to encourage conformity and a reluctance to take risk. Marginson notes that "singular rankings systems encourage institutions to reduce the emphasis on those activities that do not contribute to rankings performance; and more generally leads to convergence of behaviour between institutional types and between natural systems (and languages of use). Unless there is a broad range of rankings systems with no one system dominant, all else being equal rankings tend to work against diversity of provision. This is a serious difficulty, much remarked upon, with no solution in sight" (Marginson, 2007, p. 9).

External monitoring, both formal and informal, is therefore a powerful influence on the organisation and delivery of higher education. Both forms claim in varying ways to protect the interests of the users of higher education, most obviously students, but also, in some cases, the wider interests of government, employers and society in general. The key distinction is between approaches that are explicitly formative in nature and those that are intended to provide comparative information, either as the basis for selective resource allocation and policy development or to meet the demands of increasing marketisation; these latter forms of monitoring may have formative effects, but the process is indirect and unplanned.

Internal Monitoring

Within higher education institutions, regular monitoring of activities is now also well established. Motivated by the desire for improvement and by the need to respond to the changing external environment, universities have put in place a wide range of monitoring procedures. At institutional level, some universities have in place regular procedures for self-evaluation and/or assessment, often involving inputs and advice from external experts appointed by the university. In Finland, for example, universities systematically follow a programme of reviews, based on self-assessment and visits by specialist panels. This is an internal process, with the report and recommendations submitted to the university and the outcome pursued at the discretion of the university.

Many universities also have internal procedures for the monitoring of teaching and research, normally involving the development of a series of performance indicators. The following would be typical of many universities:

Teaching and Learning

- number of applications
- quality of entrants
- socio-economic, age, gender profiles of students
- assessment results, by stage in programme and by student profiles
- progression rates
- final assessments and levels of student achievement
- employment and student outcomes
- student feedback and evaluation
- staff feedback.

Research

- funding received, by source
- numbers of outputs, by form of output
- numbers of staff active in research
- numbers of research students
- numbers of completed research degrees.

In both cases, universities will commonly involve some element of peer review, using expert assessment drawn from either within or without the institution. Similarly, universities will often involve stakeholders in such monitoring. Student evaluation of study programmes is now familiar all over the world, assessing both content and teaching methods. Such information is usually intended for internal use, but modern web-based media and forms of communication mean that data is often more widely available. Whilst the motivation is normally concerned with quality enhancement, such monitoring is also closely associated with performance management, including both the recognition and reward of good performance and the identification and resolution of relatively poor performance or underperformance. Thus, monitoring is commonly linked to the establishment of management targets and their subsequent implementation and achievement. The results of monitoring may also be used to justify internal change and reorganisation.

The monitoring of management functions is more difficult to achieve, but many institutions have now developed performance indicators for actions such as the time taken to respond to applications, or for outcomes such as overall financial performance. Such monitoring may be implemented at different levels within the organisation, and for various organisational units, including schools, departments, service activities and teaching or research groups. In practice, monitoring is commonly taken to the level of individual members of staff. Increasingly, all categories of staff working in higher education are expected to achieve measurable outputs. Once any such activity can be measured, in either a qualitative or quantitative form, monitoring will inevitably follow, together with some form of evaluation. Monitoring is, therefore, a crucial element within staff development and human resource management, intimately linked with notions of performance and quality, and with appraisal and career development.

Whilst such monitoring will be initiated internally, it may also have an external perspective. Thus, benchmarking against key competitors is now commonly undertaken; in countries like the UK, Australia and the US, a wide range of management data is published or openly available. Combined with the growth of desktop computing power, universities have witnessed a massive growth in the potential for internal monitoring. In some cases, universities will share further information within benchmarking "clubs", intended to analyse particular activities and processes in detail, and to achieve enhanced operational efficiency or quality. For such benchmarking to be successful, a longitudinal aspect is crucial. In Australia, for example, the "Group of Eight" leading universities share monitoring data. Interestingly, these universities use this data internally to enhance their own operation, but also to achieve competitive advantage, often relative to each other. A shared interest in internal monitoring can therefore lead to both inter-institutional collaboration and competition at the same time.

Within universities, many forms of informal monitoring also exist. Traditionally, within a collegial environment, comment and criticism could flourish, ranging from friendly advice to more forthright direction. Deans, heads of department and research group leaders have a role in managing their activities, which has always involved an element of monitoring, especially of performance over time and in comparable universities. However, such monitoring has often been based on observation, word of mouth and personal contacts, rather than on more objective data. Herein lies the key criticism of such informal monitoring: a lack of any effective transparency and accountability. Informal monitoring also occurs at the level of individuals who will regularly compare their performance relative to colleagues and peers. This reflects professionalism within the university world, but also strong elements of competition between individuals, especially in research.

Conclusions

Whilst the form of monitoring may vary, there are a number of consistent techniques that recur:

- Self-evaluation, requiring those involved in the process to reflect on the relative achievement or otherwise of objectives set, and applied at the level of institution, department or source, or specific activity, such as a degree programme.
- Performance indicators, often bringing together input and output factors, and measured both over time and in comparison with a peer group of similar institutions or units of delivery. This may be refined into the identification of a smaller number of key performance indicators (KPIs).
- Targets, established through strategic and operational planning, may be monitored, by academic and professional leaders and managers; monitoring will then contribute to subsequent strategy and planning.
- Development and monitoring of a complex range of activities have stimulated the use of further techniques for higher education management, such as the balanced scorecard.
- Peer review and assessment, possibly the oldest established form of monitoring in higher education, remains a critical element within most approaches to evaluation and formative development. A key rationale to this form of monitoring is that, in academic life,

assessment and input by "experts" is more likely to be acceptable and carry authority than simple analysis of statistics and performance indicators.

Monitoring can have a deep impact on higher education, with consequences for institutions, staff, students and wider society. The conduct of monitoring therefore requires a sense of individual and corporate responsibility. In Australia, for example, the AUQA supports its methodology with a series of core values. Their approach is expected to be:

- rigorous
- supportive (recognising institutional autonomy)
- flexible (recognising institutional diversity)
- co-operative (as unobtrusive as possible)
- collaborative
- transparent
- economical (cost-effective, with minimal demands on institutions)
- open (to the public) (AUQA, 2008).

Monitoring is now a feature of higher education throughout the world. For some, it will always be seen as an intrusion, an infringement of academic freedom or of institutional autonomy. For others, it has become an essential part of ongoing improvement and development, and for some either a necessary instrument for control and direction or an essential part of competition within higher education. Such diversity of views and attitudes will probably never be reconciled.

From this short survey of monitoring, it is possible to develop an outline typology of type and motivation:

Table 17.1 Typology of Monitoring in Higher Education

Form of monitoring			Motivation
External	Formal	State Control State Supervising	Control Accountability Improvement Information Competition Change
	Informal		Information Competition
Internal	Formal		Improvement Accountability Change
	Informal		Information Improvement

There are, perhaps, also some key points that emerge from a study of the application of monitoring in higher education:

- **Transparency:** It is important that the motives for monitoring are fully articulated and understood, and that the information collected is open for challenge and comparison. Similarly, any methodology for assessment needs to be shared. Without such openness, it is clear that it is difficult to achieve any effective acceptance of conclusions reached.

- **Credibility:** It is desirable that any monitoring process carries the confidence and respect of those being monitored, such that outcomes, even if unwelcome, will carry some strength. An element of peer review is often important in this respect, always accepting that the selection of the peers themselves is a fair and open process. Credibility also often reflects the simple honesty of those participating, a characteristic that, sadly, is absent from higher education institutions in some parts of the world.
- **Simplicity:** In aiming to monitor activities across a wide range of disciplines and across many different organisational units, the need for simplicity is paramount. The rules of the exercise need to be understood by all concerned. Moreover, universities are no different from any other organisation; they will always work within a system to maximise their advantage and they will stretch rules to the limit. In such circumstances, simplicity of the monitoring process is often the best way forward.
- **Diversity:** Higher education is a highly complex area of activity, with multiple inputs and outputs. There is no simple, single end point to be measured. Institutions vary widely in their missions, disciplines vary in their requirements and outcomes, and staff vary in their interests and relative strengths and weaknesses. Monitoring systems must be sensitive to such diversity.
- **Improvement:** The most acceptable and successful forms of monitoring are associated with a sense of improvement. This does not mean that monitoring concentrates exclusively on the positive; it is equally important to identify failings and weakness. However, the broad intentions and direction of movement must be clear for all to see.
- **Accountability:** It is important that any monitoring system has safeguards built into it such that those involved are accountable for their findings and decisions.
- **Responsibility:** Finally, it is important that those involved in monitoring bear a sense of responsibility for the outcomes of the process, both planned and unforeseen. Monitoring is now crucial to the development of higher education around the world, and can play a central part in raising standards in both teaching and research. For this goal to be achieved, it is necessary for the process of monitoring to be owned and operated with proper responsibility by all concerned.

References

Australian Universities Quality Agency. (2008). www.auqa.edu.au
Brennan, J. and Shah, T. (2000). *Managing Quality in Higher Education: An International Perspective on Institutional Assessment and Change*, Buckingham: Open University Press.
Campbell, C. and Rozsnyai, C. (2002). *Quality Assurance and the Development of Course Programmes*, Bucharest: UNESCO/CEPES.
Finnish Higher Education Evaluation Council. (2007). *Audits of Quality Assurance Systems of Finnish Higher Education Institutions: Audit Manval for 2008–2011*, Tampere: Finnish Higher Education Evaluation Council.
Flint, D. (1988). *Philosophy and Principles of Auditing*, London: Macmillan.
Goedegebuure, L., Kaiser, F., Maassen, P., Meek, L., Van Vught, F. and de Weert, E. (1997). International Perspectives on Trends and Issues in Higher Education Policy, in Goodchild, L.F., Lovell, C.D., Hines, E.R. and Gill, J.L. (eds) *Public Policy and Higher Education*, Boston: Pearson.
Hartwig, L. (2003). Quality assessment and quality assurance in higher education institutions in Germany, www.ihf.bayern.de/beitraege/2003
Higher Education Funding Council for England. (2008). *Counting what is measured or measuring what counts? League tables and their impact on higher education institutions in England*, Bristol: HEFCE.
Högskoleverket. (2008). www.hsv.se/quality/qualityassurance
Marginson, S. (2007). *Global University Rankings*, Paper presented to the 32nd Annual Conference of the Association for the Study of Higher Education, November 2007, Louisville, Kentucky.
Neave, G. (1988). On the cultivation of quality, efficiency and enterprise: an overview of recent trends in higher education in Western Europe, 1986–88, *European Journal of Education*, 23(1–2) pp. 7–28.
Pile, M. and Teixeira, I. (1997). *The Importance of Quality Assessment in Higher Educational Institutions*, www.gep.inst.utl.pt/files/antigos/The_Importance_Quality_Assessment:PDF

Power, M. (1994). *The Audit Explosion*, London: Demos.

Power, M. (1997). *The Audit Society: Rituals of Verification*, Oxford: Oxford University Press.

Quality Assurance Agency. (2008). www.qaa.ac.uk

Spellings, M. (2006). *A Test of Leadership: Charting the Future of US Higher Education (the Spellings Report)*, Washington DC: US Department of Education.

Times Good University Guide 2009 (2008). London: Times Books.

US Department of Education. (2008). www.ed.gov/admins/financial/accred/accreditation

Van Vught, F. (1991). *Autonomy and Accountability in Government/University Relationships*, Paper for the World Bank Senior Policy Seminar on Improvement and Innovation in Higher Education in Developing Countries, 30 June–4 July 1991.

Yonezawa, A. (2005). The Reintroduction of Accreditation in Japan: A Government Initiative, *International Higher Education*, 40, p. 20.

18

Still Balancing Improvement and Accountability?

Developments in External Quality Assurance in the
Nordic Countries 1996–2006[1]

Trine Danø and Bjørn Stensaker

Introduction

The role and function of external quality assurance is of great importance for the development of an internal quality culture in higher education. Research has shown that external quality assurance can stimulate but also create obstacles for institutional improvement. To strike a balance between improvement and accountability is, therefore, a key issue. Although external quality assurance in the Nordic countries during the 1990s could be said to exemplify such a balance, it is questionable whether they have managed to maintain this balance over time, not least considering the introduction of various accreditation schemes in the Nordic countries as well as in the rest of Europe. This chapter presents and discusses developments in external quality assurance in the Nordic countries from 1996 to 2006 and points to key issues on how external quality assurance could also stimulate a quality culture in the "age of accreditation".

One of the key issues with respect to external quality assurance has been the debate about improvement and accountability; if a system basically created to check whether (a certain level of) quality is in place can also function as a key for stimulating institutional improvement and fostering a quality culture in higher education.

It has often been argued that improvement and accountability are incompatible and that external quality assurance tends to tilt to either side. However, with reference to Danish quality assurance procedures in the mid-1990s, Thune (1996) suggested that improvement and accountability could be seen as dimensions forming an alliance where the key elements for accomplishing this result are professionalism, careful design and implementation of evaluation methods, openness, trust, and involvement by stakeholders during the process.

Later studies have supported this assertion, suggesting that similar ways of balancing improvement and accountability have characterised the external quality assurance systems in the other Nordic countries during the 1990s (Stensaker, 1997, 1999; Askling *et al.*, 1998; Smeby and Stensaker, 1999; Fahlèn *et al.*, 2000; Karlsson *et al.*, 2002). Various types of audits and subject assessments in this period were dominating the national external quality assurance systems in these countries.

Still, in later years, and from a European perspective, there is, as a response to the Bologna

Process, a growing interest in external quality assurance methods focusing on standards and comparability and hence even more on accountability. In particular, various forms of accreditation procedures have emerged as a strong trend in quality assurance in Europe. With the introduction of new forms of evaluations, especially accreditation (-like) schemes in Europe (Schwarz and Westerheijden, 2004; Stensaker and Harvey, 2006) and in the Nordic countries (Hämäläinen *et al.*, 2001), one could question whether the "improvement– accountability" balance is still upheld in a Nordic context. Further, has this had any impact on the legitimacy of quality assurance externally at the system level and internally within higher education institutions? For example, since accreditation procedures frequently focus on checking the threshold level by using minimum standards, one could argue that the control aspect might have taken the upper hand in quality assurance (Saarinen, 2005).

Hence, the aim of this chapter is to analyse if and how current national external quality assurance systems in the Nordic countries balance the improvement–accountability dimension in the "age of accreditation", not least whether external quality assurance enhances quality culture in the institutions of higher education in the region.

The Relationship between Quality Assurance and Quality Culture

The claim that quality assurance, due to the current interest in accreditation, is tipping towards the control side of the improvement–accountability dichotomy needs further investigation. First, while accreditation is an emerging form of evaluation, established forms do not necessarily disappear as a result (Stensaker, 2003). Hence, external quality assurance is currently a multi-faceted field where it is important to analyse if and how different methods and procedures are combined and used more comprehensively to understand how the system actually functions. Second, although accreditation may signal a strong emphasis on control, one should be open to the possibility that accreditation as a method is developing, blurring the boundaries with other forms of evaluations (Stensaker, 2004; Stensaker and Harvey, 2006).

Both of these aspects may have implications for the development of a quality culture in higher education. The obvious link is related to studies showing how the design and functioning of external quality assurance schemes is closely related to what kind of institutional responses one experiences (Massy, 1999). This is not only related to formal procedures but also to how the entire process is carried out, including how meetings are set up, the types of questions asked, how they are asked, and the time reserved for discussion and feedback. In this way, the devil is indeed in the detail, since there is empirical evidence showing that much institutional dissatisfaction with visits from external review panels can be related directly to whether institutions feel they are partners in the process, and the willingness of the review panel to acknowledge and adjust to institutional perspectives and agendas (Stensaker, 1997, 1999; Karlsson *et al.*, 2002). In this process, the professionalism of the organiser of the external evaluations is of vital importance, not least in how intermediate bodies and quality assurance agencies facilitate a visit and how they enhance the professionalism of the reviewers through training activities (Askling *et al.*, 1998).

Furthermore, the emerging interest in accreditation schemes in Europe cannot be traced back to initiatives by external quality assurance agencies alone (Schwarz and Westerheijden, 2004). National policy-making, supra-national initiatives and processes such as the Bologna Process fuel an interest in evaluation methods that may support ambitions of student mobility, performance measurement and comparison of providers across national borders. Although critical comments concerning the relevance of accreditation as a means to solve all these challenges have been voiced (Haakstad, 2003; Harvey, 2004; Stensaker and Harvey, 2006), few alternatives have been suggested, which result in an increased popularity of such schemes. Given the criticism usually targeted at accreditation, it is often up to the intermediate bodies and quality assurance agencies to find practical ways to adjust accreditation, as a method, to the current political challenges facing European countries. For example, given the in-built conservatism of the accreditation method using well-established standards as the most important criteria, it may be a challenge to find ways to support the innovative dimension of higher education, although this dimension also has strong political support throughout Europe. Critical issues are related to how "accreditation" is actually implemented as a method, what kind of procedures are developed, and how these relate to institutional attempts to develop their own quality processes.

As indicated above, enhancing a quality culture is dependent on the "moments of truth" when the external quality assurance schemes confront institutions during practice. Furthermore, we would suggest that trust is not so much dependent on the evaluation method but rather a result of sensible design, including how communication takes place, the opportunities created for dialogue and the ability of external quality assurance schemes to combine their externally defined mission with responsiveness to issues high on the institutional agenda.

Data and Methods

Although this chapter attempts to analyse a general question with respect to quality assurance, the empirical data are drawn from the Nordic countries (in the current study, Iceland is excluded due to the fact that external quality assurance has mainly been a responsibility of the Ministry and also due to the lack of a more systematic effort in the area of quality assurance).

The chapter is a review of a number of studies and evaluations of Nordic quality assurance schemes. The main source of data is drawn from a recent study of the Nordic external quality assurance systems, funded by the Nordic Council of Ministers (Stensaker and Danø, 2006). By combining this study with other available research reports and studies (for example, Lindeberg and Kristoffersen, 2002; Omar and Liuhanen, 2005; Vinther-Jørgensen and Hansen, 2006), results in an analysis of developments in external quality assurance in the period 1996–2006.

Developments in External Quality Assurance in the Nordic Countries 1996–2006

Developments in Denmark

In Denmark, external quality assurance of the higher education system is divided into three different sections: a relatively comprehensive external examiner system, a number of systematic quality assurance activities operated primarily, but not exclusively, by the Danish Evaluation Institute (EVA) and a ministerial system of recognition of new study programmes. The Danish Parliament is, at the moment, debating a bill for a comprehensive accreditation system covering all of higher education from short-cycle to university programmes.

From 1992 to 1999 EVA's predecessor, the Centre for Evaluation and Quality Assurance of Higher Education (EVC), carried out evaluations of a major part of the study programmes within Danish higher education. The evaluation scheme of the 1990s was launched as part of a major reform of the Danish university system to counterbalance increased institutional autonomy. In this perspective the programme evaluations could be seen as an instrument of control. They did, however, incorporate a considerable focus on improvement (Thune, 1996). There were no direct links between evaluations and funding (Smeby and Stensaker, 1999), and few of the evaluations of the 1990s had severe effects in the sense that study programmes were closed down or severely reorganised. On the contrary, analyses of the Danish and Swedish quality assurance systems of the 1990s reveal much more subtle effects relating to discursive shifts and promotion of internal debates at the higher education institutions (Massy, 1999).

By the turn of the century, EVA experimented with a range of quality assurance approaches, such as big international and comparative evaluations and institutional evaluations. However, these projects did not provide sufficient coverage and systematic external quality assurance of the entire higher education area. Consequently EVA decided on a combined strategy to carry out accreditations of institutions and study programmes in the field of vocational higher education, while audits and programme evaluations became the main activity with regard to universities.

As mentioned, a comprehensive scheme of programme accreditations covering the entire higher education system is debated at the moment. According to the proposed structure of the new accreditation system, an accreditation board will formally make decisions about all programmes under accreditation. However, the operational aspects of the accreditation processes are likely to vary across the different fields of education. Hence, one model will be developed in regard to university education, whereas other models will be developed in other educational fields (short-cycle education and medium-cycle vocational education). Consequently, the organisations carrying out the assessments prior to formal decisions of accreditation are likely to differ in accordance with the specific field. It is, however, common to all of the accreditation processes that they should include assessments of "traditional" indicators of quality (such as organisation, syllabus, qualifications of teaching staff) as well as assessments of programmes examining such things as employability of graduates. Failure to obtain accreditation of a study programme may imply that the study programme in question will no longer be eligible for public funding.

Institutional audits, programme evaluations and other methods will remain part of EVA's activities but, given the scope of the new accreditation scheme, they are likely to play a secondary role, at least in the years to come. However, the accreditations and need for capacity-building regarding internal quality assurance will most probably result in increased needs for information and advice and thus new assignments and activities in the future for EVA as well as other actors within the field of external quality assurance in Denmark.

Developments in Finland

External quality assurance of Finnish higher education consists of two components: first, a ministerial system of governance and recognition of new study programmes and, second, evaluations, audits and accreditations of certain courses carried out by the Finnish Higher Education Evaluation Council (FINHEEC).

FINHEEC was established in 1995 with the overall mission to assist higher education institutions and the Ministry of Education in matters related to evaluation (Omar and Liuhanen, 2005). Since 1995, FINHEEC has carried out a variety of quality assurance activities including thematic evaluations, programme evaluations, evaluations for the accreditations of polytechnics (1995–2000), and audits of quality work in higher education institutions. Furthermore, FINHEEC has organised the selection of centres of excellence in education. As mentioned above, FINHEEC has accredited professional courses offered by higher education institutions. While these accreditations seem to be a continuous activity, not least since accreditation needs to be renewed every fourth year, the number of activities related to either programme evaluations, thematic evaluations or audits seems to have varied over the years. FINHEEC decides on plans of action for a three-year period, but it has to negotiate two-thirds of its budget each year. Furthermore, the Ministry of Education may direct specific assignments to FINHEEC. The accreditation of the so-called professional courses conducted by universities is an example of this.

Although FINHEEC states that in the Finnish quality assurance system improvement and assessment of the quality of education is seen as more important than accreditation (Hämäläinen *et al.*, 2001), the latter is obviously an activity included in the overall system. The accreditations of professional courses offered by universities and other higher education institutions do include a considerable element of control (Stensaker and Danø, 2006). Still, they represent a minor part of the overall activities, and other than that the focus does indeed seem to be on improvement and the stimulation of institutional quality cultures. Thus in adhering to the stated goals of the Bologna Process to integrate accreditation of certification as part of national quality assurance systems the Finnish report of 2005 refers to FINHEEC's plan to carry out cyclical audits of institutions' quality work. The audits follow general themes or criteria and failure to document sufficient quality assurance activities may lead to disapproval by FINHEEC. However, audits should support independence and diversity of institutions (Finnish Ministry of Education and Research, 2005) and the only consequence of disapproval is that a re-audit will have to be carried out.

Developments in Sweden

The Swedish National Agency for Higher Education (HSV) represents by far the biggest of the Nordic external quality assurance organisations and has a wider scope than the fellow organisations in Norway, Denmark and Finland. HSV is responsible for carrying out external quality assurance activities such as subject reviews and audits of quality assurance activities within higher education institutions. Furthermore, it handles statistics and information about and for students, recognition of foreign education, appraisal of applications for the right to award degrees, and the issuing of regulation specifying the law in higher education. Finally, HSV ensures that higher education institutions comply with the law. This takes place by way of inspection. Similar to its Norwegian counterpart, HSV is an independent authority, only with a much broader range of duties.

HSV was established in 1995 as part of a general decentralisation of the Swedish higher education sector. As mentioned above, the responsibilities of HSV are broad, comprising accountability and control as well as quality improvement, supervision and information. This may be part of the reason that quality assurance activities of the 1990s primarily focused on institutional improvement and the establishment of internal quality assurance procedures at the higher education institutions. A few thematic and programme evaluations were carried out but audits of universities and higher education institutions were the main activities. A total of 33 institutions were audited twice within the periods of 1995–1998 and 1999–2002. Based on evidence from the second round, HSV found that 70% of the higher education institutions had advanced on issues such as mission and strategies, evaluation activities, student influence, co-operation with stakeholders, internationalisation, and educational development (Omar and Liuhanen, 2005). However, no conclusions could be made at the time concerning actual effects of the activities, and since institutional audits in recent years have been replaced by a huge scheme of subject reviews, this remains to be seen.

Since 2002 most of the quality assurance activities have concentrated on the subject reviews of all study programmes at bachelor level and above. The subject reviews were launched by the Swedish government, which wished to directly assess quality of the study programmes offered (as opposed to quality assurance or quality improvement activities) (Wahlén, 2004). They serve a dual purpose by aiming at quality improvement as well as assessing if study programmes comply with the aims and legislation put down by law (Hämäläinen *et al.*, 2001). In severe cases of "quality failure", HSV can deprive the institution of its entitlement to award degrees within a certain discipline. This is one area in which the subject reviews show similarities to accreditation processes. The subject reviews also resemble accreditations in respect of the standard criteria or aspects governing each review. These aspects are, however, rather broad. They are not preset but have been developed over the years and represent general themes, which HSV regard as fundamental for higher education processes, including prerequisites, process and results of the educational programmes (Wahlén, 2004).

The subject reviews have been scheduled for a period of six years and they are currently the predominant external quality assurance activity. Other activities such as thematic evaluations of internationalisation and co-operation with stakeholders do take place but on a smaller scale. Audits of institutions' quality assurance activities have not been carried out since 2002. However, they are included and seem to regain a strong position in HSV's plans for a new cycle of activities (Vinther-Jørgensen and Hansen, 2006), and so the ball might again roll towards institutional agendas and improvement.

Developments in Norway

In recent years, Norway has witnessed reforms of the entire higher education system, particularly in regard to the institutional landscape and the legislation governing the educational institutions but also in regard to external quality assurance. The Norwegian Agency for Quality Assurance in Education (NOKUT) was established in 2003 and is responsible for most of the external quality assurance activities, except for the external examiner system, which is, compared with the Danish system, more of a responsibility of the higher education institutions themselves (Brandt and Stensaker, 2005). The main activities of NOKUT are accreditation and recognition of quality systems, institutions and course provisions and institutional audits. Furthermore, NOKUT is responsible for handling applications for recognition of foreign qualifications and occasionally, at the request of the government, it also carries out the so-called revisions (re-accreditations) of existing study programmes and other evaluations. An example of this is a huge revision process covering all bachelor and master study programmes in nursing.

NOKUT is an independent decision-making body in relation to the issuing of recognition of degrees and the accreditation of higher education institutions and new programmes of study. No other authority can modify these decisions (Omar and Liuhanen, 2005). The Norwegian institutional system is built on a basic principle of differentiation and institutional drift in the sense that institutions gain self-accrediting powers depending on their status. Thus, universities can establish bachelor, master, and PhD programmes without seeking permission by any other authority, whereas some private colleges cannot even establish new bachelor programmes without accreditation by NOKUT. By way of institutional accreditation colleges can, however, gain a "higher" institutional status and become self-accrediting, i.e. of new bachelor programmes. On the other hand, universities might lose accrediting powers in cases where audits reveal serious flaws in their internal quality assurance procedures. The Norwegian audits follow a cyclical principle and potential costs to institutions in case of negative results are more important than those of accreditations (Stensaker, 2004). The audits can in other words be seen to contain a considerable aspect of accountability and control, blurring the traditional ideas of how different quality assurance methods serve different purposes.

NOKUT replaced the earlier Network Norway Council (NNR), which had in 1998 replaced a system of scattered evaluations and no consistent national quality assurance system (Hämäläinen *et al.*, 2001). The establishment of, first, NNR in 1998 and, second, NOKUT in 2003 can be seen as both a part of and a reaction to increased autonomy of the higher education institutions in the 1990s and onwards. Evaluations and surveys indicated that institutions worked with quality issues but that the work was often insufficient in system and coherence, documentation, follow-up on decisions and linkage to management. Together with new challenges, including a rise in student numbers, international developments, new teaching methods, and rising expectations in regard to transparency and documentation, this called for a strengthening of advice as well as systematic evaluations (Omar and Liuhanen, 2005). In this perspective, the establishment of NOKUT and the introduction of an accreditation scheme can be regarded as increased focus on accountability and control. This was not the advice given by researchers in higher education policy; on the contrary, they pointed to the need for an increased focus on development and the strengthening of institutional systems for and attention to quality issues (Stensaker, 2004).

It can, however, be questioned whether the establishment of NOKUT and an accreditation scheme in Norwegian higher education does in fact lead to major changes. In this respect it is important to note that there are still no direct links between the accrediting powers of NOKUT and funding. And more importantly, the effects of accreditations seem less grave than those of audits, which do in many respects resemble the institutional evaluations carried out by NOKUT's predecessor NNR (Stensaker, 2004).

Stimulating Institutional Quality Culture in the Age of Accreditation?

As shown in the previous section, there has been considerable development in the design of external quality assurance in the Nordic countries over the last decade. In general, one can argue that the whole area has expanded introducing new methods, although the countries can be said to have their own distinct characteristics as to how the various elements are mixed. Hence the question may be whether it is possible to find a more general pattern in this complex picture related to the balancing of accountability and improvement. A comparison between the countries discloses some interesting commonalities.

Accreditation is One Approach among Others

At first sight, developments in external quality assurance activities in the Nordic countries for the last 10 years seem to reflect the general international focus on comparability, standards and quality assurance methods designed to meet the increasing global demand for transparency. Accreditation or accreditation-like practices and assessments of quality according to predefined standards and criteria are an integral part of the activities in all of the external quality assurance systems described above. Whether this does in fact imply a shift of focus and a tilt of the accountability–improvement balance towards accountability and hence control is, nevertheless, questionable.

The descriptions of the individual systems reveal that none of the quality assurance systems are completely assigned to accreditation or accreditation-like schemes. On the contrary, methods traditionally associated with improvement and the stimulation of an institutional quality culture, such as audits, are present and still quite dominant in all of the Nordic quality assurance systems. Even though the focus on accountability, transparency and comparability has increased across the Nordic countries in the past decade, there is little evidence available suggesting that it has, as a general trend, taken the upper hand. At least not in methods used.

Although accreditations and accreditation-like schemes seem to dominate in Norway, are growing in Denmark, are linked to plans of certification of institutional quality assurance schemes in Finland, and may be said to be part of the HSV duties as this agency controls the entitlement to award degrees in Sweden, the development of external quality assurance in these countries is more nuanced, as boundaries between the various methods and purposes of each method seem to blur. Thus the Norwegian audits of institutional quality assurance systems incorporate elements and consequences similar to, or even harsher than, those of the accreditations. Also, in Denmark, failure to obtain accreditation of study programmes has no immediate effect except for demands to work out follow-up plans.

Causal Links between Approach and Effects?

The potential of quality assurance activities to stimulate improvements and a quality culture cannot be limited to the label of the specific method used. Needless to say, audits might have no impact on the quality culture whatsoever, and accreditations may on the other hand fuel improvements by way of setting high standards and stimulating internal discussions on how to reach them. In this respect, responses to the Swedish accreditation-like subject reviews indicate that especially the self-evaluation processes of the reviews have contributed to self-reflection and improvement (Wahlén, 2004). The same goes for the Danish accreditations of institutions to secure University College status. Only a few institutions have obtained accreditation right away, but nevertheless most of the institutions express appreciation of the accreditation process, and following up on the results of the accreditations several representatives of the institutions have contacted EVA for advice on how to further develop aims, strategies and procedures for implementing quality assurance systems.

In discussing the potential of accreditation and accreditation-like schemes to fuel improvement and particularly to stimulate an institutional quality culture, it is, however, important to remember that accreditation schemes rarely have that focus. Accreditations are in principle carried out to assess if quality is in place in accordance with either best practice or minimum standards. In that sense, accreditation processes centre on accountability but do aim at assuring as well as improving quality. In doing so, accreditations might, however, also stimulate an institutional quality culture as implied by the Swedish and Danish experiences referred to above. Furthermore, in Norway institutional accreditation processes are dependent upon the initial audit of institutional quality assurance systems. This link creates a strong focus on internal quality processes as a condition for later accreditation.

Formulation of Criteria

It has been argued that an important factor of external quality assurance processes is the possibility for institutions to feel that they are partners in the process (Stensaker, 1997, 1999; Karlsson et al., 2002). Since accreditations are not carried out as fitness-for-purpose processes but typically follow preset standards and criteria, an important factor in promoting partnership is of course the initial formulation of criteria. In this respect, criteria of all of the Scandinavian accreditation schemes have been presented and to a varying extent debated among stakeholders. Naturally, this does not guarantee institutional acceptance and an experience of sensitivity of the criteria to specific institutional needs and agendas. On the contrary, a general characteristic of the criteria of Scandinavian systems is that, with a few exceptions, they represent broad or "soft" standards (Stensaker, 2004). Formulation of open rather than closed criteria seems to have been the goal of the Scandinavian accreditation schemes, leaving room for individual implementation (Wahlén, 2004; EVA, 2006). As such, some of the criteria used are quite similar, independent of method applied.

Nonetheless, some institutions have criticised the Danish accreditation of study programmes for being insensitive to the culture and traditions of some fields of study. Similarly, some Swedish university colleges have argued that they are evaluated according to standards that apply to universities and that particular advantages of small institutions are not always considered (Wahlén, 2004). In Norway the revisions of nursing study programmes have been criticised for the application of quantitative standards to the programmes, interpreting the criteria much further than is merited by the criteria themselves (Raaen, 2006). The criticism hints at obvious challenges of open versus closed criteria in relation to accreditations, and the argument that the interpretation of the general criteria needs to take place in the context of the institution. On the one hand, this process might rely too heavily on experts with more specialised interests, which may imply a threat to system-level criteria and needs. On the other hand, the quality assurance agency may develop standards or specific indicators of how criteria are met. While ensuring comparability and a system perspective, this may put sensitivity to institutional differences at stake. In both cases there is a risk of losing institutional trust and commitment to the process as well as legitimacy of the accreditation scheme as such.

Self-assessment

Some form of self-assessment is an integral part of the accreditation (-like) schemes in all of the Scandinavian countries. Earlier studies of effects of external quality assurance activities show that this is a focal point for the promotion of institutional reflection and improvement (PLS-Consult, 1998; Massy, 1999). Judging from the response to the Swedish subject reviews this seems to be the case for accreditations and accreditation-like practices as well (Wahlén, 2004). Institutions facing a great number of accreditations might be inclined to leave most of the work of this phase to professional administrators. While ensuring professional collection and processing of data, this may hinder internal discussion and promote an experience of the accreditation process as merely a bureaucratic exercise. However, building professional capacity in relation to accreditations may also have the opposite effect in the sense that issues of quality assurance and enhancement are put on the institutional agenda.

Meetings and Communication

Given the consequences inherent in the accreditations and accreditation-like processes, openness and dialogue about the accreditation process as such are important elements. In relation to the Danish accreditations of study programmes, representatives of the institutions are invited to a kick-off meeting at which the process, criteria and their meaning are discussed. Institutions are also given the opportunity to provide names for the expert panel and invited to comment on possible conflicts of interests: a process also common in Norway. In Sweden bilateral meetings at which various elements of the review process are described and discussed, including time frame and special needs of each subject, ensure dialogue and commitment to the process.

Apart from the initial meetings and other communication between representatives of institutions or study programmes and professionals of the quality assurance agency, site-visits are pivotal in promoting dialogue and trust (or just the opposite). A variety of competences and experience of the expert panel is of course important and criteria for the composition of expert panels are common (EVA, 2006). Furthermore, experience from the Swedish subject reviews point to the importance of peers' sensitivity and general understanding of the institution and/or study programme in question (Wahlén, 2004). Training of experts is in general considered an important element in all countries, ensuring an understanding of accreditation and evaluation processes in general and the role of the site-visit in particular. In Denmark, experts are furthermore provided with written guidelines on how to pose open questions and to avoid value judgements.

In all of the Nordic accreditation schemes, institutions or study programmes have a chance to comment on accreditation reports. In Denmark, institutions can only comment on factual errors. In Norway, institutions' comments on the accreditation report are included in the decision-making of the accreditation council. Various kinds of consulting procedures are, however, not the final point of communication related to most accreditation schemes. In Sweden, institutions are given even more opportunities to discuss the results of an accreditation. Three months after publishing decisions on each institution's right to award degrees and recommendations for the future, a national conference is held with participation of all the institutions involved in the review (Wahlén,

2004). In Denmark, many institutions and study programmes may not obtain conditional accreditation in the first place and this requires a follow-up in order to secure full accreditation at a later stage.

Conclusions, Trends and Challenges

Since our study object—external quality assurance—is still developing rapidly in the Nordic countries, it may be dangerous to draw conclusions that by tomorrow may be outdated by the latest developments. Still, when considering developments in the Nordic countries over the last decade there are three findings that can point to a continuing maintenance of the improvement–accountability balance in these countries.

First, although accreditation and accreditation-like procedures have been introduced in the Nordic countries, these systems are often integrated into a broader external quality assurance framework, reducing their potential to overrun other means and approaches to assure and improve quality. There is evidence that accreditation has brought forward tensions between the controllers and the controlled (Raaen, 2006) but, so far, this has not taken over the agenda, creating a feeling of distrust in the sector as a whole. A possible explanation for this is that external quality assurance agencies in the Nordic countries perceive their own role as that of the mediator between the government and the institutions. A related explanation is that the potential teeth of accreditation (so far) have been very moderately used, and that the scale of accreditation (-like) procedures is rather modest. For example, in Norway institutional accreditation is not given for a fixed period of time, and contains no plans for when re-accreditation should take place. Furthermore, programme accreditation is only conducted on a small scale.

Second, the integration of accreditation into a broader external quality assurance system has also led to transformation of both accreditation and more traditional methods used in the Nordic countries. The current plans in Finland to develop cyclical audits of institutional quality work and the plans in Sweden to re-establish an audit system that is leaner but also "meaner" suggests that balancing improvement and accountability may still be considered as an important dimension. Hence, in the past decade the trend has been to link accreditation (-like) procedures to the review of institutional quality assurance arrangements instead of using accreditation in a more traditional way (focusing on institutional or programme standards). However, a stronger focus on "accrediting" the quality systems of the institutions should, in principle, lead to a stronger focus on the processes that trigger quality, as these are the elements most usually checked in such systems.

Third, even though accreditation (-like) procedures have been introduced, this has not meant much change in how the external quality assurance agencies conduct their business. The traditional dialogue-based communication with the sector is still a vital characteristic of the external quality assurance process. This process includes the possibility for institutions to have a say in what criteria should be of importance, who the assessors should be, and when a visit should take place. Hence, one can identify flexibility and mutual adjustments in how work is conducted, and a softer form of application of the authority given to the controllers. This has also been a characteristic of the past, and may have created a feeling of "business as usual" at the institutions.

The trends in external quality assurance in the Nordic countries can, in other words, be summarised by the three somewhat contradictory keywords: integration, transformation and continuity. Interestingly, it might well be that it is exactly this mix of change and continuity, and adaptation and transformation that perhaps is the key to understand how this field has developed in the Nordic countries over the last decade. In this period, audit, accreditation, subject assessments, and other forms of evaluation have emerged side by side in these countries as a result of external pressure, national policy changes or more voluntary initiatives. So far, both the controlled and the controllers seem to handle the increased workload, suggesting that the current focus on accreditation does not necessarily hinder attempts to develop an internal quality culture in higher education.

This conclusion does not imply that there is no room for improvement in or lack of challenges related to the current schemes in the Nordic countries. On the contrary, there *is* room for improvement and there *are* several challenges. The main challenge is perhaps the increasing workload resulting from a more developed and expanded external quality assurance system in each country. This may be a problem for both institutions and quality assurance agencies and suggests that steps should be taken to further rationalise existing methods and procedures, creating more efficient information-gathering processes, better alignment of administrative versus academic needs in external evaluations, and perhaps integration of research in the current schemes. A related challenge is that when a country introduces a number of methods and procedures for improving and assuring quality, the significance and effect of each method might decrease as a result of less clarity concerning the purpose and implications of them. Communication, tailoring and mutual adjustments are, therefore, more needed than ever as the development of an internal quality culture in higher education institutions is more dependent on how the whole *system* for external quality assurance functions than on whether a particular *method* is being applied.

Note

1. Danø, T. and Stensaker, B. (2007) Still balancing improvement and accountability? Developments in external quality assurance in the Nordic countries 1996–2006. *Quality in Higher Education*, 13:1, 81–93. Reprinted by permission of the publisher.

References

Askling, B., Nordskov Nielsen, L. and Stensaker, B. (1998). *Mellom fag og politikk. En granskning av Evalueringscenteret og det danske evalueringssystemet for høyere utdanning* (København: Undervisningsministeriet).
Brandt, E. and Stensaker, B. (2005). *Internasjonale sensorordninger i høyere utdanning: er erfaringer fra Sverige, Danmark og England relevante for Norge?* (Oslo: NIFU STEP Arbeidsnotat 39/2005).
Eva (2006). *Akkreditering inden for det videregående uddannelsesområde—dansk og international praksis* (Copenhagen: Danmarks Evalueringsinstitut).
Fahlén, V., Liuhanen, A.M., Petersson, L. and Stensaker, B. (eds) (2000). *Towards best practice. Quality improvement initiatives in Nordic higher education institutions* (Copenhagen: Nordic Council of Ministers. TemaNord 2000: 501).
Finnish Ministry of Education and Research (2005). *National report 2004–2005* (Helsinki: Finnish Ministry of Education and Research).
Haakstad, J. (2003). "Accreditation: the new quality assurance formula? Some reflections as Norway is about to reform its quality assurance system", *Quality in Higher Education*, 7, pp. 77–82.
Hämäläinen, K., Haakstad, J., Kangasniemi, J., Lindeberg, T. and Sjölund, M. (2001). *Quality assurance in the Nordic higher education—accreditation-like practices* (Helsinki: ENQA).
Harvey, L. (2004). "The power of accreditation", *Journal of Higher Education Policy and Management*, 26, pp. 207–223.
Karlsson, O., Andersson, M.I. and Lundin, A. (2002). *Metautvärdering av Högskoleverkets model för kvalitetsbedömning av högre utbildning: hur har lärosäten och bedömare uppfattat modellen?* (Stockholm: Högskoleverket).
Lindeberg, T. and Kristoffersen, D. (eds) (2002). *A method for mutual recognition. Experiences with a method for mutual recognition of quality assurance agencies* (Helsinki: ENQA Occasional papers no. 4).
Massy, W. (1999). *Energizing quality work: higher education evaluations in Sweden and Denmark* (Stanford: National Center for Post-Secondary Improvement, Stanford University).
Omar, P-L. and Liuhanen, A-M. (eds) (2005). *A comparative analysis of systematic quality work in Nordic higher education institutions* (Helsinki: NOQA).
PLS-Consult (1998). *Undersøgelse af effekterne af uddannelsesevaluering* (Copenhagen: PLS-Consult).
Raaen, F.D. (2006). *Akkreditering og sakkyndighet. En analyse av den reviderte akkrediteringen av bachelorstudiene i sykepleie i Norge* (Oslo: Senter for profesjonsstudier, Høgskolen i Oslo).
Saarinen, T. (2005). "From sickness to cure: construction of 'quality' in Finnish higher education policy from the 1960s to the era of the Bologna Process", *Quality in Higher Education*, 11, pp. 3–15.
Schwarz, S. and Westerheijden, D.F. (eds) (2004). *Accreditation in the framework of evaluation activities. Current situation and dynamics in Europe* (Dordrecht: Kluwer Academic Press).
Smeby, J.C. and Stensaker, B. (1999). "National Quality Assessment Systems in the Nordic countries: developing a balance between external and internal needs?", *Higher Education Policy*, 12, pp. 1–12.

Stensaker, B. (1997). "From accountability to opportunity: the role of quality assessments in Norway", *Quality in Higher Education*, 3, pp. 277–284.

Stensaker, B. (1999). "External quality auditing in Sweden: are departments affected?" *Higher Education Quarterly*, 53, pp. 353–368.

Stensaker, B. (2003). "Trance, transparency and transformation. The impact of external quality monitoring in higher education", *Quality in Higher Education*, 9, pp. 151–159.

Stensaker, B. (2004). "The blurring boundaries between accreditation and audit—the case of Norway", in: Schwarz, S. and Westerheijden, D.F. (eds) *Accreditation in the framework of evaluation activities. Current situation and dynamics in Europe* (Dordrecht: Kluwer Academic Press).

Stensaker, B. and Danø, T. (2006). *Nordisk kvalitetssikring i høyere utdanning. Muligheter for gjensidig godkjenning og økt samarbeid?* (Oslo: NIFU STEP arbeidsnotat 16/2006).

Stensaker, B. and Harvey, L. (2006). "Old wine in new bottles? A comparison of public and private accreditation schemes in higher education", *Higher Education Policy*, 19, pp. 65–85.

Thune, C. (1996). "The alliance of accountability and improvement: the Danish experience", *Quality in Higher Education*, 2, pp. 21–32.

Vinther-Jørgensen, T. and Hansen, S.P. (2006). *European standards and guidelines in a Nordic perspective. Joint Nordic project 2005–06* (Helsinki: Nordic Quality Assurance Network in Higher Education. www.noqa.net).

Wahlén, S. (2004). "From audit to accreditation-like processes: the case of Sweden", in: Schwarz, S. and Westerheijden, D.F. (eds) *Accreditation in the framework of evaluation activities. Current situation and dynamics in Europe* (Dordrecht: Kluwer Academic Press).

19

A Global Survey of University Ranking and League Tables[1]

Alex Usher and Massimo Savino

This chapter presents the findings of a survey, conducted on league tables and rankings systems worldwide, including 17 standard ones and one non-standard league table. Despite the capacity of existing league tables and rankings to meet the interest of the public of transparency and information on higher education institutions, ranking systems still are in their "infancy". The authors suggest that, if international ranking schemes are to assume a quality assurance role, it would be the global higher education community that would have to identify better practices for data collection and reporting to achieve high-quality inter-institutional comparisons.

Introduction

University rankings or "league tables", a novelty as recently as 15 years ago, are today a standard feature in most countries with large higher education systems. They were originally created over 20 years ago by *US News and World Report* in order to meet a perceived market need for more transparent, comparative data about educational institutions. Reviled by critics but popular with parents, copy-cat ranking systems began popping up all over the world, usually shortly after the introduction of—or a rapid rise in—tuition fees. Wherever rankings have appeared, they have been met with a mixture of public enthusiasm and institutional unease.

One of the main causes of institutional unease is the tendency of institutional ranking schemes to use weighted aggregates of indicators to arrive at a single, all-encompassing quality "score", which in turn permits institutions to be ranked against one another. By selecting a particular set of indicators and assigning each a given weight, the authors of these rankings are imposing a specific definition of quality on the institutions being ranked. The fact that there may be other legitimate indicators or combinations of indicators is usually passed over in silence. To the reader, the author's judgement is in effect final.

Intriguingly, however, there is little agreement among the authors of these indicators as to what indicates quality. The world's main ranking systems bear little if any relationship to one another, using very different indicators and weightings to arrive at a measure of quality.

In this chapter we discuss 17 university league tables and ranking systems from around the world. Fourteen of these are "national" league tables collected from nine countries (Australia,

Canada, China, Hong Kong, Italy, Poland, Spain, the United Kingdom and the United States); three are "international" or "crossnational" league tables. Specifically, we compare these league tables in terms of their methods of data collection and their selection and weighting of indicators. We also look at an eighteenth ranking system (the German CHE rankings), which does not conform to the standard league table "rules".

What Are University Rankings and League Tables?

University rankings are lists of certain groupings of institutions (usually, but not always, within a single national jurisdiction), comparatively ranked according to a common set of indicators in descending order. University rankings are usually presented in the format of a "league table", much as sports teams in a single league are listed from best to worst according to the number of wins and losses they have achieved.[2]

Another notable aspect of league tables is that they are, for the most part, produced by commercial publishing enterprises. In part, this reflects the fact that rankings share some characteristics with "consumer guides" to various products. Although rankings are not guides to specific institutions, the publishers of individual institutional guides may incorporate ranking data as supplementary material, detailing descriptions for the purpose of providing more information to their readers. Rankings are—at least in theory—meant to be a look "under the hood" of a complex product. In many cases, the effort required to collect, collate and analyze the data required to produce the rankings is so great that their production on anything but a commercial basis is probably impossible.

University ranking systems come in two varieties: institutional ranking systems and sub-institutional ranking systems. They can be conducted either on a national or international scale. National ranking systems are ones in which all or nearly all of a country's universities are measured against one another. This was the original university ranking format, i.e. the type pioneered by *US News and World Report* in 1981 and which has been widely copied in other countries. In most cases, all universities within a country are compared, although in some cases—notably in Canada (*Maclean's* Magazine) and the United States (*US News and World Report*)—the country's universities are divided according to certain institutional characteristics and only compared to other institutions with similar characteristics, in effect creating a group of mini-league tables. It is rankings of these types that are included in this chapter.

Global institutional ranking systems are a new variation on the older idea of national rankings. There are at present only two of these: the Academic Ranking of World Universities from Shanghai's Jiao Tong University, first released in 2003, and the World University Rankings from the *Times Higher Education Supplement* of Britain (henceforth THES), first released in November 2004. The first international ranking—albeit not a global one—was actually prepared by *Asiaweek* magazine in 1997, which ranked the continent's major universities. All three of these rankings are also covered in this chapter.

Beyond institutional rankings, there are also sub-institutional rankings, which compare specific university units against similar ones at other institutions. These rankings are usually national in scope and deal with professional schools such as teaching business, law and medicine. Graduate business schools are also the subject of a number of international rankings from such organizations as *The Economist*, the *Financial Times*, the *Wall Street Journal* and *Business Week*. These types of league tables are not covered in this chapter, on the grounds that there are simply too many of them to analyze in detail. However, we will be examining one variation on the subject-specific ranking system (the CHE rankings) at the conclusion of this chapter.

There are also ranking schemes which focus on specific aspects of university activities. For instance, the Best American Research Universities ranks US institutions specifically on their research output, as, in a cruder manner, does the Centre for Science and Technology Studies in Bern, Switzerland, with its international "Champions League" tables. Similarly, *Yahoo Magazine* has ranked universities on their "connectivity", and the *Journal of Black Higher Education* has graded them on their ability to integrate students from different backgrounds in its ethnic diversity rankings. These types of ranking systems are excluded from this survey because their purposes are much more specific and limited than the general ranking systems which we wish to focus on.

How Ranking and League Tables Work

League tables, by their very nature, are meant to boil down the work of entire institutions into single, comparable, numerical indicators. In most ranking systems, this comparison is a three-stage process: first, data is collected on indicators; second, the data for each indicator is scored; and, third, the scores from each indicator are weighted and aggregated.

All ranking systems operate by comparing institutions on a range of indicators. The number of indicators in a ranking system can vary significantly, from five in the simplest case (the THES World Rankings) to several dozen in the case of the most complicated (La Repubblica or Wuhan). Specific areas of institutional activity or types of institutional output can therefore be compared across institutions, in much the same manner as is done with performance indicators.

With only a few exceptions (notably, Spain's Excelencia rankings), league table systems then take the data on each indicator and turn it into a "score". Usually, this is done by giving the institution with the highest score on a particular indicator a perfect mark of 100 and then awarding lower scores to other institutions based on how close they are to the score of the top institution. Once scores have been derived for each indicator, they are weighted, with greater weight being accorded to indicators which are believed to be of greater importance. The weighted scores from all indicators are then tallied to give a unified final score for each institution.

Clearly, the choice of indicators and the weight given to each indicator make an enormous amount of difference to the final output. Indeed, it is no exaggeration to say that publishers advertising their product as a guide to "the best" institutions, it is the publishers themselves who largely decide on which institution is the best simply through their choice of indicators and weightings. In effect, the act of choosing a set of indicators and weightings imposes a one-size-fits-all definition of quality.

The Evidentiary Basis of League Tables—How Data Is Collected

A key issue in the preparation of league tables and rankings is the method of data collection. There are three basic sources of data on institutions:

- Survey data. Surveys of the opinions or experiences of various stakeholders can be used to obtain comparable data on different institutions regarding educational quality.
- Independent third parties. Frequently, government agencies will collect and publish data on institutions in their jurisdiction, and this can be used as an objective standard by which to compare institutions. This data is very often financial in nature and is based on administrative data from bodies providing grants.
- University sources. The most complete and most detailed sources of data on universities are of course universities themselves, and they are thus potentially a very rich source of data.

The use of each source of data has advantages and disadvantages. Survey data is scientific in the sense that it records observations accurately, but to the extent that it is used to survey employers or opinion-makers on the value of degrees from various institutions, critics might reasonably question the value of such observations, as very few employers or opinion-makers are likely to have detailed views on or knowledge of every institution in question. Surveys of students and recent graduates are similarly denigrated on the grounds that while they may be able to enunciate their feelings about their own institution, they have no basis on which to compare their institution with others.

Independent third-party administrative data (usually from governments or grant-making bodies) is generally considered the "gold standard" of comparative data since it is, at least theoretically, both accurate and impartial. However, this data is not (usually) collected for the purpose of compiling league tables but rather as an administrative by-product. As a result, over-reliance on this source of data can lead to a choice of indicators simply on the availability of data rather than their contribution to appropriate/useful definition of quality.

Finally, there is data from universities themselves. In some cases, where important indicators on quality cannot be obtained via surveys or third parties, the authors of ranking schemes will address a questionnaire to institutions directly and ask for certain sets of data. The benefit of this approach is that one can—in theory—answer a number of questions about quality that cannot otherwise be answered. The main drawback is that there is no guarantee that institutions will actually report the data to the ranker on a consistent basis, as all have a clear incentive to provide data which will benefit them.

The extent to which each ranking system uses each source of data is shown below in Table 19.1.

Table 19.1 shows that surveys are the least frequently used source of data for indicators. Indeed, only Hong Kong's Education18 rankings come close to having a plurality of indicators from this source. This measure somewhat underestimates the importance of surveys, as it does not account for the weighting given to each indicator in each study. In the THES World Rankings, for instance, there is only a single survey (for "reputation"), but it accounts for 50% of the total ranking. Similarly, Canada's *Maclean's* rankings have only one survey-based indicator out of a total of 24, but this one indicator accounts for 20% of the final score.

Outside North America, third-party sources are by far the most heavily used sources of data: indeed, four of the 18 ranking schemes listed here use them exclusively. Of the remaining 14, third-party sources comprise a plurality of indicators in eight and university sources form a plurality in six. The predominance of data from universities is most understandable in the cases of the *Asiaweek* and THES rankings, as their international scope significantly reduces the possibility of third-party sources providing data on a consistent transnational basis (Shanghai Jiao Tong, the third international study in this comparison, solved this problem by relying almost exclusively on research output measures such as scientific publications and citations). In the cases of *US News and World Report*, *Maclean's* (Canada), the *Guardian* (the United Kingdom) and *Rzeczpospolita* (Poland), the explanation seems to be that the editors' definitions of "quality" could not be measured using government administrative data. This may indicate a weakness in government data collection in these countries, in the sense that information deemed important to quality measurement is not collected consistently or centrally; alternatively, it may indicate that the rankers' views of what constitutes an indicator of quality is not shared by governments or the higher education community.

What League Tables Measure—A Look at Indicators and Weightings

It should come as no surprise to learn that different ranking systems use very different indicators in order to obtain a picture of "quality". The number of individual indicators used in ranking

Table 19.1 Number of Indicators by Type of Data Source

	Raw Indicator Count	Survey Data	Third Parties	Universities
Asiaweek—Asia's Best Universities (defunct, 2000)	18	—	—	18
Daily Telegraph (2003)	1	—	1	—
Education 18.com	9	3	4	2
Excelencia, 2001	71	—	71	—
Financial Times (2003)	17	—	17	—
Guangdong Institute of Management Science	17	—	14	3
Guardian—University Guide 2005	7	—	2	5
La Repubblica	23	2	21	—
Maclean's University Rankings	24	1	5	18
Melbourne Institute—International Standing of Australian Universities	26	3	23	—
Netbig, 2004	18	1	10	7
Perspektywy/Rzeczpospolita Uniwersytet	18	1	2	15
Shanghai Jiao Tong University— Academic Ranking of World Universities	6	—	6	
The Times—Good University Guide 2005	9	—	9	—
Times Higher Education Supplement— World University Rankings	5	1	1	3
US News and World Report—America's Best Colleges 2006	15	1	3	11
Wuhan University Centre for Science Evaluation	45	2	22	21

systems worldwide runs well into the hundreds, making any kind of comparison grid too large to be useful.

In order to look at indicators and weightings in a manageable way, we have categorized them into seven larger headings, based in part on an existing model of institutional quality. Finnie and Usher (2005), in their proposal for a system of measuring quality in post-secondary education, developed a conceptual framework for quality measurement based on the following four elements:

- Beginning characteristics, which represent the characteristics, attributes and abilities of incoming students as they start their programs.
- Learning inputs, which come in two main types:
  i. resources, both financial and material, available to students and faculty for educational ends;
  ii. staff, both in terms of numbers but also the way in which they are deployed to teach and the learning environment they create, as measured by the amount of contact time students have with their teachers, the kinds of exams they face, etc.
- Learning outputs, which represent the "skill sets" or other attributes of graduates which culminate from their educational experiences, such as critical thinking, analytic reasoning and technical knowledge. They also include records relating to retention and completion.

- Final outcomes represent the ultimate ends to which the educational system may contribute, including not only such traditional measures as employment rates and incomes but also any other outcome deemed to be important to individuals and society, such as job satisfaction, being a "good citizen", etc.

These four elements or categories encompass the majority of indicators used by the ranking systems covered in this study. However, we will modify the typology in two ways: first, by making a clearer distinction between financial resources and staff, and second by including two other sets of indicators, namely "research" and "reputation".

Rankings are, however, more than just a collection of indicators; they are a weighted aggregation of indicators. It is therefore important to examine how they are put together and how each ranking system implicitly defines educational quality through the distribution of its weighting. Although the apparent differences between ranking systems are substantial, it is evident that some real and intriguing similarities exist among particular subsets of league tables.

Table 19.2 shows the differences in the indicators and weightings used by different league table systems, and in so doing, recasts much of Nina Van Dyke's work (2005) into league tables internationally. Each row listed summarizes the distribution of indicator weightings among the seven categories of indicators described in the previous section and adds up to 100%. This table clearly shows that no two ranking systems are alike and that some have virtually no areas of overlap with one another.

Despite the vastly different choices of indicators and weightings existing globally, certain patterns

Table 19.2 League Table Weightings

Publication	Beginning Characteristics	Learning Inputs-Staff	Learning Inputs-Resources	Learning Outputs	Final Outcomes	Research	Reputation
Asiaweek (India/Asia)	25	28.3	10	0	0	16.7	20
Daily Telegraph (UK)	0	100	0	0	0	0	0
Education 18.com (Hong Kong)	20	15	5	0	0	20	40
Excelencia (Spain)	0	25	25	25	0	25	0
Financial Times (UK)	9	19	15	10	27	20	0
Guangdong Institute (China)	0	0	0	57.1	0	42.1	0
Guardian University Guide (UK)	28	35	10	10	17	0	0
La Repubblica (Italy)	10	44.4	15.6	10	0	20	0
Maclean's (Canada)	15	20	44	5	0	0	16
Melbourne Institute (Australia)	11	3.5	11	12.6	4.8	40	17.1
Netbig (China)	12	21.8	6	0	0	45.2	15
Newsweek (US)	10	20	10	0	0	60	0
Perspektywy/Rzeczpospolita (Poland)	8	20.5	11.5	0	0	0	50
Shanghai Jiao Tong University (Intl/China)	0	0	0	10	0	90	0
The Times Good University Guide (UK)	3.3	53.3	6.7	3.3	3.3	30	0
Times World University Rankings (UK)	5	25	0	0	0	20	50
US News and World Report (US)	15	20	15	25	0	0	25
Wuhan (China)	10.6	8.5	16.6	3.4	0.6	48.6	11.7

do appear when the studies are grouped together geographically. For instance, studies from China—which has four different ranking projects—place much more weight on research indicators than any other study in the world. In the most extreme case—that of Shanghai Jiao Tong University's Academic Ranking of World Universities—research performance is worth 90% of the total ranking. This is followed by Wuhan, where research measures are worth 48.2% of the final ranking, Netbig (45.2%), and Guangdong (42.1%). As we have seen, much of this weighting is derived from the numbered papers and citations in bibliometric studies, studies with a heavy bias towards the hard sciences. With the exception of Guangdong, which has a major focus on learning outputs (mostly graduation rates), Chinese systems also put significant emphasis on institutional reputation. In contrast, comparatively little weight is put on either resource inputs or on final outcomes. Whether this is due to a scarcity/lack of data on these issues or to Chinese experts genuinely considering indicators of these types of less importance remains an open question.

Other regional patterns are also evident. Rankings of UK universities, for instance, completely eschew the use of reputation surveys as a means of determining quality (although THES places a 50% weighting on reputation issues). British league tables also put a comparatively high emphasis on measures of staff and staff quality: on average, they put over 40% of their weighting in this area, as opposed to an average of just 5per cent in the rest of the world's league tables combined.

The two big North American surveys, *Maclean's* rankings and *US News and World Report*, are virtually identical in the distribution of weighting, except for the fact that the Canadian version puts more weight on resource inputs and the American version puts more weight on learning output (intriguingly, the general category weightings of Italy's La Repubblica rankings are very similar in nature to those of *Maclean's* and the *US News*, even though the specific indicators used are completely different).

Table 19.2 graphically demonstrates the central premise of this chapter: different ranking systems have significantly different definitions of quality. The notion of quality in higher education is clearly a very malleable one. Some observers prefer to focus on outputs, while others focus on inputs. Among both inputs and outputs, there is very little agreement as to what kinds of inputs and outputs are important. Not only is no single indicator used across all ranking schemes, no single category of indicators is common either: remarkably, none of the seven basic categories of indicators are common to all university ranking systems.

One of the only previous comparative examinations of league tables (Dill and Soo, 2004) concluded, on the basis of an examination of four sets of league tables in four countries, that international definitions of quality were converging. Our findings, based on a larger sample, contradict their result. We acknowledge that part of the reason for the contradiction lies in the fact that we have divided indicators into seven categories instead of four and hence were always likely to find more variation. Methodological differences notwithstanding—we believe our methodology to be the more refined of the two—the results still conflict.

Consistency of Outcomes across League Tables

One might reasonably conclude from the foregoing analysis that measured institutional quality is not immutable and that an institution's ranking is largely a function of what the ranking body chooses to measure. A possible example in support of this proposition is Queen's University in Kingston, Canada. In its domestic rankings (*Maclean's*, 2005), it fares very well because it attracts good students and is reasonably well endowed and well funded. In international rankings, it fares poorly, even compared with other Canadian universities, because its small size puts it at a disadvantage in terms of non-standardized research output measures.

Due to the plethora of ranking systems that have appeared in recent years, one can now test this proposition directly. In most countries, there are at least three separate ranking "observations" made by different national and international ranking systems (those of THES and Shanghai Jiao Tong, plus one or more domestic rankings). In those instances where one can use multiple ranking schemes to look at the relative scores of institutions in a single country, we find that certain institutions invariably rise to the top: Oxford and Cambridge in the UK; Harvard, Yale, Princeton, MIT and Stanford in the US; Peking and Tsinghua in China; and the University of Toronto in Canada. Despite the very different weighting and aggregation schemes used by the domestic and international league tables, these institutions manage to consistently monopolize the top spots. Further down the ordinal ladder, the different ranking systems start to show greater variation (i.e. there is rarely any agreement between systems as to which university lies in tenth position) but regardless of the ranking scheme employed, "top universities" almost always seem to come out as top universities.

This poses a serious problem for interpretation. If rankings were absolutely inconsistent across all league tables, it would be easy to dismiss the whole idea of ranking as an intellectually worthless exercise designed simply to sell newspapers or magazines. If rankings were absolutely consistent across all league tables, then we might conclude that there are probably one or two "super" indicators which are driving the overall rankings, with the remainder of the indicators essentially being "chaff" with which to distract readers and to create false differentiations. But neither of these scenarios is true. In fact, it appears that different ranking schemes provide consistent results for some institutions and inconsistent ones for others.

The simplest explanation for this is that institutional league tables don't measure what their authors think they are measuring. League tables' authors believe that each indicator is a reasonable proxy for quality and that, suitably aggregated and weighted, these indicators constitute a plausible, holistic definition of quality. In fact, most indicators are probably epiphenomena of an underlying feature that is not being measured. That is to say, there is actually some "dark matter" exerting a gravitational pull on all ranking schemes such that certain institutions or types of institutions (the Harvards, Oxfords and Tsinghuas of the world) rise to the top regardless of the specific indicators and weightings used. A search for this "dark matter" certainly seems deserving of future research. One consideration, however, is that "age of institution", "faculty size" and "per-student expenditure" are probably excellent candidates for this "dark matter".

Rankings without League Tables: The Centre for Higher Education Development (CHE) Approach

For most of this chapter we have been describing league tables, i.e. ranking systems providing a single integrated score that allows an ordinal ranking of entire institutions. However, this is not the only possible approach to university ranking. There is, for instance, no intrinsic reason why indicators must focus solely on institutions; approaches which look at institutions at lower administrative levels (such as departments or faculties) are also possible. The *Guardian*, as of 2006, and la Repubblica both provide comprehensive departmental-level rankings across entire universities (that is to say, they provide separate rankings for each discipline), though they also synthesize the data upwards into institutional rankings, as we have explored in the previous two sections.

A different approach altogether is taken by the Centre for Higher Education Development (CHE) in Germany, which issues annual rankings jointly with a media partner (currently Die Zeit, formerly Stern). CHE conducts regular surveys of approximately 130,000 students and 16,000 faculty, covering nearly 250 higher education institutes in Germany. The student surveys are very extensive and ask a number of questions about both student experiences and student satisfaction.

The faculty survey is done in order to generate data for a special indicator known as the "insider's pick" (the survey asks professors to name the three institutions in their field of study that they would recommend to someone as the best places to study). It also has a number of indicators based on independent sources of data. Roughly two-thirds of the indicators are survey based (higher than any of the league tables listed in this study), and the remaining data points all come from third-party sources. The CHE rankings do not make use of university-sourced data.

The CHE ranking of German university departments differs from traditional league tables in two notable ways. First, as noted above, it does not weight or aggregate individual indicator scores. Each department's data on each indicator is allowed to stand independently, and no attempt is made to rank departments on an ordinal scale. CHE does not consider useful to combine widely disparate indicators into a single overall hierarchy.

This stance presents certain difficulties in presenting data in a printed format. Instead of a simple ordinal rank, all indicators must be shown for all institutions, which means that they are somewhat unwieldy and difficult to read. On the other hand, this stance has an enormous advantage when translated to the World Wide Web.[3]

Because CHE does not weight the ratings, it is possible for users themselves to in effect create their own weightings and rankings by selecting a restricted number of indicators and asking the website's database to provide comparative institutional information on that basis. In so doing, the CHE approach effectively cedes the power of defining "quality"—which, as we have seen, is one of the key roles arrogated by the authors of ranking schemes—to the consumers of the ranking system (i.e. prospective university students and their parents or sponsors).

CHE's second unique point is that, even within each indicator, no attempt is made to assign ordinal ranks. Each institution's department in a given discipline is simply classified as being in the "top third", "middle third" and "bottom third" of all institutions with respect to that specific indicator. Schools within each of these three categories are considered qualitatively equal, on the grounds that for many indicators, ordinal rankings are spurious given the small difference in measurement.

Conclusions

Based on this survey of league tables, the following conclusions arise:

- Vast differences exist between university league tables in terms of what they measure, how they measure it and how they implicitly define "quality".
- Some of these differences appear to be geographic or cultural in nature. There is notable clustering of certain types of indicators and certain types of data sources. Whether this reflects genuine differences in opinion about the definition of what constitutes "quality" in universities or cross-national differences in the collection and availability of data is unclear, although we lean towards the former explanation. The lack of common indicators across countries explains why the large international league tables (Shanghai Jiao Tong and THES) are so reliant on measures of publication outputs and on reputational surveys (respectively), as they are the only indicators that do not rely on governments or institutions to first collect and process the data.
- Despite major inconsistencies in the methodologies used to rank universities, there is a surprising level of agreement between ranking systems as to which universities in a given country are "the best". To the extent that different methodologies give differing opinions about the quality of an institution, the variance between observations grows as one moves down the ordinal rankings.

- Although the definition of "quality" is contested, league tables by definition impose a "one-size-fits-all" approach to the matter; this is precisely why they are so controversial. As the CHE approach shows, however, league tables are not the only way to approach ranking. Indeed, the spread of the World Wide Web provides collectors of institutional data with an opportunity to democratize rankings and put the power of ranking in the hands of the consumer by following an "any-size-fits-all" approach.

As Merisotis (2002) has noted, university rankings are here to stay. As imperfect as they are, they satisfy a public demand for transparency and information that institutions and governments have not been able to meet on their own. Moreover, as higher education becomes more costly for individuals and families, the demand for comparative information on universities will increase. As a means of delivering that information, however, league tables are only in their infancy, and all of them can clearly benefit from greater analysis of the assumptions implicit in their own schemes. This is particularly the case with respect to international league tables, which have a restricted range of possible indicators due to the lack of available cross-national comparative data. To the extent that international ranking schemes are taking on a quality assurance role in the growing international student market, this suggests that the global higher education community needs to begin to look at how best to collect and report data on institutions so as to permit thoughtful and responsible inter-institutional comparisons.

Notes

1. Usher, A. and Savino, M. (2007). A global survey of university ranking and league tables. *Higher Education in Europe*, 32:1, 5–15. Reprinted by permission of the publisher.
2. The term stems from UK-based chart listings that were often compared with Premier League professional soccer or football standings in England during the 1990s and can now be found in a wide variety of contexts in the United Kingdom today.
3. Available at: http://www.daad.de/deutschland/studium/hochschulranking/04690.en.html

References

Dill, D. and Soo, M. (2004). "Is There a Global Definition of Academic Quality? A Cross-National Analysis of University Ranking Systems", Public Policy for Academic Quality Background Paper. Chapel Hill: University of North Carolina.
Finnie, R. and Usher, A. (2005). *Measuring the Quality of Post-secondary Education: Concepts, Current Practices and a Strategic Plan*. Kingston: Canadian Policy Research Networks.
Maclean's Guide to Canadian Universities '05. (2005). Toronto: Rogers Publishing Limited.
Merisotis, J.P. (2002). "On the Ranking of Higher Education Institutions", *Higher Education in Europe* 27(4): 361–363.
Van Dyke, N. (2005). "Twenty Years of University Report Cards: Where Are We Now?", *Higher Education in Europe* 30(2): 103–125.

VI
System Policy

This section contains five chapters that emphasise the different aspects of system policy, and particularly changes in these elements. The chapters illuminate strong regional differences and a variety of forces driving change and reform.

In the first chapter of this section, Peter Scott reflects on the changes in higher education in Central and Eastern Europe. Obviously, reform in this part of the world has been characterised by coming to terms with steering in a post-communism context. The author takes issue with the general characterisation of Central and Eastern European higher education in terms of exceptionalism and underdevelopment. Developments in these countries are carefully put in their historical context, and a number of key themes in the reform process since 1989 are addressed. It is noted that issues dominant in the reform process are not radically different from those in Western Europe or the US.

In the second contribution to this section, Ka Ho Mok addresses policy change in higher education in another part of the world. He analyses reform and restructuring at the turn of the century in Hong Kong, Taiwan and mainland China. Common elements in these reform processes are: comprehensive reviews and fundamental reforms; policies of decentralisation; and trends of marketisation and privatisation. It should be kept in mind, however, that there are considerable differences between these countries when it comes to the drivers for change and the particular strategies adopted. The common elements do not imply that governments have retreated; on the contrary, the globalisation discourse is used to shape local agendas and to bring about (comprehensive) change in higher education.

Needless to say, the funding of the public sector has been one of the strongest tools of government (Hood, 1983). This applies to higher education as well as, in the context of changing steering approaches, governments have adjusted their funding policies. From funding models based on input to the higher education system, there have been radical shifts to output models (see e.g. Jongbloed and Vossensteyn, 2001). Dominic Orr, Michael Jaeger and Astrid Schwarzenberger discuss recent changes in funding arrangements in Germany, and particularly the increasing role of the market in these arrangements. Although indicator-based funding models have been implemented in most German states, they are often only used for a marginal part of the budget.

Theresa Shanahan and Glen Jones give us insight into policy developments in the past decade in Canadian higher education. As in the German case, two-level (federal–provincial) coordination plays an important role. Major shifts have taken place in the period under investigation. At the federal level, increased funding and competitive research support are the most striking changes. At the provincial level, increased involvement of industry and the private sector, as well as a rise of institutional diversity, are noteworthy changes. The authors use the phrase "shifting roles of government": although the market is starting to play a role, governments have also developed more coordination and control mechanisms in the system.

In the last chapter of this section, Bettina Alesi addresses changes in four European countries that have been influenced by supra-national developments. Arguably, the supra-national layer of steering and coordination has become much more important in the past decade, although analyses (see e.g. De Wit and Verhoeven, 2001) have also shown the increasing role of Europe in earlier decades. The 1989 Bologna Declaration has been an important driver, and Alesi investigates how employers in Austria, Hungary, the Netherlands and Norway respond to the emergence of first-cycle curricula and degrees. With some cautions, given the limited scope of the research and the recent reforms, the findings show a concern among employers regarding the employability of bachelor-level graduates. At the same time, the chapter indicates that a restructuring of programmes, accompanied by curricular reform and a serious look at the employability issue, may increase the willingness of employers to employ bachelor graduates.

In all, the chapters illustrate various reform and change processes in higher education across the globe. These processes are all characterised by a changing role of the government *vis-à-vis* higher education institutions. It is important to realise that this changing role is not straightforward, predictable and uniform across systems, from state regulation to autonomy and market influences. The examples (see also e.g. Gornitzka *et al.*, 2007; Huisman, 2008; Kogan and Hanney, 2000) in this section show that there is a dynamic interplay between various forces acting in specific (historical and geographic) contexts that influence the direction and profoundness of change.

References

De Wit, K. and Verhoeven, J. (2001). The higher education policy of the European Union: With or against the member states? In J. Huisman, P. Maassen and G. Neave (eds) *Higher education and the Nation State. The international dimension of higher education* (pp. 175–231). Amsterdam: Pergamon.
Gornitzka, A., Kogan, M. and Amaral, A. (eds) (2007). *Reform and change in higher education. Analysing policy implementation.* Dordrecht: Springer.
Hood, C. (1983). *The tools of government.* London: Macmillan.
Huisman, J. (ed.) (2008). *International perspectives on the governance of higher education. Alternative frameworks for coordination.* New York: Routledge.
Jongbloed, B. and Vossensteyn, H. (2001). Keeping up performances: An international survey of performance-based funding in higher education. *Journal of Higher Education Policy and Management, 23*(2), 127–145.
Kogan, M. and Hanney, S. (2000). *Reforming higher education.* London: Jessica Kingsley.

20

Reflections on the Reform of Higher Education in Central and Eastern Europe[1]

Peter Scott

Attempting to generalize about the reform of higher education in Central and Eastern Europe since the end of communism is made complicated by the difficulty in identifying clear terms of reference and points of comparison. The area and the higher education systems concerned are far from being homogeneous, for the homogeneity imposed by communism and Soviet domination did not last. When comparing Central and Eastern European higher education systems with those of the West, one is confronted with Western higher education systems that are quite heterogeneous and themselves also going through change. The routes to transition in higher education in Central and Eastern Europe are as diverse as the given systems and countries. The two standard categorizations of Central and Eastern European higher education, exceptionalism and underdevelopment, are inaccurate. Rather, Central and Eastern European higher education should be viewed as fitting into a wider effort to reorient the whole of European higher education towards the knowledge society. In this venture, Central and Eastern European higher education may possess some advantages that are not as prevalent further West.

Introduction

Two interlinked frames of reference are required to understand the reform of higher education in Central and Eastern Europe since 1989.

The first of these is that the unity of Central and Eastern Europe is an artifice, contingent on half a century of communist rule. The nation states that occupy the region bounded on the West by the Elbe and the mountains of Bohemia, on the East by the plains of Russia and on the North by the Baltic Sea and which, on the South, stretch to the Adriatic and (almost) the Aegean Seas are as heterogeneous as the nation states that occupy the West of Europe, stretching from the Arctic to the Mediterranean.

Central and Eastern Europe is both part of a larger whole, Europe, and subdivided into many regions. Its institutions, including its universities, reflect that variety. Almost certainly, despite their common experience of communism, universities in Central and Eastern Europe have less in common with each other than, for example, universities in Latin America. In any case, all universities are similar, both in terms of their historical conception and of the socio-economic and scientific-cultural pressures to which they are exposed. They are different because their administrative structures, funding regimes, and academic cultures are determined within national environments.

The second frame of reference is that because Central and Eastern Europe is an artifice (and also because the impact of communism was both more nuanced and less totalitarian than is commonly supposed), higher education in the region—like society at large—has been going through a period of transition rather than of transformation. The preferred vocabulary is revealing. "Transition" suggests a much less radical process than "transformation". Within this larger (but also more limited?) context, there are two contrasting accounts of the development of higher education in Central and Eastern Europe in its first post-communist decade. The first suggests that it has been released from a totalitarian time-warp and is consequently engaged in a process of catching up with the West that has been difficult and is still incomplete. The second suggests that higher education in Central and Eastern Europe, because it has had to cope with the collapse of values and structures associated with communist rule, has been both free and forced to flirt with privatization and other radical remedies that have been resisted by higher education in the West, certainly in Western Europe, and, as a result, has the potential to create new models of higher education in the twenty-first century.

Both are true, and both are exaggerated. There has been an element of catching-up because most Central and Eastern European higher education systems had tended to stagnate in the last two decades of communist rule. Rates of expansion, for example, slowed, while in the West, they accelerated, and scientific productivity declined. It is also broadly true that the immediate response after 1989 was to reassert a classical, even elitist, ideal of the university, which was inimical to the wider engagement with state, economy, and society, characteristic of the evolution of Western European higher education systems. Little attempt appears to have been made—at any rate, initially—to harness higher education to the urgent task of the transition to a post-communist society.

A key difference is that post-1989 reforms have been largely organizational. Although the crude Marxism–Leninism has been rubbed away, the scientific foundations of the system have remained almost intact. Central and Eastern European universities aspire to—and do—contribute to "metropolitan" scientific and broader intellectual cultures. They do not challenge these cultures from the "periphery". Even in the communist period, this scenario essentially held true.

Of course, there has also been a radical, even experimental, element in the post-1989 reconstruction of higher education. The collapse of communist-era control systems and the inadequacy of state support forced many higher education institutions to adapt or die.

This choice is apparent at many levels. In some Central and Eastern European countries, radical restructuring has taken place, even though sometimes as a result of institutional collapse rather than on a planned basis. The natural sciences and engineering, which dominated many Central and Eastern European universities between 1945 and 1989, have been displaced by business and management and information technology. Private institutions have proliferated (where the legal regime has permitted such developments), and public institutions have behaved in increasingly entrepreneurial ways (which critics have regarded as verging on the piratical). However, more recently, enthusiasm for free-market and neo-liberal prescriptions has waned—and, as a result, the pressure on Central and Eastern European higher education to provide a test-bed for radical-right reform.

Any assessment of higher education in Central and Eastern Europe at the beginning of the twenty-first century must incorporate elements of both characterizations, catching-up and radical experimentation—but must also avoid the danger of overemphasizing either. Both characterizations must be related to the wider frames of reference—first, that the idea of Central and Eastern Europe is an artifice, which has been progressively deconstructed during the past decade, and secondly, that the key motif of post-1989 higher education reforms (as of wider socio-economic reforms) has been transition rather than transformation (Hüfner, 1995). This chapter, which is based on a study of higher education reform in Central and Eastern Europe undertaken by the author on behalf of the UNESCO European Centre for Higher Education in 1999–2000 (Scott, 2000),[2] is divided into four sections:

1. A discussion of the historical context in which Central and Eastern European higher education developed until 1989.
2. An analysis of the development of modern higher education systems, and in particular, major trends which transcended the particular effects of the former division of Europe.
3. A discussion of the major themes in the development of Central and Eastern European higher education since 1989.
4. An analysis of alternative interpretations of the overall significance of the reforms undertaken since 1989, and their implications for the future direction of higher education in the region.

The Historical Context

In 1945, there were important economic and social differences within Central and Eastern Europe greatly related to the pre-war history of each country of the region.

Although communist rule tended to suppress and even to reduce these national differences, they were not eliminated entirely. The imposition of planned economies, accompanied by forced industrialization and (on a more limited scale) the collectivization of agriculture, led to a process of both levelling-up (in the case of the "peasant" economies) and eventually levelling-down (in the case of the "advanced" economies). As a result, economic differences in the region were reduced, even though they have tended to re-emerge since 1989 as given countries have been more or less successful in managing the transition to "market" economies. Social differences may also have been reduced during the period of communist rule as previously favoured social groups lost their privileges and/or were eliminated. This social levelling, however, was significantly reduced by the emergence of a *nomenklatura* under the aegis of the Communist Party.

Since the fall of communism, these differences have been partly re-established in some Central and Eastern European countries as income differentials have been widening since 1989.

Political divisions within the region were also reduced, and suppressed, by enforced membership in the Soviet-dominated Warsaw Pact. Again, accession and eligibility for membership in the European Union and/or in NATO has introduced new divisions since 1989. Ethnic differences were also overlaid by the imposed uniformity of communist rule, with the important exception of the former Yugoslavia, and ethnic homogeneity was promoted by the expulsion of German minorities in the immediate post-war period. But, again, these differences have tended to re-emerge since 1989, exposing once again the multi-ethnic and multi-confessional character of many Central and Eastern European societies.

Nevertheless, even during the period of communist rule, different historical phases can be identified, in which greater or lesser degrees of uniformity were imposed:

- In the immediate post-war period, despite the presence of Soviet troops in most of these countries, communist parties at first had to share power with other political groups.
- In the later 1940s, the onset of the Cold War and the imposition of Stalinist structures produced a period of intensely totalitarian rule, characterized by purges and repression such as had occurred in the Soviet Union in the 1930s. During this second phase, any idea

of an independent "civil society" came close to extinction. Its bare survival owed much to the quiet efforts of the universities to maintain some autonomous spaces, however restricted or discreet.

- However, a third phase quickly followed, triggered by popular resistance to Stalinist rule first in what was then the German Democratic Republic, then Poland, and finally Hungary and also by the first cautious steps towards de-Stalinization in the Soviet Union itself. Although this third phase began with the repression of these popular revolts, it eventually acquired the label of the "thaw". It corresponded with the much more dramatic social liberalization and more impressive economic growth rates in Western Europe at the same time. It culminated in the "Prague Spring" of 1968.
- The "thaw" was followed by a period of neo-Stalinism associated with the then Soviet leader, Leonid Brezhnev, or "normalization". In this fourth phase, there was no return to the wholesale terror of the second phase. Instead, its keynotes were administrative repression and economic stagnation. Again there are intriguing parallels with Western Europe. The 1970s were a difficult decade for both halves of the continent as the predominance, and preponderance, of old industries were eroded by new global challenges.
- This fourth phase was succeeded, around 1980, by a fifth and final phase, the crisis of communist rule. In some Central and Eastern European countries, significant reforms were introduced, notably in Hungary and Poland. But it was in the Soviet Union itself, subject to even greater stresses because of its status as a great power, that radical liberalization was undertaken. The Gorbachev project of *perestroika* failed, as much because of the contingencies of Soviet politics and personalities as because of its inherent implausibility. Having lost its ideological and military centre, communism collapsed/imploded at the end of the decade.

In the 1990s, understandably, there was an overwhelming temptation to regard the communist period as a deviation, an historical *cul-de-sac*. But this position proved to be neither possible nor perhaps sensible. First, there are no black holes in history. The Russian Revolution of 1917 was as much a world event as the French Revolution of 1789. Opponents and supporters are equally subject to its long-term significance. Second, the communist era was not monolithic. There were important temporal differences—such as the five phases (liberation, terror, thaw, stagnation, and crisis) which have just been outlined. Third, there were also important spatial differences. In Hungary, the period of the thaw persisted despite Brezhnevism, while in Romania neo-Stalinism lasted until the (bitter) end when the Ceausescu regime was overthrown. These differences have persisted into the post-communist period, shaping both political cultures and administrative competencies. Fourth, the two halves of the continent were not entirely disconnected during this period.[3] Both Western and Central and Eastern Europe went through processes of modernization in this half-century, one sophisticated, perhaps, and the other, crude, which nevertheless transformed social conditions. Both were subject to similar global forces. Their political and economic systems may have been different but they inhabited the same world.

The Development of Higher Education

In the middle of the twentieth century, there were three broad models of higher education available—the Humboldtian, which placed "knowledge" at the centre of the mission of the university; the "Napoleonic", which placed greater emphasis on professional formation (and was embodied most intensely in the *grandes ecoles* of France); and the Anglo-Saxon, in which pride of place was given to liberal education (albeit imparted through traditional academic forms).The dominant model in Central and Eastern Europe before 1939 was the Humboldtian one, even though "Napo-leonic" influences were also present, notably in Romania. But there were important differences, many of which persisted despite the enforced uniformity of the communist period and have re-emerged more strongly since 1989.

To the extent that traditional differences were reduced after 1945, this reduction can be attrib-uted as much to general forces, which also reshaped higher education in Western Europe, as to communist-imposed uniformity in copying the so-called "Soviet model" of higher education.

First, all higher education systems, East and West, experienced rapid growth during the post-Second World War period, culminating in the spectacular expansion of the 1960s. This growth reflected the reconfiguration of society across Europe as traditional elites lost ground before the advance of modernization. It was only in the last two decades of communist rule that growth rates diverged, as higher education in Western Europe experienced a second wave of expansion and Central and Eastern Europe stagnated politically and economically.

Second, the broadening of the social constituencies which higher education served was a com-mon feature across the continent, even if in the West it took the form of responding to democratic pressures for greater participation, and in Central and Eastern Europe, of enforced changes in university entrance policies to favour social groups according to a Marxist hierarchy ("workers" and "peasants"—and, of course, Communist Party cadres).

Third, manpower planning was a shared concern. The desire to relate the outputs of higher education to the manpower needs of the economy was pervasive. This desire was part of the wider modernization project that gripped both halves of the continent. In the West, of course, attempts at manpower planning rarely went beyond political exhortation and financial incentives to increase the production of "useful" graduates, except in fields such as medicine and teacher training. In the communist East, a more determined, but ultimately unsuccessful, attempt was made to subordinate higher education entirely to the manpower needs of a planned economy.

Fourth, across Europe, there was a general trend to develop "alternative" forms of higher educa-tion, both of institutional forms, organization of studies, and course programmes, in parallel with and sometimes at the expense of traditional universities.

Fifth, and last, across Europe, separate research institutes were established, as the development of mass higher education weakened the traditional affinities between the formation of future elites and research and scholarship and as the links between "knowledge production" and social and economic development strengthened.

As a result, it may be dangerous to overestimate the exceptionalism of the experience of higher education in Central and Eastern Europe under communist rule. It developed particular, and, on the whole, negative characteristics during this period. However, these characteristics did not elimin-ate the important differences between universities across the region that existed before 1945, nor should their significance be exaggerated at the expense of other more generic influences, which affected all European higher education systems.

This understanding is important in two senses. First, it leads us to question the historical interpretations of higher education that have grown up in Central and Eastern Europe since 1989. Continuity may be more considerable than we care to admit, not only in the sense that develop-ments during the communist period cannot simply and sensibly be ignored, but also in the sense that the communist regimes that ruled the region between 1945 and 1989 were never able to exclude, although they were able to distort, external influences, which played an important role in shaping higher education in Central and Eastern Europe during this half-century.

Even in the Stalinist period, communism was never able either to completely suppress the ideal and operation of an autonomous civil society, nor to exclude external influences entirely. Josef Jarïab has offered a salutary corrective in the case of (what was still then) Czechoslovakia:

In the sweeping political rejections of the former regime, its ugly and dehumanizing objectives were taken as results truly and generally achieved. But fortunately, they had in fact never accomplished their goals to the extent they might have thought. Due to inefficient bureaucracy and [the] rather lukewarm attitudes of many people working within the system, especially after 1968, the totalitarian educational project could not and did not fully succeed. It is also worth remembering and reminding ourselves and our Western colleagues that good teaching did not completely disappear from our schools with the introduction of communist ideology (Jarïab, 1993).

Second, such understanding suggests that it is misleading to regard universities in the region as, in any but the most superficial economic sense, underdeveloped. They were always fully "European"—before 1945 and after 1989—but also, crucially, during the years between. Until the stagnation of the communist regimes in the 1970s, the higher education systems in Central and Eastern Europe (and in the former Soviet Union) were able to produce remarkable achievements, in particular in the natural sciences, both in terms of expansion of student numbers (and so an expansion of social opportunities, sadly unaccompanied by the development of a truly democratic culture), and in terms of research, notably in the mathematical and physical sciences and in engineering.

Key Themes

Five major themes emerged from the UNESCO-CEPES study on which this chapter is based: the scale and scope of Central and Eastern European higher education, the diversity of higher education across the region, the sequencing of successive phases of higher education reform since 1989, the balance between continuities and discontinuities, and structural reforms, or the creation of new legal, administrative, and academic frameworks.

Expansion

In the 10 Central and Eastern European countries covered by the UNESCO-CEPES study, the number of students enrolled in higher education institutions increased from some 1.2 million to more than 2.1 million in 1996. And this trend still continues, even if with a reduced dynamic.

However, within this overall expansion, there have been some significant trends:

- In 1989, almost 40% of the students in Central and Eastern Europe were studying natural sciences. By 1996, the proportion had dropped 10%. During the same period, the number of students in the humanities and the social sciences increased almost three-fold, from 27% of the total to 43%. The numbers of students in education, medicine, and engineering have remained stable and have grown more slowly.
- The number of graduates has only increased by 45% despite the 66% increase in student enrolments. In some countries, there has been almost no increases, and in one, an absolute decline. The figures suggest that non-completion rates have risen across the region, which can largely be attributed to the overall expansion in student numbers and the shift towards the humanities and the social sciences.
- The number of tertiary-level teachers has increased by an even smaller amount, only 27%. However, by the standards of Western Europe and North America, staff–student ratios are still quite favourable.

Diversity or Commonality?

A major theme, which emerged from the UNESCO-CEPES analysis, was the balance to be struck between emphasizing the common characteristics of higher education systems and institutions in the region and highlighting their differences. A further complication arises from the fact that some of these common characteristics are retrospective, because they reflect the uniformity imposed during the communist era (and, therefore, might be expected to diminish in significance?), while others are prospective, because they relate to the demands to which all higher education systems in the developed world are subject (and presumably are likely to intensify). A still further complication arises because this dilemma between commonality and difference in Central and Eastern Europe is overlaid by the wider debate about whether higher education systems are converging or diverging.

The case for emphasizing difference has already been discussed. Before 1945, universities across the region had little in common, certainly no more (or less) than with universities in other parts of Europe. They included some of the oldest universities in Europe—Prague (1347) and Cracow (1364)—which long predated the development of nation states or nationalist consciousness. But the first Romanian university was not established until 1860, and the first Bulgarian university only in 1904. In both cases, the links with nation-building were explicit. It was only as a result of their forced subjection to communism that common characteristics emerged. With the collapse of communism, not only are these original differences based on traditional orientations re-emerging, but new ones are being created by the different rates of change and directions taken by post-communist developments. Some universities have been much more successful than others at adapting to the new environment of political pluralism and market engagement, in some cases because they are (literally) new foundations, in others, because they have greater room for manoeuvre, and in others, again, because their national governments have embraced change with more enthusiasm and/or success.

The case for emphasizing commonality, therefore, is twofold. First, higher education in Central and Eastern Europe was subjected for almost half a century to communist regimes which were animated by the same ideology (with some local/national peculiarities), created analogous state structures and, ultimately, had a single reference point in the sense that they were subordinate to the will of the Soviet leadership. The Conference of Ministers of Higher Education in Socialist Countries was influential in formalizing this orthodoxy. (Only Slovenia, as a republic in the former Yugoslavia, was an exception because the Titoist principle of self-management was also applied to higher education.) Second, during the 1945–1989 period, all European systems exhibited similar trends such as expansion of student numbers and consequent massification and also subordination to socio-economic requirements and greater accountability to political interests.

The collapse of communism apparently removed the first imperative for commonality—but, arguably, only to introduce another, the common dilemmas created by the transition to post-communist society across the region. So, even after communism ceased to exist, it continued to promote homogeneity. Of course, the Europe-wide—even global—trends were intensified by the collapse of communism and its replacement by democratic-capitalist regimes. As a result, universities throughout the region have had to develop policies for retraining inappropriately qualified staff and to rebalance their portfolios of academic programmes to reflect new political and social conditions, both of which are examples of post-communist adaptation, and also to develop courses in business, management, and information technology, an example of the wider impact of global forces.

Jan Sadlak has attempted to conceptualize these transitions in terms of three models of higher education in Central and Eastern Europe—pre-communist, communist, and modernized post-communist—within an analytical framework that emphasizes commonalties rather than differences (Sadlak, 1995) (see Table 20.1).

Table 20.1

	PRE-COMMUNIST Implicit and self-regulatory	COMMUNIST Centrally regulated	POST-COMMUNIST Explicit and self- regulatory
Main traits	Confidence in values of particular academic freedom	Aims, tasks, and resources in teaching and research defined by the Communist Party and allocated by the states	Competition for students funding; importance of iinstitutional/programme, academic standing; multiple forms of self-representation; adherence to academic freedom
System-wide regulation	Minimal	Compulsory and detailed party/state regulations	Preferably within a broad state regulatory role
Planning system approach	None or very limited	Comprehensive: an instrument of political control	Particularly important at Institutional level
Accountability	Limited mainly to own constituency	Mainly to political authorities (Communist Party)	Accountability towards multiple constituencies
Autonomy	Yes – but its[c] parameters were also differently defined from nowadays	Hardly any – or at the discretion of the political authorities	Determined by the degree of accountability to specific constituencies
Incentives	Reliance on intrinsic motivation in learning and research	Achievement of goals set by the party and state	Well-being of the institution and its principal constituency
Financing and budgeting	Heavily tuition-fee dependent/input-oriented line-item budgeting	Totally state-dependent but relatively "worry free"; rigid line-item budgeting	Multiple sources and instruments of financing and budgeting
Relation to labour market	Minimal and only indirect	Close co-ordination with state-set manpower planning	Significant but indirect/A result of the interaction of multiple constituencies
Internal governance and structure	Federation of relatively independent sub-units (chairs)	Externally determined and politically controlled (*nomenklatura*)	Concentration of administrative power/diversity of structure
Strategic planning	Occasionally at sub-unit level/not essential for governance	Almost none at institutional and sub-unit level	Essential for survival and/or the well-being of the institution; important approach in governance

Sadlak's broad framework emphasizes the general characteristics of higher education in Central and Eastern Europe during these three periods. There are, of course, exceptions to the rule. Peter Darvas' argument (1998) that "if there is anything peculiar about the region [Central and Eastern Europe], it is the level of complexity of changes that may exceed that which can be observed globally", may help to reconcile this apparent contradiction. Higher education in the region has followed a broadly similar post-communist trajectory—but one characterized by increasing differentiation.

Sequences of Reform

The third theme is that the reform of higher education systems in Central and Eastern Europe has already gone through two stages (and is now entering a third). The first stage was characterized by two imperatives. The first one was a desire to disengage the academic system from the very tight association with, and subordination to, the economic system that had prevailed during the communist period. The second one was to liberalize academic structures as part of a wider liberalization of political structures, with the former being largely a contingent effect of the latter.

The conclusion of a so-called Transatlantic Dialogue organized by the Pew Charitable Trusts in the early 1990s and involving both American university and college presidents and European rectors from both Eastern and Western Europe was clear: "Autonomy is the first of many steps needed to restore the university in Central and Eastern Europe to its former vitality".

The author of this article was a participant in the three seminars—at Trento, Olomouc, and Madison—which formed the Dialogue. His impression was equally clear:

> The Central and Eastern European participants insisted on a ringing restatement of this idea [of the liberal university] in purest, even absolutist, terms. The need, as the Eastern Europeans saw it, was to re-establish free universities—like free parliaments and free courts. . . . In many debates during the Dialogue, it's Central and Eastern European members seized the high moral ground, while their Western European and American colleagues were prepared to settle for the life of [the] "market and state accountability" (Scott, 1993).

However, by the mid-1990s, it had become clear that this disengagement of the academic system from the economic system and the bestowal of (formally) unrestricted autonomy on higher education had led to significant difficulties.

First, because of the strains produced by the transition from centrally planned to market economies in most Central and Eastern European countries, strains which were particularly intense in the public sector, it was not feasible to maintain this disengagement. In a negative sense, higher education was affected by the erosion of its resource base, which undermined its effective autonomy. In a positive sense, universities have clearly had a key role to play in the process of economic transition.

Second, the autonomy granted to universities was used—or perceived to be used—to block reform. Although substantial structural changes were made in all higher education systems in the region during the 1990s (including important staffing changes), few other Central and Eastern Europe higher education systems experienced the radical reconstruction experienced by the East German system following German re-unification. It has been estimated that almost half of the higher education teaching staff members in the former German Democratic Republic lost their jobs, compared with fewer than 10% in the rest of Central and Eastern Europe.[4]

Third, the liberalization of academic structures undertaken in the immediate aftermath of the collapse of communism proved in some cases to be impractical. New higher education laws were sometimes utopian in their formulations—and difficult to implement against a background of substantial continuity of personnel and significant erosion of resources. For example, rectors were granted formal powers which, in practice, they were often unable to exercise. Issues of governance and management were left undetermined.

As a result, the second phase of post-communist reform, from the mid-1990s onwards, attempted to remedy these weaknesses. Universities retreated from what could be called the "liberal absolutism" of the years immediately after 1989 when both opponents of the former communist regimes, and their passive supporters, had insisted on a high degree of institutional autonomy, but for different reasons. Autonomy, initially seen largely in terms of an absence of state power, was gradually replaced by new notions of civic and market accountability. The importance of higher education in terms of economic development, as well as political and cultural renewal, was more readily acknowledged as the emphasis switched from the subordination to the manpower needs of planned economies to engagement with a "knowledge society", albeit in the context of post-communist transition. More practical attention was paid to issues of institutional governance and management.

This second stage, therefore, was one of emerging pragmatism. After the first stage characterized by utopianism and dominated by political–cultural issues, which lasted in most countries until 1992 or 1993, the emphasis switched to the need to expand and diversify higher education to meet new socio-economic demands. The mid-1990s were dominated by these efforts. More recently, attention appears to have switched again to issues of structure—and so back to governance and management (but in much more pragmatic terms). The need for both systems and institutions to be sufficiently robust to cope with, first, the practical implications of the institutional autonomy and academic freedom granted in the immediate aftermath of 1989 and, second, with the strains of expansion and diversification that took place in the mid-1990s, is now much more readily recognized. This third stage, therefore, can be regarded as a period of normalization, but in two senses. The first is that the structures (and mentalities) needed to systematize and institutionalize post-communist reforms are now being built; the second is that the agendas of higher education in both parts of Europe, East and West, are rapidly converging.

The Lure of the West?

It is not surprising that those undertaking reform in higher education in the Central and Eastern European countries quite often emphasize the importance of Western European (and, to a lesser extent, North American) models in inspiring and in shaping the reconstruction of higher education in the region. Academic and administrative staff with a strong orientation to the West or with direct experience of higher education in the West are identified as among the most consistent supporters of reform, while those whose experience was confined to communist-dominated systems are identified as being passive, sceptical, or even resistant to reform. In some countries in the region, Western "returnees" have played an important role.

The reasons for this orientation are easy to understand. First, during the communist period, the West had been the "other" and consequently a focus for the hopes of those who opposed or resisted the former regimes. When the "Iron Curtain" was removed, it was natural that this longing for the West should be expressed through admiration and imitation of its values. Second, more concretely, the West provided examples of free institutions, which actually operated, including, of course, universities. So it was equally natural that these institutions would provide templates for the reform of the totalitarian structures inherited from the communist period. The Western template was particularly necessary in the development of business schools, which had not existed in pre-1989 universities except in the stilted form of faculties of economics, and of private higher education institutions which, of course, were not permitted during the communist period.

Third, the drive to the West was an attempt to re-link Central and Eastern European universities to what is now called, in the wake of the 1999 Bologna Declaration, "the European Area for Higher Education". The emphasis on internationalization in many Central and Eastern European universities is a concrete expression of this aspiration. However, this focus is very much on building stronger links with Western Europe and North America. As such, it is very different from the meaning attached to internationalization in universities in the West, which is already shading into something very different, globalization (Högskoleverket, 1997). Fourth, the West was seen as a source of the funding needed for reconstruction, which is another reason for the rather narrow focus of internationalization.

However, this identification with the West has encountered certain difficulties. The first, and most obvious, can be summed up in a simple question—which West? There are several models of higher education in Western Europe (which are derived from the traditional taxonomy of Humboldtian, Napoleonic, and Anglo-Saxon models evoked earlier in this chapter, but substantially readjusted by recent massification). There are also many different types of institution, university and non-university, in most Western European systems (the United Kingdom and Sweden are the only two countries with, even approximately, unified higher education systems). The second is that the Western model of higher education is not only increasingly pluralistic; it is also highly volatile. Significant reforms took place during the 1990s. To take just two examples, in England, the former polytechnics became universities in 1992 and, later in the decade, *Fachhochschulen* on the German model were developed in Austria out of a plethora of trade and craft schools.

Accordingly, as the engagement between Central and Eastern European higher education and Western European (and North American) universities has deepened, it has also become more complex. In the immediate post-communist period, higher education in the West offered a stylized—and idealized?—model. Its subordination to political authority, not simply in terms of administrative structures and funding regimes, but increasingly, in terms of quality-assurance and other performance measures as the state redefined itself as an (over-mighty?) customer; its accountability to public opinion, which forced universities to "manage" their reputations with growing professionalism; its exposure to marketing influences; its, on the whole, willing engagement with society—such characteristics were little noticed at first. Today a more nuanced relationship with the West can be observed—which can be partly explained by the continuing, even increasing, influence of reformed socialist/neo-communist parties in parts of Central and Eastern Europe, but can mainly be attributed to a better understanding of the real circumstances of higher education in the West.

Restructuring Higher Education in the Region

The fifth, and last major, theme is the scale and complexity of the restructuring of higher education systems in Central and Eastern Europe (Aaviksoo, 1997).

Higher education in the region has had to be reconstructed on a scale, and at a speed, never attempted in Western Europe. Adjustments that have required long gestation in the West have had to be accomplished within four or five years. For example, in the West, complex issues such as the relationship between universities and other higher education institutions and between higher education and research have been managed by a lengthy process of reform and negotiation stretching over several decades. In Central and Eastern Europe, such issues had to be immediately resolved after 1989.

In some countries, reconstruction has been total. It has had to proceed from first principles. Not only has the legal framework in which higher education institutions operate had to be entirely rewritten, the fundamental mission of institutions and their articulation within wider systems has also had to be reconsidered. In other words institutional restructuring has had to take place against a background of normative uncertainty—which has never been experienced in the West.

Standard solutions that could be applied across the region have not been available. The different countries in Central and Eastern Europe have been more or less successful in their attempts at economic reform (which have determined their capacity to fund and manage higher education reform), and they have taken up different stances regarding their communist pasts (which have influenced their willingness to undertake reform). Nevertheless, institutional patterns and administrative processes have varied across the region. For example, in some countries the need has been to strengthen the university as a central institution at the expense of its constituent parts; in others to decentralize power decision-making. So, even where common objectives have been pursued, different solutions have had to be found (EURYDICE, 1997, 1999).

With the exception of a minority of institutions, which have either received generous financial support from outside the region and/or have been able to charge high fees because they concentrate on courses in subjects like management and information technology, higher education in Central and Eastern Europe has been chronically underfunded (Dincaï and Damian, 1997). This underfunding has adversely affected the situation of the academic staff (often obliged to undertake multiple teaching posts, especially in private higher education institutions) and has greatly hampered attempts at institutional renewal. Although there are signs in a few countries in the region that the transition to a market economy has been (relatively) successfully accomplished, and during the 1990s the region experienced a rate of economic growth that substantially exceeded that in Western Europe, across the region as a whole economic restructuring is far from complete (and there are particular difficulties with regard to reconstituting a modern and viable public sector, which embraces most elements within higher education systems). One result has been that public institutions have become semi-privatized by depending increasingly on fee income. The "private sector" is within, not without.

Higher education systems in Central and Eastern Europe have been subject to substantial reshaping since the collapse of communism. At the system level, three general features may be particularly significant.

The first is that in some countries a significant private sector has developed (which is larger as a proportion of student numbers than in nearly every Western European country). The private sector is seen by some as more dynamic and flexible than publicly funded higher education. It is not clear whether the private sector will expand, in line with a global trend towards privatization in higher education, or contract, because if/when publicly funded institutions become more flexible and better provided with resources, private institutions will lose their comparative advantage. The largest number of private institutions is in Poland. In a few countries, such as Romania, greater obstacles have been placed in the way of developing private institutions.

The second feature is the integration of research institutes, once managed separately by academies of science or central ministries, into universities, so producing a better integration between teaching and research and also releasing additional teaching staff resources. However, although a general phenomenon, this trend towards incorporation is also uneven. The extent to which true integration has been achieved is often unclear. It appears that this situation is going to last for a while.

The third feature is that efforts have been made to create more systematic binary systems. During the communist era, non-university higher education was best described as pre- or proto-binary. Advanced education outside the universities typically took two forms: (a) specialized monotechnic institutions (often administered by other ministries apart from the Ministry of Education—or of Higher Education); and (b) higher technical schools, which were often closer in spirit to secondary education. During the 1990s, many Central and Eastern European countries decided, if not to integrate monotechnic institutions into multi-faculty universities outright, then to develop common planning frameworks; and also to upgrade higher technical schools (which sometimes, as in Hungary, involved mergers to create larger institutions).

Conclusions

The two standard categorizations of Central and Eastern European higher education are *exceptionalism* (the idea that higher education in the region is categorically different, either in a negative sense because of the debilitating experience of communist rule, or positively, because it has been able to undertake radical reforms impossible in the West); and *underdevelopment* (Central and Eastern European higher education has lagged behind higher education in the West, which provides the only model of development). However, neither categorization is satisfactory. Both only capture those elements of Central and Eastern European higher education that were most directly touched by the experience of communist rule, which are diminishing in significance at the expense of the totality.

Exceptionalism

Clearly, between 1945 and 1989, the development of higher education in Central and Eastern Europe was decisively shaped by the experience of communist rule. However, that influence was qualified in three ways:

- The experience of communist rule varied between the different countries in the region and among different periods of time.
- Higher education in Central and Eastern Europe was not hermetically sealed from external influences.
- The imperatives of modernization shaped higher education in both East and West.

Underdevelopment

The second categorization, that higher education in Central and Eastern Europe is underdeveloped, is equally unsatisfactory. Of course, there are some (limited) respects in which notions of underdevelopment may be useful. The most obvious is the slower rate of growth in student numbers after 1970, which, arguably, meant that, in a quantitative sense, higher education in Central and Eastern Europe was less mature than in Western Europe and America. As has already been pointed out, there was little difference between growth rates in the East and the West before 1970. Only with the stagnation of the last two decades of communist rule did a gap open up. Although Central and Eastern Europe experienced the first post-war wave of higher education expansion, in most countries in the region, the second was delayed until after the collapse of communism in 1989.

Arguably slower growth rates after 1970 meant that institutions had less incentive to innovate, and may have contributed to the underlying conservatism of higher education in the region (which, of course, was also a product of the political cultures and social systems that prevailed until 1989). But even the argument about the developmental effects of delayed expansion has to be treated with care. Within Western Europe there were important variations in the timing of the second wave of post-war expansion.

The issues that preoccupy higher education in Central and Eastern Europe are broadly similar to those that preoccupy higher education in Western Europe or North America: the balance within institutions between central administration and faculties, schools, or departments; the relationship between research and teaching; "distributed" delivery of higher education programmes (often linked to a regional agenda); the tension between systemic planning and institutional initiative; the maintenance of institutional diversity within increasingly "volatile" systems; new patterns of funding in which student fees and the commercial exploitation of intellectual property (in its widest sense) are of increasing importance, and state funding, less important; and the renewal of the academic profession (in terms of both recruitment and retraining).

Alternative Characterizations?

Two alternative characterizations of Central and Eastern European higher education appear to be more promising than either exceptionalism or underdevelopment. The first one emphasizes the importance of spatial dimensions and has two distinct aspects.

Although there is insufficient research evidence to contrast the experiences of "large" countries, such as Poland or Romania, with those of "small" countries, such as Lithuania or Slovenia, studies in other countries suggest that this line of approach may produce a significant effect. For example, a recent study of educational policy-making in England, Scotland, Wales and Northern Ireland (the constituent parts of the United Kingdom) highlighted the importance of scale in generating appropriate policy communities, shaping leadership cadres, and influencing policy transfers (Raffe *et al.*, 1999). One can argue that reforms and other policy initiatives are more likely to emerge in "large" countries because the plurality of interests produces a more creative environment, but that they are easier to implement in "small" countries because of the greater intimacy of political and administrative networks.

The coherence of Central and Eastern Europe was contingent on its incorporation into the communist bloc. The artificiality of this incorporation was exposed by the collapse of the communist system. First, older affinities are re-emerging—around the Baltic, in the Balkans, and even in the old nineteenth-century concept of *Mitteleuropa*. Second, wider groupings are emerging, or being extended, the best examples being the European Union, and, related to it, the project of creating, by the year 2010, a European Higher Education Area. Third, the impact of globalization is becoming more intense. Taken together, these three trends are producing significant changes in national (and individual) identities and in the orientation of all socio-economic systems, including higher education systems.

The second characterization emphasizes the developing relationship between higher education and the so-called "knowledge society". None of the main three strands within the European university tradition—Humboldtian, Napoleonic, or Anglo-Saxon—is perhaps truly compatible with a truly mass higher education project of the kind that has been attempted in the United States. All retain elements that may inhibit the full engagement of higher education with the "knowledge society". Higher education in Central and Eastern Europe and in Western Europe are alike in this respect. The "knowledge society", of course, is a hybrid phenomenon—or, more accurately, a set of interlocking phenomena. Most frequently emphasized is the growing importance of information and communication technologies and the increasing power of round-the-clock, round-the-globe markets, and the apparent triumph of neo-liberal ideology. However, other phenomena are equally, or more, important, notably (global) resistance to global markets, so-called "risk society" and, of particular significance to higher education, new and more distributed patterns of knowledge production.

In some respects, Central and Eastern European higher education may be at an advantage. For example, the decay of state authority and financial exigency may have reduced the barriers to privatization at an operational level, even if at a normative level, nostalgia for a classical ideal of the university may be an inhibition. In other respects, Central and Eastern European higher education may be at a disadvantage. For example, its exposure to globalization is much reduced, and distributed knowledge production systems are less developed. But the sum of these comparative advantages and disadvantages is likely to balance out, and, in any case, is a minor consideration judged against the larger challenges that all higher education systems face in their encounters with these novel social, economic, political and cultural forms.

Neither characterization is sufficiently developed to challenge some of the presumptions made about higher education in Central and Eastern Europe—which, despite the evidence, often still reflect characterizations of exceptionalism and underdevelopment. But both characterizations deserve further elaboration. The first, spatial, interpretation would be better for explaining the differences that are emerging in the region (and which existed, in a suppressed form, throughout the communist period). The second interpretation might offer a better explanation of the inhibitions, even the occasional conservatism, of higher education in the region—by emphasizing not the particularities of the communist experience but the commonalities within a European university tradition which may be mass in scale and structure but is elitist and hierarchical in its fundamental values (certainly in contrast to the more open American higher education system).

If either, or both, of these interpretations are seen as having any substance, the challenges facing higher education in Central and Eastern Europe appear in a different light, not as "catching up" with higher education in Western Europe, a limited (limiting?) and infinite project, but as part of a wider enterprise to reorient the whole of European higher education by reaching out beyond the elites, old and new, cultural or technical, into the diverse communities that constitute modern Europe, and by realizing the potential of the new synergies between knowledge and society and the economy, identity and culture. It is not Central and Eastern European higher education that is in transition; it is all higher education.

Notes

1. Scott, P. (2002). Reflections on the reform of higher education in central and eastern Europe. *Higher Education in Europe*, 27: 1, 137–152. Reprinted by permission of the publisher.
2. The study covered 12 institutions in the following countries: Bulgaria, the Czech Republic, Estonia, Hungary, Latvia, Lithuania, Poland, Romania, the Slovak Republic, and Slovenia. The author takes this opportunity to express his gratitude to Jean Bocock, a former colleague and Research Associate at the Centre for Policy Studies in Education at the University of Leeds, for helping him with the analysis of the case studies and by comments on this essay.
3. Such institutions as UNESCO-CEPES had played a positive role in the *rapprochement* in relation to higher education.
4. For a more detailed analysis of the issue, see K. Hüfner (1995).

References

Aaviksoo, J. (1997). "Priorities for Higher Education in Central and Eastern European Countries", *Higher Education Management*. Paris: OECD.

Darvas, P. (1998). "The Future of Higher Education in Central-Eastern Europe: Problems and Possibilities", *European Review* (October).

Dincǎi, G. and Damian, R. (1997). *Financing of Higher Education in Romania*. Bucharest: Editura Alternative.

Eurydice. (1997). *Supplement to the Study on the Structures of the Education and Initial Training Systems in the European Union: The Situation in Bulgaria, The Czech Republic, Hungary, Poland, Romania, and Slovakia*. Brussels: Eurydice.

Eurydice. (1999). *Supplement to the Study on the Structures of the Education and Initial Training Systems in the European Union: The Situation in Estonia, Latvia, Lithuania, Slovenia, and Cyprus*. Brussels: Eurydice.

Högskoleverket. (1997). "Central and Eastern Europe". In *National Policies for the Internationalization of Higher Education in Europe*. Stockholm: Högskoleverket.

Hüfner, K. (1995). "Higher Education Reform in the Context of Rapidly Changing Societies". In K. Hüfner (ed.), *Higher Education Reform Processes in Central and Eastern Europe*. Frankfurt: Peter Lang.

Jařiab, J. (1993). "Higher Education and Research in the Czech Republic", *Policy Perspectives* 51.

Raffe, D., Brannen, K., Croxford, C. and Martin, C. (1999). "Comparing England, Scotland, Wales, and Northern Ireland: The Case for 'Home Internationals' in Comparative Research", *Comparative Research* 351: 9–25.

Sadlak, J. (1995). "In Search of the 'Post-communist' University—The Background and Scenario of the Transformation of Higher Education in Central and Eastern Europe". In K. Hüfner (ed.) *Higher Education Reform Processes in Central and Eastern Europe*. Frankfurt: Peter Lang.

Scott, P. (1993). "Reflections on the Transatlantic Dialogue", *Policy Perspectives* 51.

Scott, P. (2000). "Higher Education in Central and Eastern Europe: An Analytical Report". In *Ten Years On and Looking Ahead: A Review of the Transformations of Higher Education in Central and Eastern Europe*. Bucharest: UNESCO-CEPES.

21

Globalisation and Higher Education Restructuring in Hong Kong, Taiwan and Mainland China[1]

Ka Ho Mok

Globalisation and the evolution of the knowledge-based economy have caused dramatic changes in the character and functions of higher education in most countries around the world. However, the impacts of globalisation on universities are not uniform even though similar business-like practices have been adopted to cope with competition in the global marketplace. The pressure for restructuring and reforming higher education is mainly derived from growing expectations and demands of different stakeholders in society. In the last decade, government bureaucracy, public service institutions and higher education institutions and universities have been significantly affected by the tidal wave of the public sector reform around the world. Apart from improving the efficiency and effectiveness of public services, universities are confronted with a situation in which the principles of financial accountability and responsiveness to stakeholders prevail amidst the massification stage under the condition of global economic retrenchment. In response to such pressing demands for change, policies and strategies of decentralisation, privatisation and marketisation are becoming increasingly popular measures in university governance. Reform strategies and measures like quality assurance, performance evaluation, financial audit, corporate management and market competition are adopted to reform and improve the performance of the higher education sector. This chapter examines the most recent higher education reforms and restructuring in Hong Kong, Taiwan and Mainland China, with particular reference to the issues related to globalisation of decentralisation and marketisation in higher education.

Globalisation and the Question of State Capacity

In the last decade or so, the liberalisation of national economies, the domination of supranational institutions, the disempowerment of nation-states, the prevalence of the system and culture of liberal democracy, as well as the formation of a consumer culture across the globe have made the whole world in many ways more alike (Fukuyama, 1992; Ohmae, 1990; Waters, 2001; Sklair, 1999). Scholars who support the ideas of globalisation believe that there is an inevitable convergence of human activities. The rapid globalisation and the strong demands for economic and social developments, based on national survival and growth, in both international and regional competitions, have become increasingly keen. Many globalists strongly believe that the dissolution of territorial borders and the growing interdependence and interconnectedness of different countries have made the traditional national/territorial boundary inappropriate (Gray, 1998; Held *et al.*, 1999).

It is also argued that the growing impact of globalisation has unquestionably weakened the capacity or limited the role of the nation-state in managing the public domain. Instead of assuming the role as the driver for change, modern states have to take a backseat role within the framework of rising regional economies and a global marketplace (Ohmae, 1999; Faulks, 2000). On the one hand, modern states have to compete for the huge sums of transnational capital investment. On the other hand, they have to surrender some state autonomy in exchange for a better position in the global market place. At the same time, modern states may encounter market failure since "greater international capital mobility made manipulation of the economy at the national level more difficult" (Slaughter, 1998, p. 53).

It is in such a wider socio-political and socio-economic context that notions like "wither the state" (Waters, 2001; Massey, 1997), "the decline of the state and territory" (Axford, 1995), "hollowing out of state" (Cerny, 1996); "dissolving the nation state" (McGrew, 1992) and "governance without government" (Rhodes, 1997) are employed by different scholars to conceptualise the weakening state capacity in the context of globalisation. Therefore, it is believed that individual states have to change their roles and their constitutions in order to accommodate, and not adapt to, the demands and pressures generated from external environments. "Reinventing government" (Osborne and Gaebler, 1992) and "entrepreneurial government" (Ferlie *et al.*, 1996) have become fashionable terms and the concomitant consequence is the initiation of reforms in public sector management. In order to improve the efficiency and effectiveness of public service delivery, new ways to maximise productivity and effectiveness comparable to that of the private sector are sought (Dale, 1997).

Globalisation, Changing Governance and Educational Restructuring

The questioning of state capacity and the perceived challenges generated from the processes of globalisation have driven modern states to reflect upon the ways they are managed by searching for new governance models to promote "good government". Central to the debate of governance is the changing relationship between the state and the non-state sectors and actors in terms of social and public policy provision. Unlike the classical approach of welfare state whereby the state had assumed a very dominant role in welfare provision (i.e. the primary social and public policy provider), the globalisation challenges have urged modern states to find new alternatives for governance.

In order to search for new alternatives to promote "good government", different governance modes are emerging. As Peters suggested, the market model, the participatory state model, the flexible government model and deregulated government model are alternatives to the traditional system. The emergence of these models has suggested different kinds of problems embedded in the traditional governance system, such as the self-interest of bureaucrats and the ineffective management of government (Peters, 1996). Similarly, Rhodes (1997) also argues that modern states are experiencing a "new process of governing" (p. 46) and there has been a strong need to redefine the relationship between the state and non-state sectors. During such a process of redefinition, different governance models are evolving, namely, the minimal state, corporate governance, the new public management, "good governance", socio-cybernetic system and self-organising networks (Rhodes, 1997, pp. 46–47).

Realising the state alone can never meet the pressing demands from the public in social policy provision and public management, the revitalisation process of civil society is under way, therefore co-arrangement between the state and the society is becoming a far more popular public policy trend. Emphasising the interactions between the state and society as a "two-way" traffic or bilateral model, the "one-way" "command and control model" is replaced by the "social-political governance" model (Kooiman, 1993; Cooper, 1995).

Putting the above observations related to changing governance into perspective, we can argue that the major shift of national politics from maximising welfare to promoting entrepreneurial culture, innovation and profitability in both the private and public sectors has led modern states to adopt the techniques of steering from a distance through the means of regulation, incentive and sanctions to make autonomous individuals and quasi-governmental and non-governmental institutions such as universities behave in ways consistent with their policy objectives (Marginson, 1999; Henry et al., 1999). In short, this paradigm shift is manifested by a more individualistic, competitive and entrepreneurial approach central to public management (Robertson and Dale, 2000). Such a move has inevitably transformed modern states into the "market-facilitating state" (Howell, 1993), the "market-building state" (Fligstein, 1997) or the "competitive state" (Cerny, 1996). Therefore, the role of the government/nation-state has changed fundamentally from a "provider of welfare benefits" to a "builder of markets", whereby the state actively builds markets, shapes them in different ways and regulates them (Sbragia, 2000).

In the face of global economic retrenchment and relatively weakened state capacity in social service and policy provision, there has been the pressure for restructuring and reforming education driven by growing expectations and demands of different stakeholders in society. Widespread concerns over widened access, funding, accountability, quality and managerial efficiency are perceived as prominent global trends for education. In addition, the further expansion of universities is built upon the basis of greater accountability but with lesser autonomy. Collegial processes of democracy within universities are taken over by stronger corporate management. Moreover, the role of universities has changed in such a way that they act less as critics of society but more as servants responding to the needs of the economy, while contracting its main functions to supply qualified manpower and undergoing applied research in response to market demands. In reality, universities are at a crossroad between the alleged democracy of a whimsical collegiality and the problematic efficiency of a hard-nosed managerialism (Dearlove, 1995). This chapter, as set out in this wider theoretical and public policy context, examines how educational governance modes have been changing in the Chinese societies of Hong Kong, Taiwan and mainland China.

Common Challenges to Higher Education in Greater China

The rise of the knowledge economy has generated new global infrastructures, with information technology playing an increasingly important role. The popularity and prominence of information technology has unquestionably changed the nature of knowledge, and is currently restructuring higher education, research and learning. The changes in the socio-economic context resulting from the globalised economy have inevitably led to changes in the university sector. It is in such a wider policy context that an increasing number of institutions of higher learning are being established with new missions and innovative configurations of training, serving populations that previously had little access to higher education. Major challenges common to Chinese societies include:

- the ever-increasing rate of human progress;
- the rise of the knowledge economy and the changing university;
- the growing significance of information technology in education delivery;
- the massification of higher education and the need for quality control;
- the East Asian financial crisis and the post-crisis adjustments; and

- social and political changes and the need to change higher education (Townsend and Cheng, 2000).

We have just discussed the challenges that these Chinese societies are now facing; let us now turn to how and what strategies that these Chinese societies have adopted in reforming their higher education systems in order to meet the challenges of globalisation.

Higher Education Restructuring in Greater China

Although it is difficult to make generalisations about the patterns, trends and models in higher education restructuring in these Chinese societies, since each society has its own stage and speed of development, a scrutiny of higher education reforms finds some common themes.

(1) Comprehensive Reviews of Education Systems and Fundamental Reforms

The governments of East Asian societies like Hong Kong, Singapore, Taiwan, South Korea and mainland China have conducted comprehensive reviews of their higher education systems. In Hong Kong, the University Grants Committee reviewed its higher education system in 1996 (UGC, 1996) while another comprehensive review of Hong Kong's overall education systems was completed in 2000 (Education Commission, 2000). Another round of comprehensive review of the higher education system was launched by the University Grants Committee (UGC, hereafter) in May 2001. The review covers major aspects of higher education provision, including an administrative framework for a much expanded post-secondary sector and the governance of universities. More specifically, the latest review examines issues like the definition of higher education, the role of higher education, governance structure for the higher education sector, university governance, research and identification of factors that will affect further developments of higher education in Hong Kong (UGC, 2001). After such a comprehensive review, the UGC aims to formulate new policies and governance models for the higher education sector.

In Taiwan, the government started to reform higher education following the lifting of martial law in 1987. A review of the education system was started in the mid-1990s. After the review, the government was keen to internationalise Taiwan's higher education; universities were therefore encouraged to establish links and academic exchanges with universities overseas. In addition, the Taiwan Government has attempted to introduce measures to improve the efficiency and effectiveness of higher education, particularly in terms of funding methodology, modes of provision and new management strategies (Tai, 2000; Weng, 2000; Mok, 2000b). With the changing governance philosophy, the state–education relationship has been redefined as the government has introduced the policy of "privatisation" in education. This policy reflects the revitalisation of the private sector and the mobilisation of other non-state sources to run education, through which the pressure of the state to meet the demands for higher education can be alleviated (Law, 2003; Mok, 2000a, 2002).

Similar developments can be found in mainland China. Higher education reform was started in the mid-1980s when the CCP attempted to create more opportunities for access. Following the Cultural Revolution in the mid-1970s, China had a shortage of qualified teaching staff and appropriate curricula, resources and facilities. The Chinese authorities decided to borrow knowledge, techniques and technologies from the West. Teachers were brought into universities from overseas to provide Chinese staff and students with access to foreign learning. Meanwhile, thousands of Chinese students were sent overseas to study for higher degrees. After restoration and consolidation for a few years, new reforms of higher education were launched in the mid-1980s. In the past decade or so, major reforms related to higher education were introduced with the central features of decentralisation and marketisation (Kwong, 1997; Yin and White, 1994). It is noteworthy that the comprehensive reform blueprint places emphasis on local responsibility, diversity of educational opportunities, multiple sources of educational funds, and decentralisation of power to individual higher education institutions in the governance of their own affairs despite the fact that the State Education Commission (SEC) still performs the role of "guiding" and "monitoring" the whole sector (Mok and Ngok, 2001).

(2) Policies of Decentralisation and Educational Governance

One of the changes common to these Chinese societies is the adoption of a decentralisation policy. Educational decentralisation is a popular reform of governments around the world even though diverse strategies and outcomes have resulted (Hanson, 1998). In Hong Kong, the call for quality education and the launch of university-based management were initiated within a decentralisation policy framework. Instead of "micro-control", individual universities are now given more autonomy and power in determining their daily affairs. Nonetheless, this development does not necessarily mean deregulation and retreat of the state's control. Rather, the government can exercise control through its executive arm, the UGC, to maintain a close watch over individual institutional performance. The approach to reforming the higher education system is a managerial or an executive-led model, attaching importance to the ideas of efficiency, effectiveness and economy in education (Mok and Welch, 2003). Starting with a self-monitoring assessment exercise and leading to a more formal quality assurance movement has strengthened instead of weakened the government's control (Tse, 2002; Mok, 2000a).

The fundamental changes in Taiwan's higher education sector since the late 1980s can be conceptualised as processes of denationalisation, decentralisation and autonomisation. "Denationalisation" implies that the state has begun to forsake its monopoly on higher education, allowing the non-state sector and even the market to engage in higher education provision. "Decentralisation" refers to the shift from the "state control model" to "state supervision model", whereby educational governance is decentralised from educational bureaucracies to devolved systems of schooling or universities, entailing significant degrees of institutional autonomy and a variety of forms of school-based or university-based management and administration. The term "autonomisation" refers to university academics having more autonomy to conduct research projects of any kind and far more discretion to manage and operate their institutions. The processes of "decentralisation" and "autonomisation" have become increasingly popular on the island state, but the idea of *song-bang* (liberalisation or autonomisation) should not be understood as the total withdrawal of the state. Within the educational decentralisation context, the Taiwanese Government is still the major provider of education services. The revised *University Law* stipulates that all national universities will become independent legal bodies and thus they are held accountable to the public. All state universities will be run by independent boards of directors and the state will gradually reduce its subsidy to these public universities. The proposed changes will inevitably transform the way universities are financed, regulated and managed (Law, 2003; Weng, 2001; *United News*, 28 December 1999).

Before higher education reform commenced in the 1980s, higher education governance could be characterised as a "centralised" or "state dominated" model in mainland China. Under such a governing model, the Ministry of Education (MOE) took responsibility for the design of curricula, syllabuses and textbooks, student admission and graduate job assignment and also exerted control over budgets, salary scales and personnel issues (Mok, 1996). Provincial and local education commissions and bureaus were simply mediators of national policy. In the post-Mao period, such a centralised governance model is believed to be inefficient in administration and ineffective in service delivery. In order to create greater higher education opportunities, the Chinese Government has adopted a policy of decentralisation since the 1980s to transfer authority (particularly financial) and decision making from higher to lower levels. Under the policy of decentralisation, local governments are given more flexibility and autonomy to chart the course of higher education development. This development is particularly significant for the socio-economically prosperous regions, such as the southeastern coastal areas, where the provincial or municipal governments are able to allocate more resources to finance higher education. The MOE is now charged with responsibilities to coordinate higher education development; while the central government and local government are engaged in a new relationship described by the principle of "*gongjian*" (joint administration). In "*gongjian*", local governments are charged with more responsibilities in higher education financing, provision and management while the central government only acts as regulator and coordinator. Local governments manage staff establishment, labour and wage of universities; while individual universities even enjoy far more autonomy and flexibility to run their own businesses (Mok and Ngok, 2001; Mok and Chan, 2001; Mok, 2001a, 2001b).

(3) The Marketisation and Privatisation of Higher Education

In addition to the trend of educational decentralisation, higher education developments in East Asian societies have been affected by the strong tide of marketisation and privatisation. Universities now experience pressures from governments, the main providers of higher education, to demonstrate maximum outputs from the financial inputs they are given. During a period of economic constraint, people begin to seek better use of limited public money, thus more attention is given to the issue of "value for money" and how the investment in higher education can really facilitate social and economic development (Mok and Lo, 2001; Law, 2003). In order to make the delivery of higher education more efficient and effective, there has been an increasingly popular trend of marketisation and privatisation in the higher education sector in the region (Kwong, 2000; Bray, 2000).

As with experiences in other parts of the world, these changes are closely related to the "marketisation" of education, whereby private sector principles are adopted to run education (Whitty, 1997). In order to reduce the state's financial burden, different market-related strategies are adopted such as increasing student tuition fees, reducing state allocations, strengthening the relationship between the university sector and the industrial and business sectors, and encouraging universities and academics to engage in business and market-like activities to generate revenue. Comparing the marketisation and privatisation projects of East Asian societies, it appears that for Hong Kong the reform strategies along the line of marketisation are designed to improve the efficiency and performance of the university sector rather than purely for resolving financial difficulties (Lee, 2001; Mok, 2000a).

In the midst of economic crisis, coupled with pressing demand for higher education, the Hong Kong Special Administrative Region Government has recently announced the adoption of a privatisation policy to create more learning opportunities for higher education. In 2000, Tung called for the expansion of higher education by doubling the number of associate degrees in the next 10 years. However, the problem faced by the HKSAR is understanding how to expand enrolment at this rate (Tung, 2000). One strategy is to adopt a self-financing model by the adoption of a user-charge principle. In October 2001, Fanny Law, the former Secretary for Education and Manpower, noted that the government has taken into consideration the possibility of privatising the currently publicly funded universities in Hong Kong (*Ming Pao Daily News*, 31 October 2001). In the meantime, the UGC has recently considering shedding the civil-service salary structures of the UGC-funded higher education institutions to allow salaries to reflect performance and market forces (*Ming Pao*

Daily News, 15 October 2001). These proposed measures clearly indicate that privatisation has begun to shape higher education development in Hong Kong (Mok and Lo, 2001).

The market strategies adopted in the university sector in Taiwan are not only to explore additional non-state resources to finance higher education but also to improve performance and effectiveness (Tai, 2000; Weng, 2001). With an increase in the population enrolment ratio to 40 per cent in 1998, the higher education sector in Taiwan has been expanding incessantly. In the reform context, the MOE has attempted to devolve responsibility and power to individual higher education institutions, as well as autonomy for educational financing. Multiple channels of higher education financing have been encouraged by the Taiwanese government with the MOE now providing only 75 to 80 per cent of the total budget for national higher education institutions. National universities now must search for alternative non-state sources of income to support their operational costs. With the increasing pressures of financial autonomy, Taiwanese higher education institutions are becoming more marketised and privatised amidst the policy trend of decentralisation (Mok, 2002; Mok and Lo, 2001).

In the post-Mao era, reformers have taken significant steps to privatise social welfare services in mainland China (Wong and Flynn, 2001). After the official endorsement of the socialist market system in the 1990s, strong market forces have affected educational development. Despite the post-Mao leaders' discomfort with the term "privatisation", signs of state withdrawal from the provision of social welfare are clear. In the last decade or so, the Chinese Government has allowed the rise of the market in the education sector. The emergence of private educational institutions, the shift of state responsibility in educational provision to families and individuals, the prominence of fee-charging, the growth of *minban* (people-run) colleges and universities, as well as the introduction of internal competition among higher educational institutions have clearly indicated that China's higher education is experiencing a process of marketisation. The author's field visits and field research conducted in mainland China in recent years have repeatedly confirmed that Chinese people are very concerned about higher education and there is an urgent need for more access to higher education. If reliance upon the central government alone cannot satisfy the demand for higher education, Chinese residents are willing to spend their own savings on providing their children with a university education (Zhu, 2000; Li, 2000).

Discussion: Local Autonomy vs Globalisation Pressures

There are many changes common to higher education systems in these Chinese societies, suggesting that higher education developments have been affected by similar global trends. "Hyperglobalists" have argued that the increasing connections and interactions between different nation-states and the freer and quicker interchange and movement of capital, goods, services, people, technologies, information and ideas will lead to an inevitable convergence of human activities and a receding role for the nation state (Ohmae, 1990; Fukuyama, 1992; Waters, 2001). However, some scholars have criticised the concept of global convergence as dominated by an Anglo-Saxon perception. Furthermore, the global convergence thesis is criticised as a myth by others since individual countries experience their own stages and patterns of development (Hesse, 1997, p. 117).

The preceding discussion has indicated that even though similar strategies are adopted by different countries in response to the so-called tide of globalisation, different governments may use these strategies to serve their own political purposes. As Hallak (2000) has rightly suggested, modern states may tactically make use of the globalisation discourse to justify their own political agendas or legitimise their inaction. As for Hong Kong, the call for quality control in higher education must be understood as part of the larger project of the public sector reform started since the late 1980s. The adoption of the managerial approach in university governance is designed to improve the efficiency and effectiveness of the higher education sector so that Hong Kong may be maintained as one of the more dynamic and competitive international academic centres. For this reason, the recent higher education reforms must be placed within the wider public policy reform/public management reform context in Hong Kong. Hence, reform strategies along the line of managerialism introduced in Hong Kong's higher education can be understood as simply another phase in the reengineering project under way since 1989 (Mok, 2000a).

For Taiwan, the call for higher education reforms and quality assurance has to do with the particular socio-political environment of the island-state. As Taiwan has become a more politically liberal and democratic society, university academics are eager to establish links with the external world, while the state is very keen to make the island-state more international. Thus the emphasis on the importance of international benchmarking and the significance of internationalisation can be understood as strategies to make Taiwan less isolated within the international community. In addition, the rapid expansion of private higher education in Taiwan has caused concern for improving and assuring the quality of higher education (Weng, 2001; Law, 2003).

Unlike Hong Kong or the marketisation experiences in the West, the Chinese marketisation of education has not yet entirely adopted a managerial approach whereby reforms in managing educational institutions and the introduction of control mechanisms in the university sector are believed to be the most effective ways to improve the efficiency and effectiveness of service delivery (Taylor *et al.*, 1997; Welch, 1998). What characterises the Chinese experience of marketisation is the "institutional transition", meaning a transition from a highly centralised economic planning system to the market economy (Li, 1997). In the midst of the transition, the Chinese Government has gradually retreated from the public domain, trying to mobilise non-state sectors and governments at the local level to engage in public service/policy provision. As such, market forces are being adopted to generate additional resources to run education. Thus, the marketisation of higher education in mainland China can be understood more fully by examining the interactions between the demonopolisation of the state's role in the public domain and the challenges and pressures resulting from the institutional transition. Seen in this light, the Chinese marketisation project has been locally driven rather than purely driven by the growing impact of globalisation.

Analysing the current educational developments in these societies from a public policy perspective, we find that higher education reforms are pursued within the context of managing state-building (or government-capacity) and economic growth in a state-directed (or government-directed) paradigm of governance. The introduction of higher education reforms in these societies can be interpreted as the strategies adopted by government to cope with the problems of political and bureaucratic governance rather than purely problems of economic and social difficulties no matter how severe.

Despite governments in these societies initiating policies of decentralisation in the higher education sector in recent years to allow individual universities more autonomy in their development, it is incorrect to argue that the state/government has retreated entirely from the higher education domain. Instead, the governments of these societies have taken a rather proactive approach to review their higher education systems and initiated reforms to nurture more creative and innovative citizens for national development. Even though similar patterns and trends in higher education development can be identified in these societies, the above discussion has suggested that Chinese governments are able to employ the globalisation discourse to shape a local political agenda. Most important of all, these national comparisons reveal the presence of diverse national and local agendas that give different meanings to the common management terminology and claims for so-called global trends (Cheung, 2000). If we accept diversity in domestic administrative agenda as the norm rather than the exception in global public management and governance, we may be in a better place to understand the impact of globalisation.

Conclusion

In conclusion, while there are clear globalisation trends, especially in the economy and technology, the nation-state is still a powerful actor in shaping a nation's development and in resolving global–national tensions. More importantly, the analysis of this chapter indicates that not all nations have responded in the same way to globalisation due of the specificities of their national histories, politics, cultures and economies. Therefore, the so-called global tide of market competition, non-state provision of public services, corporate governance, system-wide and institutional perform-ance management should not be treated as an undifferentiated universal trend. These different elements undoubtedly reinforce each other, though they are not equivalent or interchangeable. Instead, they may take different configurations, which remain nation-specific as well as global. Instead of simply a process of globalisation, the formulation of national policies is the result of the complicated and dynamic processes of "glocalization" (Mok and Lee, 2001). Therefore, globalisa-tion practices in higher education should not be analysed in terms of a one-dimensional move-ment from "the state" (understood as non-market and bureaucratic) to "the market" (understood as non-state and corporate). Rather, we must contextually analyse the interaction between a range of factors that are critical in shaping the local context and the impetus for change driven by global trends.

Note

1. Mok, K.H. (2003). Globalisation and higher education restructuring in Hong Kong, Taiwan and main-land China. *Higher Education Research and Development*, 22:2, 117–129. Reprinted by permission of the publisher.

References

Axford, B. (1995). *The Global System: Economics, Politics and Culture*. Cambridge: Polity Press.

Bray, M. (2000). Financing higher education: Patterns, trends and options. *Prospects*, xxx(3), 331–348.

Cerny, P.G. (1996). Paradoxes of the competition state: The dynamic of political globalization. *Government and Opposition*, 32(2), 251–271.

Cheung, A. (2000, January). *Globalization, governance and Asian values: Can there be a universal administrative paradigm?* Paper presented to the International Conference on Governance, City University of Hong Kong.

Cooper, P.J. (1995). Accountability and administrative reform: Toward convergence and beyond. In B.G. Peters and D.J. Savoie (eds) *Governance in a Changing Environment* (pp. 173–202). Montreal: Canadian Centre for Management Development.

Dale, R. (1997). The state and the governance of education: An analysis of the restructuring of the state–education relation-ship. In A.H. Halsey, H. Lauder, P. Brown and A.S. Well (eds) *Education: Culture, Economy and Society* (pp. 273–282). Oxford: Oxford University Press.

Dearlove, J. (1995). *Governance, Leadership, and Change in Universities*. Paris: UNESCO, International Institute for Educational Planning.

Education Commission (2000). *Review of Education System: Reform Proposals*. Hong Kong: Hong Kong Government Printer.

Faulks, K. (2000). *Political Sociology: A Critical Introduction*. Edinburgh: Edinburgh University Press.

Ferlie, E., Ashburner, L., Fitzgerald, L. and Pettigrew, A. (1996). *The New Public Management in Action*. Oxford: Oxford University Press.

Fligstein, N. (1997). *Markets, Politics, and Globalization*. Stockholm, Sweden: Uppsala.

Fukuyama, F. (1992). *The End of History and the Last Man*. New York: Free Press.

Gray, J. (1998). *False Down: The Delusions of Global Capitalism*. London: Granta Books.

Hallak, J. (2000). Globalization and its impact on education. In T. Mebrahtu, M. Crossley and D. Johnson (eds) *Globalization, Educational Transformation and Societies in Transition* (pp. 21–40). Oxford: Symposium Books.

Hanson, E.M. (1998). Strategies of educational decentralization: Key questions and core issues. *Journal of Educational Administration*, 36(2), 11–128.

Held, D., McGrew, A., Glodblatt, D. and Parraton, J. (1999). *Global Transformation: Politics, Economics and Culture*. Stanford, CA: Stanford University Press.

Henry, M., Lingard, B., Rizvi, F. and Taylor, S. (1999). Working with/against globalization in education. *Journal of Education Policy*, 14(1), 85–97.

Hesse, J.J. (1997). Rebuilding the state: Public sector reform in central and eastern Europe. In J.E. Lane (ed.) *Public Sector Reform: Rationale, Trends and Problems* (pp. 114–146). London: Sage.

Howell, J. (1993). *China Opens its Doors: The Politics of Economic Transition.* Boulder, CO: Wheatsheaf.

Kooiman, J. (1993). Social-political governance: Introduction. In J. Kooiman (ed.) *Modern Governance: new Government-Society Interactions* (pp. 1–6). London: Sage.

Kwong, J. (1997). The reemergence of private schools in socialist China. *Comparative Education Review, 41*(3), 244–259.

Kwong, J. (2000). Introduction. *International Journal of Educational Development, 20,* March, 79–127.

Law, W.W. (2003). Globalization, localization and education reform in a new democracy: The Taiwan experience. In K.H. Mok and A. Welch (eds) *Globalization and Educational Restructuring in the Asia Pacific Region.* Basingstoke: Palgrave Macmillan.

Lee, H.H. (2001, April). *The impacts of marketization on higher education reform in Singapore.* Paper presented at the International Conference on Marketization and Higher Education in East Asia, Shanghai.

Li, P. (1997). Institutional innovation and interest allocation under China's reform. In X.Y. Lu and P.L. Li (eds), *Report of the Social Development in New China.* Shenyang: Liaoning Renmin Chubanshe. [in Chinese]

Li, P.L. (2000). Challenging education system in the new century: Trends and future. In Ru, X., Lu, X.Y. and Li, P.L. (eds) The Analysis and Forecast of Social Development in China Year 2000. Beijing: Chinese Academy of Social Science Press. [in Chinese]

Marginson, S. (1999). After globalization: Emerging politics of education. *Journal of Education Policy, 14*(1), 19–31.

Massey, A. (1997). In search of the state: markets, myths and paradigms. In A. Massey (ed.) *Globalization and Marketization of Government Services: Comparing Contemporary Public Sector Developments* (pp. 1–16). Basingstoke: Macmillan.

McGrew, T. (1992). A global society? In S. Hall, D. Held and T. McGrew (eds.) *Modernity and its Futures* (pp. 62–113). Cambridge: Polity.

Ming Pao Daily News. 15 October 2001, 31 October 2001.

Mok, K.H. (1996). Marketization and decentralization: Development of education and paradigm shift in social policy. *Hong Kong Public Administration, 5*(1), 35–56.

Mok, K.H. (2000a). Impact of globalization: A study of quality assurance systems of higher education in Hong Kong and Singapore. *Comparative Education Review, 44*(2), 148–174.

Mok, K.H. (2000b). Reflecting globalization effects on local policy: Higher education reform in Taiwan. *Journal of Education Policy, 15*(6), 637–660.

Mok, K.H. (2001a). From state control to governance: Decentralization and higher education in Guangdong, China. *International Review of Education, 47*(1), 123–149.

Mok, K.H. (2001b). Education policy reform. In L. Wong and N. Flynn (eds) *The Market in Chinese Social Policy* (pp. 88–111). Basingstoke: Palgrave.

Mok, K.H. (2002). From nationalization to marketization: Changing governance in Taiwan's higher education systems. *Governance, 15*(2), 137–160.

Mok, K.H. and Chan, D. (2001). Educational development and the socialist market in Guangdong. *Asia Pacific Journal of Education, 21*(1), 1–18.

Mok, K.H. and Lee, H.H. (2001, April). *Globalization or glocalization? Higher education reforms in Singapore.* Paper presented at the International Conference of Cultures of Learning: Risk, Uncertainty and Education, University of Bristol.

Mok, K.H. and Lo, H.C. (2001, April). *Marketization and the changing governance in higher education: A comparative study of Hong Kong and Taiwan.* Paper presented at the International Conference on Marketization and Higher Education in East Asia, Shanghai.

Mok, K.H. and Ngok, K.L. (2001, November). *Decentralization and changing higher education governance in China.* Paper presented to the Comparative Education Society of Asia Year 2001 Conference, Taipei, Taiwan.

Mok, K.H. and Welch, A. (eds) (2003). *Globalization and Educational Restructuring in the Asia Pacific Region.* Basingstoke: Palgrave.

Ohmae, K. (1990). *The Borderless World: Power and Strategy in the Interlinked Economy.* New York: Harper Perennial.

Ohmae, K. (1999). *The Borderless World: Power and Strategy in the Interlinked Economy* (Rev. ed.) New York: Harper Perennial.

Osborne, D. and Gaebler, T. (1992). *Reinventing Government: How the Entrepreneurial Spirit is Transforming the Public Sector.* New York: Plume Books.

Peters, B.G. (1996). *The Future of Governing: Four Emerging Models.* Lawrence: University Press of Kansas.

Rhodes, R.A.W. (1997). *Understanding Governance: Policy Networks, Governance, Reflexivity and Accountability.* Buckingham: Open University Press.

Robertson, S. and Dale, R. (2000). Competitive contractualism: A new social settlement in New Zealand education. In D. Coulby, R. Cowen and C. Jones (eds) *World Yearbook of Education 2000: Education in Times of Transition* (pp. 116–131). London: Kogan Page.

Sbragia, A. (2000). Governance, the state, and the market: What is going on? *Governance, 13,* 243–250.

Sklair, L. (1999). Globalization. In S. Taylor (ed.) *Sociology: Issues and Debates* (pp. 321–345). London: Macmillan.

Slaughter, S. (1998). National Higher Education Policies in a Global Economy. In J. Currie and J. Newson (eds) *Universities and Globalization: Critical Perspectives* (pp. 45–70). London: Sage.

Tai, H.H. (2000). *The Massification and Marketization of Higher Education.* Taipei, Taiwan: Yang-Chih Book Co., Ltd. [in Chinese]

Taylor, S., Rizvi, F., Lingard, B. and Henry, M. (1997). *Educational Policy and the Politics of Change.* London: Routledge.

Townsend, T. and Cheng, Y.C. (2000). Charting the progress: Influences that have shaped education in the Asia Pacific

Region. In Y.C. Cheng and T. Townsend (eds) *Educational Change and Development in the Asia-Pacific Region: Challenges for the Future* (pp. 1–14). Lisse: Swets and Zeitlinger Publishers.

Tse, K.C. (2002). A critical review of the quality education movement in Hong Kong. In K.H. Mok and D. Chan (eds) *Globalization and Education: The Quest for Quality Education in Hong Kong* (pp. 143–170). Hong Kong: Hong Kong University Press.

Tung, C.H. (2000). *2000 Policy Address*. Hong Kong: The Printing Department.

United News, 28 December 1999.

University Grants Committee [UGC]. (1996). *Higher Education in Hong Kong*, Hong Kong: University Grants Committee.

University Grants Committee [UGC]. (2001). *Document for Open Forum on Higher Education in Hong Kong*, 23 October 2001, Hong Kong Polytechnic University.

Waters, M. (2001). *Globalization*. London: Routledge.

Welch, A. (1998). The cult of efficiency in education: Comparative reflections on the reality and the rhetoric. *Comparative Education*, 24(2), 157–175.

Weng, F.Y. (2000). Education Reform and Policy in Taiwan. In K.H. Mok and Y.W. Ku (eds) *Taiwan and Mainland China*. Hong Kong: Hong Kong Humanities Press. [in Chinese]

Weng, F.Y. (2001, April). *Towards a global trend: Decentralization or centralization in educational governance in Taiwan*. Paper presented at the Symposium on Comparative Education Policy Developments in Chinese Societies, City University of Hong Kong.

Whitty, G. (1997). Marketization, the state and the re-formation of the teaching profession. In A.H. Halsey, H. Lauder, P. Brown and A.S. Wells (eds) *Education: Culture, Economy and Society* (pp. 299–310). Oxford: Oxford University Press.

Wong, L. and Flynn, N. (eds) (2001). *The Market in Chinese Social Policy*. Basingstoke: Palgrave.

Yin, Q. and White, G. (1994). The marketization of Chinese higher education: A critical assessment. *Comparative Education*, 30(3), 217–237.

Zhu, Q. (2000). Mass consumption and consumer market in 1999. In Ru, X., Lu, X.Y. and Li, P.L. (eds) *The Analysis and Forecast of Social Development in China Year 2000* (pp. 237–264). Beijing, China: Chinese Academy of Social Science Press. [in Chinese]

22

Performance-based Funding as an Instrument of Competition in German Higher Education[1]

Dominic Orr, Michael Jaeger and Astrid Schwarzenberger

A central theme of approaches to new public management is the emulation of the market through state-induced competition. Basing state funding allocations on comparative performance is one way of setting an incentive for competitive practice amongst universities. Reforms in funding allocation have occurred in Germany at both state and university level. These have concentrated on indicator-based models, and an analysis of these procedures is the focus of this chapter. In general, it can be concluded that indicator-based models are used extensively at state and university level and that their general structure suggests a "tool box" of indicators, commonly used at both levels. In many cases, performance-based funding only determines a marginal part of total budget allocations and discretionary, incremental funding dominates. Besides being a question of allocation model construction, this has both to do with the continuing need to improve institutions' capability to compete with one another and—directly connected to this—the reluctance by many German states to complete the transition to "steering at a distance". The chapter concludes with an outlook for the future of models of performance-based funding in Germany.

Introduction

German higher education is often seen as a late starter in terms of the structural reforms and changed emphasis in governance associated with New Public Management (NPM) (Frankenberg, 2004), a goal encapsulated in the term "steering at a distance" (Braun and Merrien, 1999). The cornerstones of this approach are output-focused state steering and institutional autonomy of universities, but the state and universities in Germany still tend to be structurally intertwined in a way that inhibits a full implementation of this programme. This situation has resulted in reform initiatives with a special German character. It is not unusual that the basic programme of NPM takes on a specific local character when implemented. This has led one author to comment that if we knew what we meant by New Public Management in the 1990s, when it was largely a conceptual programme, based on the diversity of programmes to be found in the praxis, we would now find it hard to characterize the programme beyond key concepts (Toonen, 2004).

One core element of NPM is the emulation of the market through state-induced competition and the term "competition" has certainly become a key figure of the higher education reform debate in Germany (cf. Frankenberg, 2004). State funding makes up a substantial proportion of university income in Germany and a central lever for implementing competition is thus seen in the introduction of performance-based funding. Reforms in funding allocation have occurred in Germany at both state and university level, and an analysis of these reforms will be the focus of this chapter. In the second section of the chapter, the general context of current university reform initiatives is laid out and the specific structural context within which reform can be realized sketched. Sections three and four describe the performance-based allocation systems utilized at state and university level, respectively. The chapter concludes with a discussion of the German character of NPM and, on the basis of recent developments, provides an outlook for the future of models of performance-based funding in Germany.

German Context of Higher Education Reform

Not unlike its neighbours in the rest of Europe, clear pressure on German higher education has been exerted by system expansion (Teichler, 2005, p. 49 ff.). The number of new entrants into higher education in Germany rose dramatically between 1998 and 2003, with an increase of 35% from 258,000 to 347,000 students (OECD education database). This increase has been accompanied by parallel increases in the demand for academically qualified workers in the labour force (BMBF, 2005, p. 20). Despite this expansion, the new entry rate in Germany at 36% of the reference population is still below the average for OECD countries at 53% (OECD, 2005, figures for ISCED 5A 2003). However, through a combination of demographics and demand, further growth is expected, at least until 2011, and commentators have begun to talk about the imminent "student mountain" (KMK, 2005). This growth presents a quantitative challenge for German higher education. It also raises the question of the efficiency of higher education provision, since an increase in productivity will be the only way to cope with this challenge. Germany currently presents some sobering facts in this respect. According to the latest figures available, students in German higher education tend to take on average five years and four months to complete their courses, one year longer than the OECD average (OECD, 2005, data for 2002 or last year available). National statistics corroborate this fact, and indicate furthermore that while less than 25% of all students at universities complete their courses in less than five years, a further 25% require more than eight years before completion (calculation based on national statistics for 2004). Also, the survival rate of students to graduation is only 70% (OECD, 2004, data from last year available 2000). Data series show that the number of graduates actually decreased between 1998 and 2002 by 7%, which may have had a negative knock-on effect of expansion, although there are signs of a slight recovery in the 2003 data (OECD education database).

One of the inhibitors of efficiency has been seen in German *Diplom*-courses at university level. For this reason, the Bachelor's and Master's course structure promoted through the Bologna Process has been seen as one way to facilitate productivity increases. However, as one particular comparative study has shown, the actual organisational structure of a course is only one of multiple factors affecting the duration to graduation (Heublein and Schwarzenberger, 2005). Rather than trying to identify individual causes and solve them in a top-down approach, and in line with programmes in other countries, Germany has begun implementing university reform according to the steering paradigm of competition for scarce public funding. Financial initiatives are set to encourage universities to improve their performance, which is then measured in relation to the performance of their immediate competitors, that is, other universities. Since the public budget is finite, a relatively bad performance often leads to budget cuts. For this approach to be realized in Germany, two sets of reforms have been implemented:

- improvement of institutions' capability to compete
- introduction of new methods of performance-based funding.

Capability to Compete

The legal construction of the German university has changed a great deal during the past 20 years. In the first Framework Law for Higher Education from 1976, universities were defined as having a hybrid form: as both public corporation and state institution at the same time, and their right to self-administration was constrained by further legal regulations (Framework Law 1976, para. 58). This led Palandt to conclude regarding the contemporary status quo in 1993 that the self-administration model of the universities was contradictory to the core, because universities only, in effect, had the right to determine what they would teach and research (conceptual self-determination), but not the resources necessary to achieve this (material self-determination) (Palandt, 1993, p. 98). Before the idea that central planning and control was possible was called into question, this interlinkage seemed reasonable, since it was assumed that the funding-giver should be able to determine how funds were used. Palandt, however, argued critically that it was often only the courage of the heads of university administration (the so-called *Kanzler*) to interpret state regulations in a flexible manner that assured the productive operation of many universities (1993, p. 97). In fact, although this central control was far-reaching, where it ceased at local level it left room for a lot of autonomy. This had the paradoxical effect of giving faculties, and particularly individual professors, a high level of autonomy in some areas, and meant that a university was more an additive conglomeration of parts than an integrative organizational unit (p. 100).

The new approach to steering at a distance requires the university to be given a status that allows it to take responsibility for its own actions and to change concepts and resource allocation in accordance with institutional plans.[2] The state in Germany has consequently had to learn to realign its task spectrum from detailed institutional planning to system-level strategy, and institutions have had to reorganize and restructure themselves to enable them to deal with and positively translate this new responsibility into institutional management and strategy development.

A major cornerstone of this reform programme was the reformulated Framework Law for Higher Education, passed in 1998. This law was drawn up on the basis of three organisational principles: autonomy, diversity and competition, and particularly strived for deregulation to facilitate the realization of these principles (Sandberger, 2002, p. 126). Following this law, the regional states were obliged to reform their own regional higher education laws—since the *Länder* have jurisdiction in these matters—in line with these new general principles. This was indeed the litmus test for German higher education. In agreement with a number of studies (Sandberger, 2002; Stifterverband, 2002), and in contrast to Germany's neighbour Austria, which started its reform initiatives with a similar higher education framework (cf. Pechar, 2004), a preliminary conclusion can be made that these legal reforms have led to many marked changes, but the managerial autonomy of universities in Germany is still limited, which has knock-on effects for higher education funding. In reference to autonomous and competitive activities of universities, these changes and their implications for funding can be specified for the areas of leadership structure, personnel management and financial management of current expenses.

Leadership structure

In line with the hybrid institutional form, the organization of a German university was traditionally split between two structural domains: academic self-administration and administration of non-academic matters and material resources, each with its own head. The head of the latter domain, largely responsible for the procedural conformity of the budget (see also below) and personnel, was the *Kanzler* (comparable in some ways to the Registrar of British tradition). The head of academic issues was the Rector, voted for by the Senate and with the official status of *primus inter pares* among the deans and other members of the Senate. Following his/her term of office, he/she would return to his/her professorship. The collegial Senate and faculty councils had, however, substantial responsibilities for the definition of institutional goals, implementation of these goals and control of their realization. The biggest changes in leadership structure, which had begun before the new laws, but were confirmed and promoted by them, related to strengthening the central leadership, and thereby consequently weakening the collegial organs, regarded as too large and cumbersome to control such significant areas of institutional operation (cf. Kultusministerkonferenz, 1996).

Universities are now led by more influential central administrations, formed either around a rector with a rectorate or a university president supported by a presidium. The presidium includes the president, *Kanzler* (now sometimes termed vice-president for finance) and further vice-presidents for specific areas of activity, such as teaching, research, technology transfer or life-long learning, and focuses on the operation and strategic direction of the university as a whole, and therefore strives to facilitate an integrative instead of an additive organizational structure. Collegial organs, such as the Senate and specialist committees, now have little to do with executive tasks and concentrate instead on defining institutional goals and controlling (especially academic) performance. These changes on central level are also reflected at faculty level. Here the collegial faculty committees have lost influence or concerning executive functions have been replaced by the dean of the faculty or a faculty board (Sandberger, 2002, p. 148).

In summary, the reforms to university structure have increased the influence the central leadership has to steer the institution and to implement integrative strategic development. However, these reforms have also left universities with important relational issues, which have particular relevance for the operation of performance-based funding: what should be the relationship between university leadership and the state, and university leadership and faculty deans? Whilst the state has an interest in universities adopting similar allocation methods internally, so that those state objectives that are expressed, for instance, as performance indicators, can have a direct influence on professors' performance, the university leadership and, particularly, faculty deans will want to protect certain areas of activity from such an unmediated influence. In respect of performance-based funding, the question can be formulated quite pragmatically: how much influence does the faculty level have on the instruments and criteria of the funding allocation method used internally, and to what extent do internal funding instruments simply mirror state instruments?

Personnel management

Staff are a key resource of any university and equally a key expenditure, generally accounting for around three-quarters of a university's current costs. In Germany, personnel has traditionally been resourced either from a state pool, financed and administered directly by the state and, therefore, not part of the university budget, or the allocation of a personnel budget has been accompanied by a binding and detailed plan of posts (e.g. "x" posts for professors and "y" for secretaries in faculty "A"). If a university wanted to utilize the budget assigned to a professorial post for other personnel costs and leave the professorial post temporarily vacant, it would have to apply to the state ministry to do so. Equally, leaving a post free for a period and thereby nominally saving personnel costs, would have no direct consequences for the university budget. In the case of these two examples, reforms have increased the opportunities for universities to reconfigure their staffing structure and to save money by leaving posts vacant. However, a major limitation to their capacity for personnel management remains in the fact that professors and a proportion of the remaining academic and non-academic staff have civil servant status. Therefore, the university is not the ultimate employer and, subsequently, also cannot reduce personnel costs by curtailing staff contracts.

These limitations have significant consequences for performance-based funding, since the university has only limited influence over the size and structure of its personnel budget, a resource that has subsequent consequences for key university operations (e.g. teaching and research capacity). Until further flexibility within personnel budgets is possible, this particular framework condition significantly limits the possibilities for a university to react to market conditions or to the performance of its competitors. This has the pragmatic consequence for procedures of performance-based funding that small fluctuations in budget allocations will have significant effects on the part of a university's budget which is not so constrained—the current expenses.

Financial management of current expenses

Traditionally, universities in Germany have not received their current budget as a lump sum, but as a detailed catalogue of authorized expenses for specific purposes (current costs, personnel, investments). This type of budgeting is often referred to as "line-item budgeting". It affords the state a substantial transparency of university costs. At the same time, however, it systematically inhibits a university's capacity to manage its own resources, because the budget is tied to specific types of expenditure (stationery, laboratory equipment and clothing, travel, library resources, temporary staff positions, etc.) and not to specific activities. The weaknesses of a strict application of line-item budgeting have been recognized in Germany for a long time and a certain degree of flexibility to transfer budget apportions between line-items existed in many states early on in the reform process (Behrens, 1996). In line with the general principle of these new reforms, one influential organisation in Germany, the Stifterverband (2002), defined lump-sum allocations without regulations on expenditure patterns as a central objective for new laws and regulations. Although not all universities receive such lump-sum allocations, it can be summarized that the majority of universities have a very flexible budget at their discretion, with the exception of personnel (Federkeil and Ziegele, 2001).

The fulfilment of this objective does, however, entail the consequence for the state that university expenditure patterns are less transparent. For this reason, this reform has itself been seen in Germany as an additional argument for the introduction of performance-based funding at state level. In this case, funding allocations would no longer be appropriated on the basis of previous expenditure, but on the basis of performances achieved through previous funding allocations. This change can, however, also be seen from a university perspective as a move away from needs-oriented funding based on previous expenditure to performance-oriented funding. Such funding allocations tend to be made irrespective of the expenditure necessary for such performance, which is largely seen as an issue for the internal financial management of a university (Orr, 2005, p. 96). The challenge for the construction of a funding allocation method is, therefore, to balance output-based elements, which encourage a university to make its operation more efficient and thereby more competitive, with elements of stability, which assure the future operation of a university.

New Methods of Performance-based Funding

Funding allocation methods can be utilized to stimulate universities into more competitive behaviour. The reward for a better performance, at least in principle, is supplementary funding. As in many other countries (Leszczensky *et al.*, 2004a), Germany spent much of the 1990s developing and implementing new funding procedures along these lines, and the subsequent sections of this chapter will provide a systematic analysis of the various models. Before turning to the specific models, we briefly characterize the types of allocation procedures that can be applied in order to facilitate a clearer characterization of the German case. In this, state subsidies tend not to be allocated as a single block, but comprise four different components: indicator-based funding, project-based funding, mission-based funding or discretionary funding. Each of these components is characterized by a different steering approach, a different definition of performance, and, by this, a different degree of competition. Differences between countries or between historical developments are to be seen in the relative weight given to different components (Leszczensky *et al.*, 2004a, pp. 188–9; Orr, 2005, pp. 27, 93 ff.).

Indicator-based funding

The budget is based on its performance as measured by fixed indicators in a formula. Decisions on the amount of budget to be allocated to an institutional unit (e.g. university, faculty, school) are therefore automatically generated and the budget allocations rise and fall in accordance with the values of the indicators. The funding unit (e.g. state, central university management) will define indicators on the basis of the activities it wants to stimulate or which it feels most adequately represent the workload of the unit to be funded. Whilst in the latter case, indicators may be used, for instance, to represent the number of professors employed within the institutional unit, only those indicators which measure performance in a previous period (i.e. *ex post*) are truly performance dependent (e.g. number of graduates). Most procedures are used to distribute a fixed budget between institutional units and the resulting subsidy is therefore dependent both on the performance of individual units and the performance of their direct competitors. Of the four possible components of funding allocation, this component has the highest potential for introducing competitive behaviour, but also for budget instability.

Project-based funding (earmarked grants)

The basis of this allocation can be diverse. Either the funding unit develops a programme initiative or the institutional units apply to the funding unit for financial support on the basis of proposals, which are then evaluated, and following an affirmative judgement, funded. In the former case, this allocation method can be used to encourage certain units to provide specific services or programmes endorsed by the funding unit. In the latter case, institutional units have the opportunity to define programmes themselves. The criteria for judging a proposal can be a combination of previous performance and a formative judgement on the proposed project. In both cases, institutional units are in competition with other grant applicants.

Mission-based funding

This instrument for funding allocation is based on a consensus between state and an individual university or between university administration and a faculty on future policy and institutional goals. Funding for the achievement of these goals is normally laid down in a contract-like agreement made up of both qualitative and quantitative criteria and valid for a given number of years. The ultimate achievement of these goals may, or may not, be measured at the end of the agreement period. In the former case, a budget adjustment may be made. Competition between institutions for allocations within this component is not transparent and usually marginal.

Discretionary incremental funding

This component does not facilitate competition between institutions since it is based on individual agreements with institutions, which are not formalized in any of the above ways. The extent of central state control within this component depends on whether the grant is allocated as a line-item budget with fixed expenditure categories or as a block grant. In the latter case, state control is minimal. The basis for this funding was traditionally the respective previous year's budget, which was carried forward and at times increased to take account of inflation (incrementalism) or corrected on account of general budget constraints. As higher education reform often entails abolishing line-item budgeting, this method of allocating a state subsidy has become increasingly inappropriate, since the basis of the allocated amount cannot be latterly reconstructed and is not transparent. Many higher education systems retain at least a small proportion of their budget for distribution via this method because it provides a certain financial stability for the institutions.

Indicator-based allocation models, therefore, entail the most direct form of competition between institutional units and a high transparency, whilst discretionary incremental funding entails the least. Project-based and mission-based funding are methods that can be implemented to improve the transparency of funding allocations, whilst not being dependent on the definition of unambiguous, quantitative indicators that cannot be applied to all university activities. Reforms of funding in Germany have unsurprisingly concentrated on indicator-based funding, although discretionary funding still dominates funding allocations in many *Länder*. Experiments have also begun with mission-based agreements. However, until now, these have largely been used to justify or frame discretionary funding allocations (e.g. in Berlin, cf. Leszczensky *et al.*, 2004b; and in Bremen, cf. Jaeger and Leszczensky, 2005) and have yet to become separately distinguishable funding instruments.

Indicator-based Funding Models in Germany at State Level

The state grant to universities in Germany is a very significant source of their income. It accounts for about 80% of their total income (the other sources: 18% from third-party funding and only 2% from operating income). For this reason, it is seen by states as an important lever of higher education policy and allocation methods have been reformed greatly since the 1990s. As mentioned earlier, each of the 16 German *Länder* (i.e. the federal states) have jurisdiction over higher education matters in their region, and although all states are largely following the same paradigm and reform programmes described above, they do implement different funding models based on their own political agenda and regional context. This is why no single German model of funding allocation can be determined.

Besides regional differences, Germany also has two types of higher education institutions (HEI)—universities (strictly speaking) and so-called *Fachhochschulen* (universities of applied sciences, formerly called polytechnics)—and in some states different funding models for each type of HEI have been introduced on account of the different expectations for each type of institution. Currently, roughly three-quarters of all students study at universities. Therefore, and in line also with the subsequent section on internal allocation models, the results presented in this section refer only to models applied in the university sector, irrespective of whether they also apply to *Fachhochschulen* or not.

The first states introduced their models in the early 1990s, and by 2004, 11 out of the 16 German states were using formula funding as an element of their university funding models. As shown in Figure 22.1, there is a marked diversity between the states concerning the percentage of state subsidy allocated through indicator-based funding to universities (here the state subsidy was adjusted to

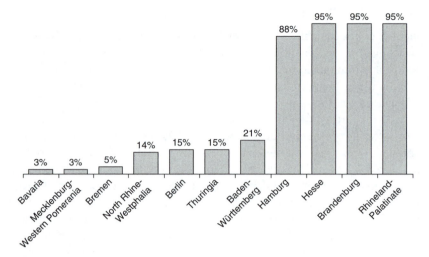

Figure 22.1 State Procedures of Indicator-based Funding, 2005 (as percentage of total state subsidy).

Source: Updated data from Leszczgnsky and Orr (2004).

exclude medicine and funding reserved for construction projects). Some states—e.g. Hesse and Brandenburg—allocate 95% of their budget via indicators, whilst others—e.g. Mecklenburg-West Pomerania and Bavaria—distribute no more than 5% of the state subsidy in this way. The remaining proportion of the funding allocation tends to be based on discretionary incremental allocations.

The total proportion of a grant allocated by indicators can be further analysed on the basis of the character of the indicators used, since (particularly in Germany) most of the models encompass a number of different indicators. Not all of these are necessarily directly performance dependent and they can be classed by their relationship to performance. The difference is particularly striking in states such as Hamburg and Hesse: in Hamburg, only some 7%, and in Hesse only 15%, of the total state subsidy is based on performance-dependent (*ex post*) indicators, although nearly 90% and 95% of the subsidy respectively is indicator based. In Hesse target numbers for enrolled students are agreed between the state and the individual universities, and in Hamburg target numbers for graduates are used. As these target numbers are based on actual numbers from previous years, there is a relation to past performance, yet the indicator cannot be labelled *ex post*, since the target numbers may or may not be achieved. It can be said instead that such indicators have an *ex ante* orientation.

The use of *ex ante* indicators, such as target numbers or input values (e.g. number of professors), has the function of both promoting future performance and reducing the extent of allocation fluctuations within indicator-based allocation models. A high proportion of indicator-based funding, therefore, does not necessarily equate to extensive reallocations of funds. A further method to cushion dramatic budgetary effects is to use average values over several years. This method is frequently applied by the *Länder* for those indicators that may fluctuate considerably between years, such as the amount of third-party funding. Additionally, many *Länder* have implemented tolerance bands beyond which budget effects are not realized (e.g. 5% in Berlin). Such tolerance bands usually refer to maximum losses only. Even when there are no percentage thresholds for budget gains, as the total budget is usually a fixed amount, limiting losses of some institutions consequently affects the potential gains of highly competitive institutions.

In practice, studies have shown that changes of more than 2% of the state subsidy are quite rare (Leszczensky *et al.*, 2004b; Jaeger and Leszczensky, 2005). However, whilst a change of just 2% may seem negligible at first sight, one has to bear in mind two factors: first, universities are highly dependent on state subsidies, which make up the bulk of their income, and secondly, universities' opportunities to influence their spending situation (especially concerning personnel) are very limited. Therefore, even a seemingly minor change of 2% of the state subsidy may have dire consequences for a university.

In view of the comments above on the expansion of the higher education system in Germany and on the need to improve productivity, it is interesting to note that until now all the implemented models of indicator-based funding in Germany concentrate on teaching rather than research. However, a further reason for this may be quite pragmatic: performances in teaching can be measured more easily than in research. Besides teaching and research, many of the models include some indicators that target gender equality.

Teaching

The indicators most commonly used to measure a university's teaching-related performance are the number of students and the number of graduates. The variations on these two indicators are manifold—e.g. the number of students within their first semester, within a certain number of semesters or only those who are still within the "regular study duration", a normative prescription for expected study time by field of study.[3] Likewise, sometimes only those graduates who get their degree within this regular study duration are counted in an indicator. Teaching-focused indicators that reflect *internationalization* are also used, such as the number of foreign students (or graduates) as a percentage of the total number of students (or graduates).

Research

Research indicators focus mainly on the amount of third-party funding which a university earns; this may be weighted by funding source—e.g. public sources are given priority over private sources. A further research-related indicator, which can be found frequently, is the number of doctorates and so-called *Habilitationen* (post-doc qualifications to teach in higher education). Only in one case are publications used as an indicator (in Bavaria, newly introduced in 2005).

Gender Equality

Equality indicators tend to determine only a small share of the indicator-based allocations, but are frequently included in models. They are based on the share of female students or professors in relation to the respective total number. Performance is either compared between institutions or over time.

Allocation Models in Germany at Institutional Level

Reform initiatives at state level are aimed at improving the productivity of universities and at both facilitating and stimulating their strategic management of teaching and research within the whole institution. Just as at the state level, universities too are implementing new methods of funding allocation as levers of reform at institutional level. In this, institutions have to develop a funding strategy which balances the needs of the internal units (especially faculties) with the need to compete with other institutions for state grants on the basis of specific indicators—e.g. by increasing the number of students and the volume of third-party funding. So the central questions are:

- Whether German universities have adopted indicator-based funding methods for their internal resource allocation?
- To what extent allocations to faculties are indicator based?
- To what degree the models applied internally either reflect institutional strategy or mirror state models?

These aspects were analysed on the basis of a national questionnaire on the internal use of formula-based models and target agreements in German state universities by the Higher Education Information System (HIS) in 2004 (Jaeger *et al.*, 2005).

In order to enable the newly strengthened faculty level to realize its responsibilities for leadership and management of research and teaching provision at discipline level, central university administration has to decentralize at least a part of its state grant down to this institutional unit. In this, the university is not only confronted with the same questions of model design, but must firstly determine the appropriate degree of decentralization—i.e. the degree of funds that should be administrated autonomously on faculty level. The current practice in Germany is, in this respect, very diverse, with proportions ranging from 1.3% to 68%, although the majority of universities (74%) do not currently decentralize more than 10% of their state subsidy.[4] That means that staffing costs are rarely included in internal decentralization and thus are still centrally administrated.

Indicator-based allocation components are found in almost every university's decentralized budgets. In fact, many universities introduced indicator-based funding components into their internal budgeting framework before their respective *Länder* had established models at state level.

As indicated in Figure 22.2, by 1996 nearly half of all universities had such components. This proportion rose to three-quarters by 2003, with the rest of the universities planning an implementation for the near future. Up to half of all universities either have or are planning to implement "target agreements". However, an analysis of the current agreements leads to the conclusion that, in line with the state models, these components do not fully determine allocations to faculties, but are often supplementary to discretionary incremental allocations, which continue to dominate internal allocation procedures.

As indicated in Figure 22.3, only one in ten universities uses indicator-based instruments for the internal allocation of more than 7% of their state grant. The average share of indicator-based components in the internal distribution of the total state grant is about 4%, so the relevance of these

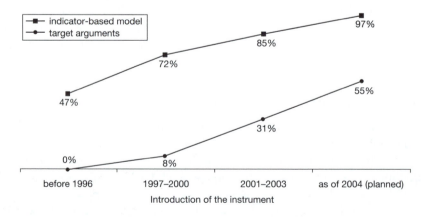

Figure 22.2 Implementation of internal instruments of budget allocation in Germany.

Source: Adapted from Jaeger *et al.* (2005).

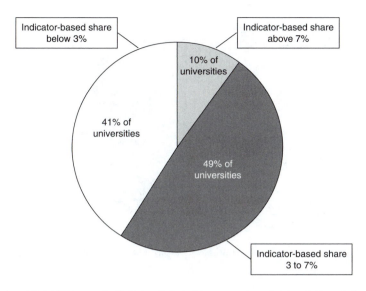

Figure 22.3 Indicator-based Models' Relevance for the University Budget (as a percentage of state subsidy, excluding hospitals).

Source: Adapted from Jaeger *et al.* (2005).

models for the faculties is quite low. If one concentrates only on the share that is given on the basis of performance-based (*ex post*) indicators—i.e. without *ex ante* indicators such as the number of staff, the budget relevance of indicator-based models is even lower: For most of the universities, the indicator-based share is below 3%.

Furthermore, nine in ten universities that apply indicator-based allocation models use these to allocate budgets for current costs, but not for personnel, which is often administered centrally or funded through discretionary allocations. This is conformation of the generally retrictive effect that framework conditions can have on the design of these models.

Concerning the selection of indicators for internal procedures, there are general similarities between the models, which are used at state level and internally. They include *ex ante* and *ex post* indicators, and the latter, performance-dependent indicators, tend to dominate. Furthermore, there is a higher emphasis on teaching indicators than research indicators. As in state-level models, the majority of universities focus on student numbers and the number of graduates as indicators for teaching, and on the third-party funding volume and the number of doctorates and *Habilitationen* as indicators for research. Only one-sixth of universities have integrated indicators related to publication volume into their models. It appears that this remains a contentious indicator with a restricted application, mainly because of the difficulty of finding consensual definitions of publications and agreeing on the appropriate weighting of different types of publication (refereed articles, books, co-authorship, etc.).

An analysis of the data shows that there are two direct links between state and university funding allocation models. First, universities in states with an indicator-based funding model tend to apply such models for internal purposes more frequently than universities in states without indicator funding. Secondly, when asked about the relationship between their internal funding models and the respective state procedures of the *Länder*, the majority of universities considered this relation to be quite close (see Figure 22.4).

There are considerable differences between the states in this respect. In some states, for example Berlin, North-Rhine-Westphalia and Rhineland-Palatinate, the internal university procedures are closely related to the state models, whereas in other states, for instance, in Hesse,

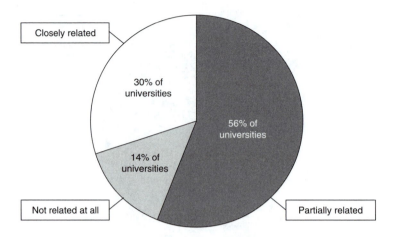

Figure 22.4 Degree of Relatedness between Internal Indicator-based Allocation Procedure and State Model.

Source: Adapted from Jaeger *et al.* (2005).

the allocation systems of some universities differ considerably from the state systems. The reasons for the different relations between the internal models and the state model can be seen in three aspects:

1. *The degree of appropriateness of the state model for the internal resource allocation:* some states use funding models that can easily be transferred on the level of internal budget allocation. For example, the state allocation procedure in Berlin uses a multitude of indicators to reflect the individual profiles of different institutions. In contrast, the models of other states are not to a comparable degree applicable for internal budget allocation, because they focus on singular aspects of performance. The Hessian model, for instance, focuses on student numbers.
2. *The degree of permanence and reliability of the state allocation model:* the transfer of the state model to the internal level only makes sense when the state model is handled transparently and is not being modified from year to year to correct unanticipated effects.
3. *The date of implementation of the state model:* in states where the state model was introduced very recently, the universities have often already developed internal allocation procedures that they can only gradually adapt to the state model.

Discussion: The German Character of Performance-based Funding in Higher Education

Frequency of Indicator-based Models and Their Financial Relevance

As reported, the adoption of formula-based funding procedures is already widely spread in the *Länder* as well as in the German universities: 11 of the 16 *Länder* use such procedures to allocate funding to universities, and almost all German universities apply formula-based funding systems for the internal budget allocation or plan to do so in the near future. In view of this popularity, it is surprising that, in most cases, models are only relevant for marginal parts of the respective budgets. This is especially the case for internal budget allocation, where only five universities allocate more than 7% of the state subsidy by formula. On the state level, only four *Länder* allocate high budget shares (more than 80% of the state subsidy) by means of performance indicators. Reasons for this low financial relevance, particularly from the perspective of universities, may be the following:

- German universities have only low flexibility in handling personnel costs, which amount to nearly 80% of their total expenditure. Thus, reallocations between universities must be restricted (e.g. 1% to 2% of state subsidy) because high losses cannot be absorbed by universities in the short to medium term due to these "fixed" costs.
- On the level of university internal budget allocation, the inclusion of higher budget shares inevitably implies the decentralization of personnel costs. Since in most *Länder* the preconditions for decentralizing the staff costs were introduced by the state only recently, a lot of universities are presently concerned with the decentralizing process, which is very complex for all parties and often takes several years.

With the continuance of decentralizing processes within universities, it can be anticipated that the relevance of formula-based allocation procedures will rise in the next years. Already, several universities (e.g. the Free University of Berlin) are experimenting with the inclusion of staff costs in their internal allocation procedures. Also, at state level the budget shares that are allocated by formula are increasing, as can be noted, for example, in Berlin and North Rhine-Westphalia. However, it should be noted that the steering potential of performance-based funding via indicators is also limited, so that the budget relevance of such procedures should not be raised at any cost. This applies especially for the level of internal budget allocation, as it is only possible to a limited degree to reflect the different subject characteristics within formula-based procedures.

Model Design

Indicators and model architecture

In respect of the design of formula-based funding procedures in German higher education, two facts seem conspicuous:

- First, with regard to the range and definition of performance indicators, there is a basic homogeneity between the adopted funding procedures, at state as well as at institutional level. At both levels, the procedures usually apply the same set of standard indicators: student numbers and numbers of graduates as indicators for performance in teaching, and third-party funding as well as numbers of doctorates and *Habilitationen* as indicators for research-related efforts. Furthermore, at state as well as at internal level, teaching-related indicators are usually weighted higher than research-related parameters. This leads to the following conclusions: (1) the fact that the procedures usually consist of the same "tool box" of standard indicators suggests that the design of procedures is usually not directly related to strategic goals on state or on university level. Rather, pragmatic aspects, such as practicability and measurability seem to be frequently more important for the definition of indicators; and (2) the emphasis on teaching performance in most of the funding models can presumably be ascribed to the dominance of teaching problems in the higher education policy discourse (e.g. study duration, dropout rates, etc.). Furthermore, as some authors (e.g. Ziegele and Handel, 2005) argue, the higher emphasis on teaching performance compared to research performance makes sense in view of the consideration that the reputation of professors in Germany depends particularly on efforts in research and not so much on their teaching-related activities. This one-sided incentive structure can be balanced out by a higher emphasis on teaching performance in formula-based funding models.

• Secondly, on the level of precise design and model architecture of the funding procedures, there are remarkable differences between the funding models. This is especially striking with regard to the formula-based procedures on state level. In view of developments over the past decade, at least two aspects seem to be relevant here. *(1) Regional diversity of the higher education systems:* in terms of both the number of students in each regional system, the size of the university and *Fachhochschule* sectors and the average size of institutions, there are significant differences. For example, both the university sectors in Berlin and Lower Saxony account for 6% of all students in Germany. However, Berlin has only three universities and Lower Saxony has 11. This diversity has inevitable effects on the construction of funding mechanisms and on the question of whose performance should be compared with whom and on what basis. *(2) Regional development of allocation models:* in each state the design of allocation models is usually the result of cooperation between the local ministry of science and the rectors' conference. This has a lot to do with a strategy for change management, whereby the central actors in a field of reform are involved in the development of the reform programme. The importance of cooperation between actors became evident in Baden-Württemberg, when the universities refused to accept the new allocation model with the argument that too many reforms were being implemented simultaneously and, therefore, that financial predictability was necessary. In contrast, in Berlin the state has developed an allocation model in close cooperation with the universities and *Fachhochschulen*. In this, it is apparent that regional actors have different opinions in respect of, *inter alia*, how much of a budget can be allocated by formula (between 1% and 95%), how many indicators are necessary (between few indicators for a clear steering effect and many indicators to reflect different institutional profiles) and whether different higher education sectors should compete together or separately (unified allocation or sector-specific allocation systems). Comparative reports, such as those carried out by HIS Higher Education Information System (see references below), aim to facilitate and inform such decisions, but regional policy and practice will always play a significant role.

Relation between internal and external allocation models

In most of the German universities, internal formula-based funding models are to a high degree related to the respective state models (where such a model is used). Exceptions are the universities in particular states, where specific features of the state procedure make it unattractive for universities for internal budgeting. Irrespective of the general appropriateness of the state funding procedures, the alignment between internal and external funding procedures should be carefully considered by a university:

• If the formula-based funding model is to be used as an instrument of strategic management, it must be primarily related to the strategic goals of the university. The construction of the model and the definition of indicators should be deduced from the strategic goals of the university and only in the second instance from efforts towards alignment with the state model.

• Nevertheless, a university must find ways of legitimizing and procedures for implementing budget adjustments caused by the state allocation procedure. This means that components of a state model are likely to be adopted internally.

The interplay between these two factors would explain the general finding that only a minority of universities have allocation systems not related to state procedures.

Effects of Current Allocation Models

In view of the multitude of practices, the question can be raised as to the role which competition via performance-based allocation systems is playing as an instrument for steering and coordination in Germany. It must, however, be stated that many of the allocation systems currently being applied at state and university level are still very new and that the situation can be characterized as still in a phase of experimentation. However, a number of factors can be identified which affect the acceptance and impact of performance-based funding at the present:

- *General budget cuts*: in many *Länder* cuts have been made to total university budgets of up to 10% despite increasing numbers of students (HRK, 2004). This has the effect that performance-based funding cannot reward high performers with additional funding, but only with less funding cuts than their lower performing counterparts. This has a strong negative effect on both the external (state) and the internal (university) indicator-based allocation models.
- *Inconsistent handling of indicator-based procedure*: in Hesse, for example, the reallocations between universities according to the indicator-based procedure were not, in fact, realized consistently. Instead, they were further adjusted to take account of additional factors, which were not made transparent and had the character of discretionary decisions.
- *Discretionary funding*: in some states, for instance, Lower Saxony, the effects of an allocation model based on performance have been undermined by secondary funding decisions realized through discretionary allocations, thereby neutralizing the impact of the indicator-based funding procedure (cf. Handel *et al.*, 2005).
- *State initiative to restructure university systems*: according to the principle of "steering at a distance", restructuring effects will be the consequence of performance-based funding. However, in a number of *Länder* states have initiated restructuring through policy programmes. Illustrative for current actions is Lower Saxony. In September 2003 the so-called "Higher Education Optimization Concept" (HOK) was announced, which resulted in a reduction in the number of HEIs (from 19 to 18) and the number of locations (from 32 to 29). Many of the changes involved moving or merging faculties from two different locations. This programme is a clear example of state-led steering in a top-down manner and is evidence that performance-based funding is only one element in the steering framework.

Outlook

This review of performance-based funding as an instrument for competition in German higher education has shown that the current models are widely used, but that their budget relevance is marginal. Current developments point to a number of trends for the future:

- In a number of *Länder*, the autonomy of universities and *Fachhochschulen* is being increased. This will lead to a greater capability to compete and facilitate the extension of performance-based funding on state and institutional levels. Examples are pilot institutions in Saxony (Dresden Technical University) and Hesse (Darmstadt Technical University).
- The scope of performance-based funding may be increased by the implementation of

target agreements. These instruments are being applied in nearly all the German *Länder* at state level and increasingly at institutional level as well. Practice shows that these agreements are not being introduced as alternatives to indicator-based systems, but as complementary mechanisms with a different steering character (e.g. longer validity period, consideration of quality and context). In states such as Baden-Württemberg, Berlin and North-Rhine Westphalia they are used as secondary steering instruments, whereas in Bremen and Hamburg they are in fact the primary methods of steering and funding allocation.

- The imminent introduction of student fees in Germany (as early as winter 2006 in some *Länder*) may be seen as another way of increasing competition between institutions through funding. Those institutions that can attract students will profit from the fees they bring. For the future it will be necessary to assure that both funding through tuition fees and performance-based state funding are integrated into a consistent steering framework, since certain overlaps between both funding models are likely, such as an overemphasis on student demand and on teaching-based indicators.

Notes

1. Orr, D., Jaeger, M. and Schwarzenberger, A. (2007). Performance-based funding as an instrument of competition in German higher education. *Journal of Higher Education Policy and Management*, 29:1, 3–23. Reprinted by permission of the publisher.
2. Ziegele (2004) provides a more detailed discussion of the interdependence between financing and organizational autonomy under the term "institutional economics".
3. For each course of study, there is a fixed amount of semesters that is set as the "regular study duration" (*Regelstudienzeit*), this relates to the expected amount of time required by a student to complete the course (e.g. it is longer for medicine students and shorter for students of business studies). Many students, however, exceed this time for a number of different reasons.
4. To improve the comparability of data, decentralization and the importance of various allocation components are expressed here as a proportion of the state subsidy, which universities receive. This sum has been adjusted to exclude any grants for capital, medical faculties and facilities.

References

Behrens, T. (1996). *Globalisierung der Hochschulhaushalte—Grundlagen, Ziele, Erscheinungsformen und Rahmenbedingungen [Globalisation of university budgets—foundations, goals, models and framework conditions]*. München: Luchterhand.

Braun, D. and Merrien, F.-X. (1999). Governance of universities and modernisation of the state. In D. Braun and F.-X. Merrien (eds), *Towards a new model of governance for universities?* London: Jessica Kingsley.

Bundesministerium für Bildung und Forschung (BMBF). (2005). *Bericht zur technologischen Leistungsfähigkeit Deutschlands 2005 (Zusammenfassung) [2005 Report on Germany's Technological Performance (Summary)]*. Retrieved October 6, 2006, from http://www.bmbf.org/pub/zusammenfassung_TLF-Bericht2005.pdf.

Federkeil, G. and Ziegele, F. (2001). *Globalhaushalte an Hochschulen in Deutschland. Entwicklungsstand und Handlungsempfehlungen. Gutachten im Auftrag der CDU-Fraktion des Sächsischen Landtags [Lump-sum budgeting in German universities. State of development and recommendations for implementation]*. Gütersloh: Centrum für Hochschulentwicklung.

Frankenberg, P. (2004). *17 Thesen zur Hochschulreform—Strategien einer ganzheitlichen Hochschulentwicklung in Deutschland [Strategies for a comprehensive development of higher education]*. Stuttgart: Ministry for Science, Research and Arts.

Handel, K., Jaeger, M. and Schmidlin, J. (2005). Evaluation der formelgebundenen Mittelvergabe für die niedersächsischen Fachhochschulen [Evaluation of performance-based funding allocation for Fachhochschulen in Lower Saxony]. *Beiträge zur Hochschulforschung, 27*, 72–89.

Heublein, U. and Schwarzenberger, A. (2005). *Studiendauer in zweistufigen Studiengängen—ein internationaler Vergleich [Study duration in two-cycle courses—an international comparison]*. Hanover: HIS Kurzinformation.

Hochschulrektorenkonferenz (HRK). (2004). *Press release: Im Brennpunkt: Die Hochschulfinanzierung [Hot topic: Higher education funding]*. Retrieved October 6, 2006, from http://www.hrk.de/de/brennpunkte/112.php

Jaeger, M. and Leszczensky, M. (2005). *Evaluation der leistungsbezogenen Mittelvergabe auf der Ebene Land-Hochschulen in Bremen [Evaluation of performance-based funding allocation at state level in Bremen]*. Hanover: HIS Kurzinformation.

Jaeger, M., Leszczensky, M., Orr, D. and Schwarzenberger, A. (2005). *Formelgebundene Mittelvergabe und Zielvereinbarungen als Instrumente der Budgetierung an deutschen Universitäten: Ergebnisse einer bundesweiten Befragung [Formula-based *funding and target agreements as instruments of budgeting in German universities: Results of a national survey].* Hanover: HIS Kurzinformation.

Kultusministerkonferenz (KMK). (1996). *Leitungsstrukturen im Hochschulbereich [Leadership structures in higher education].* Retrieved October 6, 2006, from http://www.hopo-www.de/ konzepte/kmk-leitung.html

Kultusministerkonferenz (KMK). (2005). *Prognose der Studienanfänger, Studierenden und Hochschulabsolventen bis 2020 [Prognosis for new entrants, students and graduates until 2020].* Retrieved October 6, 2006, from http://www.kmk.org/ statist/dok176.pdf.zip

Leszczensky, M. and Orr, D. (2004). *Staatliche Hochschulfinanzierung durch indikatorgestützte Mittelverteilung. Dokumentation und Analyse der Verfahren in 11 Bundesländer n [State higher education funding through indicator-based allocations. Documentation and analysis of procedures in 11 German states].* Hanover: HIS Kurzinformation.

Leszczensky, M., Schwarzenberger, A., Orr, D. and Weitz, B. (2004a). *Staatliche Hochschulsteuerung durch Budgetierung und Qualitätssicherung: Ausgewählte OECD-Länder im Vergleich [State higher education steering through budgeting and quality assurance: Selected OECD countries in comparison].* Hanover: HIS Hochschulplanung.

Leszczensky, M., Jaeger, M. and Orr, D. (2004b). *Evaluation der leistungsbezogenen Mittelvergabe auf der Ebene Land-Hochschulen in Berlin [Evaluation of performance-based funding allocation at state level in Berlin].* Hanover: HIS Kurzinformation.

OECD. (2004). *Education at a glance.* Paris: OECD.

OECD. (2005). *Education at a glance.* Paris: OECD.

OECD. (n.d.). *Education database.* Retrieved October 6, 2006, from http://www1.oecd.org/scripts/ cde/members/ linkpage.html

Orr, D. (2005). *Hochschulsteuerung und Autonomie englischer Universitäten—Hochschulfinanzierung und Qualitätssicherung aus einer Verfahrensperspektive [Steering higher education and autonomy of English universities—higher education funding and quality assurance as organizational procedures].* Münster: Waxmann.

Palandt, K. (1993). *"Wozu sind Sie der Boss?" Probleme mit der Selbstverwaltung der Hochschulen ["What are you the boss of?" Problems with the self-administration of universities].* In W. Körner (ed.) *Der Ausbau der Hochschulen oder der Turmbau zu Babel.* Wien: Passagen Verlag.

Pechar, H. (2004). Austrian higher education meets the knowledge society. *Canadian Journal of Higher Education,* 34(3), 55–72.

Sandberger, G. (2002). Organisationsreform und -autonomie: Bewertung der Reformen in den Ländern [Organizational reform and autonomy: Evaluation of the reforms of the German states]. *Wissenschaftsrecht,* 35, 125–150.

Stifterverband für die Deutsche Wissenschaft. (2002). *Qualität durch Wettbewerb und Autonomie—Landeshochschulgesetze im Vergleich [Quality through competition—state laws of higher education in comparison].* Essen: Stifterverband.

Teichler, U. (2005). *Hochschulsysteme und Hochschulpolitik: Quantitative und strukturelle Dynamiken, Differenzierungen und der Bologna-Prozess [Quantitative and structural dynamics: Differentiation and the Bologna Process].* Münster: Waxmann.

Toonen, T. (2004, September). *Public sector reform in the knowledge-based economy: (Higher) education in institutional perspective.* Keynote paper at the CHER Annual Conference, Twente.

Ziegele, F. (2004). Finanzierung und Organisation von Hochschulen. Wie Veränderungsprozesse ineinander greifen [The funding and organization of universities. How change processes interact]. *Die Hochschule,* 1, 74–86.

Ziegele, F., and Handel, K. (2005). Anreizsysteme im Hochschuleinsatz [Incentive systems used in higher education]. In W. Benz, J. Kohler and K. Landfried (eds) *Handbuch Qualität in Studium und Lehre.* Berlin: Raabe.

23
Shifting Roles and Approaches
Government Coordination of Post-Secondary Education in Canada, 1995–2006[1]

Theresa Shanahan and Glen A. Jones

This chapter analyses changing approaches to system-level governance in Canadian post-secondary education from 1995–2006. A review of major policy initiatives reveals a shift in provincial and federal government roles in and approaches to the coordination of post-secondary education. The federal government has strategically invested in post-secondary education, increasing its direct and indirect support for research and development and, at the same time, retreating from other areas of support. Provincial governments have expanded post-secondary systems and increased institutional diversity and the role of the market in post-secondary education while simultaneously developing more mechanisms of coordination.

Introduction

This chapter is about the changing role of the state in post-secondary education in Canada. Our objective is to provide a critical analysis of changes to system-level governance in Canadian post-secondary education during the past decade (1995–2006). We do this by examining major government policy initiatives and highlighting policies that signal a departure in the state's relationship with post-secondary education. We begin by providing an overview of policy changes at the federal and provincial levels of authority. We conclude with observations on the developments, dynamics and pressures that have emerged in the governance of Canadian post-secondary education.

The Federal Context

Canada is a federal constitutional monarchy and a parliamentary democracy. The country is made up of ten partially self-governing provinces and three autonomous territories. Governing power is shared between the provincial and federal levels of government. The constitution outlines the division of powers between the provincial and federal governments. Section 93 of the Constitution Act, 1867, specifically gives the provincial legislatures the exclusive power to make laws in relation to education. Consequently, the provinces have the direct and central role in developing legislation, regulating and coordinating post-secondary education, as well as providing operating support to post-secondary institutions.

The federal government has no direct role in shaping or coordinating post-secondary education, and Canada is the only industrialized country without a federal office or department of education. In the absence of a central government agency, there is no clear mechanism for national policy development.

As a consequence of the constitutional division of powers, historically, in Canada, education systems have developed within each province independently of one another, with each provincial government shaping its own education system to meet the needs of its region. Different arrangements have evolved in each province and territory for the coordination and regulation of post-secondary education.

The Changing Role of the Federal Government

Although the federal government has no direct role in coordinating or regulating post-secondary education, it has a powerful role in other areas of state governance that intersect with post-secondary education. Under section 91 of the Constitution Act 1867, the federal government has jurisdiction over national defence, Indian affairs, national security (including crime and prisons), external affairs, economic development, the territories and any other areas of national interest. All of these areas intersect with post-secondary education. For example, the government of Canada operates a military college, supports educational programming in Canadian prisons, funds international scholarship programs, and operates a number of programs and initiatives designed to address the need for further education of Canada's aboriginal peoples, including support for First Nations University of Canada. While the participation rates of Canada's aboriginal populations have been increasing, they are still dramatically lower than the Canadian average (Holmes, 2006), and Canada's overall record in aboriginal policy issues has been abysmal.

While the federal government is involved in a wide range of policy areas that intersect with post-secondary education, recent changes in the role of the federal government are particularly evident in four policy areas: federal–provincial transfers, skills development, research and development, and student financial assistance.

Federal–provincial Transfers

The federal government makes transfer payments to the provinces to support post-secondary education. These transfer arrangements involve cash transfers, tax point transfers, and equalization payments to the poorer provinces. These transfer arrangements have been modified over time, but they were significantly reformed under the Chretien Liberal government. As part of a broader strategy to reduce the federal deficit, the new government's 1995 budget drastically reduced financial transfers to the provinces for health, education and welfare. The provinces lost $14 billion. At the same time, the government created a new mechanism to transfer the funds called the Canada Health and Social Transfer (CHST), in place from 1996/97 to 2004/05. This program aimed at further reducing the federal government's spending and the provinces lost another $6 billion (Fisher et al., 2005, p. 48). Finally, in an effort to provide greater accountability and transparency for federal health funding, the CSHT was split in April 2004 into the Canada Health Transfer (CHT) and the Canada Social Transfer (CST) covering post-secondary education and welfare. Health receives 62% of the transfer funds, while post-secondary education and welfare share the remaining 38% of the transfer.

A number of provinces were already reducing their funding to post-secondary education amid a recession, and most provinces responded to the dramatic cuts in transfer payments by simply further reducing post-secondary education spending and, in some provinces, increasing or deregulating tuition fees. When reductions in the portion of the transfer going to post-secondary education are calculated against student enrolment, it has been estimated that per student funding during the period 1994/95 to 2004/05 decreased by almost 50% (Fisher *et al.*, 2005). In the context of deficit reduction, the federal government essentially decreased its role in providing operating support for post-secondary education by unilaterally modifying its transfer arrangements, and many provincial governments responded by asking institutions to make financial cuts and allowing institutions to increase tuition fees.

Skills Development

The federal government has had a long history of involvement in labour market skills training and development programs and services in colleges, government institutions and the workplace. Beginning in the mid-1980s the federal government shifted away from supporting labour market training programs in community colleges and government facilities and moved towards supporting private industry, voluntary sector and employer-sponsored skills training under the Canadian Job Strategy (CJS). This shift represented a privatization of training provision, away from public community colleges and government centres. Beginning in the mid-1990s, much of the responsibility and funding for training devolved to the provinces and territories through negotiated Labour Market and Development Agreements (LMDAs) between the two levels of government. The federal government retained its responsibility for labour mobility across Canada, and continues to fund national youth, aboriginal, persons with disabilities, at-risk youth, immigrants, apprenticeship and literacy programs (Fisher *et al.*, 2005).

Changes in the mechanisms for the funding and delivery of skills development programming have increased the presence and influence of the private sector in this area, arguably devolving to the private sector the power to shape labour market training. The federal retreat from this area has allowed regional industry groups to take a more active role in fashioning their own training policy programs that meet the needs of their catchment area.

Research and Development

The federal government has long been the major source of funding for university research and development, but when the federal deficit turned into a federal surplus, significant new investments were directed towards a range of initiatives as component parts of the government's new "innovation" strategy (Wolfe, 2002). The federal government has expanded funding to the three traditional granting councils[2] that support investigator-initiated research programs selected on the basis of peer review. In 1999 the government reorganized the Medical Research Council (MRC) into the multi-disciplinary Canadian Institute of Health Research (CIHR) and doubled its funding.

The federal government also expanded the National Centres for Excellence program that had emerged in 1989 under the prior Conservative government's science policy. These applied and strategic science networks link researchers across the country in virtual networks and are funded by both the public and private sector. Their mandate is to turn university research into marketable technologies and increase Canadian global competitiveness in a knowledge-based economy. In 1997 the Liberal government expanded the program, with a focus on addressing the research needs of the private sector, increasing knowledge transfer, and advancing the government's economic and applied science agenda. By 2001, there were 29 networks that had been funded (Fisher *et al.*, 2005).

In addition to expanding existing programs, the federal government made substantive investments in entirely new initiatives. In 1997 it created the Canada Foundation for Innovation (CFI), an independent public foundation to fund research infrastructure through partnerships with the private and voluntary sectors, as well as with provincial governments. Aimed at supporting the research infrastructure needs of universities, colleges, hospitals and other not-for-profit institutions, the Canadian Foundation provides partial matching support in order to leverage private-sector and provincial government contributions. This has become the major source of financial support for research infrastructure in Canadian higher education.

The federal government also created the Canada Research Chairs (CRC) program, an initiative designed to create eventually 2,000 government-supported research chairs in Canadian universities. This phased program of direct government investment in human resources has focused on the creation of new tier 1 (senior) and tier 2 (junior) chairs, allocated to universities on the basis of past success in research council competitions. Some chairs are internal university appointments designed to provide status and retain major Canadian scholars, while others are external and designed to attract leading world scholars. For the first time, institutions were required to develop and submit an institutional research plan in order to obtain support under the CRC program. Preference has been given to health and natural and applied sciences, which dominate the chairs (and only 20% have been awarded to women).

Other new initiatives have included the creation of the Canada Learning Council in 2004, and the substantive expansion of the Canadian Graduate Scholarships program in 2003, but perhaps the most symbolically important initiative has been the federal government's agreement, after decades of lobbying from the sector, to provide some support for the overhead or indirect costs associated with research funded by the federal government. From the outset, the federal granting councils had only provided support for the direct costs of research, and institutions essentially subsidized indirect costs through operating grant support. Some one-time-only support for indirect costs was provided in 2001, and in 2003 the government established the Indirect Costs Program with the objective of eventually providing 40% overhead support for research. Ironically the program has been phased so that institutions with modest levels of research activity currently receive a higher percentage of overhead support than the most research-intensive universities.

Student Financial Assistance

The federal government has played an important role in student financial assistance since the creation of the Canada Student Loan Program (CSLP) in 1964. The program is operated in collaboration with and administered by the provinces through provincial student assistance offices, and its basic structure remained largely unchanged since its inception until 1994, except for changes in the amount of assistance available and the conditions of repayment.

In 1994 the program was overhauled and a new Canada Student Financial Assistance Act was passed. This legislation increased loan limits for both full-time and part-time students; increased maximum loan levels; changed payment provisions; created a new Special Opportunity Grant for students with disabilities, needy and part-time students, and women in doctoral programs; changed assessment mechanisms; and created new mechanisms for financing student loans through the private sector (Meloshe, 1994).

By the late 1990s, the rising levels of tuition in several provinces were beginning to raise difficult national political issues concerning the adequacy of Canada's student financial assistance mechanisms and the increasing level of student debt loads. In 1998 the federal government took steps to provide additional support for specific groups, such as students with disabilities and part-time students with high financial needs, through the Canadian Opportunities Strategy, and encourage families to save for their children's post-secondary education through a registered education savings program (RESP). Interest on RESP contributions is not taxed, and the government provides a top-up Canada Education Savings Grant of 20% (up to $400) on annual contributions.

These funds can only be used to support the costs of post-secondary education.

The federal government also created the Canada Millennium Scholarship Foundation (CMSF), a private non-profit entity, and provided the foundation with a substantive endowment. Its ten-year mandate is to provide needs-based student grants and some merit-based scholarships. The foundation is now a major source of student grants in a student financial system dominated by federal and provincial loan programs.

Finally, the federal government has, rather enigmatically, increased the level of tax credits associated with tuition, books and student maintenance costs. The creation of an expanded, universal tax credit program has been very expensive, and a number of policy analysts have noted that the universal nature of the program is regressive. The fact that individual benefits are obtained long after the initial expenditure does little to encourage participation in post-secondary education (Neill, 2006).

Retreats in some areas and advances in others characterize shifts in the federal government's role in post-secondary education. Change in fiscal arrangements (federal–provincial transfer payments) mark the end of federal transfers as a major source of support for post-secondary education in Canada. Through the Canadian Job Strategy Program we see the retreat from publicly funded skills training and development and a shift towards privatized training shaped by industry groups. In student assistance we see increasing assumptions about family contributions to the costs of post-secondary education, accompanied by new government mechanisms to encourage family savings and tax credits for post-secondary expenditures. Grant support in student financial assistance has shifted from universal programs to support for targeted groups. At the same time, the federal government has taken on a more direct approach in post-secondary education—getting funds directly into the hands of institutions, researchers and students. It has accomplished this by investing in various ways in the direct and (for the first time) indirect costs of research and by increasing student grants, scholarships and tax credits associated with the costs of student education.

Provincial Government Coordination

The constitutional division of powers in Canada provides that the provincial governments are directly responsible for the funding, regulation and coordination of post-secondary education. In each province a government ministry has been assigned responsibility for post-secondary education, and decisions related to funding and coordination take place within the political context of the province. The Council of Ministers of Education Canada provides a forum for the sharing of information across provincial jurisdictions, but each province has its own regulatory framework, its own policy mechanisms and its own unique institutional structures and arrangements.

Perhaps the clearest trend in provincial government coordination in Canada during the past decade is that the provinces are moving in quite different policy directions in terms of their approaches to the regulation and control of higher education. The sudden reduction in federal transfers in the mid-1990s led to idiosyncratic provincial responses, but there have been common themes associated with changes in provincial coordination, especially in terms of increasing institutional diversity, system-level coordination, increasing institutional competition and the use of market-like mechanisms, and changes in accountability arrangements.

Institutional Diversity

Historically, Canadian higher education has been described as having a binary structure involving universities and non-degree-granting post-secondary institutions commonly referred to as community colleges. Regardless of the province, post-secondary education has been a state-regulated, secular, publicly funded enterprise characterized by a high level of institutional autonomy for universities. Described as a public monopoly (Skolnik, 1987), degree-granting has been strictly controlled by the provincial governments in Canada. Provincial governments have in the past treated universities equally with regards to the distribution of grants and resources. This equality of treatment has made for a relatively homogeneous university system of post-secondary education without the formal stratification of institutions found elsewhere. State authority over universities is delegated to a corporate board made up of government appointees overseeing the administration of the university, and a senate primarily made up of faculty as the governing body responsible for academic issues. There is little interference or regulation by provincial governments in the internal day-to-day university decision-making. The main areas of intrusion occur in relation to funding and accounting for funds. Otherwise, universities control their own hiring, curriculum and admissions (Jones, 2006).

By contrast, community colleges are generally subject to greater government regulation and control than universities. Colleges vary by function and features across the provinces (Dennison, 1995). In some provinces colleges are comprehensive, applied, technical institutes running parallel to the universities without a university-transfer function (e.g., Ontario). In other provinces (for e.g., British Columbia, Alberta and Quebec) they serve as feeder institutions for universities, with an explicit transfer process built in. In either case, the colleges have a vocational education function and serve the needs of the labour market. The Quebec *Colleges d'enseignement general et professional* (CEGEP) are comprehensive, public institutions that offer a two-year pre-university program (which is required for admission to university) and a three-year career or technical program. In New Brunswick the provincial college is essentially operated directly by the provincial ministry, while in most provinces community colleges have individual governing boards operating under sector-wide legislation.

In the 1990s a number of provinces took steps to increase the level of institutional diversity, largely in an attempt to increase the range of options available to students and, ostensibly, to address accessibility. British Columbia created a network of university colleges by selectively expanding the mandate of a number of existing community colleges to include full undergraduate degree programs. More recently, Alberta, British Columbia and Ontario have revised legislation and expanded degree-granting authority, with some restrictions, to community colleges, specialized art colleges and private universities. In Alberta and Ontario college degree-granting is limited to applied degrees, but, across all three provinces, mechanisms have been developed for reviewing applications for authority to grant degrees, and for considering applications from private institutions seeking provincial recognition. Manitoba and Saskatchewan have approved the creation of new degree-granting institutions, including First Nations University, Canada's first university focusing on the needs of aboriginal populations, in Saskatchewan, and a new publicly supported Mennonite university and northern university in Manitoba.

There are implications for system organization and system governance associated with increased institutional diversity, and the once clear distinction between the university and non-university sector is blurring, altering the traditional binary nature of post-secondary education in Canada. New types of hybrid institutions that do not fit neatly into existing classification systems are emerging, along with innovative institutional partnerships across the university and non-university sectors. System regulation has been affected by these changes and we see provincial governments attempting to address the challenges of expansion and differentiation through the promotion of transfer arrangements between sectors, and the creation of new intermediary bodies in some provinces to review applications for new universities or new programmatic arrangements.

There are also unresolved issues related to the ways in which these new institutions and degree programs will be recognized by the more established institutions. There has never been a national accreditation or program assessment mechanism in Canada, in large part because of an assumption that Canadian universities were roughly equal in terms of standards. With the increasing expansion of degree-granting, and the rise of hybrid programmatic and institutional arrangements, there may be a need for some form of national mechanism.

System-wide Coordination

Given the binary institutional structure of higher education in most provinces, coordination structures and policies have tended to be sector-specific. Intermediary bodies with executive decision-making authority over the system have not been a dominant characteristic of Canadian post-secondary education. However, there appears to be a growing tendency towards the creation of coordination mechanisms or approaches that are system-wide, rather than focusing only on the university or community college sectors. Some provinces are revisiting the use of intermediary bodies or other agencies to advise the provincial ministries of education on planning, reviews and the assessment of new programs. Sector-specific intermediary bodies were created and abandoned in most provinces, including British Columbia, Alberta, Saskatchewan, Manitoba and, most recently, Ontario (in 1996) and Quebec (in 1993). In Nova Scotia, New Brunswick and Prince Edward Island provincial intermediary bodies were replaced by a regional Maritime Provinces Higher Education Commission that provides advice to all three provinces.

Most provinces have moved towards the development of cross-sector, system-wide approaches to coordination. Alberta and British Columbia have a long history of facilitating transfer and credit recognition between sectors through system-wide councils. Manitoba created a system-wide post-secondary council in 1996, whereas Newfoundland created in 1992 the Newfoundland and Labrador Council on Higher Education (Jones, 2006). Other provinces have created committees to facilitate articulation arrangements between sectors, or develop transfer guides to encourage greater transparency in terms of the possibilities for student mobility between sectors. Ontario has recently created the Higher Education Quality Council of Ontario, an independent agency that is mandated to conduct research on quality, participation and accessibility, and advise the government on the best ways to measure performance in this large post-secondary system (Shanahan et al., 2005). While these intermediary bodies play a role in system coordination, they are essentially advisory; only Manitoba's Post-secondary Council has executive authority over some aspects of post-secondary policy.

Competition and Marketization

In the early 1990s the political economy in Canada dramatically shifted. The effects of an economic recession for provincial governments were exacerbated by federal cuts in transfer payments. Provincial governments were searching for ways to reduce expenditures and raise income to finance post-secondary education. Provincial governments responded to the federal cuts in various ways, depending on the ideology of the government in power. In Ontario, British Columbia and Alberta neoliberal government policies prevailed. These included using fiscal strategies that employed market mechanisms and market principles to allocate resources, generate revenues, and address accessibility and accountability (Young, 2002; Jones and Young, 2004; Shanahan et al., 2005). Tuition was deregulated, or partially deregulated, and increased; operating grants were decreased, and key performance indicators were attached to a portion of institutional funding (see Alberta, 2005). Rationalization and planning of post-secondary education came to the forefront, driven by fiscal restraint. In some provinces, such as Ontario, "planning" amounted to "reacting to" economic pressures, and fiscal policies were used deliberately to shake up the system instead of providing it with much-needed coherence and direction (Shanahan *et al.*, 2005). In other provinces, such as Quebec, provincial governments held fast to tuition freezes and low tuition policies, while succumbing to funding attached to performance measures (Trottier and Bernatchez, 2005).

It is perhaps in the area of tuition fee policies that the clearest differences between provincial approaches can be found. While in some provinces tuition fees have escalated dramatically (British Columbia, Ontario, Nova Scotia), in others provincial governments have taken steps to freeze or even reduce them (Manitoba, Quebec, Newfoundland and Labrador). Across all provinces, however, one can discern an increased use of targeted grant mechanisms and matching fund schemes, frequently designed to encourage competition for funds within the sector and increase a market presence in the system. These arrangements are over and above the highly competitive nature of the federal government's approach to funding research and development.

Accountability

Institutions of higher education are subjected to increasing requirements for accountability, both in terms of changing approaches to accountability within post-secondary policy and of broader public sector accountability requirements that have an impact on post-secondary institutions. Accountability is far from a new aspect of provincial policy arrangements, but there seems to be an increasing emphasis on the development of structures that focus on a direct accountability relationship between the individual institution and government, rather than more holistic, sector-wide approaches. The development of institutional contracts between universities and government in Quebec, for example, is designed to document institutional obligations. Ontario is now moving towards multi-year, institution-specific, enrolment and accountability agreements with government. In some other provinces new money comes with requirements that universities submit accountability plans to spell out improvements to be made and specific results that will be achieved with the funds.

In many of the provinces the growth in the private career college sector has triggered reviews of the legislation relating to this sector. Though this sector has to date been largely invisible in terms of government regulation and national data systems, concerns over the need for increased consumer protection and a desire on the part of government to determine the conditions under which students attending private career colleges are eligible for student financial assistance have led to increased regulation and institutional accountability.

Public institutions are increasingly held accountable under the terms of broad, public-sector arrangements, and institutions of higher education are increasingly viewed as member institutions within this broader public sector. Institutions of higher education must provide accessibility services to address the needs of disabled populations under provincial human rights codes or disability acts. As major contractors with federal government agencies and councils, higher education institutions must fulfil the federal government's employment equity accountability requirements. Institutions of higher education are increasingly covered by provincial freedom of information and protection of privacy acts that mandate that institutions provide access to information under specific conditions, but also hold institutions accountable for ensuring that private information is protected.

Across Canada changes in the provincial government's role in coordinating post-secondary education have been driven by the policy priorities of accountability, quality, accessibility and efficiency. However, each province has taken different approaches to achieving these priorities. There is an overall trend towards the use of market mechanisms in fiscal policies, private-sector partnerships, institutional diversity, system-wide coordination and an increasing emphasis on accountability exercises.

Conclusion

There have been major shifts in role since 1995 at both the federal and provincial levels of government in the coordination of higher education in Canada. The federal government was the major source of financial support for the post-war massification of higher education in Canada through a system of formulaic provincial transfers that included an equalization component. The federal government's approach to provincial transfers was frequently modified, but the 1995 federal budget essentially changed the entire arrangement. The approach since then has shifted away from indirect funding of post-secondary education through transfer payments and towards providing support for research-intensive institutions in order to further the government's innovation agenda and addressing student financial support issues through a rather enigmatic combination of grants, initiatives designed to encourage family savings, and universal tax credits. The shift in funding has increased the federal government's influence over Canadian post-secondary education.

The federal government's mammoth investments in research and development signal a dramatic change in its role and approach. The federal government has shifted from simply sponsoring research activity, to providing major support for institutional and human resource research infrastructure. Research-intensive universities have been major beneficiaries of these new initiatives, but given the amount of money involved, almost all institutions of higher education have been planning strategically to strengthen their research infrastructure and productivity. A further consequence of the federal government's research policies has been to increase diversity within the post-secondary sector, based on research capacity. The reduction in importance of the federal block transfer and the increase in competitive research support have led to gender, disciplinary, institutional and regional disparities across the country. Women, the humanities, liberal arts institutions and the Atlantic and Prairie provinces have not been the largest beneficiaries (Shanahan *et al.*, 2005; Jones, 2006).

Also, the federal government's decision to create and endow private foundations as a mechanism to deal with post-secondary policy issues has been an interesting innovation in coordination during the period. In an era of large government surpluses, this approach has allowed the government to devote major resources in a single year to specific causes without making ongoing commitments. On the other hand, these foundations may represent a new form of government intermediary with somewhat ambiguous accountability relationships to both government and the sector that they have been asked to serve.

At both levels of government we see the increased involvement of industry and the private sector in post-secondary education. Federal and provincial governments have adopted market mechanisms in allocating resources and generating revenue, perhaps devolving some regulatory influence, if not authority, to the private sector or market. Provincial governments appear to be shifting the balance between university autonomy, state control and the market (Bruneau and Savage, 2002).

The traditional binary structures of Canadian higher education are becoming increasingly blurred in many provinces by an expansion in the range of institutions that have the authority to grant degrees, and by increased opportunities for experimentation in institutional partnerships and articulation arrangements. Provincial post-secondary systems are expanding. Provincial coordinating structures and approaches have shifted focus from the "sector" level (college or university sector) to the "system" level. Governance and regulation are increasingly viewed from a cross-sector, system-wide perspective. Provincial governments are interested in increasing access to higher education, but also in increasing mobility within higher education by facilitating transfer between and within sectors. The government of Alberta's rebranding of its provincial higher education system in terms of "Campus Alberta" provides an excellent example of a shift to a system-wide approach.

There are clear governance implications at the system and institutional levels of all these changes, which, combined, have created an increasingly complex policy environment. At the institutional level there are "more ties that bind", more targets to be met, more funds to be matched, more partners to be found and more accountability plans to be submitted, as the government expands its mechanisms of control. While there are substantive differences by province, the institutional environment is generally far more competitive and increasingly viewed as stratified. The most research-intensive universities now meet regularly as a group to discuss common issues and develop lobbying strategies; a Canadian association of "polytechnics" has been created to further the interests of elite community colleges that offer applied degrees and differentiate these institutions from others within the sector.

Over the past decade in Canada, at both levels of government, we see the state exerting stronger influence on post-secondary education. The federal government has used fiscal policy and its legitimate authority over the national economy to strengthen its role in post-secondary education. Provincial governments have expanded post-secondary systems and increased institutional diversity. At the same time, they have developed more mechanisms for controlling and shaping the coordination of the system. Clearly changing government roles have resulted in new intrusions and new innovations by both levels of government in the post-secondary domain, shifting post-secondary education a little closer towards the market in a country where post-secondary education has historically been a public enterprise. All of this has been accomplished without massive reform of the governance of post-secondary education in Canada.

Notes

1. Shanahan, T. and Jones, G.A. (2007). Shifting roles and approaches: government coordination of post-secondary education in Canada, 1995–2006. *Higher Education Research and Development*, 26(1), 31–43. Reprinted by permission of the publisher.
2. The Social Sciences and Humanities Research Council of Canada (SSHRC); the Natural Sciences and Engineering Research Council of Canada (NSERC); and the Medical Research Council.

References

Alberta. (2005). *A learning Alberta: Advanced education—a cross-jurisdictional overview of accessibility, affordability and quality*. Edmonton: Government of Alberta.
Bruneau, B. and Savage, D. (2002). *Counting out the scholars: The case against performance indicators in higher education*. Toronto: Lorimer.
Dennison, J.D. (ed.) (1995). *Challenge and opportunity: Canada's community colleges at the crossroads*. Vancouver: University of British Columbia Press.
Fisher, D., Rubenson, K., Clift, R., MacIvor, M., Meredith, J., Shanahan, T., Jones, G., Trottier, C. and Bernatchez, J. (2005). *Canadian federal policy and post secondary education*. New York: Alliance for International Higher Education Policy Studies.
Holmes, D. (2006). *Redressing the balance: Canadian university programs in support of aboriginal students*. Unpublished report, Association of Universities and Colleges of Canada, Ottawa.
Jones, G.A. (2006). Canada. In J.K. Forest and P.G. Altbach (eds) *International handbook of higher education*. Dordreht: Kluwer Academic Publishers.
Jones, G.A. and Young, S.J. (2004). Madly off in all directions: Higher education, marketization and Canadian federalism. In P. Teixeira, B. Jongbloed, D. Dill and A. Amaral (eds) *Markets in higher education: Rhetoric or reality?* Dordrecht: Kluwer Aademic Publishers.
Meloshe, M. (1994). *Reforms to Canada student loans program*. Ottawa: Human Resources Development Canada.
Neill, C. (2006). *Tax credits*. Paper presentation at the Conference on "Enhancing Access to Post-secondary Education: Recent Progress and Future Challenges", Canada Millennium Scholarship Foundation, Ottawa, September.
Shanahan, T., Jones, G., Fisher, D. and Rubenson, K. (2005). *The case of Ontario: The impact of post-secondary policy on Ontario's higher education system*. New York: Alliance for International Higher Education Policy Studies.
Skolnik, M. (1987). State control of degree granting: The establishment of a public monopoly in Canada. In C. Watson (ed.) *Governments and higher education—the legitimacy of intervention* (pp. 56–83). Toronto: Higher Education Group, OISE.

Trottier, C. and Bernatchez, J. (2005). *Higher education policy in Quebec: A case study.* New York: Alliance for International Higher Education Policies Studies.

Wolfe, D.A. (2002). Innovation policy for the knowledge-based economy: From the red book to the white paper. In G.B. Doern (ed.) *How Ottawa spends, 2001–2002.* Toronto: Oxford University Press. Retrieved November 30, 2006, from http://www.utoronto.ca/progris/pdf_files/Wolfe_InnovationPolicy.pdf

Young, S. (2002). The use of market mechanisms in higher education finance and state control: Ontario considered. *Canadian Journal of Higher Education, 32*(2), 79–102.

24

Bachelor Graduates on the Labour Market

A Cross-National Comparison of the Employers' Viewpoint[1]

Bettina Alesi

One of the most vehemently discussed questions in the process of restructuring traditional long study programmes according to the Bachelor/Master model is how to develop first-cycle curricula and degrees which are a meaningful preparation for a following Master programme as well as for the labour market—as stressed in the Bologna Declaration. It remains to be seen for which occupational levels undergraduate programmes will prepare and how these new degrees will be assessed on the labour markets in different countries in Europe. The chapter focuses on the employers' viewpoint, giving an overview of the assessment of Bachelor degrees in four countries: Austria, Hungary, the Netherlands and Norway. As it is a very early stage to provide in-depth analyses because so far there are hardly any Bachelor graduates on the labour markets, the chapter illustrates from a more analytical perspective what factors might influence their transition to the world of work and the development of their further careers.

Introduction

When the Ministers of Education of 29 European countries came together in Bologna in 1999 to sign the Bologna Declaration with the purpose of creating a "European Higher Education Area" until 2010, two driving forces were estimated to be in the background of this process: the enhancement of academic quality on the one hand and the employability of graduates on the other (see Reichert and Tauch, 2003, p. 8). Additionally, these two aims were seen to be compatible when two years later in Prague the:

> Ministers expressed their appreciation of the contributions toward developing study programmes combining academic quality with relevance to lasting employability and called for a continued proactive role of higher education institutions (Prague Communiqué, 2001).

Although placing the employability issue at the top of the agenda, the Bologna Declaration, as well as the subsequent Communiqués of Prague, Berlin and Bergen, does not offer a precise definition of the term. With regard to the undergraduate cycle, the Bologna Declaration only stresses:

The degree awarded after the first cycle shall also be relevant to the European labour market as an appropriate level of qualification (Bologna Declaration, 1999).

On one hand, this is a clear statement that higher education institutions should develop Bachelor programmes which do not only have a preparatory function for a following Master programme but also enable the graduates to enter work life (see Teichler, 2004). On the other hand, the Bologna Declaration does not substantiate for which occupational levels undergraduate programmes shall prepare for and how Bachelor graduates should be trained in order to meet the requirements of the labour market.

In many countries in Europe, single-tiered study programmes were predominant before the Bologna-related reforms. Therefore, one of the most delicate and exciting questions in the process of restructuring these programmes is how to develop first cycle curricula and degrees which are also a meaningful preparation for the labour market (Teichler, 2005).

It is still unclear which "solutions" will be chosen and will prevail in the different higher education systems across Europe in order to adjust to the goals of the Bologna Declaration. What remains to be seen is:

- whether Bachelor programmes will prepare in principle for similar occupations like traditional single-tiered programmes or whether they will prepare for occupations between the traditional academic professions and vocational occupations;
- what amount of specialisation and specific preparation for the world of work will be imparted in undergraduate programmes;
- how the ongoing reforms will affect the identities of universities and non-university higher education institutions and whether Bachelor degrees from both types of institutions will converge or diverge in the long run.

Looking at the employment system on the other hand, the reform of study structures poses again a series of yet unanswered questions:

- How will a new "intermediary" type of degree be assessed on labour markets used to two main types of degrees, more theoretically oriented university degrees and more practically oriented degrees from non-university higher education institutions such as *Fachhochschulen* in Austria and Germany or *hogescholen* in the Netherlands?
- Which degree of specialisation in undergraduate programmes is desirable? Are companies willing to offer additional training or more time to develop for Bachelor graduates with a rather general background?
- Which level of study or degree will turn out to be the formal prerequisite for many professional occupations: the Bachelor or the Master degree?
- How will first or early jobs determine subsequent careers? Does, for example, a Bachelor graduate employed at first in a middle-level position have a realistic chance to move to a high-level occupation in later stages of his or her career? Will first-job salary differences between Bachelor and Master graduates shrink in the course of a professional career or not?

It thus becomes clear that the question of acceptance of Bachelor degrees—which is nowadays in the focus of the public debate—is not exclusive but only one of several issues when thinking about how the ongoing reforms might affect the relationship between higher education and the world of work.[2] At the same time it becomes clear that the transition of these new graduates to the labour market is intertwined with other dimensions of the relationship between higher education and work, like for example the curricular arrangements of the new programmes and the specific features of graduate recruitment and human resource management in companies.

In this chapter, the employers' point of view on the employment chances as well as subsequent career prospects for new Bachelor graduates in four countries—Austria, Hungary, the Netherlands and Norway—will be illustrated.

The employers' standpoint was investigated in the framework of an internationally comparative study commissioned by the German Federal Ministry of Education and Research and carried out by the Centre for Research on Higher Education and Work at the University of Kassel in 2004/05 (see Alesi *et al.*, 2005a, 2005b).[3] Besides the employers' viewpoint, the study included a cross-national analysis of structural and curricular strategies in the process of implementing Bachelor and Master programmes in different European countries.[4] Further, the acceptance of the new two-tiered system by students and staff in universities and non-university higher education institutions was also a major theme of the study.

The specific focus in the following chapter, namely the *employers' view* on the *first cycle* of study programmes and degrees has been chosen because:

- firstly, concerns about the labour market acceptance of the new degrees pertain mainly to Bachelor degrees, while Master degrees are normally considered to be similar to traditional university degrees, and
- secondly, compared with other studies on the Bologna Process, such as for example the Trends IV Study (see Reichert and Tauch, 2005), the Bachelor/Master Stocktaking Study has put a strong emphasis on the employers' viewpoint.

Methods

The illustration of the employers' point of view is based on the analysis of:

- relevant documents (e.g. policy papers of employers' associations) and empirical studies;
- country reports provided by national experts on the basis of detailed guidelines;
- interviews with decision-makers in human resource departments in different sectors of the labour market and representatives of employers' associations—usually persons responsible for education or research policy—(see Table 24.1) and an interview with a representative of the Austrian Council for Economic and Social Questions.[5]

Without exception, all companies were large companies, playing a leading role on both national and international markets and having a high level of attractiveness for graduates as well as recruiting significant numbers of them. The selection of the interview partners was carried out together with national experts in the included countries.

The interviews took place in November and December 2004, mainly *in situ*, and lasted between 45 and 60 minutes. They were carried out in German and English, sometimes with the help of interpreters, and were based on interview guidelines.

When analysing the empirical material it seemed meaningful to categorise the employers' assessments on the basis of two main aspects:

Table 24.1 Overview of the Interviewees' Institutions/Corporations

Country	Interviewees' institutions/corporations
Austria	IT company (one interview) Media organisation (one interview) Employers' association (one interview)
Hungary	Telecommunications company (one interview) Pharmaceutical company (one interview) Employers' association (one interview)
Netherlands	Oil company (one interview) Construction (ships) company (one interview) Employers' association (one interview)
Norway	Aluminium and oil company (one interview) Oil and gas company (one interview) Employers' association (one interview)

- firstly, the interviewees in the personnel departments—who in general did not have experience with the new Bachelor or Master graduates because so far there hardly are any graduates on the labour markets—named a series of decisive factors for the question, whether a Bachelor degree will be accepted as an appropriate level of qualification for highly qualified positions or not. These factors will be presented in detail in the following section;
- secondly, on the basis of actual deployment practices, employers assessed possible entrance positions and salaries for Bachelor graduates compared to traditional graduates and Master graduates as well as possible modes of career development. The opinions to this subject will be presented in the section afterwards.

Decisive Factors for the Acceptance of New Degrees

A commonality of the countries referred to in this chapter is the former differentiation of study programmes and degrees along two types of institutions: universities and non-university higher education institutions. Thus, these countries as well as other countries in Europe with similar higher education traditions face similar challenges in the process of converting their longer single-tiered study programmes to the Bachelor/Master model: they have to find a way to connect the former idea of the binary system with different levels of study programmes and degrees.

According to the findings of the Bachelor/Master Stocktaking Study, until now universities have mainly kept their academic orientation in both Bachelor and Master programmes and have not put too much effort into implementing Bachelor programmes which prepare for the labour market as well as for a consecutive Master programme—as stressed in the Bologna Declaration. A majority of students continue their studies after the Bachelor and this corresponds with the view of academic staff, who tend to believe that a higher academic degree is necessary for many professional and managerial occupations.

This is different in non-university higher education. Professors at these institutions regard their Bachelor degrees as attractive for the labour market because graduates:

- have practical experience and some specialisation which makes them employable without too much additional training; and

- might have a competitive advantage compared to traditional graduates taking into account that (at least in some countries) they are younger and probably more trainable according to the employers' needs.

In the following, these views shall be contrasted with the employers' perceptions on the subject. Research on the relationship between study and subsequent employment indicates that the question, whether new credentials like the Bachelor degrees will be accepted on the labour market or not, has to be investigated in a broader context, including:

- the design and quality of the new programmes, respectively;
- the qualification profiles of the new graduates; and
- the specific features of graduate recruitment and human resource management in companies.

Design and Quality of the New Programmes

In general, the interviewed employers stated that whether a new type of degree will be accepted on the labour market or not depends foremost on the specific content of the respective study programme. As proof for this argument, an Austrian interview partner remembered quite a similar discussion that took place 10 years ago in Austria, when the *Fachhochschul*-sector was introduced:

In Austria we had a very similar discussion concerning the acceptance of titles with the introduction of *Fachhochschulen* (. . .) where the question was raised: Will it have a value at all, will it be accepted and in which way will it differ from a university degree. Ten years later, the acceptance is not a question at all anymore. Some *Fachhochschul* graduates even had temporarily better chances on the labour market than university graduates and they probably even do so today. The "A" and "B" value [university degrees are classified by an A and *Fachhochschul*-degrees by a B in the public service in Austria] is another issue. The question is if here [in the Bachelor programmes] the qualifications can be obtained which are needed by the industry. (. . .) The acceptance will be decided by the quality of the supply of Bachelor programmes. You can observe the same thing with respect to *Fachhochschul*-programmes: Those which are good are accepted. And it doesn't matter if the "FH" [abbreviation for the addendum *Fachhochschule* in academic titles in Austria] is added to the title or not. I can imagine a similar development now and I think that we are following a wrong track in the discussion if we are talking about a "yes" or a "no"—in contrary, the question is: How good is he/she [the Bachelor graduate]?[6]

As an overall idea, the interviewed persons in the human resource departments as well as the representatives of the employers' associations in the selected countries had a positive attitude towards the Bologna reforms. Especially in some countries like Austria and Norway, employers have been concerned for many years about the long duration of studies and the high drop-out rates at universities. The reform of study structures, which is sometimes linked to more comprehensive reforms like reforms that provide more institutional autonomy and require more attention to quality in higher education, is seen as a step in the right direction. It is seen to enhance quality and flexibility, both for students and the needs of the labour market. Employers therefore emphasise that it is important how the Bologna reforms are being implemented: they plead for a real reform and not for a simple relabelling of traditional programmes as well as for a speedy and a more or less complete restructuring of traditional programmes.[7]

They see a chance that especially university education becomes more relevant to the needs of the labour market. Nevertheless, this should not be interpreted in a way that employers expect universities to transform into *hogescholen* or *Fachhochschulen*. In contrast, scenarios of a possible convergence of the binary system due to the Bologna reforms have been met with reluctance because certain educational attainments and certain job positions or work assignments actually reflect each other to a quite high extent. Although there are tasks which can be equally fulfilled by university as well as by non-university graduates there are also positions in the labour market for which companies like to recruit:

- specialised graduates from non-university higher education who are able to start working more or less immediately within a given setting and have a good problem-solving competence;
- graduates from universities with a more universal competence combined with critical judgement and a deep theoretical knowledge base.

The employers requested that universities should keep their academic approach as a distinguishing feature from non-university higher education but take more into account that they are preparing a majority of their students for careers outside the academia and that they would enable a smoother transition to the labour market if they would encourage students to deal more with practical problems, for example by writing a Bachelor or Master thesis on a question which has a practical origin or impact in companies.

The employers did not anticipate acceptance problems for Bachelor degrees resulting from a shorter duration of the first cycle compared with traditional long-study programmes. In contrast, if Bachelor programmes would concentrate on the core qualifications of the certain disciplines, they could be regarded as a more or less focused version of traditional programmes. With respect to the question, how general or specific curricula should be in the first cycle, the employers' statements were again very similar: They preferred rather broad curricula but with a certain amount of specialisation, as the following interview statement shows:

> Education or qualification is becoming more and more specific and this specificity is determined by ever shorter life cycles. Therefore it is getting more and more important (. . .) to go in the direction of core competences. If my assumption is correct then higher education institutions will rather go for core competences on the Bachelor level because these competences don't change so quickly and I need exactly these competences to add a specialisation in a life-long perspective, either as a renewal or a completion or a broadening of the knowledge base. Without these core competences it will be very difficult later to add specialised knowledge. (. . .) The question is in how far the transmission of core qualifications leaves space for the transmission of specialisation as well and I think that would probably be an adequate answer but this answer can be only given by each discipline separately: How much core qualifications do certain disciplines have and how much room for specialisation do they allow already on the Bachelor level? It is important to specify these core competences which allow to enter professional life.[8]

Specific Features of Graduate Recruitment and Human Resource Management

The evaluation of a Bachelor degree as an appropriate higher education degree depends further on the specific features of recruitment and human resource management in different companies or sectors of the labour market. The analysis of the empirical material suggests that, amongst others, the following aspects have to be taken into account:

- the differences in the handling of formal prerequisites in different professions;
- the variation in the selection criteria according to specific characteristics of the companies, such as, for example, their degree of attractiveness for graduates (e.g. companies located in metropolitan vs. in rural areas);
- the differences in the ability to offer continuing education according to the companies' size, for example; and
- the differences concerning the interpretation of credentials by human resource management decision-makers.

Differences in the handling of formal prerequisites

Regarding the two main employment sectors which were chosen for investigation in the presented study, namely the industrial and the media sector, a greater openness for graduates with a Bachelor degree could be observed in the latter. The different views concerning the labour market value of a Bachelor degree result from a different handling of formal prerequisites in the selection and hiring process: entrance positions for journalists are generally less strongly linked to certain fields of study or specific credentials than many professional occupations in the industrial sector, where one can often find divided labour markets not only for different study fields but also for university and non-university higher education graduates. As expressed in the interviews, in times of shortage of university graduates with certain specialisations it is more usual to search for these specialists abroad than to hire graduates from a local *hogeschol*, for example, and offer them some additional training.

This is different in the media sector where—as the following citation shows—skills are required that are rather related to talent (e.g. a good feeling for language) than to qualifications in a narrow sense which can be obtained in a formal learning process:

> Whether somebody is suitable as a journalist or not, does not depend on the educational attainment. Individuals have these required competences or not and this is tested by the colleagues in the assessment centre. I think that if you don't have the basic requirements, e.g. a good feeling for language, you can't obtain them while studying at university but what you obtain here is rather special techniques and knowledge.[9]

According to this interview partner, it is a common phenomenon in journalism that students find attractive occupations before completing their studies, thus entering work life without a degree at all. Quite often these students without graduation are the more talented ones, but officially they count as drop-outs and failures. The new Bachelor/Master system will offer these students better chances to leave university with a degree after a shorter period of study, which was highly welcomed by the interviewed person in the human resource department of a media organisation.

Variation in the selection criteria

As mentioned above, the selected companies for the Bachelor/Master Stocktaking Study were in general employers with a high degree of attractiveness for graduates. While talking to the decision-makers in the personnel departments of these companies it became quite clear that because they are able to select the best-qualified graduates from a big pool of applicants they enforce more severe hiring standards than the average company. One interview partner illustrated this by the following relation: Having a capacity of 25–30 trainee places per year at the headquarters of his company, he is confronted annually with about 5,000 applications. This makes it easy to carry out a negative selection of those applicants who do not have at least a university (equivalent) degree. But better chances for Bachelor graduates were expected in the regional branches, which sometimes have difficulties finding good graduates. Additionally, the introduction of a tiered degree system could enhance the qualification level in rural areas because more individuals might feel encouraged to study at a university or a college.

Differences in the ability to offer continuing education

Some of the interviewed employers feared that Bachelor graduates from the university sector will have more difficulty being accepted on the labour market than Bachelor graduates from non-university higher education. This view was especially expressed in the Netherlands and in Hungary where the Bologna reforms have mainly affected the university sector, whereas the new Bachelor programmes at non-university higher education institutions have in general the same duration as their predecessor programmes (mainly three years in Hungary and four years in the Netherlands). Therefore the employers expect a similar qualification level from Bachelor graduates from non-university higher education and entrance positions and salaries will not vary too much.

This is different in Austria and Norway where Bachelor programmes at universities and non-university higher education institutions are shorter than traditional programmes in both tracks and in general have the same duration (mainly three years). But even in these countries there are no serious concerns about the employability of Bachelor graduates from the non-university higher education sector because employers estimated that the practical orientation of this education will be kept in the new Bachelor programmes.

Employers were in general not familiar with Bachelor graduates from universities. These graduates were seen sometimes as "semi-finished products", probably lacking specialised knowledge which is regarded to be necessary for starting a professional career in the countries that were in the focus of this study. It was therefore expected that these graduates would need additional training or continuing education in order to be adequately employed, e.g. in positions requiring an academic degree. Employers expected that Bachelor graduates from universities will have better chances to start in a large company because here they might have wider possibilities for continuing education (inside the company or by working part-time and attending a Masters programme).

What becomes clear in these statements is that the employability issue is frequently discussed one-sidedly: it is often regarded as a desirable attribute of the job applicant but not as part of the employers' personnel development strategy as well. When asked about similar or different qualification requirements for Bachelor and Master graduates, both variants were expressed in the framework of the interviews: While some companies would not make a difference between these two types of graduates, others would give Bachelor graduates more time to develop than Master graduates.

Differences in the interpretation of credentials

The last factor which seems to have an impact on the question of whether Bachelor degrees will be accepted as an appropriate level of qualification for highly qualified occupations or not is the way in which personnel managers tend to interpret credentials or, speaking with Spence (1973), the signalling effect of credentials.[10] In some interviews it became clear that the traditional university education carries a strong signal for employers, indicating that the graduate has proven to be willing and capable to learn and to work independently—from which employers infer a high performance capacity.

Two points of the "hidden curriculum" of traditional university education were expressed in interviews:

- the Humboldtian concept of the unity of teaching and research offering a high degree of autonomy to students with regard to the organisation of their learning schedule;[11]
- the character of the final thesis in the traditional university education—regardless of whether or not the specific content is relevant for the later occupation.

Employers presumed that if a certain individual has managed to organise his/her learning schedule independently and to work on a given question in the final thesis independently he/she has acquired important skills for the later occupation where self-discipline, problem-solving abilities and the ability to deal with uncertainty are required. University education is furthermore expected to train flexibility as the following extract of an interview with an Austrian employer shows:

> I believe that especially university education has a headstart compared to *Fachhochschul*-education. Because a university student has to organise everything more or less by him(her)-self and he/she has to see how he/she gets his/her learning material. At *Fachhochschulen* you are confronted more with a school-like system that has other advantages like specialised and practically oriented knowledge. But I think that the university has the advantage that you have to learn to be flexible: "There are no places in certain classes anymore, I have to reorganise myself". With this problem the student at a *Fachhochschule* is not confronted: he/she has his/her learning schedule and he/she attends classes.[12]

It is not yet clear what we can conclude from this for the employment chances of Bachelor graduates, taking into account the trend to develop more structured curricula/learning schedules in the undergraduate cycle and to reduce the volume and scientific approach of the Bachelor thesis compared to the traditional final thesis.

Deployment and Career Prospects for the New Graduates

Surveys on graduate employment have indicated for a longer time that there are an increasing number of graduates who do not manage to enter traditional academic careers because, amongst others, the number of highly qualified jobs has increased to a lesser extent in the past decades than the number of graduates. Therefore, higher education experts consider that the introduction of shorter programmes can be regarded as an adequate answer to the challenges which occur in the process of the expansion of higher education (see e.g. Teichler, 2006). Especially the traditional focus of university education—the preparation for research and top careers in industry and administration—is regarded to be too narrow to cope with the increasing diversity of talents, professional aspirations and career prospects of the students. If the ongoing reforms would be taken as an opportunity to develop shorter programmes with a more specific orientation towards the world of work, a better training for occupations below traditional academic professions could be imparted in these shorter programmes than in traditional highly theoretical long university programmes.

Employers interviewed in the framework of the Bachelor/Master Stocktaking Study expected that the medium level between vocational occupations and academic professions will eventually end up in occupations for Bachelors in about 5–10 years' time. Comparing entry positions for Bachelor and Master graduates, the interviewees considered that there is a range of job positions where it simply does not make sense to apply with only a Bachelor degree because in the past these positions have been mainly reserved for university graduates with at least a degree equivalent to a Master, which are, for example, occupations in:

- research and development (in particular all natural sciences);

- partly technical and engineering fields; and
- law departments in companies.

However, there is a wide range of occupations which nowadays are open for both graduates from universities as well as graduates from non-university higher education and which in the future could be open for Bachelor graduates as well, such as occupations in:

- production and logistic fields;
- qualified sales, distribution and consulting services (for example, sales representatives for pharmaceutical products);
- fields where applied informatics, statistics or mathematical knowledge is required (there could be a need for mathematicians with a Bachelor degree in insurance agencies, for example, being responsible for the calculation of statistical models while the development of new models would be delegated to mathematicians with a Master degree or a PhD); and
- journalism, as mentioned before.

The interview partners generally did not have precise ideas about the entrance wages of Bachelor graduates as the following citation shows:

> Where will the salaries lie? I think that there will be a difference between Bachelor and Master graduates because the competence is differing. But it also depends very much on the question how somebody performs in his/her competence and you can observe nowadays that you get paid according to your function and competence and not any more according to your educational attainment. That means: the further you are away from finishing your first education, the less it is relevant for the payment. Crucial is the continuing education. And we have a great challenge in this respect. And the investment in my continuing education will be decisive for my payment or position.[13]

This possible equalisation of wages after several years of work as well as the equalisation of career opportunities was a trend observed in all included countries: Wages and careers are becoming more and more a function of the performance of the individuals and are less dependent on the educational attainment than it used to be some years ago.

However, the employers expected that—generally speaking—Master degrees will lead to different levels of professional careers than Bachelor degrees. It was assumed that—as an average— Master graduates will not only have a higher knowledge level but also a higher ability and willingness to learn and to invest in their continuing education than graduates from shorter study programmes.

Conclusion

Although the study cannot be generalised in a statistical or quantitative sense, a number of common elements in the selected countries were observed which could be relevant for other European countries as well, especially for those with a similar higher education tradition like the countries that were in the focus of this study. The employers' views can be summarised as follows.

There is a greater concern about the employability of Bachelor graduates from the university sector than from the non-university higher education sector because the former might be educated too generally and lack some specialisation which is regarded to be—in general—indispensable on labour markets in Northern and Central Europe.

Employers are at present rather in favour of the "survival" of the binary system because of traditionally established modes of deployment for university and non-university graduates. The idea behind the Bologna Declaration that the duration of study cycles should function as a yardstick for the professional value of a study programme and that duration should slowly replace the significance of different types of institutions (see Teichler, 2006) was not yet reflected by the interviewees.

It is too early to state what occupations Bachelor graduates will have after graduation or how their careers will develop in the course of their professional life. But it seems that the link between the formal educational attainment and the occupational status is lowering and that the performance in comparison to the educational background is getting more and more decisive for careers. This is especially true for labour market sectors characterised by a higher flexibility of graduate deployment. A Bachelor degree can in principle be a door-opener for highly qualified positions, especially if the respective graduate will continue studies.

As it is still a very early stage to give elaborate answers to some of the questions raised above, the emphasis in this chapter was put on a more analytical view, trying to show what factors might influence the acceptance of new degrees: curricular characteristics of Bachelor programmes seem to be the key for a successful transition to the labour market and for further careers. If the restructuring of study programmes is accompanied by curricular reforms and especially if the universities are taking the employability task seriously, then the employers do not expect acceptance problems. There were no concerns that shorter programmes will lack sufficient time to impart the necessary general and specialised knowledge of certain disciplines in order to be able to cope with typical professional assignments. Employers, however, did not make precise statements whether they will evaluate a Bachelor graduate from a three-year programme differently than one from a four-year programme, for example. It should be remembered though that the vagueness of the employers' statements is related to the fact that at the time of our study the interviewees—especially the decision-makers in the personnel departments of the selected companies—had little information about the ongoing reforms and hardly had experiences with Bachelor graduates from the new restructured programmes. For more in-depth-analyses further studies are necessary, when large cohorts of graduates from the new study programmes will enter professional life.

Notes

1. Alesi, B. (2007). Bachelor graduates on the labour market: a cross-national comparison of the employers' viewpoint. *Tertiary Education and Management*, 13:2, 85–98. Reprinted by permission of the publisher.
2. For the different dimensions of this relationship see Brennan, Kogan and Teichler (1996).
3. The study will be addressed in the following by the acronym "Bachelor/Master Stocktaking Study" while the official name is "Bachelor and Master Courses in Selected Countries Compared with Germany".
4. The countries analysed were Austria, France, Germany, Hungary, the Netherlands and Norway. Additionally, the study included an analysis of the British involvement in the Bologna Process. Interviews with employers only took place in Austria, Hungary, the Netherlands and Norway.
5. The Bachelor study programmes set up in the first phase of the study structure reform in Austria were required to seek expert advice about their professional relevance from the Austrian Council for Economic and Social Questions (Der österreichische Beirat für Wirtschafts- und Sozialfragen) before they could be submitted to the Ministry for approval.
6. Translated into English from the German original by the author of this chapter.
7. While in Hungary, the Netherlands and Norway higher education legislation envisages a more or less comprehensive introduction of tiered study programmes and degrees, this is not the case for Austria: the implementation of tiered study programmes has only reached about 25% of the total amount of study programmes by the time the study was conducted.

8. Translated into English from the German original by the author of this chapter.
9. Translated into English from the German original by the author of this chapter.
10. Spence assumes that employers can use two main factors in order to infer the future productivity and performance of job applicants: signals and indices. While indices stand for fixed attributes like gender or age, signals stand for attributes which can be influenced by the applicant like educational attainments and job experiences, for example.
11. On the other hand, this lowly structured study system has often been criticised and made responsible for high drop-out rates and long study periods, for example, in Austria (see Pechar and Pellert, 2004).
12. Translated into English from the German original by the author of this chapter.
13. Translated into English from the German original by the author of this chapter.

References

Alesi, B., Bürger, S., Kehm, B.M. and Teichler, U. (2005a). *Bachelor- und Master-Studiengänge in ausgewählten Ländern Europas im Vergleich zu Deutschland. Fortschritte im Bologna-Prozess.* Bonn and Berlin: BMBF.

Alesi, B., Bürger, S., Kehm, B.M. and Teichler, U. (2005b). *Bachelor and Master Courses in Selected Countries Compared with Germany.* Bonn and Berlin: BMBF.

Bologna Declaration (1999). *The European higher education area. Joint declaration of the European Ministers of Education of 19 June 1999.* Available online at: http://www.bologna-berlin2003.de/ pdf/bologna_declaration.pdf (accessed 30 September 2005).

Brennan, J., Kogan, M. and Teichler, U. (1996). Higher education and work: a conceptual framework. In J. Brennan, M. Kogan and U. Teichler (eds), *Higher education and work* (pp. 1–24). London: Jessica Kingsley.

Pechar, H. and Pellert, A. (2004). Austrian universities under pressure from Bologna. *European Journal of Education,* 39, 317–330.

Prague Commuiqué (2001). *Towards the European higher education area. Communique of the meeting of European Ministers in charge of higher education in Prague on 19 May 2001.* Available online at: http://www.bologna-berlin2003.de/pdf/ Prague_communiquTheta.pdf (accessed 30 September 2005).

Reichert, S. and Tauch, C. (2003). *Trends 2003. Progress towards the European higher education area.* Brussels: European University Association. Available online at: http://www.eua.be/eua/jsp/en/ upload/Trends2003final. 1065011164859.pdf (accessed 30 September 2005).

Reichert, S. and Tauch, C. (2005). *Trends IV: European universities implementing Bologna.* Brussels: European University Association. Available online at: http://www.bologna-bergen2005.no/ Docs/02-EUA/050425_EUA_TrendsIV.pdf (accessed 30 September 2005).

Spence, M. (1973). Job market signaling. *Quarterly Journal of Economics,* 87, 355–374.

Teichler, U. (2004). *Changes in the relationship between higher education and the world of work on the way towards the European higher education area.* Keynote speech at the EUA Conference "University and Society: Engaging Stakeholders", in Marseille, 1–3 April 2004.

Teichler, U. (2005). Berufliche Relevanz und Bologna-Prozess. In U. Welbers and O. Gaus (eds), *The shift from teaching to learning* (pp. 314–320). Bielefeld: W. Bertelsmann Verlag (Blickpunkt Hochschuldidaktik, Bd. 116).

Teichler, U. (2006). *Berufliche Relevanz und berufliche Orientierung des Studiums im Wandel.* Beitrag zum Workshop der Österreichischen Forschungsgemeinschaft: Studienzulassung und Studienqualität: Gute Studierende brauchen gute Universitäten und gute Universitäten gute Studierende, 10–11 März 2006. Available online at: http://www.oefg.at/text/ veranstaltungen/ studienzulassung_qualitaet/Beitrag_Teichler.pdf (accessed 7 April 2006).

VII
Institutional Management

The issue of institutional management has become of increasing importance in higher education as both institutions, and the national systems of which they are part, have expanded to accommodate more and more students and activities. Whereas it might have been possible formerly to rely on untrained academics themselves, supported by a limited number of administrators, to direct the work of our universities and colleges, now an increasing number of specialist managers and trained academic-managers are required.

Key issues here, then, include how higher education institutions are organised and managed, both centrally and departmentally (Becher and Kogan, 1992), and how they relate to the economy (Clark, 1998; Deem, 2001: Slaughter and Leslie, 1997) and the wider community.

In the first of five chapters in this section, Colin Pilbeam examines the contemporary structures of higher education institutions. Different perspectives on organisations and institutions are presented, and two model classifications are considered—McNay's typology of collegium, bureaucracy, corporation and enterprise; and Olsen's similar, but independently derived, categorisation of the university as a community of scholars, an instrument for national political agendas, a representative democracy or a service enterprise embedded in competitive markets. The influence of design, institutional pressures and environmental challenges (e.g. research assessment, the knowledge economy, the development of "third stream" funding) on each of these models is then examined.

The second chapter, by Jenny Lee, focuses on a key level of institutional management, but one which is accorded relatively little attention when compared with the levels of the university and government: namely, the department. Lee's concern is with how the twin forces of the institution and the discipline impact on departmental culture, an arena in which, at least in recent history, the discipline has been regarded as stronger. She pursues this interest by carrying out a factor analysis of a large American data set containing information on academics' assumptions, beliefs and values. Lee concludes that the discipline and the institution have impacts of similar magnitude, but varying in terms of the dimension of departmental culture being examined.

Colin Green and Geraint Johnes examine the evidence on economies of scale and mergers in higher education. Having outlined the theory and methodology behind studies in this area, they summarise the state of existing research: science teaching is more expensive than non-science teaching; most higher education institutions are already fairly efficient; further expansion of many higher education systems might better proceed through creating new institutions rather than expanding the existing ones; but, at the same time, it might be more efficient to concentrate particular aspects of higher education provision in particular institutions.

Green and Johnes then move on to consider the extent to which mergers of higher education institutions are motivated by economic factors, and whether they lead to cost efficiencies. They conclude that rationalisation is difficult to achieve in higher education settings, and that the evidence of actual cost savings being achieved in practice is limited.

Iryna Lendel, Phil Allen and Maryann Feldman take a rather different economic perspective, in looking at the impact universities have on economic growth in their regions. Having reviewed the available theory, they consider the evidence on knowledge spillovers and agglomeration effects, and the role of the university in encouraging innovation. While much public investment is justified on the basis that such effects will impact on the local economy, the evidence is that this impact is by no means certain, with much depending on the regional economy's capacity to make use of the benefits a local university can offer.

Finally in this section, Matthew Hartley and David Soo switch the debate to consider the relationships between universities and their local communities, with a particular focus on the civic engagement of students and staff. Older ideas of university service have clearly undergone challenge in the American system, resulting in renewed initiatives at national and institutional levels to promote service learning. While much has been achieved, more remains to be done, not least in developing similar initiatives in other countries.

References

Becher, T. and Kogan, M. (1992). *Process and Structure in Higher Education.* London: Routledge, 2nd edition.

Clark, B. (1998). *Creating Entrepreneurial Universities: organisational pathways of transformation.* New York: Elsevier.

Deem, R. (2001). Globalisation, New Managerialism, Academic Capitalism and Entrepreneurialism in Universities: is the local dimension still important? *Comparative Education,* 37, 1, pp. 7–20.

Slaughter, S. and Leslie, G. (1997). *Academic Capitalism.* Baltimore, MD, Johns Hopkins University Press.

25

Institutional Structures

Where Legitimacy and Efficiency Meet

Colin Pilbeam

Introduction

Organizations are shaped by the environment in which they operate and universities are no exception to this. Broadly, the environment can be classified as either technical or institutional (Scott and Meyer, 1991). Both may be represented to a greater or lesser extent in any single environment, giving rise to a typology of four organizational environmental types. Universities are typically found in environments which are institutionally strong but technically weaker. As a consequence, organizational structures, and their antecedents in this environment, may be different from those found in technically strong but institutionally weak environments (like manufacturing firms), or where both are strong (like banks) or both are weak (like restaurants).

To understand organizational structures it is, therefore, necessary to use tools that can aid interpretation of both the technical and the institutional environments. These are different because the technical environment is primarily concerned with issues of resource, and is dominated by the questions of efficiency and effectiveness, while the institutional environment addresses the question of legitimacy, and focuses on rules, roles and beliefs, or cultural and symbolic aspects of the organization.

Structures within organizations are created from the interplay between these two environmental settings. Moreover, as environments change, so the structures will change to create new forms. These transitions may create conflict within an organization as new structures are necessarily, but perhaps awkwardly, superimposed or juxtaposed to existing forms.

This chapter draws on two different perspectives on organization to explain both the variety and similarity of forms found in universities. Having briefly summarized these two perspectives, they will be applied to two models of university organization, highlighting which elements of either perspective the models appeal too. Finally, the impact on organizational structures of three different drivers for change in universities will be explored using the perspectives previously outlined. This will illustrate the causes of tension and the difficulties associated with responding to environmental changes.

Perspective 1: Organizational Design

Structures within an organization reflect the tasks that the organization needs to perform, and the mechanism of coordination required to accomplish these activities. Certain tasks can only be performed in particular ways, and some of these ways will be more effective than others. Similarly, some mechanisms of coordination may be more appropriate for some tasks but not others, so that for effective and efficient organizational performance there needs to be a consistency between the task to be performed and the mechanisms for its coordination.

Mintzberg (1979) suggests that there are five principal ways in which organizations coordinate their work. The first of these ways, mutual adjustment, uses informal communication to coordinate activities. As work becomes more complex and requires more operators, then an individual may take responsibility for the work of others. Such direct supervision requires individuals to issue instructions and to monitor activity. By standardizing the process, the outputs or the inputs, these two coordination mechanisms can be circumvented. Work processes may be standardized by speci-fying the content of the work. For example, course designs with intended learning outcomes attempt to standardize the process. Alternatively, the outputs may be standardized. Much of the debate surrounding the implementation of the Bologna Process has to do with standardizing outputs, so that similar degrees from institutions in different countries are comparable, and those students who complete them have identical skill and knowledge sets. Finally, coordination may be effected through the standardization of inputs (or skills). Specifying the training required before a particular task can be undertaken ensures that individuals who deliver the task know what is required of them. Coordination in this case is thus indirect. Over the past 50 years, universities have come to assume that individuals possessing a doctorate are able to lecture.

As organizations tackle a variety of tasks there will inevitably be a mix of coordinating mechan-isms in any single organization. Nevertheless, as the environment in which the organization oper-ates becomes more complex, so direct supervision gives way to standardization of work (processes, outputs and inputs), and finally succumbs once more to mutual adjustment. Conversely, as environmental instability increases, standardization gives way to direct supervision or mutual adjustment, depending on the level of environmental complexity.

In addition to these five coordinating mechanisms, Mintzberg also identified five basic com-ponents of an organization. An operating core performs the basic work of the organization related to the production of products or services. In the case of the modern university, the academic staff lecture and research. This is the basic work of a university. The strategic apex has overall responsibil-ity for the organization, and is "charged with ensuring that the organization serves its mission in an effective way and also that it serves the needs of those who control, or otherwise have power over the organization" (Mintzberg, 1983, p. 13). These may be the members of the senior management team of a university, including the vice-chancellor, the pro-vice-chancellors, registrar, finance dir-ector and so on. Linking the strategic apex to the operating core is the middle line. In a university context these are the deans and heads of school/departments. The other two components—the technostructure and the support staff—sit outside of this axis but support its activities. Individuals in the technostructure serve the organization by affecting the work of others through standardiza-tion of processes, outputs or inputs. They also assist the organization in adapting to its environ-ment. For example, personnel in university registries operate processes to monitor the progress of students across the whole university. Others in human resources may initiate training to ensure that categories of staff of particular grades have comparable skills, while those in accounts provide order to the financial outputs of the university. A fifth component is the support staff, who support the functioning of the operating core, and include staff in the library, marketing department and international office.

While every organization may contain all of these five basic components, the prominence given to any particular component will influence the configuration of the organization and the specific coordination mechanism that is emphasized within it. As noted, the technostructure aims to standardize the work processes of others, and pulls the organization towards a machine bureaucracy. By contrast, members of the operating core resist this, wishing to work autonomously, and relying on standardization of skills to integrate their activities in a professional bureaucracy. Those in the strategic apex seek to control all decision making, relying on direct supervision which creates a simple structure. As individuals in the middle line gain power either from above—the strategic apex—or below—the operating core—for their own units, so the organization takes on a divisionalized form, in which each unit standardizes its own outputs. Finally, when support staff become more influential, the organization becomes more collaborative and requires mutual adjustment adopting a configuration described by Mintzberg as an adhocracy. Within the adhocracy groups may form and disband as tasks require. Typically these are highly organic (as opposed to mechanistic) structures that lend themselves to innovation, by bringing together professionals with complementary skills who coordinate their activities by mutual adjustment rather than through standardization.

Each configuration of principal component and dominant coordination mechanism is congruent with a particular environmental condition. Simple structures are often found in simple dynamic environments, while simple stable environments favour the machine bureaucracy. With an increasingly complex environment, professional bureaucracies are found in stable circumstances, while adhocracies are found in unstable circumstances. Where the units of a divisionalized form experience different environments they can operate autonomously and allow the organization to cope with different circumstances.

Effective organizations not only adopt configurations that are internally consistent and are congruent with their environmental circumstances, but also need to balance a series of five competing influences that impact on any organization (Mintzberg, 1991). Each of these influences is attractive to a particular component of an organization and will tend to favour a particular configuration. The five influences are direction, efficiency, proficiency, concentration and innovation. These appeal respectively to the strategic apex, the technostructure, the operating core, the middle line and the support staff, and therefore seem congruent with the simple structure, the machine bureaucracy, the professional bureaucracy, the divisionalized form and the adhocracy.

Perspective 2: An Institutional View

Of course the foregoing discussion does presume that the coordination and control of activity are the critical dimensions for organizational success. Meyer and Rowan (1977) challenge that view, by noting that the structural elements and the activities of an organization are often loosely coupled (Weick, 1976). Instead, Meyer and Rowan suggest that, because organizational structures arise in institutionalized contexts, "organizations are driven to incorporate the practices and procedures defined by prevailing rationalized concepts of organizational work and institutionalized in society" (p. 340). In other words, by conforming to the expectations that other actors (commonly the state or the professions) have of organizations and work, the legitimacy and so survival of an organization is increased irrespective of whether the organization performs its work efficiently. This suggests that an alternative, institutional, perspective on organizational structures merits consideration.

In describing the three "pillars" of institutions, Scott defined institutions as consisting "of cognitive, normative and regulative structures and activities that provide stability and meaning to social behaviour. Institutions are transported by various carriers—cultures, structures and routines—and they operate at multiple levels of jurisdiction" (Scott, 1995, p. 33). These institutional structures and their associated processes obtain an apparently inviolable rule-like quality (Zucker, 1987), which specify appropriate courses of action in particular circumstances. They are also deeply embedded in formal structures, and so lie beyond the discretion of specific individuals to change them. Consequently, they are not easily changed or challenged, and may be considered as the taken-for-granted assumptions underpinning the culture of an organization (e.g. Schein, 1996).

While aspects of each of the three elements of institutions may be present in a single organization, it is helpful for the purpose of understanding institutional forms in universities to examine the structures and processes of each element separately. For each of them has a different origin and may result in different outcomes. As one dominates the other two, so the structures and processes in an organization adopt a particular and distinctive yet stable pattern.

Accepting that, irrespective of structure or process, one of the defining properties of institutions is to constrain behaviour, the regulative pillar gives particular prominence to the rules, laws and sanctions, both formal and informal, that guide, monitor and reward different behaviours. Actors comply because, according to the calculus of rational choice, it is in their self-interest to conform. This emphasizes the dependent nature of one organization upon another, and suggests that one organization is able to bring formal and informal pressure to bear upon another to affect action. Clearly, conforming to legal requirements falls within this element. However, gaining access to resources by complying with the requirements of a sponsor is also a response to the coercive forces characteristic of this pillar e.g. DiMaggio and Powell, 1983). In England, one of the streams of funding for universities is on the basis of student numbers. Contract ranges are agreed between the university and the Higher Education Funding Council for England (HEFCE), and financial penalties are imposed on universities for over- or under-achieving the target.

Institutional stability may be achieved not by rules and monitoring, but through social beliefs and norms that are both internalized and imposed by others (Scott, 1995). This is the normative pillar. A normative system defines appropriate goals and legitimate ways of achieving them. These are generated according to values and norms that inform aspects of social life. Values describe what is desirable and provide a mechanism for evaluating actual performance, while norms specify how things should be done. Clearly, a normative system may constrain action, but it also empowers and enables, providing direction for appropriate action. Unlike the instrumental logic of the regulative pillar, a logic of appropriateness underpins the normative pillar. Actors conform by considering "what is expected of them in the circumstance". The normative pillar provides the basis for developing and defining roles, each with expected patterns of behaviour. In general academics may be expected to conform to the values and norms established for the particular discipline in which they specialize (Becher, 1989). In particular, the incumbents of the vice-chancellor or pro-vice-chancellor roles in a university will be expected to represent their institution externally and to demonstrate leadership (e.g. Smith *et al.*, 2007).

A third pillar is the cognitive system, which critically depends on actors interpreting the environment according to "rules that constitute the nature of reality and the frames through which meaning is made" (Scott, 1995, p. 40). Reality is socially constructed, so that meaning arises and is maintained through social interaction. The resulting symbolic systems and cultural rules affect behaviour by orientating and guiding actions according to taken-for-granted conventions. In many cases behaviour is mimetic; an actor copies the behaviour of another. According to DiMaggio and Powell (1983), this is particularly prevalent in those circumstances identified by Cohen *et al.* (1972) of goal ambiguity, environmental uncertainty, or when technologies are poorly understood. Actors attempt to behave conventionally in order to gain or retain legitimacy. As an example, a key aspect of the experience of doctoral education is the socialization of the individual student into the academic world (Delamont *et al.*, 2000), so that he/she becomes fluent in the use and interpretation of the symbols and artefacts associated with academic life generally, and his/her particular discipline specifically.

Two Models of Universities

Some of the principles from these two organizational perspectives may be useful in interpreting and explaining university structures found in different environmental settings. The two perspectives outlined emphasize respectively organizational efficiency and organizational legitimacy. The importance of either focus for organizational sustainability and success varies with different aspects of the environment in which the organization is situated. Some environments, for example markets, demand that efficiency is prioritized, while others, for example regulated environments, require legitimacy through conformity. Universities across the globe are found in a diversity of environmental contexts, where the demands for efficiency or for legitimacy vary to a greater or lesser extent, and both may vary independently from each other. In some countries, like the USA and UK, market conditions are more prominent, while in other countries, such as those in central Europe, the state plays a dominant role in the organization of the university, and universities are highly institutionalized.

Two models of university organization capture and differentiate some of this environmental variation. Each describes key features of universities found in different situations. Using these typologies it is possible to explore how universities in different circumstances are designed and coordinated to achieve efficiency, and what processes and practices are adopted to obtain legitimacy.

McNay (1995) categorized universities into four organizational types according to their position along two orthogonal dimensions. The first dimension described the definition of policy for the whole organization as being loose or tight. In other words, universities may operate more or less autonomously, and more or less independently of the expectations of the state for organizations in the higher education sector. The second dimension described the internal control over the activities of the university (or the implementation of any policy) as either loose or tight. At one end of the continuum, individuals or units (including departments) have freedom to pursue their own interests irrespective of the wishes of the central authorities within the university, while at the other extreme activities are tightly prescribed and monitored. This created a typology of universities with distinct labels (collegium, bureaucracy, corporation and enterprise) and characteristics.

A decade later, and seemingly without reference to McNay's work, Olsen (2005) provided an alternative model, again categorizing the organization of universities along two orthogonal dimensions, first whether university operations and dynamics are governed by internal or external factors, and second whether actors (both internal and external to the university) have shared or conflicting norms and objectives. This matrix provided four stylised visions of what a university is for and the circumstances under which it will best perform. These are:

- the university as a community of scholars;
- the university as an instrument for national political agendas;
- the university as a representative democracy; and finally
- the university as a service enterprise embedded in competitive markets.

The descriptive similarity in the labelling between the two models suggests that they may be congruent with each other. Both refer not only to a collegium or self-governing community of scholars, but also to a service enterprise embedded in a competitive market or, more succinctly, an enterprise university, where customers and professionals, with skills and the knowledge to meet clients' requirements, come together.

In McNay's model the policy definition dimension may indicate the extent to which external factors (e.g. state intervention) influence or control the activity within a university. This has similarities with the dimension in Olsen's model where university operations and dynamics are governed either by internal or environmental factors. Environmental factors (i.e. those external to the university) are commensurate with tight policy control, where government (or other significant stakeholders) influence the actions of a university. This allows the collegium and the bureaucracy, which occur under loose policy definition in McNay's model, to be equated with the two visions in Olsen's model where university operations are governed by internal factors, namely the university as a self-governing community of scholars and the university as a representative democracy. Similarly, where policy definition is tight (the corporation and enterprise quadrants of McNay's model), external environmental factors may influence university operations and dynamics so that, according to Olsen, universities are instruments for national political agendas or service enterprises embedded in competitive markets.

In contrast to these similarities, control of implementation and the possession of shared or conflicting norms are not identical, although they may have the same outcomes. Where control of implementation is loose there may be little forced interaction between actors, such that it appears as though they share the same norms and objectives. Under loose control of implementation, actors that do not share the same norms and objectives need not interact, as there is no requirement for them to work together, and so expose their differences. In circumstances of loose control it may, therefore, be difficult to discover whether norms and objectives are shared between actors, or whether they conflict. Conversely, under tight control, actors are required to work together, and this may reveal circumstances not only where actors share norms and objectives, and so activity occurs, but also where they do not.

Nevertheless, it seems probable that the self-governing community of scholars equates with the collegium, and that the bureaucracy is similar to the representative democracy, because, in both of these, actors will have norms and objectives that are congruent. While there are obviously similarities between Olsen's description of a university as a service enterprise embedded in capital markets and McNay's enterprise university, it is perhaps less obvious that the university as corporation equates to Olsen's description of a university as an instrument for national political agendas. However, with an appropriate university governance structure which acts to ensure organizational support for, and conformity with, the political aspirations of the state, there may be congruence between the two models.

University Structures: How They Are Influenced by Design and Institutional Pressures

It seems reasonable to conclude that, within either model, each of the four quadrants is sufficiently dissimilar from the other three to be distinct, and to represent a particular model of university organization. Moreover, it seems likely that there is sufficient similarity between the two organizational models to permit a quadrant from one model to be aligned with one in the other. Each of these four organizational types has widely different organizational and institutional characteristics, and so may respond to the challenges of efficiency and legitimacy in different ways, which will now be explored.

Collegium

In the collegium, or self-governing community of scholars, the operating core of academics dominates the organization, leading to a professional bureaucracy, and coordination of activity is through the standardization of skills along disciplinary lines (Becher, 1989). Typically, the management style is consensual, drawing on the taken-for-granted assumptions that the main purpose of the university is to pursue knowledge, and that those suitably qualified should be free to pursue any lines of enquiry deemed appropriate. There is a "shared commitment to scholarship and learning, basic research and search for truth, irrespective of immediate utility and applicability, political convenience or economic benefit" (Olsen, 2005, p. 8). By adhering to the tenets of a particular discipline, each member of the academic community has a meaning system that can influence his/her behaviour. Allegiance is typically to the discipline and not to the institution. Cognitive structures therefore dominate the institutional forms in this type of university organization. Consequently, regulative structures in the institutional environment, for example the processes of the Quality Assurance Agency in the UK which regularize and systematize the delivery of teaching materials and feedback, and so give more authority to the technostructure in the configuration of organizational activities, creates tensions within this type of organizational structure.

Bureaucracy

The university as a bureaucracy emphasizes the importance of external regulatory bodies in determining the activities of the university. External monitoring of university performance, to ensure compliance with externally developed standards and the achievement of set targets, demands the creation of an internal mechanism that mirrors the external one in order to achieve the desired outcomes. For example, the Research Assessment Exercise in the UK (HEFCE, 2001), which evaluates and rewards universities according to their research performance, encourages individual universities, departments or units to set up their own monitoring processes. Characteristically, these mechanisms seek to control and monitor task performance (i.e. output) and standardize work processes. A trivial, but nonetheless impactful, example within the university is the use of standard templates for delivering lecture materials. So long as the teaching material is packaged demonstrably in the "correct" way, then learning will follow inevitably! Such practices call for a technostructure which will monitor and evaluate the performance of the operating core, as in the machine bureaucracy. Olsen (2005) argues that giving power to technical and administrative staff in a university, for example through the creation of such technostructures, is justified by their contribution to the performance of the university. Clearly, these are regulatory structures that coerce universities to conform to rules in return for rewards.

A structure that conforms to rules, either imposed by external stakeholders or developed internally, and standardization of work processes, may not be able to respond to circumstances that require flexibility and novelty. In particular, research and teaching that is transdisciplinary may create difficulties for the organization, because it may not conveniently fit into standard work processes. Similarly, activities that demand atypical activities, for example "mode 2" research (Gibbons *et al.*, 1994), which engages with practice and does not conform to conventional research practices, may require organizations to develop new organizational practices to monitor and evaluate work performance, but these will not sit easily in a bureaucracy.

Corporation

Both the university as corporation, and as an instrument for political agendas, suggests that external policy-makers have considerable influence over the organization and activities within the university. External political agendas affect funding sources, which in turn influence the behaviours within the university, with activity being monitored with a range of performance indicators. Scholarly purposes are subordinated to purposes dictated by political support and funding opportunity (Olsen, 2005). Appropriate organizational structures are suggested by external review, and normatively adopted. For example the evolution of the vice-chancellor as the appointed chief executive officer of the university, with considerable decision-making power, began in the UK with the Jarratt Report (Committee of Vice-Chancellors and Principals, 1985) and was further developed in the Dearing Report (National Committee of Inquiry into Higher Education, 1997), so that by the time of the Lambert Review (Lambert, 2003), the idea of a small appointed senior management team to lead UK universities was widely adopted in practice. Preoccupied with securing resources for their university, the senior management team is directive in their leadership style, expecting that members of the university will deliver required outputs efficiently and effectively. In many cases this generates a divisionalized organizational structure, where each division performs a core function, and is headed up by a member of the senior management team. A common example is the separation of teaching and research, most obviously illustrated by the creation of separate pro-vice-chancellor roles. These are augmented by other senior roles, such as the pro-vice-chancellor responsible for enterprise. Delivering the core functions in this way creates divisions, which encourage the appointment of managers to oversee activities according to operating plans. The organizational focus is on the delivery of outputs. The divisionalized university structure is born with the emergence of clearly defined roles. Both the incumbent and others have normative expectations of what the performance of the role requires.

Enterprise

The enterprise university, or the university as a service organization embedded in competitive markets, focuses on packaging research and teaching into products and services that can be purchased by consumers. Information and knowledge are sources of competitive advantage that can be combined in multiple ways to meet particular market needs. The ability to "mix and match" effectively requires individuals and units to work together. In many cases this gives a more prominent role to support staff who can mediate these interactions. Moreover, the formal hierarchy of a university breaks down, as teams combine and re-combine to pursue specific opportunities. This structure resembles the adhocracy in which there is mutual adjustment to coordinate and control the activities of participating individuals. As the fiscal position of universities in many countries has deteriorated, so universities have increasingly adopted an entrepreneurial stance in order to generate additional income and create some autonomy from governmental control (Clark, 1998). This orientation has been actively encouraged by governments, especially in Europe (e.g. Department for Education and Skills, 2003), so that universities are socially obliged to commoditize their activities for sale to individuals and organizations in both the private and public sectors. This creates a normative expectation upon universities to fulfil this function, and routines develop within the university to support this. Many universities, particularly in the UK, have developed specialist business development offices that facilitate knowledge transfer—a relatively recent discourse in the activity of universities—and links to industry (HEFCE, 2003). However, as normative expectations increase, and entrepreneurial behaviour is seen as an acceptable and appropriate practice for academics, so individuals and institutions copy the practice of others, especially if the practices are novel and the circumstances ambiguous. Consequently, the enterprise university draws on both cognitive and normative patterns to inform its practices. However, the demands for interdisciplinarity and opportunism that underpin the activity of an enterprise university challenge the collegial and disciplinary focus of most departments.

Table 25.1 summarizes key elements of each of the four university types from both an organizational design and an institutional perspective. In each case legitimacy is sought in different ways, reflecting the relative power of, and prominence given to, external stakeholders. Where these are important, regulative structures appear. In circumstances where external stakeholders have less

Table 25.1 Key Elements of Four University Types from an Organizational Design and Institutional Theory Perspective

University Type	Key Part of the Organization	Coordination of Activity	Configuration of the Organizational Form	Influences on Organizational Form	Prominent Institutional Pillar	Characteristic of Environment
collegium	operating core	standardized skills	professional bureaucracy	proficiency	cognitive	stable, complex
bureaucracy	technostructure	work processes	machine bureaucracy	efficiency	regulative	stable, simple
corporation	strategic apex	direct supervision and outputs	divisional forms	concentration	normative	pockets of stability in complex environment
enterprise	support staff	mutual adjustment	adhocracy	innovation	cognitive/ normative	dynamic, complex

power, or are internal to the university, the legitimacy is achieved through normative or mimetic mechanisms. Efficiency is clearly a priority of the whole university, where it is characterized as a bureaucracy. Equally it may drive the activity of divisions within a university, as a corporation, or the parts within the university, as an enterprise, but it may not be a driver for the integrated activity of the whole university in these two cases. Each part may be efficient, but as each pursues different goals so the whole may become less efficient. Considerations of efficiency have little or no place in the university as collegium.

How Might Environmental Challenges Affect Institutional Structures?

None of the four types of university exist in a pure form, rather a university comprises a mix of some or all of these elements. Obviously, this creates a tension within the institution as it strives to organize to meet the, perhaps conflicting, demands of multiple stakeholders. These tensions may be heightened by changes in the environment which challenge the status quo, so that the structures that had developed in one circumstance are no longer appropriate and must change as a consequence of wider political or market forces. Three discourses that surround universities in the UK, and which appeal respectively to one of the three institutional perspectives, and which better fit one of the particular approaches to organizational design, will be examined. In each case, how the institutional and organizational perspectives might respond to these discourses will be discussed briefly.

Research Assessment

Academics in UK universities have undergone a number of periodic peer-review assessments of research quality over the last two decades. The significance of these assessments has been to influence the level of funding available for research from funding councils to universities in the UK. Generally, the higher the quality grading the greater the level of financial support, although in more recent assessments several of the lower grades received no financial support for research. Support for research has been concentrated increasingly, therefore, on those departments and universities that have the highest quality grades. Within the UK higher education sector this has created a labour market for academics with demonstrable capability in research, as institutions seek to enhance their organizational performance and so garner greater financial resources.

From an institutional perspective the state has imposed a process of assessment and evaluation on universities, with the sanction of loss of funding for poor performance. The rules of the assessment process have been made clear, and this can easily inform institutional-level decision making. Those choices that enhance research performance are supported, while those that do not are contested or rejected. Organizational units in this context behave instrumentally, coerced into compliance by an imposed regulative framework, and incentivized to do so by the prospect of financial reward. Nevertheless, such regulative structures conflict with the cognitive structures typically found in a university where the values of academic freedom dominate. Often individual academics struggle intellectually, although perhaps not practically, to comply with the externally imposed requirements to produce sufficient research output that exceeds a particular perceived quality. However, for staff who have not known an alternative work environment, there may be a normative acceptance that producing enough research output of sufficient quality to be acceptable by an RAE review panel is an appropriate goal. The organization gains legitimacy as a university by complying with the explicit rules of the RAE: nevertheless, the legitimacy of this activity may, or may not, be contested within each institution by the academic staff.

In an organizational form—a professional bureaucracy—where the operating core dominates and the imposed requirements conflict with the expected behaviour, then tensions are inevitable and inefficiencies probable. However, if the university is conceptualized as a corporation, led by a small but powerful senior management team, the existence of a regulative framework, imposed by a dominant stakeholder with clear financial rewards, makes decision making more straightforward, and subsequent activities more focused and efficient. In this organizational form there is a tendency to create divisional structures based on particular activities and outputs, thereby enhancing efficiency; for example the position of pro-vice-chancellor (research) and a research services division, which might support the pursuit of funding for research. Moreover, the strategic apex (or senior management team) may draw on the expertise of the technostructure to monitor research performance of individuals and departments within the university, and so tend towards the conceptualization of a university as a bureaucracy. Reports of research metrics are requested and produced at different levels of detail, and work processes are monitored. These take on a significance that exceeds their impact on actual research-related activities. Clearly, this uses additional resource, and can create inefficiencies overall, within the university. Nevertheless, the existence of these monitoring structures may legitimate both the activity—research assessment—and the university, for behaving as universities might be expected to in these circumstances.

Knowledge Economy

Following the Lisbon declaration, governments in Europe increasingly have sought ways to exploit the scientific knowledge base more effectively in the pursuit of enhanced economic performance. Universities are perceived to be an important stakeholder in meeting this challenge, being involved in the production of new knowledge through research, in the transmission of knowledge through education and training, and in its dissemination through information and communication technologies (Commission of the European Communities, 2003). This is evident in the UK, where both science and higher education policies focus on universities conducting more immediately applicable research (Department for Education and Skills, 2003; HM Treasury et al. 2004), and engaging more effectively with industry so that knowledge can be exploited for national economic wealth creation.

Harnessing universities closely to wealth creation, as these policies do, creates a new normative expectation. It is seen to be increasingly appropriate for the activities of universities in the UK to be evaluated according to criteria of relevance to end-users and impact (House of Commons Science and Technology Committee, 2006; Sainsbury Review, 2007). This utilitarian view of academic output conflicts with a prior normative view of knowledge for its own sake (e.g. Delanty, 2001), and may create tensions within the academic community, where the disciplinary values which prioritize the academic pursuit of knowledge may be strongly adhered to. A change within a single institutional perspective (in this case the normative one) may be as disruptive and challenging as a change from one perspective to another, for example from the cognitive to the regulative, as in the previous exemplar caused by research assessment.

While the operating core of the university, which plays a dominant role in the university as collegium, may not accept the objective to marry academic activities to economic impact, the senior management team (strategic apex, emphasized in the university as corporation) may do so with greater enthusiasm, in order to preserve the legitimacy of the university. Consequently, activities are developed and structures emerge that demonstrate that the particular university is actively supporting this normative expectation. For example, knowledge transfer offices represent conformity to this normative expectation. Roles are also created for the technostructure and the support staff. UK government funding (e.g. Higher Education Innovation Fund) encourages engagement with industry, but this requires a change in work processes and outputs, which are features of the university as corporation or bureaucracy but not collegium. Such changes to standard activities require adjustment, and so the involvement of other members of the university staff, including those in the technostructure, to design new models of working and monitor outputs, and through the support staff to access resources and prepare outputs in different formats. Within this discourse academics are encouraged increasingly to tailor their outputs to meet the needs of the end-users, often believed to be small and medium-sized enterprises (Sainsbury Review, 2007). This requires individuals with diverse skills to interact in smaller teams to meet particular objectives. This is characteristic of an organization designed as an adhocracy, and resembles the enterprise university, which packages outputs appropriately to meet the needs of different stakeholders.

Meyer and Rowan (1977) observed that organizational structures that offered legitimacy may not increase efficiency. So it is in this case, none of these university structures may be particularly efficient in making contributions that meet industry needs, yet each may serve to legitimize the university as contributing to the creation and development of a "knowledge economy".

Third-stream Funding

Universities have been increasingly resource-constrained (Shattock, 1995; Marginson and Considine, 2000). While absolute levels of funding from central government may have increased, funding per student has fallen. In order to bridge this funding deficit, universities are encouraged to pursue alternative sources of funding, commonly known as "third stream" funding (e.g. Shattock 2003). Most often this involves the university exploiting its physical or technical assets (Warner and Leonard, 1997). Less often, but perhaps more significantly, does it involve the commercialization of the skills and expertise of its academic staff.

There is evidence (e.g. Pilbeam, 2006) that expertise in generating "third stream" funding is neither discipline- nor university-specific. Different disciplines in different universities display significant variation in their ability to attract "third stream" funding. Some groups or departments in some universities generate considerable sums of money, while the same disciplines in other universities do not. Competence seems to reside in particular teams, and is not shared even within the same university. These relatively small units, with a customer orientation that draws together individuals and groups with complementary skills, typify an adhocracy and are characteristic of the enterprise university. This particular organizational format runs counter to the university conceptualized either as a bureaucracy or as a corporation, because the activities are transient and localized. As a consequence systems to monitor activity cannot easily be developed centrally, moreover the structures to organize this activity cannot be easily centralized—as in the bureaucracy. Similarly, the responsiveness required of teams in an enterprise university is not easily found within a corporation, where decisions are made by a small senior management team. Clearly, the university conceptualized as a bureaucracy, or as a corporation, may not be an effective design for generating "third stream" funding. Nevertheless, within the higher education sector in the UK there is an increasing understanding, especially amongst senior figures in the university, that the pursuit of third-stream funding is desirable, and should be encouraged, so that it is becoming an accepted part of academic practice in most UK universities. What is less clear is how this is best put into practice, particularly in relation to commercializing academic expertise, which may have uncertain outcomes. The result is that individual academics and universities copy one another, in order to legitimize their activities in this "new" domain of academic life.

Each of these three examples illustrates a different causal argument that links organizational structures to the institutional setting (Scott, 1995). In the case of research assessment, structures were imposed. UK universities needed to conform in order to secure funding for research. This is not so for the knowledge economy. Universities are not obliged to incorporate the fulfilment of this objective into their missions, but have voluntarily chosen to do so, in order to gain approval from the funding agencies and the state. By contrast, the financial inducements obtained from "third stream" funding encourage universities to recognize the financially constrained reality in which they exist, and to adapt their organizational structures to fit a revised institutional setting, which permits commercial exploitation of knowledge and skills. The examples also illustrate, respectively, regulative, normative and cognitive structures that orient the organization of universities and influence the forms that they may take.

Conclusions

Neither McNay nor Olsen assume that the university is a pure form of one (or another) of their proposed types, but rather is a mixture of several, if not all, of these types, reflecting a variety of responses to diverse environmental pressures. In common with the developing managerial agenda in public sector organizations (e.g. Deem *et al.* 2001), questions of effectiveness and efficiency are increasingly prominent in UK universities, which demand a technical response in terms of organizational structures. Consequently, universities, although still positioned in a strongly institutional environment, are also found in a strengthening technical environment too. Increasing emphasis is being placed on performance and impact as the exemplars show. In order to accommodate these changes, the design of universities is shifting away from the collegium model, where the operating core dominates and coordination is achieved by standardization of skills/inputs, towards a bureaucracy or corporation, where work is coordinated and controlled, respectively, by standardizing work processes through a technostructure, or through a small management team (the strategic apex). This shift gives greater prominence to centralized monitoring and evaluation structures, with direction from a small senior management team, often along functional lines. There have also been parallel changes in the institutional environment so that normative and regulative structures, rather than cognitive ones, underpin many of the recently developed activities now embraced by universities as part of their core business.

Changes in structure to meet the demands of an increasingly technical environment are nevertheless tempered by the strongly institutionalized setting of the higher education sector. So, while increasing emphasis is placed on becoming efficient and effective, universities need to also recognise that responding only to these demands militates against fulfilling the needs, or expectations, of the institutional environment. Meyer and Rowan persuasively argue that, by promoting efficiency, organizations may sacrifice the legitimacy and support that is derived from conformity to the institutional environment, or more tersely, "conformity to institutionalized rules often conflicts sharply with efficiency criteria" (1977, p. 340). Universities are set within a highly institutionalized environment, and many of their resources come from, or are controlled by, stakeholders in this environment, primarily the state. In order to remain legitimate within this environment, universities must continue to appear and behave like universities. Structurally, this may be achieved by decoupling the technical activities of the university from its formal structures. By ensuring that the interface with the key institutional stakeholders is maintained, the activities within the university can diversify to meet a widening range of technical demands. The technostructure and strategic apex play a significant role here in protecting the activities of the operating core, which is the engine of all universities.

Universities have a long history, and an enduring identity that is widely recognized, having been fashioned in response to a stable institutionalized environment. These university structures are, however, changing as the environment, where the pursuit of legitimacy was paramount, accommodates the forces of efficiency and effectiveness. The future challenge for universities lies in developing coherent structures at an institutional level that retain legitimacy with key stakeholders, while simultaneously demonstrating efficiency in their activity. Creating structures at an organizational level that achieve such a balance in a stable environment is not easy, either legitimacy or efficiency is prioritized, but this is even more problematic in a turbulent environment where conflicting policy drivers may appeal more strongly to either institutional or efficiency perspectives. Consequently, structures may become incoherent and incompatible, and perhaps ultimately fragment into smaller autonomous units that serve one or other of these agendas. The foregoing exemplars imply a tendency towards this. Evidently, universities are a crucible in which efficiency meets legitimacy. Unfortunately, although the reaction has begun, it has not yet finished and so, aided by the tools of organizational design and institutional theory, this chapter has explored some of the possible reactions and suggested some of the products or institutional structures that may result.

References

Becher, T. (1989) *Academic tribes and territories: intellectual enquiry and the cultures of disciplines*. Milton Keynes: Open University Press.
Clark, B.R. (1998) *Creating entrepreneurial universities: organizational pathways of transformation*. Oxford: Pergamon.
Cohen, M.D., March, J.G. and Olsen, J.P. (1972) A garbage can model of organizational choice. *Administrative Science Quarterly 17*, 1–25.
Commission of the European Communities (2003) *The role of the universities in the Europe of Knowledge*. 58 Final. Luxembourg: European Commission.
Committee of Vice-Chancellors and Principals (1985) *Steering committee for efficiency studies in universities*. London: CVCP.
Deem, R., Fulton, O., Hillyard, S., Johnson, R.N., Reed, M. and Watson, S. (2001) *New managerialism and the management of UK universities*. Swindon: Economic and Social Research Council.
Delamont, S., Atkinson, P. and Parry, O. (2000) *The doctoral experience: success and failure in graduate school*. London: Falmer Press.
Delanty, G. (2001) The university in the knowledge society. *Organization 8*, 149–153.
Department for Education and Skills (2003) *The future of higher education*. London: HMSO.
DiMaggio, P.J. and Powell, W.W. (1983) The Iron Cage revisited: Institutional isomorphism and collective rationality in organizational fields. *American Sociological Review 48*, 147–160.
Gibbons, M., Limoges, C., Nowotny, H., Schwartzman, S., Scott, P. and Trow, M. (1994) *The new production of knowledge: the dynamics of science and research in contemporary societies*. London: Sage.
Higher Education Funding Council for England (2001) *2001 Research Assessment Exercise: The Outcome*. Bristol: HEFCE.
Higher Education Funding Council for England (2003) *Higher Education-Business Interaction Survey 2000–2001*. Bristol: HEFCE
HM Treasury, Department for Trade and Industry and Department for Education and Skills (2004) *Science & Innovation Investment Framework 2004–2014*. London: HM Treasury.

House of Commons Science and Technology Committee (2006) *Research Council Support for Knowledge Transfer: Government Response to the Committee's Third Report of Session 2005–06.* London: House of Commons.

Lambert, R. (2003) *Lambert Review of Business–University Collaboration.* Norwich: HMSO.

Marginson, S. and Considine, M. (2000) *The Enterprise University: Power, Governance and Reinvention in Australia.* Cambridge: Cambridge University Press.

McNay, I. (1995) From the collegial academy to corporate enterprise: the changing cultures of universities. In: T. Schuller (ed.) *The Changing University?*, pp. 105–115. Buckingham: Open University Press.

Meyer, J.W. and Rowan, B. (1977) Institutionalized organizations: formal structure as myth and ceremony. *American Journal of Sociology 83*(2): 340–363.

Mintzberg, H. (1979) *The structuring of organizations: a synthesis of the research.* Englewood Cliffs, N.J.: Prentice-Hall.

Mintzberg, H. (1983) *Structure in Fives: Designing Effective Organizations.* New Jersey, USA: Prentice-Hall International Editions.

Mintzberg, H. (1991) The effective organization: forces and forms. *Sloan Management Review 32*(2):54–67.

National Committee of Inquiry into Higher Education (1997) *Higher Education in the Learning Society.* London: HMSO.

Olsen, J.P. (2005) *The institutional dynamics of the (European) University.* University of Oslo: Centre for European Studies.

Pilbeam, C.J. (2006) Generating additional revenue streams in UK universities: an analysis of variation between disciplines and institutions. *Journal of Higher Education Policy and Management 28*, 335–349.

Sainsbury Review (2007) *The Race to the Top: A review of Government's Science and Innovation Policies.* Norwich: HMSO.

Schein, E.H. (1996) Culture: the missing concept in organization studies. *Administrative Science Quarterly 41*, 229–240.

Scott, W.R. (1995) *Institutions and Organizations.* Thousand Oaks: Sage.

Scott, W.R. and Meyer, J.W. (1991) The organization of societal sectors: propositions and early evidence. In: W.W. Powell and P.J. DiMaggio (eds) *The New Institutionalism in Organizational Analysis*, pp. 108–140. Chicago: The University of Chicago Press.

Shattock, M. (1995) The university of the future. *Higher Education Management 7*, 157–164.

Shattock, M. (2003) *Managing Successful Universities.* Maidenhead: Open University Press.

Smith, D., Adams, J. and Mount, D. (2007) *UK Universities and Executive Officers: the changing role of Pro-Vice-Chancellors.* London: Leadership Foundation for Higher Education.

Warner, D. and Leonard, C. (1997) *The income generation handbook. A practical guide for educational institutions.* 2nd edn. Buckingham: Open University Press.

Weick, K.E. (1976) Educational organizations as loosely coupled systems. *Administrative Science Quarterly 21*, 1–19.

Zucker, L.G. (1987) Institutional theories of organization. *Annual Review of Sociology 13*, 443–464.

26

The Shaping of the Departmental Culture

Measuring the Relative Influences of the Institution and Discipline[1]

Jenny J. Lee

Despite its fundamental role in the structure and function of higher education, departmental culture has received little attention from higher education scholars and virtually no research has been done on how departmental culture is shaped by the larger disciplinary and institutional cultures. This study demonstrates the extent to which different aspects of departmental culture can be attributed to the influence of institutional and disciplinary cultures.

Introduction

The academic department is a fundamental component in American higher education. Over the past century, academic disciplines have become increasingly specialised, and thus scholars describe the academic department as, "the basic organizational element" (Austin, 1990, p. 63), the "basic operating unit [of the organization]" (Clark, 1987a, p. 259), and "the central building block—the molecule—of the American university" (Trow, 1977, p. 12). The possible reasons are many. The academic department is notably the "home" where the academic in an institution lives (Harrington, 1977, p. 54); it signifies a local grouping for the varied academic disciplines in the academy. While departments make up the institution, they also run independently, as they function to coordinate and manage the academic process (Tucker, 1984). Departments are allocated (and, in many cases, generate) their own power and resources; they contain their distinct curricula, financial budgets, and administrative leadership. Moreover, academic departments are powerful and significant structures of influence. Virtually all colleges and universities rely on individual departments to change course offerings and content, appoint and promote teaching and administrative staff, and manage services needed by both professors and students on behalf of the larger institution (Andersen, 1977; McHenry, 1977; Trow, 1977; Edwards, 1999). Therefore the academic department is a critical unit of analysis in higher education.

These units, however, are highly idiosyncratic and complex. Within a single institution as many as 50 or more separate departments coexist. Departmental structure (i.e. organisation, policies, standards, etc.) varies from one unit to another. In a typical research university, for example, the department of chemistry allocates a substantial portion of its resources to laboratory research, whereas the department of fine arts concentrates on creative performance and production. Both the chemistry and fine arts professors depend on favourable peer reviews for promotion and tenure, but they must fulfil very distinct sets of criteria. Such departmental differences are not limited only to academic roles and rewards, but extend also to teacher–student interactions, instruction and evaluation methods, curricular requirements, and more.

These observable structural variations represent an expression of multiple values from various influences. In other words, the external rules and procedures of a given department reflect internal ideas, values and goals about its role in the institution and in larger society. These departmental differences are attributable to the relative influences both of the *institution* and of the *discipline* to which the department belongs (Light, 1974; Trow, 1977; Clark, 1984; Clark, 1987a; Ruscio, 1987b; Edwards, 1999). For this reason, the academic department is often referred to as the intersection between the larger discipline and the local institution (Clark, 1987a). Understanding the extent to which these two major forces shape the academic department is the goal of this study.

Organisational Culture as an Appropriate Lens

The academic department can be understood best as an *organisational culture*. Anthropologists originally conceived of culture as distinct, self-contained societies with unique practices and beliefs that distinguished one group from another. Sociologists more fully developed the notion of sub-cultures, or a culture within a culture (Arnold, 1970; Peterson, 1979; Becker, 1982). For the past three decades, higher education scholars have increasingly applied such notions to the educational field, considering culture as a fundamental attribute of a given organisation (Chafee and Tierney, 1988; Kuh and Whitt, 1988) because the concept of culture helps to explain organisational behaviours and policies. Thus, each academic department certainly can be characterised by its distinctive practices and beliefs.

The academic department also can be understood as an organisational *subculture* because it exists in the intersection of two broader cultures: of the institution and of the discipline. Whereas the institutional culture and disciplinary culture have been studied by higher education scholars (Ladd and Lipsett, 1975; Clark, 1980, 1987a, 1987b; Becher, 1987; Smart *et al.*, 2000), the departmental culture has been less researched (McHenry, 1977). As Walvoord and her colleagues (2000) suggest, the academic department is "a flexible [conveyor] belt, not the rigid cog that translates intellectual knowledge into multiple kinds of service to multiple constituencies" (p. 25). In a sense, the academic department represents the cultural union between the marriage of the institution and the discipline.

Since the academic department simultaneously belongs to an institution and an academic discipline, the external forces from these larger organisational cultures influence their shared subculture, the academic department. Furthermore, these forces are not necessarily equal, depending on the relative status of the discipline and the institution, each with its own culture (Ruscio, 1987a). Perhaps as a consequence of these complex interconnections between the larger cultures and sub-culture, the relative influence of the institutional culture and the disciplinary culture on the departmental culture has been left uninvestigated.

Departments as Organisational Cultures

Although the problems surrounding academic departments are readily identifiable, how the problems are to be understood and addressed are less clear. Austin (1990) warns that conflicts occur when the traditional values of the disciplinary culture differ from those of the local institutional culture, leading to problems in areas such as career development, professorial productivity, the reward system, and institutional morale. As such, perhaps the best way to begin untangling the complexities of the modern academic department is by examining its values (Kennedy, 1997;

Walvoord *et al.*, 2000), or what I and others refer to as "culture" (Peterson *et al.*, 1986; Wilber, 1998; Astin and Lee, forthcoming). This study formally defines culture as: *the persistent patterns of shared values, beliefs and assumptions among individuals within a group.* More than attending to the external manifestations of group ideals, this study rests on the notion that internal beliefs serve as the basis of outward behaviours (Schein, 1992). The following three principles further guide this cultural analysis of academic departments in the broader study of organisational culture.

First, the study of organisational culture involves more than policies, practices and behaviour, as has already been well demonstrated in previous research (Hofstede, 1991; Smart, and Hamm, 1993; Smart *et al.*, 1997). While academic workload, productivity and organisational effectiveness are essential concerns, reformers need to look beyond managerial studies towards the shared values and beliefs that drive college academic behaviour. In other words, a failure to understand the broad scope of organisational culture (beyond issues of workload and effectiveness) severely hinders one's ability to address the range of challenges facing higher education (Chafee and Tierney, 1988).

Second, fundamental reform in academic policies is also problematical without first widening the focus from individual professors to their departmental cultures (Wergin, 1993). To study college professors as a single group is misleading as many researchers agree that the so-called independent and isolated scholar is a false notion (Light, 1974; Becher, 1987; Metzker, 1987).

Third and most important, a department's academic staff is not as an isolated organisational culture, but part of the larger academic cultures defined by both the institution and the discipline (Clark, 1980). And while a single college's (or discipline's) culture can be viewed as unique and distinctive, it is also composed of multiple subcultures (Trice and Beyer, 1993). Academics should thus be viewed as interconnected groups or members of multiple organisations and cultures. Quite often, these cultures within a culture (sometimes referred to as subcultures) can hold opposing ideologies and values, as in the case of different departments within an institution (or within a discipline).

Therefore, the academic department is best understood as an organisational culture, defined by a unique set of values, beliefs and assumptions, which is a part of other larger cultures. Even with the best intentions towards departmental (and organisational) reform, an examination of departmental culture should not be solely limited to its performance and effectiveness. Rather, a more encompassing view allows one to observe the less obvious hindrances to reform that can be gained through a fuller understanding of departmental culture. In so doing, one should examine multiple dimensions of departmental culture as parts of other wholes. In other words, scholars would benefit by viewing academic values in a given department not merely as characteristic of that department but also as potentially a reflection of the values of the larger discipline and institution of which that department is part.

Conceptual Framework

Given these guiding principles, Clark's (1984) conception of departmental culture appears to be most appropriate. He explains that academics are members of the academic profession at large, the national system, the college, and the discipline. The two latter arenas are most critical:

Academics are caught up in various matrices, with multiple memberships that shape their work, call upon their loyalties and apportion their authority. Central among the matrices is the most common fact of academic work: the academic belongs simultaneously to a discipline, a field of study, and an enterprise, a specific university or college. These primary modes of organisation crisscross each other . . . crossing of these two lines of membership provides the master matrix of the higher education system (Clark, 1984, p. 112).

Clark then goes on to state, "the discipline and the enterprise converge . . . in the operating units of universities and colleges, a department . . . is simultaneously an arm of a discipline and a part of an enterprise" (p. 115). Analysts concur that the two main branches of the academic department are the institution and the discipline, using such metaphors as "the central link between the university and discipline" (Trow, 1977, p. 13) and the "organizational nexus where institution and discipline meet" (Light, 1974, p. 20). Both branches are essential, as the department serves as the disciplinary representatives as well as the administrative leads of the institution.

A Venn diagram showing the relation between the institutional culture and the disciplinary culture and their intersection, the departmental culture, is shown in Figure 26.1. Here, the institutional culture intersects with the disciplinary culture, forming the departmental culture. Although the institutional and disciplinary cultures are represented as relatively similar in influence (i.e. the same size), the relative effects of the institutional culture and disciplinary culture may vary. For instance, should the institution exert a more powerful cultural force on the department than the discipline, the institutional culture would be depicted as much larger than the disciplinary culture. In this case, the professors in such a department would show greater affinity with the local institution, commonly referred to as "locals", unlike those "cosmopolitans" who would identify themselves more with the discipline (Gouldner, 1957; Merton, 1957). Locals and cosmopolitans are not necessarily found in equal numbers within similar types of institutions or disciplines, however. Rather, "a subtle, intricate interaction with many nuances occurs as we move through the various disciplines and across the many institutions, each with its own culture" (Ruscio, 1987a, p. 329).

Indeed, past research has identified various combinations of locals and cosmopolitans, depending on the cultural dimension in question (i.e. reactions to students and staff, perceptions of one's institution, and participation in governance (Lammers, 1974)). Differences in relative effects of the institutional culture and the disciplinary culture also come into play in determining what constitutes "prestige". For the local institution, prestige appears to be mostly based on assigned rankings for the administrative members within the institution. In the larger discipline, prestige tends to be determined by the quality and level of one's scholarship to a given field. The varying interpretations of what is "prestigious" come into conflict when considering who has

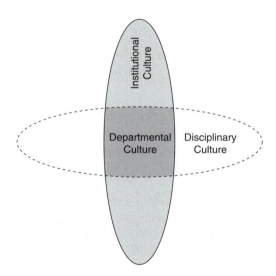

Figure 26.1 Adaptation of Clark's Conception of the Academic Department.

the higher rank. Is it the dean of student affairs or the highly published assistant professor? Such conflict can weaken administrative authority and the ability to carry out institutional change (Birnbaum, 1988).

In sum, any effort to get departments to share more responsibility in institutional change would be facilitated by a better understanding of how the different institutional cultures have helped to shape each department's culture. Among other things, the relative power of these two forces helps to differentiate locals from cosmopolitans. And while researchers commonly agree that the institution and discipline define the academic department, the degree to which these forces shape the culture of any given department is at present unknown. Therefore, my major research questions are: to what extent is departmental culture shaped by the culture of the larger institution? To what extent is the departmental culture shaped by the discipline? To what extent is it a combination of both disciplinary and institutional culture? My sub-questions are as follows: which aspects of departmental culture are more dependent on institutional culture? Which aspects of departmental culture are more dependent on disciplinary culture?

Data Source

The primary data source for this study was generated from a national survey of over 55,000 academic staff collected as part of the Cooperative Institutional Research Program (CIRP), which is sponsored by the American Council on Education and the Higher Education Research Institute (HERI) at the University of California, Los Angeles. The academic staff data were collected using the 1998 Faculty Survey (Sax *et al.*, 1999). The survey instrument includes demographic and bio-graphical information, and is especially focused on academic procedures and practices, professional priorities, opinions and perceptions of the institution, and satisfaction. Appendix 26.1 presents the distribution of institutions and academic staff by institutional type.

Ninety-six survey items were identified reflecting the assumptions, values and beliefs of college professors regarding their work, their institution and their profession. Each of these items was assessed to reflect the values, beliefs and perceptions of individual professors. By aggregating professors" responses to these items within a given department, institution or discipline, it is possible to obtain an estimate of the professorial "culture", by which I mean their *shared* values, beliefs, perceptions and assumptions (Lee, 2004).

In order to obtain measures on each of the 96 items that would reflect the culture of a given department, restrictions were made in determining the minimum number of individuals that would be required to constitute a "culture" (Lee, 2004). One could argue that as long as there are at least two or more individuals, there is a culture. Indeed, in some small colleges an entire department might consist of two or three persons. However, one can also argue that the greater number of people used to define a single culture, the more reliable the cultural measures. In keeping with these arguments, and following a series of methodological analyses to see how the reliability of the measures was affected by varying the minimum number of professors per department, departments with less than three survey respondents were eliminated from the data-file. The number of respondents per department was also examined across stratification cells, in order to maintain as much representation across institutional types as possible. In some cases, especially among the larger disciplines (e.g. business, English, psychology), departments with fewer than five respondents were also eliminated, leaving 4,202 departments and 34,847 professors in the entire sample with the number of respondents per department averaging slightly more than eight.

In order to identify composite variables reflecting various dimensions of academic culture, an exploratory principal components factor analysis with varimax rotation was conducted using the mean departmental scores on each of the 96 academic culture variables. Thus using the individual department as the unit of analysis, 13 dimensions of academic culture were identified. The resulting scales (obtained by a simple summing of the highest loading items), together with Cronbach alphas (in parentheses) were as follows: *Collegiality* (0.87), *Commitment to diversity* (0.88), *Commitment to scholarship and scholarly recognition* (0.82), *Commitment to students' affective development* (0.93), *Commitment to teaching* (0.71), *Dissatisfaction with collegiate culture* (0.63), *Governance stress* (0.72), *Instrumental orientation* (0.64), *Job satisfaction* (0.85), *Multicultural orientation* (0.71), *Prestige orientation* (0.82), *Student centredness* (0.86), and *Valuing professional autonomy* (0.66) (Lee, 2004).

Measures of "departmental culture" were obtained by computing mean scores for each department separately on each of the 13 academic culture variables. Measures of "disciplinary culture" consisted of 13 parallel mean scores based on responses of all professors within a given discipline (i.e. across institutions) with 47 different sets of scores (i.e. one set for each discipline). For the analyses to be conducted for the present study, these disciplinary means have been merged with their appropriate departmental means so that each of the 8,514 departments has 13 overall "disciplinary culture" scores as well as its own 13 departmental culture scores. Finally, measures of "institutional culture", which were obtained by computing means on the 13 academic culture variables separately for each of the 429 institutions (i.e. across disciplines) were also merged with the appropriate departmental data, so that each of the 8,514 departments has 39 cultural scores: 13 each for the department, 13 for its institution, and 13 for its discipline. In addition, variables representing institutional characteristics (i.e. type, size, selectivity, location, etc.) have been added to the data for each department. Next, the contribution of a given department's professors was removed from the disciplinary means used for *that* department in order to eliminate experimental dependence between each department's mean scores and the mean scores of its corresponding discipline (Lee, 2004). If left uncorrected, the data from both the discipline and the department would have been duplicated, thus artificially inflating the correlations between each institutional department's means and its corresponding disciplinary means.

Data Analyses

The data analyses involved a series of blocked, stepwise linear regression analyses to determine the extent to which the "departmental culture", as defined by the mean scores of the 13 cultural dimensions in an individual department, is shaped by the larger disciplinary culture as opposed to the overall institutional culture. This methodology allows one to observe the effects of each stepwise block of variables on the dependent variable, while simultaneously observing changes in the effects of the other blocks of variables (those already in the equation as well as the "potential" effects of those not yet entered). Changes in the beta coefficients for each variable can thus be compared on a step-by-step basis.

Variables

The unit of analysis in all regressions was the individual department, and the dependent variables were each of the 13 culture composite variables: *Collegiality, Commitment to diversity, Commitment to scholarship and scholarly recognition, Commitment to students' affective development, Commitment to teaching, Dissatisfaction with collegiate culture, Governance stress, Instrumental orientation, Job satisfaction, Multicultural orientation, Prestige orientation, Student centredness,* and *Valuing professional autonomy*. Given that there are 13 measures of departmental culture, 13 regressions were conducted to assess the effect of disciplinary culture on departmental culture. The first block of independent variables were the 13 disciplinary culture measures. The second block of independent variables were the 13 institutional culture measures. By placing institutional culture as a separate block, following disciplinary culture, one can note how much institutional culture adds to the effects of the disciplinary culture on departmental culture.

Since the first block of variables has a unique advantage as to the extent of its relative contribution to the dependent variable, the analyses were repeated inverting the order of the blocks just described (thus comprising 13 additional regression analyses). This reflects the amount of variance a given set of independent measures accounts for in the dependent variable, and the *increase* in R^2 reflects the amount of *additional* variance attributable to the next set of independent measures.

Findings

Consistent with Clark's (1984) conception, both the institution and the discipline shape the academic department. Across each of the regression analyses, the institutional mean beta and the disciplinary mean beta independently accounted for at least 0.14 (and up to 0.73) in predicting the departmental mean score. Findings further indicate that neither the discipline nor the institution uniformly accounts for a greater portion of departmental culture. Rather, the stronger influence of the discipline or the institution depends on the dimension of culture being examined.

Greater Institutional Effects

The institution accounts for much more of the departmental culture (than of the disciplinary culture) on *Prestige orientation, Student centredness, Dissatisfaction with collegiate culture, Commitment to diversity, Commitment to scholarship and scholarly recognition, Job satisfaction, Collegiality,* and *Governance stress.* According to Table 26.1, the institutional culture has a strong effect on the department's *Prestige orientation* and related *Scholarship and scholarly recognition,* whereas the disciplinary culture has very little effect. The largest difference among all the institutional and disciplinary culture comparisons occurs with *Prestige orientation* (β difference = 0.70). Moreover, the disciplinary influence substantially drops (from $\beta = 0.12$ to $\beta = 0.02$) after controlling for the institutional influence. While this heavy dependence on institutional culture may, in part, be an

Table 26.1 Comparing Institutional Culture and Disciplinary Culture Effects on Departmental Culture (in order of strongest difference in effects)

Cultural dimension	Mean cultural variable	Total R^2	β	β difference*
Prestige orientation	Institutional Disciplinary	0.53	0.72/0.02	+0.70
Student centredness	Institutional Disciplinary	0.66	0.78/0.18	+0.60
Dissatisfaction with collegiate culture	Institutional Disciplinary	0.63	0.75/0.22	+0.53
Commitment to diversity	Institutional Disciplinary	0.35	0.57/0.17	+0.40
Commitment to scholarship and recognition	Institutional Disciplinary	0.54	0.62/0.28	+0.34
Job satisfaction	Institutional Disciplinary	0.27	0.48/0.18	+0.30
Collegiality	Institutional Disciplinary	0.35	0.44/0.14	+0.30
Governance stress	Institutional Disciplinary	0.19	0.37/0.23	+0.14

*β difference = Institutional β—Disciplinary β.

Note: $N = 4{,}202$ departments.

artefact (in the sense that the professors are being asked about the institution's priorities), the same cannot be said of the cultural items that comprise *Scholarship and scholarly recognition*, which also showed a much stronger institutional (as opposed to disciplinary) effect (β difference = 0.34). The disciplinary effect on this factor also substantially drops (from $\beta = 0.42$ to $\beta = 0.28$) when the institutional effect is taken into account. Colleges and universities (unlike larger disciplines) are often distinguished by their degree of commitment to furthering scholarly knowledge through research (the most obvious contrast being the research university versus the small liberal arts college). As such, it is no surprise the institutional values of prestige and scholarship cut across the disciplines.

The institutional culture also strongly affects departmental perceptions of students ($\beta = 0.78$) and their collegiate culture ($\beta = 0.75$). Such findings indicate institutional views of students strongly pervade despite disciplinary differences, while disciplinary-specific views are far less influential. Indeed, one can readily identify entire institutions prioritising student development, whereas disciplines hardly possess a universal approach to students (with the possible exception of Education). Similarly, the value of research is also a strong institutional effect, as colleges and universities are often distinguished by commitment to furthering scholarly knowledge through research. Thus, the institutional value of having a strong national reputation also transpires across the disciplines.

The institution is also largely responsible for departmental job satisfaction ($\beta = 0.48$), collegiality ($\beta = 0.44$), and governance stress ($\beta = 0.37$). As one might expect, the institution determines teaching loads, committee work, and other professorial responsibilities, thus affecting departmental perceptions of professorial work and related governance duties. Departmental collegiality is also an institutional byproduct for which the disciplinary culture has less influence.

Perhaps among the more unexpected findings is the institutional influence of a department's commitment to diversity ($\beta = 0.57$). This finding indicates departmental perceptions of recruiting diverse teaching staff, administrators and students are not as affected by the discipline as by the institution. One may have anticipated, rather, that some disciplines would share a more critical view, and thus influencing the departmental culture, of creating a more multicultural environment. However, the much smaller disciplinary effect ($\beta = 0.17$) shows such disciplinary views are not as prominent as overall institutional views towards diversifying the local campus.

Greater Disciplinary Effects

Among the 14 regressions, two regressions indicated the far greater effect of disciplinary culture over institutional culture. The discipline was relatively more powerful in a department's *Instrumental orientation* and *Multicultural orientation*. According to Table 26.2, utilitarian views (i.e. increasing students' earning power, use of computers, preparing students for employment, etc.) of a given department are largely affected by its disciplinary affiliation ($\beta = 0.71$). One can ascertain disciplines that more likely embrace such views (i.e. business, computers, engineering) and other disciplines that do not (i.e. humanities). Moreover, one can also identify disciplines that are more homogeneous in regard to its multicultural orientation, explaining its strong disciplinary effect.

Table 26.2 Comparing Institutional Culture and Disciplinary Culture Effects on Departmental Culture (in order of strongest difference in effects)

Cultural dimension	Mean cultural variable	Total R^2	β	β difference*
Multicultural orientation	Institutional Disciplinary	0.51	0.37/0.58	−0.21
Instrumental orientation	Institutional Disciplinary	0.58	0.21/0.71	−0.50

*β difference = Institutional β—Disciplinary β.

Note: $N = 4,202$ departments.

This particular finding, nonetheless, appears at first contrary to an earlier finding showing the stronger effect of the institution on a department's diversity orientation. Given the different variables to comprise these cultural dimensions (Lee, 2004), however, views of institutional priorities in diversity are not necessarily synonymous with multicultural opinions. An orientation towards a diverse college population that solves social problems is thus conceivably a stronger disciplinary opinion than an institutional one.

Similar Effects

As shown in Table 26.3, both the institution and the discipline contribute relatively similarly in departmental cultures as they pertain to *Commitment to students' affective development*, *Commitment to teaching*, and *Valuing professional autonomy*. The latter two findings are rather surprising given the obvious institutional structures that determine academic autonomy and teaching responsibility (which would be indicated by a high institutional beta). Often, institutions dictate academic independence and teaching load regardless of the discipline to which the department belongs. However, in both cultural dimensions, the discipline carries a slightly higher effect. One possible explanation may be that some disciplines are markedly similar in their approach to teaching (i.e. education and humanities). Other disciplines may be similar in how they value autonomy, particularly the disciplines where work in the for-profit sector is a viable option (i.e. business, engineering and computer science). These within-field similarities may thus contribute to the higher than expected disciplinary beta weight. The relatively similar effects of both the institution and the discipline may also indicate that teaching commitments and valuing autonomy are universal (and perhaps fundamental) to the academic profession across all institutions and disciplinary fields.

The institutional culture is only slightly greater than the effect of disciplinary culture when it comes to the department's *Commitment to students' affective development* (β difference = 0.08). It is interesting to note that although departmental *Student centredness* and *Satisfaction with collegiate culture* are both determined mostly by the institutional culture, departmental *Commitment to students' affective development* as well as *Commitment to teaching* are jointly shaped by the institutional and disciplinary cultures. One may infer, thus, that while the institutional culture substantially influences all aspects of the department's views about students, the effect of the disciplinary culture is confined primarily to the department's commitment to teaching and priority given to students' affective development.

Conclusion

This study has attempted to unravel the conception of the academic department being situated in two larger cultures: the institutional culture and the disciplinary culture. While scholars have emphasised the powerful role of the discipline on college professors (Biglan, 1973a, 1973b; Becher,

Table 26.3 Comparing Institutional Culture and Disciplinary Culture Effects on Departmental Culture (in order of strongest difference in effects)

Cultural dimension	Mean cultural variable	Total R^2	β	β difference*
Commitment to students' affective development	Institutional Disciplinary	0.58	0.55/0.47	+0.08
Commitment to teaching	Institutional Disciplinary	0.30	0.36/0.38	−0.02
Valuing professional autonomy	Institutional Disciplinary	0.27	0.31/0.38	−0.07

*β difference = Institutional β—Disciplinary β.

Note: $N = 4,202$ departments.

1987; Austin, 1990), the study argues that, in many respects, the institution plays a more influential role. Thus, one must consider the aspect of culture being examined in order to determine the extent to which the two cultures shape the academic department. Particularly, as it relates to departmental perceptions of students, research, and professional workload and responsibilities, the institution determines a greater degree of such values. Disciplinary differences do exist but such differences form less of the departmental culture than do institutional differences. In regard to ideals of the institution, namely multiculturalism and instrumentalism, the views are more disciplinary related. In some cases, when observing departmental autonomy and teaching, both the institution and discipline share similar effects.

The findings of this study enlighten previous work in disciplinary and institutional differences. Austin and Gamson's (1983) review suggests that institutional size and complexity are strongly related to academic autonomy, which they define as "the ability of [professors] to set institutional goals and to structure the organisation to maximize professional concerns". While this study also finds that autonomy is related to the institution, it further reveals that autonomy is also almost equally related to disciplinary fields.

Braxton and Hargens's (1996) review proposes research orientations are readily discernable by "high-consensus fields" (i.e. chemistry, physics) and "low-consensus fields" (i.e. social sciences). The related finding of the current study—a commitment to research as largely a function of the institution than the discipline—demonstrates that although disciplinary differences in research subsist, the overall effects are actually more attributable to the institution. Clark's (1987a) research affirms that professors in research universities show more interest in research than do professors in other types of institutions (doctoral granting, comprehensive, liberal arts, and two-year colleges).

For policy implications, this study suggests that some cultural values are more susceptible to institutional change than others. Professors' perceptions of students and the collegiate culture are notably characteristic of the local institution. Though some disciplinary-related biases may affect the values of the department, the findings here show that institutions can successfully shape (or reshape) departmental opinions about students. Professors' commitment to creating a diverse college environment, commitment to research, and collegiality is also within the greater control of the immediate college or university. Other departmental values, namely orientation towards multi-culturalism and instrumentalism, ought to be a greater responsibility of the larger discipline.

Future studies should consider how these findings are specifically related to institutional factors (size, selectivity and institutional type), as well as how the degree of institutional influence differs from one disciplinary field to another. While the pervasiveness of disciplinary culture is evident within large research institutions (Ruscio, 1987a; Austin, 1990), whether the discipline maintains such a strong influence in community colleges, for example, has not been established. Given that this study assumed all such forms, the exact impact of particular institutional characteristics remains uninvestigated.

Note

1. Lee, J.J. (2007). The shaping of the departmental culture: measuring the relative influences of the institution and discipline. *Journal of Higher Education Policy and Management*, 29:1 41–55. Reprinted by permission of the publisher.

References

Andersen, K.J. (1977). In defense of departments. In D.E. McHenry (ed.) *Academic departments: Problems, variations, and alternatives.* San Francisco, CA: Jossey-Bass.

Arnold, D. (1970). A process model of subcultures. In D.O. Arnold (ed.) *The sociology of subcultures.* Berkeley, CA: Glendessary.

Astin, A.W. and Lee, J.J. (forthcoming). *A taxonomy of faculty cultures across the academic disciplines.*

Austin, A.E. (1990). Faculty cultures, faculty values. In W.G. Tierney (ed.) *Assessing academic climates and cultures* (New Directions for Institutional Research No. 68). San Francisco, CA: Jossey-Bass.

Austin, A.E. and Gamson, Z.F. (1983). *Academic workplace: New demands, heightened tensions* (ASHE-ERIC Higher Education Research Report No. 10). Washington, DC: Association for the Study of Higher Education.

Becher, T. (1987). Disciplinary shaping of the profession. In B.R. Clark (ed.), *The academic profession: National, disciplinary, and institutional settings.* Los Angeles, CA: University of California Press.

Becker, H.S. (1982). Culture: A sociological view. *Yale Review,* 71, 513–527.

Biglan, A. (1973a). The characteristics of subject matter in different academic areas. *Journal of Applied Psychology,* 57(3), 195–203.

Biglan, A. (1973b). Relationships between subject matter characteristics and the structure and output of university departments. *Journal of Applied Psychology,* 57(3), 204–213.

Birnbaum, R. (1988). *How colleges work: The cybernetics of academic organization and leadership.* San Francisco, CA: Jossey-Bass.

Braxton, J.M. and Hargens, L.L. (1996). Variation among academic disciplines: Analytic frameworks and research. In J.C. Smart (ed.) *Higher education: Handbook of theory and research,* Vol. 11 (pp. 1–46). New York: Agathon Press.

Chafee, E.E. and Tierney, W.G. (1988). *Collegiate culture and leadership strategies.* New York: Macmillan Press.

Clark, B.R. (1980). *Academic culture.* New Haven, CT: Yale University, Higher Education Research Group.

Clark, B.R. (1984). The organizational conception. In B.R. Clark (ed.) *Perspectives on higher education.* Los Angeles, CA: University of California Press.

Clark, B.R. (1987a). *The academic life: Small worlds, different worlds.* Princeton, NJ: The Carnegie Foundation for the Advancement of Teaching.

Clark, B.R. (ed.) (1987b). *The academic profession: National, disciplinary, and institutional settings.* Los Angeles, CA: University of California Press.

Edwards, R. (1999). The academic department: How does it fit into the university reform agenda? *Change,* 31(5), 17.

Gouldner, A.W. (1957). Cosmopolitans and locals: Toward an analysis of latent social roles. *Administrative Science Quarterly,* 2, December, 281–306.

Harrington, F.H. (1977). Shortcomings of conventional departments. In D.E. McHenry (ed.) *Academic departments: Problems, variations, and alternatives.* San Francisco, CA: Jossey-Bass.

Hofstede, G.L. (1991). Culture and organizations. *International Studies of Management and Organization,* 10, 15–41.

Kennedy, D. (1997). *Academic duty.* Cambridge, MA: Harvard University Press.

Kuh, G.D. and Whitt, E.J. (1988). *The invisible tapestry: Culture in American colleges and universities* (ASHE-ERIC Higher Education Report No. 1). Washington, DC: Association for the Study of Higher Education.

Ladd, E.C. and Lipsett, S.M. (1975). *The divided academy: Professors and politics* (New York: McGraw-Hill).

Lammers, C.J. (1974). Localism and cosmopolitanism, and faculty response. *Sociology of Education,* 47(1), 129–158.

Lee, J.J. (2004). Comparing institutional relationships with academic departments: A study of five academic fields. *Research in Higher Education,* 45(6), 603–624.

Light, D. (1974). Introduction: The structure of the academic professions. *Sociology of Education,* 47(1), 2–28.

McHenry, D.E. (ed.) (1977). *Academic departments: Problems, variations, and alternatives.* San Francisco, CA: Jossey-Bass.

Merton, R.K. (1957). *Social theory and social structure.* Glencoe, IL: The Free Press.

Metzker, R.P. (1987). Academic profession in the United States. In B.R. Clark (ed.) *The academic profession: National, disciplinary, and institutional settings.* Los Angeles, CA: University of California Press.

Peterson, M.W., Cameron, K.S., Mets, L.A., Jones, P. and Ettington, D. (1986). *The organizational context for teaching and learning: A review of the research literature* (ED 287 437). Ann Arbor, MI: National Center for Research to Improve Postsecondary Teaching and Learning.

Peterson, R.A. (1979). Revitalizing the culture concept. *Annual Review of Sociology,* 15, 137–166.

Ruscio, K.P. (1987a). The distinctive scholarship of the selective liberal arts college. *Journal of Higher Education,* 58(2), 205–222.

Ruscio, K.P. (1987b). Many sectors, many professions. In B.R. Clark (ed.) *The academic profession: National, disciplinary, and institutional settings.* Los Angeles, CA: University of California Press.

Sax, L.J., Astin, A.W., Korn, W.S. and Gilmartin, S.K. (1999). *The American college teacher: National norms for the 1998–1999 HERI faculty survey.* Los Angeles, CA: Higher Education Research Institute, UCLA.

Schein, E.H. (1992). *Organizational culture and leadership.* San Francisco, CA: Jossey-Bass.

Smart, J.C., Feldman, K.A. and Ethingon, C.A. (2000). *Academic disciplines: Holland's theory and the study of college students and faculty.* Nashville, TN: Vanderbilt University Press.

Smart, J.C., Kuh, G.D. and Tierney, W.G. (1997). The roles of institutional cultures and decision approaches in promoting organizational effectiveness in two-year colleges. *Journal of Higher Education,* 68(3), 256–281.

Smart, J.C. and Hamm, R.E. (1993). Organizational culture and effectiveness in two-year colleges. *Research in Higher Education,* 34(1), 95–107.

Trice, H.M. and Beyer, J.M. (1993). *The cultures of work organizations.* Englewood Cliffs, NJ: Prentice-Hall.

Trow, M. (1977). Departments as contexts for teaching and learning. In D.E. McHenry (ed.) *Academic departments: Problems, variations, and alternatives.* San Francisco, CA: Jossey-Bass.

Tucker, A. (1984). *Chairing the academic department: Leadership among peers* (2nd edn). New York: Macmillan Press.

Walvoord, B.E., Carey, A.K., Smith, H.L., Soled, S.W., Way, P.K. and Zorn, D. (2000). *Academic departments: How they work, how they change* (ASHE-ERIC Higher Education Report No. 27(6)). San Francisco, CA: Jossey-Bass.

Wergin, J. (1993). Departmental rewards. *Change*, 25, July–August, 24.
Wilber, K. (1998). *The marriage of sense and soul: Integrating science and religion.* New York: Random House.

Appendix 26.1 Number of Institutions and Faculty, by Institutional Type

Institutional Type	Institutions Total	Institutions Sample	Faculty Total	Faculty Sample
All institutions	2,618	429	440,850	13,946
All four-year institutions	4,489	380	336,832	12,858
Universities				
Public	124	28	106,488	2,913
Private	72	29	41,779	1,594
Four-year colleges				
Public	390	85	108,713	4,298
All Private	903	244	79,852	4,053
Non-sectarian	375	86	36,012	1,555
Catholic	174	33	16,099	817
Protestant	354	99	27,741	1,681
All two-year institutions	1,129	49	104,018	1,088

Note: Adapted from Sax *et al.* (1999).

27

Economies of Scale and Mergers in Higher Education

Colin Green and Geraint Johnes

Introduction

The structure of an industry, like the structure of a firm, is determined in large measure by the nature of technology. In some industries, such as heavy manufacturing, substantial investments in machinery are needed in order to engage in production, and so firms need to produce high levels of output in order to recoup their investment costs. Hence such industries are characterised by a small number of large firms. In some other industries, different types of large investments, such as advertising, are necessary—and so we see, for example, small numbers of large supermarket chains. In yet other sectors, the technology is much smaller scale, and so are the firms populating the industry. So many plumbers, for instance, operate on a self-employed basis in "firms" comprising just one worker.

Technology shapes costs. It would be possible for a small firm to produce small quantities of steel—but it would not be able to do so at a unit cost that is as low as that achievable by large steel producers, simply because the technology would not allow that. Economies of scale dictate that, in some industries, large firms enjoy substantial advantages over small producers.

These arguments extend to the case of the education sector. In the case of primary and secondary education, markets are for the most part local, and this (if nothing else) restricts the size of schools. In higher education, markets are much larger. There is a long history of young people moving away from their parental homes to undertake a university education, so that the market footprint of a higher education institution has been regional, national or (increasingly) global. Meanwhile, another major function of universities is to produce research that pushes out the frontiers of knowledge and understanding on a worldwide scale. Universities tend therefore to be larger than schools.

Over recent years, higher education policies in many countries have encouraged universities to engage increasingly in competitive behaviour. Marketing the higher education institution on a global stage has become key to the institution's sustainability. It is likely that such changes in the environment within which universities operate have led to change also in the nature of economies of scale, rendering smaller institutions more financially vulnerable than they once were. In some cases this has led to merger activity.

As is the case in many other industries, universities produce a multiplicity of products. A full consideration of cost structures needs, therefore, to take into account the way in which these various products relate to and interact with one another. If, for example, it is more efficient (other things being equal) to produce physics graduates in an institution which has a mathematics department than in institutions that do not, then that is something that should be reflected in the analysis. Indeed, we should expect that synergies, or economies of scope, of this sort are quite common. It would explain why we see a proliferation of universities that are comprehensive in their disciplinary provision (even though most students specialise), and universities that produce both teaching and research.

In this chapter we shall review recent work on cost structures, economies of scale and economies of scope in the university sector. In essence this updates another survey on university costs provided by Cohn and Cooper (2004). This is followed by a consideration of developments in the literature on merger activity in the higher education sector. We conclude by drawing the threads together and suggesting some possible avenues for future research.

Cost Structures, Economies of Scale and Economies of Scope

The underpinnings of the modern literature on university costs are to be found in the work of Baumol et al. (1982). Their study examines the role of contestability as a means of achieving socially optimal outcomes in a market economy, and focuses on the role of organisations, that (could potentially) produce a multiplicity of outputs, as agents that can, by the mere threat of entry into highly concentrated industries, curtail the market power of monopolies. As a by-product of this analysis they provide a conceptual framework within which economies of scale and of scope in a complex multiproduct organisation can be understood.

For the specific case of higher education, the pioneering empirical work of Cohn et al. (1989), using the concepts developed by Baumol et al., has been key to all subsequent studies. The approach taken by Cohn et al. is to use statistical regression analysis in order to estimate the parameters of a cost equation. A characteristic of this equation is that it should have a functional form that satisfies a number of desiderata, amongst which are that the data (and not any assumption made by the analyst) should decide whether or not economies of scale or of scope exist. There are several possible functional forms, but the simplest is known as the quadratic. In a particularly simple case where a university produces two outputs—teaching, T, and research, R—costs, C are estimated by the equation:

$$C = \alpha + \beta T + \delta R + \gamma T^2 + \varphi R^2 + \lambda TR \qquad (1)$$

Here the Greek letters are the parameters of the model that are to be estimated by regression. They may be positive or negative. Note that this is not a straightforward linear regression; the presence of the squared terms (T^2 and R^2) and the interaction term (TR) means that a change in the level of output of either teaching or research has quite a complicated impact upon expected costs.

Estimating the values of the parameters of this equation is, in principle at least, quite a simple exercise. Data (which may be cross-section or longitudinal) are collected about the costs and outputs of a number of universities, and estimates of the parameter values can then be obtained using standard statistical software. Defining measures that can be used to represent costs, and especially teaching and research activity, can be contentious, however. Costs are ideally defined to include both current expenditures and an annualised measure of capital spend, but to exclude spending that is related to non-educational aspects of universities' provision (such as "hotel" costs associated with student residences and catering). Teaching outputs are usually measured by numbers of graduates at various levels (such as undergraduate, postgraduate). Some commentators have, however, highlighted the desirability of including a quality dimension in the teaching measure, and so include in their analysis an indicator of educational value added (Johnes et al., 2005). The measurement of research activity is particularly fraught with difficulty, but most studies use research income from grants as an indicator which is related to the market value of the (quantity and quality of) research produced.

These measurement issues are, for the most part, matters of detail. Various cost measures are highly correlated with one another. Likewise, although publications data or peer reviews of research are necessarily retrospective, while research funding is forward looking, the correlation between these measures is high (though of course not perfect).

In practice, it is unusual for a cost equation for higher education institutions to be as simple as the one discussed above. Universities produce a plethora of outputs. These include teaching at different levels (foundation, bachelors, graduate certificates and diplomas, masters, doctorates) and in a wide variety of different subjects, conducting research in these same subject areas; and, increasingly, engagement in "third mission" work, which may take the form of executive education and lifelong learning activities, community outreach, consultancy, joint ventures and other partnerships with business. For statistical reasons (which include problems of multicollinearity and the availability of degrees of freedom) it is not possible to include separate measures of all these outputs in a cost equation. But it has become usual to employ at least some disaggregation of outputs by level (undergraduate, postgraduate) and subject (science, non-science) for the teaching outputs. This means that the equation that is to be estimated becomes longer, but the principles are the same: outputs influence costs, and they do so in a way that allows for the possible existence of both economies of scale and economies of scope.

While many early estimates of cost equations such as those discussed here are based on ordinary least squares (OLS) regression, some more sophisticated estimation techniques have more recently been introduced into the literature. Johnes (1996) was the first to employ stochastic frontier methods in this context. These are based on the observation that best-fit methods (such as OLS) are inappropriate for the estimation of a cost curve, which is in essence an envelope drawn around observations for universities which are not all necessarily equally efficient. As a by-product, the stochastic frontier method allows estimates of each university's technical efficiency to be obtained. Stochastic frontier methods have since been used to analyse costs or production in higher education by a number of authors, including Cooper and Cohn (1997), Izadi *et al.* (2002), and Stevens (2005).

More recently, Johnes and Johnes (2008) have exploited the opportunity that longitudinal (or "panel") data afford to estimate stochastic frontier models that have random parameters. This allows, in effect, a separate cost equation to be estimated for each university, hence recognising the fact that some institutions might, for perfectly legitimate reasons, have higher unit costs than others. For instance, ancient universities with the responsibility of maintaining buildings of historical importance, or universities located in areas where land prices are high, may have unusually high costs, without this meaning that they are in any way inefficient. Equations of this type have been estimated for a number of countries, including England (Johnes and Johnes, 2008), Spain (Johnes and Salas-Velasco, 2007), Italy (Agasisti and Johnes, 2008) and Germany (Johnes and Schwarzenberger, 2007).

Despite these methodological innovations, the basic idea remains simple. Costs are modelled in the form of an equation which links outputs of teaching and research (and possibly other things) to expenditures. The functional form of the equation allows for (but crucially does not impose) the possible existence of scale and scope economies.

We are now in a position to say something more precise about how these scale and scope economies can be measured. Baumol *et al.* (1982) note that, in a single product organisation, economies of scale can be measured as the ratio of average costs to marginal costs, and they extend this concept to the multiproduct setting by defining analogous measures of overall (or "ray") returns to scale and product-specific returns to scale. Both the average and marginal costs can be calculated using the estimated cost equation discussed earlier. It is usual for measures of returns to scale and to scope to be reported for a typical university, that is, for an institution that produces average levels of all outputs. In principle, however, it is possible to use the information provided by the cost equation to evaluate measures of returns to scale and scope that are distinct for each individual institution. Finding that, on average, universities are "too small" does not mean that every university is "too small". Nevertheless, as we shall see, some useful lessons can be learned by examining the case of a representative institution.

If the measure of ray returns to scale exceeds one, then an institution can realise economies of scale by expanding all of its provision. In this case, the institution may be thought of as being "too small", in the sense that it does not produce enough to exploit fully the opportunity that technology affords to bring down unit costs (we recognise that this is a narrow, and purely economic, interpretation of what it means to be "too small"). In such a scenario, mergers might be regarded as a means of capturing the scale economies that remain available. If, on the other hand, ray economies of scale are less than one, the institution is experiencing diseconomies of scale. Likewise, if our measure of the product-specific returns to scale associated with, say, arts teaching, exceeds one, then economies of scale exist that remain underexploited. It would be possible to expand the number of arts students at a given university and, as a direct consequence, achieve lower unit costs. If product-specific returns to scale are less than one, on the other hand, diseconomies of scale are experienced, and unit costs would fall if the university reduced its output of this type.

Economies of scope are measured by using the cost equation to compare the expected cost of producing a given set of outputs (usually the average across all universities) at a single institution with the expected cost of producing the same outputs, but this time in separate, single-product institutions. If the latter exceeds the former, then economies of scope are present. Otherwise institutions experience diseconomies of scope. It is usual, again following Baumol et al. (1982), to define a measure of returns to scope that is positive in situations where scope economies are present, and negative otherwise.

Numerous studies of university costs have been conducted over the last 20 years. In addition to those mentioned above, we are aware of studies conducted for Australia (Lloyd et al., 1993), Japan (Hashimoto and Cohn, 1997), Turkey (Erk, 1989; Lewis and Dundar, 1995), the United Kingdom (Glass et al., 1995a, 1995b; Johnes, 1997, 1998; Johnes et al., 2005), and the United States (de Groot et al., 1991; Getz et al., 1991; Nelson and Hevert, 1992; Dundar and Lewis, 1995; Koshal and Koshal, 1995, 1999, 2000; Koshal et al., 2001). In most cases these studies are based upon a cross-section of data obtained by comparing universities in a single country at a given point in time (there are exceptions: Nelson and Hevert, for example, study costs *within* a single institution). As might be expected, the results provide conclusions that differ across countries, and—within each country—across different periods. Nevertheless, especially in the latest generation of studies, many of the results suggest some consistent patterns, and these form the basis of the discussion that follows.

First, for a typical institution, it is more costly to provide science teaching than non-science teaching. This is unsurprising in view of the laboratory facilities needed for most science subjects. More disaggregated analysis of subject-specific costs is unusual in the literature, but they indicate that the provision of medical tuition is (far) more costly than is teaching in the other sciences (Johnes et al., 2005). Again this is unsurprising, since medical education is typically jointly provided with expensive hospital facilities. Another common finding is that postgraduate teaching is more costly than undergraduate teaching, this likely being due in part at least to smaller class sizes in the former. Findings on the costs associated with doctoral students vary from country to country; where such students are used extensively to teach undergraduates, their net costs are low in comparison with those of other postgraduates, owing to the contribution that they make to the overall teaching effort.

Secondly, the technical efficiency of higher education institutions is generally quite high. The example of German universities studied by Johnes and Schwarzenberger (2007) is typical. Of 72 universities, they found that 54 have efficiency scores in excess of 80%. However, international studies do suggest that there may be patterns that explain efficiency differences across institutions. Universities in economically depressed (often peripheral) regions tend to have lower efficiency scores than do those in more prosperous areas (Agasisti and Johnes, 2008). Universities with multiple campuses located distant from each other tend to have lower efficiency scores (Johnes and Salas-Velasco, 2007). And small, often highly specialised, institutions often appear to have lower efficiency than do others (Johnes et al., 2005). These last two observations are instructive in the context of the debate on institutional mergers, since they suggest that such mergers might results in an improvement in overall *technical efficiency* (that is, how far institutions are from their cost frontier).

Thirdly, in many countries, ray economies of scale are (just) exhausted for an institution of typical size (Agasisti and Johnes, 2008; Johnes and Johnes 2008; Johnes and Schwarzenberger, 2007). This means that further expansion of existing institutions could lead to diseconomies, and that any increase in the size of the higher education system as a whole should involve the creation of new institutions. Note, however, that this finding does not apply to all countries.

Fourthly, where it applies, the above result appears to be due primarily to the exhaustion of economies of scope. Care needs to be taken in interpreting this finding. Few people would doubt that there are indeed synergies between teaching and research (both of which need information resources and administrative support), or between disciplines. The finding that economies of scope are exhausted refers to the *further expansion* of the typical university not yielding *further* economies of scope.

The last two findings need to be qualified, however, by the observation that these results have been obtained using frontier methods that evaluate the shape of institutions' cost curves as they would be if the institutions were technically efficient—not the cost curves that actually pertain. If educational policy is made on the premise that institutions should operate efficiently, then that is all well and good. If, on the other hand, the authorities accept that some amount of inefficiency is inevitable, it may be the case that the fixed costs associated with the creation and subsequent operation of new institutions are sufficient to reverse these findings.

Another important caveat that attaches to these findings is that they refer to a university of average size. For smaller institutions, ray returns to scale may be positive. As an example, Johnes et al. (2005) provide evidence of how ray returns to scale for English institutions of higher education decline as the size of the university increases from 50% to 200% of average size. This means that mergers of smaller institutions could realise an improvement in *allocative efficiency* (that is, how appropriate the allocation of student places and research activity is across institutions).

Fifthly, despite the exhaustion of ray economies of scale, product-specific scale economies remain to be exploited. In Germany and Spain, for example, increased concentration of provision of all outputs (undergraduates in sciences, undergraduates in other subjects, postgraduates, and research) could result in economies (Johnes and Salas-Velasco, 2007; Johnes and Schwarzenberger, 2007). This would involve transferring student places and research resources, over time, between universities in such a way as to increase the degree to which various institutions specialise in the production of specific types of output. An early study by Johnes (1997) suggested that such a policy could also result in system-wide savings in the UK, and the most recent findings for England (Johnes and Johnes, 2008) suggest that this remains the case, at least for postgraduate education and research. Policies to encourage concentration of provision in these areas have been in place for many years; for the UK, these have included selective research council funding of postgraduate studentships, and the financial implications of the research assessment exercises.

At various points in the discussion above, we have highlighted the implications of economies of scale and of scope for institutional mergers. In the next section, we discuss these implications in greater depth, with specific reference to merger activity that has been observed in various countries over recent years.

The Link Between Costs and Merger Activity

While mergers have been the source of much attention and analysis in economics, there has been little economic analysis of mergers in higher education. This is despite the prevalence of merger activity within this industry. For instance, Rowley (1997) suggests that some 200 mergers occurred involving a higher education partner in the 1970s and 1980s in the UK alone (many involving the release of further education colleges from local authority control, or of health training facilities from the National Health Service). Other jurisdictions such as Australia, Germany, the Netherlands and Sweden have also experienced widespread merger activity in the higher education sector (Goedegebuure and Meek, 1991; Mahony, 1992; Skodvin, 1999).

Those mergers in higher education that are of higher profile fit the mould of a case where there would appear to be clear gains in terms of cost efficiencies in administration and other non-academic parts of higher education provision. For instance, the recent amalgamation of two major universities in Manchester is a clear case where efficiency gains from merger would be expected, and where these are assisted by their very close geographic proximity. Furthermore, these two large institutions produced product mixes prior to amalgamation that were, in part, distinct from one another. This suggests a role for scope economies. However, these factors also make this a fairly special case, comparable but also in many ways distinct from the amalgamation of the institutions that comprise the University of London. More typical cases of merger in, for instance, the UK or Australia have involved the amalgamation of institutions that may vary markedly in size, and operate in geographically distinct areas, where some overlap in initial product mix may be present, where one institution may have very specialised teaching outputs, and where one or both of the initial institutions may not operate in the higher education sector prior to merger. In Australia, much of this merger activity can be considered as linked to the move to a unitary higher education system (Mahony, 1993), and has incorporated the movement of the teaching of newly "professional-ised" occupations (such as teaching and nursing) into the university sector. Hence, whilst economic factors may influence merger decisions there are clearly other institutional forces involved.

Here we seek to examine to what extent merger activity in the higher education sector is conditioned by economic factors, and in particular the likelihood of merger leading to cost efficiencies. This latter point is critical as, in the absence of cost efficiencies, merger will in theory lead to an increased market share and higher prices (Farrell and Shapiro, 1990). There are a number of challenges in the economic analysis of merger generally and particularly within the higher education sector. First, we are dealing with multi-product firms; whilst the product portfolio of each firm may overlap they are unlikely to be identical. Furthermore, even where overlap of product offerings occurs, these products are likely to be differentiated. Unlike mergers in other sectors, university mergers often involve institutions of vastly different size. Rowley (1997) suggests that the typical difference in pre-merger institution scale is 10 to 1. Hence, evaluating the impact of any merger in higher education on market outcomes is difficult. A further general problem in the evaluation of cost efficiencies generated by mergers is whether these savings could or would have been achieved by individual institutions in the absence of merger. Applying this counter-factual criterion focuses the analysis on cost efficiencies that are merger-specific, rather than just a comparison of pre- and post-merger cost structures.

We examine a number of potential sources of cost efficiencies that are typically considered in the industrial organisation literature on mergers, and discuss the issues and impediments to realisation of these cost savings in the context of higher education. These can be grouped into two broad areas. First, we might expect merger to allow the opportunities for cost savings to be realised (so-called rationalisation savings). Second, there may be merger-specific spill-overs that increase efficiency. We consider each in turn.

Rationalisation

To aid discussion, consider an even simpler version of the university cost function than that set out in (1). There are two universities, both produce the same outputs but have distinct cost functions. Initially we further assume that there are no complementarities between teaching and research. The cost functions that attach to each of two universities may then be written as:

$$C(y_1) = \alpha_1 + \chi T_1 + \theta R_1 \qquad (2)$$

$$C(y_2) = \alpha_2 + \rho T_2 + \eta R_2 \qquad (3)$$

If the universities' cost structures differ, then by construction each university has comparative advantage in either the production of research or teaching. Assume that university 1 has comparative advantage in teaching, whilst university 2 has comparative advantage in research. In this case, cost savings can, in theory, be gained post-merger by a reallocation of resources in line with comparative advantage. Hence site 1 (formerly university 1) specialises in teaching and site 2 (university 2) specialises in research. This will lead to lower unit costs of overall production of research and teaching in the merged university. In this way merger may allow cost efficiencies through a reallocation of resource that would not have been possible with two distinct universities. Furthermore, these cost efficiencies are not necessarily related to economies of scale or scope.

There are a number of reasons why, in reality, these simple cost efficiencies may not be realised. First, as set out in (1), research and teaching may be complements. Hence if $\lambda < 0$ this undermines the separation of teaching and research into separate "plants". For instance, Dundar and Lewis (1995) demonstrate significant economies of scope in the joint production of teaching and research within the same department. Their results suggest that splitting departments into teaching units and research centres would result in higher unit costs in the production of both teaching and research.

More complex issues relate to product differentiation. At its simplest if, instead of the two cost functions above, we have two institutions that produce distinct research and teaching outputs (consider for instance an ex-teaching college merging with a science-based institution), then the simple transfer of resources across campus may not be possible. This is because the labour, capital and other inputs that underlie each institution's cost function may not be substitutable for one another. For instance, academics specialising in educational research may not be readily used in the production of science teaching outputs. Even in the extreme case where labour inputs are perfectly substitutable, there may be issues related to imperfect labour mobility that may reduce the potential to gain cost efficiencies from specialisation. Both institutions will enter the merger with pre-existing labour forces, with many workers likely to be on permanent contracts. In the case where the institutions are not geographically proximate, individual workers may be unwilling to commute to, or move near, a new campus.

A final point to keep in mind is that the teaching products may be differentiated across the institutions due to location. In this sense both institutions supply teaching outputs to separate regional markets, and teaching production across these two institutions will not be substitutable.

Together, these provide some of the reasons why the typical post-merger sources of cost savings through rationalisation may not be readily achievable in a higher education setting.

Merger, Economies of Scale and Scope

In terms of economic factors likely to influence merger activity in the higher education sector, one might expect a significant role for economies of scale and/or scope. However, previous evidence for the UK and Australia suggests only a limited role for scale and scope economies as a driver of merger. Johnes (1997) demonstrates that, while large unexhausted economies of scale exist in the UK higher education system, only a relatively minor part of this could be exploited via the merger of existing institutions. Lloyd et al. (1993) find some evidence of post-amalgamation reduction in costs in Australia, where this is associated primarily with economies of scale where larger universities merged with small colleges. They also note that even these cost savings are predicated on an assumption that increases in scale did not affect quality of teaching outputs (for instance, through larger class sizes). However, they also demonstrate only modest gains from economies of scope, and only where one or more of the pre-merger institutions was a college of advanced education. The largest estimate of scope economies was only 3.1% (Lloyd et al., 1993, p. 1089). Furthermore, in some cases they found diseconomies of scope as a result of merger. Meanwhile, Rowley (1997), in an analysis of 30 UK mergers with a higher education partner, reports that only one reported post-merger cost efficiencies.

If then, as set out earlier, the production of higher education is characterised by both economies of scale and scope, with many institutions operating at small scale and many mergers involving at least one small institution, why do mergers not result in cost efficiencies? In addition, there is an argument that certain high-cost teaching activities, such as physical sciences and postgraduate education, should be more concentrated than other teaching production. For instance, Johnes (1997) suggests that concentration of these activities will enhance overall efficiency. Furthermore, it has been demonstrated that substantial unexhausted economies of scale are most likely to occur in institutions of very small size (Brinkman and Leslie, 1986). These considerations further the expectation that merger of higher education institutions could lead to the realisation of scale economies. However, a difficulty in linking these considerations directly to a case for merger is that these economies could, in theory, be achieved through unilateral expansion of existing institutions—at least where there are no institutional rigidities that prevent this from happening. This is an important caveat. Institutional rigidities can result from a wide variety of sources, including government control of the sector. Also some institutions may not wish to expand to realise economies of scale or scope because this might compromise quality.

There is a more general argument (Farrell and Shapiro, 2001) that mergers should only result in cost efficiencies through economies of scope, rather than scale. Essentially the question is: why does it pay the merged institution to increase production when it did not pay to increase production prior to the merger? Farrell and Shapiro argue that any economies of scale in production resulting specifically from merger are likely to be small in magnitude, and that greater competition between firms is a more significant driver for them to reach minimum efficient scale. Instead, any cost efficiencies from mergers are likely to be in the form of synergies (i.e. scope economies) from the interaction of the two firms post-merger, synergies that would not be possible with the two firms operating as separate, competing entities. It is worth noting, as an aside, that in principle any of the synergies that could occur due to a merger could also, in principle, be achieved with a sufficiently complex contract (Farrell and Shapiro, 2001). However, in reality many of these may not be realistic in the presence of competition between the two institutions. Furthermore, the extent to which it is more beneficial to realise these economies through merger relates to the level of transaction costs associated with cross-institution contracting.

Synergies from merger must be of the form that the combination of the two institutions generates a cost function that is in effect superior to that of the two initial institutions' cost functions—superior, that is, in the sense that holding production constant, costs fall. In effect this means that the merging institutions combine their hard-to-trade factors of production in a novel manner that leads to lower costs or improved product quality (Farrell and Shapiro, 1990). In the higher education context a number of potential synergies can be envisaged.

Large and diverse institutions may be associated with lower unit costs (Lloyd et al., 1993). Individuals enrolled in the merged institution may have access to a larger portfolio of subject choices than that offered by the pre-merged institutions. This may have the effect of increasing student demand for courses offered by the merged institution, driving unit costs down. These scope economies could conceivably be achieved without merger through, for instance, joint teaching agreements across institutions. However in this case, some of the cost benefit may be lost through coordination and contracting costs across the institutions.

There are reasons why there may be scope economies in any productive input that covers many teaching and/or research units. For instance, consider the marketing of teaching products in a simple case where there are two institutions producing two distinct teaching product mixes, and each has a marketing unit that seeks to increase demand for teaching (i.e. increase student numbers) through the provision of information in the marketplace. If the minimum efficient scale of marketing production is larger than that needed to market the individual institutions' teaching products, then merger may lead to a reduction in per unit marketing costs, and hence scope economies in marketing across the merged institutions' range of teaching products. This type of scope economy clearly fits the mould of a synergy that would not readily be achievable without merger. There is also an argument that, with the increasing move away from local to global education markets, the minimum efficient size of marketing production may have increased. This may provide an increase in the incentive for merger of smaller education institutions.

More generally, if there are economies of scale in administration that can be only realised with a larger institution then this could drive down average administrative costs post-merger. A factor likely to affect this latter case is that many mergers occur between institutions at geographically distant sites. In this case, distance and the need for local administration staff may provide a limiting factor to the achievement of cost savings. A further issue is the potential for diseconomies due to difficulties in merging disparate management styles within one institution (White, 1987). Institutions have different codified and tacit rules. Merging these into one coherent operating approach is likely to be difficult. This is likely to be more problematic still in the case where one of the merger partners was not previously operating in higher education, but rather was operating under a different regulatory framework.

Mergers in higher education may lead to research synergies. For instance they may lead to increased academic integration and collaboration across disciplines (Skodvin, 1999). This is essentially an argument that merger may promote increased sharing of complementary skills across institutions.

This section has provided a discussion of the potential for cost efficiencies to be achieved in higher education through the merger of institutions. It has been argued that many of the typical rationalisation economies associated more generally with merger are difficult to realise in a higher education setting. Furthermore, for merger to be viewed as the best approach to realise unexhausted economies of scale a case needs to be made as to why these institutions could, or would, not expand unilaterally to drive their own unit costs down. It is argued that scope economies are the most likely source of cost efficiencies via merger in the higher education sector. However, the limited number of econometric analyses of the cost effects of higher education merger casts some doubt even on this source of cost savings.

Conclusion

Merger activity in all business sectors is common. It is often motivated by economic considerations, especially where competition is fierce. In higher education markets work imperfectly, and there are many institutional factors that serve either to encourage or hinder mergers. In general, however, competition between higher education institutions is becoming increasingly aggressive as the market for their services covers a wider geographical area, and as private financing comes to represent an increasing share of their income. At the same time, costs that are fixed in nature— most notably those associated with marketing and the development of a brand—are increasing. These trends suggest that the minimum efficient size of a higher education institution is likely to rise somewhat over the coming few years. As an academic exercise, it will be interesting to compare cost structures of the recent past with those that will obtain in, say, a decade's time. On a more practical level, the trends noted above suggest that it is likely that mergers in higher education will become more common than has been the case in the past. Higher education has never been more exciting.

References

Agasisti, T. and G. Johnes (2008) Heterogeneity and the evaluation of efficiency: the case of Italian universities, *Applied Economics*, forthcoming.

Baumol, W.J., J.C. Panzar and R.D. Willig (1982) *Contestable Markets and the Theory of Industry Structure*, San Diego, CA: Harcourt Brace Jovanovich.

Brinkman, P. and L. Leslie (1986) Economies of scale in higher education: sixty years of research, *Review of Higher Education*, 10, 1–28.

Cohn, E., S. Rhine and M. Santos (1989) Institutions of higher education as multi-product firms: economies of scale and scope, *Review of Economics and Statistics*, 71, 284–290.

Cohn, E. and S. Cooper (2004) Mulitproduct cost functions for universities: economies of scale and scope. In G. Johnes and J. Johnes (eds) *The International Handbook on the Economics of Education*, Cheltenham: Edward Elgar.

Cooper, S. and E. Cohn (1997) Estimation of a frontier production function for the South Carolina education process, *Economics of Education Review*, 16, 323–327.

de Groot, H., W. McMahon and J. Volkwein (1991) The cost structure of American research universities, *Review of Economics and Statistics*, 73, 424–431.

Dundar, H. and D. Lewis (1995) Departmental productivity in American universities: economies of scale and scope, *Economics of Education Review*, 14(2), 119–144

Erk, N. (1989) The economics of higher education and tests of equity criteria in Turkey, *Higher Education*, 18, 137–147.

Farrell, J. and C. Shapiro (1990) Horizontal mergers: an equilibrium analysis, *American Economic Review*, 80, 107–126.

Farrell, J. and C. Shapiro (2001) Scale economies and synergies in horizontal merger analysis, *Antitrust Law Journal*, 68, 685–710.

Getz, M., J. Siegfried and H. Zhang (1991) Estimating economies of scale in higher education, *Economics Letters*, 37, 203–208.

Glass, C., D. McKillop and N. Hyndman (1995a) Efficiency in the provision of university teaching and research: an empirical analysis of UK universities, *Journal of Applied Econometrics*, 10, 61–72.

Glass, C., D. McKillop and N. Hyndman (1995b) The achievement of scale efficiency in UK universities: a multiple-input multiple-output analysis, *Education Economics*, 3, 249–263.

Goedegebuure, L. and L. Meek (1991) Restructuring higher education: a comparative analysis between Australia and the Netherlands, *Comparative Education*, 27, 7–22.

Hashimoto, K. and E. Cohn (1997) Economies of scale and scope in Japanese private universities, *Education Economics*, 5, 107–115.

Izadi, H., G. Johnes, R. Oskrochi and R. Crouchley (2002) Stochastic frontier estimation of a CES cost function: the case of higher education in Britain, *Economics of Education Review*, 21, 63–71.

Johnes, G. (1996) Multi-product cost functions and the funding of tuition in UK universities, *Applied Economics Letters*, 3, 557–561.

Johnes, G. (1997) Costs and industrial structure in contemporary British higher education, *Economic Journal*, 107, 727–737.

Johnes, G. (1998) The costs of multi-product organizations and the heuristic evaluation of industrial structure, *Socio-Economic Planning Sciences*, 32, 199–209.

Johnes, G. and J. Johnes (2008) Higher education institutions' costs and efficiency: taking the decomposition a further step, *Economics of Education Review*, forthcoming.

Johnes, G. and M. Salas-Velasco (2007) The determinants of costs and efficiencies where producers are heterogeneous: the case of Spanish universities, *Economics Bulletin*, 4(15), 1–9.

Johnes, G. and A. Schwarzenberger (2007) *Differences in cost structure and the evaluation of efficiency: the case of German universities*, mimeo, Lancaster University.

Johnes, G., J. Johnes, E. Thanassoulis, P. Lenton and A. Emrouznejad (2005) *An exploratory analysis of the cost structure of higher education in England*, Nottingham: Department for Education and Skills.

Koshal, R. and M. Koshal (1995) Quality and economies of scale in higher education, *Applied Economics*, 27, 773–778.

Koshal, R. and M. Koshal (1999) Economies of scale and scope in higher education: a case of comprehensive universities, *Economics of Education Review*, 18, 269–277.

Koshal, R. and M. Koshal (2000) Do liberal arts colleges exhibit economies of scale and scope?, *Education Economics*, 8, 209–220.

Koshal, R., M. Koshal and A. Gupta (2001) Multi-product total cost function for higher education: a case of bible colleges, *Economics of Education Review*, 20, 297–303.

Lewis, D. and H. Dundar (1995) Economies of scale and scope in Turkish universities, *Education Economics*, 3(2), 133–157.

Lloyd, P., M. Morgan and R. Williams (1993) Amalgamations of universities: are there economies of scale or scope?, *Applied Economics*, 25, 1081–1092.

Mahony, D. (1992) Establishing the university as the sole provider of higher education: the Australian experience, *Studies in Higher Education*, 17, 219–236.

Mahony, D. (1993) The construction and challenges of Australia's post-binary system of higher education, *Oxford Review of Education*, 19, 465–483.

Nelson, R. and K. Hevert (1992) Effects of class size on economies of scale and marginal costs in higher education, *Applied Economics*, 24, 473–482.

Rowley, G. (1997) United we stand: a strategic analysis of mergers in higher education, *Public Money and Management*, 17(4), 7–12.

Skodvin, O-J. (1999) Mergers in higher education—success or failure?, *Tertiary Education and Management*, 5, 65–80.

Stevens, P. (2005) The determinants of economic efficiency in English and Welsh universities. *Education Economics* 13, 355–374.

White, L. (1987) Anti-trust and merger policy: a review and critique, *Journal of Economic Perspectives*, 1, 13–22.

28
University-based Economic Growth

Iryna Lendel, Phil Allen and Maryann Feldman

Introduction

Many public policies are based on the popular assumption that investment in university research and infrastructure benefits regional economies. After all, we live in a knowledge economy and universities are seen as a core element of a regional intellectual infrastructure—an essential factor in building technology-based industries and competitive firms. This argument is attractive to many politicians who seek to promote economic growth, and economic development has become the third mission of universities (Etzkowitz, 2003). Still, there are skeptics who doubt the ability of universities to promote economic development (Feller, 1990) and who worry about the effect of this emphasis on the integrity of the academic enterprise (Slaughter and Leslie, 1997). Leaving normative concerns aside, this chapter examines the relations between higher education, industry and economic development. We provide a review of the literature with emphasis on how universities impact economic development and technological change with specific emphasis on the places where they are located.

A body of empirical work concludes that universities are necessary but not sufficient for positive regional economic outcomes. The operative question is under which circumstances universities affect economic growth; specifically, what characteristics of universities promote knowledge transfer and what characteristics of places promote knowledge absorption? While we debate the merits of increased emphasis on commercial activity, universities are moving aggressively into active technology transfer and engagement with commercial activity. The operative question here is how to best manage these relationships to ensure that all of society's goals are met.

This chapter begins by introducing the student of higher education to the theoretical background of university-based growth, including major concepts of increasing returns to scale and institutional economies. The following section looks at the ways universities affect regional economies and addresses the literature that presents the concepts of tacit and codified knowledge and agglomeration economies to explain the mechanisms of knowledge spillovers from universities to companies and industries. The concept of regional innovation systems (RIS) helps to place universities within regional economies and makes a framework to observe the evolution of the universities' role in the regional economy from the concept of *learning regions* to the model of *university products*, where universities are presented as endogenous to the regional systems. The conclusions in the chapter synthesize the thoughts behind the literature on economic development theories and the knowledge spillovers concept, suggesting the major hypothesized systems linking universities with regional growth: mechanisms of knowledge spillovers due to agglomeration economies of scale and specific economic environments where the knowledge spillovers occur.

Framing the Problem

As a field, regional economic development is a complex topic that incorporates theories from different disciplines. The notion of how wealth is generated and distributed has been a topic in economics beginning with Adam Smith's (1776) theory of the market economy. Joseph Schumpeter (1934) was the first economist to study innovation and entrepreneurs as the actors who create innovation in the economy. Olson (1982) and North (1955), in discussing institutional economies, highlighted the importance of public environments and their effect on economic growth. The social capital theory of Putnam *et al.*, (1993) and Granovetter (1985) draw attention to social relationships in the process of creating innovation. Increasingly there is a recognition that geography provides a platform on which to organize economic activity in ways that are more efficient and productive.

Innovation, after all, is a social process. Cities are centres of economic activity that provide externalities that result from the co-location of firms (Audretsch and Feldman, 1996). Externalities are defined by economists as the unintended effects of market transactions that are difficult to capture through the price mechanism. The classic example is the bee keeper and the fruit orchard—both gain from co-location but it would be difficult to imagine how they might compensate one another. Agglomeration economies are the external effects associated with the spatial concentrations of resources. In dense urban environments, linkages between firms, either forwards to the market or backwards to suppliers, work more efficiently, producing more revenue per unit of resources. The concentration of activity in cities allows for increased specialization and a deeper division of labor among firms. The observed benefits of agglomeration not only lowered the costs, but also created better opportunities for innovating and designing new products and services. Moreover, co-location creates greater opportunities for interaction, lowering the costs associated with gathering information. Economists say that agglomeration economies lower transaction costs and thus knowledge-based activity is enhanced. A number of scholars, including Weber (1929), Tiebout (1956), Nelson (1986), Chinitz (1961), and Young (1999), established the positive effect of externalities, characteristics of agglomeration economies, phenomena of the increasing returns to scale, deepened specialization of production, and increased elasticity of supply. These scholars tried to understand the variation of economic performance among regions. Technology is key to this effort.

Robert Solow's Nobel Prize-winning work on the technological residual is credited with emphasizing technology-based economic development. Solow (1957) empirically tested the relationship between economic growth and capital stock, or the presence of physical plant and equipment. The growth that could not be explained by the model was called the residual and is associated with technological change. The presence of the residual implied a contribution of technology advances other than a simple industrialization of economy through the substitution of labour for capital. Solow's residual stood for technology shocks over the business cycle frequencies and was a very important input into the emerging new growth theory.

In the late 1980s, Paul Romer built upon Young's concept of increasing return and Solow's technological residual and formulated a set of principles that established his new growth theory—the main theoretical basis for technology-based regional strategies (Romer, 1986). The new growth theory places its main emphasis on endogenous growth based on industries that generate increasing returns to scale. These industries have a high accumulation of knowledge in the form of new technologies: "the model here can be viewed as an equilibrium model of endogenous technological change in which long-run growth is driven primarily by the accumulation of knowledge by forward-looking, profit-maximizing agents" (Romer, 1986, p. 1003). The model is based on three main elements: externalities of new knowledge, increasing returns in the production of output, and decreasing returns in the production of new knowledge. In his later work, Romer illustrated the historical origins of developing a new growth model into a neoclassical growth model rooted in Marshall's concept of increasing returns that are external to a firm but internal to an industry (Marshall, 1890), and Young's basis of increasing returns through increasing specialization and division of labor. Romer further developed Solow's concept of exogenous technological residual and argued Arrow's (1962) view of knowledge as a purely public good, and he resolved optimization problems by applying a competitive equilibrium with externalities derived from a partially excludable nature of new knowledge to a new dynamic growth model. Romer introduced and analytically evaluated three important premises of the new growth theory: (1) "The first premise . . . implies that growth is driven fundamentally by the accumulation of partially excludable, nonrival inputs"; (2) "The second premise implies that technological change takes place because of the action of self-interested individuals, so improvements in the technology must confer benefits that are at least partially excludable";[1] and (3) "The third premise . . . implies that that technology is a non-rival input" (Romer, 1990, p. S74).

Romer argued that excludability is a function of the technology and the legal system, and therefore prevents anyone other than the owner from using new knowledge to create quasi rents. "The advantage of the interpretation that knowledge is compensated out of quasi rents is that it allows for intentional private investments in research and development. . . . What appeared to be quasi rents are merely competitive returns to rival factors that are in a fixed supply." (pp. S77–S78). He emphasized the importance of human capital in the research process and pointed to agglomeration economies that occur at the intersection of highly specialized firms and a diverse environment that encourages innovations. His theory also states that simple urbanization and specialization itself can only create an economy predisposed to innovation, but what actually creates that economy is the immense investment in research and development combined with a supporting infrastructure of transportation, communication, information, and education.

The concept of increasing returns implies the existence of knowledge spillovers and the benefits of the co-location for innovative activity (Feldman, 1994). Known alternatively as the new industrial geography (Martin and Sunley 1996; Martin, 1999) or the new economic geography (Krugman, 1991, 1995, 1998, 1999; David, 1999), there has been an active intellectual effort to study the relationship of location to economic growth.

The Real Effects of Academic Research

The production function approach suggests that firms that are located in a region with large stocks of private and public research and development (RandD) expenditures are more likely to be innovative than those located a greater distance from such stocks. This advantage is due to benefits from knowledge spillovers and agglomeration effects. Many studies combine geography (distance from the source of knowledge) and innovation (tacit nature of knowledge leakages) within the knowledge production function developed by Griliches (1979). These studies imply that innovative inputs (RandD expenditures) produce innovative outputs (patent or innovation counts) due to localization of RandD spillovers. Moreover, in the early 1980s, a popular hypothesis discussed in the literature relates the spatial distribution of knowledge to its core generator, the university. Jaffe modified the Cobb-Douglas production function to incorporate the influence of technology spillovers on productivity or innovation (Griliches, 1979; Jaffe, 1986, 1989). Using the state as the level of analysis, Jaffe (1989) classified patents in technological areas and showed that the number of patents is positively related to expenditures on university RandD, after controlling for private RandD and the size of the states. He interpreted these positive relationships as localized technological spillovers from academic institutions to local firms. Moreover, his model established the importance of a research university to the location of industrial RandD and inventive activity.

In the mid-1990s the Griliches-Jaffe knowledge production function became a major framework for modelling the impact of universities on separate industries and whole regions (Acs *et al.*, 1991, 1994a, 1995; Almedia and Kogut, 1994; Audretsch and Feldman, 1996; Audretsch and Stephan, 1996; Acs, 2002). Feldman (1994) and co-authors, in a series of papers, extended this analysis to consider innovative activity. In 1994, Acs, Audretsch, and Feldman differentiated the production function for large and small firms, finding that geographic proximity to universities is more beneficial for the small firms, as university RandD may play a substitution role for firms' internal RandD, which is too costly for small firms (Acs, Audretsch and Feldman, 1994b). Feldman and Florida (1994) used the knowledge production function to study 13 three-digit SIC industries[2] on a state level and reach conclusions regarding the influence of agglomeration through the network effect: "Concentration of agglomeration of firms in related industries provide a pool of technical knowledge and expertise and a potential base of suppliers and users of information. These networks play an especially important role when technological knowledge is informal or of a tacit nature ..." (p. 220). Using less aggregated industrial classification (four-digit SIC sectors), Audretsch and Feldman (1996) found that the geographical concentration of the innovation output is positively related to the industrial RandD, which proves the existence of knowledge spillovers within the industrial cluster.

This literature, however, often looks at the single link that channels knowledge created in a university to a specific industry, but never assesses the comprehensive impact of all university products on a regional economy. Jaffe (1989) is very careful in interpreting his research, noting: "It is important to emphasize that spillover mechanisms have not been modeled. Despite the attempt to control for unobserved 'quality' of universities, one cannot really interpret these results structurally, in the sense of predicting the resulting change in patents if research spending were exogenously increased" (p. 968). Varga (1997) confirmed this position in his literature survey "Regional Economic Effects of University Research: A Survey." He reviewed the literature on the impact of university research in four areas: (1) the location choice of high-tech facilities, (2) the spatial distribution of high-tech production, (3) the spatial pattern of industrial research and development activities, and (4) the modeling of knowledge transfers emanating from academic institutions. Varga found that:

> Regarding the effect of technology transfer on local economic development, the evidence is still vague. Its main reason is that no appropriate model of local university knowledge effects has been developed in the literature. Studies either test for a direct university effect on economic conditions or focus on academic technology transfer, but none of them provides an integrated approach (p. 28).

Audretsch (1998) also expressed his caution regarding the interpretation of knowledge spillovers in several empirical studies:

> While a new literature has emerged identifying the important role that knowledge spillovers within a given geographical location plays in stimulating innovative activity, there is little consensus as to how and why this occurs. The contribution of the new wave of studies ... was simply to shift the unit of observation away from firms to a geographic region (p. 24).

The other major stream of literature (sometimes using the knowledge production function as well) was established by Jaffe, Trajtenberg and Henderson (1993) by using patent citations data as knowledge flows that can reveal the relationships between innovation in terms of geography, time, and sequence. These scholars found that innovative firms more often quote research from local universities, as compared to the universities that conduct similar research in a more distant place. Almedia, Kogut, and Zander in their multiple studies concluded that localized knowledge builds upon cumulative ideas within regional boundaries and depends on the ability of the local labour market to accommodate engineers, scientists, and workers who hold the knowledge (Kogut and Zander, 1992, 1996; Almedia and Kogut, 1994). The Almedia and Kogut (1997) study of the semi-conductor industry finds that knowledge spillovers from university research to private companies are highly localized. Other studies draw similar conclusions using different levels of geography and different industries (Maurseth and Verspagen, 1999; Verspagen and Schoenmakers, 2000; Kelly and Hageman, 1999).

Many scholars explored the agglomeration effect of urbanization on the efficiency of university knowledge spillovers. Utilizing Polanyi's concept of tacit knowledge (Polanyi, 1962, 1967) and Innis's concept of encoding personal knowledge (Innis, 1950, 1951), scholars classified knowledge as either tacit or codified and then related them to the process of learning and the spatial distribution of knowledge.

Using these concepts of tacit and codified knowledge, Lucas (1988), Caniels (2000), and Audretsch and Feldman (1996), among others, emphasized that knowledge is neither evenly distributed nor equally accessible in every location. The accumulation of tacit knowledge has regional boundaries while the utilization of codified knowledge depends more on the susceptibility of the recipient to accumulate and employ it. Feldman and those who contributed to the stream of research initiated by Adams and Jaffe (Feldman, 1994; Adams and Jaffe, 1996; Adams et al., 2000; Adams, 2001, 2002, 2004), focused on the localization of university spillovers and found significant evidence that knowledge flows travel a certain geographical distance within regions. While studying commercialized academic research, Agrawal and Cockburn (2002), among others, found strong evidence for the co-location of upstream university research and downstream industrial RandD activity at the level of metropolitan areas.

Agglomeration effects result not only in localized knowledge but also in creative ideas that combine different types of knowledge as a result of urbanization effects or the co-location of a large number of firms in different industries. The line of reasoning is that local diversification stimulates the occurrence of different types of knowledge and their innovative combinations (Harrison et al., 1996; Adams et al., 2000; Adams, 2001; Desrochers, 2001).

Many scholars acknowledged the differences in regional performance and they attributed these differences to the patterns of knowledge spillovers and regional absorption of innovation. Döring and Schnellenbach (2006) surveyed the latest theoretical concepts of knowledge spillovers and concluded that "despite its public good properties, knowledge does not usually diffuse instantaneously to production facilities around the world. Regional patterns of knowledge diffusion, as well as barriers to the diffusion of knowledge, can therefore feature prominently in explaining the differential growth of production and incomes between regions".

There are two major obstacles to knowledge spillovers. The first obstacle arises from the proprietary rights for explicit (codified) knowledge at some phase of its development (patenting innovation). At the same time, exclusive rights for new knowledge cannot ensure its total secrecy—for example, publishing scientific articles and presenting at conferences require disclosing information at the phase prior to patenting. The second obstacle is the cognitive abilities of individuals who can utilize tacit knowledge. Some regions might not have enough scientists with the specific skills or knowledge needed to comprehend and utilize new information. That is, the recipients of knowledge spillover might not be able to absorb the information made available to them. If human capital is sophisticated enough to absorb technical knowledge, then the positive benefits for knowledge spillovers may be realized. Few studies paid attention to path dependencies and the impact of existing industry mix, production culture, and other legacies of a place on current regional economic outcomes.

The University as an Important Regional Player in Regional Innovation Systems

Since the 1980s, studies have analyzed innovation processes within geographical systems (Edquist, 1997; Freeman, 1991; Freeman and Soete, 1997; Lundvall, 1992; Maskell *et al.*, 1998). This stream of research started with identifying national innovation systems (NIS) in Europe, assuming that the occurrence of innovation depends on the structure and organization of industries and companies within a nation, institutions and existing social networks, size of the region, and infrastructure (physical, financial, cultural). The model recognizes universities as institutions supportive to innovation. The role of universities is seen as either direct—through the education of students and production of ideas—or indirect—through knowledge spillovers from research and education.

Over time, the locus of innovative activity changed from the national level to regional economies. Certainly, part of this attention was due to the idea of clusters (Porter, 1990). Yet the literature differentiates between the location of production and the location of innovation (Audretsch and Feldman, 1996). Precise attention of scholars to the regional innovation systems only emphasized the role of universities as regional institutions that matter most to innovative activity.

In the 1990s, through the introduction of the concept of learning regions, social scientists looked at universities as endogenous to the regional systems (Morgan, 1997; Florida, 1995; Lundvall and Johnson, 1994; Hudson, 1999; Keane and Allison, 1999). They concentrated on the creation of knowledge and its absorption by local firms through the social and organizational networks mainly at the regional level. The increased interest in regional information systems (RIS) was triggered by the regionalization of production and the growing importance of a region in global competition. Forced to compete globally, regions were striving for developing regional competitive advantage.

The necessity for continuous innovation with the purpose of developing or retaining a regional competitive advantage changed the whole paradigm of learning. Universities started to see a new client—spatial clusters and relational networks of small and medium-sized firms that substituted for large corporations (Chatterton and Goddard, 2000). The dynamic of learning shifted from a model where learning occurs at universities and knowledge is then applied at the workplace, to a model where interactive learning occurs throughout the lifetime—at the university, workplace, and networking functions.

In late 1990s and early 2000s, the concept of RIS has been widely studied and empirically tested, especially in Europe (Amin and Thrift, 1995; Braczyk and Heidenreich, 1998; de la Monthe and Paquet, 1998; Cooke, 1998; and Hassink, 2001). Scholars have developed a typology to assess structural differences of RISs (Cooke, 1998, p. 19–24) and conducted comparative analyses of regional information systems (Hassink, 2001, p. 224). Iammarino and McCann (2006) classified industrial clusters within four different stages in the evolution of technological innovation systems. Each life-cycle stage of innovation systems has a corresponding knowledge base, a distinctive type of industrial regime, is based on a different phase of knowledge spillovers, and has different requirements in the presence of knowledge-generating institutions within the regional system of innovation.

The concept of differentiating phases of innovation systems within the technological life-cycle is consistent with the stream of research on innovation systems and their spatial and knowledge components by Oinas and Malecki (Oinas and Malecki, 1999, 2002; Malecki, 1997). Analyzing the knowledge component of innovation systems, along with local conventions (e.g. tolerance toward failure, risk-seeking, enthusiasm for change and rapid response to technological change), they emphasize the increasingly important role of regional creativity within the context of regional knowledge.

Acknowledging different types of regional institutions, Etzkowitz (2003) introduced the Triple Helix[3] model that conceptualizes university–industry–government relations. This model describes changes in relationships among three main regional players: academia, business, and government. With the growing importance of knowledge, and as the production of knowledge transforms into economic enterprise, the university is given a more prominent role in the regional economy. The university develops an organizational capacity not only to produce knowledge, but also to deploy knowledge into the regional economy or to sell the products derived from new knowledge outside the region. This process is consistent with an innovation being changed from an internal process of a single firm into one that takes place among many firms and knowledge-producing institutions. These changes trigger a transformation in the relationships among university, industry, and government (Figure 28.1) from a "statist" model of government controlling academia and industry (1),[4] to a "laissez-faire" model, which separates the roles of industry, academia and government, interacting only modestly across strong boundaries (2), and, finally to the Triple Helix model with each institutional sphere maintaining its identity while taking on the role of each of the others (3).

With each of the three players, industry, state, and academia, partially taking on the roles of the others, the established match of an institution to its traditional role and functions is outmoded. The Triple Helix model implies interactions across university, industry, and government; and the interactions are mediated by organizations such as industrial liaisons, university technology transfer offices, university contract offices, and other entities. These mediators have a mission to ease legal and organizational barriers in the interaction of the three players to benefit the deployment of innovation within the region or to benefit the profitable sale of the knowledge products resulting in benefits to the region through a multiplier effect.

According to Pires and Castro, Gulbrandsen, and Leydesdorff and Etzkowitz, as the Triple Helix model evolves, each of the three institutions begin to assume the traditional roles of the others in the technology transfer process (Gulbrandsen, 1997; Pires and Castro, 1997; Leydesdorff and Etzkowitz, 1998). For example, the university performs an entrepreneurial role in marketing knowledge, in creating companies, and also assumes a quasi-governmental role as a regional innovation organizer.

Direct Effects of University Research

In 1980, the United States Congress passed the Bayh-Dole Act and the intellectual property landscape in the U.S. changed dramatically. Universities were allowed to retain intellectual property

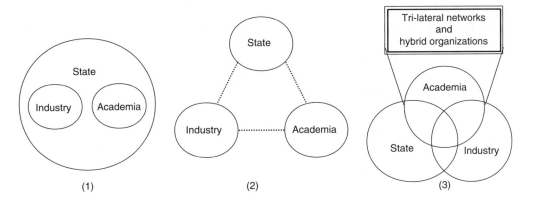

Figure 28.1 "Anthropology" of Triple Helix Model.

Source: Etzkowitz, H. (2003). Innovation in innovation: the Triple Helix of university-industry-government relations. *Social Science Information*, 42(3), 302.

rights and to pursue commercialization even though the basic research had been funded by the federal government. In the late 1990s, technology transfer activities of research universities began to be recognized as important factors in regional economic growth. Scientists started to look at the different factors and mechanisms stimulating transfer of new technology from university to industry (Cohen *et al.*, 1994; Campbell, 1997; Lowen, 1997; Slaughter and Leslie, 1997; DeVol, 1999). Discussing the benefits of such technology transfer, Rogers, Yin, and Hoffmann (2000) hypothesized that "research universities seek to facilitate technological innovations to private companies in order to: (1) create jobs and contribute to local economic development, and (2) earn additional funding for university research" (p. 48). They illustrated the potential impact of university research expenditures on jobs and wealth creation through the process of simple technology transfer.

Beeson and Montgomery (1993) tested the relationship between research universities and regional labor market performance. They assessed a university's impact on local labour market conditions by measuring quality in terms of RandD funding, the total number of bachelor's degrees awarded in science and engineering, and the number of science and engineering programs rated in the top 20 in the country (p. 755). Beeson and Montgomery identified four ways in which colleges and universities may affect local labor markets: (1) increasing skills of local workers (together with rising employment and earnings opportunities), (2) increasing the ability to develop and implement new technologies, (3) affecting local demand through research funds attracted from outside the area (a standard multiplier effect), and (4) conducting basic research that can lead to technological innovations (p. 753).[5]

Link and Rees (1990) emphasized the important role of graduates to a local labour market, particularly for new start-ups and the local high-tech market, assuming they do not leave the region. Gottlieb (2001) took this idea further in his Ohio "brain-drain" study, emphasizing that exporting graduates is a sign of long-run economic development problems for a region. In their study of 37 American cities, Acs, FitzRoy and Smith (1995) tested university spillover effects on employment, and, like Bania, Eberts and Fogarty (1993), tried to measure business start-ups from the commercialization of university basic research. These studies produced mixed results, showing that university products are statistically significant in their impacts in one case and insignificant in others.

Following Adams' findings about the positive effect on industrial research from the geographical proximity to university research (Adams *et al.*, 2000; Adams, 2001), many studies (Audretsch and Feldman, 1996; Audretsch and Stephan, 1996; Cortright and Mayer, 2002) found that for most industries, activities that lead to innovation and growth take place within only a few regions nationally or globally. Whether it was the impact of universities on regional labor markets or the impact of university RandD and technology transfer on the growth of employment or per capita income, a broader framework was needed to measure the impact of all products created in universities.

Each university interacts with the regional economy as represented by local businesses, government agencies, and the region's social and business infrastructure. The actual interaction is based on its set of products and their value to the region. The university can create sources of regional competitive advantage and can significantly strengthen what Berglund and Clarke (2000) identify as the seven elements of a technology-based economy: (1) regional, university-based intellectual infrastructure—a base that generates new ideas, (2) spillovers of knowledge—commercialization of university-developed technology, (3) competitive physical infrastructure, including the highest quality and technologically advanced telecommunication services, (4) technically skilled workforce—an adequate number of highly skilled technical workers, (5) capital creating adequate information flows around sources of investments, (6) entrepreneurial culture—where people view starting a company as a routine rather than an unusual occurrence, and (7) the quality of life that comes from residential amenities that make a region competitive with others.

The university's influence on these factors is of interest to economic development because each university product can be an asset used by a regional economy or can be sold outside the region, generating regional income. Each university makes a choice about what product will be a priority to produce and sell, assigns its resources, and creates policies to implement its goals.

Many studies are focused solely on showing the impact of university presence using the multiplier effect of university expenditures. These studies are confusing the impact of university products (which we identify as purposefully created outcomes according to a university mission) and the impact of university presence in a region (which depends on university expenditure patterns). In the traditional multiplier-effect studies, the models usually take into account two factors of university impact: (1) the number of university students and employees (which is a non-linear function of university enrollment) and the impact of their income through individual spending patterns and (2) a pattern of university expenditures via a university budget. These two factors (sometimes called university products) are indirect functions of enrollment and endowments and are highly collinear with university size. While normalized to per-capita indicators, they highly correlate with university reputation and, apart from the reputation, are to a large degree uniform across regions.

Morgan (2002) tried to bridge the gap between two concepts of university products and create a conceptual model of the two-tier system of higher education institutions in the United Kingdom. Using Huggins' (1999) and Phelps' (1997) concept of the globalization of innovation and production in regional economies, he discusses two models of direct and indirect employment effects—the elite model and the outreach/diffusion-oriented model (Figure 28.2). Morgan emphasizes the increased role of universities in developing local social capital by acting as "catalysts for civic engagement and collective action and networking" and "widening access to cohorts from lower socio-economic backgrounds" improving local social inclusion (pp. 66–67).

Bringing elements of globalization into understanding the role of universities for the local economy is widely emphasized in the MIT Industrial Performance Center's study led by Richard

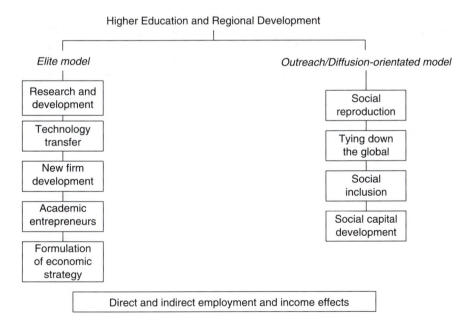

Figure 28.2 Universities and Regional Development: Two Paradigms.

Source: Morgan, B. (2002) Higher education and regional economic department in Wales: an opportunity for demonstrating the efficacy of devolution in economic development, *Regional Studies*, 36(1), 66.

Lester. The 2005 report "Universities, Innovation, and the Competitiveness of Local Economies" discusses an important alignment of the university mission with the needs of the local economy, emphasizing that this alignment is affected by the globalization of knowledge and production and depends on "the ability of local firms to take up new technologies, and new knowledge more generally, and to apply this knowledge productively".

Through the different roles played by universities, this study acknowledges diverse pathways of transferring knowledge from universities to local industries (Figure 28.3). Some of these pathways are common to economies with different core industries, and some are unique to the regions. For example, *education/manpower development* is as valuable for the economy as *industry transplantation* and *upgrading mature industry economy*. *Forefront science and engineering research* and *aggressive technology licensing policies* are unique and critical for *creating new industries economies*, and *bridging between disconnected actors* is as distinctive for the economy as *diversifying old industry into related new industry*.

These unique and common pathways for economies with different industrial structures imply existence of universities' products that, besides teaching and research, include faculty consulting, publications, and collaborative research.

The discussion about the role of a university in the regional economy has been enriched by a model created by Louis Tornatzky, Paul Waugman, and Denis Gray (Tornatzky *et al.*, 1995, 1997, 1999, 2002). These researchers advocate the importance of research universities for regional economic development and examine whether the influence of a university on a local economy differs geographically. The authors conclude:

> While we agree with skeptics who argue this [university's impact on a local economy] is not easily accomplished and that some universities and states appear to be looking for a quick fix, we believe that there is enough evidence to demonstrate that universities that are committed

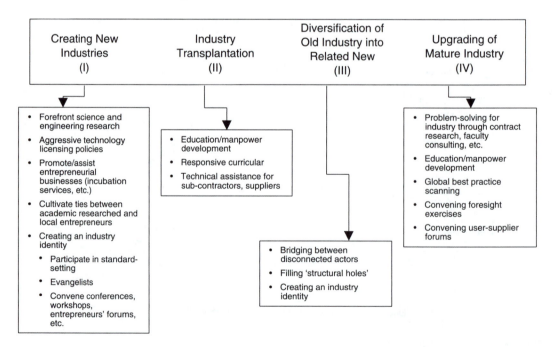

Figure 28.3 University Roles in Alternative Regional Innovation-led Growth Pathways.

Source: Lester, R. (2005) *Universities, Innovation, and the Competitiveness of Local Economies*, Industrial Performance Center, MIT, p. 28.

and thoughtful can impact their state or local economic environment in a number of ways (Tornatzky *et al.*, 2002, pp. 15–16).

Tornatzky's hypothesis of the ways that universities can affect regional economies is presented in Figure 28.4.

The research team identified 10 "dominants" of institutional behavior that enable the university's external interactions with industry and economic development interests and lie beneath organizational characteristics and functions that facilitate those interactions. Tornatzky *et al.*, (2002) group these dominants, or interactions, characteristics, and functions into the three broad groups depicted in Figure 28.4. The first group (1) represents partnering mechanisms and facilitators identified as "functions, people, or units that are involved in partnership activities that allegedly have an impact on economic development" (Tornatzky *et al.*, 2002, p. 16). The list of programs or activities in this component includes, but is not limited to, industry research partnerships, industry education and training, and other activities.

The second group (2) includes institutional enablers (university mission, vision, and goals, and faculty culture and rewards) that facilitate partnering through the "relevant behavior of faculty, students, and administrators [that] are supported by the values, norms, and reward systems of the institution" (Tornatzky *et al.*, 2002, p. 18). The third group is represented by two boundary-spanning structures and systems: formal partnerships with economic development organizations (labelled (3) in the figure) and industry-university advisory boards and councils (labelled (4)). They are positioned to link the university system to the economic development intermediaries and business community. As a result of communication between all of the components, the framework captures locally generated technological outcomes (5), such as new knowledge and technologies that trigger economic development.

Tornatzky, Waugman and Gray (2002) acknowledged that, while the local economic environment of universities is complex, only universities that are actively involved in extensive industry partnerships can successfully transfer their products into local economies. Such universities will

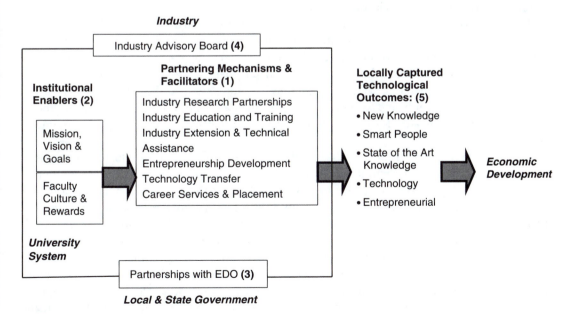

Figure 28.4 Innovation U.: New University Roles in a Knowledge Economy.

"tend to adopt language in mission, vision, and goal statement that reflects that emphasis. They [universities] also tend to incorporate different versions of those statements in reports, publications, press releases, and speeches directed at the external world" (p. 19).

Paytas *et al.*, (2004) tested this hypothesis in their case studies of eight universities by examining the scope of universities' economic engagement in local economies. They assessed the breadth of involvement of universities with their regions and local communities and concluded that, for a university to play an important role in the development of industry clusters, it "must be aligned with regional interests and industry clusters across a broad spectrum, not just in terms of technical knowledge. . . . The characteristics of the clusters are as important, if not more important than the characteristics of the university" (p. 34).

Goldstein *et al.*, (1995) developed a set of university outputs that is also broader than the traditional understanding of university products, which includes only *skilled labor* and *new knowledge*. Their framework identifies eight university products and among them distinguishes between knowledge creation and co-production of knowledge infrastructure, human capital creation, capital investment and technological innovation and technology transfer. This model adds a new and very important understanding of leadership value and regional milieu. According to the framework, these university outputs impact regional productivity and business innovation, enable business start-ups, increase regional capacity for sustained development, and spark off regional creativity. The spending pattern of university reflected in capital investment creates direct and indirect multiplier-type impact regional economy. This framework was operationalized by Goldstein and Renault (2004) and tested with the modified Griliches-Jaffe production function.

A similar approach is used by Porter (2002) in a report for the Initiative for a Competitive Inner City. He studied six primary university products using a multiplier-effect approach. Porter identifies the main impacts on the local economy through the university's (1) employment, by offering employment opportunities to local residents; (2) purchases, redirecting institutional purchasing to local businesses; (3) workforce development, addressing local and regional workforce needs; (4) real estate development, using it as an anchor of local economic growth; (5) advisor/network-builder, channeling university expertise to local businesses; and (6) incubator provider, to support start-up companies and advance research commercialization.

These approaches mix university products—goods and services that are produced by universities according to the university mission—with university impacts—results of university influence on surrounding environments. For example, universities influence appreciation of surrounding real estate value without including this in their mission statement. Lester's study acknowledges that "working ties to the operating sectors of economy are not central to the internal design of the university as an institution, and as universities open themselves up to the marketplace for knowledge and ideas to a greater degree than in the past, confusion over mission has been common" (Lester, 2005, p. 9).

According to Hill and Lendel (2007), higher education is a multi-product industry with seven distinct products: (1) education, (2) contract research, (3) cultural products, (4) trained labor, (5) technology diffusion, (6) new knowledge creation, and (7) new products and industries. These products become marketable commodities that are sold regionally and nationally or they became part of a region's economic development capital base. Growth in the scale, quality, and variety of these products increases the reputation and status of a university. An improved, or superior, reputation allows universities to receive more grants and endowments, attract better students, increase tuition, conduct more RandD, and develop and market more products. This reinforcing mechanism between a university's reputation and university products transforms universities into complex multi-product organizations with a complicated management structure and multiple missions. A university manages its portfolio of products as defined in the university's mission statement and expressed through the university's functions and policies.

Conclusions

The new growth theory and the concepts of increasing returns to scale, knowledge spillovers and knowledge externalities form a basis for creating a framework for technology-based regional economic development. They enable an understanding of the factors that influence regional knowledge creation and implementation of an innovation into regional economic system.

The studies on knowledge spillovers and agglomeration effects apply a variety of approaches and methodologies to studying the impacts of knowledge. Even as they lead to a better understanding of the impact of universities, the results are often fragmented to specific industries and extracts of geographies, primarily due to constraints on data availability. However, even with this fragmentation the empirical results prove the significance of university-based research effects on follow-up industry RandD, increased numbers of intermediate results such as patents, start-up companies, growing employment and wages. It is evident that the positive role of the university in regional economic performance cannot be ignored.

However, the effect of university products on regional economic outcomes is not evident. New knowledge and innovation directly create only intermediate results, such as patents, spin-off companies, graduates, new products and technologies, and new economic, social, and cultural regional environments. Deployed within regional economies, these effects create local competitive advantage. Positive externalities of agglomeration economies of scale allow knowledge spillover and explain the mechanism that enables both, creating the intermediate results of university products and deploying them into regional economies.

Synthesis of thoughts behind the literature on economic development theories and the knowledge spillovers concept suggests that there are two major hypothesized systems linking universities with regional growth: (1) mechanisms of knowledge spillovers due to agglomeration economies of scale, and (2) specific economic environments where the knowledge spillovers occur. The environment of knowledge spillovers and deployment of the results of knowledge spillovers into regional economies can be described by characteristics that reflect the intensity of agglomeration economies and their qualitative characteristics, such as quality of the regional labor force, level of entrepreneurship, intensity of competition in a region, structural composition of regional economic systems and industries, and social characteristics of places, such as leadership and culture.

Notes

1. Paul Samuelson developed the theory of public goods where he assigned all goods to four categories by their two essential characteristics: rivalry and excludability. Knowledge is a public good, which is non-rivalrous and non-excludable. However, developing applications of new knowledge in a form of practical value for the market benefits developers who are earning a profit from selling the applications. The self-interests of developers make the new knowledge of improving technology to become partially excludable goods.
2. Established in the 1930s, the Standard Industrial Classification (SIC) is a United States government system for classifying industries by an up to four-digit code. In 1997, it was replaced by the six-digit North American Industry Classification System (NAICS).
3. The discussion on this model is led by Henry Etzkowitz—associate professor of sociology at Purchase College and Director of the Science Policy Institute at the State University of New York. He is co-convener of the bi-yearly International Conference on University-Industry-Government Relations: "The Triple Helix".
4. This model is more relevant to European systems of education.
5. Also discussed by Nelson (1986).

References

Acs, Z. (2002). *Innovation and the growth of cities.* Northampton, MA: Edward Elgar.
Acs, Z., Audretsch, D. and Feldman, M. (1991). Real effects of academic research: comment. *American Economic Review, 81,* 363–367.
Acs, Z., Audretsch, D. and Feldman, M. (1994a). RandD spillovers and innovative activity. *Managerial and Decision Economics, 15,* 131–138.
Acs, Z., Audretsch, D. and Feldman, M. (1994b). RandD spillovers and recipient firm size. *Review of Economics and Statistics, 76,* 336–340.
Acs, Z., FitzRoy, F.R. and Smith, I. (1995). High technology employment, wages and university RandD spillovers: evidence from U.S. cities. In P. Reynolds *et al., Frontiers of Entrepreneurship.* Wellesley, MA: Babson College.
Adams, J.D. (2001). Comparative localization of academic and industrial spillovers. *NBER Working Paper, 8292.* Retrieved from NBER (National Bureau of Economic Research) Working Papers database: http://www.nber.org.
Adams, J.D. (2002). Comparative localization of academic and industrial spillovers. *Journal of Economic Geography, 2*(3), 253–278.
Adams, J.D. (2004). Learning, internal research, and spillovers evidence from a sample of RandD laboratories. *Rensselaer Working Papers in Economics 0409.*
Adams, J.D., Chiang, E.P. and Starkey, K. (2000). Industry-university cooperative research center. *NBER Working Paper, 7943.* Retrieved from NBER Working Papers database.
Adams, J.D. and Jaffe, A. (1996). Bounding the effects of RandD: an investigation using matched establishment-firm data. *NBER Working Paper, 5544.* Retrieved from NBER Working Papers database.
Agrawal, A. and Cockburn, I. (2002). University research, industrial RandD, and the anchor tenant hypothesis. *NBER Working Paper, 9212.* Retrieved from NBER Working Papers database.
Almedia, P. and Kogut, B. (1994). Technology and geography: the localization of knowledge and the mobility of patent holders. *Working Paper.* Philadelphia, PA: The Wharton School, University of Pennsylvania. Retrieved September 7, 2003, from http://www.wharton.upenn.edu.
Almeida, P. and Kogut, B. (1997). The exploration of technological diversity and the geographic localisation of innovation. *Small Business Economics, 9,* 21–31.
Amin, A. and Thrift, N. (1995). *Globalization, institutions, and regional development in Europe.* Oxford: Oxford University Press.
Arrow, K.J. (1962). The economic implications of learning by doing. *Review of Economics Studies, 29,* 155–173.
Audretsch, D. (1998). Agglomeration and the location of innovative activity. *Oxford Review of Economic Policy, 14*(2), 18–29.
Audretsch, D. and Feldman, M. (1996). RandD spillovers and the geography of innovation and production. *American Economic Review, 86,* 630–640.
Audretsch, D. and Stephan, P. (1996). Company-scientist locational link: the case of biotechnology. *American Economic Review, 86,* 641–652.
Bania, N., Eberts, R. and Fogarty, M. (1993). Universities and the start-up of new companies: can we generalize from route 128 and Silicon Valley? *The Review of Economics and Statistics, 75,* 761–766.
Beeson, P. and Montgomery, E. (1993). The effects of colleges and universities on local labor markets. *The Review of Economics and Statistics, 75*(4), 753–761.
Berglund, D. and Clarke, M. (2000). Using research and development to grow state economies. Washington D.C.: National Governors' Association.
Braczyk, H-J. and Heidenreich, M. (1998). Regional governance structures in a globalized world. In Brabzyk, H-J., Cooke, P., Heidenreich, M. (eds) *Regional innovation systems: the role of governances in a globalized world.* London: UCL Press.
Campbell, T.I.D. (1997). Public policy for the 21st century: addressing potential conflict in university-industry collaboration. *Review of Higher Education, 20*(4), 357–379.
Caniels, M.C.J. (2000). *Knowledge spillovers and economic growth: regional growth differentials across Europe.* Cheltenham: Elgar.
Chatterton, P. and Goddard, J. (2000). The response of higher education institutions to regional needs. *European Journal of Education, 35*(4), 475–496.
Chinitz, B. (1961). Contrasts in agglomeration: New York and Pittsburgh. *The American Economic Review, 51*(2), 279–289.
Cohen, W., Florida, R. and Goe, W.R. (1994). *University-industry research centers in the U.S.* Pittsburgh, PA: Center for Economic Development, Carnegie Mellon University.
Cooke, P. (1998). Introduction: origins of the concept. In Braczyk, H.J., Cooke, P., Heidenreich, M. (eds) *Regional innovation systems. the role of governance in a globalized world.* London: UCL Press.
Cortright, J. and Mayer, H. (2002). *Signs of life: the growth of biotechnology centers in the U.S.* Washington, DC: The Brookings Institute.
David, P.A. (1999). Krugman's economic geography of development. NEGs, POGs and naked models in space. *International Regional Science Review, 22,* 162–172.
de la Mothe, J. and Paquet, G. (1998). Local and regional systems of innovation as learning socio-economies. In de la Mothe, J. and Paquet, G. (eds) *Local and regional systems of innovation* (pp. 1–16). Boston, MA: Kluwer.
Desrochers, P. (2001). Local diversity, human creativity, and technological innovation. *Growth and Change, 32*(3), 369–394.

DeVol, R.C. (1999). *America's high-tech economy: growth, development, and risk for metropolitan areas.* Santa Monica, CA: Miliken Institute.

Döring, T. and Schnellenbach, J. (2006). What do we know about geographical knowledge spillovers and regional growth?: a survey of the literature. *Regional Studies, 40,* 375–395.

Edquist, C. (1997). Systems of innovations approaches—their emergence and characteristics. In Edquist, C. (ed.) *Systems of innovations: technologies, institutions and organizations.* London: Cassell.

Etzkowitz, H. (2003). Innovation in innovation: the Triple Helix of university-industry-government relations. *Social Science Information, 42*(3), 293–337.

Feldman, M.P. (1994). The university and economic development: the case of Johns Hopkins University and Baltimore. *Economic Development Quarterly, 8*(1), 67–76.

Feldman, M.P. and Florida, R. (1994). The geographic sources of innovation: technological infrastructure and product innovation in the United States. *Annals of the Association of American Geographers, 84*(2), 210–229.

Feller, I. (1990). Universities as engines of RandD-based economic growth: they think they can. *Research Policy, 19*(4), 335–348.

Florida, R. (1995). Towards the learning region. *Futures, 27*(5), 527–536.

Freeman, C. (1991). The nature of innovation and evolution of the product system. In *Technology and productivity: the challenge for economic policy.* Paris: Organization for Economic Co-operation and Development.

Freeman, C. and Soete, L. (1997). *The economics of industrial innovation.* Cambridge, MA: The MIT Press.

Goldstein, H.A., Maier, G. and Luger, M. (1995). The university as an instrument for economic and business development: U.S. and European comparisons. In Dill, D. and Sporn, B. (eds) *Emerging patterns of social demand and university reform: through a glass darkly. Issues in higher education.* Tarrytown, NY: Elsevier Science Inc.

Goldstein, H.A. and Renault, C. (2004). Contributions of universities to regional economic development: A quasi-experimental approach. *Regional Studies, 38*(7), 733–746.

Gottlieb, P. (2001). *The problem of brain drain in Ohio and northeastern Ohio: what is it? how severe is it? what should we do about it?* Center for Regional Economic Issues, Weatherhead School of Management, Case Western Reserve University, Cleveland, Ohio.

Granovetter, M. (1985). Economic action and social structure: A theory of embeddedness. *American Journal of Sociology, 91,* 481–510.

Griliches, Z. (1979). Issues in assessing the contribution of RandD to productivity growth. *Bell Journal of Economics, 10,* 92–116.

Gulbrandsen, M. (1997). Universities and industrial competitive advantage. In Etzkowitz, H. and Leydesdorff, L. (eds) *Universities in the global economy: a Triple Helix of university-industry-government relations* (121–131). London: Cassell.

Harrison, B., Kelley, M. and Gant, J.P. (1996). Innovative firm behavior and local milieu: exploring the interaction of agglomeration, firm effects, and technological change. *Economic Geography, 72*(3), 233–258.

Hassink, R. (2001) Towards regionally embedded innovation support system in South Korea: Case-studies from Kyongbuk-Taegu and Kyonggi. *Urban Studies, 38,* 1373–1395.

Hill, E. and Lendel, I. (2007). The impact of the reputation of bio-life science and engineering doctoral programs on regional economic development. *Economic Development Quarterly, 21*(3), 223–243.

Hudson, R. (1999). "The learning economy, the learning firm and the learning region": a sympathetic critique of the limits to learning. *European Urban and Regional Studies, 6,* 59–72.

Huggins, R. (1999). Embedding inward investment through workforce development: experience in Wales. *Papers in Planning Research.* Cardiff: Department of City and Regional Planning, University of Wales.

Iammarino, S. and McCann, P. (2006). The structure and evolution of industrial clusters: Transactions, technology and knowledge spillovers. *Research Policy, 35*(7), 1018–1036.

Innis, H.A. (1950). *Empire and communications.* Oxford: Oxford University Press.

Innis, H.A. (1951). *The bias of communications.* Toronto: University of Toronto Press.

Jaffe, A. (1986). Technological opportunity, spillovers of RandD: evidence from firms' patents, profits, and market value. *American Economic Review, 76,* 984–1001.

Jaffe, A. (1989). Real effects of academic research. *The American Economic Review, 79*(5), 957–970.

Jaffe, A.B., Trajtenberg, M. and Henderson, R. (1993). Geographic localisation of knowledge spillovers as evidenced by patent citations. *Quarterly Journal of Economics, 108,* 577–598.

Keane, J. and Allison, J. (1999). The intersection of the learning region and local and regional economic development: analyzing the role of higher education. *Regional Studies, 33*(9), 896–902.

Kelly, M. and Hageman, A. (1999). Marshallian externalities in innovation. *Journal of Economic Growth, 4,* 39–54.

Kogut, B. and Zander, U. (1992). Knowledge of the firm, combinative capabilities, and the replication of technology. *Organization Science, 3,* 383–397.

Kogut, B. and Zander, U. (1996). What firms do? Coordination, identity and learning. *Organization Science, 7*(5), 502–518.

Krugman, P. (1991). *Geography and trade.* Cambridge, MA: MIT Press.

Krugman, P. (1995). *Development, geography and economic theory.* Cambridge, MA: MIT Press.

Krugman, P. (1998). What's new about economic geography. *Oxford Review of Economic Policy, 14*(2), 7–17.

Krugman, P. (1999). The role of geography in development. *International Regional Science Review, 22,* 142–161.

Lester, R. (2005). *Universities, innovation, and the competitiveness of local economies: summary report from the local innovation project.* MIT: Industrial Performance Center. (MIT-IPC-05-010)

Leydesdorff, L. and Etzkowitz, H. (1998). The Triple Helix as a model for innovation studies. *Science and Public Policy, 25*(3), 195–203.

Link, A.L. and Rees, J. (1990). Firm size, university based research, and the return to RandD. *Small Business Economics*, 2, 25–31.

Lowen, R. (1997). *Creating the Cold War university: the transformation of Stanford*. Berkeley, CA: University of California Press.

Lucas, R.E. (1988). On the mechanics of economic development. *Journal of Monetary Economics*, 22, 3–42.

Lundvall, B. (1992). *Introduction*. In Lundvall, B. (ed.) *National systems of innovations: towards a theory of innovation and interactive learning*. London: Pinter.

Lundvall, B. and Johnson, B. (1994). The learning economy. *Journal of Industry Studies*, 1(2), 23–42.

Malecki, E.J. (1997). *Technology and economic development: the dynamics of local, regional and national competitiveness*. Boston, MA: Addison Wesley Longman.

Marshall, A. (1890). *Principles of economics*. London: Macmillan.

Martin, R. (1999). Critical Survey. The new "geographical turn" in economics: some critical reflection. *Cambridge Journal of Economics*, 23, 65–91.

Martin, R. and Sunley, P. (1996). Paul Krugman's "Geographical Economics" and its implications for regional development theory: a critical assessment. *Economic Geography*, 72(3), 259–292.

Maskell, P., Eskelinen, H., Hannibalsson, I., Malmberg, A. and Vatne, E. (1998). *Competitiveness, localised learning and regional development: specialisation and prosperity in small open economies*. London: Routledge.

Maurseth, P.B. and Verspagen, B. (1999). Knowledge spillovers in Europe. A patent citation analysis. Paper presented at the CRENOS Conference on Technological Externalities and Spatial Location, University of Cagliari, 24–25 September.

Morgan, K. (1997). The learning region: Institutions, innovation and regional renewal. *Regional Studies*, 36(5), 491–503.

Morgan, B. (2002). Higher education and regional economic department in Wales: An opportunity for demonstrating the efficacy of devolution in economic development. *Regional Studies*, 36(1), 65–73.

Nelson, R. (1986). Institutions supporting technical advance in industry. *The American Economic Review*, 76(2), 186–189.

North, D.C. (1955). Location theory and regional economic growth. *The Journal of Political Economy*, 63(3), 243–258.

Oinas, P. and Malecki, E. (1999). *Making connections: technological learning and regional economic change*. Aldershot: Ashgate.

Oinas, P. and Malecki, E. (2002). The evolution of technologies in time and space: from national and regional to spatial innovation systems. *International Regional Science Review*, 25(1), 102–131.

Olson, M. (1982). *The rise and decline of nations*. New Haven, CT: Yale University Press.

Paytas, J., Gradeck, R. and Andrews, L. (2004). *Universities and the development of industry clusters*. Pittsburgh, PA: Center for Economic Development, Carnegie Mellon University.

Phelps, N. (1997). *Multinationals and European integration: trade, investment and regional development*. London: Jessica Kingsley.

Pires, A.R. and Castro, E.A. (1997). Can a strategic project for a university be strategic to regional development? *Science and Public Policy*, 24(1), 15–20.

Polanyi, M. (1962). Tacit knowledge: Its bearing on some problems of philosophy. *Reviews of Modern Physics*, 34, 601–616.

Polanyi, M. (1967). *The tacit dimension*. New York: Doubleday.

Porter, M. (1990). *Competitive advantage of nations*. New York: The Free Press.

Porter, M. (2002). Leveraging colleges and universities for urban economic revitalization: an action agenda, initiative for a competitive inner city and CEOs for cities. Retrieved September 4, 2005 from http://www.cherrycommission.org/docs/Resources/Economic_Benefits/EDA_University_based_partnerships2004.pdf

Putnam, R.D., Leonardi, R. and Nanetti, R.Y. (1993). *Making democracy work*. Princeton, NJ: Princeton University Press.

Rogers, E.M., Yin, J. and Hoffmann, J. (2000). Assessing the effectiveness of technology transfer offices at U.S. research universities. *The Journal of the Association of University Technology Managers*, XII, 47–80.

Romer, P.M. (1986). Increasing returns and long-run growth. *Journal of Political Economy*, 94, 1002–1037.

Romer, P.M. (1990). Endogenous technological change. *Journal of Political Economy*, 98, 72–102.

Schumpeter, J. (1934). *The fundamental phenomenon of economic development*. Cambridge, MA: Harvard University Press.

Slaughter, S. and Leslie, L. (1997). *Academic capitalism: politics, policies, and the entrepreneurial university*. Baltimore, MD: Johns Hopkins University Press.

Smith, Adam. (1776). *Wealth of Nations*, C.J. Bullock (ed.). Vol. X. The Harvard Classics. New York: P.F. Collier and Son, 1909–14; Bartleby.com, 2001. www.bartleby.com/10/.

Solow, R.S. (1957). Technical change and the aggregate production function. *Review of Economics and Statistics*, 39, 312–320.

Tiebout, C. (1956). A pure theory of local expenditures. *Journal of Political Economy*, 64(5), 416–424.

Tornatzky, L.G., Waugaman, P.G. and Bauman, J.S. (1997). *Benchmarking university-industry technology transfer in the South: 1995–1996 data*. Research Triangle Park, N.C.: Southern Growth Policies Board, Southern Technology Council.

Tornatzky, L.G., Waugaman, P.G. and Casson, L. (1995). *Benchmarking university-industry technology transfer in the South: 1993–1994 data*. Research Triangle Park, N.C.: Southern Growth Policies Board, Southern Technology Council.

Tornatzky, L.G., Waugaman, P.G. and Gray, D. (1999). *Industry-university technology transfer: models of alternative practice, policy, and program*. Research Triangle Park, N.C.: Southern Growth Policies Board, Southern Technology Council.

Tornatzky, L.G., Waugaman, P.G. and Gray, D. (2002). *Innovation U.: new university roles in a knowledge economy*. Raleigh, Research Triangle Park, N.C.: Southern Growth Policies Board, Southern Technology Council.

Varga, A. (1997). Regional economic effects of university research: a survey. *Research Paper, 9729*. Retrieved March 5, 2002, from West Virginia University, Regional Research Institute.

Verspagen, B. and Schoenmakers, W. (2000). The spatial dimension of knowledge spillovers in Europe: evidence from patenting data. Paper presented at the AEA Conference on Intellectual Property Econometrics, Alicante, 19–20 April.

Weber, A. (1929). *Theory of the location of industries*. Chicago IL: The University of Chicago Press.

Young, A.A. (1999). *Money and growth: selected papers of Allyn Abbott Young*. London: Routledge.

29

Building Democracy's University

University–Community Partnerships and the Emergent Civic Engagement Movement

Matthew Hartley and David Soo

Introduction

Colleges and universities have deep civic roots. Their founding documents and current mission statements underscore the imperative of cultivating in students the manners and means of assuming leadership positions within society (Morphew and Hartley, 2006). In the U.S. context (which is the one with which we are most familiar, and which constitutes the central thrust of this chapter), the early colonial colleges focused their attentions on the sons of wealthy patrons of particular towns or cities. Yale, for example, was conceived as an institution "wherein youth may be instructed in the arts and sciences, who through the blessing of Almighty God, may be fitted for public employment, both in Church and civil State". In the decades following the Revolution, the notion of a democratic purpose for higher education began to grow. As higher education historian Frederick Rudolph observes, "A commitment to the republic became a guiding obligation of the American college" (1962, p. 61).

From their inceptions, colleges and universities have also played an important role as institutions that provide cultural enrichment, and function as economic and social anchors. The Brown brothers, businessmen who provided capital for their namesake institution in Providence, Rhode Island, made the pragmatic argument that "building the college here will be the means of bringing great quantities of money into the place, and thereby greatly increasing the markets for all kinds of the country's produce, and consequently increasing the value of estates to which the town is a market" (Cochran, 1972). Indeed, many towns established private colleges as a strategy for drawing people to them. This role continues today. In many locales, universities are the largest private employers and have an important role to play in upholding the economic stability of these areas (Harkavy and Zuckerman, 1999).

Despite this rich civic legacy, in the 1980s many had come to feel that institutions of higher learning had lost their way. Utilitarian and economic aims were seen as trumping loftier purposes. Critics charged colleges and universities with serving the interests of disciplinary-bound professors, rather than actively trying to solve pressing real-world problems (Smith, 1990; Sykes, 1989). What then occurred was the launching of a multiplicity of efforts aimed at re-asserting the civic purposes of American higher education. In this chapter we examine why and how this occurred. Then, we survey the current landscape and note some of the predominant forms of engagement that have emerged. Finally we underscore the emergent trend that is taking place, which is shifting the emphasis from community-based learning and university–community partnerships to a civic engagement aimed at reclaiming democratic ideals.

Reclaiming Higher Education's Civic Purposes

What gave rise to this resurgent effort to promote the civic purposes of American colleges and universities? The early 1980s were troubled times. A faltering economy produced intense fiscal pressures on colleges and universities (Thelin, 2004). A demographic decline in the number of 18- to 22-year-olds threatened tuition-dependent institutions (Crossland, 1980). Some experts predicted that within a decade as many as a third of all colleges and universities would merge or close (Keller, 1983). Many colleges and universities responded by adopting a market-centered mind-set—student-as-customer—and what the customer wanted was jobs (Bloom *et al.*, 2006). In 1969, 80% of incoming freshmen indicated that developing a meaningful philosophy of life was an important goal in life; by 1996 the proportion had dropped to 42%. In 1971, half of all students (49%) said they were attending college "to be able to make more money"; by 1991 that had climbed to three-quarters (75%) (Astin, 1998).

Many institutions began developing pre-professional and occupational programs, which proved quite popular with students (Breneman, 1994; Delucchi, 1997; Knox *et al.*, 1993). Breneman notes, "For all colleges, professional degrees awarded rose from 33% in 1972 to 54% in 1988" (p. 139). However, this shift in academic mission exacted a price. Faculty morale on many campuses suffered. Boyer, in the prologue of his influential book, *College: The Undergraduate Experience in America*, pointedly observed, "[s]crambling for students and driven by marketplace demands, many undergraduate colleges have lost their sense of purpose" (1987, p. 3).

There also emerged concerns over the political disengagement of young people. A front page article in the *Miami Herald* in 1983, typical of the time, described college students as "optimistic about themselves but cynical about the world, concerned about their careers and involved with the care of their bodies. Competitive, well-groomed, they are also practical and status-conscious" (Veciana-Suarez, 1983). In his landmark study of American college students, Levine likened them to "passengers on a sinking ship, a Titanic if you will, called the United States or the world" (1980, p. 104).

> [T]oday's fatalism fuels a spirit of justified hedonism. There is a growing belief among college students that if they are doomed to ride on the Titanic, they ought at least to make the trip as pleasant—make that as lavish—as possible and go first class, for they assume there is nothing better (ibid, pp. 104–5).

It was a troubling image that found resonance in the academy.

At nearly the same time Frank Newman, then-director of the Education Commission of the States, wrote an influential report entitled *Higher Education and the American Resurgence* (1985), which outlined the challenges facing American higher education. One of the central issues Newman pointed to was civic disengagement. He concluded: "If there is a crisis in education in the United States today, it is less that test scores have declined than it is that we have failed to provide the education for citizenship that is still the most significant responsibility of the nation's schools and colleges" (p. 31). Of particular concern was rampant political disaffection. In 1989, the American Political Science Association's Task Force on Civic Education for the 21st Century concluded: "We take as axiomatic that current levels of political knowledge, political engagement, and political enthusiasm are so low as to threaten the vitality and stability of democratic politics in the United States" (http://www.apsanet.org/section_463.cfm). Among the hundreds of thousands of college freshmen surveyed by the Higher Education Research Institute at UCLA, the percentage who agreed that it is "important for me to keep up to date with political affairs" declined from 58% in 1966 to 26% by 1998 (Sax *et al.*, 1999).

From Community Service to Service-learning

Newman's report caught the attention of the presidents of Brown, Georgetown and Stanford Universities. They too were concerned about the failure of college and universities to instill in students a sense of social and civic responsibility. This meeting led to the founding in 1986 of Campus Compact, a presidential organization aimed at promoting civic engagement. Within a year it had 113 members, by 1995 its membership had swelled to 520. In its first few years, Campus Compact focused its attention on promoting student volunteerism or community service. However, several individuals (most notably Stanford president, Donald Kennedy, who was a Campus Compact board member) began arguing that such an emphasis would relegate these efforts to a sideshow within the academy. This work had to be linked to the academic core.

This occurred in two ways, the first of which focused on re-conceptualizing scholarship. In 1990, Boyer offered a broader conception of faculty work in *Scholarship Reconsidered* (1990), one of the most influential higher education texts of the twentieth century (Braxton *et al.*, 2002). According to Boyer's close collaborator, Rice, the book:

> reframed the issues so that we could get beyond the old teaching-versus-research debate, rise above the theory/practice hierarchy plaguing the discussion of scholarship, and begin to think in new ways about the alignment of faculty priorities and institutional mission (2005, p. 17).

The impetus behind Boyer's ideas was the sense that "what is needed [for higher education] is not just more programs, but a larger purpose, a larger sense of mission, a larger clarity of direction in the nation's life" (Boyer, 1994). The force of his message was multiplied through the near-simultaneous launching (in 1991) of the annual Forum on Faculty Roles and Rewards, which was sponsored by the American Association for Higher Education (AAHE) and Carnegie (Miller, 2005). As a result, thousands of discussions were launched across the country regarding faculty roles and the definition of scholarship.

A second thrust of this work emphasized the curriculum. In 1990, the National Society of Internships and Experiential Education (NSIEE) published *Combining Service and Learning: A Resource Book for Community and Public Service* (Kendall, 1990). The book offered readings that pragmatically explained how service might be incorporated into the curriculum, and why such work was consonant with academic work. It also reflected the consensus that had emerged among practitioners of service-learning (which is what the pedagogy came to be called), as codified in the Principles of Best Practices for Combining Service and Learning in 1989. The preamble of this document makes an explicit link between service-learning and civic engagement: "We are a nation founded upon active citizenship and participation in community life. We have always believed that individuals can and should serve" (http://www.johnsonfdn.org/principles.htm).

Some of these shared principals were:

- engaged learning is a legitimate pedagogical strategy and is as effective (if not more so) than traditional methods for certain learning situations;

- engaged learning allows students to grasp the complexity (and messiness) of real-world problems;
- engagement is an effective means of learning collaborative skills and engaging in collective problem solving;
- engaged learning shifts the emphasis of service from personal charitable voluntary acts (community service) to efforts aimed at understanding root causes of social problems; and
- engaged learning opportunities should be developed through the formation of committed partnerships where community partners define their own needs.

In 1991, Campus Compact launched the Integrating Service with Academic Study (ISAS) initiative, funded by the Ford Foundation. Over the next three summers ISAS worked with five-person teams from 60 institutions, helping them integrate service-learning into their curricula. The initiative also funded 130 service-learning workshops nationwide, and developed a host of written materials and sample syllabi from a wide range of disciplines. Service-learning initiatives received a significant boost after President Clinton signed legislation in 1993 creating the Corporation for National and Community Service. The Higher Education component, Learn and Serve America (LSAHE), became one of the most important funding sources for "enhance[ing] students' civic skills through service-learning" (http://www.learnandserve.org/about/programs/higher_education.asp).

A 1999 RAND report indicates that:

> LSAHE awarded approximately $10 million in direct grants to about 100 higher education institutions and community organizations for each of the three years from Fiscal Year 1995 through Fiscal Year 1997. Through subgranting, these funds reached close to 500 higher education institutions—nearly one of every eight colleges and universities nationwide (Gray et al., 1999).

These funds were an extremely important lever for securing the support of senior administrators for community and civic engagement initiatives on many campuses. The growth of service-learning as a pedagogy in part is reflected in Campus Compact's rising membership (since service-learning was the principal thrust of the organization's work during the 1990s).

As service-learning proliferated, important ideological differences began to emerge among its proponents. A few prominent leaders of the wing that emphasized democratic education (e.g. Richard Battistoni, Harry Boyte, Ira Harkavy, e.g.) called for explicitly tying community-based work to democratic and civic (citizenship) skills—encouraging students not just to see themselves as participants in a local community, but as part of a wider polity in which political awareness is a requisite for understanding how to enact systemic change. Boyte in particular became critical of service-learning, arguing that in practice it often "neglects to teach about root causes and power relationships, fails to stress productive impact, [and] ignores politics" (2004, p. 12).

However, the vast majority of practitioners saw service-learning primarily (and pragmatically) as a powerful pedagogy. They held that, unless service-learning was linked to disciplinary interests, it would fail to secure widespread legitimacy. Edward Zlotkowski, one of the most thoughtful of these advocates, forcefully argued:

> Until very recently the service-learning movement has had an "ideological" bias; i.e., it has tended to prioritize moral and/or civic questions related to the service experience. Such a focus reflects well on the movement's past but will not guarantee its future. What is needed now is a broad-based adjustment that invests far more intellectual energy in specifically academic concerns. Only by paying careful attention to the needs of individual disciplines and by allying

itself with other academic interest groups will the service-learning movement succeed in becoming an established feature of American higher education (Zlotkowski, 1995, p. 123).

This pragmatic stance proved so successful that, by the end of the 1990s, one pioneer, Naddine Cruz, was shocked to find herself having to defend social justice as a *possible* outcome of service-learning at an association meeting (Stanton *et al.*, 1999).

A number of efforts were made specifically aimed at legitimizing service-learning. AAHE sponsored a monograph series focusing on the use of service-learning as a means of advancing disciplinary knowledge (eventually 21 volumes were produced), under the editorial leadership of Zlotkowski. This wildly successful series (which continues to be published by Stylus Press after the demise of AAHE) demonstrated how service-learning was being creatively used by many faculty members in a range of disciplines. There was progress on the research front as well. A growing number of studies on the impact of service-learning on students provided important empirical confirmation of its efficacy as a pedagogy (Astin, 1998; Astin *et al.*, 2000; Eyler, 2000; Eyler and Giles, 1999). In addition, several outlets for research on engaged teaching and scholarship emerged during the 1990s.

Where's the "Civic" in Civic Engagement?

One event that helped reanimate the discourse on civic engagement and citizenship preparation was the work of the National Commission on Civic Renewal, co-chaired by William J. Bennett and Senator Sam Nunn, which pointed to the decline in political and civic participation, as well as the "stirrings" of "a new movement". The Commission's final report stated:

> Within the neighborhoods, the towns, the local communities of America are the stirrings of a new movement of citizens acting together to solve community problems. It is a nonpartisan movement that crosses traditional jurisdictions and operates on a shoestring. It is a movement that begins with civic dialogue and leads to public action. It has gone largely unnoticed, unappreciated, and unsupported (1997, p. 9).

Conspicuously absent in the 57-page document was any mention of higher education. Despite the development of service-learning efforts on many college and university campuses, many of these activities received scant attention. Then-Executive Director of Campus Compact, Elizabeth Hollander, wrote in an editorial:

> [W]e need to do a better job in spreading the word about the good work campuses are doing in educating students about their civic responsibilities . . . When was the last time you saw a major article in the *Chronicle of Higher Education* on this topic? (Hollander, 1998).

Hollander also underscored that recent research by Astin found that the impact of community-based learning on the "social conscience and political activism" of students was "not encouraging". Service-learning, though a powerful pedagogy, tended to be directed at goals other than political awareness and civic consciousness. That was an oversight that needed to be addressed. What was needed was a broader conception of this work—a more robust civic engagement

The American Council on Education (ACE) established the ACE Forum on Higher Education in cooperation with several other associations, including the Association of American Universities, AAHE, Association of American Colleges and Universities (AACandU), Campus Compact, and the New England Resource Center for Higher Education. The first conference was held in 1998 at

Florida State University. ACE President, Stanley O. Ikenberry, explained its purpose: "The quality of civic life in our country, and the strength of our democracy, is in some trouble . . . we have a role to play in improving it, through the opportunities we offer our students and the service we render to the community" (ACE, 1998). In December of that year a group of university presidents, provosts, deans, faculty members and representatives of foundations and associations met at the Wingspread conference center in Wisconsin, and they convened again in July 1999. The product of those two meetings was the Wingspread Declaration on Renewing the Civic Mission of the American Research University, written by Harry Boyte and Elizabeth Hollander. Evoking the words of Charles Eliot, the declaration provocatively asked: How might students, faculty, staff, and administrators become "filled with the democratic spirit?" The statement asserted that faculty ought to:

> . . . take responsibility for a vibrant public culture at their institutions. Such a public culture values their moral and civic imaginations and their judgments, insights, and passions, while it recognizes and rewards their publicly engaged scholarship, lively teaching, and their contributions through public work (p.10—http://www.compact.org/initiatives/research_universities/wingspread_declaration).

This was a call for colleges and universities to kindle the civic imaginations of students and to re-imagine their own civic roles.

In addition, Campus Compact convened 51 university presidents at the Aspen Institute in July 1999 to establish an agenda to promote of civic engagement. What resulted was the "Presidents' Declaration on the Civic Responsibility of Higher Education", drafted by Thomas Ehrlich, a senior scholar at the Carnegie Foundation for the Advancement of Teaching, and Elizabeth Hollander. As the work was disseminated over the next few months, the document was signed by 539 college and university presidents. Of particular note is the following passage:

> We are encouraged that more and more students are volunteering and participating in public and community service, and we have all encouraged them to do so through curricular and co-curricular activity. *However, this service is not leading students to embrace the duties of active citizenship and civic participation.* We do not blame these college students for their attitudes toward the democracy; rather, we take responsibility for helping them realize the values and skills of our democratic society and their need to claim ownership of it (emphasis added: http://www.compact.org/resources/declaration/about).

The declaration underscored the failure of many community engagement or service-learning efforts to demonstrate any impact on civic outcomes, such as voting or knowledge of political issues. It was a call for radical restructuring of the engagement movement around the formation of civic skills.

A second widely circulated document on engagement was also published in the same year. "Returning to Our Roots: The Engaged Institution" was developed by the Kellogg Commission on the Future of State and Land-Grant Universities, a group of 24 land grant presidents as well as foundation and corporate representatives. Pointing to "enrollment pressures", "a growing emphasis on accountability and productivity from trustees, legislators, and donors", the document defined "engagement" as "institutions that have redesigned their teaching, research, and extension and service functions to become even more sympathetic and productively involved with their communities, however community may be defined" (p. 9: http://www.cpn.org/topics/youth/highered/pdfs/Land_Grant_Engaged_Institution.pdf). The document called for a renewed commitment to the historic land-grant ideal of service to the state and wider society, and provided a series of 11 portraits of institutions that illustrated seven principals: responsiveness to communities, regions and states; respect for partners; academic neutrality; accessibility to "outsiders"; integration or interdisciplinary work; coordination of institutional efforts; and the commitment of resources to these ends.

Other efforts began to emerge. The American Association of State Colleges and Universities (AASCUs) launched the American Democracy Project in 2003, which promotes curricular and programmatic development around political engagement. The project currently has more than 200 participating institutions (http://www.aascu.org). Project Pericles, founded in 2000 by entrepreneur Eugene Lang, is a network of 21 colleges and universities (all but one private) that have made a demonstrated institutional commitment to civic engagement, including a board resolution to that end, comprehensive programming, defined outcomes, and the provision of a program director (http://projectpericles.org). With the support of the Fund for Postsecondary Improvement, the Bonner Foundation is working with four institutions to pilot a Civic Education Academic Certificate program (Meisel, 2007).

AASCU has done important conceptual work teasing out the civic dimension of a liberal education, and its president Carol Schneider argues that "fostering social responsibility and civic engagement" is one of three key areas that comprise the "New Academy" (Schneider, 2005). Although she uses service-learning and community-based research as examples, she also makes clear that "We have to put Big Questions from our society directly into the college curriculum" (p. 12). Since 2000, the Kellogg Forum on Higher Education for the Public Good, based at the University of Michigan, has sponsored conferences and initiatives aimed at countering the "minimalist transactional view of the academy" and encouraging colleges and universities to take up "the responsibility to provide transforming civic leadership" (Burkhardt and Chambers, 2003).

The Current Landscape

What does the current engagement landscape look like? A useful starting point for addressing this question is member data gathered by Campus Compact. In 2006, Campus Compact had 1,008 members, approximately a quarter of all post-secondary institutions in the United States. Data provided by the 506 respondents reveal widespread civic efforts. Arguably the most prevalent civic strategy remained service-learning. Fully 91% reported offering an average of 35 such courses in the past year (http://www.compact.org/about/statistics/2006/service). Another national survey of 32,840 faculty found that one in five (22%) had taught a service-learning course in the past two years (Lindholm *et al.*, 2002). Institutional infrastructure was also in place to support these efforts—80% indicated that they had at least one office or center dedicated to coordinating service-learning, and/or civic engagement efforts. One-third (31%) of these institutions reported having multiple offices (often attached to different schools within a university or focused on academic or co-curricular service).

However, the Campus Compact data also reveal considerable variation among member institutions. Indeed, the association likens the landscape to a pyramid, in which a comparatively small group of institutions have fully developed programs and a larger proportion have made fewer inroads (http://www.compact.org/faculty/specialreport.html). A mere 7% of Compact members offered 100 or more service-learning courses per year, 12% offered between 51 and 99 courses, 45% between 11 and 50, and 28% offered 10 or fewer courses per year (http://www.compact.org/about/statistics/2006/service). Another important marker of institutional commitment to civic engagement is its faculty rewards system. Only a third (34%) of Compact members reported rewarding community-based research or service-learning in faculty review, tenure and/or promotions. In a recent national survey of 729 chief academic offices, two-thirds (68%) indicated that their institution had developed policies or engaged in efforts to encourage and reward a broader definition of scholarship (O'Meara and Rice, 2005). However, the prevailing academic norms continue to hold the scholarship of discovery and pure research as the gold standard.

In 2006, the Carnegie Foundation for the Advancement of Teaching unveiled a new community engagement classification. This elective designation defined community engagement as "the collaboration between institutions of higher education and their larger communities (local, regional/state, national, global) for the mutually beneficial exchange of knowledge and resources in a context of partnership and reciprocity", and 76 applied for and received the classification. Each of these institutions submitted a report to Carnegie detailing their engagement activities. An analysis of reports from 63 of these institutions (those willing to share their application materials with us) reveals important insights into the kinds of engagement activities occurring at these colleges and universities.

Perhaps most notable was that institutions tended to point to a similar set of engagement activities, especially service-learning and volunteer service. Much of the work involves partnering with direct-service agencies (activities in schools, such as tutoring, and serving marginalized populations such as the homeless were common efforts). The vast majority of these institutions had a coordinating structure (an office or center or several centers) supporting these activities. However, they varied in size from one staff member to 22, and in budgetary allotments from the thousands of dollars to the millions. The scope of their activities ranged from a single person coordinating university–community partnerships to well-staffed centers that coordinated all aspects of a university's engagement, from community outreach to coursework to service activities. A few campuses had no centre at all, but instead relied on standing committees or less formalized groups of individuals to coordinate engagement work.

Institutional type seems to influence how engagement is conceptualized. For example, liberal arts colleges, which tend to describe themselves as providing a formative educational experience, underscored the importance of preparing future civic leaders. Using language typical for this group, one college stated that it seeks to "encourage students to be responsible citizens who provide service to and leadership for an increasingly interdependent world". By contrast, large research universities were more likely to talk about serving by producing knowledge or, as one put it, "serving [the state], the nation, and the world community. The discovery and dissemination of new knowledge are central to [our] mission".

David Maurrasse (2001) has suggested a number of indicators of institutional commitment that could be used to judge a university's community engagement efforts, without which, he writes, "community partnerships run the risk of being marginalized" (p. 185):

- Do partnerships involve more than one person or a small number of people at the institution, and are various efforts across campus coordinated?
- Does the administration place a high priority on engagement activities, including by substantially including engagement activities in promotion and tenure?
- Is engagement a part of both the academic and economic missions of the institution?
- Is service-learning conceived of both as a tool for student learning and genuine engagement with the community? (paraphrased from pp. 184–185)

In nearly every case, the applications of these institutions could respond with a resounding "yes". There is no doubt that these institutions believe in the importance of being civically engaged. There were ample examples of academic leaders stating their support of and commitment to these efforts. Rewards and ceremonies recognizing such efforts were fairly common. However, service-learning courses accounted for only 6% of total courses on average. While not an inconsequential number, it hardly represents a major curricular feature of institutions that are arguably among the most engaged in the US. Despite calls for greater institutional responsiveness (most recently by the Spellings Commission), institutional policies (e.g. faculty roles and rewards) are often at odds with community engagement. Disciplinary orientation continues to dominate academic activities (Benson *et al.*, 2005). Further, it is important to note that only one in five of these institutions made any mention whatsoever to engagement activities with any political dimension at all. Most often, these references came from involvement in association initiatives such as AASCU's American Democracy Project or Project Pericles. Community engagement activities on campus are largely apolitical in nature. Despite language about preparing "citizens" or serving democratic purposes, what we see is a largely apolitical "civic" engagement.

An International Movement

Internationally, the engagement movement is beginning to become more widespread, and it is here that an increasing emphasis on democratic engagement is developing. There have been numerous calls to define the place of the university, not only in promoting activities such as service-learning but in preparing future citizens. Hollister (2006: http://activecitizen.tufts.edu/?pid=421) characterizes the growth of civic engagement and social responsibilities by international institutions as a "recent dramatic upsurge", and notes that an "invisible revolution is underway in higher education on all continents—a growing movement to educate active citizens and to apply university resources to community needs". Organizations around the world are addressing the issue and individual universities are engaged in efforts on campuses throughout the world.

Statements exploring the concept of university engagement and the university's social role have been published by groups including the Association of Commonwealth Universities, with 500 university members, the Australian Consortium for Higher Education, Community Engagement and Social Responsibility, and by policymakers in South Africa. One of the largest projects is the International Consortium for Higher Education, Civic Responsibility and Democracy, which was started in 1999 as a collaboration between the Council of Europe and three U.S. organizations (Benson *et al.*, 2007). A research project is exploring the activities performed on campuses across the world that further democratic values and practices, and will help to promote these activities both on campuses and in wider society. International consortia, the growing number of international conferences, and expanding networks promise to allow developments in community engagement to spread and gain synergies from worldwide practices.

Australia is illustrative of the growing international movement toward engagement. At the same time as market pressures have increased commercialization and caused higher education to be viewed as a private good in Australia, there have also been increasing commitments to community engagement (Hartley *et al.*, 2005). The Australian Consortium for Higher Education, Community Engagement and Social Responsibility released a report (2004—http://www.tufts.edu/talloiresnetwork/downloads/AustralianConsortiumpaper.pdf) in which it sought to begin to gather "ideas and representations of community engagement which draw on a range of voices from a range of university, government, and community contexts" (p. 3). On the institutional level, the University of Queensland has balanced market pressures with a significant increase in engagement with its local community. It has committed to seeking partnerships with the local community, collaborations with businesses and industries, research that will lead to improved education and health, and ways to offer direct services to the community. One way of working toward these goals is a recently formed office called the UQ Boilerhouse, which addresses the needs of the western region of Brisbane on the newly established UQ Ipswich campus. "The Center strategically integrates research, teaching, and learning in service and engagement to the needs and aspirations of the university's local communities" (Hartley *et al.*, 2005, p. 39). Australia continues to develop its community engagement at both the national and institutional levels. Presumably, the growing international conversation around engagement will continue to enrich and be enriched by such efforts.

Conclusion

Colleges and universities are continuing to grapple with the issue of how they might best fulfill their civic roles. The current growth of university–community partnerships and engaged institutions are just the latest manifestation of a tradition centuries old. Many questions remain. How can the university contribute to society, both locally and beyond? What is the most appropriate way to serve the society, be it through preparing knowledgeable and engaged citizens, performing direct service and application of knowledge to society's problems, or simply through performing basic research and other knowledge that may indirectly help society? Other questions are new. What are the best ways to engage communities in the knowledge-creation process, and how can this be done in light of power differentials between large institutions and individuals? How can a university overcome the legacy of neglect and paternalism in their past relationships with their communities? Colleges and universities will continue to engage with these questions, and the diversity of higher educational institutions ensures that there will be myriad answers and solutions. Thoughtful individuals, aided by networks and communities of others thinking about similar issues, promise to allow institutions around the world to meet their civic obligations in the years ahead.

References

American Council on Education. (1998, July 27). ACE Conference Explores the Role of Colleges in Promoting Civic Responsibility. *Higher Education and National Affairs, 47,* 1, 3.

Astin, A. (1998). The Changing American College Student: Thirty-year Trends, 1966–1996. *The Review of Higher Education, 21*(1), 115–135.

Astin, A., Sax, L.J. and Avalos, J. (2000). *Long-term effects of volunteerism during undergraduate years.* Los Angeles, CA: Higher Education Research Institute, UCLA.

Benson, L., Harkavy, I. and Hartley, M. (2005). Integrating a Commitment to the Public Good into the Institutional Fabric. In A.J. Kezar, T. Chambers and J. Burkhardt (eds) *Higher Education for the Public Good: Emerging Voices from a National Movement* (pp. 185–216). San Francisco, CA: Jossey-Bass.

Benson, L., Harkavy, I. and Puckett, J. (2007). *Dewey's Dream: Universities and Democracy in an Age of Education Reform.* Philadelphia, PA: Temple University Press.

Bloom, D., Hartley, M. and Rosovsky, H. (2006). Beyond Private Gain: The Public Benefits of Higher Education. In P.G. Altbach and J. Forrest (eds) *International Handbook of Higher Education* (pp. 293–308). Dordrecht, Netherlands: Springer.

Boyer, E. (1987). *College: The Undergraduate Experience in America.* New York, NY: HarperCollins.

Boyer, E. (1990). *Scholarship Reconsidered.* Princeton, NJ: The Carnegie Foundation for the Advancement of Teaching.

Boyer, E. (1994, March 9). Creating the New American College. *The Chronicle of Higher Education.*

Boyte, H.C. (2004). *Everyday Politics: Reconnecting Citizens and Public Life.* Philadelphia, PA: University of Pennsylvania.

Braxton, J., Luckey, W. and Holland, P. (2002). *Institutionalizing a broader view of scholarship through Boyer's four domains.* San Francisco, CA: Jossey-Bass.

Breneman, D.W. (1994). *Liberal Arts Colleges: Thriving, Surviving, or Endangered?* Washington, D.C.: Brookings Institute.

Burkhardt, J. and Chambers, T. (2003). Kellogg Forum on Higher Education for the Public Good: Contributing to the Practice of Democracy. *Diversity Digest, 7*(1, 2), 1–2.

Cochran, T.C. (1972). *Business in American Life: A History.* New York: McGraw-Hill.

Crossland, F.E. (1980). Learning to Cope with a Downward Slope. *Change, 12*(5), 18–25.

Delucchi, M. (1997). "Liberal Arts" Colleges and the Myth of Uniqueness. *Journal of Higher Education, 68*(4), 414–426.

Eyler, J. (2000). Studying the Impact of Service-Learning on Students. *Michigan Journal of Community Service Learning,* Fall, 11–18.

Eyler, J. and Giles, D.E., Jr. (1999). *Where's the Learning in Service-Learning?* San Francisco, CA: Jossey-Bass.

Gray, M.J., Ondaatje, E.H., Geshwind, S., Fricker, R., Goldman, C., Kaganoff, T., *et al.* (1999). *Combining Service and Learning in Higher Education: Evaluation of the Learn and Serve America Higher Education Program.* Santa Monica, CA: Rand Education.

Harkavy, I. and Zuckerman, H. (1999). *Eds and Meds: Cities' Hidden Assets.* Washington, D.C.: The Brookings Institute.

Hartley, M., Winter, A., Nunery II, L.D., Muirhead, B. and Harkavy, I. (2005). Factors Influencing Civic Engagement at Australian and U.S. Research Universities: Two Illustrative Examples. *Journal of Higher Education Outreach and Engagement, 10*(2), 25–47.

Hollander, E. (1998, October-November). Civic Education: Is Higher Ed Losing? *Compact Currents, 12,* 2.

Keller, G. (1983). *Academic Strategy: The Management Revolution in Higher Education.* Baltimore, MD: The Johns Hopkins University Press.

Kendall, J.C. (ed.) (1990). *Combining Service and Learning: A Resource Book for Community and Public Service.* Raleigh, NC: National Society for Experiential Education.

Knox, W.E., Lindsay, P. and Kolb, M.N. (1993). *Does College Make a Difference?: Long-term Changes in Attitudes and Activities.* Westport, CT: Greenwood Press.

Levine, A. (1980). *When Dreams and Heroes Died: A Portrait of Today's College Students.* San Francisco, CA: Jossey-Bass.

Lindholm, J.A., Astin, A.W., Sax, L.J. and Korn, W.S. (2002). *The American College Teacher: National Norms for 2001–2002.* Los Angeles, CA: Higher Education Research Institute, UCLA Graduate School of Education and Information Studies.

Maurrasse, D. (2001). *Beyond the Campus: How Colleges and Universities Form Partnerships with Their Communities.* New York: Routledge.

Meisel, W. (2007). Connected Cocurricular Service with Academic Inquiry: A Movement Toward Civic Engagement. *Liberal Education, 93*(2), 52–57.

Miller, M. A. (2005). AAHE's Legacy. *Change.*

Morphew, C. and Hartley, M. (2006). Mission Statements: A Thematic Analysis of Rhetoric across Institutional Type. *Journal of Higher Education, 77*(3), 456–471.

National Commission on Civic Renewal. (1997). *A Nation of Spectators: How civic disengagement weakens America and what we can do about it.* College Park, MD: National Commission on Civic Renewal.

Newman, F. (1985). *Higher Education and the American Resurgence.* Princeton, NJ: The Carnegie Foundation for the Advancement of Teaching.

O'Meara, K. and Rice, R.E. (eds) (2005). *Faculty Priorities Reconsidered.* San Francisco, CA: Jossey-Bass.

Rice, R.E. (2005). Scholarship Reconsidered: History and Context. In K. O'Meara and R.E. Rice (eds) *Faculty Priorities Reconsidered: Rewarding Multiple Forms of Scholarship* (pp. 17–31). San Francisco, CA: Jossey-Bass.

Rudolph, F. (1962). *The American College and University: A History.* New York: Alfred A. Knopf.

Sax, L.J., Astin, A., Korn, W.S. and Mahoney, K.M. (1999). *The American Freshman: National Norms for Fall 1999.* Los Angeles, CA: Higher Education Research Institute.

Schneider, C.G. (2005). Making Excellence Inclusive: Liberal Education and America's Promise. *Liberal Education, 91*(2), 6–17.

Smith, P. (1990). *Killing the Spirit: Higher Education in America.* New York, NY: Viking Press.

Stanton, T.K., Giles, D.E., Jr. and Cruz, N.I. (1999). *Service Learning: A Movement's Pioneers Reflect on Its Origins, Practice and Future.* San Francisco, CA: Jossey-Bass.

Sykes, C. (1989). *Profscam: Professors and the Demise of Higher Education.* New York, NY: St. Martin's Press.

Thelin, J.R. (2004). *A History of American Higher Education.* Baltimore, MD: Johns Hopkins University Press.

Veciana-Suarez, A. (1983, October). On Campus, Students Eye Bottom Line Materialism, Status Take Hold at Colleges. *Miami Herald,* p. 1A.

Zlotkowski, E. (1995). Does Service-Learning Have A Future? *Michigan Journal of Community Service Learning,* (Fall), 123–133.

VIII
Academic Work

Academic work is basically about the activities described by Clark (1983, p. 12) as the "manipulation of knowledge", whether it relates to "efforts to discover, conserve, refine, transmit" or "apply it".

This seemingly clear-cut definition around the central concept of knowledge becomes more fluid, and even messy, when looking at current day-to-day activities of academics. First of all, the balance of discovering (research) and transmitting (teaching) knowledge may differ considerably between and within higher education systems, institutions and departments. Second, it can be argued that the changing contexts of higher education (massification, globalisation, marketisation, individualisation) have changed the nature of the knowledge creation and dissemination processes and, consequently, the nature of academic work (see also Section IX, particularly Merle Jacob's chapter). Third, Clark aptly identifies the core tasks of academics, but leaves aside borderline activities: that is, those activities that clearly involve academic expertise, but are often considered as "second-tier" activities. This set of activities includes, for example, the work of those involved in quality assurance, organising educational content for virtual learning, and those occupied with staff development. In all, one could argue that academic work has become much more diversified and fragmented. This should not necessarily be considered as something negative: the increasing diversity and flexibility arguably offer more opportunities for academic careers in higher education (see e.g. Enders and Weert, 2004). Despite this, the negative consequences of these developments dominate the current literature, with clear concerns about the academic identity and academic freedom (see e.g. Henkel, 2000).

The issue of fragmentation is picked up by Kerri-Lee Krause in the first chapter in this section. She explores the key factors that shape academic roles and identities in contemporary higher education. In this, she makes a clear distinction between factors that stem from the broader international and policy context, and those that emerge from the higher education institutions (mission, priorities) themselves. She then moves on to focus in depth on the tensions created by the key factors described and the teaching–research–service triad. A number of alternative paradigms are presented that potentially overcome these tensions, and a plea is made to seriously discuss these alternatives in relation to a reconsideration of academic identities.

In the second chapter of this section, Ranald Macdonald discusses the topic of academic development, which can be considered as being part of "second-tier" work. Following Hounsell (1994), a general definition of academic development would be those activities that sustain and enhance the quality of learning and teaching within higher education institutions. After having described trends in academic development in different countries, Macdonald addresses the nature of academic development activities, whether this task should be conceived of as "academic practice", how academic developers are organised and what their impact is (unnecessary overhead or quality improvement?). Finally, further challenges for academic developers are presented.

In the third chapter in this section, Jan Currie and Lesley Vidovich address the changing nature of academic work, and—as Krause did in her chapter—allude to issues of fragmentation and loss of identity. They address a wide range of interlinked factors: the impact of changing demographics and working conditions; the role of e-technology; the influence of marketisation and privatisation; the impact of managerialism; and the role of internationalisation. The (potential) effects of these trends are illustrated with empirical findings from various studies. Currie and Vidovich conclude that markets and governments have assumed greater powers over academics, leading to polarisation and cultural shifts. They warn—based on a recent international survey—of irreparable damage to job satisfaction and academic freedom.

That topic, academic freedom, is central to the final contribution to this section. Gerlese Åkerlind and Carole Kayrooz first address the meaning of the concept, and then present findings from a survey of social science academics in Australia. These findings particularly address how these social scientists made sense of academic freedom. Åkerlind and Kayrooz identify five different ways of understanding academic freedom, and present two themes representative of this variety: the types of constraints on academic activity, and the role of internal and external factors in creating freedom. They conclude with the argument that these different ways of understanding allow for "greater clarity, precision and comprehensiveness in debate".

References

Clark, B.R. (1983). *The higher education system. Academic organization in cross-national perspective*. Berkeley, CA: University of California Press.

Enders, J. and Weert, E.D. (2004). Science, training and career: Changing modes of knowledge production and labour markets. *Higher Education Policy*, *17*, 135–152.

Henkel, M. (2000). *Academic identities and policy change*. London: Jessica Kingsley.

Hounsell, D. (1994). Educational development. In J. Bocock and D. Watson (eds) *Managing the university curriculum* (pp. 89–102). Buckingham: Open University Press.

30

Interpreting Changing Academic Roles and Identities in Higher Education

Kerri-Lee Krause

Introduction

The evolution of academic roles represents an instructive socio-historical barometer of changing higher education priorities and goals over time. Change has characterised institutions of higher learning since their inception, but the last decade provides a particularly interesting snapshot of ways in which universities as organisations have transformed in response to changing social, economic, political and policy imperatives. Of particular interest in this chapter is the changing nature of academic labour, and the factors shaping academic identities in this inconstant environment. Discussion is limited to Anglo-Saxon higher education systems, with full acknowledgement that the research–teaching–service configuration does not necessarily apply globally, and that this has not always been the predominant academic work paradigm in universities. Nevertheless, it proves a useful vehicle for interpreting some of the changes taking place in academic roles and identities, and the implications of these for the sector.

Academic roles and identities are multi-faceted and differentially influenced by the interaction of an array of factors, both within and beyond the individual, the department and the institution. As these roles become increasingly complex, there is a growing scholarly interest in analysing ways in which they also appear to be fragmenting. Rowland (2006, p. 62) identifies a number of ever-widening "fault lines" contributing to the fragmentation of academic work. These include fault lines in relation to disputed views on the purposes of higher education, fault lines between teaching and research, and the fragmentation of knowledge. A number of factors are reinforcing these fault lines, including higher education funding policies, institutional reward and promotion structures, the performativity agenda (Macfarlane, 2007), and institutional policies on specialisation of academic roles, for example "research-only" or "teaching-only" positions.

Paradoxically, while widening fault lines are evident in the higher education landscape, there is a simultaneous blurring of boundaries (Henkel, 2007; Musselin, 2007), resulting from various approaches to integration of the many dimensions of academic work and the structures supporting it. At the macro level, Bleiklie and Kogan (2007) observe that there has been a trend towards more integrated university structures, with a tightening of the links between the different parts of the university to make them more efficient and accountable. Meanwhile, at the micro level of the academic worker, Rowland (2006, p. 62) points out that "academic work" increasingly spans traditional boundaries, and now potentially forms part of many roles, including those of academic developer, multimedia specialist, educational technologist and learning adviser (see also Kogan and Teichler, 2007). Other factors contributing to boundary blurring in academic work include: the broadening of the notion of "service" to include leadership and community engagement; the impact of emerging technologies, and the evolution of "bricks and clicks" hybridised forms of higher education (Adelman, 2000); the growing interest in fostering academic leaders and know-ledge workers, who perform a range of academic and administrative roles across traditional university elements; and the imperative to engage in third-mission knowledge-exchange activities with community and industry. These are just some of the more recent developments that have led many academics to perceive themselves as "boundary spanners". The boundaries are increasingly blurred between the research–teaching–service triad that has tended to typify conceptualisations of academic work in the Anglo-Saxon higher education sector since the nineteenth century. At one end of the spectrum, fragmentation of academic work is evident, while at the other, there are imperatives to integrate and span academic role boundaries, particularly at the institutional level.

The lack of stability in the configuration of higher education institutions and their roles—as a result of constant changes in national policies, market forces, globalisation, third-mission impera-tives and technological advances—means that academic workers face challenging times, as they seek to come to terms with their role in this volatile environment. These "vectors of change" (Schuster and Finkelstein, 2006, p. 12) represent powerful forces that do not necessarily propel in a single direction, thus setting up significant and, some may argue, unresolvable tensions. Everything is "in play" as the higher education sector experiences what Schuster and Finkelstein so aptly describe as "acceler-ating metamorphosis" (p. xvii), which is affecting every aspect of the academy. In particular, these researchers comment on the metamorphosis of the academic profession, which is the principal focus of this discussion.

The chapter explores some of the key factors shaping academic roles and identities, including national policies and international higher education trends, institutional missions, disciplinary, departmental and individual factors. It acknowledges that the lenses through which one interprets academic work significantly influence one's view of academic roles, and the relationships between the somewhat contested and problematised tripartite configuration of research, teaching and ser-vice. Interpretations of learning and teaching in higher education have tended to rely heavily on psychological frameworks. However, there is growing recognition of the inherent value in examining the multi-dimensionality of academic work through a socio-cultural lens (e.g. see Fanghanel and Trowler, 2007), which accounts for the influences of history, politics and culture in shaping academe. The chapter then proceeds with discussion of the ways in which key drivers of change, and selected contextual factors, are reshaping academic roles and identities. It concludes with implica-tions for policy and practice in international, national and local higher education contexts.

Approaches to Interpreting Academic Work

Analysis of the factors shaping academic work, and understandings of their relative significance, depend to a large extent on one's assumptions and frameworks of interpretation. A comprehensive and informed interpretation of academic life is one that takes account of historical, theoretical and philosophical perspectives, and a recognition of the need to adopt a bigger picture perspective of the implications of changes in academic work for the academic profession, the academy and the society in which that academy functions (Schuster and Finkelstein, 2006, p. 354). Moreover, it is important to consider the assumptions underpinning such an analysis. For instance, Hughes (2005) identifies several myths and assumptions about the connection between research and teaching in higher education. These include the myth of the mutually beneficial relationship between research and teaching, and the assumption of the superiority of lecturer as researcher (p. 16). Such assumptions need to be acknowledged for the ways in which they shape interpretation of the academic role, and the value, or otherwise, of attempts to connect the various dimensions of academic labour.

The importance of contextualising analysis of academic work in the context of socio-cultural, socio-political and socio-historical processes is supported by Fanghanel and Trowler (2007), who argue that the context of academic practice is highly significant. These authors support a move away from simple technical–rational models of change to socio-cultural theories that take account of the structural context of practice, and of communities of practice theoretical frameworks, such as those proposed by Engestrom (2001) and Lave and Wenger (1991). A socio-cultural theoretical frame-work focuses on university environments with attention to the structures and communities within them. Such an emphasis places the spotlight on how individuals operate in the various communities within and beyond the university, while acknowledging the undeniable influence on academic work and identity of macro (institutional) and meso (departmental) missions, traditions and values, and of individual beliefs and modes of operation (Fanghanel and Trowler, 2007).

Having recognised the influence of one's assumptions, and the frames of interpretation through which one views academic work, and having advocated the benefits of a holistic approach that recognises the influence of social, cultural and historical contexts on academic communities, atten-tion now turns to analysis of a range of factors contributing to the shaping and reshaping of academic roles in higher education.

Key Factors Shaping Academic Roles and Identities

Multiple factors shape academic roles and identities. Musselin (2007, p. 1) contends that there is no ideal, commonly agreed or "stable state" of the academic profession. Rather, it is a dynamic profes-sion adapting and evolving in response to changing external factors. These factors include: national policies and international trends; institutional factors such as the university mission and priorities; departmental and disciplinary factors; and individual beliefs and values. These will be discussed in turn.

International Trends and National Policies

Questioning the role of the university

Internationally, significant questions are being raised about the fundamental role and purpose of higher education in post-industrial societies (Peters and Humes, 2003). While this trend is not a new one, it may be argued that the factors prompting these questions, and the implications of the responses given, may have more serious consequences for the future of higher education than in previous generations. Bleiklie and Kogan (2007, p. 483) contend that the change catalysts now facing universities represent attempts to alter the "organisational characteristics that used to be regarded as essential to universities". As far back as 1983, the Organisation for Economic Cooper-ation and Development-sponsored Intergovernmental Conference on Policies for Higher Education observed an internal crisis of purpose in universities (Peters, 1998, pp. 76–77). Schuster and Finkel-stein go so far as to say that, while change has always been a characteristic of higher education, the changes now being experienced are unprecedented in terms of number and rapidity (2006, p. 3).

Massification, marketisation and globalisation

Key reasons for changes in higher education include the massification of the sector, and the strengthening of the higher education market in a global context. Universities are now as sensitive as any other organisation to global shifts and trends in the higher education market. The well-documented increases in cross-national movements of international students over the last two decades, along with the noteworthy growth of the higher education sector in south and east Asia—specifically, China and India—have intensified the competition between and within nations for the international student dollar.

The massification of higher education, developments in information and communication technologies, and quantum leaps in the nature of and access to knowledge mean that the future of universities and their academic staff is increasingly difficult to predict. The nature of academic work has not been immune from the influences of globalisation and marketisation. As Bottery (2006) observes, economic globalisation paradoxically increases demands for standardisation and predictability rather than flexibility. Academic staff are now more likely to be expected to satisfy greater demands from students, particularly when notable proportions of performance-based funding rely on measures of student satisfaction.

The expectations of students, industry groups, governments and communities now represent significant forces shaping such areas of academic work as course offerings, curriculum design, modes of delivery, assessment standards and professional development needs. These changes have shaped academics' approaches to teaching, selection of curriculum content, and the types and volume of administrative and service tasks in which they engage on a daily basis. There is evidence, too, that, as universities seek to gain the competitive edge in international ranking exercises, such as that of the Jiao Tong Index or the Times Higher, pragmatic decisions are being made about which academic staff will be "research active" and which will be more teaching-focused in their work. There is growing pessimism in some quarters about the ultimate impact on academe of the increase in research-only and teaching-only positions in many institutions. As universities seek to make their mark in the competitive global market of higher education, the nature of academic work is inevitably transformed.

Performativity

The inevitable outcome of global competitiveness and marketisation in the higher education sector is that universities, and all who work in them, are now required to provide evidence of optimal performance across a range of activities, including research, teaching and service. The rapid rise of third-mission activities, and reliance on private sector funding, has led to a greater need for accountability to a range of industry and community stakeholders. Performativity—the principle of optimal performance (Lyotard, 1984, p. 44), requiring maximisation of output against minimisation of input—has been the result. In such an environment, the outcome of academic work is increasingly judged in terms of its contributions to economic performance. Ball (2000, p. 1) contends that performativity is a mode of regulation that employs judgement and demonstrable comparisons to control activity and to bring about change. The promulgation of performativity in higher education has significant implications for academic work, and how academics perceive themselves and their role in the production of knowledge.

Teaching and research separated by national policy frameworks and funding practices

The fractualisation of academic work along teaching and research lines is reinforced by national higher education policy frameworks and funding schemes that conceptualise research and teaching as mutually exclusive endeavours, addressed by distinctly separate policies and funding arrangements. In countries like the UK, New Zealand and Australia, for example, national funding schemes have tended to polarise academic work around what are increasingly portrayed as two distinct sets of activities: high-quality, high-impact research that contributes to the relevant national research schemes, and high-quality teaching that results in high levels of student satisfaction, and thus contributes to positive performances that are rewarded via schemes such as the Learning and Teaching Performance Fund (Australia) and the Teaching Quality Enhancement Fund (UK).

Zukas and Malcolm (2007, p. 62) contend that separate policies for teaching and research have worked to maintain distinctions between them, and further to promote what Trowler and colleagues (2005, p. 439) have termed "policy paradoxes, shaping practices in contradictory ways and setting up incommensurable goals". These paradoxes, and the trend towards segregation of research and teaching at the national level, necessarily filter through to institution-level policies and practices underpinning academic work.

Casualisation and stratification of the academic workforce

Another significant factor shaping academic roles and identities is the internationally observed trend towards the casualisation and increased stratification of the academic workforce, resulting from flexible, often non-permanent, work pattern configurations. These changes in the nature and configuration of academic appointments have increased the number of specialist, single-function roles—the majority of which appear to be in teaching. Schuster and Finkelstein (2006) express deep concern at the resultant stratification in the US academic workforce. Academic activities appear to be narrowing, with teaching and research forming a "dyadic core", and "academic citizenship" relegated to the periphery (p. 123). Similar trends have been noted in Australia (Kimber, 2003) and in the UK (Fanghanel, 2007a). The rapid growth in the proportion of casual academic staff also contributes to the danger that the relationship between the academic staff member and the university is weakened in such areas as commitment to the institution and its mission, and service loyalty, as the workforce becomes more contingent (Schuster and Finkelstein, 2006, p. 326).

Institutional Factors: The Mission, Priorities and Context of the University

National and international developments have a powerful influence on institutional missions and priorities. As universities become more reliant on funding from sources other than government, so they are compelled to raise revenue, to be competitive in attracting students—particularly international and graduate students—and to be responsive to the needs and expectations of a range of stakeholders, including students, community groups, industry and funding bodies. The role of these factors in shaping the nature of academic work cannot be underestimated. There is a growing body of literature examining ways in which academic staff are managing these changes. The spotlight has fallen on such areas as academic citizenship, the notion of the third mission, and the impact of the triple helix of university–industry–government relations (Etzkowitz and Leydesdorff, 2000) on academic work.

Knowledge transfer, third mission and community engagement

The focus on institutional priorities such as knowledge transfer, third mission and community engagement has had a significant impact on how academic staff perceive their roles in higher education (e.g. see Henkel, 2007; Musselin, 2007). Hatakenaka (2005, p. 8) observes that these third-stream activities originally were defined as activities that took place beyond the core businesses of teaching and research. Yet, as these links with external bodies have developed across the sector, the value of integrating them with the core work of teaching and research has emerged. Krause (2007) identifies the need for a language and theorising that forges connections among the activities of learning, teaching, research and third-stream endeavours, in order to avoid what currently appears to be the case, the inevitable demarcation of operational and intellectual zones of academic enquiry. The challenge of integrating core activities pertaining to academic enquiry in higher education remains substantial when separate funding models continue to drive national policy.

The notion of "public scholarship" has attracted growing interest for its attempt to integrate various facets of academic work and enquiry in higher education. It challenges the assumption that academic work constitutes a range of separate tasks. It is a holistic model of academic work that conceives of the scholarly domains as integrated, while respecting their interdependent contributions (Colbeck and Michael, 2006a). Yapa (2006, p. 73) defines public scholarship as:

> . . . scholarly activity generating new knowledge through academic reflection on issues of community engagement. It integrates research, teaching and service. It does not assume that useful knowledge simply flows outward from the university to the larger community. It recognises that new knowledge is created in its application in the field, and therefore benefits the teaching and research mission of the university.

The public scholarship movement emerged from US land grant university priorities of developing, sharing and applying knowledge, with a view to contributing to democracy and encouraging democratic citizenship (Cohen, 2001). It has also been underpinned by Boyer's (1990) reconceptualisations of academic work (Colbeck and Michael, 2006b). While it has its roots in US higher education, the principles of public scholarship are of relevance to the UK and Australian higher education sectors, as universities face the challenge of drawing together the more traditional academic activities of teaching and research in the context of imperatives to locate academic work in the public domain.

The values inherent in the public scholarship model are challenging to operationalise, both from the academic staff perspective and from the institutional viewpoint, given that institutional policies typically tend to reflect the separation of teaching and research activities in response to national funding structures. Nevertheless, as the sector looks for positive ways to reconceptualise the complex work of academics, an integrated approach such as that of public scholarship may prove a fruitful avenue for future exploration.

Policies on the teaching–research nexus

University policies on the relationship between teaching and research play a key role in shaping academic work. Hughes (2005) reflects on the dearth of compelling empirical evidence to support the strategic and policy significance of research–teaching linkages; yet belief in the fundamental reciprocal value of these linkages in the work of academics remains one of the most "passionate allegiances" (Ramsden and Moses, 1992, p. 273) in higher education. A web-based analysis, of the ways in which Australian universities depict the connections between teaching and research in their public policy documents (Krause, 2007), revealed that all but two Australian universities made statements about the link between research and teaching in their policy statements. However, the nature and extent of these connections varied considerably. Just under half of Australian universities espoused the value of alignment, integration or complementarity between research and teaching in their institutions. One in five universities made the connection between teaching–research linkages and knowledge transfer, and only one stated that teaching informed research in their university. Krause observes that these policy statements were typically aspirational, and notably lacking in operational objectives.

The relatively limited and unsophisticated treatment of the connection between teaching and research in university policy statements is problematic for the future of academic work and how it is conceived. Jenkins and Healey (2007) caution that institutional policies for research may be fracturing the potential links between teaching and research in the lives of academics, and in the experience of students, particularly at undergraduate level (p. 119). Despite increasing attention being paid to the links between research and teaching, through such national bodies as the Higher Education Academy (UK) and the Carrick Institute for Learning and Teaching (Australia), the move to disaggregate these activities into two more distinctly manageable spaces that can be demarcated, scrutinised and measured has been a significant one. National research assessment exercises, coupled with national performance-based funding measures for learning and teaching, have tended to increase the likelihood of segregation rather than integration of these activities. It is also true that there is no clear intellectual agreement or conclusive empirical evidence as to the appropriate extent or nature of linkages between teaching and research.

Institutional reward and recognition structures

Institutional reward and recognition structures typically reflect a tendency to segregate and fragment academic work. Ingraham and Ingraham (2006, p. 118) note that the intervention of bureaucracy, and the values associated with its methodologies, are seen by the academic profession as largely unnecessary and, fundamentally, undermining. The drive towards institutional accountability, bureaucratisation of teaching (Barnett, 2003), and performance-based funding has led to the exteriorisation of what were once internal principles and values, and typically private practices. Ingraham and Ingraham observe that the drive to codify academic practice has alienated academic staff (2006, p. 102). The higher education sector is witness to ongoing tensions with respect to academic promotions policies and criteria, and the relative valuing and rewarding of research and teaching performance. Moreover, minimal attention has been given to the need for promotion criteria that reflect the wide-ranging activities that seem to now be included in the "service" dimension of academic work.

Departmental, Disciplinary and Individual Factors

The powerful role of disciplinary and departmental factors in shaping academic work and identities cannot be ignored. The work of Becher and Trowler (2001) has been most influential in raising awareness of the significance of academic and disciplinary cultures. The department is typically the site of academic decision-making, career planning and performance review. The research of Schuster and Finkelstein (2006) highlights that, in the US, many academic staff experience a disjunction between their departmental and institutional spheres of influence. According to their study, faculty members perceive that they are "losing their grip on institutional affairs while they continue and even reinforce their focus on their own department" (p. 107). Similarly, Fanghanel's study (2007a) of 18 UK academics reiterates the crucial role of the departmental and disciplinary unit, and its impact on academic practice.

Failure to take account of local departmental differences and disciplinary specificities is contributing to fragmentation in the institutional landscape (Fangahanel, 2007b) and, arguably, in the identities of academic workers. Fanghanel concludes that the ways in which teaching–research linkages are conceived in the institution have a significant impact on how academic staff relate to the university, to the discipline, to the department and to academic labour, arguing that these linkages function as a filter that permeates other filters through which academic staff may see their role.

In Fanghanel's (2007a) study, academic staff felt that teaching took second place after research. This perception is well documented, and confirms the findings of Krause and colleagues (2007), who interviewed 31 academic staff across a range of disciplines in eight Australian universities. The Australian academics identified several impediments to their capacity to connect their discipline-based research with their teaching, including: organisational structures of universities that appear to represent teaching and research as separate activities, and a perception that academic staff hiring decisions are based on research outputs not teaching ability. Several interviewees also commented on the key role of the department in fostering a culture that values both teaching and research. Activities such as hosting regular departmental teaching forums, to parallel the regular depart-mental research seminars, were identified as important for conveying departmental values in relation to research and teaching. The majority of interviewees also expressed concern that the Australian-based research assessment exercise (formerly the Research Quality Framework—RQF—now the Excellence in Research for Australia—ERA) would only serve to reinforce the value of research over teaching.

The UK academics in Fanghanel's (2007a) study expressed concern at what they perceived as institutional "agenda swapping", creating zones of conflict and insecurity due to movement between a focus on teaching and a focus on research funding. As a result, staff felt that their attention was constantly oscillating between two poles of research and teaching, with little integra-tion of the two. Fanghanel concludes that the disjointedness of initiatives, and the lack of cohesion between teaching and research policy and practice, contributes to a sense of disempowerment and trivialisation of academic labour. A more sophisticated approach to analysing the changing nature of academic labour is advocated, "so that newcomers to academia . . . can evolve a coherent identity within their domains of competence" (p. 18).

Closely connected to disciplinary affiliation are the individual ideological and pedagogical beliefs and values that underpin how academic staff conceive of their work, and the reciprocal relations between teaching and research in the discipline. Rowland (2006) argues that intellectual love, a love of the subject matter, lies at the centre of academic practice. In his view, developing a culture of enquiry is the key to linking research and teaching in the disciplines. Further, he proposes that reinforcing of enquiry-based approaches to learning in higher education may go some way towards addressing the common complaints that students are no longer motivated by a love of their subject.

The Contested Triad

While the teaching–research–service triad is a well-entrenched one with a strong history in higher education (see, for example, Cummings, 1998), alternative paradigms have also been proposed to capture the evolving nature of academic work. For instance, in the US the Kellogg Commission on the Future of the State and Land-Grant Universities (2000) proposed that academic work in the twenty-first century is more appropriately captured by the terms "learning, discovery and engagement". This follows Boyer's seminal depiction of academic work as comprising four distinct yet related functions of discovery, integration, application and teaching (Boyer, 1990, p. 16). Meanwhile Laredo (2007), acknowledging the reality and importance of "third mission" activities in higher education institutions, proposes that the tripartite configuration of academic roles and university functions be conceived as: undergraduate teaching (or mass tertiary education); profes-sional specialised higher education research, with a focus on problem-solving research and mode 2 knowledge (Gibbons et al., 1994); and academic training and research. Laredo argues that each institution will have a unique mix of these three functions and, concomitantly, the third-mission activities and the shape of academic roles will be determined by the configuration of these activities

The utility and relevance of the familiar teaching–research–service triad is being questioned and challenged. Some have observed, for example, that the tripartite role of the university academic appears to be shrinking as the work of academics becomes increasingly unbundled (Kinser, 1998;

Macfarlane, 2005; Schuster and Finkelstein, 2006). The result of this unbundling, it is argued, is that universities now comprise a myriad of specialised roles, including teaching-only or research-only positions, instructional designers, community engagement specialists and many more. One obvious result of this unbundling process has been the separation of teaching, research and service activities, leading to what Schuster and Finkelstein (2006, p. 192) call a "largely silent redefinition of faculty work roles", and a concomitant stratification of the academic workforce along gendered and contingent workforce lines:

> Teaching, research and service specialists are emerging, yet no one is debating the medium to long-term effects and implications for higher education (p. 232)

How one interprets these changes is framed by the assumptions and conceptual frameworks one uses to interpret the relationship between teaching, research and service in academe. On the one hand, many academics may embrace these changes as opportunities for reframing their work. These opportunities could include the promise of greater career flexibility, increased scope for entrepreneurial behaviour (Duberley *et al.*, 2007), a more open and collaborative approach to knowledge, and mutually beneficial relationships with communities and industry. On the other hand, Churchman (2006) observes that academic interviewees in her Australian study experienced considerable role strain, as they sought to come to terms with reconciling their existing understandings of academia and those more corporate and commercialised values promoted by the institution. Academic staff in higher education face an important watershed, as they seek to come to terms with who they are and what they do.

One important area of academic work that tends to be left out of account, in the ongoing debate about the relative importance of research and teaching, is that of "service" in academe. Macfarlane (2005) contends that the concept of academic service has shifted and been reinterpreted over time. Notably, in Musselin's (2007) analysis of the transformation of academic work, there is no overt acknowledgement of the service component of academic work—only teaching and research are mentioned, along with "new missions" which are presented as synonymous with third-mission activities.

Macfarlane (2005) argues that competitive individualism has supplanted communitarian and collegial values, hence degrading the value of service in the triad of academic activities. This devaluing of service also tends to be evident in academic promotion policies, where teaching and research are clearly privileged over service components of the academic role, with the latter perceived to be most highly regarded. Service, then, is not typically interpreted as a "good investment" in terms of academic career advancement (Macfarlane, 2005, p. 175; see also Knight, 2002). This view is further reinforced by Schuster and Finkelstein (2006), who observe that the narrowing of the scope of academic staff activities in US universities has led to a shift in emphasis from a triadic to a dyadic core of activities, namely teaching and research, with activities such as administration and academic citizenship being relegated to the periphery of academic functions. They observe that there are fewer and fewer opportunities for academic staff to operate as academic citizens, and that, when these opportunities arise, they are rarely rewarded in the form of promotions criteria.

Yet, as Macfarlane points out, service roles are increasingly critical to the efficient functioning of the university. In teaching, roles such as peer mentoring, peer observation of teaching, curriculum design, development and review may all arguably be conceived as service to the discipline. Moreover, the range of service roles related to research has also increased, in the form of increased service demands, and opportunities to support newly established journals, or to mentor junior researchers. Shils (1997) supports this argument, contending that academic citizenship is a key role that should be seen as integral and complementary to teaching and research activities. In an attempt to theorise academic service and citizenship more rigorously, Macfarlane (2007) proposes a five-tiered academic service pyramid, including service in support of students, colleagues, the institution, the discipline and professional bodies, and the community. The key, however, is whether or not these contributions are valued and rewarded.

Reshaping the Teaching–Research–Service Debate

In response to the simultaneous trends of the blurring of boundaries and the unbundling and fragmentation of academic work, some theorists are encouraging an alternative, more integrated view of academic work. At one level, scholars such as Brew (2006) argue that we need to move beyond the traditional divide between research and teaching, to a more inclusive approach that emphasises academic work as integral to "scholarly knowledge-building communities of practice" (p. 180). In this way, activities relating to research and teaching become inseparable and suffused into the idea of knowledge work (Lucas, 2007).

Going one step further, proponents of public scholarship argue that this is a powerful way to blend all the domains of "intellectual activity into a distinctive whole" (Ramaley, 2000, p. 11). Public scholarship goes well beyond the service learning paradigm to emphasise "scholarly work as it is grounded in disciplined elements of scholarship, that is . . . peer reviewed . . . shared and available to others" (Cohen and Yapa, 2003, p. 6). As such, it prioritises mode 2 knowledge production (Gibbons *et al.*, 1994) and its role in the student learning experience. It presents learning as a process of discovering how one might contribute to society using scholarly knowledge and processes. These processes might include how to formulate, solve and share a research problem using disciplinary knowledge (Janke, 2006, p. 53). Such scholarly processes are inherent to the well-documented teaching–research nexus literature, but they take the nexus one step further into the domain of community engagement. These priorities of knowledge exchange, and ecological and political awareness, among both students and staff are identified as critical for those working in a globalised higher education context (Bottery, 2006).

In summary, the concept of public scholarship brings under a single lens the range of activities constituting academic enquiry, emphasising that, together, they constitute the core business of responsible and responsive institutions of higher education in the twenty-first century. Colbeck and Michael (2006b) contend that, rather than being another dimension of academic work, public scholarship *is* academic work that is reframed as a unified whole.

While alternative paradigms to existing and increasingly fragmented views of academic work may be on offer, they require a number of conditions to succeed. Suggesting alternative ways of conceiving academic labour also has significant implications for academic staff and how they view themselves and their work.

Implications for Policy and Practice

This chapter has outlined some of the ways in which the shape of academic work appears to have changed in recent years, with particular attention given to changes inherent in the contested triad of teaching, research and service. It has identified key factors contributing to these changes, and has explored some of the international developments taking place as part of the reshaping of academic work and identities. The changes in academic labour have significant implications for policy and practice in the higher education sector. A number of pertinent questions now need to be addressed. For instance, in the light of the purpose of higher education, one may ask who should do academic work, and is there an optimal configuration of responsibilities that simultaneously adds value to student learning, individual academic careers, disciplinary research, institutional missions and community needs? There is also considerable scope for challenging current higher education policies and funding regimes for the ways in which they typically separate the core activities of research and teaching, with a notable tendency to favour the former. At the institutional level, an important question pertains to the medium- to long-term effects and implications for higher education institutions of the changes in academic work and careers.

It is critical that the fragmentation and unbundling of academic work not be accepted as a mere inevitability of progress. Rather, alternative approaches to the reshaping of academic work need to be considered in rigorous and scholarly ways that engage all members of the academic community, including academic and professional staff—and boundary-spanners who fit neither category neatly—students, policy-makers, key stakeholder groups and community members. When it comes to reframing academic work, and considering implications for academic career paths and reward structures, it is essential that academic staff be included in these decision-making processes, to inform policy in this regard, and to be encouraged to take an active role in reshaping the work that lies at the heart of who they are. Their voices must be heard above the resounding call for universities to be more efficient, competitive and commercialised. To facilitate such empowerment among academic staff, it is important for university leaders and communities to create opportunities that encourage scholarly debate about the longer-term implications of changes to academic labour (Peters *et al.*, 2005). Such enabling settings should be characterised by professional development and support for staff, and a collegial approach to discussions about the nature and purpose of higher education, and the communities that it comprises. Success lies in an ongoing and strengthened partnership between informed, consultative and responsive policy-makers and academic staff, who are actively engaged in institution-wide dialogue about their changing roles and who are supported and empowered to manage ongoing role and identity transformations.

References

Adelman, C. (2000). A parallel universe: Certification in the Information Technology Guild. *Change, 32*(3), 20–29.

Ball, S.J. (2000). Performativities and fabrications in the education economy: Towards the performative society. *Australian Educational Researcher, 17*(3), 1–24.

Barnett, R. (2003) *Beyond all reason: Living with ideology in the university*. Buckingham: Open University Press.

Becher, T. and Trowler, P.R. (2001) *Academic tribes and territories* 2nd edn. Buckingham: Open University Press.

Bleiklie, I. and Kogan, M. (2007). Organisation and governance of universities. *Higher Education Policy, 20*, 477–493.

Bottery, M. (2006). Education and globalisation: Redefining the role of the educational professional. *Educational Review, 58*(1), 95–113.

Boyer, E.L. (1990). *Scholarship reconsidered: Priorities of the professoriate*. Princeton, N.J.: Carnegie Foundation for the Advancement of Teaching.

Brew, A. (2006). *Research and teaching: Beyond the divide*. London: Palgrave Macmillan.

Churchman, D. (2006). Institutional commitments, individual compromises: Identity-related responses to compromise in an Australian university. *Journal of Higher Education Policy and Management, 28*(1), 3–15.

Cohen, J. (2001). Public scholarship: serving to learn. In M.E. Kenny, L.K. Simon, K. Kiley-Bradeck and R.M. Lerner (eds) *Learning to serve: Promoting civil society through service learning* (pp. 235–255). Norwood, MA: Kluwer.

Cohen, J. and Yapa, L. (2003). Introduction. In J. Cohen and L. Yapa (eds) *A blueprint for public scholarship at Penn State*. University Park: Pennsylvania State University.

Colbeck, C.L. and Michael, P.W. (2006a). Individual and organizational influences on faculty members' engagement in public scholarship. In R.A. Eberly and J. Cohen (eds) *Laboratory for Public Scholarship and Democracy. New Directions for Teaching and Learning, No. 105*. San Francisco, CA: Jossey-Bass.

Colbeck, C.L. and Michael, P.W. (2006b). Public scholarship: Resynthesizing Boyer's four domains. In J.M. Braxton (ed.) *Delving Further into Boyer's Research on Scholarship. New Directions for Institutional Research, No. 129*. San Francisco, CA: Jossey-Bass.

Cummings, W.K. (1998). The service university movement in the US: Searching for momentum. *Higher Education, 35*, 69–90.

Duberley, J., Cohen, L. and Leeson, E. (2007). Entrepreneurial academics: Developing scientific careers in changing university settings. *Higher Education Quarterly, 61*(4), 479–497.

Engestrom, Y. (2001). Expansive learning at work: Toward an activity theoretical reconceptualisation. *Journal of Education and Work, 14*(1), 133–156.

Etzkowitz, H. and Leydesdorff, L. (2000). The dynamics of innovation: From national systems and "Mode 2" to a triple helix of university–industry–government relations. *Research Policy, 29*, 109–123.

Fanghanel, J. (2007a). *Investigating university lecturers' pedagogical constructs in the working context.* Higher Education Academy Report. Retrieved April 25, 2008 from www.heacademy.ac.uk/assets/York/documents/ourwork/research/fanghanel.pdf.

Fanghanel, J. (2007b). Teaching excellence in context: drawing from a sociocultural approach. In A. Skelton (ed.) *International perspectives on teaching excellence in higher education* (pp. 197–212). London: Routledge.

Fanghanel, J. and Trowler, P. (2007). *New academic identities for a new profession?: Situating the teaching dimension of the academic role in a competitive enhancement context.* Paper presented at the RESUP International Conference, Paris. Retrieved April 24, 2008 from http://www.resup.ubordeaux2.fr/manifestations/conferenceinternationaleparis2007/Actes/FANGHANEL%20et%20TROWLER_RESUP2007.pdf.

Gibbons, M., Limoges, C., Nowotny, H., Schwartzman, S., Scott, P. and Trow, M. (1994). *The new production of knowledge: the dynamics of science and research in contemporary societies.* London: Sage.

Hatakenaka, S. (2005). *Development of third stream activity: Lessons from international experience.* Higher Education Policy Institute Report. Retrieved April 24, 2008 from http://www.hepi.ac.uk/pubdetail.asp?ID=196andDOC=seminars.

Henkel, M. (2007). Can academic autonomy survive in the knowledge society? A perspective from Britain. *Higher Education Research and Development, 26*(1), 87–99.

Hughes, M. (2005). The mythology of research and teaching relationships in universities. In R. Barnett (ed.) *Reshaping the university: New relationships between research, scholarship and teaching* (pp. 14–26). Buckingham: Open University Press.

Ingraham, B.D. and Ingraham, S.M. (2006) eQuality: A dialogue between quality and academia, *E-Learning, 3*(1), 112–122.

Janke, E.M. (2006). The promise of public scholarship for undergraduate research: Developing students' civic and academic scholarship skills. *Higher Education in Review, 3*, 51–68.

Jenkins, A. and Healey, M. (2007). Critiquing excellence: undergraduate research for all students. In A. Skelton (ed.) *International perspectives on teaching excellence in higher education* (pp. 117–132). London: Routledge.

Kellogg Commission on the Future of State and Land-Grant Universities. (2000). *Renewing the covenant: Learning, discovery, and engagement in a new age and different world.* Washington, DC: National Association of State Universities and Land-Grant Colleges. Retrieved April 24, 2008 from www.nasulgc.org/publications/Kellogg/Kellogg2000_covenant.pdf.

Kimber, M. (2003). The tenured "core" and the tenuous "periphery": The casualisation of academic work in Australian universities. *Journal of Higher Education Policy and Management, 25*(1), 41–50.

Kinser, K. (1998). Faculty at private for-profit universities: The University of Phoenix as a new model? *International Higher Education, 13*, 13–14.

Knight, P. (2002). *Being a teacher in higher education.* Buckingham: Open University Press.

Kogan, M. and Teichler, U. (eds) (2007). *Key challenges to the academic profession.* UNESCO Forum on Higher Education. Retrieved April 24, 2008 from www.uni-kassel.de/incher/v_pub/cap1.pdf.

Krause, K. (2007). *Knowledge transfer, engagement and public scholarship: Emerging possibilities for an integrated approach to academic enquiry.* Paper presented at International Policies and Practices for Academic Enquiry: An international colloquium, Marwell. Retrieved April 24, 2008 from www.griffith.edu.au/__data/assets/pdf_file/0007/39265/KrauseMarwell2007.pdf.

Krause, K., Arkoudis, S. and Green, A. (2007). *Teaching–research linkages: Opportunities and challenges for practice and policy.* Paper presented at the Carrick Institute for Learning and Teaching Forum on the Teaching–Research Nexus, Adelaide, 2007. Retrieved April 24, 2008 from www.carrickinstitute.edu.au/carrick/webdav/users/siteadmin/public/dbi_forum_trnexus_07_paper_krause.pdf.

Laredo, P. (2007). Revisiting the third mission of universities: Toward a renewed categorisation of university activities? *Higher Education Policy, 20*, 441–456.

Lave, J. and Wenger, E. (1991). *Situated learning: Legitimate peripheral participation.* Cambridge: Cambridge University Press.

Lucas, L. (2007). Research and teaching work within university education departments: Fragmentation or integration? *Journal of Further and Higher Education, 31*(1), 17–29.

Lyotard, J-F. (1984). *The postmodern condition: A report on knowledge.* Manchester: Manchester University Press.

Macfarlane, B. (2005). Placing service in academic life. In R. Barnett (ed.), *Reshaping the university: New relationships between research, scholarship and teaching* (pp. 165–177). Buckingham: Open University Press.

Macfarlane, B. (2007). Defining and rewarding academic citizenship: The implications for university promotions policy. *Journal of Higher Education Policy and Management, 29*(3), 261–273.

Musselin, C. (2007). *The transformation of academic work: Facts and analysis.* eScholarship Repository, University of California. Retrieved April 24, 2008 from http://repositories.cdlib.org/cshe/CSHE-4-07.

Peters, M. (1998). Cybernetics, cyberspace, and the politics of university reform. In M. Peters and P. Roberts (eds) *Virtual technologies and tertiary education* (pp. 74–92). Palmerston North, NZ: Dunmore Press.

Peters, M. and Humes, W. (2003). Editorial: Education in the knowledge economy. *Policy Futures in Education, 1*(1), 1–19.

Peters, S.J., Jordan, N.R., Adamek, M. and Alter, T.R. (eds) (2005). *Engaging campus and community.* Ohio: Kettering Foundation Press.

Ramaley, J.A. (2000). Embracing civic responsibility. *AAHE Bulletin, 52*, 9–13.

Ramsden, P. and Moses, I. (1992). Associations between research and teaching in Australian higher education. *Higher Education, 23*, 273–295

Rowland, S. (2006). *The enquiring university: Compliance and contestation in higher education.* Maidenhead: Open University Press.

Schuster, M. and Finkelstein, M. (2006). *The restructuring of academic work and careers: The American faculty.* Baltimore: The Johns Hopkins University Press.

Shils, E. (1997). *The calling of education: The academic ethic and other essays on higher education.* Chicago: University of Chicago Press

Skelton, A. (ed.) (2007). *International perspectives on teaching excellence in higher education: Improving knowledge and practice.* Oxford: Routledge.

Trowler, P., Fanghanel, J. and Wareham, T. (2005). Freeing the chi of change: The Higher Education Academy and enhancing teaching and learning in higher education. *Studies in Higher Education, 30,* 427–444.

Yapa, L. (2006). Public scholarship in the postmodern university. In R.A. Eberly and J. Cohen (eds) *Laboratory for Public Scholarship and Democracy. New Directions for Teaching. No 105.* San Francisco, CA: Jossey-Bass.

Zukas, M. and Malcolm, J. (2007). Teaching, discipline, network. In A. Skelton (ed.) *International perspectives on teaching excellence in higher education* (pp. 60–73). London: Routledge.

31
Academic Development

Ranald Macdonald

Introduction

A consideration of "academic development" inevitably begins with issues of definition, as different terms are used in different countries and educational sectors to refer to the same or similar activities. Whether it is academic development in Australia and New Zealand, staff or educational development in the UK, faculty, instructional or organisational development in the US, "academic development" has become ubiquitous in many higher, tertiary or post-compulsory education systems, at least in more developed countries. "Professional" and "academic staff" development are also used in various contexts (Macdonald, 2002). For convenience, and perhaps because of its growing use in the main journal in the field—the *International Journal for Academic Development* (IJAD)—and in the author's home country, the UK, the term "academic development" is used as all-encompassing for what will be seen to be a great variety of roles and activities.

The academic background of the individual academic developer, their status and where they are located within the organisation, the formal and informal roles they undertake and the extent to which this relates to how they see themselves, and the way they interact within and between institutions and countries, are amongst the aspects to be considered in this chapter. However, as well as the contention that academic development may have become a legitimate "academic tribe with its own territory" (Macdonald, 2003; Bath and Smith, 2004), there are those who take a more critical stance, such as Land (2004), Clegg (2003) and Rowland (2006) from the UK, and the Challenging Academic Development (CAD) Collective (Peseta, 2005), with representatives primarily from Australia, Canada and New Zealand as well as the UK.

Academic developers may not feel a pull to either "compliance or contestation", as characterised by Rowland (2006), but have a sense of purpose and perhaps pragmatism that enables them to address equally the needs of individuals, the institution and national agendas. However, many academic developers may not dwell very much on the perceived tensions between working directly with individual academic staff and meeting the wider, and perhaps conflicting, needs of the institution.

This account is largely taken from the author's British perspective, informed by his contacts with academic developers and the literature in Australia, Hong Kong, New Zealand, Singapore, Sri Lanka, the US and a number of other European countries. Where possible, examples are drawn from elsewhere, but readers from other countries may have to translate the examples and principles to their own contexts. After a brief introduction to what is meant by "academic development", and to the development of networks internationally, the nature of academic development activity is examined, together with the contention that it is a form of academic practice. There then follows some discussion of the organisation and impact of academic development, before concluding with some current issues, such as the nature of identity within the profession and some challenges for the future.

What is Academic Development?

There is some debate as to whether academic development is what people "know" or what they "do", and whether it is a profession or an activity (Macdonald, 2003). The following quotes, whilst not necessarily fully inclusive of those engaged in the field or the activities in which they engage, may prove a useful starting point:

> ... academic development is taken to mean practices designed to enhance the academic performance of an institution of higher education. For purposes of convenience, this is assumed to subdivide into staff (often in North America, faculty) development, where the focus is on enhancing the professional competence of academic faculty members; and educational development, which includes curriculum development and instructional design, as well as input to policies governing the design, delivery, evaluation and recognition of teaching (Candy, 1996, p. 17).
>
> ... an academic developer is any person who has a role in which they are explicitly expected to work with academics to assist them to reflect upon their academic role in relation to teaching, research, scholarship, leadership, funding applications and supervision of students. An academic developer may also work at a departmental/institutional level in a developmental role (Fraser, 2001, p. 55).
>
> Academic/educational/faculty development refers to the numerous activities which have to do with the professional learning of academics in post-compulsory, tertiary or higher education. Since academics perform a variety of roles, and are engaged on a variety of contracts, the scope for academic development is wide (Brew, 2004, p. 5).

Immediately a number of potential tensions are revealed: what do people engaged in the area call themselves, to what extent are they "real" academics and what is their primary focus—the individual or the institution? Editorials in IJAD, arguably the house journal of academic developers worldwide, continually reflect these questions, as it considers "who" the academic developers are, "what" they do, "where" they are located within the organisational structure, "how" they go about their work, and "with what effect" their activities provide evidence of making a difference (Knapper, 1997). Further editorials in IJAD, perhaps reflecting a continual questioning of ourselves, have begun with the following titles: "Is academic development a profession?" (1998), "The changing face of academic development" (2002), "The scope of academic development" (2004), "Making sense of academic development" (2006) and "Evaluating academic development in a time of perplexity" (2007). Rowland (2007) reflects this uncertainty or ambiguity about academic development by observing that a third of the articles in IJAD over a six-year period (2001–2006) "focused on the role and identity of academic (or educational) developers" (p. 9).

Choosing to use the term "staff development", Webb (1996a) delineates the area as including "the institutional policies, programmes and procedures which facilitate and support staff so that they may fully serve their own and the institution's needs" (p. 1). The tension between fully serving "their own and the institution's needs" continues to reverberate in the literature. Following from Webb's definition, academic development is taken by many to be activities that are concerned with "sustaining and enhancing the quality of learning and teaching within the institution" (Hounsell, 1994). What also begins to become clear are the origins of the area in the quality agendas since the 1970s, particularly in relation to improving the quality of teaching and learning through staff development (Hicks, 2007) and a focus on individuals and their "development", itself a contentious issue for some (Webb, 1996b).

Some Short Histories and Goals of Academic Development

Much of the accessible published work on the history of academic development is in English and, as such, does not give a complete picture of the world-wide nature of the phenomenon, though English-speaking academic developers working with departments in other countries have collaborated on accounts of practice in IJAD. However, a few short accounts of national developments and their respective networks gives a useful picture of the ways in which different political, educational and other agendas have promoted, and sometimes worked against, academic development. Beginning with the largest network, in the US, and then by contrast the UK and Sri Lanka, together with an international umbrella network, some sense of diversity and similarity begins to emerge.

The United States

In a brief history of faculty development in the United States, Lewis (1996) notes that its origins were in higher education institutions supporting academics to develop expertise in their discipline, through research and undertaking higher qualifications, sabbaticals and travel to professional meetings. In the late 1960s and early 1970s there were student protests against poor teaching and irrelevant courses, resulting in development programmes to improve both teaching or instruction and the curriculum, often funded by grants from private foundations or public agencies (Fletcher and Patrick, 1998). As economic conditions worsened and academic life became more stressful during the 1980s, there was a growth in more "holistic" development activities to provide personal support in preparation for retirement or career changes, as well as just coping with day-to-day pressures. The 1990s saw the growth of faculty development programmes and centres, partly as a response to public calls for greater accountability and a recognition that they contributed to the vitality of the institution.

In his 2006 Presidential Address to the Professional and Organizational Development Network in Higher Education (POD), Groccia (2006) set the organisation in its historical context, outlined its current activities and looked to the future, echoing moves already begun in other networks to look to the professional development of the faculty developers, and explored in an extensive survey of US faculty developers by Sorcinelli *et al.*, (2006). POD was founded in 1975 and draws most of its nearly 1,800 membership from the US and Canada. Its aim is to "foster human development in higher education through faculty, instructional and organizational development" (http://www.podnetwork.org/). The three aspects of development provide a focus for its various activities including conferences, publications, consulting and networking, as well as fulfilling a national advocacy role.

United Kingdom

As with all national post-compulsory education systems, the United Kingdom has seen dramatic change since the 1970s (Ashwin 2006): in terms of the numbers and diversity of students; a move from a binary system of universities and polytechnics to a unified university sector, though with considerable difference between individual institutions; reductions in real spending per student and an increase in the ratio of students to teachers; moves to modularised curriculum structures; and changing government aims in relation to the economy. There has also been a significant increase in government regulation as well as, more recently, an increase in funded special initiatives to support developments in learning and teaching.

One aspect of this greater interest in learning and teaching has been the move to professionalise and accredit teaching in higher education, with the Staff and Educational Development Association (SEDA) at the forefront of these developments (Beaty, 2006). SEDA was formed in the UK in 1993 by the merger of two organisations, which take its history back to 1974. SEDA is a professional association committed to improving all aspects of learning, teaching and training in higher education through staff and educational development, and its activities fall under five main headings: professional development, conferences and events, publications, research and services to members. An aspect of its work has been the development of teacher accreditation programmes across many UK and other universities, and the official taking up of this approach through the National Committee of Inquiry into Higher Education in 1997. SEDA subsequently developed a professional development framework, which provides named awards for a wide range of academic and related roles such as learning technologies, student support and guidance, and supervising postgraduate research (Brand, 2007—http://www.seda.ac.uk).

Sri Lanka

Following student-led unrest as a result of poor graduate prospects, and the closure of universities for two years in 1986–1987 (Ekaratne, 2003), there was a recognition that there had to be improvements in the quality of both teaching and the learning experience, together with greater employability prospects for graduates through skills they acquired during their courses. The Sri Lankan University Grants Commission required all new staff to receive training in teaching and learning from 1995 and the establishment of staff development centres in all the universities. The result was a need for more staff developers and the development of a "Training the Trainers" programme, led by the University of Colombo in 1997. The Sri Lanka Association for Improving Higher Education Effectiveness (SLAIHEE) was founded in 2005 as an association "of Higher Education professionals dedicated to improving teaching and learning effectiveness by actively supporting educational developers and leaders in higher education in Sri Lanka". It has annual conferences and a website and newsletter to communicate with its growing membership (http://www.slaihee.org).

The International Consortium for Educational Development (ICED)

The ICED was formed in 1993 to promote academic development in higher education across the world. By forming a network, whose members are national organisations or networks concerned with promoting good practice in higher education, it was intended to provide an opportunity to support new networks or those in countries without networks. With around 20 member networks, ICED has annual Council meetings, a bi-annual international conference and publishes IJAD (http://www.osds.uwa.au/iced/).

Despite its efforts, ICED's membership is predominantly in Europe, North America and Australia/New Zealand. Some "emergent" networks have been members but, in essence, it remains a body of large, well-organised and administered organisations in Australasia, Canada, Germany, the UK and the USA and smaller, looser networks, including Belgium, Denmark, Finland, the Netherlands, Norway and Sweden. There are also networks in other countries, such as Croatia, Estonia, India, South Africa and Sri Lanka, and, though ICED states its commitment "to support educational development in higher education in developing countries" or where no network exists, promoting the development and maintenance of new networks remains a significant challenge.

The Nature of Academic Development Activity

In analysing how academic developers go about their work, Gosling (1997) conceptualised five broad approaches: "reflective practitioner", "educational researcher", "professional competency", the "human resources" or "managerial" approach, and the educational developer as a consultant or expert with the role of disseminating best practice. These approaches may be adopted individually, together or be seen as phases in an individual's career or personal development (Macdonald, 2003). However, a number of other studies have categorised or conceptualised academic development in somewhat different ways.

Drawing on an empirical study of UK institutions, Land (2004) identifies 12 orientations to academic development, or "variations in practice": managerial, political strategist, entrepreneurial, romantic, vigilant opportunist, researcher, professional competence, reflective practitioner, internal consultant, modeller-broker, interpretive-hermeneutic and discipline-specific. The orientation(s)— "which include the attitudes, knowledge, aims and action tendencies of academic developers in relation to the contexts and challenges of their practice" (p. 13)—to be effective, will need to be congruent with the organisational culture in which the developer finds him or herself. Land locates these orientations within a framework comprising two axes which represent polarised tendencies— the needs of the individual as against those of the institution, and practice, which might be characterised as domesticating as it fits with the purpose or mission and prevailing culture of the institution, rather than liberating and running counter to these factors. He further elaborates these polarities as systems/person orientation and adherence to policy/emancipatory critique, and superimposes a series of organisational cultures onto the model as the basis for examining how academic developers might respond to different models of change.

Recognising that academic development has, in recent years, moved from the margins to the mainstream in many institutions, Candy (1996) contrasts the role of staff and educational development in industrial organisations—"fundamentally deficit-oriented, designed to remedy shortcomings in people's current level of skill" (p. 8)—with knowledge-based organisations, where the nature of the work is non-repetitive, non-standardised, and involves problem-solving (p. 9). In the latter case, where it is those who are able to develop non-standardised solutions to non-recurrent problems who are valued most, it is investment in this expertise that gives the organisation its competitive advantage. Arguing that staff development in higher education should meet the needs of a learning organisation, Candy (p. 11) develops what he terms the CAREER model of staff development:

Comprehensive and embrace the total spectrum of academic work;
Anticipatory rather that reactive;
Research-based and theoretically rigorous;
Exemplary in terms of modelling best practice especially in teaching/learning methodologies;
Embedded in the institutional culture and context;
Reflective and encourage reflective awareness of practice; and
Geared towards the notion of *lifelong personal and professional development.*

Similarly, Gosling (2001), in his follow-up survey of the activities of educational development units in the UK, identifies specific activities such as improvements of teaching and assessment practices, curriculum design and learning support; professional development of academic staff; organisational and policy development; and learning development of students. Quoting the work of Badley and Webb, who note, respectively, that much of the writing on educational development offered no place for research or scholarship and that "development" itself is a contested term, Gosling (p. 75) adds two further elements to the definition of higher educational development: "Informed debate about learning, teaching, assessment, curriculum design, and the goals of higher education; and promotion of the scholarship of teaching and learning and research into higher education goals and practices".

A perpetual dilemma for academic developers is that, when working with others—including academics, administrators and managers—each has different expectations or understandings of the relevant power or authority they possess. Further, they may all have different approaches to, or conceptions of change and risk-taking. Stefani and Matthew (2002) note the tensions between "directive, task-based approaches" and "developmental, process-based approaches", where the former may be less effective in leading to real change, and the latter may take more time, and thus cost more, but are more likely to lead to lasting and effective change.

There is also the implication here of different approaches to change—simplistically contrasted as either "top–down" or "bottom–up", though D'Andrea and Gosling (2001) characterise this as "vertical" and contend that "horizontal" activities across organisational structures are important. The latter would include working with human resources, developing staff timetables to focus on student learning as an outcome rather than teaching hours as an input, engaging with estates strategies to ensure appropriate rooms and learning environments, and ensuring that institutional information and learning and teaching strategies are aligned. The reality may be that change emerges from wherever productive conversations are enabled to take place in what are highly complex organisations—higher education institutions (Macdonald and Joughin, 2008).

Academic Development as Academic Practice

A major issue in the literature has been the extent to which academic developers are "real" academics. Candy (1996) contends that academic developers should be identified, not as para-professionals, but as meta-professionals, who are academics *par excellence* and, given that their clients are academics themselves, there needs to be absolute congruence between their actions and their recommendations—"they must practice what they preach" (p. 17). Further, their effectiveness in changing individual attitudes and institutional culture "is dependent on being, and on being seen to be, reputable academics whose area of research and teaching happens to be higher education itself" (p. 16).

The debate also extends to whether academic development is a profession, with Harland and Staniforth (2003) arguing that, as a profession, it should reflect all the characteristics of academic practice, not least that the work is grounded in research and theoretical knowledge. Building on Macdonald's (2003) contention that it may well now be "time for academic development to receive recognition as an academic tribe with its own territory", Bath and Smith (2004) defend the propositions that academic developers are, by the nature of their work, academic, and that higher education is a legitimate academic discipline in its own right (p. 9). Whilst they do concur with Andresen (1996) that academic developers' academic work may not always be seen as "regular", they see more similarities than differences, with many of the hallmarks of other disciplines, such as professional associations and journals, co-location in departments or units, and a growing research and scholarly tradition. In a survey of UK academic development units in 2006, Gosling (2008) reports that 72.5% of those responding see undertaking or contributing to pedagogic research as part of their function, and a similar picture of engagement in and with research can be observed in other countries, with a growth in masters and doctoral candidates in academic development.

Taking this further, Andresen (1996) argues that academic developers are professional because "we are academics: we do academic work by pursuing and advancing scholarship within our own field in (and sometimes outside of) higher education institutions" (p. 44). "Our own field" may be our original discipline, a transdisciplinary notion, or higher education studies—an area also identified by Candy (1996) and Rowland (2006). In arguing "for the health of their profession and the enhancement of its contribution to the whole academic enterprise", Andresen (1996) suggests that "academic developers must continue to participate in relevant discourse about their theory and practice. They should develop their capacity to hand on their practices and discourse, learning from and contributing to appropriate academic disciplines (e.g. the study of Higher Education) and engaging in pragmatic self-criticism" (p. 47).

Based on 20 interviews with academic developers from six countries, and drawing on Rowland's (2006) contention that all academic work is fragmented in some way, Harland and Staniforth, (in press) observe the field to consist of many sub-groups "that have little in common with each other". Further, they may come from very different backgrounds and experiences, with different skills and qualifications.

Arguing that academic development, as with any academic practice, should be critical, Rowland (2006) explores the ways in which academics can develop their teaching. He suggests three models of academic development—atheoretical, educational and critical interdisciplinarity—Table 31.1 summarises the approaches and how the developers' roles or approach would change with each.

Whilst the approaches may not be exclusive, they do require academic developers to recognise their own disciplinary identity and engage in the practices of any academic—research, scholarship, teaching and engaging with their community, and in service to the university and beyond, including professional associations.

How Academic Developers Are Organised

Academic or faculty development has conventionally been located in central departments or units, whether academic or administrative. However, this often results in the academic developers either working generically through workshops, courses and events, or more specifically with individuals or small groups of enthusiasts. A particular challenge has always been for academic development to be valued at the subject or discipline level, where academics have their primary allegiance, and for developers to be aware of the departmental cultures which may differ

Table 31.1 Teaching Development and Approaches to Academic Development

Teaching in Higher Education	Academic Development
craft/skill—atheoretical — 'how'	trainers addressing practical problems of teaching developing competence
educational approach, more holistic view of academic practice — 'why'	theorise, conduct research, produce findings making educational judgements
critical interdisciplinarity; closer relationship between research and teaching — 'what' — 'being a . . .'	sharpen disciplinary identity contestation between different views about the nature of the subject

Based on Rowland (2006)

significantly within the same institution (Gibbs, 1996). The notion of situated learning and communities of practice (Lave and Wenger, 1991; Wenger, 1998) has helped to focus attention on where professionals learn, which, in the case of academics, is in their academic department. Successful central units may adopt more hybrid forms of engagement, recognising the need to provide discipline-relevant development as the context for their activities. Using a two-dimensional framework, with central/local and generic/discipline-specific as the dimensions, to analyse Australian academic development, Hicks (1999) identifies a number of models of development: central, dispersed, mixed and integrated. Acknowledging the challenge or risk to central units, McAlpine (2006) argues that more local approaches, as have been used in medical education for some time, might "serve as a constructive counter-weight or counter-balance to institutional pressures for generic top-down development initiatives" (p. 126). Whether institutional managers would be persuaded by this argument is a moot point, particularly where departments are not operating in ways they would wish.

However, whilst acknowledging the need for central units and the dangers of promoting more departmentally based academic development, Boud (1999) observes that academic development work happens, often informally, in the departments, professional settings and research sites where academics spend most of their time. He argues that more formal approaches should also be located in these settings, where academic identity is largely formed. Using examples from his own institution of teaching development projects and a writing for publication group, academic development is seen as part of the day-to-day activity of academic life, though often "rendered invisible or subordinate by centralizing preoccupations" (p. 7). Orzech (1998) gives an account of a departmental project in mathematics in which, though there was contact with the university's small Instructional Development Centre, which was unable to act in anything more than a supportive role, it was largely local actions that sought to balance collaboration, individual initiatives and strategic goals. The central unit had a role in directing the project teams to the appropriate literature, and providing advice on approaches to project management, monitoring and evaluation, but the need to take ownership and responsibility locally led to the emergence of departmental academic developers who would probably never use that term to describe themselves.

Recognising that much of the organisational focus in many institutions is based around disciplines, Healey and Jenkins (2003) and Baillie (2003) illustrate how national and even international networks have grown to support more discipline-based academic development. Though many enhancement initiatives have focused on more generic issues such as assessment or large-group teaching, the development in the UK of the Higher Education Academy Subject Centre Network (http://www.heacademy.ac.uk/) has provided a more culturally specific context for many discipline-focused activities, including academic development. Similarly, Healey and Jenkins (2003) note examples in the US and Australia, and organisations such as the International Society for the Scholarship of Teaching and Learning (ISSoTL) providing opportunities for the development and dissemination of disciplinary-focused scholarly initiatives. Jenkins (1996) also recognises the role of generic academic development in promoting inter-disciplinary learning, but stresses that it is only by working at a disciplinary level that the mass of academics will engage.

In the UK there is more of a tradition of academic (more often called "educational") development in the former polytechnic sector, where learning and teaching had been afforded higher priority. However, recent government and funding body initiatives have encouraged more research-intensive institutions to produce learning and teaching strategies, recognise teaching excellence, bid for Centres for Excellence in Teaching and Learning (CETLs) and require new academics to undertake accredited teaching courses as a condition of a permanent contract (Gibbs, 2005). Similar initiatives in Australia, New Zealand, Sweden and the US, amongst others, have engaged academics in research-led institutions in professional development, though often with a focus on the relationship between their research and teaching, or on notions of scholarship as articulated by Boyer and others (Boyer, 1990; Glassick *et al.*, 1997).

The Impact of Academic Development

An issue of ongoing concern for academic developers is that there are those in their institutions who view them as either an unnecessary overhead intruding into their professional practice as teachers, or as a diversion of funding away from the true business of a university—research. This raises challenges when academic development departments are asked to be accountable, or to evaluate the impact of their activities, in particular when they are required to show how their activities have contributed to strategically defined outcomes, and not just whether they are in line with strategic objectives (Brew, 2007).

There have been few studies of the impact of academic development, though notable exceptions include those by: Gibbs and Coffey (2004) on the impact of training of university teachers on their teaching skills, their approach to teaching and the approach to learning of their students; Rust (1998) on the impact of educational development workshops on teachers' practices; Rust (2000) on the impact of initial training courses on university teaching; Piccinin and colleagues on the impact of individual consultations on student ratings of teaching (1999), and on the teaching of younger versus older faculty (2002); and Stes *et al.*, (2007) on the long-term and institutional effectiveness of a faculty training programme. Krebber and Brook (2001) present a model for more effective evaluation of programmes, moving beyond the so-called "happy sheets" of participant satisfaction, arguing that there needs to be appropriate alignment of the evaluation strategy with both the nature of the intervention and the level at which the impact is to be assessed, based on the principle of meaningful or constructive alignment.

The New Zealand Ministry of Education commissioned a team from Massey University to undertake a systematic review on the impact of academic staff development on student outcomes (Prebble *et al.*, 2004). The report came up with two propositions concerning the relationship between academic development and student learning outcomes: good teaching has positive impacts on student learning; and teachers can be assisted to improve the quality of their teaching through a variety of academic interventions (p. 12). With respect to the second proposition, the study reviewed and summarised the impact of five types of academic development interventions: short training courses; *in situ* training; consulting, peer assessment and mentoring; student assessment of teaching; and intensive staff development (p. 26). The findings were thought to support further investment in the development of the professional practice of teaching, though with varying evidence to support the various approaches. The report recommended further research in New Zealand, and a successful bid was subsequently made to the Ministry of Education's Teaching and Learning Research Initiative. The three-year project began in 2006, involving partnerships between academic developers with teachers on large first-year courses in all eight New Zealand universities, to improve student learning through enhancement initiatives. The outcome will be a range of empirically identified academic development strategies and approaches that directly enhance student success and learning outcomes (http://tlei.massey.ac.nz/index.htm).

Whilst there are undoubtedly other impact evaluations being undertaken, it is notable that a government department is directly supporting this initiative.

Issues of Identity and "Thinking Otherwise"

For a over a decade there has grown up a tradition of critiquing the practice and principles of academic development, beginning perhaps with Webb (1996a), and including Clegg (2003), Land (2004) and Rowland (2006) in the UK. More recently the Challenging Academic Development (CAD) Collective, which grew out of a conference symposium in 2004, has provided a focus through conference presentations, a discussion list (http://mailman.ucc.usyd.edu.au/mailman/listinfo/itl-cad) and publications to "think otherwise"—"to turn away from the norm, from expected or authorised thinking" (Holmes and Grant, 2007).

A special edition of IJAD in 2007 (Volume 12, No. 1) brought together a group of the CAD advocates and two commentators—Maryellen Weimer and Stephen Rowland—to offer their own critique of the positions taken by CAD. A common issue raised in the critiques is that of identity—"the conception of self in relation to others" (Trowler and Cooper, 2002). Clegg (2003) reflects that where developers are located in the institution is "likely to strongly influence how they are seen and their standing", an issue also raised by Harland and Staniforth (2003). Tensions arise between adopting scholarly and professional stances (Holmes and Grant, 2007), challenges from the post-colonial notion of "unhomeliness", and engaging in academic development "ambivalently" rather than as a "foot soldier of university management" (Manathunga, 2007), and reflecting on "mourning" and different relationships with the Other (Grant, 2007).

From a different perspective come Handal (2008), who proposes the "critical friend" as a possible unifying professional identity for academic developers, and Land's (2008) notion of a paradoxical identity, "involving both domestication and critique, perceived as powerful and powerless, modernist and postmodern, both with and sometimes against the work of colleagues" (p. 135).

Where Next for Academic Development?

As with any group making a claim for professional, including academic, status, academic developers need to look to their own initial and continuing professional development; how does one become an academic developer and remain in good standing? The UK Staff and Educational Development Association's Fellowship scheme provides professional accreditation for those who present a portfolio and undertake an interview, based on descriptions and reflections of their professional practice and the values on which it is based. Different approaches may be adopted in other countries, such as the requirement that all academic developers have, or be working towards, a PhD. In other contexts academic developers may not be on academic contracts, providing a tension between administrative and academic status for individuals (Harland and Staniforth, 2003)

"Development" is too often viewed as what we do to change people rather than how we change the system, processes and cultures in which individuals can locate their practices (Webb, 1996a), further indicating the need to be more strategic (Gibbs, 2005). However, as higher education becomes more competitive, institutions may choose to focus on a particular niche, which, together with government pressures to develop particular student attributes and improve teaching or for universities to engage in specific activities, may result in academic and other staff having to take on particular characteristics (Hicks, 2007). This will have implications for academic developers in their academic staff development roles, and further blur the distinction between individual and institutional needs.

A further challenge for academic developers is Webb's (2004) contention that our work "from the perspective of senior managers, is a tiny and non-critical part of the operation of the enterprise. . . . it does not have a risk factor attached to it" (p. 174). From the developer's perspective, the improvement of learning and teaching may be paramount yet, whilst this is undoubtedly important, it is only one aspect of an institution's process and purpose. Having experienced the move from a development to more senior management role, Webb advises academic developers to recognise the need to compromise their positions at times in sharing the strategic positioning of the university, and maintain a valued voice based on their appreciation of the complexity of the organisation and ability to deal with multiple perspectives. In agreeing with the broad sentiment of this position, Knapper (2003) reminds us that "we have played a vital role in keeping universities honest by drawing attention to the central *educational* mission of higher education at a time when our colleagues seem preoccupied with other matters" (p. 7). One implication of this is that academic developers should ensure they acquire a central role in the university community, through membership of committees, policy development, engagement with consultations and having a loud and clear voice in promoting a more holistic approach to the development of academic practice.

Drawing on reports from the member networks of ICED, Brew (2006) notes the growing involvement of a number of networks in national policy and planning, in relation to issues such as initiatives to accredit courses and set standards for teaching and supporting learning, establishing national centres for excellence in learning and teaching, and working with other organisations to establish the position of higher education research. These moves require academic development to show confidence and the courage of its convictions to contribute to institutional and national (and even international) developments in both an academic and professional manner. The growing evidence-based culture will require us not just to theorise about our practices but also to research and evaluate them (Brew, 2003).

Lee and McWilliam (2008) suggest that "too much anxiety and inward-looking self-examination will limit the field moving forward in the most productive way" (p. 75), and call for academic development to take a more "leaderly disposition" as higher education moves further into the twenty-first century. That is perhaps the major challenge for the profession in the future.

References

Andresen, L. (1996). The work of academic development—occupational identity, standards of practice and the virtues of association, *International Journal for Academic Development*, 1(1) pp. 38–49.

Ashwin, P. (2006). The development of learning and teaching in higher education: the changing context, in Ashwin, P. (ed.) *Changing Higher Education: The development of learning and teaching*. Routledge: London.

Baillie, C. (2003). Development in the disciplines, in Kahn, P. and Baume, D. (eds) *A Guide to Staff and Educational Development*. Kogan Page: London.

Bath, D. and Smith, C. (2004). Academic Developers: an academic tribe claiming their territory in Higher Education, *International Journal for Academic Development*, 9(1) pp. 9–27.

Beaty, L. (2006). Towards professional teaching in higher education: the role of accreditation, in Ashwin, P. (ed.) *Changing Higher Education: The development of learning and teaching*. Routledge: London.

Boud, D. (1999). Situating academic development in professional work: using peer learning, *International Journal of Academic Development* 4(1) pp. 3–10.

Boyer, E.L. (1990). *Scholarship Reconsidered: Priorities of the professoriate*, The Carnegie Foundation for the Advancement of Teaching. San Francisco, CA: Jossey-Bass.

Brand, A. (2007). The long and winding road: professional development in further and higher education, *Journal of Further and Higher Education* 31(1) pp. 7–16.

Brew, A. (2003). The future of research and scholarship in academic development. In Eggins, H. and Macdonald, R. (eds) *The Scholarship of Academic Development*. Buckingham: Open University Press.

Brew, A. (2004). Editorial: The scope of academic development, *International Journal for Academic Development*, 9(1) pp. 5–7.

Brew, A. (2006). Editorial: Making sense of academic development, *International Journal for Academic Development* 11(2) pp. 73–77.

Brew, A. (2007). Editorial: Evaluating academic development in a time of perplexity, *International Journal for Academic Development*, 12(2) pp. 69–72.

Candy, P. (1996). Promoting lifelong learning: academic developers and the university as a learning organisation, *International Journal for Academic Development*, 1(1) pp. 7–19.

Clegg, S. (2003). Problematising ourselves: continuing professional development in higher educaiton, *International Journal for Academic Development*, 8(1/2), pp. 37–50.

D'Andrea, V. and Gosling, D. (2001). Joining the dots: reconceptualizing educational development, *Active Learning in Higher Education* 2(1) pp. 64–80.

Ekaratne, S. (2003). Take one country . . ., in Edwards, H., Baume, D. and Webb, G. (eds) *Staff and Educational Development: Case studies, experience and practice from higher education.* London: Kogan Page.

Fletcher, J.J. and Patrick, S.K. (1998). Not JUST workshops anymore: the role of faculty development in reframing academic priorities, *International Journal for Academic Development*, 3(1) pp. 39–46.

Fraser, K. (2001). Australian academic developers' conceptions of the profession, *International Journal for Academic Development* 6(1) pp. 54–64.

Gibbs, G. (1996). Supporting educational development within departments, *International Journal for Academic Development*, 1(1) pp. 27–37.

Gibbs, G. (2005). Being strategic about improving teaching and learning in research-intensive environments, *Keynote address to Higher Education Research and Development Society of Australia Conference 2005.* Available at http://conference.herdsa.org.au/2005/gibbs.cfm Last accessed 6 March 2008.

Gibbs, G. and Coffey, M. (2004). The impact of training of university teachers on their teaching skills, their approach to teaching and the approach to learning of their students, *Active Learning in Higher Education*, 5(1), pp. 87–100.

Glassick, C.E., Huber, M.T. and Maeroff, G.L (1997). *Scholarship Assessed: Evaluation of the professoriate.* San Francisco, CA: Jossey-Bass.

Gosling, D. (1997). Educational development and institutional change in higher education, in Gokulsing, K. and Da Costa, C. (eds) *Usable Knowledge as the Goal of University Education.* Lewiston, NY: Edwin Mellen Press.

Gosling, D. (2001). Educational development units in the UK—what are they doing five years on? *International Journal for Academic Development*, 6(1) pp. 74–90.

Gosling, D. (2008). *Educational Development in the United Kingdom: Report for the Heads of Educational Development Group.* Available at: http://www.hedg.ac.uk/documents/HEDG_Report_final.pdf. Last accessed 10 March 2008.

Grant, B.M. (2007). The mourning after: academic development in a time of doubt, *International Journal for Academic Development*, 12(1) pp. 35–43.

Groccia, J.E. (2006). POD and the Riddle of the Sphinx. *Presidential Address to the 2006 POD Network Annual Conference*, 26 October 2006.

Handal, G. (2008). Identities of academic developers: critical friends in the academy?. In Barnett, R. and Di Napoli, R. (eds) *Changing Identities in Higher Education: Voicing perspective.* London: Routledge.

Harland, T. and Staniforth, D. (2003). Academic development as academic work, *International Journal for Academic Development*, 8(1/2) pp. 25–36.

Harland, T. and Staniforth, D. (in press). A family of strangers: The fragmented nature of academic development, *Teaching in Higher Education.*

Healey, M. and Jenkins, A. (2003). Discipline-based educational development, in Eggins, H. and Macdonald, R. (eds) *The Scholarship of Academic Development.* Buckingham: Open University Press.

Hicks, M. (2007). *Positioning the Professional Practice of Academic Development: An institutional case study.* University of South Australia, unpublished EdD thesis.

Hicks, O. (1999). Integration of central and departmental development: reflections from Australian universities, *International Journal for Academic Development*, 4(1) pp. 43–51.

Holmes, T. and Grant, B. (2007). Editorial: Thinking otherwise in academic development, *International Journal for Academic Development*, 12(1) pp. 1–4.

Hounsell, D. (1994). Educational development, in Bocock, J. and Watson, D. (eds) *Managing the University Curriculum: Making common cause*, pp. 89–102. Buckingham: Open University Press.

Jenkins, A. (1996). Discipline-based educational development, *International Journal for Academic Development*, 1(1) pp. 50–62.

Knapper, C. (1997). Editorial: Five questions about academic development, *International Journal for Academic Development*, 2(1) pp. 5–7.

Knapper, C. (2003). Editorial: Three decades of educational development, *International Journal for Academic Development* 8(1/2) pp. 4–9.

Krebber, C. and Brook, P. (2001). Impact evaluation of educational development programmes, *International Journal for Academic Development*, 6(2) pp. 96–108.

Land, R. (2004). *Educational Development: Discourse, identity and practice.* Buckingham: SRHE and Open University Press.

Land, R. (2008). Academic development: identity and paradox. In Barnett, R. and Di Napoli, R. (eds) *Changing Identities in Higher Education: Voicing perspectives.* London: Routledge.

Lave, J. and Wenger, E. (1991). *Situated Learning: Legitimate peripheral participation.* Cambridge: Cambridge University Press.

Lee, A. and McWilliam, E. (2008). What game are we in? Living with academic development, *International Journal for Academic Development*, 13(1) pp. 67–77.

Lewis, K.G. (1996). Faculty development in the United States: a brief history, *International Journal for Academic Development*, 1(2) pp. 26–33.

Macdonald, R. (2002). Educational development: research, evaluation and changing practice in higher education, in Macdonald, R. and Wisdom, J. (eds) *Academic and Educational Development: Research, evaluation and changing practice in higher education.* London: Kogan Page.

Macdonald, R. (2003). Developing a scholarship of academic development: setting the context. In Eggins, H. and Macdonald, R. (eds) *The Scholarship of Academic Development.* Buckingham: SRHE/Open University Press.

Macdonald, R. and Joughin, G. (2008). What does it take to improve assessment in support of learning?. In Joughin, G. (ed.) *Assessment, Learning and Judgement in Higher Education: Critical issues and future directions.* Dordrecht: Springer.

Manathunga, C. (2007). "Unhomely" academic developer identities: more post-colonial explorations, *International Journal for Academic Development*, 12(1) pp. 25–34.

McAlpine, L. (2006). Coming of age in a time of super-complexity (with apologies to both Mead and Barnett), *International Journal for Academic Development*, 11(2) pp. 123–127.

Orzech, M. (1998). A departmental perspective on educational development, *International Journal for Academic Development*, 3(1) pp. 19–23.

Peseta, T. with Hicks, M., Holmes, T., Manathunga, C., Sutherland, K. and Wilcox, S. (2005). The Challenging Academic Development (CAD) Collective, *International Journal for Academic Development*, 10(1) pp. 59–61.

Piccinin, S., Cristi, C. and McCoy, M. (1999). The impact of individual consultation on student ratings of teaching, *International Journal for Academic Development*, 4(2) pp. 75–88.

Piccinin, S. and Moore, J-P. (2002). The impact of individual consultation on the teaching of younger versus older faculty, *International Journal for Academic Development*, 7(2) pp. 123–134.

Prebble, T., Hargraves, H., Leach, L., Naidoo, K., Suddaby, G. and Zepke, N. (2004). *Impact of Student Support Services and Academic Development Programmes on Student Outcomes in Undergraduate Tertiary Study: A synthesis of research.* Ministry of Education, New Zealand.

Rowland, S. (2006). *The Enquiring University: Compliance and contestation in higher education.* Buckingham: Open University Press.

Rowland, S. (2007). Academic development: a site of creative doubt and contestation, *International Journal for Academic Development*, 12(1) pp. 9–14.

Rust, R. (1998). The impact of educational development workshops on teachers' practice, *International Journal for Academic Development*, 3(1) pp. 72–80.

Rust, C. (2000). Do initial training courses have an impact on university teaching? The evidence from two evaluative studies of one course. *Innovations in Education and Training International*, 37(3) pp. 254–262.

Sorcinelli, M.D., Austin, A.E., Eddy, P.L. and Beach, A.L. (2006). *Creating the Future of Faculty Development. Learning from the past, understanding the present.* Boston, MA: Anker Publishing Company.

Stefani, L. and Matthew, B. (2002). The difficulties of defining development: a case study, *International for Academic Development*, 7(1) pp. 41–50.

Stes, A., Clement, M. and Petegem, P.V. (2007). The effectiveness of a faculty training programme: long-term and institutional impact, *International Journal for Academic Development*, 12(2) pp. 99–110.

Trowler, P. and Cooper, A. (2002). Teaching and learning regimes: implicit theories and recurrent practices in the enhancement of teaching and learning through educational development programmes, *Higher Education Research and Development*, 21(3) pp. 221–240.

Webb, G. (1996a). *Understanding Staff Development.* Buckingham: Open University Press.

Webb, G. (1996b). Theories of staff development: development and understanding, *International Journal for Academic Development*, 1(1), pp. 63–69.

Webb, G. (2004). Development and beyond, in Baume, D. and Kahn, P. (eds) *Enhancing Staff and Educational Development.* London: RoutledgeFalmer.

Wenger, E. (1998). *Communities of Practice: Learning, meaning and identity.* Cambridge: Cambridge University Press.

32
The Changing Nature of Academic Work

Jan Currie and Lesley Vidovich

Academic work is increasingly located within the complex interplay between global, national and local contexts, pushing and pulling in different directions. Universities, whose "core business" is knowledge production, have become more important for nations in today's global economy, where knowledge is often treated as a commodity that moves quickly around the world. This sharper focus on universities in a nation's economic fortunes has resulted in significant policy changes that are rapidly transforming the working conditions of academics and their professional identities.

This chapter discusses the changing nature of academic work, with a particular focus on the last decade, which has seen universities and academics altering their mission statements and strategic plans to integrate themselves into the global knowledge economy. It draws on empirical studies, including our own, that highlight the impact of corporate managerialism and new accountability mechanisms on academic work. Building upon the benchmark Carnegie international survey of the academic profession across 14 countries in the early 1990s (Altbach, 1996), this chapter provides a follow-up based on the preliminary results of academics surveyed in two of the 20 countries during 2007—the United Kingdom (UK) and Australia—about the consequences of funding constraints, expansion of higher education, greater competition and pressures to be more business-like and become more international (Universities UK, 2007; Coates *et al.*, 2008).

The ideology of neo-liberal globalisation underpins many of these drivers of change. It emphasises market forces to lever universities out of their conservative traditions. Many academics have resisted these changes; others have embraced them. In the end, the technical and ideological dimensions of globalisation have necessitated that academics become more internationalised, entrepreneurial and computer-savvy.

The invention of e-technology has effectively compressed time and space, thereby significantly augmenting instantaneous communications to create a more highly networked society, including those networks involving academics. As with other workers dealing with information and data, computers have become their workstations and affected every aspect of their profession, from teaching to research to community service, and reaching into their private spaces and time. The ideological dimension of globalisation has forged restructuring and re-culturing deep within the academic heartland of universities. In particular, economic-driven agendas and neo-liberal ideologies underpinning privatisation, marketisation, instrumentalism, managerialism and inter-nationalisation have reshaped the higher education landscape. Funding issues permeate all of these policy trends.

The global nature of these trends has meant that most academics have been swept along with the current; but what has been the impact on academic work? Many have argued that such changes have challenged traditional notions of academic autonomy, collegiality, collaboration and trust (Gappa et al., 2007). Others have highlighted the intensification of academic work and loss of security of academic tenure, which in turn has an impact on stress, morale, and work–life balance (Anderson et al., 2002; Cataldi et al., 2005; Schuster and Finkelstein, 2006). While the impact of changes is likely to vary between countries, as well as within countries (both between and within individual universities), our argument here is that there are identifiable and significant "global" patterns in the changing nature of academic work.

This chapter is organised into sections based on the major technical and ideological elements of globalisation identified, and the impact that they have on the lives of academics. The primary focus is the impact of neo-liberalism on academic work, as it is seen as the integrating rationale for most of the major changes. Institutions can no longer operate outside of the influence of globalisation, as Marginson and Van der Wende (2007) argue:

> In a networked global environment in which every university is visible to every other, and the weight of the global dimension is increasing, it is no longer possible for nations or for individual higher education institutions to completely seal themselves off from global effects . . . Nations, and institutions, have space in which to pilot their own global engagement. But this self-determination operates within limits, that constrain some nations and institutions more than others, and complete abstention by national systems of higher education is no longer a strategic choice (p. 5).

This chapter looks at the impact that this global environment has had on academics, and the degree to which their work lives have been affected. It begins with a brief overview of the changing demographics of the academic and student populations of universities, as such demographics not only provide a useful contextual background, but they are intimately bound to the key ideological shifts, as explored further in the chapter. Next, the impact of e-technology is considered, followed by a series of neo-liberal phenomena (privatisation, marketisation, instrumentalism and managerialism) and then internationalisation. Finally, a meta-analysis of the changing balance between constraint and agency for academics brings the chapter to a close. It should be noted, however, that, although the chapter is subdivided into separate themes, the consequences emanating from these ideological shifts overlap.

Changing Demographics and Working Conditions

In many countries higher education has moved from being an elite to a mass system in the last two decades; this was more noticeable in Europe, where some countries, like Norway, surpassed the United States, which was thought of as the leader in mass higher education. Even in the US, over the past 25 years student enrolments increased by almost 50%, to around 17 million, (Gappa et al., 2007). Those countries with over 55% of the age cohort in higher education are Australia, Canada, France, Finland, Korea, Norway and the US. The OECD average in 2001 was 52%. Outside of the OECD countries, enrolments have increased at an even more dramatic pace, though these countries still may not have achieved massification. China, India and Brazil are still below 15% enrolment, even though a country like China had 15 million students in 4,000 institutions in 2005 (Robinson, 2008). The desire for a university education has grown exponentially in these countries, and the supply cannot keep up with the demand. Thus, many of the surplus students travel overseas for their educations.

What have these increases meant for academic staff? If funding does not increase with student numbers, academics' workloads keep climbing. Students are becoming more diverse (in terms of age, ethnicity, race, socio-economic status, nationality, culture and language), forcing academics to change their teaching styles, and adding hours to their already heavy teaching commitments to cater for these different needs.

Many academics around the world feel that their working conditions have deteriorated as their working hours have increased. A recent Australian study (Coates *et al.*, 2008) found that on average academics spent 50 hours per week on their jobs, and almost two-thirds believed that their working conditions had deteriorated. Academics were most critical of the lack of secretarial, teaching and research support. The average workload in many parts of the world is variously reported to be between 49 and 55 hours per week. Universities UK (2007) reported that, with increased fees and familiarity with the use of technology, students are increasingly being regarded as consumers "who demand up-to-date information about educational 'goods', '24/7' access to facilities, quality services and personalised treatment" (p. 10). The pace of work is relentless, and Gappa *et al.* (2007) use the term "racheting" to describe the multifaceted demands on US academics' time:

> External calls for greater accountability and demonstrable outcomes, institutional pressure for faculty to generate revenue, and the necessity of keeping up with the never-ending expansion of new knowledge all conspire to create seemingly endless demands and expectations of faculty members (p. 17).

Harman found similar changes in academic staff roles in Australia across a 20-year period, based on survey data gathered in 1977 and 1997 (2001, 2002, 2003). Respondents reported high satisfaction with academic components of their jobs, while expressing criticism of their work environments, including the level of stress on the job and increasing workloads. These types of changes often lead to much discussion about workload formulae (e.g., Houston *et al.*, 2006, in New Zealand; Burgess *et al.*, 2003, in the UK), which can create divisive faculties. Changing workload formulas have not solved heavy workloads; it's like "shifting deck chairs on the Titanic"!

Lang (2005), writing about his life on the tenure track in a small American college, describes the difficulty of keeping his body and soul together. He had a heavy teaching load of four courses one semester and three the next, two young children and an ambitious writing schedule, which he constantly had trouble meeting. Gappa *et al.* (2007) report the increasing expectations for higher levels of productivity, with finding enough time to do their work one of the most frequently mentioned sources of stress among early-career faculty (Rice *et al.*, 2000). In Canada, Fisher and Rubenson (1998) found that academics were experiencing an intensification of work practices, a loss of autonomy, closer monitoring and appraisal, less participation in decision-making and a lack of personal development through work.

This loss of autonomy may be related to the "unbundling", or specialisation and differentiation of academic work, another development that is largely a result of the demand for institutions to be more efficient and cost-effective (Schuster and Finkelstein, 2006; Gappa *et al.*, 2007). For example, teaching work is often divided between curriculum designers, technology specialists, teachers and evaluators. In Australia academics who teach distance education (about 25%) experience a degree of unbundling of their work that is quite noticeable. The principal academic provides the content, someone else designs the course product, a tutor does the assessment and is in contact with the students via e-mail, a technologist provides the computer support and a teaching and learning specialist evaluates the course. As a result, academics experience less control over designing and engaging with the teaching experience.

Another characteristic of academics is their bifurcation into those on continuing employment or tenure track and those who are off tenure track, on contracts and increasingly insecure in their employment. Schuster and Finkelstein (2006) report that, as of 2003, 65% of the US total faculty were off tenure track, and described this as a movement towards becoming a contingent work-force. Gappa *et al.* (2007) reiterate this, stating that a bifurcated faculty consists of those with full-time tenure track appointments who are more likely to enjoy the traditional benefits of professorial work—respect, autonomy, collegiality and opportunities for professional growth—while the others receive few of these benefits. The result is greater inequities in conditions, a loss of a sense of commitment, and underutilisation of the intellectual capital of many academics. Schuster and Finkelstein (2006) were concerned as to whether the "corporate faculty will simply wither away, to be displaced by a more variegated, more specialized, less cohesive academic body" (p. 363).

A similar bifurcation of academic staff is noted in Anglo-Saxon countries like Australia, Canada, the UK and New Zealand. For example, in the UK only 55% of academics were employed on a permanent basis (Universities UK, 2007). The shift to a more contingent staff is not as dramatic in European countries; however, the trend is still noticeable in many of them. In China the "iron rice bowl", or guaranteed employment with associated benefits such as housing and health care, is disappearing as the government is determined that universities become more efficient (Yang, 2005). Similarly in Hong Kong, substantiation (or tenure) has almost disappeared (Petersen and Currie, 2007). The working conditions in non-OECD countries are extremely insecure and require many academics to "moonlight" in other jobs. The precarious nature of academic work and the declining working conditions often lead academics to consider changing jobs. For example, 75% of Australian academics in a 2007 study (Coates *et al.*, 2008) said they were considering changing jobs, even though they were quite satisfied overall with the work that they did. Universities UK (2007) reported that academics were less satisfied with their jobs than those in the general UK workforce, and those on fixed-term contracts were significantly more dissatisfied.

In many countries the academic profession is ageing as recruitment into permanent jobs declines. For example, in the UK the proportion of staff aged over 50 has risen from 34% to 41% in the last 10 years (Universities UK, 2007). At the same time women are entering into the profession at an increasing rate, even though their promotion to the top positions does not reflect their numbers yet. Schuster and Finkelstein (2006) worry that the increasing "feminization" of US academics may carry a hint of declining social power and prestige. Yet, the gendered nature of universities has not been broken: universities continue to be segregated horizontally and vertically by gender, with women more often found in certain jobs and disciplines, and more often located in entry-level positions (Currie *et al.*, 2002). In the UK, 42% of academics are women, and are more likely to be on fixed-term contracts than men. The proportion of women holding professorial posts is only 16% (Universities UK, 2007), equal to that in the US. Finland boasted the highest propor-tion of women among professors (18%) of 15 European Union countries (Osborne, 1998). In Ireland at that time just over 5% of the professoriate were women (O'Connor, 2000), whereas Australia recorded 11% (Ward, 2000). In China, in 2000, 15% of full professors were women (Yang, 2005).

Students and staff have become more mobile, creating fears of a brain-drain for many countries as academics depart for overseas positions, while many international students gain residency in the countries where they study, never to return home. For example, in the UK non-nationals made up 13% of core academic staff in 2004/05, up from 8% in 1995/96. Many of these are Chinese and Indian nationals who gain research contracts (Universities UK, 2007). Minorities have also joined the ranks of academe in increasing numbers in the US, Canada and Australia.

E-technology

A global market for university education and knowledge exists, and has increasingly been filled by virtual universities, for-profit organisations that teach by e-technology, and off-campus teaching by many universities seeking additional revenue from trans-national and distance teaching. In the process academics produce e-learning, e-books and e-journals. Wired and wireless campuses, a laptop on every desk, e-lectures and PowerPoint teaching are common just about everywhere in the world. For academics, this means that they have to learn new software programs, with institutions relying on them to develop their technological skills with little training to manage student records and carry out other administrative tasks (such as entering grades electronically and corresponding to students and colleagues through e-mails) that previously would have been done by secretaries.

Not all universities have a good technological infrastructure, and, even within the OECD, there is great variation in the amount of teaching done through technological innovations. In a study (Currie *et al.*, 2003) in 1998/99 of four universities in four different countries (France, the Netherlands, Norway and the US), at Boston College and the University of Twente the use of e-mail for teaching purposes was taken for granted, but at Oslo and Avignon fewer academics followed this practice. A Boston College academic said: "With a click I can e-mail a class of 293 students. That's quite effective." Technological support was available to academics at Boston College to make it easy: they were provided with a list of students' e-mail addresses. The negative side of e-mails was expressed by a University of Twente academic: "Yes, I think it has increased the workload because now we get questions we wouldn't have gotten in the past. So there's more communication." Despite the expectation that more academics will be teaching via information communication technologies, the majority of all academics interviewed preferred face-to-face teaching. There were also national differences, with the Dutch and American academics more readily taking up the new technologies in their teaching than the French and Norwegians.

Academics, like other professionals, have experienced the penetration of information technologies (laptop computers, mobile phones and personal digital assistants) into their lives no matter where they are working. This allows them to work just about anywhere, anytime. A new term has been coined for this situation—the "portable humanoid office" (Challenger, 2002). The boundaries that separated work from other spheres of academics' lives are disappearing. E-technology has been the chief cause of the blurring of work and home (Eveline and Currie, 2006); however, the permeability of the work–family border goes almost always one-way, to facilitate the transfer of work into the home (Edwards and Wacjman, 2005).

In a 2005 study of academics with children 12 years or under at one Australian university, Eveline and Currie (2006) found that having a computer at home was both a blessing and a curse. It definitely meant that fewer boundaries existed between home and work, but it also allowed many parents to care for their young children and continue working. At the same time, they found a clash between getting work done and spending time with their families. The comments of a full-time academic woman indicate how intensification (urgency and speed demands) connects with extensification (increased workload, work hours and working away from the office): "E-mail requests have a sense of urgency to me and I often think, 'It will be quicker to just deal with this e-mail now, rather than later.' So I spend time with e-mail rather than doing what I had planned earlier. Ultimately, this increases my workload and working hours." As not all countries will have as much access to these technologies, some academics may not be plagued by this extensification and intensification of workloads, although the increased number of university students enrolled in countries outside of the OECD means that their workloads are likely to have intensified as well.

Privatisation, Marketisation and Instrumentalism

A shift in the prevailing ideology in public sector management generally—and more specifically in higher education—occurred in the 1980s, although the timing and degree of the shift varied across different countries. Most commentators observed this neo-liberal ideology continuing into the new millennium. Privatisation, marketisation and instrumentalism in higher education are key expressions of this neo-liberal ideology accompanying the phenomenon of globalisation. As governments have struggled with the burden of funding universities, especially with the massification of higher education, attention has turned to private funding sources. Privatisation has been defined by Marginson (1993, p. 177) as "the transfer of production or assets from the public (government or state) to the private (non-government) sector", although others (e.g. Whitty and Power, 2000) have maintained that it also includes supplementation with private funds—such as student fees, charging for services, contracting out and industry sponsorship.

Privatisation might be seen more as an ongoing process than a fixed state, where there is a transition from less public ownership to more private ownership. It might also be envisaged as a political as well as an economic strategy, with the former identified in terms of a shift in the balance of power between different interest groups, and, therefore, the issue for academics becomes the extent to which privatisation empowers or disempowers them in relation to other groups. As privatisation has accelerated, debates about the relative balance between higher education as a public or private good have come to the foreground. Tierney (2006, p. 182) explains that "a public good provides public benefits; otherwise there would be no reason for an investment of public funds in the undertaking". However, with privatisation and marketisation, the emphasis shifts towards individual benefits rather than the social benefits that have traditionally been associated with higher education, thereby repositioning academics and their work within society.

Marketisation or "creeping privatisation", according to Whitty and Power (2000), involves a combination of enhanced institutional autonomy and customer choice to establish a marketplace with varying degrees of government regulation and public accountability. Arguably, marketisation has had a more profound effect on academics than full privatisation, as a central platform of marketisation is competition, which has been pivotal in changing the nature of academic work. Competition has come to prevail as a primary *modus operandus* of higher education sectors; universities, faculties, departments, disciplines and individual academics compete for scarce resources and status. As a result, competition fragments the academic corps, forcing wedges both vertically and horizontally through universities. Despite competition pervading (higher) education, policy discourses concurrently highlight collaboration and cooperation, and these contradictory discourses add to the tension and confusion for academics, who are now required to engage with "the market" as never before. One significant vehicle for promulgating markets and competition in higher education is league tables—especially international rankings—as each institution is rendered highly publicly visible to a wide range of "customers". Marginson (2007, p. 10) describes the Shanghai Jiao Tong University's (SJTU) international rankings as "a proxy mapping of the world-wide field of research universities . . . [where] the top 20 and top 100 identify the superleague and 'wannabes' ", and he maintains that SJTU has "earned the right to mediate the market though its data quality". Such rankings are now central components of the marketisation of higher education.

In the teaching domain, privatisation and marketisation have forged the reconstruction of students as customers, changing the nature of the teacher–student relationship more towards one of economic exchange. In research, funding partnerships and sponsorships have challenged the independence of some research, and tended to foster applied projects with short-term outcomes. The latter is evidenced, for example, in the 2007 Australian survey of academic work (Coates *et al.*,

2008), when respondents reported that they were increasingly involved in applied rather than basic research.

The neo-liberal, market ideology has also invaded the curriculum, where instrumentalism is replacing the liberal humanist orientation, resulting in a privileging of applied knowledge. There has been a trend towards more funding going to vocationally oriented courses that attract larger student numbers. Further, some academic departments that are more distant from short-term market possibilities have closed (e.g. philosophy, history and physics). Whitty and Power (2002) used the term "corporate curriculum" to describe the greater corporate penetration of the curriculum by businesses and industries, promoting consumerism and marketing their own products, even if indirectly. Overall, instrumentalism has led to a narrowing of teaching and research programmes, potentially challenging academic freedom to pursue wider directions.

Altogether, the expression of neo-liberal ideology has required academics to be more entrepreneurial than ever before to fill a void in funding left by governments, and this does not always sit comfortably with them. Academics are not only engaging more with business/industry as sources of funds, but also adapting to structures and cultures imported from the corporate world.

Managerialism

As universities scramble for "world class" status in the international marketplace, they are increasingly importing corporate structures and cultures in a drive to enhance efficiency and effectiveness, and thereby gain a competitive edge. With this corporate managerialism, two apparently contradictory processes are occurring simultaneously: increasing devolution and increasing accountability. On the one hand, policy discourses highlight devolution of power for enhanced autonomy of localised decision-making (or is it more responsibility than power?); but, on the other hand, this autonomy is strictly circumscribed and regulated by a requirement for enhanced accountability to central authorities, who prescribe the outcomes to be achieved. These twin processes represent "decentralised centralism" (Karlsen, 2000) and "steering at a distance" (Kickert, 1991).

Corporate managerialism, riding on the barrow of neo-liberal ideology penetrating universities, represents a new style of governance for universities, driven by external forces (Deem, 2003). Geurts and Maassen (2005, p. 35) looked at issues of governance in universities as the "rules, structures and enforcement mechanisms . . . to do with the preparation of the decisions, the actual decision-making process and the implementation of the decisions taken" in relation to the Carnegie study of academic work in the early 1990s (Altbach, 1996). While they found significant national differences in academics' views of the efficiency and effectiveness of their governance structures, they found major similarities in academics' "control-seeking behaviour". Academics across the different countries reported a high level of cognitive control over their basic teaching and research activities, but they also reported a relatively low level of normative and regulative control over their working environment. They were dissatisfied with their lack of involvement in institutional governance, and wanted to be more involved.

In the follow-up 2007 Australian survey of academic work (Coates *et al.*, 2008), respondents reported that their universities were strongly characterised by top–down management styles, cumbersome administrative processes and a performance orientation, whereas they were weak on collegiality and communication between management and academics. These traits were seen as "a characterisation that is often associated with managerialism" (Coates *et al.*, 2008, p. 8). It is clear that managerialism is seen as being in tension with collegiality for academics. The growing gap in salaries, benefits and cultures between "professional managers" (especially those with corporate rather than academic backgrounds) and grassroots academics reported elsewhere is also evident amongst the Australian respondents.

A decade earlier we (Currie and Vidovich, 1998) examined growing managerialism in American and Australian universities, and reported academics' perceptions of changes in university governance from more collegial towards more corporate managerial models, including smaller and often less representative decision-making bodies. Managerial styles were described variously by our participants as autocratic, bureaucratic and top–down, which they contrasted with earlier more prevalent consultative, participatory styles. They may have been alluding to the "golden age" that is often depicted by academics, who reminisce nostalgically about a time in the past when academic life was rosier. Arguably, there is no clear dichotomy between collegiality and corporate managerial decision making, and there is likely a complex interplay between the two, although evidence suggests that the general trend over time has been towards the latter, with potential implications of a progressive silencing of academic voices in universities.

As an integral component of managerialism, academics have been subject to increasing amounts and types of accountability, defined by Ranson (2003, p. 462) as "a *social practice* pursuing particular purposes, defined by distinctive relationships and evaluative procedures". According to Burke (2005, p. ix), "The 1990s became known as the decade of accountability for higher education in the United States"—and commentators in other countries have agreed. Accountability for academics takes many forms, including annual performance management reviews, prescribed performance indicators, quality audits, teaching portfolios, graduate surveys, student evaluations, and research and teaching assessment exercises. It is now a decade since we (Vidovich and Currie, 1998) reported on changing accountability and autonomy at the "coalface" of academic work in Australia, and noted the augmenting power of governments over academics with the introduction of new forms of accountability. Changes in Australia were paralleling those in many other parts of the world, and were of deep concern to academics. Arguably, the last decade has seen an acceleration of these trends. For example, in 2005 Welch observed that:

> . . . the professoriate is also being pressured to account for their activities, including ways in which they expend their resources, in more detailed ways. This has given rise to something of an international cottage industry of developing and implementing so-called quality assurance mechanisms in higher education, although in practice many academics see little if any positive relationship between such exercises and gains in quality (p. 206).

Welch's comment about a "cottage industry" points to the growing presence in the higher education field of both national and international quality assurance agencies and associations, suggesting to some commentators a convergence of particular forms of accountability in university sectors across the globe (e.g. Henry *et al.*, 2001; Vidovich and Slee, 2001; Vidovich, 2004).

An Australian Research Council study by Currie *et al.*, investigated the impact of globalisation on accountability mechanisms in the Asian regions of China, Hong Kong and Singapore (Vidovich *et al.*, 2007; Yang *et al.*, 2007; Currie *et al.*, 2008). We found that there were some striking similarities with accountability trends in the West, and that policy borrowing was clearly evident, especially from the US and UK (countries which dominate international league tables of universities), in the quest to compete in the global marketplace. Hong Kong had experienced the strongest shifts towards neo-liberal corporate accountability of the three regions, with direct policy borrowing (for example the Research Assessment Exercise—RAE) from its former British colonial master. In the words of one of our Hong Kong participants: "There is nothing that feels good about it [RAE] . . . they take it to mean countability not answerability. You have to prove your merit to a bureaucracy that can only credit countable items." The costs of accountability in terms of time, money, stress and morale were expressed in similar ways in each Asian region to the West, but in addition there were deep concerns about Western hegemony, especially in relation to distorting research away from local priorities. Our research over the last decade has revealed strong evidence for what others have called a "sophisticated network of surveillance" (Webb, 2005), and the "terrors of performativity" (Ball, 2003) created by accountability policies, and these have deeply impacted on the working lives of academics. Arguably, accountability has caused a "distortion of 'authentic' educational quality due to disconnection from 'grassroots' educational values and practices" (Vidovich, 2008, forthcoming).

Together, managerialism and accountability are in tension with professional autonomy, academic freedom and trust. Trust has been eroded by the constant surveillance of neo-liberal practices in education generally, and universities in particular, and a growing chorus of commentators have been calling for trust to be re-established (Ranson, 2003; Olssen *et al.*, 2004; Tierney, 2006). Despite general trends in managerialism and accountability, changes are not even across the globe, with, for example, some European countries taking a "lighter touch" to accountability, enabling greater respect for institutional autonomy and academic freedom (Massy, 1999; Huisman and Currie, 2004). However, the degree of convergence of forms of corporate management and accountability across different jurisdictions with very different contexts is a matter of concern for academics.

Internationalisation

To compensate for reductions in government subsidies, Australian, Canadian, UK and US universities, in particular, have aggressively recruited full-fee-paying students from East and Southeast Asia (Snider, 2003). As Welch (2000) describes it, ". . . when international students are mentioned, Vice Chancellorial eyes . . . increasingly light up, seeing them as one means to strengthen the institution's bottom line" (p. 15).

Since 1980 the number of international students has doubled, with the vast majority of the 2.5 million students in 2006 going to four countries: US (22%), UK (12%), Germany (10%) and France (10%). Germany and France gained many of their students through the ERASMUS student exchange scheme, and for France also from its former colonies. Most Western European countries do not charge high fees for overseas students, thus gaining revenue is not a principal goal for them. In contrast, many English-speaking countries have prioritised recruiting international students in an attempt to raise revenue, such as Australia, which was a destination for 7% of all international students in 2006 (UNESCO, 2006). The average proportion of international students in Australian universities was 15%, with some universities having as many as 25%. There is concern that this will reduce the access to a university education for domestic students, especially the disadvantaged. Since some universities in Australia have become dependent on international students for their financial survival, they are even more vulnerable when there are fluctuations in the recruitment of overseas students, such as occurred after the Asian meltdown in the late 1990s (when currencies plummeted in South Korea, Thailand, Malaysia, the Philippines and Indonesia when foreign investors withdrew their money suddenly), and after 9/11 in 2001.

In addition to the competition for international students, academics compete for research collaborators and research funding beyond their borders. This is particularly the case in the European Union, but increasingly nations are emphasising having international partners on research grant applications. As a result of an emphasis on overseas collaboration and publications, there are often conflicts in trying to balance the international with the local, the regional and the national. Research assessment exercises, like the one in the UK over the past 20 years, have emphasised international excellence, so having international collaborators strengthens research teams (Universities UK, 2007).

English-speaking countries have the advantage of English as the international language of choice, and this enables them to be a magnet for many international students. As a result of attracting many students from non-English-speaking backgrounds, academics are faced with more work to integrate international students into their campuses, especially if they are from non-English-speaking backgrounds. Academics also have to cater for different styles of learning and pay more attention to internationalising their courses (Burgess *et al.*, 2004). The extra time it takes to prepare courses for an international clientele is often not taken into account in the calculation of teaching workloads. Furthermore, there are some academics, particularly in US universities, who are unenthusiastic about internationalising the curriculum, and are rather insular in their attitudes towards other countries (Altbach, 2005). As universities increase the number of students on their campuses, they often create international offices and directors. These additional staff members are more likely to be there to support students, and only rarely to assist staff to cater for the extra work they do to teach international students (Luijten-Lub, 2007).

Conclusion

Academics have always been part of an international community in their pursuit of creating new knowledge for the betterment of humankind. They are more connected now in a globalised world, and confront many common changes in the nature of their academic work. The similar challenges they face are diminished government funding concurrent with massification of higher education, work intensification, pressures towards privatisation, marketisation and instrumentalism (in teaching and research), importation of corporate managerial structures and cultures, increased accountability, new demands associated with accelerated internationalisation, dwindling collegiality and trust, decreased autonomy and challenges to academic freedom (Altbach, 2005; Currie *et al.*, 2006). All of these changes have to some extent been caused by the neo-liberal ideological shift accompanying globalisation, which has spurred governmental cutbacks in education. These changes, however, are not even across countries or institutions; localised contexts remain important in defining the nature of academic work. That is, both convergences and divergences are evident in trends in academic work across different countries.

Overall, there has been a shift in locus of power upwards and outwards from universities, creating winners and losers. In particular, markets and governments have assumed greater power over academics. Arguably, globalisation and the various manifestations of the ideological shift, which privileges discourses of the market in higher education, have further polarised academic communities by exacerbating vertical hierarchies and associated differentiation, both between and within institutions. Further, the changes have heralded a cultural shift with a greater emphasis on external rather than internal motivation, and with rewards that are increasingly materialistic in nature ("money makes the world go round", even in the academy!). However, research (e.g. Forgasz and Leder, 2006; Houston *et al.*, 2006) has shown that academics value intrinsic motivators such as autonomy and, therefore, if trends continue and academics face a decline in those elements which offer them the greatest job satisfaction, this career choice will become even less popular for subsequent generations.

Although it is too early at the time of writing in early 2008 for the cross-national comparisons from the 2007 survey of academic work in 20 countries, or for comparisons with the Carnegie survey in the early 1990s (Altbach, 1996), preliminary findings of the Australian and UK 2007 surveys (Coates *et al.*, 2008; Universities UK, 2007) indicate worrying trends. Even though Australian academics still rate their academic work as reasonable on job satisfaction and relative autonomy, three out of four academics have considered major changes to their jobs. In the survey of academics in UK universities, less than half said that their overall job satisfaction was high or very high. One of the researchers suggested that these changes were a result of the "late industrialisation" of academia, and wondered "How far can this go before it irreparably damages the self-motivated, self-regulated academic community that many argue is necessary for scholarly endeavour?" Other worrying results were that only a third of academics believed that their administration supported academic freedom, while three in four academics believed that pressures to increase research productivity were threatening the quality of research (Gill, 2008). If these trends continue into the future, there are "clear and present dangers" about the type of universities our nations are creating, and whether they will have the ability to recruit and retain the "best and brightest" to renew the academic profession.

References

Altbach, P. (1996). (ed.) *The International Academic Profession: Portraits of Fourteen Countries.* Princeton, NJ: Carnegie Foundation for the Advancement of Teaching.

Altbach, P. (2005). Academic Challenges: The American Professoriate in Comparative Perspective. In A. Welch (ed.) *The Professors: Profile of a Profession.* Dordrecht, The Netherlands: Kluwer Press, pp. 147–165.

Anderson, D., Johnson, R. and Saha, L. (2002). Changes in academic work. Retrieved 15 March 2008 from: http://www.dest.gov.au/archive/highered/otherpub/academic_work.

Ball, S. (2003). The teacher's soul and the terrors of performativity. *Journal of Education Policy, 18*(2), 215–228.

Burgess, M., Currie, J. and Maor, D. (2004). Cross-Cultural Issues in Technology-Mediated Teaching and Learning: The Case of Australian Offshore Education. In C. Vrasidas and G. Glass (eds) *Current Perspectives on Applied Information Technologies: Online Professional Development for Teachers.* Greenwich, CT: Information Age Publishing, pp. 159–176.

Burgess, T., Lewis, H. and Mobbs, T. (2003). Academic workload planning revisited. *Higher Education, 46,* 215–233.

Burke, J. (2005). Preface. In J. Burke (ed.) *Achieving Accountability in Higher Education.* San Francisco: John Wiley & Sons.

Cataldi, E.F., Bradburn, E.M., Fahimi, M. and Zimbler, L. (2005). 2004 National Study of Postsecondary Faculty. (NCES 2006–176). Washington, DC: National Centre for Education Statistics.

Challenger, J. (2002). Extending working hours in Australia. *Labour and Industry, 13*(1), 91–110.

Coates, H., Goedegebuure, L., van der Lee, J. and Meek, L. (2008). *The Australian Academic Profession in 2007: A First Analysis of the Survey Results.* Melbourne and Armidale: Australian Council for Education Research and Centre for Higher Education Management and Policy, University of New England, March, Retrieved March 21, 2008 from: http://www.une.edu.au/pdal/research/chemp/projects/cap.

Currie, J., DeAngelis, R., de Boer, H., Huisman, J. and Lacotte, C. (2003). *Global Practices and University Responses.* Westport, CN: Greenwood Press.

Currie, J., Petersen, C.J. and Mok, K.H. (2006). *Academic Freedom in Hong Kong.* Lanham, Maryland: Lexington Books.

Currie, J., Thiele, B. and Harris, P. (2002). *Gendered Universities in Globalized Economies: Power, Careers and Sacrifices.* Lanham, Maryland: Lexington Books.

Currie, J. and Vidovich, L. (1998). Microeconomic reform through managerialism in Australian and American universities. In J. Currie and J. Newson (eds) *Universities and Globalization: Critical Perspectives.* Thousand Oaks and London: Sage, pp. 153–172.

Currie, J., Vidovich, L. and Yang, R. (2008). "Countability not answerability": Accountability in Hong Kong and Singaporean universities. *Asia-Pacific Journal of Education, 28*(1), pp. 67–85.

Deem, R. (2003). New managerialism in UK universities: Manager-academic accounts of change. In H. Eggins (ed.) *Globalisation and Reform in Higher Education.* Berkshire: Open University Press.

Edwards, P. and Wacjman, J. (2005). *The Politics of Working Life.* Oxford: Oxford University Press.

Eveline, J. and Currie, J. (2006). *E-Technology, Networked Homes and Knowledge Workers in Globalized Economies: Impact on Life Balance.* Paper presented at the International Sociological Association Congress, Durban, 18 July.

Fisher, D. and Rubenson, K. (1998). The Changing Political Economy: The Private and Public Lives of Canadian Universities. In J. Currie and J. Newson (eds) *Universities and Globalization: Critical Perspectives.* Thousand Oaks: Sage, pp. 77–98.

Forgasz, H. and Leder, G. (2006). Academic life: Monitoring work patterns and daily activities. *The Australian Educational Researcher, 33*(1), 1–22.

Gappa, J., Austin, A. and Trice, A. (2007). *Rethinking Faculty Work: Higher Education's Strategic Imperative.* San Francisco: John Wiley & Sons.

Geurts, P. and Maassen, P. (2005). Academics and institutional governance. In A. Welch (ed.) *The Professoriate.* Dordrecht, Netherlands: Springer, pp. 35–58.

Gill, J. (2008). Researchers believe results culture puts quality at risk, *Times Higher Education.* Retrieved 10 April 2008 from: www.timeshighereducation.co.uk/sotry.asp?sectioncode=26&storycode=40142.

Harman, G. (2001). Academics and institutional differentiation in Australian higher education. *Higher Education Policy, 14,* 325–342.

Harman, G. (2002). Academic leaders or corporate managers: Deans and heads in Australian higher education, 1977 to 1997. *Higher Education Management and Policy, 14,* 53–70.

Harman, G. (2003). Australian academics and prospective academics: Adjustment to a more commercial environment. *Higher Education Management and Policy, 15,* 105–122.

Henry, M., Lingard, B., Rizvi, F. and Taylor, S. (2001). *The OECD, Globalisation and Education Policy.* Oxford: Pergamon.

Houston, D., Mayer, L. and Paewai, S. (2006). Academic staff workloads and job satisfaction: Expectations and values in academe. *Journal of Higher Education Policy and Management, 28*(1), 17–30.

Huisman, G. and Currie, J. (2004). Accountability in higher education: Bridge over troubled waters? *Higher Education, 48*(4), 529–552.

Karlsen, G. (2000). Decentralised centralism: framework for a better understanding of governance in the field of education. *Journal of Education Policy, 15*(5), 525–538.

Kickert, M. (1991). *Steering at a distance: A new paradigm of public governance in Dutch higher education.* Paper presented at the European Consortium for Political Research, University of Essex.

Lang, J.M. (2005). *Life on the Tenure Track: Lessons form the First Year.* Baltimore: The Johns Hopkins University Press.

Luijten-Lub, A. (2007). *Choices in Internationalisation: How Higher Education Institutions Respond to Internationalisation, Europeanisation, and Globalisation.* Enshede, Netherlands: CHEPS, University of Twente.

Marginson, S. (1993). *Education and Public Policy in Australia.* Cambridge: Cambridge University Press

Marginson, S. (2007). Global position and position taking: The case of Australia. *Journal of Studies in International Education, 11*(1), 5–32.

Marginson, S. and Van der Wende, M. (2007). *Globalisation and Higher Education.* OECD Discussion Paper, Paris.

Massy, W. (1999). Energising quality work; Higher education quality evaluation in Sweden and Denmark. *Project 6, Quality and Productivity in Higher Education.* Stanford, CA: Stanford University, National Centre for Post-secondary Improvement.

O'Connor, O. (2000). *Resistance in academia.* Paper presented to NAWE International Conference on Women in Higher Education, New Orleans, Louisiana.

Olssen, M., Codd, J. and O'Neil, A. (2004). *Education Policy.* London: Sage.

Osborne, M. (1998). *Facts and figures still show little room at the top for women in science in most EU countries.* Paper presented to the European Union Women and Science Conference, Brussels, April.

Petersen, C.J. and Currie, J. (2007). Higher Education Restructuring and Academic Freedom in Hong Kong. *The Journal of Comparative Asian Development, 6*(1), 1–21.

Ranson, S. (2003). Public accountability in the age of neo-liberal governance. *Journal of Education Policy, 18*(5), 459–480.

Rice, R., Sorcinelli, M. and Austin, A. (2000). *Heeding new voices: Academic careers for a new generation.* New Pathways Working Paper series, No. 7. Washington, DC: American Association for Higher Education.

Robinson, S.P. (2008). *Higher Education in China: The Next Super Power is Coming of Age.* Washington DC: American Council on Education.

Schuster, J.H. and Finkelstein, M.J. (2006). *The American Faculty: The Restructuring of Academic Work and Careers.* Baltimore: The Johns Hopkins University Press.

Snider, P. (2003). *Exploring the Relationships between Individualism and Collectivism and Attitudes Towards Counselling Among Ethnic Chinese, Australian and American University Students.* PhD Thesis, Murdoch University, Perth, Australia.

Tierney, W. (2006). *Trust and the Public Good.* New York: Peter Lang.

UNESCO (2006). *Open Doors 2006: Report on International Educational Exchange.* Paris: UNESCO.

Universities UK. (2007). *Research Report: The changing academic profession in the UK: setting the scene.* London: Universities UK.

Vidovich, L. (2004). Global-national-local dynamics in policy processes: A case study of "quality" policy in higher education. *British Journal of Sociology of Education, 25*(3), 341–354.

Vidovich, L. (2008, forthcoming). "You don't fatten the pig by weighting it": Contradictory tensions in the "policy pandemic" of accountability infecting education. In M. Simons, M. Olssen and M. Peters (eds.) *Re-reading Education Policies: Studying the Policy Agenda of the 21st Century.* Sense Publishers (Handbook Series).

Vidovich, L. and Currie, J. (1998). Changing accountability and autonomy at the "coalface" of academic work in Australia. In J. Currie and J. Newson (eds) *Universities and Globalization: Critical Perspectives.* Thousand Oaks: Sage, pp. 193–211.

Vidovich, L. and Slee, R. (2001). Bringing Universities to Account? Exploring Some Global and Local Policy Tensions. *Journal of Education Policy, 16*(5), 431–453.

Vidovich, L., Yang, R. and Currie, J. (2007). Changing Accountabilities in Higher Education as China "opens up" to globalisation. *Globalisation, Societies and Education, 5*(1), 89–107.

Ward, B. (2000). *The female Professor: A rare Australian species—the who and how.* Paper presented at the European Conference on Gender and Higher Education, ETH, Zurich, September 12–15.

Webb, T.P. (2005). The anatomy of accountability. *Journal of Education Policy, 20*(2), 189–208.

Welch, A. (2000). *Internationalising Australian universities in a time of global crisis.* In Educational reforms and teacher education innovation for the 21st century. Presented at Waseda International Symposium, Tokyo, March.

Welch, A. (2005). Conclusion: New millennium, new milieu? In A. Welch (ed.) *The Professoriate.* Dordrecht, Netherlands: Springer, pp. 205–215.

Whitty, G. and Power, S. (2000). Marketisation and privatisation in mass education systems. *International Journal of Educational Development, 20*(1), 93–107.

Whitty, G. and Power, S. (2002). The overt and hidden curricular of quasi-markets. In G. Whitty (ed.) *Making Sense of Education Policy.* London: Paul Chapman Publishing, pp. 94–106.

Yang, R. (2005). The Chinese professoriate in comparative perspective: Self-perceptions, academic life, gender differences and internal differentiation. In A. Welch (ed.) *The Professors: Profile of a Profession.* Dordrecht, The Netherlands: Kluwer Press, pp. 179–192.

Yang, R., Vidovich, L. and Currie, J. (2007). University accountability practices in Mainland China and Hong Kong: A Comparative Analysis. *Asian Journal of University Education, 2*(1), 1–21.

33

Understanding Academic Freedom

The Views of Social Scientists[1]

Gerlese S. Åkerlind and Carole Kayrooz

The current debate about academic freedom has been marked by a lack of clarity and consistency as to what academic freedom actually means. Sometimes it is described solely in terms of individual freedoms; at others in terms of an interplay between individual, collegial and institutional freedoms. Sometimes it is presented as a set of rights; at others, as a pairing of rights and responsibilities. This chapter presents an empirical investigation of the range of understandings of academic freedom experienced amongst social scientists in Australian universities. The investigation was undertaken from a phenomenographic perspective and five different ways of understanding academic freedom were constituted, based on two primary dimensions of variation in views: the types of constraints regarded as an appropriate part of academic freedom; and the role of self and other (i.e., peers, institution, society) in creating academic freedom. The structural relationships found between different ways of viewing academic freedom in this study provides a broader framework within which to interpret the range of views found in the literature and public debate.

Introduction

From the 1980s there has been growing debate about the role of academic freedom in university life (e.g. Tight, 1988a; Slaughter and Leslie, 1995; Marginson, 1997; Vidovich and Currie, 1998; Marginson and Considine, 2000), accompanied by frequent suggestions that academic freedom is becoming increasingly constrained in modern universities. Some warn that constraints on academic freedom will lead to a deterioration in the quality of public debate and the practices of pluralistic democracy (e.g. Melody, 1997). Preliminary research findings also suggest that constraints on academic freedom may be a factor in falling teaching and student standards and an emphasis on "safe" rather than speculative or contentious research (Kayrooz *et al.*, 2001; Kayrooz and Preston, 2002; Tierney, 2001).

This concern with the deterioration of academic freedom has arisen in response to widespread changes in the nature of higher education resulting from increasing fiscal pressures and constraints on universities throughout the 1980s and 1990s, following the international economic downturn of the 1970s. These fiscal pressures have been accompanied by a growing societal and governmental concern with accountability and evaluation of academic performance, as well as increasing pressures and trends towards marketisation and commercialisation of university teaching and research (Schuller, 1995; Smyth, 1995; Kogan *et al.*, 1994). As such, the debate about academic freedom forms part of a larger debate as to the nature of academia and academic work today (Cuthbert, 1996; Martin, 1999; Taylor, 1999; Coaldrake and Stedman, 1999; Marginson, 2000).

The Meaning of Academic Freedom

Despite the wide-ranging debate about academic freedom in recent times, there is little consensus between parties as to what academic freedom actually means. The existing literature shows that the concept is open to a range of interpretations and has been used at times to support conflicting causes and positions (Kaplan and Schrecker, 1983; Tight, 1988b; Worgul, 1992). Despite this lack of clarity, some common themes can be found in the literature, as will be described below, though they emerge with varying degrees of frequency.

At its most basic, academic freedom is frequently presented as a negative right of individual academics—that is, the right to non-interference in their activities:

> the freedom of the teacher or research worker in higher institutions of learning to investigate and discuss the problems of his (sic) science and to express his conclusions, whether through publication or in the instruction of students without interference from political or ecclesiastical authority or from the administrative officials of the institution in which he is employed, unless his methods are found by qualified bodies of his own profession to be clearly incompetent or contrary to professional ethics (Arthur Lovejoy, quoted in Worgul, 1992, p. 4).

This type of definition emphasises the concept of academic freedom as a freedom *from*, i.e., freedom from interference. Others see academic freedom as being more about a freedom *to*, i.e., a freedom to engage in appropriate academic activities. This represents a shift in the interpretation of academic freedom from being a negative right to a positive right of academics. In addition, the "freedom to" interpretation has associated implications for the role of institutions of higher education, by way of indicating a responsibility on their part to provide the appropriate support for academic activities required to enable academic freedom (O'Hear, 1988). This goes beyond the simple absence of interference from institutions implied by a "freedom from" interpretation.

The interpretation of academic freedom as a right often also leaves open the question of what areas this right should apply to: "whether academic freedom should apply only to the acknowledged special interests of academics or whether it should instead be extended indefinitely to cover any teaching, scholarship, research or publication which any academic chooses to engage in" (Tight, 1988b, p. 118). In other words, is it a freedom which applies to *any* activity in which an academic chooses to engage, or only to *particular* activities—and if the latter, selected according to what criteria?

Other descriptions of academic freedom include reference to the underlying goals or purposes of academic freedom, with these being seen as an *inherent* component of its meaning. This type of interpretation positions academic freedom as a means to an end, not as an end in itself (O'Hear, 1988; Hawkesworth, 1988), bringing with it certain responsibilities as well as rights:

> Academic freedom refers to the freedom of individuals to study, teach, research and publish without being subject to, or causing undue interference. Academic freedom is granted in the belief that it enhances the pursuit and application of worthwhile knowledge, and as such is supported by society through the funding of academics and their institutions. Academic

freedom embodies an acceptance by academics of the need to encourage openness and flexibility in academic work, and of their accountability to each other and to society in general (Tight, 1988b, p. 132).

The interplay of rights and responsibilities present in the above description is taken further by some, such as Turner (1988), who emphasises obligations above rights in the distinction he draws between freedom of speech and academic freedom. He argues that, unlike the general public, academics have no "right to silence":

> Mr. Raymond Honeyford was not obliged to publish articles criticising the child-raising practices of the patrons of his school. But lecturers in sociology are under some obligation to speak their minds on social policy: dissembling motivated by fear would be corrupt and expedient silence interpretable as culpable non productivity (Turner, 1988, p. 105).

Others further extend and elaborate the notion of responsibility by appealing to various forms of accountability, including professional accountability to peers, democratic accountability to the general community, managerial accountability to the employing university and market accountability to customers (Russell, 1993; Vidovich and Slee, 2001). Others contest the notion of accountability itself, referring to a legitimation crisis—who decides what knowledge is and who knows what needs to be decided? (Lyotard, 1993).

However, all of these descriptions so far emphasise academic freedom as a concept primarily relevant to individual academics. In contrast, in other interpretations, collegial/disciplinary and institutional aspects of academic freedom are also highlighted:

> Academic freedom for an *institution* [author's italics] usually includes autonomy or self government according to the terms of its constitution, with power to determine academic policies, the balance between teaching and research, staffing ratios, the appointment, promotion and discipline of students, curricula, standards, examinations and the conferring of degrees and diplomas; and with the control over the material resources needed to undertake these activities . . . Academic freedom for the *academics* [author's italics] is generally assumed to include the right to participate in the government of the institution and its policy-making, freedom in what and how to teach, choice of research topics, and freedom to travel and to communicate with colleagues (Rendel, 1988, pp. 74–75).

It is clear from this literature review that there is substantial variation in views as to the meaning of academic freedom. Although this lack of consensus is typically acknowledged in scholarly writing about academic freedom, the full range of variation has not been explored in a comprehensive way, nor the relationships between different views elaborated. In public debate (which is inevitably less scholarly) the situation is more worrying, as each party's definition of academic freedom is rarely described and the existence of varying views hardly acknowledged. Given the rising debate about academic freedom, this kind of variation in meanings and definitions can lead to debate at cross purposes.

To date, public debates and scholarly discussions about the nature of academic freedom have been marked by a lack of empirical data. What empirical research has been conducted has focused on perceived changes in academic freedom or academic autonomy over time and academics' ways of responding to those changes—though even this research is limited in nature. For instance, within Australia, where the research reported in this chapter was conducted, there have been only a handful of empirical studies investigating aspects of academic freedom (Vidovich and Currie, 1998; Anderson and Johnson, 1998; Slaughter and Leslie, 1995), and none of these have examined the underlying meanings of academic freedom amongst participants in the studies.

In response to the rising concern about the role of academic freedom in modern universities, the lack of clarification as to what different researchers mean by academic freedom, and the paucity of empirical research in the area, we undertook an empirical investigation of the range of meanings of academic freedom amongst social scientists in Australian universities. The findings are reported below.

Methodology

The data on which this chapter is based were originally collected as part of a larger study investigating Academic Freedom and Commercialisation in Australian Universities (see Kayrooz *et al.*, 2001). The original study involved a web-based questionnaire survey of 165 social science academics from 12 universities in Australia (representing a 20% response rate to the original questionnaire). One item from the questionnaire was selected for further analysis for this chapter. This item requested respondents' written comments in response to the following prompt:

> Academic freedom is not a well defined concept. We would like to know what academic freedom means to you.

Responses to this item were analysed using a phenomenographic approach (Marton, 1981, 1986; Marton and Booth, 1997). While phenomenographic research is more commonly based on interview data, the use of alternative forms of data, including written comments in response to open-ended questions, is well accepted (Prosser, 1994; Russell and Massey, 1994; Marton and Booth, 1997; Åkerlind and Jenkins, 1998).

As with all phenomenographic research, the aim was to investigate variation in the underlying meaning of, or ways of understanding, a phenomenon—in this case, academic freedom. The desired outcome was constitution of a structured "space" of variation, representing key aspects of the qualitatively different ways of viewing academic freedom represented amongst the group of academics surveyed. The structure of the resulting "outcome space" is based on the relationships between those different views, in terms of the critical aspects of variation which both link and separate the different meanings to and from each other.

Highlighting the relationships between different ways of experiencing academic freedom provides a way of looking at the phenomenon holistically, despite the fact that it may be experienced differently by different individuals, and by the same individuals at different points in time and context (Marton and Booth, 1997). The aim is to simultaneously portray the whole as well as the parts in a single outcome space of variation. This is achieved by taking a collective view of the range of ways of understanding academic freedom across the sample group of academics—collective in that each category of experience is defined in relation to the others, not independently, and there is a focus on identifying critical dimensions of variation which run throughout the sample of written responses, not on the specific complexity of individuals' responses.

The academics surveyed were selected to represent as much variation in views of academic freedom as possible, within the parameters of being social scientists in Australian universities. To the extent that the variation within the sample reflects the variation within the desired population—in this case, university academics in the social sciences—it is expected that the *range* of meanings within the sample will be representative of the *range* of meanings within the population (Marton and Booth, 1997; Francis, 1996; Booth, 1992).

This is a different type of representativeness to that commonly used in social research, and thus deserves further elaboration. As the aim of phenomenographic research is to capture the range of variation in ways of experiencing or understanding a phenomenon, the sample selected should be as heterogeneous as possible along lines that are likely to be associated with such variation. However, there is no expectation that the sample will be representative of the population quantitatively, in terms of the *frequency* distribution of particular ways of experiencing within the group, only that the *range* of ways of experiencing should be representative. Consequently, the researcher needs to ensure variation within the sample along key demographic criteria that one would expect to be associated with variation in experience; however, there is no expectation that the frequency distribution of such demographic criteria within the sample will match the distribution within the population.

Respondents were selected from varied disciplines within the social sciences, with varying levels of experience as an academic, on varying classifications and types of appointment, and engaged in different degrees of entrepreneurial activity and types of research. They were also selected to ensure a range of institutional types in which respondents were located, using the commonly accepted institutional groupings developed by Marginson (Marginson and Considine, 2000), i.e., "Sandstones" (pre-1970 universities), "Gum Trees" (post-1960 universities), "New Universities" (ex-colleges) and "Unitechs" (universities of technology). These groupings are primarily based on the age, disciplinary foci and research-intensive nature of the universities.

The sample is further elaborated below:

- *Institutional Location*—24% from Sandstone universities, 18% from Gum Trees, 14% from New Universities, 17% from Unitechs;
- *Discipline*—18% economics/commerce, 16% management, 15% education, 14% sociology, 11% media studies/communications, 10% political science, 17% other social sciences;
- *Academic Classification*—5% Level A appointments, 42% Level B, 34% Level C, 14% Level D, 5% Level E (where A represents the most junior and E the most senior level of academic appointment in Australia);
- *Nature of Appointment*—93% continuing appointment, 6% non-continuing;
- *Gender*—58% men, 42% women;
- *Academic Experience*—5% less than 2 years, 15% 2–5 years, 21% 6–10 years, 31% 11–20 years, 28% more than 20 years;
- *Sources of Research Funding*—38% no funding, 44% competitive funding, 6% private industry, 11% other.

The data were analysed in an iterative manner, involving repeated readings of respondents' written comments, comparing and contrasting them for similarities and differences, searching for groupings of comments which produced maximum variation between groupings and minimum variation within groupings, and looking for key relationships, or dimensions of variation, which related as well as distinguished the groupings of written comments to and from each other. (See Bowden and Walsh, 1994, for more detailed descriptions of approaches to phenomenographic analysis.) This continued until a consistent set of groupings, represented as the following "categories of description", eventuated. Each category represents a qualitatively different meaning or way of understanding academic freedom.

Outcomes

Five qualitatively different ways of understanding academic freedom emerged during the data analysis, with academic freedom variously seen as:

1. An absence of constraints on academics' activities.
2. An absence of constraints, within certain self-regulated limits.
3. An absence of constraints, within certain externally regulated limits.
4. An absence of constraints, combined with active institutional support.
5. An absence of constraints, combined with responsibilities on the part of academics.

The five categories are marked by variation along two key themes, or "dimensions of variation", which serve both to link and separate the different ways of understanding academic freedom. The two themes represent variation in perceptions of:

- *types of constraints* regarded as part of academic freedom, ranging *from* a focus on the total absence of constraints *to* include certain externally regulated constraints; and
- the *role of internal and external factors*, i.e., self versus other, in creating academic freedom—in terms of the interplay between what others do and what the academic him/herself does in creating academic freedom. This ranged *from* perceptions of academic freedom as an entirely externally determined occurrence *to* one involving a mixture of factors, both external and internal to the academic concerned.

The five different ways of viewing academic freedom are outlined in more detail below, represented as the following "categories of description".

Category 1: An Absence of Constraints on Academics' Activities

Within this category, academic freedom is seen as a situation of unlimited freedom for academics, with a focus on there being no controls on or reprisals for the activities that an academic may engage in. Relevant academic activities were variously described as research and publication, teaching, control over time and workload, freedom of speech and expression of ideas, intellectual enquiry and the pursuit of knowledge, and the challenging of accepted paradigms. For example:

- Ability to speak freely, in any forum, on any topic without fear of reprisal from University where employed.
- The right to undertake research of my choosing and the right to choose what and how I teach.
- Ability to research, publish and teach in areas without any control from the government and management.
- Academic freedom means the freedom to choose the subjects I offer to students, what areas of research I pursue and what public pronouncements I make. It also means the freedom to determine my own time allocation to the various tasks required.
- To have unlimited control over my research work.

Although the different written comments emphasise different activities that academics might engage in, what they all have in common is an emphasis on the right of the academic to choose and engage in the selected activity without interference or fear of reprisals.

Category 2: An Absence of Constraints, within Certain Self-regulated Limits

As with the previous category, the way of understanding academic freedom represented by this category also emphasises an absence of constraints, but this time within certain limits, i.e., within areas of academic expertise, areas of enquiry that are important for society, and/or areas of enquiry that are important for academic disciplines. However, the emphasis is on self-regulation in these areas and self-determination as to which areas are important. For example:

- To be able to research, publish and teach in those areas I consider to be of importance in terms of their social implications.
- It means the ability for me to set the direction of my research outcomes based on what I believe to be the salient research developments in my disciplinary field.
- That it is my choice, as a professional academic, to do the research and teaching that I believe will advance my profession . . .
- It is not the freedom to do whatever you want. It should be the freedom to speak and publish as an academic (on the basis of expertise) without fear or favour.
- Academic freedom means being able to pursue the research areas which I regard as important to society and being able to openly express them . . .

The main distinction between this category, or way of viewing, academic freedom and the previous one is that in this case some limits on the areas of academic freedom have been set, although they have been set by the academic concerned.

Category 3: An Absence of Constraints, within Certain Externally Regulated Limits

The understanding of academic freedom represented by this category incorporates the two primary aspects of academic freedom which emerged in the previous two categories, that is, the absence of interference in academic activities and the setting of certain limits on the areas of non-interference. However, the sense of appropriate limits is extended beyond self-regulated limits to include some externally regulated criteria or constraints. Appropriate external constraints were variously seen as including: the requirement to meet scholarly standards of activities, such as appropriate balance and rigour in academic work; to work in areas or ways regarded as appropriate by one's peers or colleagues; to work within appropriate ethical guidelines; and to meet appropriate quality assurance guidelines. For example:

- The ability and freedom to be able to define one's topic of research and to undertake that research (within the confines of public ethical constraints).
- Academic freedom means being able to mount, teach and administer course content which, while subject to peer scrutiny, is not subject to managerial consideration of revenue raising, or political considerations. It means being able, without fear of political or man- agerial reprisal and for the public good, to make public your judgments on matters within the purview of your expertise . . .
- Academic freedom relates principally to my research, teaching and my relationship with my employers. First, it means that I should be able to undertake research of my choosing and publish the results without gaining permission from my employment or an external agency. Second, it means that the only constraints on my teaching should be the broadly accepted understandings of academia in general and my field of study in particular. That is, academic freedom does not mean that I can teach whatever I like, how I like, rather that

the constraints are set by collegiality and the commonly accepted standards of balance and scholarly enquiry. Third, that my employment relationship, including job security, promotion and normal academic benefits, should be unaffected by my personal and scholarly expression.

- The privilege (for which I am accountable), made possible by the trust bestowed in me and my colleagues by the tax paying general public, to exercise my discretion in creating and disseminating knowledge which I deem to be of benefit to, and in the service of, the wider society of which I am a member.

Although different comments emphasise different areas of constraints as legitimate or appropriate, what all comments have in common is the emphasis on the freedom to undertake activities of the academic's choosing, but within broad constraints of one sort or another, including external constraints.

Category 4: An Absence of Constraints, Combined with Active Institutional Support for Academics' Activities

The focus of the categories so far has been on non-interference in academic activities, with different degrees of constraints being seen as appropriate. In this category, academic freedom is seen as requiring not only the absence of interference but the presence of supports to enable the exercise of academic freedom. These supports are primarily seen in terms of the requirement to provide the funding, resources and infrastructure necessary to enable appropriate academic activities. For example:

- It means the opportunity, supported by institutional resources, to pursue teaching and research and to participate as a public intellectual in societal debates.
- To my mind academic freedom connotes the existence of institutional and social conditions in which a person trained in teaching/researching has time and opportunity to think and to communicate ideas, regardless of the apparent costs or benefits, in financial or political terms, of those ideas and that communication. Constraints upon such freedom must be the intrinsic academic requirements of openness to reasoned argument, critique and authentic intellectual curiosity, not extrinsic limits or directions set by (apparent) economic, political or moral necessity.
- Self-directedness and the capacity to critique established theory and practice and to be supported in this by the apparatus of the University and the broader national and international intellectual, scholarly and research networks.
- Academic freedom refers to the capacity (time, space and resources) to undertake intellectual work, both knowledge generation and dissemination, in a climate that is free of interference by vested interests external and internal to the academic community, and in which the control of the processes and products of such work is retained and exercised by members of the academic community in accordance with democratically determined ethical principles, standards and procedures.

Category 5: An Absence of Constraints, Combined with Responsibilities on the Part of Academics

Categories 1 to 4 have emphasised academic freedom as being primarily an externally determined occurrence, by way of an absence of external interference and a presence of external supports. In category 5, there is a significant expansion in the perceived features of academic freedom to include the presence of internal responsibilities on the part of academics themselves. This includes the responsibility to actually exercise the freedom available to them, by way of participating in social debates and undertaking research and teaching, and to do so wisely and appropriately. For example:

- The responsibility to engage in open and informed debate without fear or favour. The responsibility of implementing, to the best of one's ability, decisions that have been democratically reached and agreed upon. The right to continually challenge such decisions.
- Academic freedom means the ability and integrity to conduct research for the public good without fear or favour. It means the freedom to be able to research and make public comment on important matters of social significance without concern (fear of repercussions) of the consequences of such action. Academic freedom is the obligation of academics to make social and political commentary.
- This refers to the personal integrity possessed by an academic, together with freedom of thinking and freedom of speech and advocating or disseminating their professional knowledge or findings of research results. An academic should also honour their research autonomy (i.e. is to be free from intervention or suppression from authorities, or business or political organisations) so that the society can benefit from their contributions.
- It means that the University for which I work has no direct say in what I write and what I teach . . . It also means that academics exercise their freedom. Conditions of freedom in the above respect are worthless if academics hide behind the idea of freedom and become intellectually lazy or follow conventions or pursue their careers. Institutional freedom by itself guarantees nothing intellectually speaking and maybe a hindrance to intellectual pursuits . . .

Relationships between the Categories

Categories 1 to 5 are seen as representing the key qualitatively different ways of understanding academic freedom present in the sample of academics surveyed. However, the five categories are not independently constituted, but are linked in a hierarchical relationship based on inclusivity (see Table 33.1). That is, the understanding of academic freedom represented by categories higher in the hierarchy includes awareness of the aspects of academic freedom represented by categories lower in the hierarchy, but *not* vice versa. This finding is in accordance with the phenomenographic view that different ways of understanding a phenomenon would typically be internally related, due to the inherently related nature of human experience (Marton and Booth, 1997). This leads to the

Table 33.1 Increasing Complexity across Different Ways of Understanding Academic Freedom

	Categories of different ways of understanding academic freedom				
Inclusive foci of the categories	Freedom without constraints	Freedom within self-regulated constraints	Freedom within external constraints	Freedom, constraints and supports	Freedom, constraints and responsibilities
Freedom from interference	1	2	3		
Freedom from interference and *freedom to* engage in appropriate activities				4	
Freedom from interference and responsibility *to* engage in appropriate activities					5

expectation that the qualitatively different ways of understanding a phenomenon constituted during a phenomenographic analysis would typically represent more and less complex and complete understandings of the phenomenon, rather than different and unrelated understandings.

The five qualitatively different ways of understanding academic freedom described above were marked by expanding complexity along the following two themes or dimensions of variation in awareness of different aspects of academic freedom:

1. *The types of constraints* regarded as an appropriate part of academic freedom—with a varying focus across categories *from* the importance of having no constraints or only self-imposed constraints *to include* a sense of appropriate externally imposed constraints;
2. *The role of internal and external factors* in creating academic freedom—with a varying focus across categories *from* perceiving the presence or absence of academic freedom as an entirely externally determined occurrence (i.e., determined by the presence or absence of collegial, institutional and social supports and constraints) *to include* the perception that academic freedom is at least partially internally determined by individual academics themselves (in terms of whether academics exercise their responsibility to use academic freedom appropriately). Where academic freedom is seen as externally determined, there is a focus on academic rights to non-interference (categories 1–3), or both rights and requirements for support (category 4). These rights and requirements may then be met or not met, but this is a decision which is made externally to individual academics, by the institution, government, etc. Where academic freedom is seen as internally determined, there is a focus on the role played by academics themselves in determining academic freedom, through meeting or not meeting their responsibilities.

The hierarchically inclusive nature of the relationship between categories is dialectically reflected in these two dimensions of variation (see Table 33.2). Understandings of academic freedom which are *lower* in the hierarchy are marked by a focus on: freedom without constraints or with constraints which are entirely self-imposed; and the role of external factors in creating academic freedom, by way of an absence of external interference and a presence of external supports. Understandings of academic freedom which are *higher* in the hierarchy are marked by an expansion in focus to include: freedom within certain externally regulated constraints; and the role of factors internal to the academic in creating academic freedom, by way of responsibilities on the part of the academic.

The hierarchical nature of the relationships between Categories 1 to 5 and the ordering of categories within the hierarchy emerged through an iterative process, involving interactive alternation between searching for logical and empirical evidence of inclusivity. Empirical evidence of inclusivity included the observation that, *as a group*, the written comments from which particular categories of description were constituted showed some reference to aspects of academic freedom present in categories lower in the hierarchy, but *not* vice versa.

The descriptions of different meanings or ways of understanding academic freedom presented here may create the impression of each meaning being experienced as an accumulation of key aspects or features of academic freedom. By contrast, it is important to acknowledge that experience occurs holistically. Consequently, although each category may be presented as consisting of a combination of different aspects, this is for descriptive and analytic purposes. The understanding or meaning represented by each category of description would be a holistic one, and necessarily different to the sum of its parts or aspects. Furthermore, as noted above, the categories are not attempting to portray the complexity of human meaning, but rather the critical aspects of different ways of understanding or experiencing the same phenomenon. This focus on critical aspects of experience is seen as having a powerful heuristic value in aiding our understanding of academic freedom.

Table 33.2 Key Dimensions Marking the Inclusive Nature of Relationships between Categories

Dimensions	Categories				
	1	2	3	4	5
Types of constraints considered consistent with academic freedom	No constraints	Self-imposed constraints only	Self and externally-imposed constraints	Self and externally-imposed constraints	Self and externally-imposed constraints
Perceived role of internal and external factors in creating academic freedom	Academic freedom as entirely externally-determined (a focus on rights)	Academic freedom as entirely externally-determined (a focus on rights)	Academic freedom as entirely externally-determined (a focus on rights)	Academic freedom as entirely externally-determined (a focus on rights *and* requirements)	Academic freedom as internally *and* externally-determined (a focus on *rights and* responsibility)

NB: *External factors* are those external to the academic him/herself, and may include supports and constraints from disciplinary colleagues, the institution in which the academic is located and/or a larger community or society of which the academic is a part. *Internal factors* are those internal to the academic, primarily an individual sense of responsibility to exercise academic freedom appropriately.

Discussion

In this chapter we have undertaken an empirical analysis of the range of ways of understanding academic freedom, as experienced by social science academics. An inclusive hierarchy of awareness of different aspects of academic freedom emerged from the analysis, based on two primary dimensions of variation: the *types of constraints* regarded as an appropriate part of academic freedom; and the *role of internal and external factors* in creating academic freedom. Five qualitatively different ways of understanding academic freedom emerged, represented as the following five categories:

1. An absence of constraints on academics' activities.
2. An absence of constraints, within certain self-regulated limits.
3. An absence of constraints, within certain externally regulated limits.
4. An absence of constraints, combined with active institutional support.
5. An absence of constraints, combined with responsibilities on the part of academics.

It is instructive to compare the different understandings of academic freedom which emerged from this study with those that emerged in the literature overviewed in the introduction to this chapter. Although this study was empirically based and previous literature on the meaning of academic freedom has been primarily historically, comparatively and conceptually based, there was a substantial overlap in themes. This is regarded as providing support for the findings of the study reported here, as one would expect to see clear relationships between the outcomes of different ways of exploring the meaning of academic freedom.

Key themes which were identified in the literature and also emerged in this study included: an emphasis on academic freedom as a right to non-interference in academic activities; the distinction between academic freedom as a "freedom from" interference as opposed to a "freedom to" engage in appropriate academic activities (implying associated institutional support); and the role of responsibilities and obligations, in addition to rights, in creating academic freedom. Looking at the different ways of understanding academic freedom which emerged from this study, the understandings represented by Categories 1–3 focused primarily on academic freedom experienced as an absence of constraints and interference, in line with the "freedom from" interpretation of academic freedom. Category 4 focused on the need for appropriate institutional *support*, in line with the "freedom to" interpretation. While the first four categories emphasised academic freedom as a *right* of academics, the fifth and final category focused on the concomitant responsibilities that right places upon academics, in line with interpretations from the literature which emphasise academic freedom as involving obligations and accountability.

Another issue which emerged in the literature on academic freedom is the distinction between individual autonomy, collegial or disciplinary autonomy and institutional autonomy. This study presents a unique picture of the interplay between these three autonomies in academics' understandings of academic freedom. The focus across all of the categories which emerged in this study is on academic freedom as a right of academics as *individuals*. However, in Categories 1 and 2, individual rights are the sole focus of the understanding, while in Category 3 there emerges a sense in respondents' comments that these rights are appropriately constrained by the standards or criteria of an academic's colleagues, discipline or professional body. In addition to these constraints, in Category 4, an emphasis on the role of the institution, and to a certain extent society, in providing appropriate supports for academic freedom emerges. Category 5, which emphasises the responsibilities inherent in academic freedom, includes awareness of responsibilities to an academic's colleagues/discipline, institution and society.

It should be noted that not every written comment that fell into Categories 3–5 emphasised each type of external constraint or support as being appropriate. For instance, it was possible for a comment to emphasise the meeting of peer-based standards as appropriate to academic freedom without emphasising the meeting of social standards. Nevertheless, at the point at which external constraints become an accepted part of one's understanding of academic freedom, the possibility for various types of constraint emerges and was found amongst the group of written comments representing each category, as a whole. Similarly, although all areas of responsibilities need not emerge in any one written comment, variation across the areas was found in the group of written comments, as a whole.

A final theme which was identified in the literature and on which this study can cast further light is the question of to which academic activities academic freedom should apply, that is, is it relevant only to particular activities of academics or to any activity in which an academic might engage? The social scientists surveyed in this study described academic freedom as applying to one or more of the following areas of activity: research, teaching, freedom of speech and expression, and/or the pursuit of knowledge and truth to inform social debate and social good. This was in addition to the view that academic freedom applied to *any* activity of an academic.

An interesting finding is that this variation in views as to which activities are appropriate was found in *each* of the ways of understanding academic freedom which emerged in this study, and did not distinguish between them consequently. This means that whether one is talking about teaching, research or the pursuit of truth, one can experience academic freedom with regard to that activity as being a simple absence of constraints or a mixture of constraints, supports and responsibilities. In other words, based on the analysis reported in this chapter, the type of activity to which academic freedom is seen as relevant is not a critical aspect of the meaning of academic freedom, as the range of possible activities was found equally in each category and did not distinguish between them. Another way of thinking about this is to regard them as independent sub-categories of each way of understanding academic freedom, which do not contribute to the structure of the relationships between the different understandings.

The focus taken in this chapter on the structural relationships between different understandings of academic freedom has practical implications for future debate and discussion of issues around academic freedom. To date, this debate has been muddied by a lack of clarity as to what academic freedom means and as to which interpretation any one party in a debate is using. Further, there is often little awareness that different interpretations of academic freedom exist. For example, in a debate about a recent discussion paper on the future of universities, the two key contributors clearly spoke from different understandings of academic freedom (Kinnear, 2001). One contributor discussed academic freedom from the perspective that it should involve a complete absence of constraints; the other saw academic freedom as involving an absence of constraints, but with clear academic responsibilities.

Similarly, in two recent studies of the impact on academic freedom of recent changes in Australian higher education, both studies defined academic freedom by referring to both individual *and* institutional freedoms (Vidovich and Currie, 1998; Slaughter and Leslie, 1995). At the individual level, academic freedom was thought to be the right to exercise professional judgement without fear of retribution; and at the institutional level, it was perceived to be the right of institutions to be self-governing. While the assumed meaning of academic freedom appeared to be similar in the two studies, neither explored the interplay between rights and responsibilities in academic freedom, nor the varying levels of rights and responsibilities. Furthermore, they did not problematise the issue of varying understandings of academic freedom or responsibility.

In summary, as far as we are aware, this study represents not only the first empirical investigation of the meaning of academic freedom, but the first attempt to elaborate the full range of variation in meanings, at least as experienced amongst social scientists. The chapter also explores the logical relationships between the different meanings that emerged, which provides a way of looking at academic freedom holistically, even though it may be understood in different ways by different individuals in different situations and circumstances.

By exploring the logical relationships between different ways of understanding academic freedom, this study enables an understanding of which aspects of academic freedom are being focused on or not focused on in the different interpretations which arise in the literature and in public debate. This provides a valuable opportunity to clarify where any disagreement between different debaters lies and precisely which aspects of academic freedom are regarded as most under threat due to the current changes in the higher education system. While no one way of experiencing academic freedom is regarded as *inherently* better than another, the inclusive nature of the relationships between the categories indicates that those higher in the hierarchy represent a more complex and inclusive awareness of the various aspects of academic freedom. Such distinctions should lead to greater clarity, precision and comprehensiveness in debate.

Acknowledgments

The data on which this chapter is based were originally collected as part of a larger study investigating "Academic Freedom and Commercialisation in Australian Universities" and funded by the Australia Institute, Canberra ACT. For a full report of the larger study, see Kayrooz *et al.*, 2001.

Note

1. Åkerlind, G.S. and Kayrooz, C. (2003). Understanding academic freedom: the views of social scientists. *Higher Education Research and Development*, 22:3, 1. Reprinted by permission of the publisher.

References

Åkerlind, G. and Jenkins, S. (1998). Academics' views of the relative roles and responsibilities of teachers and learners in a first-year university course. *Higher Education Research and Development*, 17, 277–289.
Anderson, D. and Johnson, R. (1998). *University autonomy in twenty countries*. Evaluations and Investigations Program, Canberra: Higher Education Division, Department of Employment, Education, Training and Youth Affairs.
Booth, S. (1992). *Learning to program: A phenomenographic perspective*. Sweden: ACTA Universitatis Gothoburgensis, 89: 1992.
Bowden, J. and Walsh, E. (eds) (1994). *Understanding phenomenographic research: The Warburton Symposium*. Melbourne: EQARD, RMIT.
Coaldrake, P. and Stedman, L. (1999). *Academic work in the twenty-first century: Changing roles and policies*. Canberra: Department of Education, Training and Youth Affairs, Higher Education Division.
Cuthbert, R. (1996). *Working in higher education*. Buckingham: SRHE and OU Press.
Francis, H. (1996). Advancing phenomenography—Questions of method. In G. Dall 'Alba and B. Hasselgren (eds) *Reflections on phenomenography: Toward a methodology?* (pp. 35–48). Gothenburg, Sweden: Goteborg Studies in Educational Sciences 109, ACTA Universitatis Gothoburgensis.
Hawkesworth, M. (1988). Human rights and academic freedom. In M. Tight (ed.) *Academic freedom and responsibility* (pp. 17–30). Buckingham: SRHE and OU Press.
Kaplan, C. and Schrecker, E. (eds) (1983). *Regulating the intellectuals: Perspectives on academic freedom in the 1980s*. New York: Praeger.
Kayrooz, C., Kinnear, P. and Preston, P. (2001). *Academic freedom and commercialisation in Australian universities: A study of social scientists*. Australia Institute Discussion Paper No. 37, Canberra: Australia Institute.
Kayrooz, C., and Preston, P. (2002). Academic freedom: Impressions of Australian social scientists. *Minerva*, 40, 341–358.
Kinnear, P. (ed.) (2001). *The idea of a university: Enterprise or academy?* Australia Institute Discussion Paper No. 39, Canberra: Australia Institute, 49–50.
Kogan, M., Moses, I. and El-Khawas, E. (1994). *Staffing higher education: Meeting new challenges*. London and Pennsylvania: Kingsley Publishers.
Lyotard, J. (1993). *The postmodern condition: A report on knowledge*. Minneapolis: University of Minnesota Press.
Marginson, S. (1997). How free is academic freedom? *Higher Education Research and Development*, 16, 359–369.

Marginson, S. (2000). Rethinking academic work in the global era. *Journal of Higher Education Policy and Management*, *22*, 23–35.

Marginson, S. and Considine, M. (2000). *The entrepreneurial university: Power, governance and reinvention in Australia.* Cambridge: Cambridge University Press.

Martin, E. (1999). *Changing academic work.* Buckingham: SRHE and OU Press.

Marton, F. (1981). Phenomenography—Describing conceptions of the world around us. *Instructional Science, 10*, 177–200.

Marton, F. (1986). Phenomenography—A research approach to investigating different understandings of reality. *Journal of Thought, 21*, 28–49.

Marton, F. and Booth, S. (1997). *Learning and awareness.* Hillsdale, NJ: Lawrence Erlbaum Ass.

Melody, W. (1997). Universities and public policy. In A. Smith and F. Webster (eds) *The postmodern university?* (pp. 72–84). Buckingham: SRHE and OU Press.

O'Hear, A. (1988). Academic freedom and the university. In M. Tight (ed.), *Academic freedom and responsibility* (pp. 6–16). Buckingham: SRHE and OU Press.

Prosser, M. (1994). Using phenomenographic research methods in large-scale studies of student learning in higher education. In R. Ballantyne and C. Bruce (eds) *Phenomenography: Philosophy and practice* (pp. 321–332). Brisbane: QUT Publications and Printing.

Rendel, M. (1988). Human rights and academic freedom. In M. Tight (ed.) *Academic freedom and responsibility* (pp. 74–87). Buckingham: SRHE and OU Press.

Russell, A. and Massey, G. (1994). Comparison of three data collection methods for phenomenographic analysis. In R. Ballantyne and C. Bruce (eds) *Phenomenography: Philosophy and practice* (pp. 333–342). Brisbane: QUT Publications and Printing.

Russell, C. (1993). *Academic freedom.* London: Routledge.

Schuller, T. (1995). *The changing university?* Buckingham: SRHE and OU Press.

Slaughter, S. and Leslie, L. (1995). In J. Smyth (ed.) *Academic work: The changing labour process in higher education* (pp. 112–128). Buckingham: SRHE and OU Press.

Smyth, J. (1995). *Academic work: The changing labour process in higher education.* Buckingham: SRHE and OU Press.

Taylor, P. (1999). *Making sense of academic life.* Buckingham: SRHE and OU Press.

Tierney, W. (2001). Academic freedom and organisational identity. *Australian Universities Review, 44*, 7–14.

Tight, M. (1988a). *Academic freedom and responsibility.* Buckingham: SRHE and OU Press.

Tight, M. (1988b). So what is academic freedom? In M. Tight (ed.) *Academic freedom and responsibility.* Buckingham: SRHE and OU Press.

Turner, J. (1988). The price of freedom. In M. Tight (ed.) *Academic freedom and responsibility* (pp. 104–113). Buckingham: SRHE and OU Press.

Vidovich, L. and Currie, J. (1998). Changing accountability and autonomy at the "coalface" of academic work in Australia. In J. Currie and J. Newson (ed.) *Universities and globalisation: Critical perspectives* (pp. 193–211). Thousand Oaks, California: Sage Publications.

Vidovich, L. and Slee, R. (2001). Bringing universities to account? Exploring some global and local policy tensions. *Journal of Education Policy, 16*, 431–453.

Worgul, G.S. (ed.) (1992). *Issues in academic freedom.* Pittsburgh: Duquesne University Press.

IX
Knowledge

This, the final section of the handbook, contains four chapters on the theme of knowledge. Under this general heading, the chapters address the nature of academic research, the consequences of disciplinarity, the impact of changing forms of knowledge, and the continuing significance of the liberal ideal to our understanding of the nature of the university.

Arguably, this theme gets to the heart of what higher education and, in particular, the long-lasting but continually adapting institution we know as the university are all about. A consideration of knowledge raises fundamental questions about what we know, how we know it, and what we then do with it.

These are questions which have engaged many of our foremost researchers over the years, as in Becher's (1989; Becher and Trowler, 2001) work on disciplinary tribes and territories, Clark's (1984, 1993) comparative studies of higher education, Gibbons *et al.*'s discussions about the changing nature of research (Gibbons *et al.*, 1994; Nowotny *et al.*, 2001), and Barnett's (1990, 1997) contributions to the debate—which has continued virtually since universities were first established—on the "idea" of the university.

They are also questions which range over the artificial boundaries we have necessarily imposed upon the organisation of this handbook, coming up also, for example, in Krause's chapter—discussing the links between the roles of research, teaching and service—in the section on academic work.

In the first of the four chapters in this section, Angela Brew examines the nature of academic research in contemporary society. After discussing the definition(s) and purposes of research, she considers a series of in-built conflicts or contradictions in its practice: between the different interests involved; between the imagination required to undertake meaningful research and others' desire to control it; and in the values held by researchers, their employers and funders. Underlying her argument is the recognition that academic research is embedded within society, no longer something carried out, if it ever was, in an "ivory tower".

Ruth Neumann considers disciplinarity in parallel to knowledge. Starting again with some definitions, she reviews the development of disciplinary forms through history and their current proliferation, with the rise of trans- and inter-disciplinary concerns. She notes the impact of these developments on the structuring of knowledge and the internal organisation of universities. And she considers how the different characteristics of disciplines affect research and teaching.

Merle Jacob takes as his topic the redefinition of the role of higher education and research, focusing on recent experience in Western European countries. His concern is with how changes in the ways that higher education and research are organised and funded impact upon the production, dissemination and value accorded to knowledge. With the funding and evaluation of teaching and research now increasingly separated, universities, which have long valued the interaction between the two activities, face new challenges as they seek to define their future missions.

Finally, Tony Harland discusses the university, neoliberal reform and the liberal educational ideal, noting the tensions between the last two of these terms. He reviews the neoliberal challenge to the older liberal ideas embodied in the university, and their effects on organisation, culture and knowledge. The continuing existence of the liberal ideal, however, suggests much about its essential value and importance.

References

Barnett, R. (1990). *The Idea of Higher Education*. Buckingham: Open University Press.
Barnett, R. (1997). *Higher Education: a critical business*. Buckingham: Open University Press.
Becher, T. (1989). *Academic Tribes and Territories: intellectual enquiry and the cultures of disciplines*. Milton Keynes: Open University Press.
Becher, T. and Trowler, P. (2001). *Academic Tribes and Territories: intellectual enquiry and the culture of disciplines*. Buckingham: Open University Press, 2nd edn.
Clark, B. (ed.) (1984). *Perspectives on Higher Education: eight disciplinary and comparative views*. Berkeley, CA, University of California Press.
Clark, B. (ed.) (1993). *The Research Foundations of Graduate Education: Germany, Britain, France, United States, Japan*. Berkeley, CA, University of California Press.
Gibbons, M., Limoges, C., Nowotny, H., Scott, P., Schwartzmann, S. and Trow, M. (1994). *The New Production of Knowledge: the dynamics of science and research in contemporary societies*. London: Sage.
Nowotny, H., Scott, P. and Gibbons, M. (2001). *Re-thinking Science: knowledge and the public in an age of uncertainty*. Cambridge: Polity Press.

34
Academic Research in Contemporary Society

Angela Brew

Considerations of research in contemporary society are inevitably tied to theories of that society and the academy as an institution within it. Yet research creates the very theories which explain society. So, paradoxically, research is positioned inside and outside theories of contemporary society. In order to understand the nature of research in society, we must first consider what academic research is and does. This is by no means straightforward. At every turn, contradictions confront us. This chapter explores these contradictions, first by examining the competing interests that academic research serves, and exploring the ways in which power is exercised within universities. It then goes on to examine how creativity and fiction are embedded in research policy and practice. Specifically, the chapter explores how research is sustained by the ways in which society, universities and individuals create fictions about themselves and their work. Conflicts in values are then explored. The chapter discusses the preservation of elitism within the academy alongside espousal of democratic values, and the way values of inclusivity are denied through power. Finally, the chapter shows what research could look like if person-centred values were dominant. It examines the role of reflexive awareness, and suggests that researchers face the risks of coping with the complexity and ambiguity of a contemporary globalised society by minimising their reflexive awareness and focusing on more immediate concerns.

So what is research? Nowotny *et al.* (2001) argue that the definition of research is affected by such things as the increasing number of contexts in which it is carried out, the proliferation of demands for knowledge in specific contexts, and the mix of practices, methods and beliefs which now constitute it. Within this context, they suggest that the rules of engagement are fuzzy and being made up as we go along: "There is a high degree of uncertainty, there is no clear-cut direction but many competing ideas, theories and methods, and no one is in overall charge" (p. 115). Not only are there so many more political, social, economic and individual factors having a say in how research should be organised and conducted, but greater contextualisation within society is affecting ideas about what constitutes "objective knowledge" and how the reliability of research knowledge is assessed. Nowotny *et al.* argue that powerful individuals, groups and institutions present ways through this ambivalence, but they cannot articulate its full complexity, nor can they present the best or even the most appropriate ways forward in many contexts. Indeed, they are part of the complexity and simply add to the ambiguity. This presents a paradox for this very chapter. Saying anything about research in contemporary society is inevitably going to fail to articulate the full extent of its complexity.

If we are to understand the nature of research in contemporary society, we must have some ideas about what we mean by contemporary society. This will depend on the theoretical perspective we adopt. Contemporary theories of higher education have tended to talk in terms of the responses of academics to neo-liberalism (Marginson, 2007; Marginson and Considine, 2000; Slaughter 1993). Such theories suggest that research pursues performative agendas, designed to meet the needs of governments who exercise increasing levels of surveillance over the academy.

Rather than being confined to one particular theoretical tradition, I prefer to take an eclectic approach, focusing on ideas that illuminate aspects of society in ways that enable the drawing out of what I like to call the "ironic turn" in theories of research. I use this term to cover the contradictions, paradoxes, and incongruities that emerge when we look closely at research policy and practice. In this chapter I highlight many ways in which policies and practices have opposite effects to those that are intended.

Explanations of research in terms of responses to neo-liberalism do not take account of the complexities and ambiguities, and the rate of change in universities and society. We need theories that do take account of the fluidity and pace of change. For this reason, I am drawn to Bauman's (2006, p. 1) idea of "liquid modernity". He defines this as: "a society in which the conditions under which its members act change faster than it takes the ways of acting to consolidate into habits and routines". I like this idea because it suggests a role for creativity, and places intentionality in the hands of all who are involved in research policy and practice (including researchers) in any way, shape or form. We shall see how this plays out in relation to research agendas later.

I am also drawn to Giddens' (1999) notion of a "runaway world". As well as expressing speed of change, there is, in this concept, the expectation that actions go beyond the actions of individual governments to take account of the globalised arena. This is very important when we come to talk about the nature of research in contemporary society. Giddens reminds us that society is a world-wide society. This speaks of the interconnectedness of our contemporary concerns, even if different people live very different kinds of lives.

Both of these theories in their different ways express something about our living in a period of transitions. They both say something about the nature of those transitions; that they are fast-paced and multifaceted. Barnett's (2000) concept of super-complexity underscores this notion.

So in these fast-paced, supercomplex and multifaceted contexts, what can we say of research in a general sense? Let me make some suggestions. Research is clearly designed to enhance understanding. Through academic research discoveries are made, new knowledge is generated, and new ideas and concepts come to light. I have argued elsewhere that the purpose of research is to teach; not in the narrow sense of teaching students, but to teach people in society in the sense of providing ways of understanding the world (Brew, 2006). Indeed, there is not a single aspect of contemporary daily life which has not been informed in some way by academic research in one form or another.

Research has to be capable of being shared in some way; not only in the sense of products or artifacts, but also its processes. New research is only possible if the knowledge that is generated, as well as how the research was done, are communicated to others. An important part of academic research is peer review. Research has to stand up to critical scrutiny by others. These elements were identified by Glassick et al., (1997), on the evidence of criteria for evaluation used by some 800 organisations (universities, funding bodies, foundations etc.), as being important aspects of scholarly work. A further important component that they identified is that we have not only to develop new knowing, enhancing understanding, but we have to have some insight into what it is we have done. This is what they call a reflexive critique. Perhaps more contentious is the idea that research has to have something to do with developing knowing; not just knowledge as a quantity of information, but inner personal knowing as well—developing wisdom perhaps. I want to argue, too, that there is a coherence between the knowing, the understanding we have developed, how we came to that understanding and who we have become.

When we come to look at the many agendas which research is required to address, it is clear that these definitional statements present some conundrums. The agendas of governments, of research councils, of publishers, of the media, and the personal agendas of researchers, suggest a series of contradictions which are exhibited in the many ways in which research is pursued, interpreted and used within contemporary society. Research clearly occupies contested space (Brew, 2001a), and that space is transitory, ambiguous, global and super-complex.

Doing research is a creative pursuit. Research traditions are the result of acts of the creative imagination. Research policies, too, require creativity. Indeed, acts of creativity are embedded in every aspect of research, whether at the policy level, the level of research communication, the process of engaging in a particular research project, or in the consciousness of the researcher. It is this which makes research so fascinating to study, because here lies the irony. Research defines a social space wherein particular kinds of creativity are pursued. This is logically implied by Bauman's idea of liquid modernity; that the world is forever being created anew. Before habits and routines have consolidated actions into rules and procedures, the creative process has moved on. For Bauman, this is a description of society in the postmodern era. Research is a key vehicle for the advancement of what Bauman (2006) calls "liquid life". Yet creativity does not come out of a vacuum. The creativity of researchers is likely to be stimulated by creative acts of earlier researchers: "the shoulders of giants". Some acts of creativity are experienced as constraints which inhibit acts of creativity. For example, policies at governmental or institutional levels require creativity for their development, but they are often viewed as constraints on academics. Indeed, there are a number of discussions in the academic literature about the ways in which policies, built on economic rationalist principles, are constraining academics in terms of the types and levels of publication, and so on. Yet these very policies are making possible new fields of study. Ironically, therefore, although constraints may inhibit, they can also stimulate new kinds of creativity. Witness, for example, the ways in which government policy in Australia has opened up national security as a new subject for study, or the ways in which in the UK the Thatcherite policy to encourage the development of "enterprise", through what became the Enterprise in Higher Education initiative was colonised by academics into a different kind of agenda, one that opened up new kinds of scholarship into graduate attributes. Furthermore, creative acts in research may result from resistance to what are perceived as constraints, such as the increase in research and practice in integrating research and teaching, as a response to policy initiatives to separate the teaching and research roles of academics.

Just as dictating to a painter or a sculptor how to create a particular picture or artefact is likely either to inhibit the creative process, or to turn the artist's creativity in another direction, so attempts to steer research in particular directions either stultifies research or results in creative responses in terms of new ways of seeing the world, developing new understandings. In the past, I have argued for the need for research to be transformed to help us live in a complex society characterised by uncertainty, ambiguity and unpredictability (Brew, 2001a, 2007). In this chapter I want to suggest that these ironic twists in the nature of research as a creative pursuit define the scenario through which the relationship of research to contemporary society must be viewed. For it is in negotiating their ways through these that everyone associated with research makes a contribution to the kind of society that will result in the future.

Interests

Research is required to serve many different interests. It is of prime national and international significance. So government investment in research is important, both the amount of investment and the type of investment, with high-level, complex scientific and medical research being at the pinnacle of esteem. Governments are interested in funding research that has some kind of national benefit. Investment in research also signals to other nations what level of understanding, even of civilisation, a particular nation has reached (Campbel, 2003). Ironically, pursuing national benefit may be at the expense of solving global problems. For example, large, long-term international teams are needed to solve the problems of climate change. Nationally funded research projects that focus on short-term, relatively local, concerns may be counterproductive to this.

Governments' attempts to control research agendas through research councils with government-appointed directors, through mechanisms for assessing research quality and quantity, in defining priority areas for research, backed by output-driven funding regimes often considered punitive, pose particular challenges for certain kinds of research. This is because government research assessment and accountability requirements imply views of the nature of knowledge, and how knowledge is constructed, that assume that knowledge can be packaged; that projects with a defined life-span carried out by the same person or team can be viewed and presented as intellectually separate from each other. This view of research assumes that it is possible to somehow "manage" research by defining research outcomes in advance of doing the research. So, for example, research grant applications make statements about outcomes and impacts of research, in the academic discipline and the society more generally. Requirements for writing such grants make assumptions about what can be known prior to the research being done. Such projects may also be required to contribute to the economy in some way, and the researcher may have to describe their project in terms that will appeal to a general educational audience, not just an audience of their colleagues, who are likely to know the subject. In Australia, for example, research project applications have to include a summary that will be capable of being understood, not just by academics, but also by politicians. In other words, researchers are buying into a whole culture of ideas about what research is, and how to define it.

Clearly defined objectives within clearly bounded projects are not only viewed as "marketable" within neo-liberalism, they appear to be a way of controlling an uncontrollable system. Defining projects suits some disciplinary areas better than others. For example, research that involves participants in decision-making, such as participatory action research or collaborative inquiry, qualitative interdisciplinary research, performances, creative works, exhibitions, research in industrial and professional secondments, clinical practice, and social scientific or education research that uses new methodologies such as autoethnography, do not easily lend themselves to such measures. Indeed, most areas of investigation are complex and multifaceted. What is interesting is that these forms of research have developed alongside the development of performative agendas. I am not suggesting that they have developed as a response to such agendas. However, it is worth reflecting on the ways in which definitions of research have continued to go beyond performative requirements, as a complex array of alternative theories to neo-liberalism play themselves out.

There is a difference between research carried out to address accountability agendas, and coming to know through a more organic process of inquiry which does not presume the outcomes. Neo-liberal ideas rest on a set of assumptions about the nature of knowledge that do not readily fit notions of research as a creative, organic process with a life of its own (see e.g. Brew, 2001a). Researching something interesting to know about, following where the research leads at the time at which it leads, without the need to wait until a particular project is ended before going on to the next project, is much more organic than the research grant treadmill would allow. There are particular dilemmas faced by a researcher with a predisposition to carry out speculative, or what has become known as "blue skies", research, and there are disjunctions between economic performative views of research and ideas which arise from changing understandings of the nature of knowledge. In scientific areas, speculative research is becoming almost impossible because of the high cost of scientific equipment. What is most troublesome, perhaps, is that managerialist views of research have made "blue skies", speculative, or new forms of research difficult to justify and even more difficult to publish. Yet, ironically, as control of research funding and accountability requirements appear to tighten, there has been an intellectual loosening of what is methodologically possible.

Research councils, which may or may not be funded by governments, also have their own interests which may or may not coincide with the interests of governments. Industry also has a huge interest in funding academic research, and this can skew research in academic departments towards particular projects. Nowotny *et al.* (2001) draw attention to how academics are becoming increasingly involved in multidisciplinary teams, involving experts from different areas of society, including government ministers, consultants, lawyers, industrialists, members of non-governmental organisations and end-users. The interests of all of these may differ. The research is required to steer a course between conflicting interests, and may end up satisfying none.

Increasingly, the media is interested in research and this influences institutional managers. It has a vested interest in the bizarre, in "sexy" topics, i.e. ones which capture the imagination or provide graphic interest when presented, for example, in television programmes. There is now a variety of opportunities for disseminating research findings due to increased interest in research by the public (Nowotny *et al.* 2001). Media presents research in a variety of ad hoc ways. These are not predictable by researchers prior to the work being done. Media interest in a particular project may conflict with the interests of the researcher, and may portray the research in unintended ways, some of which may not be flattering. Yet researchers are constantly heard on the radio and viewed on television and in electronic and print media.

Finally, there are the inherent interests of the academics themselves. These interests are frequently circumvented through the need to obtain funding from government, research councils or industry. However, they are fundamental to the research enterprise for, without the intrinsic interests of academics in diverse fields of study, much research would simply be impossible. Extrinsic rewards in terms of advancement and/or promotion are also important to the research interests of academics, and feed government and other agendas. However, much research requires long hours of painstaking work and persistence, and a willingness to overcome setbacks, which can only be driven by researchers' intrinsic interest in the topic. In many cases, research achievements in varied domains of knowledge are the result of academics researching issues which interest them personally. The quest for academic truth in many disciplines is an altruistic pursuit, in that it has an underlying intention to benefit society, but, ironically, it has often been attained through the self-interested study by individuals and groups who identify an area that requires investigation (Kogan and Henkel, 1992). Policy-makers and politicians have tended not to appreciate this (Brew, 2007).

The point I have been endeavouring to highlight in relation to these varied and different interests is that they frequently conflict. It is perhaps at the level of the individual academic or research team that the contradictions appear to be most acute. It is the individual academics who are having to do a balancing act between what they would most like to do and what is possible to do, given the levels of, and competition for, funding. As well as thinking about the topics and issues that need to be explored in the field, researchers have to think about how they, and their institution, might get some research credit or funding, or how they can work effectively with others who may have financial backing. With the current pressure on academics that has come about through a mass higher education system, projects that are not funded are difficult to complete, and they are not as prestigious as funded ones. Indeed, the fierce competition brought about by research assessment in some countries has created a situation where there can be conflict between the research that individuals would like to pursue and what they are permitted by their university or faculty to do. This suggests lower levels of commitment, and may result in failure to research issues of fundamental importance. Indeed, it is known to have resulted in a shift away from basic research to research of an applied or strategic nature (Lucas, 2006).

However, this is not an orderly, rational process. Nowotny *et al.* (2001) describe the coming together of different interests, projects and expectations as an "agora", a kind of free-floating marketplace with "transaction spaces", where ideas emerge from negotiations between different interests and groups. This is akin to the watery metaphors which Bauman (2006) talks about. Research defines not only a contested space, it defines a continuously shifting, ambiguous, super-complex interplay of interacting, overlapping, competing and conflicting, as well as cooperative, interests.

Important in this scenario are relationships of power and patronage, which often go unrecognised and unchecked. The ways in which power is used by different groups and individuals in influencing research directions, processes and outcomes is not well documented. Power operates to define the nature of research and what is valued in particular contexts. It dictates particular views of how a given institution operates or should operate both within itself and in relation to external forces. Particular sections of academia are closely allied to powerful outside groups (Slaughter, 1993). These groups can exploit research opportunities and undermine individual creativity by the growth of cross-disciplinary collaborative projects, which are directed and evaluated not by scientific peers but by experts chosen by governments or research councils (Nowotny *et al.* 2001). This can skew the depth of understanding in particular areas which are over-researched, and leave others relatively untouched. Powerful organisations can also utilise research outcomes for political ends. An example is the ways in which the tobacco industry managed, for years, to suppress research findings in relation to the health effects of smoking, or the ways in which, more recently, the Bush government in the USA attempted to suppress or discredit evidence of climate change (Harris, 2003). Indeed, the very use of the term "climate change" is a consequence of powerful attempts to minimise the need to take the kinds of actions which are implied in the use of the alternative term "global warming".

Imagination

A critical element in the relationship of research to society is the role of the creative imagination. This may take the form of unsubstantiated supposition, on the part of governmental and funding bodies, that what they fund is what they get. It may take the form of creative representations of the research capacity or achievements of their staff on the part of universities, and it may take the form of creative responses to policy on the part of researchers.

Within the neo-liberal view, governments attempt to control research communication through, for example, funding requirements and research assessment schemes. These mechanisms of control can be rationally supported through appealing to ideas of positivist research based on notions of detachment and non-involvement. Yet, at the same time, as we are seeing an increase in strategies put about by governments to measure research, to define research priority areas and dictate research agendas, so too we are seeing a proliferation of different ways of doing and communicating research. Attempts to measure and control academic research always have to be seen in the context of the existence, and perhaps growth, of ways of knowing which come from much more intricate and multifaceted thought. The generation of knowledge will not be controlled in the way that governments believe it will. The complex, fast-paced interplay between research and contemporary society means that, before mechanisms of control are devised, intellectual progress has made them outmoded. This is a consequence of what Nowotny *et al.* (2001) call "mode-2ishness". Mode 2 society arises, they argue, not through the existence of any one causal dimension of late modernity such as the dominance of the "market", or through the pervasive use of communication technologies, or globalisation. It arises through a number of processes underlying any or all of these: the generation of uncertainties, new kinds of economic rationality (e.g. what is likely to be funded), the role of expectations (the future being viewed as an extension of the present), what they call the "flexibilisation" of distance (both physical and social), and increasingly flexible and permeable social structures with a capacity for self-organisation. This echoes Bauman's idea that structures and systems are outmoded before they are established. Yet this too creates a paradox. Society creates a fiction about research in universities, and this is fed by media images. The view of research and the use of individual researchers and research teams to comment on matters of importance, to sit on expert panels and to officiate in public inquiries is often unconnected to the ways in which countries may view higher education institutions more generally.

One of the effects of governmental performative requirements in regard to research outputs is that the numbers of active researchers within universities has become known. For example, in the UK, 66% of academics were defined by their university as not sufficiently "research active" to be entered into the 2001 RAE (McNay, 2003). This means that myths about all academics on teaching and research contracts engaging in research are seen as just that: myths. Further, we know from research on research productivity that researchers do not inhabit a level playing field where research performance is concerned. There are many factors that contribute to productive research. These include institutional factors, for example the type and size of institution, the departmental climate—including the level of publication of colleagues and existence of post docs, level and type of funding, size of laboratories—and the academic discipline (Caroyol and Matt, 2006; Smeby and Try, 2005). Research productivity is also affected by the type and level of appointment, the number of years researchers have held tenure track positions, their age, their gender and their childcare responsibilities (Fox, 2005; Stack, 2004). Individual capabilities such as self-efficacy and confidence to carry out research also affect researcher productivity (Fisher, 2005; Toma, 1999), as do factors such as workload, time spent on research and on teaching, how many collaborators they have, how specialised the research is, the number of graduate assistant hours and doctoral supervision completions (Leahey, 2006; Lee and Bozeman, 2005). All of these factors will, in turn, affect academics' career progression. Yet the rhetoric in many universities assumes that researchers are all the same (Åkerlind, 2008). Each institution operates within imaginative fictions about its role and reputation in regard to research. Such fictions, often expressed in terms of mission statements or strategic plans, provide clues as to the kind of institution it believes itself to be, and give guidance about directions for the future.

There is a curious irony that so often a course of action taken by governments turns out to result in its opposite. So, in responding to a rationally driven political directive, researchers are required to create an imaginative but plausible fiction about where their research is likely to lead, knowing that research is full of surprises; that it is the unexpected finding that is likely to be the most revealing, or even to have the most impact. In order to operate within an academic environment, each person creates a fiction about the field of study in which they are involved, and their role and reputation within it. Research agendas cannot do without such fictions. They include the imaginative pursuit of new areas which seem to be promising, the creative specification of expected research outcomes and the narratives of track records researchers may be asked to produce. All of these are presented as rational responses to the situations in which researchers find themselves. Academics are dependent on fiction at the same time as privileging the rational.

Values

At the root of all that we say and do in relation to any aspect of research are sets of values which define what is considered important intellectually and to society. Academic research is caught up in a crisis of values. Most particularly, it is located within contradictory values. These are enshrined within decision-making, policies and strategies.

Research is traditionally an elite activity. It depends on the application of some of the most able minds in the world putting themselves to work to solve fundamental problems of human existence and survival. The demands of that society, as we saw above, are such that increasing numbers of experts other than those in universities are being called upon to explore issues, and society is increasingly "talking back" to experts. Research is thus becoming more democratic. However, democratic ideals sit uneasily with elitism. Nowotny *et al.* (2001) express a similar idea. They suggest there is a tension between enhancing "excellence" in research quality and productivity, and satisfying pressures from people in society to participate within knowledge production. This leads to "an inescapable contradiction between the university's scientific and social roles" (p. 87).

Universities are organised to develop and preserve elites through hierarchical structures. Indeed, power operates in a range of different ways to preserve research for the elite. Mass higher education, which is based on democratic ideals of education for all, has, paradoxically, led to elitist structures being reinforced. Undergraduate students increasingly have been distanced from academics. In Australia, for example, it is possible for students to go through their entire degree without ever knowing a tenured faculty member. Within university hierarchies there are unwritten but clear rules that define who is and who is not allowed, or capable of, or permitted to do, research. By and large, within universities, research is preserved for academics and for the higher years, and particularly for postgraduates, as if it were a kind of reward for hard work and academic achievement.

While there is frequently media attention given to discoveries made by undergraduate (and sometimes even school) students, and clearly a need in all areas of contemporary life for creative responses to the problems facing the world, governments and funding councils in the Western world, while espousing democratic values, not only preserve but also encourage research elites. Values conflicts are nowhere more stark than in relation to the setting up and funding of undergraduate research. Undergraduate students tend to be alienated from the research culture (Zamorski, 2002; Lindsay *et al.*, 2002), and consider it to be conducted behind closed doors (Robertson and Blackler, 2006). There is growth in inquiry-based modes of learning, but this generally takes place separately from the research activities of academics. Moves to introduce research in the early years of undergraduate education are resulting in students engaging in "research tasters". However, schemes to encourage undergraduate students to engage in research alongside academics require institutional, or at the very least departmental, schemes to be set up, and are non-existent in many countries. In some, they are almost considered taboo. Funding such programmes is a key stumbling block, and at national levels it is dependent upon research councils taking seriously the potential contribution to each university's research effort of undergraduate students. This is evident in the values and the work of the National Science Foundation in the USA, but it is by no means universal.

Values conflicts uphold practices in universities that define students as "other", exclude undergraduates, and also general staff and some academics from the research community, and preserve mechanisms that support and sustain particular views of research and views of students and what they are capable of. I borrow the idea of the "other" from post-colonial theorists such as Bhabha (1996), who explain that creating an identity for any group or culture inevitably creates an "other": those who are outside the group (Manathunga, 2006). Bourdieu (1988, pp. 88–9) argues that the academy is built on patronage, that the academic is required to wait until those with academic power permit them to go on to the next stage. This exercise of patronage means that those without academic power are required to engage in "submissive waiting":

> The exercise of academic power presupposes the aptitude and propensity, themselves socially acquired, to exploit the opportunities offered by the field: the capacity to "have pupils, to place them, to keep them in a relation of dependency" and thus to ensure the basis of a durable power, the fact of "having well-placed pupils" . . . implies perhaps above all the art of

manipulating other people's time, or, more precisely, their career rhythm, their curriculum vitae, to accelerate or defer achievements as different as success in competitive or other examinations, obtaining the doctorate, publishing articles or books, appointment to university posts, etc. And, as a corollary, this art, which is also one of the dimensions of power, is often only exercised with the more or less conscious complicity of the postulant, thus maintained, sometimes to quite an advanced age, in the docile and submissive, even somewhat infantile attitude which characterises the good pupil of all eras (Bourdieu, 1988, p. 88).

Researchers will follow a particular way of doing things if they are dependent upon the patronage of those with power who are likely to make decisions about them and about their future progress.

Closely related to democratic ideals are notions of inclusivity. Once again, values conflicts are evident. I have argued elsewhere that we need to develop universities as inclusive, scholarly, knowledge-building communities (Brew, 2006). This idea suggests expanded definitions and conceptions of teaching, of research and of knowledge. It involves considering how learning occurs for both academics and students, and reconsidering what research is and who generates it. It asks us to think about the kind of knowledge that is being generated and by whom; in other words, to seriously question who the scholars are in higher education. The notion of inclusive, scholarly, knowledge-building communities suggests that academics and students are engaged in a shared enterprise. It challenges us to think about what kinds of communities universities are and to consider the kinds of relationships between people in universities, specifically the kinds of relationships between academics and students. The democratisation of research implies universities setting as goals the inter-relationship of students as participating scholars and breaking down barriers to this, perhaps through collaborative research projects. Through the concept of inclusive, scholarly, knowledge-building communities the university becomes a partnership, where all take part in its growth and development through inquiries at different levels. This is not to say that everyone has equal strengths or equal knowledge. It does not mean that everyone is equally powerful. But it does mean that there is more of an awareness of issues of power and how power is exercised.

Such an ideal is based on a set of person-centred values that stress cooperation, inclusivity and mutual respect; the dispositions that Brookfield and Preskill (1999) suggest are central to democratic discussion. In contrast, the highly competitive nature of the grant applications process, shortage of research funding, and restrictions in the numbers of high-level university positions, means that the process of research can be extremely competitive. The intensity of this competition is heightened by the use of sporting and sometimes warlike metaphors in research policy (Brew 2001a, 2007).

Competition and cooperation are in a dialectical relationship in relation to research. Both are needed for it to be successful. Too much competition stifles cooperation. Shortage of funding encourages competition, yet research teams are needed for success in much research. In Big Science, international cooperation is essential because of the high cost of equipment. Often researchers are working in the context of international collaboration, ironically, when competing for scarce national resources within their own country.

In a study of the views of researchers (Brew, 2001b), it was found that some presented research as if the researcher was absent from, or incidental to, their awareness. In other words, the researcher as a person was not a focus of attention. For others the person of the researcher, their ideas and way of being was the main focus of attention when presenting ideas about the nature of research or talking about their research (Brew, 2001b). In one view (called the trading view) it is the career of the researcher, their reputation and how it is growing that is the focus of attention. In another (the journey view), in the centre of a researcher's awareness are the personal issues and dilemmas that perplex them, and how these concerns relate to the disciplinary issues that are the subjects of the research.

When researchers treat the person of the researcher as if absent from, or incidental to, awareness, writing about research in a detached, impersonal way presents few problems. Argument is viewed as an accepted and integral component of research. "Attacking" and "destroying" an argument is an accepted part of academic life. Treating ideas as if detached from persons allows this kind of behaviour. Researchers are expected to learn to "pick themselves up" after an "attack" on their ideas, or after being "knocked back" with a grant proposal or article submitted for publication.

This view of research embodies a different set of values to the view that places the person of the researcher as an integral part of the research. Fortunately, in many disciplinary areas there is a noticeable trend towards viewing research as a participative process; a conversation where each person makes sense of the research findings for themselves. This is to recognise that ideas are the ideas of people, that different people will have different perspectives, and that these different perspectives need to be respected and listened to. However, while academics can choose to conduct research and communicate research findings in collaborative ways, they are at the same time subject to the pressure of funding regimes and research assessment frameworks that require particular forms of expression and publication outlets which may take a more combative stance.

Reflexivity

Academics' views of research, then, are situated in multifaceted contexts in which competing interests and values cannot be reconciled but do have to be lived with. In writing about disciplines, Pinch (1990) draws attention to their rhetorical nature, to the ways in which academics are continually defining their disciplinary area in the normal course of doing academic work. The idea of a discipline, or belonging to a discipline, is a continual subject for critical reflection and appraisal. The concept of research is not like this. While academics may reflect on particular methodologies of research or particular techniques of investigation, what research is, as a phenomenon in higher education, is more often than not assumed. Academics deal in their research teams and departments with the minutiae of day-to-day responses to the different pressures and interests that I have described in this chapter, but by and large the meta-level reflexivity is missing. This is evident when we look at the academic literature on the nature of research and how it is understood by academics. There is a good deal of discussion about the nature of "science" from philosophical and empirical perspectives, and research is a subject for those whose discipline area is higher education policy and practice, but subject specialists are not concerned by and large with questions about what research is. This is similar to the situation that existed with regard to teaching until Boyer's (1990) notions of the scholarship of teaching raised questions about academics critically reflecting on teaching, and established a discourse amongst practitioners about its theory and practice. Arguably time pressures make this an impossibility for many academics, but critical reflection on teaching in higher education has led to the establishment of practice-based literatures, and the spread of ideas about university teaching in many disciplines. The same is not yet true of academic research.

Indeed, what is surprising to anyone interested in understanding the nature of research is how little research on research existed in the academic literature until about six or seven years ago. Although, as we have seen, university research is of central political, cultural and economic importance for nations, surprisingly little has been published that critically examines the ways that research is experienced within institutions of higher education (Åkerlind, 2008; Brew, 2001a, 2001b). Therefore, within the super-complexity of the relationship of research and society, we have relatively unsophisticated ways of understanding the many different ways in which academics think and act. Åkerlind (2008, p. 30) has recently highlighted the "hidden nature of the variation" in academics' ways of experiencing research. Disciplinary variation has long been used as an explanation for differences in ways of thinking about research. Yet we now know that this provides insufficient explanations (Brew, 2001b). Research has, until recently, been silent on understanding the varied responses of individuals within the academy to the neo-liberal agendas of governments, and the changing patterns of research activity and communications, contextualised within a fast-paced global society. It has been left to individual researchers and research teams to carve out ways of responding, without understanding how these fit into a more general theoretical framework. The result is that researchers coming from different perspectives on research fail to communicate effectively (Brew, 2001a).

This tells us something about the nature of research—that researchers are not, by and large, thinking about Research with a capital "R". Their focus is more often than not on the specific research they are engaged in, not on the relationship of research to society. Åkerlind (2008) identified four categories of variation in academics' views of "being a researcher". Three of these looked inwards to what the researcher was doing: fulfilling academic requirements, establishing oneself in the field, developing oneself personally. Only the fourth category—enabling broader change—looks outwards to society. In the context of the argument of this chapter, this is curious. It is another example of the paradoxical nature of the relationship of research to contemporary society. I have argued, following Nowotny et al. (2001), that academics are having to balance competing interests and values, and that society is developing an intimate relationship with research and researchers. So how is it possible that many academics' understandings of being a researcher do not take account of society?

Bauman provides an explanation:

> Unable to slow the mind-boggling pace of change, let alone to predict and control its direction, we focus on things we can, or believe we can, or are assured that we can influence: we try to calculate and minimise the risk that we personally, or those nearest and dearest to us in that moment, might fall victim to the uncounted and uncountable dangers which the opaque world and its uncertain future are suspected to hold in store for us (Bauman, 2007, p. 11).

Giddens (1999), too, draws attention to the ways in which globalisation has resulted in focusing attention on local concerns, witnessed in the move to devolution in countries like the UK, and a focus on "family values". Both Bauman and Giddens see this as a process of minimising risk. As far as academic research is concerned, it is a reminder that every act of wanting to know within a research context implicates an act of not wanting to know. Ironically, in conditions of supercomplexity, ambiguity and fluidity in the interrelationship of research and society, global problems can only be addressed, as far as academic researchers are concerned, by focusing on what is, at a particular moment and in a particular context, clear, simple and immediate.

Conclusion

This chapter has explored a range of different ironic responses in relation to research in contemporary society. I have examined competing interests served by academic research, and traced the ways in which governmental neo-liberal agendas have developed alongside an intellectual freeing up of methodologies and ways of doing research. I have pointed to the ways in which, by trying to meet competing agendas, academics may fail to satisfy them. I have noted ways in which power is exercised within universities, and have explored how research is sustained by the ways in which society, universities and individuals create fictions about themselves and their work in relation to research agendas. I have examined the conflicts in values relating to research in society. In particular,

I have explored the ways in which elitism is preserved within the academy, while democratic values are espoused. I have also examined the ways in which the values of inclusivity are denied through power. I have provided a glimpse of what research might look like if person-centred values were dominant, and identified conflicts with current practice. Finally, I have suggested that researchers face the risks of coping with the complexity and ambiguity of a contemporary globalised society by minimising their reflexive awareness and focusing on their immediate concerns.

At every turn, contradictions have been noted. This is inescapable, owing to the ambiguous, pluralistic, supercomplex world in which we live, and the creativity associated within the very heart of what we understand as academic research. We do not know what new ideas will yet emerge to challenge and explain society, and we do not know where such ideas may come from; whether they may be creative responses to what has been discovered before, or resistances to initiatives, policies and strategies devised by politicians and bureaucrats. What is clear is that there is no going back to the ivory tower. Academic research will continue to be integrated with society, and will continue to find ways to explain it. Importantly, the relationship of research to contemporary society will continue to challenge the creativity of those whose concern is with discovering new understandings of aspects of reality, and also those whose creative concern is with providing policies and resources to support it.

References

Åkerlind, G. (2008). An academic perspective on research and being a researcher: an integration of the literature. *Studies in Higher Education, 33*(1), 17–31.

Barnett, R. (2000). *Realizing the University in an Age of Super-complexity*. Buckingham: Open University Press.

Bauman, Z. (2006). *Liquid Life*. Cambridge: Polity Press.

Bauman, Z. (2007). *Liquid Times: Living in an age of uncertainty*. Cambridge: Polity Press.

Bhabha, H. (1996). The other question: Difference, discrimination, and the discourse of colonialism. In H. Baker, M. Diawara and R. Lindeborg, *Black British cultural studies: A reader* (pp. 87–106). Chicago: University of Chicago Press.

Bourdieu, P. (1988). *Homo Academicus*. Translated from the French by P. Collier. Cambridge: Polity Press.

Boyer, E.L. (1990). *Scholarship Reconsidered: Priorities of the Professoriate*. Princeton, NJ: Carnegie Foundation for the Advancement of Learning.

Brew, A. (2001a). *The Nature of Research: Inquiry in Academic Contexts*. London: RoutledgeFalmer.

Brew, A. (2001b). Conceptions of Research: A phenomenographic study. *Studies in Higher Education, 26*(2), 271–285.

Brew, A. (2006). *Research and Teaching: Beyond the Divide*. London: Palgrave Macmillan.

Brew, A. (2007). Academic autonomy and research decision-making: the researcher's view. In M. Tight, C. Kayrooz and G.S. Åkerlind (eds), *International Perspectives of Higher Education Research, Vol 4—Autonomy in Social Science Research: The view from United Kingdom and Australian Universities* (pp. 47–64). Oxford: Elsevier.

Brookfield, S. and Preskill, S. (1999). *Discussion as a Way of Teaching: Tools and Techniques for University Teachers*. Buckingham: Open University Press.

Campbel, D.F.J. (2003). The evaluation of university research in the United Kingdom and the Netherlands. In P. Shapira and S. Kuhlmann (eds) *Learning from Science and Technology Policy Evaluation* (pp. 98–131). Cheltenham: Edward Elgar Publishing.

Caroyol, N. and Matt, M. (2006). Individual and collective determinants of academic scientists productivity. *Information Economics and Policy, 18*, 55–72.

Fisher, R.L. (2005). *The research productivity of scientists: how gender, organisation culture and the problem choice process influence the productivity of scientists*. Oxford: University Press of America.

Fox, M. (2005). Gender, family characteristics, and publication productivity among scientists. *Social Studies of Science, 35*(1), 131–150.

Giddens, A. (1999). *Runaway World: How Globalisation is Reshaping Our Lives*. London: Profile Books.

Glassick, C.E., Huber, M.T. and Maeroff, G.I. (1997). *Scholarship Assessed: Evaluation of the Professoriate*. An Ernest L Boyer Project of the Carnegie Foundation for the Advancement of Teaching. San Franscisco, CA: Jossey-Bass.

Harris, P. (2003). Bush covers up climate research. *The Observer*. Accessed 28 April 2008 from http://www.guardian.co.uk/environment/2003/sep/21/usnews.georgewbush/print

Kogan, M. and Henkel, M. (1992). Constraints on the individual researcher. In T.G. Whiston and R.L. Geiger (eds) *Research and Higher Education* (pp. 112–116). Buckingham: Open University Press.

Leahey, E. (2006). Gender differences in productivity: Research specialization as a missing link. *Gender Society, 20*, 754–780.

Lee, S. and Bozeman, B. (2005). The impact of research collaboration on scientific productivity. *Social Studies of Science, 35*(5), 673–702.

Lindsay, R., Breen, R. and Jenkins, A. (2002). Academic research and teaching quality: the views of undergraduate and postgraduate students. *Studies in Higher Education, 27*(3), 309–327.

Lucas, L. (2006). *The Research Game in Academic Life.* Buckingham: Open University Press.

Manathunga, C. (2006). Doing educational development ambivalently: Applying post-colonial metaphors to educational development? *International Journal for Academic Development, 11*(1), 19–29.

Marginson, S. (2007). Freedom as control and the control of freedom: F.A. Hayek and the academic imagination. In M. Tight, C. Kayrooz and G.S. Åkerlind (eds) *International Perspectives of Higher Education Research, Vol 4—Autonomy in Social Science Research: The view from United Kingdom and Australian Universities* (pp. 67–104). Oxford: Elsevier.

Marginson, S. and Considine, M. (2000). *The Enterprise University: Power, Governance and Reinvention in Australia.* Cambridge: Cambridge University Press.

McNay, I. (2003). Assessing the assessment: an analysis of the UK Research Assessment Exercise, 2001, and its outcomes, with special reference to research in education. *Science and Public Policy, 30*(3), 1–8.

Nowotny, H., Scott, P. and Gibbons, M. (2001). *Re-thinking Science: Knowledge and the Public in an Age of Uncertainty.* Cambridge: Polity Press.

Pinch, T. (1990). The culture of scientists and disciplinary rhetoric. *European Journal of Education, 25*(3), 295–304.

Robertson, J. and Blackler, G. (2006). Students' experiences of learning in a research environment. *Higher Education Research and Development, 25*(3), 215–229.

Slaughter, S. (1993). Beyond basic science: research university presidents; narratives of science policy. *Science, Technology and Human Values, 18*(3), 278–302.

Smeby, J.C. and Try, S. (2005). Departmental contexts and faculty research activity in Norway. *Research in Higher Education, 46*(6), 593–619.

Stack, S. (2004). Gender, children and research productivity. *Research in Higher Education, 45*(8), 891–920.

Toma, I.D. (1999). Understanding why scholars choose to work in alternative inquiry paradigms. *Research in Higher Education, 40*(5), 539–569.

Zamorski, B. (2002). Research-led teaching and learning in higher education: a case. *Teaching in Higher Education, 7*(4), 411–427.

35
Disciplinarity

Ruth Neumann

Knowledge is the core business of universities. In its different forms and structures, knowledge provides the underlying basis for how a university is organised and how it conducts its teaching and research. Disciplines, or "bundles of knowledge" (Clark, 1983), embody different knowledge forms reflecting both epistemological approaches and the social aspects of knowledge communities. However, knowledge is not static. As knowledge increases, changes and becomes more specialised, the number of disciplines continues to increase. This dynamic nature is reflected in the differing organisational structures of knowledge within universities over time and across countries. While disciplines form the most important basis underpinning academic organisation, there is an ever more complex array of fields of study and sub-disciplines, as well as emerging areas of interdisciplinary knowledge and inquiry. Knowledge boundaries are contestable and flexible.

The word "discipline" is by definition an association between knowledge and learning and instruction within an organisation, typically a university. This organisational structure is conducive to learning, and forms a protective boundary for teaching and research, yet is sufficiently flexible to accommodate change originating from both within the institution and from external influences. Closely intertwined with the notion of disciplines and learning is the conception of research. In the discussion of disciplinarity in this chapter, three key turning points in the conception of research are evident. The first is the notion of "research" as the critical interpretation of existing, accepted knowledge combined with original thought. The second is the discovery and advancement of new knowledge, resulting in our present distinction between research and scholarship. The third, with reference to differing modes of knowledge production, is the investigation of problems of social significance combining and applying knowledge and method from more than one discipline.

Understanding disciplinarity is a fascinating story which unfolds in the sections below. The first part examines the nature and structure of knowledge, the second reviews organisational structures within universities to accommodate disciplines, and the third discusses the role of disciplines in teaching and research.

The Structure of Knowledge

The Nature of Disciplines and Knowledge Forms

Disciplines are organisational structures of knowledge and different disciplines are composed of different forms of knowledge. Kockelmans (1979) traces the origins and changing meanings of the word discipline from the Latin "disciplina". From its beginnings, the word discipline was associated with the process of instruction and learning, with usage from the late Middle Ages onwards denoting the process of instruction in specific subject matter. Thus, discipline is "the educational process associated with one of the branches of scientific knowledge" (Kockelmans, 1979, p. 17). It is also a "recognised branch or segment of knowledge within rational learning, with certain generally agreed upon canons and standards" (Kiger 1923, quoted in Swoboda, 1979, p. 52). The Oxford English Dictionary (2002) provides six definitions and usages of "discipline", which span training from ways of behaving and thinking to branches of learning and instruction. These definitions cover knowledge content, epistemology and social aspects of knowledge communities. As our understanding of disciplines deepens, it is increasingly understood that students' formal learning and specialisation in specific disciplines involves not only knowledge of specific subject matter, but also participation in a social, cultural process of ways of thinking and approaching learning.

Disciplines comprise a number of accepted features. A discipline encompasses a general body of knowledge, with some agreed logical taxonomy, and accepted basic literature which defines its parameters. A discipline has its own specialised vocabulary and an accepted body of theory. A discipline also has a sense of sequence, which enables researchers to discuss gaps in disciplinary knowledge, theory and research. There are accepted techniques and methods of theory testing, revision and generation, and recognised techniques for replication and (re)validation of research. Disciplines have established communication methods, which include professional associations, conferences and journals with peer-reviewed publications. There is a recognised progression of experiences and preparation for the development of researchers and teachers in the discipline.

Disciplines display differing levels of maturity, and there is a recognised positioning in relation to other disciplines, as well as linkages and lineages between disciplines. Becher's (1989) landmark study of disciplinary enquiry and cultures highlights the high status accorded physics among the sciences, and the higher recognition of history compared with geography. Within disciplines, Becher notes a further pecking order where "mathematical economists were considered the *crème de la crème* within the discipline; 'messy' areas such as labour economics were generally given a low rating" (1989:57). Within this hierarchy of disciplines, those that are more theoretical are accorded a higher status than the more practical disciplines, a tradition that can be traced to Aristotle's knowledge hierarchy of theoretical, practical and productive. The highest status was accorded to the theoretical subjects of theology, mathematics and physics. Philosophy has long been seen as the key discipline, uniting and transcending other knowledge forms. Seen as a discipline with a unified form of knowledge, it has incorporated many now separate disciplines: psychology, sociology, science and mathematics (Moran, 2002).

This discussion has highlighted the evolution of the term "discipline" and its connection of a body of knowledge with learning and instruction, particularly within a university. Through its origin from the Latin "disciplina", it is argued that the learning within a discipline implies a hierarchy and the operation of power, where there is specialised and valued knowledge possessed by some but not by others. Thus, intertwined in "discipline" are specialised knowledge and accepted processes in relation to that knowledge form, located within a formal learning institution which prepares students for a profession.

Disciplinary Developments: An Historical Overview

Taking an historical perspective, the academics of the early universities were comparatively unspecialised, practising a holistic and unitary view of knowledge. The purpose of the curriculum was to prepare students for careers in the church, law, medicine, public administration and education, while at the same time forming the basis of learning for a well-educated and well-rounded "man".

Within the early universities of the twelfth to fourteenth centuries, knowledge was organised into what were termed the seven liberal arts. These comprised the trivium, the disciplines of grammar, rhetoric, and dialectic, and the quadrivium, consisting of arithmetic, astronomy, geometry and music (Perkin, 1984). This medieval curriculum stemmed from the world of learning of ancient Greece, and the organisation of knowledge into these disciplines in the medieval university forms the basis of many academic disciplines today. Learning was grouped into four faculties: arts, and the three higher ("superior") faculties of law, medicine and theology (Rudy, 1984). These university disciplines remained essentially unchanged for several hundred years. The Renaissance period brought some additional disciplines into the arts faculty: Greek literature, languages such as Hebrew and ancient Greek, poetry, history, and a widening of philosophy to include Platonic as well as Aristotelian philosophy (Rudy, 1984).

During the Enlightenment the range of disciplines within universities expanded to include applied science, medical science, economics, animal husbandry, agriculture and public finance (Rudy, 1984). In a few German universities science and research in scientific disciplines was introduced into the curriculum and the university mission, paving the way for more far-reaching changes in disciplinarity and knowledge-creation within universities. The period of the Enlightenment emphasised the "progress of human knowledge through the powers of reason and rationality. This pursuit of reason was underpinned by the development of clearer procedures and methodologies within disciplines, and greater specialisation of learning, changes that were most keenly felt in the sciences and mathematics" (Moran, 2002, p. 5).

However, until 1800 much of the growth in disciplines, especially science disciplines, took place outside of universities in academies, societies and specialised institutions such as the Accademia Secretorum Natura in Naples and the Royal Society in England (Redner, 1987). Within universities the medieval curriculum remained dominant, continuing to prepare students for careers in law, public administration and medicine. During the late eighteenth and early nineteenth century, university learning and its curriculum became revitalised, forming the basis of the modern university in terms of disciplines, research and teaching. Among the important changes were the institutionalisation of science (Redner, 1987) into universities, as well as the introduction of our current notion of research as the discovery of new knowledge as a core university function. Research involved not only the re-interpretation of knowledge but the creation of new knowledge, with a consequent increase in the number of disciplines within universities. During the nineteenth century there was a veritable explosion of knowledge, leading to a broadened definition of both university learning and the range of disciplines taught within universities. The German education reforms of Wilhelm von Humboldt and the creation of the University of Berlin became the prototype for the modern research university. This fundamental development, the introduction of the science disciplines in universities, gradually spread across Europe, the US and Japan.

The development and expansion of university disciplines in the period to the late eighteenth century was stronger in the humanities and professional areas such as law than in scientific disciplines. Until the pioneering example of German universities, such as Halle and Goettingen, the scientific disciplines remained stronger outside the university than within. The University of Goettingen, however, offered an expansive range of disciplines, spanning history, literature, archaeology, science, medicine, chemistry, metallurgy and agriculture, with superb library and laboratory resources (Rudy, 1984). The development of learning through seminars, and the productivity of Goettingen's teachers and students in contributing to scientific knowledge, provided the context for von Humboldt's vision of a university, epitomised in the formation of the University of Berlin in 1810. From the nineteenth century onwards the university, its disciplinary range and revitalised teaching and research approaches was reformed and re-instituted (Redner, 1987).

Importantly the university organisation provided the environment to "professionalise knowledge", with its continuous tradition of debate and disputation in teaching, and a reasonable degree of political autonomy and independence (Redner, 1987; Leff, 1968). In structural terms the new disciplines were accommodated within the existing loose framework of faculties. However, learning moved from broad general education by multidisciplinary faculties to learning within specialised disciplines (Swoboda, 1979).

Disciplinary Proliferation and Beyond

The shift from the notion of research as the critical engagement with accepted knowledge to research as the creation of "new" knowledge, discovery and experimentation revolutionised universities in all countries. In addition, the institutionalisation of science within universities proliferated knowledge and hence disciplines. By the early twentieth century these changes had been adopted in all countries with established universities. The impact was profound. By the latter half of the twentieth century there was a still increasing array of disciplines and sub-disciplines, as well as the emergence of moves to counteract the increasing specialisation and fragmentation of knowledge through interdisciplinary and other forms of working.

The expansion in knowledge from the nineteenth century onwards has shown that disciplines change continually. They can evolve, grow and decline. What is a discipline is not necessarily straightforward and is open to discussion. There are temporal dimensions, and there may also be national and institutional dimensions. Disciplines consist of conglomerates of individuals and specialist groups, connected by subject matter and shared methodological approaches. Within disciplines specialisms or specialisations can become quite substantial in size, often diverging or becoming increasingly independent from the main discipline, in terms of cultural and methodological approaches, with alternate communication channels through the establishment of new journals and conferences for meeting and networking. There are essentially four ways that new disciplines are formed. They can arise through forces internal to disciplines or through external social forces (Becher, 1989).

When changes arise internally differentiation and separation can occur either through fission or fusion. In the former process an increasingly larger and independent specialism establishes an autonomous existence, breaking away from the parent discipline. The case of computing separating from mathematics is one such example. The establishment of a new discipline through fusion, as in the case of biochemistry, results from the merging of two overlapping specialisms in different disciplines, namely biology and chemistry. Institutional processes in such separations do not necessarily occur with ease, and generally span quite some time. There may be a progression of moving the specialisation or emerging discipline into a research institute, or to establish connections with teaching programmes beyond the discipline. These steps do not involve strong commitments by institutions and represent an incomplete differentiation. A later step would be the establishment of a new department which includes undergraduate instruction. The formation of a new, separate department represents "an almost irreversible differentiation, for universities are strongly committed to departments of instruction" (Hagstrom, 1965, p. 123).

There are other forms of disciplinary formation which derive from external societal stimulus. For example, the introduction of professional fields such as accounting, management and nursing are responses to market demand. From their beginning, universities have prepared students for professions and public administration. Among the earliest examples are law and medicine. Since then many professions have been included, and the establishment of university study in vocational areas forms part of the formation of their professional identity and professionalisation. In such developments the vocational areas add to their applied focus more theoretical elements, in a process of "intellectualisation". A second form of responding to external forces is the establishment of disciplines (and departments) in technical areas which fulfil specific social functions. Some recent examples are aeronautical engineering, biotechnology and medical physics. These involve the reorganisation of existing knowledge and technical specialisations to form a newly identified area of study and research. Non-technical areas, such as peace and conflict studies and women's studies, may also be placed in this category.

There is also disciplinary decline. A global analysis of science disciplines in the twentieth century shows that disciplines characterised as fixed-categorical fields, such as astronomy, botany and zoology, declined precipitously, while those disciplines characteristised as dynamic-network fields, such as geology, biology, chemistry, physics and mathematics, did not (Gabler and Frank, 2005). Disciplines or areas of study introduced via external forces for change can also decline, reflecting social changes in the priorities of specialisation, or through (re-)incorporation into a parent discipline.

The discussion highlights not only the explosion of disciplines in a relatively short period of time, but also draws attention to how this proliferation occurs, and the constant change that helps to underline the fluid nature of disciplinary boundaries. With the rapid expansion of knowledge have come concerns that so much specialised knowledge results in fragmentation of knowledge. By the mid-twentieth century the expansion of universities, students, learning and disciplines produced calls to focus on solving social problems, not only problems arising from the discipline.

The two types of problem-solving or research were termed mode 2 and mode 1 respectively (Gibbons et al., 1994). The distinction attempts to capture the diversified types and sites of knowledge production within the context of mass access to higher education. Mode 1 knowledge production distinguishes the "traditional" disciplinary approach to knowledge and its production, while mode 2 knowledge production is focused on the context of application, reflecting issues of social and economic concern. By its very nature, mode 2 is described as transdisciplinary, utilising a range of theoretical perspectives and practical methodologies in solving problems. It is not interdisciplinary in drawing on existing disciplines, nor is it a process of leading to the formation of new disciplines.

This discussion is an important one, which highlights that the forms of knowledge production have further diversified, reflecting the variety of problems and the central role of knowledge in modern societies. The discussion relates not only to research but also to teaching and learning, where there are debates about the need to integrate knowledge and avoid fragmentation. This discussion moves beyond the disciplines and introduces the ideas of interdisciplinarity, multidisciplinarity and transdisciplinarity, all serving in different ways to counter the specialisation of disciplinarity.

The term interdisciplinary can be traced to the 1920s, becoming more prevalent across the social sciences and humanities post-World War II (Moran, 2002). Discussions of interdisciplinarity relate to the structure of knowledge and of education. The notion of interdisciplinarity involves two or more disciplines interacting in research or learning, and together producing an outcome (Rowntree, 1982; Gordon and Lawton, 1993). Thus, interdisciplinarity addresses issues and problems for which there are not solutions within an existing discipline alone, thus requiring dialogue and interaction between two or more disciplines. The ambiguity of the prefix "inter" has been noted as allowing interpretations of interdisciplinary as a means of creating connections between different disciplines, or as a means of forming a space between or beyond the disciplinary boundaries. It can thus also be described as transdisciplinary, anti-disciplinary, or post-disciplinary. However, Moran (2002, p. 17) argues that the very nature of the term interdisciplinary "assumes the existence and relative resilience of disciplines as modes of thought and institutional practices".

Interdisciplinary can be distinguished from multidisciplinary, which refers to the co-existence of several disciplines. In the former case, there is not necessarily any interaction between disciplines or disciplinary perspectives. Multidisciplinarity exists where several disciplines are offered as part of a combined degree, or in courses that are team-taught by members of different disciplines. The connection is one of proximity rather than interaction or integration between the disciplines (Rowntree, 1982).

Transdisciplinary can be used interchangeably with interdisciplinary to convey the notion of going beyond or transcending disciplinary boundaries. The prefix "trans" may be seen as less ambiguous than the prefix "inter". Essentially, transciplinarity is a new form of learning and solving complex problems, requiring cooperation among academics and stakeholders external to the university (Klein, 2004). The emphasis is on practice and current social problems, which involve the full range of research approaches from basic, through applied and problem-oriented, and involve multiple stakeholders in problem investigation and solution. Transdisciplinary research is demand-driven from outside the discipline. Hence, the focus is strongly on inclusion of researchers and problem-solvers beyond and outside of the university, as in the mode 2 definition of Gibbons *et al.*, (1994). By its very nature, transdisciplinarity focuses on ever-changing problems to be solved, and is a mode of operating which is not intended to create new disciplines or longer-term areas of study.

Categorisation of Knowledge Types or Taxonomies of Knowledge

By the mid-twentieth century the proliferation of disciplines was such that researchers became increasingly interested in the epistemological and social nature of disciplines. In addition, the "massification" of higher education produced a growing number of scholars interested in studying higher education, including its organisational and cultural aspects. Together, these trends produced models and frameworks for the categorisation and characterisation of knowledge, and the application of these frameworks to examining higher education.

The examination of differences and relations between disciplines has an established history in philosophy and the sociology of knowledge and science. Particularly powerful has been the work on paradigms and paradigm development within fields of knowledge. Work in this tradition discusses knowledge fields as theoretical or empirical, restricted and unrestricted, mature-effective and immature-ineffective, and pre-paradigmatic and paradigmatic (see discussions of Conant, Pantic, Ravetz and Kuhn in Becher, 1989, and Braxton and Hargens, 1996). Among the more influential frameworks are those of Kolb (1984) and Biglan (1973a, 1973b), subsequently adapted by Becher in empirical research on disciplines and their cultures (1989; Becher and Trowler, 2001; see also Table 35.1). Central to these approaches are the appreciation of the multi-dimensional nature of disciplines (Trowler, 1998), and the incorporation of both the epistemological attributes and the social features which comprise disciplines.

Biglan's typology of disciplines consists of three dimensions:

1. Hard–soft: the degree to which there is a shared inquiry paradigm.
2. Pure–applied: the concern for application to practical problems.
3. Life–non-life: the extent of orientation to living organisms.

These three dimensions can be arranged into eight categories: hard–life–pure; hard–non-life–pure; soft–life–pure; soft–non-life–pure; hard–life–applied; hard–non-life–applied; soft–life–applied;

Table 35.1 A Schematic Presentation of the Discipline Classifications

Becher/Biglan	Kolb	Disciplinary areas
Hard–pure	Abstract–reflective	Natural sciences
Soft–pure	Concrete–reflective	Humanities & social sciences
Hard–applied	Abstract–active	Science-based professions
Soft–applied	Concrete–active	Social professions

Source: Becher, 1994, p. 152.

soft–non-life–applied. This typology has been replicated and applied in numerous subsequent investigations, and found to be robust across institutions as well as at the individual and department levels (e.g. see Braxton and Hargens, 1996; Creswell and Bean, 1981; Creswell and Roskens, 1981; Creswell *et al.*, 1981; Smart and Elton, 1982; Stoecker, 1993).

The usefulness of such disciplinary categorisations is that they are differentiated and sufficiently subtle to enable meaningful comparisons across the various disciplines without "losing the wood for the trees". Broad knowledge categorisations can be argued to blur or neglect subtle variations at the more micro-level; however, there is the advantage that through its apparent simplification the most significant features are highlighted and clarified. The categorisation recognises that knowledge-based structures are of fundamental significance, and that the epistemological cannot be separated from the social. The central features of these knowledge classifications will now be outlined (Neumann, 2003a, pp. 225–226).

Hard–pure knowledge (typically sciences such as physics or chemistry) is typified as having a cumulative, atomistic structure, concerned with universals, simplification and a quantitative emphasis. Knowledge communities tend to be competitive but gregarious, and joint or multiple authorship is commonplace. Soft–pure knowledge (such as history and anthropology) is in contrast reiterative, holistic, concerned with particulars and has a qualitative bias. There is no sense of superseded knowledge, as in hard–pure fields. Scholarly enquiry is typically a solitary pursuit, with a limited overlap of interest between researchers.

Hard–applied knowledge (as in engineering and agriculture) derives its underpinnings from hard–pure enquiry, is concerned with mastery of the physical environment, and geared towards products and techniques. Soft–applied knowledge (such as education, law and management studies), in its turn, is dependent on soft–pure knowledge, being concerned with the enhancement of professional practice and aiming to yield protocols and procedures. Applied knowledge communities, especially hard–applied ones, are also gregarious, with multiple influences and interactions on both their teaching and research activity (Biglan, 1973b).

Knowledge forms can be seen as a continuum, with disciplinary boundaries somewhat arbitrary and contestable. Most disciplines have a diversity of research styles and epistemological characteristics. Further, disciplines, and the sub-disciplines within them, can be seen to straddle discipline groups. Economics, for example, can be argued to contain a spectrum from hard–pure to soft–pure; while geography comprises physical geography, a hard knowledge categorisation, and human geography, a soft one. Some parts of engineering may be seen as less applied and closer to the pure end of the spectrum than others.

The Organisation of Knowledge and Learning within Universities

Universities and their internal organisational structures have been identified as a crucial component of the successful housing of disciplines. These structures have provided legitimate authority and effective protection for the core teaching and research functions of the university. At the same time, they have been sufficiently flexible and adaptable to accommodate change, both from within and from outside the university. In effect, the structures have become increasingly diversified and specialised, reflecting the changing view of knowledge, from complete and universal to provisional and hypothetical.

In the broadest of designations, university structures prior to the eighteenth century can be described as pre-disciplinary, those of the nineteenth and twentieth centuries as disciplinary. Universities have moved from teaching a small number of elite subjects, taught by a relatively unspecialised academic profession able to teach all subjects, to highly specialised knowledge enterprises. It is the disciplines that provide the main institutional organising base and the avenue of authority, work and belief (Clark, 1984). Disciplines, established as departments or similar academic organisational units, thus provide the major structuring for the academic work roles of research and teaching. This disciplinary organisation strongly conditions how duties and responsibilities are allocated, while Clark's master matrix of organisation insightfully captures the dynamic relationship between discipline and institution. As Clark observes:

> . . . the concentration on knowledge is what academics have most in common. But what they have least in common is common knowledge, since the bundles they tend are specialized and separated one from another (1984, p. 107).

From the mid-twentieth century it can be argued that there has been a development of post-disciplinary structures. The nature of knowledge and the types of questions being asked within disciplines increasingly requires alliances beyond the immediate discipline or department. Similarly, there is greater pluralism in the locations of knowledge production and knowledge use, requiring differing combinations of disciplinary knowledge to be drawn on (Weingart and Stehr, 2000). There is simultaneously the push to further specialisation, for which the departmental structures have been well suited, as well as increasing cross-disciplinary needs to form and maintain informal alliances for teaching and research programmes (Straus, 1973). Institutional responses enable the offering of courses and programmes combining different departmental teaching programmes, and the establishment of large research centres and institutes arranged around a cluster of connected disciplines, or related to specific problems.

There is a need for structural flexibility. Departments are efficient means for teaching, learning and research, and hence provide strong counters for interdisciplinary initiatives in universities. The advancement of knowledge requires specialisation and departmentalisation, as well as the opportunity for free and easy cross-fertilisation. However, the dynamics of institutionalisation are overwhelmingly disciplinary and have transformed previous potential interdisciplinarities, such as education, into disciplines proper (Swoboda, 1979). Interdisciplinary structures are likely to remain temporary or isolated phenomena, resulting in termination or absorption into existing disciplines. The solution of problems within mode 2 forms, by their very nature, will require flexible but temporary structures (Gibbons et al., 1994). The co-evolution of knowledge and structure highlight the complexity of academic organisation. Nevertheless, highly specialised disciplinary organisation remains the hallmark of what is the "modern university".

Clark's organisational master matrix represents the intersection between the discipline and the local institution. Hence the academic department can be seen as an organisational subculture, representing the junction between the two broader cultures of the discipline and the institution. The cultural forces contributed by the institution and the discipline to the department are not necessarily shared, and reflect both the status of the discipline and the status of the institution (Lee, 2007). Lee's study of departmental culture, utilising a large US national data set, finds that in many ways the institution forms a more influential role within the department than the discipline. The crucial factor is the degree to which a university is teaching- or research-oriented. A commitment to research is largely a function of the university not the discipline, and the pervasiveness of disciplinary cultures appears particularly evident within large research institutions (Lee, 2007; Ruscio, 1987; Clark, 1987).

Continuity and Change in Formal Organisational Structures

Structural change within universities tends to be additive and the total elimination of structural units rare (Gumport and Snydman, 2002). Thus, the investigation of disciplinarity and organisational structure over time will inevitably find enduring organisational features and structural elements which connect the present to the past.

Five forms of structural change have been proposed (Gumport and Snydman, 2002):

1. Knowledge differentiation: such as the separation of engineering into multiple, new entities—electrical, industrial, civil, mechanical, chemical.
2. Knowledge promotion: the labelling change from "department" to "school", "division" or "college", to reflect the expansion in overall academic programme structure or programme offering at postgraduate level. Examples include the change from department of nursing to school of nursing, or department of business to graduate school of management.
3. Knowledge evolution: name changes which signal substantial change in the knowledge associated with the area and/or change in professional legitimacy. An example would be the transformation of the librarianship department to the department of library sciences and later library information sciences.
4. Knowledge consolidation: evident through departmental mergers and consequently often name changes. For example six initial departments in a school of business were consolidated into three, and later these three departments underwent further name changes (marketing, management information systems, decision sciences). Such consolidation and name changes reflected changes in business school programmes nationally.
5. Knowledge stability: where no change may have occurred for a period of time, reflecting structural persistence.

The different changes outlined translate across nations. Indeed, the names of university departments reveal how we organise and codify knowledge. In a cross-national analysis of academic departments or units involved in both teaching and research functions across three Commonwealth countries (the UK, Australia and Nigeria), Tight (2003a, 2003b) highlighted that, while departmental names are reflective of the disciplinary area/field, there can be peculiarities related to national systems, as well as considerable diversity within a country (e.g. German, German Language and Literature, German Studies, Germanic Studies). However, it is noted that long-established disciplines, such as law, physics, philosophy and chemistry, display less variety in terms of departmental titles. Highlighting the strength of disciplinary structures, compared with interdisciplinary ones, Tight's analysis found little evidence of thematic departments created by massification. Similarly, a global analysis of science departments, based on academic staff composition over the twentieth century, while highlighting changes and trends within science, still found that throughout the world the vast majority of basic natural sciences continue in the well-established disciplines: mathematics, physics, chemistry, biology, astronomy, botany, geology, zoology (Gabler and Frank, 2005).

Variations across Time and Types of University

The knowledge-based organisation of universities is fluid rather than "hard-wired", influenced by university type, time and space. The continual subdivision and re-combination of discipline-based organisational units provides a map or directory of the world of learning (Storer and Parsons, 1968). For example, electronics, nuclear engineering and astronomy are all spawned from physics, while cell biology, neuroscience, pharmacology and biochemistry had their origins in biology.

The flexibility of institutional organisational divisions can be seen in the various branches of learning within departments (Becher, 1989, 1983; Neumann, 2003a, p. 221). Material science, for example, can be located in physics or in chemistry. Astronomy may be incorporated within a physics department or form a department on its own. Theoretical physics is closer to mathematics than solid state physics, which can also be located in chemistry, while electronics and hydraulics form part of the applied end of the spectrum, forming connections with branches of engineering. Engineering has itself diversified, drawing on changes within physics, chemistry and biology. Disciplines also change in their epistemology. Economics, for example, is recognised to have moved from the social science end of the spectrum to being more mathematical in character.

Institutional context can influence disciplinary perspective. The case of law in Australia shows that some universities have drawn attention to conservative curricula focusing on the more formal aspects of law ("black-letter law"), while others have more radical and critical emphases (McInnis and Marginson, 1994; Pearce *et al.*, 1987). Conventional universities will house departments of history, while more recently established universities will incorporate history in cultural studies. Church (1976) illustrates the changes in history over time and space by comparing the development of the discipline in Britain and France, and argues the importance of the wider social and cultural context. A global analysis of history across 89 countries during the twentieth century maintains that history has shifted from a concentration on great civilisations to examining nation-states as "societies" with common identities and problems. It is argued that the history curriculum globally reflects worldwide changes in models of "society" (Frank *et al.*, 2000).

Disciplines and Their Role in University Teaching and Research

An academic's identity is entwined in their discipline (Henkel, 2000; Silver, 2003). Strength of commitment to the discipline forms the basis for career, activity and identity. Clearly it also impacts and is reflected in the research and teaching roles. The influence of disciplinary cultures in research is encompassed in the definition of discipline: there are different epistemological stances, procedures for data collection and verification, and communication styles and forms. Studies in psychology, sociology and, increasingly, in the field of higher education, have focused on these disciplinary influences and expressions in research activity. Within the sociology of knowledge and of science the focus of researchers has been on the experimental sciences, with important studies of physics (e.g. superconductors) and molecular biology (e.g. work on viruses and DNA). Biglan's work in psychology and Becher's in higher education are notable for the understandings gained across all disciplinary types. Their research highlights differing patterns of collaboration, communication and publication patterns across the disciplinary groupings.

Researchers in hard fields tend to collaborate with more people, report working in groups rather than individually, and publish through journals rather than books or monographs, when compared to the softer disciplines. Disciplines concerned with application and those connected to professional areas will publish technical reports, and may have a product or invention as an outcome of their research. Thus the discipline groups reflect differing rates, frequency and types of publications. Citation patterns and external research grant awards also reflect these differing epistemological characteristics. Preferences for the teaching and/or research roles of academic work have also been of interest. Academics in pure and hard disciplines have been noted as indicating preferences for research, while activities relating to professional and service areas are of stronger interest to academics in applied disciplines.

Universities also educate students, inducting them not only into subject matter but more importantly into a way of thinking, tradition and style of inquiry. Each discipline provides a cognitive map with its own language and socialisation processes of discovering, understanding and discussing knowledge. Until recently, the role and influence of disciplines in university teaching and learning processes has been all but neglected (e.g. see Hativa and Marincovich, 1995; Neumann, 2001).

Examinations of disciplinary cultures in graduate and doctoral education are still relatively sparse. Doctoral students can be seen as early career researchers undergoing a process of disciplinary socialisation and enculturation. Graduate education is highly discipline-specific, and students are primarily socialised into the discipline and not the institution. However, it has been noted that closer attention to disciplinary cultures is needed to assist our understanding of the evolution and change occurring within doctoral education (Turner *et al.*, 2002), and the role of institutional climate and disciplinary culture in doctoral student socialisation (Hirt and Muffo, 1998). There are some large-scale studies that can be built on. For example, different writing styles and patterns closely relate to disciplinary groups of doctoral theses (Parry, 2007, 1998); the discipline foremost, and the institution to a much lesser extent, determines the structure of doctoral programmes (Neumann, 2003b, 2005); while supervisory patterns and communications are also connected to the nature of the discipline (Becher *et al.*, 1994).

The study of disciplinary differences and influences on undergraduate teaching and learning is by comparison embryonic. Kolb (1984) has been influential with his analysis and theorising on learning styles (see also Table 35.1), maintaining that different styles are found across the different types of disciplines. Some theoretical work (Neumann, 2003a) has examined the application of the Biglan disciplinary classifications in relation to the epistemological characteristics of teaching and learning (Table 35.2), and their social and cultural characteristics (Table 35.3) at the undergraduate level.

Table 35.2 The Epistemological Characteristics of Teaching and Learning

	Epistemological		
	Subject matter/curriculum	Assessment	Main cognitive purpose
Hard–pure (natural science and mathematics)	• linear/hierarchical • atomistic • cumulative	• examinations • numerical • limited marking guides	• understanding theory • reasoning • disciplinary-related skills
Soft–pure (humanities, social science)	• "spiral" • reiterative • holistic	• continuous assessment • essays • marking guides	• broad knowledge • critical skills • synthesis • creativity
Hard–applied (science-based professions)	• sequential • application	• examinations • numerical • application	• problem-solving • career preparation • practice-related skills
Soft–applied (social professions)	• current research • application	• essays • short answers • practice-related	• broad knowledge • application • practice-related skills

The epistemological features in the table are an indicative and not exhaustive list.

Source: Neumann, 2003a, p. 228.

Table 35.3 The Social and Cultural Characteristics of Teaching and Learning

	Social		
	Teacher characteristics	Teaching methods	Learning characteristics
Hard–pure (natural science, mathematics)	• prefer research • collaborative • low SET*	• lecture • laboratory • field work	• numerical • memorisation • problem-solving
Soft–pure (humanities, social science)	• prefer teaching • individualistic • high preparation time • high SET*	• lecture • seminar/tutorial	• critical thinking • oral/written expression
Hard–applied (science-based professions)	• collaborative • high face-to-face • low SET*	• lecture • laboratory • field work	• memorisation • application • problem-solving
Soft–applied (social professions)	• prefer teaching • collaborative • high SET*	• lecture • seminar • case study	• oral/written expression • case studies • application

The social features in the table are an indicative and not exhaustive list.

* SET—student evaluation of teaching ratings.

Source: Neumann, 2003a, p. 231.

The framework outlined in Tables 35.2 and 35.3 is derived from existing studies of undergraduate teaching and learning across English universities in the UK, Australia, Canada and the US. Conceptually the framework presents similarities and differences on the knowledge-related and socially related aspects of teaching and learning. Other recent studies at the undergraduate level have examined the integration of disciplinary knowledge in specialised undergraduate writing (Carter, 2007), and the interaction between student motivation and disciplinary course content in the determination of student achievement and successful course performance (Breen and Lindsay, 2002).

Another emerging area is that of the scholarship of teaching and learning within the disciplines. This focus recognises that teaching, curriculum, assessment and communication practices within the disciplines vary, and that there is equally a need for members of the disciplines to research and better understand the teaching and learning focus of their disciplines. There is a need to understand "the power of the particular in a world where the general or the universal way" is most highly valued (Shulman, 2002, p. vi). There are traditions of, for example, engineering education and chemical education, including their own journals as communication channels. It is argued that genres, topics and methods are still being invented and that this is an area where the power of disciplinary styles influence studies and investigations into teaching and learning (Huber, 2002; Huber and Morreale, 2002). Equally, it is argued that professional development for academics in teaching needs also to be couched within the disciplines, rather than adopting a generic, one-size-fits-all approach (Healey and Jenkins, 2003).

Finally, in addition to considering the influence of disciplinary variations on the core academic work roles of teaching and research, there is growing awareness that academic behaviours and practices in leadership, management and administration may also reflect their disciplines (Kekale, 1999, 2002; Blackmore, 2007).

References

Becher, T. (1983). The cultural view. In: Clark, B.R. (ed.) *Perspectives on Higher Education: Eight Disciplinary and Comparative Views*. Berkeley, CA: University of California Press.

Becher, T. (1989). *Academic Tribes and Territories.* Buckingham: Open University Press.

Becher, T. (1994). The significance of disciplinary differences. *Studies in Higher Education, 19*(2), 151–161.

Becher, T., Kogan, M. and Henkel, M. (1994). *Graduate Education in Britain.* London: Jessica Kingsley.

Becher, T. and Trowler, P. (2001). *Academic Tribes and Territories.* Buckingham: Open University Press, 2nd edition.

Biglan, A. (1973a). The characteristics of subject matter in different scientific areas. *Journal of Applied Psychology, 57*(3), 195–203.

Biglan, A. (1973b). Relationships between subject matter characteristics and the structure and output of university departments. *Journal of Applied Psychology, 57*(3), 204–213.

Blackmore, P. (2007). Disciplinary differences in academic leadership and management and its development: a significant factor? *Research in Post-Compulsory Education, 12*(2), 225–239.

Braxton, J.M. and Hargens, L.L. (1996). Variation among academic disciplines: analytical frameworks and research. In: Smart, J.C. (ed.) *Higher Education: Handbook of Theory and Research.* Vol. XI. New York: Agathon Press. 1–46.

Breen, R. and Lindsay, R. (2002). Different disciplines require different motivations for student success. *Research in Higher Education, 43*(6), 693–725.

Carter, M. (2007). Ways of knowing, doing, and writing the disciplines. *College Composition and Communication, 58*(3), 385–418.

Church, C. (1976). Disciplinary dynamics. *Studies in Higher Education, 1*(2), 101–118.

Clark, B. (1983). *The Higher Education System: Academic Organization in Cross-National Perspective.* Berkeley, CA: University of California Press.

Clark, B. (1984). The organizational conception. In: Clark, B. (ed.) *Perspectives on Higher Education: Eight disciplinary and comparative views.* Berkeley, CA: University of California Press. pp. 106–131.

Clark, B. (1987). *The Academic Life: Small worlds, different worlds.* Princeton, NJ: The Carnegie Foundation for the Advancement of Teaching.

Creswell, J.W. and Bean, J.P. (1981). Research output, socialization, and the Biglan model. *Research in Higher Education, 15* (1), 69–91.

Creswell, J.W. and Roskens, R.W. (1981). The Biglan studies of differences among academic areas. *The Review of Higher Education, 4*(3), 1–16.

Creswell, J.W., Seagren, A.T. and Henry, T. (1981). Professional development training needs of department chairpersons: a test of the Biglan model. *Planning and Change, 10*, 224–237.

Frank, D., Wong, S., Meyer, J. and Ramirez, R. (2000). What counts as history: A cross-national and longitudinal study of university curricula. *Comparative Education Review, 44*(1), 29–53

Gabler, J. and Frank, D. (2005). The natural sciences in the university: Change and variation over the 20th century. *Sociology of Education, 78*, July, 183–206.

Gibbons, M., Limoges, C., Nowotny, H., Schwartzmann, S., Scott, P. and Trow, M. (1994). *The New Production of Knowledge: The dynamics of science and research in contemporary societies.* London: Sage.

Gordon, P. and Lawton, D. (1993). *Dictionary of Education.* London: Hodder & Stoughton.

Gumport, P.J. and Snydman, S.K. (2002) The formal structure of knowledge: An analysis of academic structure. *The Journal of Higher Education, 73*(3), 375–408.

Hagstrom, W.O. (1965). The differentiation of disciplines. In: Barnes, B. (ed.) (1972). *Sociology of Science: Selected readings.* Harmondsworth: Penguin. pp. 121–125.

Hativa, N. and Marincovich, M. (eds) (1995), *Disciplinary Differences in Teaching and Learning: Implications for Practice.* No. 64 Winter. San Francisco, CA: Jossey-Bass.

Healey, M. and Jenkins, A. (2003). Discipline-based educational development. In: Eggins, H. and Macdonald, R. (eds) *The Scholarship of Academic Development.* Buckingham: Open University Press. pp. 47–57.

Henkel, M. (2000). *Academic Identities and Policy Change in Higher Education.* London: Jessica Kingsley.

Hirt, J. and Muffo, J. (1998). Graduate students: Institutional climates and disciplinary cultures. *New Directions for Institutional Research, 92*, 17–33.

Huber, M. (2002). Disciplinary styles in the scholarship of teaching: Reflections on the Carnegie Academic for the Scholarship of Teaching and Learning. In: Huber, M. and Morreale, S. (eds) *Disciplinary Styles in the Scholarship of Teaching and Learning.* Washington, DC: American Association for Higher Education and The Carnegie Foundation for the Advancement of Teaching. pp. 25–44.

Huber, M. and Morreale, S. (2002). Situating the scholarship of teaching and learning: A cross-disciplinary conversation. In: Huber, M. and Morreale, S. (eds). *Disciplinary Styles in the Scholarship of Teaching and Learning.* Washington, DC: American Association for Higher Education and The Carnegie Foundation for the Advancement of Teaching, pp. 1–24.

Kekale, J. (1999). "Preferred" patterns of academic leadership in different disciplinary (sub)cultures. *Higher Education, 37*, 217–238.

Kekale, J. (2002). Conceptions of quality in four different disciplines. *Tertiary Education Management, 8*(1), 65–80.

Kiger, J. (1971). Disciplines. *Encyclopedia of Education.* New York: Philosophical Library.

Klein, J.T. (2004). Interdisciplinarity and complexity: An evolving relationship. E: CO Special Double Issue 6, No. 1–2, pp. 2–10.

Kockelmans, J. (1979). Science and discipline: Some historical and critical reflections. In: Kockelmans, J. (ed.) *Interdisciplinarity and Higher Education.* London: Pennsylvania State University Press, p. 11–48.

Kolb, D. (1984). *Experiential Learning. Experience as the Source of Learning and Development.* Englewood Cliffs, NJ: Prentice-Hall Inc.

Lee, J. (2007). The shaping of the departmental culture: Measuring the relative influences of the institution and discipline, *Journal of Higher Education Policy and Management, 29*(1), 41–55.

Leff, G. (1968). *Paris and Oxford Universities in the Thirteenth and Fourteenth Centuries: An institutional and intellectual history*. Sydney: John Wiley & Sons.

McInnis, C. and Marginson, S. (1994). *Australian Law Schools after the 1987 Pearce Report*. Canberra: Australian Government Publishing Service.

Moran, J. (2002). *Interdisciplinarity*. London: Routledge.

Neumann, R. (2001). Disciplinary differences and university teaching. *Studies in Higher Education, 26*(2), 135–146.

Neumann, R. (2003a). A disciplinary perspective on university teaching and learning. In: Tight, M. (ed.) *Access and Exclusion*. Oxford, Elsevier. pp. 217–245.

Neumann, R. (2003b). *The Doctoral Education Experience: Diversity and complexity*. Canberra: Department of Education, Training and Science.

Neumann, R. (2005). Doctoral differences: PhDs and professional doctorates compared. *Journal of Higher Education Policy and Management, 27*(2), 173–188.

Parry, S. (1998). Disciplinary discourse in doctoral theses. *Higher Education, 3*, 273–299.

Parry, S. (2007). *Disciplines and Doctorates*. Dordrecht: Springer.

Pearce, C., Campbell, E. and Harding, D. (1987). *Australian Law Schools: A discipline assessment for the Commonwealth Tertiary Education Commission*. Canberra: Australian Government Publishing Service.

Perkin, H. (1984). The historical perspective. In: Clark, B. (ed.) *Perspectives on Higher Education: Eight disciplinary and comparative views*. Berkeley, CA: University of California Press.

Redner, H. (1987). The institutionalization of science: a critical synthesis. *Social Epistemology, 1*(1), 37–59.

Rowntree, D. (1982). *A Dictionary of Education*. Totowa, NJ: Barnes and Noble Books.

Rudy, W. (1984). *The Universities of Europe, 1100–1914: A history*. Rutherford, NJ: Associated University Presses.

Ruscio, K. (1987). The distinctive scholarship of the selective liberal arts college. *Journal of Higher Education, 58*(2), 203–222.

Shorter Oxford English Dictionary. (2002). Oxford: Oxford University Press.

Shulman, L. (2002). Foreword. In: Huber, M. and Morreale, S. (eds) *Disciplinary Styles in the Scholarship of Teaching and Learning*. Washington, DC: American Association for Higher Education and The Carnegie Foundation for the Advancement of Teaching, pp. v–ix.

Silver, H. (2003). Does a university have a culture? *Studies in Higher Education, 28*(2), 157–169.

Smart, J.C. and Elton (1982). Validation of the Biglan model. *Research in Higher Education, 17*, 213–229.

Stoecker, J. (1993). The Biglan classification revisited. *Research in Higher Education, 34*(4), 451–464.

Storer, N. and Parsons, T. (1968). The disciplines as a differentiating force. In: Montgomery, E. (ed.) *The Foundations of Access to Knowledge—A symposium*. Syracuse, NY: Syracuse University.

Straus, R. (1973). Departments and disciplines: stasis and change. *Science, 182*, 895–989.

Swoboda, W. (1979). Disciplines and interdisciplinarity: A historical perspective. In: Kockelmans, J. (ed.) *Interdisciplinarity and Higher Education*. London: Pennsylvania State University Press, pp. 49–92.

Tight, M. (2003a). The organisation of academic knowledge: A comparative perspective. *Higher Education, 46*, 389–410.

Tight, M. (2003b). Naming academic knowledge; What is included within the university? In: Tight, M. (ed.) *Access and Exclusion*. Oxford: Elsevier, pp. 247–268.

Trowler, P. (1998). *Academics Responding to Change: New higher education frameworks and academic cultures*. Bristol, PA, USA: Open University Press.

Turner, J., Miller, M. and Mitchell-Kernan, C. (2002). Disciplinary cultures and graduate education. *Emergences, 12*(1), 47–70.

Weingart, P. and Stehr, N. (2000). *Practising Interdisciplinarity*. Toronto: University of Toronto Press.

36
Out with Humboldt and in with the Knowledge Society
On the Consequences of the Redefinition of the Role of Higher Education and Research

Merle Jacob

Introduction

Several observers have noted that higher education and research are increasingly being subjected to a number of external forces that, taken together, have the effect of redefining the mission of the institutions within the sector (Bleiklie, 2003; Clark, 1998; Etzkowitz, 2003; Neave, 1988). One such force is the new trend that higher education and research should contribute directly to innovation or economic development, while another is that higher education institutions themselves should become quasi-market organizations. A corollary to the changing position of higher education and research in society is the introduction of a new regime of governance, sometimes described as multi-level governance or alternatively as an open method of policy coordination. Multi-level governance refers to higher education and research institutions now being subject to different types of accountability or measures of evaluation from different groups. Thus, apart from national steering imperatives, there are also guidelines laid down by the European Union, for example, which entail some coordination between the national and the international (e.g. the European Science Foundation calls).

The novelty of this approach to the evaluation of higher education and research is greater or lesser, depending on whether one takes the long or the short view of the relationship between higher education and research and the state. The dominant position in the debate over the role of higher education and research in society has been that evaluation in terms of value added to specific user groups, contribution to economic development, etc. is novel and potentially problematic (Van der Meulen, 2008). One of the most significant criticisms raised in this respect is that the implementation of evaluation through demonstrated utility to society, via meeting the needs of certain specified groups, creates a democratic deficit. Another is that, seen from a political point of view, higher education and research funding has always been treated as expenditure that had to be justified in terms of well-defined outcomes. The current state of affairs, according to Neave (1988), is merely a reflection of the state's progress towards developing steering mechanisms that are more appropriate to the initial goals. Neave's observation is noteworthy, in that it shows that the developments we are discussing were already manifest as trends more than two decades ago, which implies that they should now be regarded as stable phenomena.

Nowotny *et al.* (2001) and Gibbons *et al.* (1994) have argued, both implicitly and explicitly, that changes in the organization of knowledge production have implications for the way in which knowledge is evaluated. This chapter elaborates on this somewhat controversial claim to make the argument that the regime(s) of governance for higher education and research in Western Europe that have been evolving since the 1980s have epistemological consequences. Here, I define epistemology as a coherent set of arguments about "what is knowledge?", "how is knowledge acquired?" and "what do people know?" This position will be elaborated in an argument that may be summarized in four points. First, the new governance imperatives for higher education and research both differentiate and unite research and education by regarding them as having the same output: knowledge. This focus on knowledge is reflected in the use of indicators such as relevance, user involvement, contribution to economic development (innovation) and skill acquisition as suitable for evaluating higher education and research. Second, taken together, these indicators have the potential to exacerbate extant tensions between research and higher education that may lead to a radical separation of the two activities. Third, the replacement of learning and education, with skill acquisition and learning outcomes, has the potential of normalizing all education to a model that closely resembles that of the natural sciences and/or engineering. Fourth, excessive focus on instrumental outcomes has inadvertently created the underpinnings of a system in which academic knowledge production is subjected to a value hierarchy, in which knowledge that can be easily commodified or commercialized is rated most highly.

The chapter takes the system of higher education and research in Western European countries as its primary empirical referent. The reason for this is that, while many of the tendencies reported here are no doubt relevant to other contexts, higher education and research, and research and innovation policy are two areas that defy generalizations and overarching descriptions. Thus, while the same set of policies, steering mechanisms, etc. may be applied in several countries, further study almost always reveals significant micro-level differences in definition of the terms of reference, implementation and, last but not least, outcomes. Mindful of this, I have tried to limit myself to those areas which have the highest degree of comparability and whose idiosyncrasies are fairly well known to me.

Differentiating Research and Education

There is a burgeoning academic discussion about the pros and cons of the rising tide of new public management routines in higher education and research management (Court, 2004; Deem *et al.*, 2007). While the tide of opinion among academics is definitely against the managerial ethic that is being applied to universities, opinions are much more muted with respect to the shift in the definition of the mission of the public university to include economic development. The majority of the research produced on this topic is focused on describing the impact of measures to promote entrepreneurialism. The emphasis in this literature is on evaluating output in terms of patents, licenses and number of firms (Shane, 2004; Siegel *et al.*, 2003). There is a small but growing interest in understanding the impact of the new demands on scientific careers (Duberley and Cohen, 2007), as well as some research focused on inscribing the new mission of the university into the history of the institution (Etzkowitz, 2003; Gibbons *et al.*, 1994). One example of the latter is the hypothesis that the university's new role in economic development is the result not of a policy-directed process, but an outcome of an " 'inner logic' of academic development that previously expanded the academic enterprise from a focus on teaching to research" (Etzkowitz, 2003, p. 109). Another is the Gibbons *et al.* (1994) thesis that academic knowledge production has undergone a qualitative shift, from mono-disciplinary, research-led knowledge production agendas to interdisciplinary research performed in collaboration with actors outside of academe.

European higher education and research is between a proverbial rock and a hard place in the face of the impact of the redefinition of its role in society. On the one hand, there is the notion that science proceeds best when left to its own devices, and, on the other, we have the exponentially rising costs of research and the expectation that these will be funded from the public purse. To complicate matters further, academic freedom is often used to protect research, but seldom to defend academic sovereignty over curricular development and content. This is a fairly long and well-established state of affairs, at least for the European public university system, as one finds Kant in his essay *The Conflict of the Faculties* conceding that disciplines such as theology and law should be submitted to state control over curricula, but making an exception for philosophy. Kant's argument suggests that the battle for control over curricula was decided long before Bologna.

What is important from the point of view of this chapter is that teaching is already subordinated to a regime of governance, one that takes its point of departure in an expectation of more involvement by the governing bodies than there has been in research. Given that teaching is already an "ordered" object, this begs the question as to what is qualitatively different about the new governance regime that could further exacerbate existing tensions. To begin with, the argument could be made that the point at which research and teaching meet naturally is in postgraduate education. I am here mindful that the dominant ideology in European higher education remains one which argues that all teaching should be research-based, but I focus on postgraduate rather than undergraduate education because postgraduate education is equivalent to research training in many disciplines. Thus, this activity is the one in which it is most likely that research-active staff would be engaged in teaching.

The indicators for evaluating education focus almost exclusively on students as output, while research is subjected to an evaluation logic which has dissemination as its main interest. Ironically, this evaluation regime manages to work to the disadvantage of all parties concerned, since it ignores students as the single most important factor in the dissemination of academic knowledge. Hence, policy-makers are caught in an increasing search for new ways of promoting knowledge dissemination, because, as long as they exclude student output as a measure of dissemination, higher education and research institutions will always appear to be lagging behind. Further, indicators of knowledge transfer, such as mobility, cannot be fully operationalized if we treat graduates of the university system as carriers of knowledge only after they have got their first job and moved on to another. This would be to imply that the average university graduate has no knowledge on graduation.

From the point of view of the university, the policy system's tendency to overlook the role of students as conduits for disseminating knowledge from the university creates a dissonance, between the internal logic of the university as an organization and the auditing measures used by its external stakeholders to evaluate its performance. One reason for this is that it puts into question a number of efforts that have been made to realize a more coherent system of evaluation for research and education at the level of individual performance evaluation. Academic career development has long been acknowledged to have an internal tension, in that research and teaching are hierarchically related in the performance evaluation system. Put differently, a scholar who excels in research, but has little teaching experience, is more likely to be successful at getting senior positions than her colleague, who has little or no publication record but a large portfolio of outstanding course evaluations. This is an everyday reality that is rife with tension, not only because of its implications for the individual academic's choice, but because it suggests that instead of the assumed harmony between research and teaching implied in the Humboldtian vision, there is instead an inherent conflict between these two activities that has to be managed both institutionally and individually.

The separation of indicators of evaluation for education and research may, arguably, be said to convey the reality of the individuality of the two activities. It, however, presents problems for university management at all levels, since every head of department must encourage his or her staff to strive to embody the Humboldtian ideal of teacher-researcher, since specialization in teaching will only lead to frustrated ambitions. Specialization in research will attract attention, and even funding, but student income is still the most stable source of funding for most European public universities.

Entrepreneurship research and education is a good illustrative example of this argument, since it embodies the tensions outlined. Furthermore, since entrepreneurship research and education are associated with the so-called "third" mission, this is an area which provides some insight as to how the third mission interacts with the core missions. Entrepreneurship research and education at once exemplifies and explains the increasing separation of research and teaching, as well as the privileging of certain forms of academic knowledge over others. For those who are not familiar with this area of research and education, entrepreneurship education provides students with the skills necessary to create and manage a firm. Although, in most cases, one will find entrepreneurship research located within the business school, it is surprisingly often not co-located with entrepreneurship education, which, particularly in Western Europe, tends to be most often sited within the engineering or natural science faculties.

Unlike many other knowledge areas, entrepreneurship research and education are not necessarily developing within the same community, but, in many cases, the educational agenda has a strong vocational focus, while the research agenda seems to be oriented towards understanding and explaining the phenomenon of entrepreneurship. In addition, entrepreneurship education has a strong missionary or imperialistic element, in that it often has an ambition to embed itself in all other disciplines. This mission is an outcome of the need to justify educational offerings in terms of their ability to contribute to the employability of students. In its most ambitious incarnation, entrepreneurship education aims to inspire entrepreneurial thinking and cultivate entrepreneurial leadership in all organizations and society (mission statement of the Arthur Blank Center for Entrepreneurship at Babson College: see http://www3.babson.edu/eship/). This discourse and its ambitions were also reflected in the enterprise movement in the UK. Entrepreneurship education may, arguably, be said to be an almost too illustrative example of the intimate connections between the discourse about the changing role of higher education and research in society and the nature of research and education. However, processes such as the Bologna reform in the European Union, taken together with national reforms, have given rise to similar developments, in so far as they blur the boundaries between different forms of tertiary education by emphasizing skills and learning outcomes rather than education.

From Higher Education and Research to Knowledge Production and Dissemination

Research is the activity that is most immediately called upon to demonstrate its utility via proof of dissemination. The indicators used to demonstrate dissemination are predominantly of a bibliometric character. Increasingly, Western European countries are moving towards national evaluation systems similar to the UK's Research Assessment Exercise. This type of assessment is primarily directed towards evaluating the dissemination of research within the research community itself via publication. In many countries, this bibliometric trend gains additional legitimacy and warrant, as it is often touted as equivalent to measuring excellence and/or benchmarking the national research system against other national research systems. This has meant that quality in research is operationalized in terms that are more or less defined by the international science citation index—a development that continues apace despite complaints of linguistic bias and protest from disciplines with other types of publication patterns. Moreover, peer-reviewed journal articles are gradually taking precedence over monographs and anthologies. The focus on counting, taken together with the hierarchy of publications and the insistence on applying these measures to all disciplines, suggests that research evaluation is part of the same trend observed with higher education. Just as the rewriting of curricula, to present skills as the learning outcomes of a period of study, had the inadvertent effect of ordering all disciplines into a model that resembles that of the natural and engineering sciences, so too does the increasing preoccupation with citation counts, and the formalization of the hegemony of peer-reviewed publications versus other types. In summary, just when we have accepted the claim that science is home to several epistemic cultures, the procedures for organizing and governing science are now gradually promoting a mono episteme.

One of the markers of the new role ascribed to higher education and research is that they are now more often than not referred to by their outcomes rather than as activities in themselves. Thus, research is often referred to as knowledge creation or production, while teaching is treated as knowledge development. The pervasiveness of knowledge as a descriptor for higher education and research institutions and activities is not an insignificant development, if we take our point of departure in the premise that language is often revelatory of intent. One superficial analysis would be to treat the new "knowledgespeak" as a logical development of the dominance of the knowledge society/economy worldview. Another view is that the term knowledge is a better descriptor for inscribing the activities of the higher education and research sector into market logic than education and research.

Nowotny *et al.* (2001) and Ziman (2000) are the authors who have devoted the most attention to the problem of what, if any, are the qualitative shifts in the nature of knowledge occasioned by contemporary changes in the organization of knowledge creation at universities. Large parts of the discussion in the Nowotny *et al.* (2001) volume are a debate with Ziman about the changing nature of knowledge. The thesis outlined by Gibbons *et al.* (1994), and developed by Nowotny *et al.* (2001), is that science—and here the authors are primarily referring to research—is moving from a set of criteria for the evaluation of its knowledge which focused on reliability to social robustness. Socially robust knowledge differs in that it is strongly contextualized, or perhaps local, knowledge. The claim that knowledge developed in a specific practical context for a specific application, by a well-defined community of users and researchers, is superior or more robust than the received view of knowledge is controversial. The first source of suspicion is, of course, that it seems to be an epistemology tailor-made for the current fashion in research and innovation policy, which has it that research has to demonstrate relevance. Relevance is defined in terms of a variation of witness testimony, i.e. specific groups in society attest to the relevance of the knowledge via making the claim that they can or have used it to achieve some specific end.

The received criteria for what is good knowledge include specification of the range of validity of the claims, reliability, etc. In addition, it is understood that the quality of the knowledge is directly proportional to the breadth of the range of validity of the knowledge claim. Nowotny and her colleagues spend a great deal of time addressing this particular issue, and that of reliability, because these are the two issues at which policy dictates have the most implications for how knowledge is justified in science. This is also a debate which is difficult, because it requires that we move the discussion between two different realms of analysis, without running the risk of confusing it with ought. On the normative side, we have two claims: one is the policy claim that science needs to demonstrate relevance through, for want of a better term, contextualization—i.e. picking problems that are already identified in society, forming coalitions with groups outside the research world. The claim from science policy scholars, such as Nowotny and her colleagues, is that these policy dictates are compatible with the requirements for creating good scientific knowledge, since science is itself revising these requirements in the light of the new types of problems. The empirical response is that the conditions for producing knowledge have to be protected from day-to-day social and political realities if science is to maintain its neutrality.

More importantly, several reports from the Mode 2 trenches suggest that the reality is far from the collective struggle for providing good answers to shared questions (cf. Rappert, 1999; Ram, 1997), which Nowotny and colleagues sketch in such unproblematic terms. Many researchers report that their research has been unable to reach groups that they believe would find it useful, because of the nature of the coalition that funded the research in the first place. More importantly, while the rhetoric of higher education and research policies emphasizes knowledge transfer and making science more accountable to society, the reality is that science is only accountable to those groups who can afford to meet the costs of conducting research.

Thus far, we have focused on research and teaching, and the implications of new governance mechanisms for the way in which these activities are now enacted, what kinds of outcomes they are required to produce, etc. If we look at the institutions of higher education and research, there are also some important changes being taken. The European system of higher education and research was initially quite functionally differentiated, with most countries having several different types of institutions. For example, the polytechnics, *fachhochschulen* and other vocational schools formed one tier, while universities formed another, and it was assumed that these institutions were distinguished by the breadth of disciplines on offer and the existence of doctoral education. It is not uncommon now for universities to have a limited offering of disciplines, and that professional or vocational training could be included in that curriculum.

More importantly, reforms such as the Bologna Process have had implications for curriculum development, which have tended to reinforce this tendency for the university to be a set of functions rather than a specific type of institutional setting (Teichler, 1996). To add to this complexity, some countries, such as Denmark, have merged research institutes with universities, and are promoting critical mass rather than diversity. A similar proposal for the merger of universities and university colleges was recently outlined in Norway (Ministry of Education and Research, Norway 2008: 3). What this suggests is that the predictions and expectations of pluralism that characterize the arguments outlined in the mode 2 and Triple Helix (university/industry/government: see Etzkowitz and Leydesdorff, 2000) theses are more complex than these narratives suggest. On the one hand, one might argue that pluralism is occurring because we can no longer say, with any given certainty, to what type of institution the term university may refer. On the other hand, there is a certain convergence or homogenizing effect, which may be attributed to the increasing internationalization of national higher education and research systems, as a result of the influence of actors such as the Organisation of Economic Cooperation and Development and the European Union.

Discussion

The initial premise of this chapter, that changes in the way one organizes and funds higher education and research would affect what knowledge is produced and how it is valued, is one that may appear at once intuitive and controversial. On the one hand, we know that governance signals do have implications for content; and, on the other, that science has always operated with the assumption that its methods are more or less outside the purview of social and political interference. We have argued that demands such as relevance, social responsibility, economic development and employability all converge to give priority to some kinds of knowledge as opposed to others. My intention is not to indicate that this type of knowledge is inferior or less desirable than that which accompanied the old systems of governance. Research in higher education has shown that many of our standard assumptions about pedagogy, for instance, are premised on particular assumptions about learning and the learner that are in themselves culturally informed. This creates problems when the learner does not share the characteristics assumed in these pedagogies. Similarly, the sociology of science has shown that science is not a neutral affair. The point is that neither research nor education was neutral before the introduction of "knowledgespeak".

Given this, it is surprising how few of the discussions about the changing role of science in society attempt to flesh out the power implications of the new governance regime. Kogan (2005) is one of the only examples known to this author, and he concludes that the relations between the cognitive and relational aspects of power are "tendencies" rather than determinants. This is a fairly safe type of conclusion to draw, given that it remains unclear which disciplines have achieved the status of producing socially robust knowledge. However, it says little about the other power relations that issue from the current order of things.

Two issues leap to mind once we switch focus to the power implications of the new knowledge order. The first arises from the stakeholder notion of society inherent in third mission and mode 2 talk, and the second stems from the changing balance of power between research and teaching, as a result of the focus on commodified forms of knowledge transfer and other measurables.

Nowotny and others have suggested socially robust knowledge as a way of keeping science "straight" (for which, read "relevant"); however, the concerns for democracy and relevance that drive the proposal of socially robust knowledge are rooted in a naïve view of politics and power. In other words, relevance and social responsibility are not inherently compatible. Marginalized groups in society have no greater access to mode 2 science than they do to its predecessor. Their situation may have actually been worsened in the context of mode 2, where, in order to get science to address one's interests, one is expected to be able to collaborate not only in terms of meeting part of the costs, but also be able to specify one's knowledge needs in terms that could be translated into science. Even groups that are used to collaborating with science have difficulty with the latter, let alone those who do not. Further, as Harland notes (in this volume), some parts of science contribute to the common weal by acting as a critical voice, speaking up for marginalized groups and those without a voice, as well as creating a space for reflection on the taken for granted. How this research sector is to prove the social robustness of its knowledge remains uncertain within the current frame of accountability.

Decades of being subjected to separate governance and evaluation regimes have meant that research and education have developed parallel research communities. In addition, the assumption that the profile of the average academic is that of teacher-researcher or researcher-teacher is observed in the breach rather than in practice. This means that, seen from the point of view of university workers, teaching and research have little to do with each other. From the point of view of the university as an organization, however, it is their interaction and the synergies that they can create for the institution that gives the university meaning. Are we therefore at an impasse? Is there something to be gained from informing the micro perspectives of mainstream research on higher education with the macro- and meso-level concerns of research and innovation policy?

It is important to bear in mind that research on higher education has always had a number of scholars who have made regular border crossing to research policy by virtue of their focus on the university rather than on higher education (cf. Becher, 1989; Rothblatt and Wittrock, 1993; Trow 1979; Trow and Nybom, 1991). However, for the most part the two communities exist in isolation from each other, and this isolation has increased as research and science policy have become increasingly integrated with innovation policy. This development has meant that the few possibilities for building bridges are fast disappearing, as research and innovation policy scholars become more entrenched in the ideological work of constantly maintaining the research component in research and innovation policy. The result is that scholars of research and innovation policy are inadvertently becoming the front-line agents of the neo-liberalist agenda of change for higher education and research. Harland (in this volume) captures this succinctly by pointing out that, although much is being made of what is being done to the academy by external agents, little is said about the lack of any thoroughgoing critique, or about the greater effort being expended on adjusting to the new regime rather than resisting it.

Part of the reason for this response is that there is really very little support in terms of alternative organizational models and leadership solutions that are tailor-made for the academy. Ongoing efforts to sew corporate clothing on academic bodies have given rise to ill-fitting suits, and have exacerbated institutional tensions. This type of knowledge could be created if higher education and research policy scholars were to join forces, and create a common research agenda, aimed at understanding and developing new knowledge on how to more effectively manage the newly emerging challenges resulting from the redefinition of the role of higher education and research in society. Three issues might be included in such an agenda.

One point to which we could devote more attention would be to consider the issue of the university as an organizational actor. Universities have conventionally seen themselves, and are perceived, as arenas for students and scholars to engage in the common enterprise of learning and creating knowledge. Recently, governments have become insistent on forcing universities to act as organizations (Krücken and Meier, 2006; Whitley, 2008), through a process of delegating autonomy to the university level, and increasing pressure on universities to take responsibility for creating and implementing strategies, identifying suitable stakeholders and meeting their needs. The evolution of the university as an organizational actor is a process that will require a new type of expertise, since the natural space for the university as organization would be on the meso-level, i.e. between national research/innovation policy (macro) and the department/unit level within the university (micro). This type of expertise can be developed through the combined forces of research on higher education and research policy.

A second issue is related to the problem of profiling and reintegrating research and education. The new ideology of accountability does not regard students as important agents in the transfer of knowledge from universities to the rest of society. This is in several respects problematic, but the most significant point is that the organizational life, routines and norms of universities are shaped to a large extent by the student body. Even without the neo-liberalist framing of students as customers of higher education, universities have had to become more responsive to students' needs as a result of a series of occurrences, such as the 1968 student revolts, state-driven educational reform and, last but not least, changing pedagogy. Thus, students were treated as stakeholders in university education prior to the new public management era, and in that capacity the student body participated in nearly every aspect of university life through membership of all types of committees.

A third issue would be to attempt to focus together on the impact of the redefinition of the mission of higher education and research to function as an engine of economic development. A number of dichotomies emerge from this view of education and research as activities to be valued, in so far as they have the capacity to effect socio-economic change. These may be summarized as "knowledge for all versus knowledge for socio-economic change", "technology versus science", "training for jobs versus education for citizenship", "research versus education", and last but not least "open access knowledge production versus intellectual property". The policy panacea for reconciling these dichotomies is institutional profiling, and in this is another opportunity for border crossing between research on higher education and that on research and innovation policy. By this I mean that, if institutions are going to profile themselves, they will need insight into both types of activities and the synergies that they create or lose in co-location or separation.

References

Becher, T. (1989) *Academic Tribes and Territories*. Buckingham: Open University Press.

Bleiklie, I. (2003) Hierarchy and Specialisation: on the institutional integration of higher education systems. *European Journal of Education*, 38(4), pp. 341–355.

Clark, B. (1998) *Creating Entrepreneurial Universities: Organizational Pathways to Transformation*. Oxford: Pergamon.

Court, M. (2004) Talking Back to New Public Management Versions of Accountability in Education. *Educational Management Administration & Leadership*, Vol. 32(2), 171–194.

Deem, R., Hillyard, S. and Reed, M. (2007) *Higher Education, and the New Managerialism: The Changing Management of UK Universities*. Oxford: Oxford University Press.

Duberley, J. and Cohen, L. (2007) Entrepreneurial Academics: Developing Scientific Careers in Changing University Settings. *Higher Education Quarterly*, Vol. 61(4), pp 479–497.

Etzkowitz, H. (2003) Research groups as "quasi-firms": the invention of the entrepreneurial university. *Research Policy*, 32: 109–121.

Etzkowitz, H. and Leydesdorff, L. (2000) The dynamics of innovation: from National Systems and "Mode 2" to a Triple Helix of university–industry–government relations, *Research Policy*, 29: 109–123

Gibbons, M., Limoges, C., Nowotny, H., Schwartzman, S. and Scott, P. (1994) *The New Production of Knowledge: The dynamics of science and research in contemporary societies*. London: Sage.

Kogan, M. (2005) Modes of Knowledge and Patterns of Power. *Higher Education*, 49, 9–30.

Krücken, G. and Meier, F. (2006) Turning the University into an Organizational Actor. In G. Drori, J. Meyer and H. Hwang (eds) *Globalization and Organization: World Society and Organizational Change*. Oxford: Oxford University Press, pp. 241–257.

Ministry of Education and Research, Norway (2008) *Sett under ett: Ny struktur i høyere utdanning*. Norwegian Ministry of Education and Research, Oslo, Norway. (Available in Norwegian only at http://www.stjernoe.no/get/565).

Neave, G. (1988) On the cultivation of quality, efficiency and enterprise: an overview of recent trends in higher education in Western Europe, 1986–1988. *European Journal of Education*, 23, pp. 7–23.

Nowotny, H., Scott, P. and Gibbons, M. (2001) *Re-Thinking Science: Knowledge and the public in an age of uncertainty*. Cambridge: Polity.

Ram, M. (1997) The Politics of Research: Local Consultation in a City Challenge Context. *Sociology*, 29, 275–292.

Rappert, B. (1999) The uses of relevance: Thoughts on a reflexive sociology. *Sociology*, 33(4) 705–723.

Rothblatt, S. and Wittrock, B. (1993) *The European and American University Since 1800*. Cambridge: Cambridge University Press.

Shane, S. (2004), Encouraging university entrepreneurship? The effect of the Bayh-Dole act on university patenting in the United States. *Journal of Business Venturing*, 19(1), 127–151.

Siegel, D.S., Waldman, D.A., Atwater, L.E. and Link, A.N. (2003) Commercial knowledge transfers from universities to firms: improving the effectiveness of university-industry collaboration. *Journal of High Technology Management Research*, 14(1), 111–133.

Teichler, U. (1996) The changing nature of higher education in Western Europe. *Higher Education Policy*, 9(2) pp 89–111.

Trow, M. (1979) Elite and Mass Higher Education: American Models and European Realities. In *Research into Higher Education: Processes and Structures*, pp. 183–219. Stockholm, National Board of Universities and Colleges.

Trow, M. and Nybom, T. (1991) *University and Society: Essays on the Social Role of Research and Higher Education*. London, Jessica Kingsley.

Van Der Meulen, B. (2008) Interfering Governance and Emerging Centres of Control: University Research Evaluation in the Netherlands. In R. Whitley and J. Gläser (eds), *The Changing Governance of the Sciences*, 191–203, Dordrecht, Springer Verlag.

Whitley, R. (2008) Universities as Strategic Actors: State delegation and changing patterns of evaluation. In R. Whitley and J. Gläser (eds), *The Changing Governance of the Sciences*, 191–203, Dordrecht, Springer Verlag.

Ziman, J. (2000) *Real Science: What it is and What it Means*. Cambridge, Cambridge University Press.

37

The University, Neoliberal Reform and the Liberal Educational Ideal

Tony Harland

Introduction

The history of the university shows that both ancient and modern institutions have undergone radical change from time to time, and that foundational ideas about knowledge and the purposes of a higher education have been transformed. We are presently experiencing such a period of transition, which has its origins in the neoliberal political and economic reforms of the 1960s and 1970s. In this chapter, I set out to provide a view on how neoliberalism has impacted on aspects of the cultural and intellectual life of the university. It is a story largely about constant adjustment in an unsettled academy, but, set against this is the idea that there is also something secure about the modern university that has been resistant to the reform agenda. One of the enduring qualities is the liberal educational ideal, which is essentially a post-enlightenment educational philosophy, rather than a political or economic project. It is characterized by concepts of freedom of thought and expression, and for those who inhabit the academy there appears to be something almost instinctive about holding these values (the common use of the word "liberal" in both ideas can seem confus-ing: the term neoliberal represents the current reform agenda and liberal education represents a particular philosophy; neoliberal is not "new liberal" in the educational sense).

Many commentators on higher education have serious concerns about the current changes to institutions, the problems faced by academics and the threats to liberal education (Axelrod, 2002; Barnett, 2000). The university is in "ruins" (Readings, 1996), there is a "crisis of identity" (Malcolm and Tarling, 2006) and higher education is "beyond all reason" (Barnett, 2003). However, as much as I can see why these and other similar accounts have been written, my own experiences and observations of university life allow me some optimism for the future, even if that future is likely to be different. If I draw upon Robert Pirsig's remark about New York City; the university has always been going to hell but somehow it never gets there (1991, p. 274).

In any commentary about higher education, it is difficult to generalize, as no two institutions seem to share the same characteristics. However, I will try to make observations that reflect the sector more generally. It is inevitable that I also draw on my work as an academic staff developer and researcher in the field of higher education. I have worked closely with many academics and students from around the world, particularly in universities in the United Kingdom, New Zealand and Malaysia, and their experiences have helped me frame this chapter. I will start by giving a brief overview of the concepts of liberal education and neoliberalism, before examining the impact of neoliberal reform on higher education.

The Liberal Project

A liberal educational philosophy is encapsulated by the post-enlightenment understanding that knowledge can be its own end, and that the university can be a site of pure reason with free enquiry for both teachers and students. It empowers individuals through knowledge and the development of critical skills and values. The grand claim of liberal education is that it frees those with such an education to contribute to social change, and perhaps make the world a better place to live in. Importantly, free and open debate seems to be the only way of preserving our modern Western liberal democracies (Harris, 2005). Those who teach and learn in New Zealand's universities, for example, are charged by the state "that they accept a role as critic and conscience of society" (Education Act, 1989).

There is a more pragmatic conception of the liberal ideal that originated in Germany in the nineteenth century, when the position of research in the modern university first became recognized. Certain liberal characteristics from this time have been well maintained and are still valued as foundational, both by higher education and the wider society. These qualities include critical thinking and skills development as the basis of intellectual advancement. Axelrod (2002) suggests that:

> Liberal education in the university refers to activities designed to cultivate intellectual creativity, autonomy and resilience; critical thinking; a combination of intellectual breadth and specialized knowledge; the comprehension and tolerance of diverse ideas and experiences informed participation in community life; and effective communication skills. (p. 34)

Such a liberal vision is often reflected in the ivory tower metaphor, or seen as a romantic notion from some mythical golden age of the university, or for some, far too elitist (Beck, 1999). It is easy to see why, because liberal aspirations can appear removed from the realities of academic practice, the experiences of students and the world outside the university. However, even though some of the early claims of liberal education were never realistic or practical, the general idea is alive and well. Higher education still wants those who take part to be able to think critically, and it is recognized that higher learning includes both an epistemological and an ontological project. Values, such as tolerance of diverse ideas or contributing to social change, have a rightful place in the disciplines, and the idea of the academic as a public intellectual is seldom contested.

Higher education is still committed to the pursuit of knowledge, but what is currently being questioned is the sort of knowledge that has a place in our institutions. Furthermore, outside of the Western model, liberal educational values may be irreconcilable with other cultural systems: for example, if these systems are predicated on certain religious worldviews or politics outside of the liberal democracies. In such systems, questioning of fundamental ideas or authority may not be encouraged or tolerated. However, liberal ideas about education may also be incompatible with particular neoliberal values that have recently emerged in Western higher education.

Neoliberalism

Despite resistance, neoliberal political and economic reform has had a major impact on higher education. Neoliberalism is founded on a belief in the supremacy of the market over state intervention, and it seeks to bring about societal changes by creating conditions that allow free competition. Neoliberalism is underpinned by a belief that self-determination and individual rights better guarantee economic efficiency through competition. Such a move requires the state to withdraw from many economic and social activities, and assume a new role of ensuring that the market can operate efficiently. Governments can then concentrate on the provision of public goods such as health and education. Neoliberal ideology reached a critical point with the major reforms of the Thatcher government in the UK and the Reagan government in the USA in the late 1980s (Giroux, 2002).

A difficulty arose with the reform process when public institutions, such as hospitals, schools and universities, were included in the neoliberal project. A new era of full or partial privatization of state services began, and public institutions that could not be partly or wholly sold off to the private sector were reorganized, with new forms of control and governance based largely on public accountability and compliance that, for example, created new competition between public institutions. Such neoliberal strategies were very different to the reform of the private sector, which laid down conditions to maximize freedom of action, individual rights and liberty. With respect to higher education, new legislation aimed to ensure that it would be organized and operated in an ideologically acceptable manner. However, in doing so, previously held freedoms and rights were taken away. Marginson (1997) uses the term "regulated autonomy" for the simultaneous devolution and central control of higher education. Institutions are now highly regulated, which challenges the neoliberal emphasis on deregulation (Davies *et al.*, 2006). Neoliberal reform has affected the public higher education sector, and there is evidence that it is now a worldwide phenomenon (Giroux, 2005, Marginson and Rhoades, 2002).

Large-scale changes in higher education throughout the 1980s and 1990s in the United Kingdom and New Zealand, for example, included new systems of government funding, political interference with institutional management, new control mechanisms of audit and the assessment of core activities such as research and teaching. These changes were coupled with a relentless drive to mass higher education, as more and more students were encouraged to participate. Knowledge became recognized as a commodity that could provide economic wealth and also be traded. Higher education institutions were seen through a new lens of "enterprise", and would primarily serve the economy with students taking on a new identity as customers purchasing a product in a new service industry. The outcome of reform has been a shift in the ways in which higher education operates and thinks about its various purposes, and, in particular, there have been major transformations of research, teaching and higher education's relationship with society. All Western higher education institutions are now characterized to some extent by new arrangements for accountability and organization, which impact on the primary knowledge project.

Although many changes have come about during the higher education reforms of the past 30 years or so, two stand out as having a particular impact on liberal educational values. Firstly, changes to university organization and culture have required new forms of accountability and the measurement of academic work. Secondly, as the nature of academic work changes, so do the knowledge structures of a higher education.

Changes to Organization and Culture

The neoliberal project was seen to shift power from the public sphere to the private sphere (Chomsky, 2003) and, in doing so, it marginalized a relatively autonomous academic community (Lynch, 2006). In this struggle for power the boundaries between the public university and the private sector become blurred, and now public institutions are without doubt an instrument of the state that largely serve the needs of business and the economy. Knowledge is increasingly becoming a privatized commodity, and there are systems of education that have embraced this notion by situating institutions directly *in* the market. For example, in Malaysia, recent initiatives by government and the private sector have resulted in the building of a state university whose purpose is to directly meet a strategic economic need for professional training, with government as a major shareholder, and a new private university whose curriculum is largely dictated by the end-users of its services in the private sector. Serving such different constituencies in this manner marginalizes the values of the public university and the liberal ideal.

In the West, the key instrument for directing neoliberal change in established institutions has been that of public accountability for state funding. Governments decide on what higher education should be doing, and then hold each institution accountable for how they measure up. And "measure" is the correct term here for determining value, despite the many functions of a university defying reasonable measurement and each institution being unique. Individuals and organizations are typically subject to standard national schemes that are designed to suit the sector, and this tends to result in measuring only what is possible, which leads to distorted ideas about competency and endless argument. There is no automatic link between compliance schemes and the quality of higher education, and what is measured can seem far removed from the realities of academic life. Accountability is dressed up with ethical arguments, and we are told that its purpose is to achieve transparency and improve quality. Transparency appeals to a benevolent side but it also has an invisible tyrannous side (Strathern, 2000), and quality has now become a metaphor for managerial control (Codd, 2005).

Regulatory systems of evaluating and accounting for practice are now a major part of every academic's working life, and it is the academic who bears the brunt of the financial cost of the audit culture. A consequence of this neoliberal control mechanism is that all those who work in higher education have a new activity of "being accountable" to sit alongside teaching and research, and being held to account requires substantial effort and time. Accountability is not just imposed by governments and other outside bodies, but is also internalized and generated within institutions (Davies *et al.*, 2006). Yet, when academics (or their institutions) do not value compliance, the task can be treated with disdain or even subverted (Trow, 1996). Avoidance of truth and levels of subversion must depend on what is at stake, but the stakes are often very high. Transparency disappears and in the accountability game each party mistrusts the other; institutions and government or academics and managers. Misinformation gets dressed up as evidence and overall there may be no positive gain from the process. Certain forms of internal accountability can undermine the work that was previously done in a collegiate and trusting environment. O'Neill (2002) makes the point that:

> Much professional practice used to centre on interaction with those whom professionals serve: patients and pupils, students and families in need. Now there is less time to do this because everyone has to record the details of what they do and compile evidence to protect themselves. (p. 50)

Accountability leads to appeals to standards that are external to the individual and, therefore, to what Ranson (2003) calls "inauthentic selves". For enacting liberal educational values we may need to remain authentic and avoid the distorting effects of imposed standards. However, there is always a risk in trusting others, as they can let us down. For example, students were, by and large, trusted not to plagiarize. Now there is an assumption that it will happen, energy is spent actively seeking the evidence to hold students to account, and a different relationship between teachers and students is created. Yet, the new era of plagiarism stems from the increased class sizes of the neoliberal institution with its overloaded students, easy-to-mark assignments and the electronic means to copy and paste.

The complex impacts of neoliberal reform cannot be predicted with any certainty, and any unforeseen consequences of accountability are typically dealt with by another reporting mechanism. A simplified illustration is the introduction of the Research Assessment Exercise in the UK, which tended to move academics away from teaching, and then the later insistence on assessing teaching quality, which was seen, in part, as an attempt to restore some balance. Auditors create auditees who themselves wish to become auditors as part of the intensification of accountability (Strathern, 2000). I recently enjoyed taking part in the audit of a university audit process, and the thought occurred to me that we could have an endless process of auditing the auditors. Where would one stop?

Levin (2006) recognizes that academics can be agents of neoliberalism even while they oppose it, and be tempted to adopt the management practices that they are subject to. New ways of thinking creep into the academy. It seems much easier for governments, vice chancellors and heads of departments to insist that an academic be publicly accountable for a certain number of research publications, rather than to trust them to do quality research. Liberal educational philosophy requires collegiality, openness and trust to operate effectively, and accounting systems, particularly those that focus on the individual, serve to weaken the collective bonds of the academy (Barnett, 2003). However, academics have been known to break trust by not fulfilling their obligations to teaching, research and colleagues. In such cases accountability mechanisms can make practices more public and help institutions deal with problems. The difficulty seems to be that measures introduced to catch a few recalcitrant staff are usually applied to whole departments, institutions or education systems.

Changes to Knowledge

The nature of academic work is changing significantly, and the trinity of teaching, research and service has disintegrated, with many university lecturers expected to spend a considerable part of their time engaged in other activities (Barnett, 2000). Neoliberal-driven practices are more inclusive of a variety of roles and the academic may take advantage of new business opportunities, private consultancy, patents, corporate collaborations and research activities that would have previously been done by commerce or industry. These changes in emphasis have led to a distortion of university activities towards research and development and income generation, and the market clearly wants a piece of higher education. In this new context, academic work becomes increasingly casualized, and old disciplinary allegiances shift as researchers form partnerships outside the university or move into new knowledge areas. All higher education institutions have to take advantage of new market opportunities to finance their business, and intellectual activity is seen as intellectual capital. The university has become a key element of the wider global knowledge economy, with the expectation that knowledge production is responsive to society's economic, social and political needs.

Knowledge can no longer be contained within the higher education community and new forms of knowledge are seeking a place in higher education. This breakdown of traditional knowledge boundaries can be partly explained by changes in the nature of the research process. According to Gibbons *et al.* (1994), traditional disciplines have become less secure as knowledge is generated within transdisciplinary spaces, in which university researchers spend time sharing their territory with others outside of their institutions. These authors call this "Mode 2" knowledge, and it is neither pure nor applied by definition, but created in the context of practice. Furthermore, it may not necessarily result in the usual research products, such as journal articles, but is reflexive and encoded within the expertise of the researcher and the research team. At present, the legitimacy of such knowledge production is unclear, and Mode 2 activities appear to be both encouraged and discouraged at the same time. Nowotny *et al.* (2003) use the example of nurse researchers embracing Mode 2 knowledge concepts: however, they are also pulled in the opposite direction by tradition and accountability. New professions entering higher education still need to defer to the established academic community, and in particular to the dominant forms of research accountability which rely on clear definitions of research quality. While evaluation and measurement of research products rather than process remains the norm, the place of conventional ways of organizing knowledge will be assured.

We are also told that students now have an understanding that they are largely purchasing their education to enable them to enter the world of work. Universities, in particular, respond by introducing applied courses in new knowledge areas to attract these students, and this partly explains the shift from subjects that have no immediate commercial value to those that do, mainly in the sciences and health sciences. New industries want higher education to meet their needs, and to provide training and education opportunities that enable students to be competent employees. Yet why should a public university expend its effort on behalf of a company's shareholders? Of course, universities have traditionally trained doctors, lawyers and engineers, and society needs good medical care and so on. So why not do the same in the new fields such as biotechnology? Societies also need economic stability, but there is still a widely accepted view that higher education has to be more than training for work. Barnett (1997) argues that education, including professional training, needs both a foundation of knowledge and skills and the capacity for critical thought and critical action. In this view, "critical being" is seen as the essential project of higher education, and such critical forms of knowledge equip students to live in a complex and changing neoliberal world and constantly renewing society.

Knowledge to be bought and sold, and students as customers, are concepts that do not sit well with liberal educational traditions. The liberal ideal requires a self-critical community of teachers and students, and the university is finding it more difficult to provide spaces for this. Not all students will identify with knowledge as capital, and they too need to be aware of neoliberal change and be prepared to question the academy as they share a responsibility to shape education and its purposes:

> . . . higher education . . . is one of the few public places left where students can learn the power of questioning authority, recover the ideals of engaged citizenship, re-affirm the importance of the public good and expand their capacities to make a difference (Giroux, 2002, p. 450).

The liberal university also has the double responsibility of being "critic and conscience of society". As an epistemological idea this has always been a difficult concept, but Barnett (2000) offers a possible understanding in his thoughts on the importance of critique:

> . . . we find hope that higher education can offer a countervailing force in society, distinct from and, if necessary, in opposition to the dominant voices of the day (p. 54).

Such a service to the democratic project is not perfect, and standing outside of higher education, society or the state is not always possible, particularly in a neoliberal world. Furthermore, universities have not necessarily had a good record of serving society. In the 1960s Neil Postman suggested that education in schools was failing America for its lack of critical edge (see Postman and Weingartner, 1969). The list of societal problems identified then seem to be just as relevant and as complex to solve today and higher education needs to remember its responsibilities, as institutions and their graduates will play their part, sometimes unwittingly, in the maintenance of old problems and the creation of new ones. Higher education must take some responsibility for equipping graduates not only to cope with a changing world, but also the capacity to contribute to this world. It seems sensible that every discipline that finds a home in our institutions should make room for the critic and conscience concept. However, for many teachers and subjects, such ideas lack substance and practical realization.

Table 37.1 summarizes the key neoliberal and liberal characteristics discussed so far, and the way in which they are regulated in higher education. Laying one set of ideas alongside the other in such a manner is designed to show the paradigm shift for each concept. However, this is not to claim that ideas can be separated so easily in practice.

A Nearly Reasonable Idea

I recently came across the phrase "nearly reasonable" in an article on "risk" by Erica McWilliam (2007), and it helped me make sense of the neoliberal project. It is puzzling why neoliberal ideas can often appear both reasonable and unreasonable at the same time, and why they are remarkably difficult to argue against (Strathern, 2000). To take one example from Table 37.1, it seems reasonable that higher education should be accountable for its public funding. However, if accountability also transfers power to a new hidden elite, results in debilitating compliance regimes and is detrimental to teaching and learning, can it still be reasonable? Giroux (2002) suggests that "neoliberalism wraps itself in what appears to be an unassailable appeal to common sense" and, as a consequence, it remains largely unchallenged in the academy. Neoliberalist thinking has also become so embedded in our professional and private lives that any alternative becomes unthinkable (Strathern, 2000; Lynch, 2006). An academic born after 1960 may have spent their whole university life as student and teacher swept along on the tide of neoliberal reform, and it is no wonder that it all seems so normal.

The general absence of challenge may also be due to self-interest in the academy and complacency towards wider educational issues. Bourdieu (1988) observes that academics tend to be conformist in nature, and because they are also competitive and have their first loyalty to their subject discipline rather than an institution (Becher, 1989), individual or collective action to contest reform is less likely. It is also unusual for academics to critique their own working practices, and Freire (1994) comments that they have always had trouble looking at themselves. Every area of knowledge can be studied in a university, but there is relatively little interest (for those outside of the subject) in the study of higher education (Rowland, 2006). Simply speaking out on issues can mark

Table 37.1 Neoliberal and Liberal Characteristics

Neoliberal characteristics	Liberal characteristics
Competition	Collegiality
Accountability	Public openness
New forms of legislation, power and control	Values of trust, evidence, honesty and truth
Fragmented and private	Democratic
Control mechanisms	*Control mechanisms*
Research Assessment Exercise	Self-critical community
Teaching Quality Assessment	Internal standards
Audit	Peer review
Intellectual capital	Critic and conscience

a staff member as a rebel or a whistleblower, but Rowland provides a recent example in which a university would only allow its higher education researchers to research in subjects permitted by the senior management, so that research outcomes would have institutional utility. Yet, the only way to understand and unravel the complexities of the places in which we work is through an educative inquiry process free from constraint. However, Chomsky (2003) suggests that "there will undoubtedly be an effort to repress the activism that is a natural outgrowth of serious enquiry" (p. 159). At present we can still have open debate but not serious contestation and, according to Chomsky, critique is confined to tactical questions that arise within the system. Neoliberal changes have caused a subtle shift in the intensity of subordination and control, and academics can easily be manipulated.

Now that the main ideological thrust of neoliberalism has become embedded in our thinking about higher education, the academy appears to simply adapt to each new change thrust upon them. There is good evidence that we now find it difficult to envision a world without compliance, and may even depend on it because the alternatives are feared. In the continuing debate about the possible abolition of the Research Assessment Exercise in the UK, there appears to be a consensus that some form of assessment is now necessary. Those who do well out of the competition have little incentive to move to alternative ways of funding research, despite recognizing the pernicious and distorting effects that the exercise can have on knowledge, research and teaching. And, of course, there will be those in higher education who have thought carefully about neoliberalism and see it as an acceptable ideology and a completely reasonable idea.

The Limits of Neoliberalism

The other story is that neoliberal ideology has not entirely succeeded. Universities in particular are resilient organizations, and tend to resist change *per se*. Examples of neoliberal resistance are easily found. Furthermore, there are parts of practice that reform finds it harder to touch, and these include liberal educational values. For example, knowledge and research may be redirected to serve economic needs but the thinking and work that is done often needs to find an international audience, and standards of quality are protected by the disciplines and the judgment of peers. The best research is published in the top journals in that field and, despite the imperfections of peer review, there is wide agreement in the academic community that it provides a valuable service to the quality of knowledge. Similarly, teaching postgraduate students and the examination procedures for their research also provide a space where liberal values still have a strong foothold. Disciplinary ideologies and the professions in higher education have always been anti-liberal, in the sense that they tend to serve themselves and re-enforce hegemonic authority (Chomsky, 2003). However, they also serve a key role in preserving the liberal educational project.

Furthermore, governments and markets recognize value in liberal education, and certain liberal forms of knowledge are seen to have economic utility. Critical thought and action are required to handle knowledge in the new knowledge economies, and graduates are also recruited on the basis of their critical capacities. Liberal education remains the foundation of the elite universities such as Harvard and Oxford, where there is still a place for the un-measurable in teaching and academic life. However, for the majority of less powerful institutions, the problems of reform are much more fundamental. The sheer scale of the current mass higher education enterprise seems to leave little space or time for liberal educational experiences, particularly at the undergraduate level. We now have a situation in which most of teaching is done in larger classes, and by staff who have less time to teach and even less time to think about this activity.

In contrast, there are still plenty of examples of educational experiences that can be understood in more traditional liberal terms, and numerous illustrations are written about in the higher education literature. Such neoliberal resistance is partly due to there being an epistemological and ontological bottom line for individual academics that will rarely be crossed. Barnett (2003) contrasts a biotechnology initiative for profit with teaching critical reflection-in-action in nursing. His point is to argue for multiple and competing forms of life in the university but it is clear from his account that liberal education can still be one of them. Liberal avenues are not closed off and these spaces or "pockets of resistance" ensure that a higher education can still be an end in itself.

A Life of Reason under New Management

"A life of reason under new management" (Barnett, 2000, p. 78) might be a fitting epitaph to the modern university and the position of liberal education within it. In today's institutions many of the original values of the liberal ideal hold fast, even though changes to organization and control may be hostile to this type of activity. Both new management and liberal values seem to have their place.

As for the neoliberal project, continued homogenization of economic and political systems across the world will ensure that it is not seriously challenged (Fukuyama, 1992). We are still firmly in the grip of neoliberal thinking. The higher education sector has largely embraced reform and individual reactions have made little difference to this (Readings, 1996; Giroux, 2002; Strathern, 2002). Barnett (2003) talks about a conspiracy of silence in the academic community, particularly when new policies are devoid of values; the ends are stated and the means worked out but no one contests the ends. Instead of values we have accountability. Yet a desire to be so accountable would be unusual in other parts of our lives and, except in extreme instances, how much evidence does anyone really need? How many of the billions of words of justification are ever read and how much is acted upon, either by those who impose compliance or by those who desire to learn from the process? What neoliberal reform does, however reasonable it might seem, is to drive our compliance behaviours, take us away from teaching and research, and subtly shift power from individuals, the disciplines and institutions to the state and private enterprise.

There is no logical reason why higher education should be exempt from such sweeping change, and academics do take advantage of new freedoms that neoliberalism brings, particularly in new knowledge areas and research opportunities in science, technology and health. Many academics also do well under the new management, and would have little interest in challenging the status quo. From management's perspective, everyone now knows a lot more about what is going on in our institutions. Yet, if an academic has been around for a while they will have experienced the shift from being a trusted professional to being closely managed and even mistrusted. If this change was just about grumpy old men (mostly) complaining about filling in forms and reminiscing about the good old days, then time would have sorted them out, and the economic and political reform of academic life would have been largely complete by now. However, a life of reason and the liberal ideal are not foreign, even to the new generation of academics, and questions about knowledge, teaching and student learning are still important. What experiences do we want for students and what sort of education might be needed for a changing world?

Academics can see the liberal ideal carefully written into every mission statement, and Lynch (2006) suggests that this at least gives permission for certain foundational ideas. However, institutions can stand for certain values even if they don't perform these as services (Beck, 1999; Giroux, 2002). To seriously engage with such complex ideas academics need to understand the current and historical arguments around what it means to have a higher education. Without such a theory any debate will be shallow, yet the sector continues to recruit teachers who, for the most part, have no professional preparation for the task of teaching. In research-intensive universities academics are still recruited on the basis that they have completed a research project. Of course, they can learn to teach as they go, but with all the other expectations of them, they may not have the time nor inclination to seriously develop a personal theory of teaching, or a philosophical perspective on the purposes of a higher education.

Neoliberalism has ensured that self-interest is the order of the day, and it is not uncommon to find academics and students who are generally disinterested in or unaware of the possibilities of a liberal education. Alongside this, higher education partly understands itself as a liberal project, and this is enacted authentically in many of our research communities, and can still be found in undergraduate teaching and courses. There is something essential about human nature that equips us for the intellectual life, and academic identities are founded and sustained on liberal values that will be as difficult to remove as the countervailing neoliberal ideologies. And liberal educational values may have found a new ally, because neoliberalism has also latched onto the economic benefits of such an education. If these liberal educational attributes do prove their worth in the knowledge economy, recovery of older aims and purposes may be rapid, particularly for the undergraduate student. Either way, higher education as a liberal project will remain with us. To what extent will be decided by those who control our institutions and, perhaps more importantly, by the private choices made by the individual academic within the system.

Acknowledgements

I would like to thank Toni Tidswell for her enthusiatic support and perceptive comments on this chapter.

References

Axelrod, P. (2002). *Values in conflict: the university, the marketplace and the trials of liberal education.* Montreal & Kingston: McGill-Queen's University Press.

Barnett, R. (1997). *Higher education: a critical business.* Buckingham: Open University Press.

Barnett, R. (2000). *Realizing the university in an age of supercomplexity.* Buckingham: Open University Press.

Barnett, R. (2003). *Beyond all reason. Living with ideology in the university.* Buckingham: Open University Press.

Becher, T. (1989). *Academic tribes and territories: intellectual enquiry and the cultures of disciplines.* Buckingham: Open University Press.

Beck, J. (1999). Makeover or takeover? The strange death of educational autonomy in neo-liberal England, *British Journal of Sociology of Education, 20*(2), 223–238.

Bourdieu, P. (1988). *Homo Academicus.* Cambridge: Polity Press.

Chomsky, N. (2003). *Chomsky on democracy and education.* New York: RoutledgeFalmer.

Codd, J. (2005). Teachers as "managed professionals" in the global education industry: the New Zealand experience, *Educational Review, 57*(2), 193–206.

Davies, B., Gottsche, M. and Bansel, P. (2006). The rise and fall of the neo-liberal university, *European Journal of Education, 41*(2), 305–319.

Education Act (1989). Part 14 Establishment and disestablishment of tertiary institutions, 162, 4(a)(v), New Zealand Government.

Freire, P. (1994). *Paulo Freire on higher education.* New York: State University of New York Press.

Fukuyama, F. (1992). *The end of history and the last man.* London: Penguin Books.

Gibbons, M., Limoges, C., Nowotny, H., Schwarzman, S., Scott, P. and Trow, M. (1994). *The new production of knowledge: the dynamics of science and research in contemporary societies.* London: Sage.

Giroux, H.A. (2002). Neoliberalism, corporate culture, and the promise of higher education: the university as a democratic public sphere, *Harvard Educational Review, 72*(4), 425–463.

Giroux, H.A. (2005). The terror of neoliberalism: rethinking the significance of cultural politics, *College Literature, 32*(1), 1–19.

Harris, S. (2005). Rethinking academic identities in neo-liberal times, *Teaching in Higher Education, 10*(4), 421–433.

Levin, J.S. (2006). Faculty work: tensions between educational and economic values, *The Journal of Higher Education, 77*(1), 62–88.

Lynch, K. (2006). Neo-liberalism and marketisation: the implications for higher education, *European Educational Research Journal, 5*(1), 1–17.

Malcolm, W. and Tarling, N. (2006). *Crisis of identity? The mission and management of universities in New Zealand* (Wellington: Dunmore Publishing).

Marginson, S. (1997). Steering from a distance: power relations in Australian higher education, *Higher Education*, *34*, 63–80.

Marginson, S. and Rhoades, G. (2002). Beyond national states, markets, and systems of higher education: a glonacal agency heuristic, *Higher Education*, *43*(3), 281–309.

McWilliam, E. (2007). Managing "nearly reasonable" risk in the contemporary university, *Studies in Higher Education*, *32*(3), 311–321.

Nowotny, H., Scott, P. and Gibbons, M. (2003). Mode 2 revisited: the new production of knowledge, *Minerva*, *41*(3), 179–194.

O'Neill, O. (2002). *A question of trust.* Cambridge: Cambridge University Press.

Pirsig, R.M. (1991). *Lila: an inquiry into morals.* New York: Bantam.

Postman, N. and Weingartner, C. (1969). *Teaching as a subversive activity.* New York: Delacorte Press.

Ranson, S. (2003). Public accountability in the age of neo-liberal governance, *Journal of Education Policy*, *18*(5), 459–480.

Readings, B. (1996). *The university in ruins.* Harvard, MA: Harvard University Press.

Rowland, S. (2006). *The enquiring university.* Buckingham: Open University Press.

Strathern, M. (2000). The tyranny of transparency, *British Educational Research Journal*, *26*(3), 309–321.

Trow, M. (1996). *Trust, markets and accountability in higher education: a comparative perspective* (Berkley: University of California, Centre for Studies in Higher Education, Research and Occasional Paper Series 1.96).

Index